Computing with Words
in Information/Intelligent Systems 1

Studies in Fuzziness and Soft Computing

Editor-in-chief
Prof. Janusz Kacprzyk
Systems Research Institute
Polish Academy of Sciences
ul. Newelska 6
01-447 Warsaw, Poland
E-mail: kacprzyk@ibspan.waw.pl

Vol. 3. A. Geyer-Schulz
Fuzzy Rule-Based Expert Systems and Genetic Machine Learning, 2nd ed. 1996
ISBN 3-7908-0964-0

Vol. 4. T. Onisawa and J. Kacprzyk (Eds.)
Reliability and Safety Analyses under Fuzziness, 1995
ISBN 3-7908-0837-7

Vol. 5. P. Bosc and J. Kacprzyk (Eds.)
Fuzziness in Database Management Systems, 1995
ISBN 3-7908-0858-X

Vol. 6. E.S. Lee and Q. Zhu
Fuzzy and Evidence Reasoning, 1995
ISBN 3-7908-0880-6

Vol. 7. B.A. Juliano and W. Bandler
Tracing Chains-of-Thought, 1996
ISBN 3-7908-0922-5

Vol. 8. F. Herrera and J.L. Verdegay (Eds.)
Genetic Algorithms and Soft Computing, 1996,
ISBN 3-7908-0956-X

Vol. 9. M. Sato et al.
Fuzzy Clustering Models and Applications, 1997,
ISBN 3-7908-1026-6

Vol. 10. L.C. Jain (Ed.)
Soft Computing Techniques in Knowledge-based Intelligent Engineering Systems, 1997, ISBN 3-7908-1035-5

Vol. 11. W. Mielczarski (Ed.)
Fuzzy Logic Techniques in Power Systems, 1998,
ISBN 3-7908-1044-4

Vol. 12. B. Bouchon-Meunier (Ed.)
Aggregation and Fusion of Imperfect Information, 1998
ISBN 3-7908-1048-7

Vol. 13. E. Orłowska (Ed.)
Incomplete Information: Rough Set Analysis, 1998
ISBN 3-7908-1049-5

Vol. 14. E. Hisdal
Logical Structures for Representation of Knowledge and Uncertainty, 1998
ISBN 3-7908-1056-8

Vol. 15. G.J. Klir and M.J. Wierman
Uncertainty-Based Information, 1998
ISBN 3-7908-1073-8

Vol. 16. D. Driankov and R. Palm (Eds.)
Advances in Fuzzy Control, 1998
ISBN 3-7908-1090-8

Vol. 17. L. Reznik, V. Dimitrov and J. Kacprzyk (Eds.)
Fuzzy Systems Design, 1998
ISBN 3-7908-1118-1

Vol. 18. L. Polkowski and A. Skowron (Eds.)
Rough Sets in Knowledge Discovery 1, 1998,
ISBN 3-7908-1119-X

Vol. 19. L. Polkowski and A. Skowron (Eds.)
Rough Sets in Knowledge Discovery 2, 1998,
ISBN 3-7908-1120-3

Vol. 20. J.N. Mordeson and P.S. Nair
Fuzzy Mathematics, 1998
ISBN 3-7908-1121-1

Vol. 21. L.C. Jain and T. Fukuda (Eds.)
Soft Computing for Intelligent Robotic Systems, 1998
ISBN 3-7908-1147-5

Vol. 22. J. Cardoso and H. Camargo (Eds.)
Fuzziness in Petri Nets, 1999
ISBN 3-7908-1158-0

Vol. 23. P.S. Szczepaniak (Ed.)
Computational Intelligence and Applications, 1999
ISBN 3-7908-1161-0

Vol. 24. E. Orłowska (Ed.)
Logic at Work, 1999
ISBN 3-7908-1164-5

continued on page 518

Lotfi A. Zadeh
Janusz Kacprzyk (Eds.)

Computing with Words in Information/Intelligent Systems 1

Foundations

With 135 Figures
and 22 Tables

Springer-Verlag Berlin Heidelberg GmbH

Prof. Lotfi A. Zadeh
Berkeley Initiative in Soft Computing (BISC)
Computer Science Division and
Electronics Research Laboratory
Department of Electrical and Electronics
Engineering and Computer Science
University of California
Berkeley, CA 94720-1776
USA
E-mail: zadeh@cs.berkeley.edu

Prof. Janusz Kacprzyk
Systems Research Institute
Polish Academy of Sciences
ul. Newelska 6
01-447 Warsaw
Poland
E-mail: kacprzyk@ibspan.waw.pl

ISBN 978-3-662-11362-2

Cataloging-in-Publication Data applied for
Die Deutsche Bibliothek – CIP-Einheitsaufnahme
Computing with words in information/intelligent systems: with 22 tables / Lotfi A. Zadeh, Janusz Kacprzyk (ed.)
1. Foundations. – 1999
(Studies in fuzziness and soft computing; Vol. 33)
ISBN 978-3-662-11362-2 ISBN 978-3-7908-1873-4 (eBook)
DOI 10.1007/978-3-7908-1873-4

Originally published by Physica-Verlag Heidelberg New York in 1999
Softcover reprint of the hardcover 1st edition 1999

Hardcover Design: Erich Kirchner, Heidelberg

SPIN 10728854 88/2202-5 4 3 2 1 0 – Printed on acid-free paper

Foreword

These two volumes consisting of *Foundations* and *Applications* provide the current status of theoretical and empirical developments in „computing with words".

In philosophy, the twentieth century is said to be the century of language. This is mainly due to Wittgenstein who said:

> „The meaning of a word is its use in the language game".
> „The concept *game* is a concept with blurred edges".

In the first phrase, „the language game" implies the everyday human activity with language, and in the latter, „game" simply implies an ordinary word. Thus, Wittgenstein precisely stated that a word is fuzzy in real life.

Unfortunately this idea about a word was not accepted in the conventional science. We had to wait for Zadeh's fuzzy sets theory. Remembering Wittgenstein's statement, we should consider, on the one hand, the concept of „computing with words" from a philosophical point of view. It deeply relates to the everyday use of a word in which the meaning of a word is fuzzy in its nature.

On the other hand, „computing with words" can be considered in the perspective of history of computing with language in computer science and also in artificial intelligence. We can go back to the 1950s when an attempt to machine translation started. As we know, this computer scientific adventure to computing with language terminated in 1965 when the US Air Force pronounced machine translation a failure. Researchers continued their activities in computing with language under different titles such as parsing, question-answering or expert systems and the like in the setting of artificial intelligence. There was, however, a strict line between natural language processing and computing, as pointed out by Halliday. Computing was not intelligent in any sense. It was considered just as a tool to realize an intelligent system.

A breakthrough was made in the 1990s by Zadeh's idea of „computing with words". The history of computing with language has now made a revolutionary turn. We have entered the true age af computing with language. Computing itself is now viewed from a perspective of human intelligence. Human cogitation is nothing but „computing with words" as Zadeh points out. Cogitation is essentially connected with recognition. In human recognition, we see the world with words. We articulate the physical world with Wittgenstein's blurred words. According to Zadeh, this articulation is a „fuzzy granulation".

As such, fuzzy logic is a promising tool to play a very important role in intelligent computing. From now on, we will be able to view any computing as „computing with words". This idea would become a main stream to create „an artificial brain".

This volume, Part 1: *Foundations*, includes introductory papers related to various basic aspects of, and approaches to „computing with words".

I wish to congratulate the editors, Professors Zadeh and Kacprzyk for these volumes for their great success. In particular, I wish to acknowledge Professor Janusz Kacprzyk who has been mainly the driving force behind this project.

Tokyo, March 1999

Michio Sugeno
President
International Fuzzy Systems Association (IFSA)

What is Computing with Words?

Lotfi A.Zadeh[1]

The label „Computing with Words (CW)" lends itself to misinterpretation. There are some who say „What is new? Isn't this what we have been doing all along?" The answer is: No, not really. Then, what is it?

Historically, computing was focused on manipulation of numbers. With the passage of time, the meaning of computing became much more encompassing. Today, computing is a term that is applied to manipulation of a wide variety of data ranging from numbers and symbols to signals, sounds, images, and text. Thus, computing with numbers – as in numerical analysis – is far less prevalent today than processing of a text drawn from a natural language, as in machine translation, spelling correction, interfaces, and summarization. Although such operations do involve manipulation of words, what should be underscored is that they are not representative of what is in the mainstream of computing with words.

The intended meaning of computing with words is reflected in the content of the papers included in this volume. More concretely, the meaning of computing with words is conveyed by examples of problems drawn from its mainstream.

Representative of such problems are the following:

a) solution of a system of linear equations with linguistic rather than numerical coefficients,
b) operations on functions which are defined by fuzzy if-then rules with linguistic values. Example: interpolation or maximization of a function defined by a fuzzy rule set, e.g.:

   if X is small then Y is small
   if X is medium then Y is large
   if X is large then Y is small

c) computation of linguistic probabilities;

   Example:

   A box contains balls of various sizes. Most are large and a few are small.

[1] Professor in the Graduate School and Director, Berkeley Initiative in Soft Computing, University of California, Berkeley, CA 94720-1776

What is the probability that a ball drawn at random is neither large nor small?

d) syllogistic reasoning;

Example:

Most young men are healthy
Robert is young
What is the probability that Robert is healthy?

e) Dispositional reasoning:

Example:

Slimness is attractive
Cindy is slim
What can be said about Cindy's attractiveness?

What we see is that problems of this type do not lend themselves to solution by conventional methods drawn from logic, probability theory and numerical analysis. They do fall within the province of Computing with Words (CW).

It is helpful to distinguish between two types of problems in computing with words:

- level 1 problems (CW1) are those in which members are replaced with words, as in examples (a), (b), (c), and (d),
- level 2 problems (CW2) in which the premises are propositions drawn from natural language whose meaning cannot be simply defined, as in example (e).

There are four principal rationales for computing with words:

1. **The don't know rationale**

   Values of variables are not known with sufficient precision to justify the use of numbers.

2. **The don't need rationale**

   Precision is not needed.

3. **The can't solve rationale**

   A problem cannot be solved or a task cannot be performed through the use of numbers.

4. The can't define rationale

A concept is too complex for numerical definition.
Examples: causality, relevance, summary.

Since the objects of computation in computing with words are propositions drawn from a natural language, it is necessary to have in computing with words a means of defining meaning in a way that makes semantics amenable to computation. In computing with words, this is accomplished through the use of constraint-centered semantics of natural languages (CSNL). In this semantics, the meaning of a proposition is represented as a generalized constraint on an implicit variable. The constraint-centered semantics of natural languages has a much higher expressive power than conventional meaning-representation systems based on predicate logic.

The high expressive power of the constraint-centered semantics of natural languages makes it possible to use computing with words as a foundation for what may be called the computational theory of perceptions (CTP). This theory suggests many new applications for the basic methodology of computing with words.

In essence, the computational theory of perceptions is inspired by the remarkable human capability to perform a wide variety of physical and mental tasks without any measurements and any computations. Everyday examples of such tasks are: parking a car, driving in heavy traffic, playing golf, balancing a pole and summarizing a story. Underlying this capability is the brain's ability to manipulate perceptions – perceptions of time, distance, speed, force, direction, color, likelihood, intent and truth, among others.

An essential difference between measurements and perception is that, in general, measurements are crisp whereas perceptions are fuzzy. In the computational theory of perceptions, the point of departure is a description of perceptions as propositions expressed in a natural language as, e.g., Robert is very honest, overeating causes obesity, it is very unlikely that there will be a significant decline in the price of oil in the near future, etc. Once perceptions are described as propositions, the machinery of computing with words may be employed to reason with them. This, in essence, is the key idea underlying the computational theory of perceptions.

It is a long-standing tradition in science to accord more respect to numbers than to words. But it is becoming increasingly clear that the remarkable human ability to manipulate words and perceptions without any measurements and any computations plays a key role in human intelligence. In the final analysis, the role model for computing with words and the computational theory of perceptions is the human mind.

Berkeley, February, 1999. Lotfi A. Zadeh

Contents

Foreword v
M. Sugeno

What is Computing with Words? vii
L.A. Zadeh

1. INTRODUCTORY SECTIONS

Fuzzy Logic = Computing with Words 3
L.A. Zadeh

Performing Approximate Reasoning with Words? 24
D. Dubois, L. Foulloy, S. Galichet and H. Prade

Approximate Reasoning as a Basis for Computing with Words 50
R.R. Yager

What is Intelligent Measurement? 78
L. Reznik

2. COMPUTING WITH WORDS: LINGUISTIC ASPECTS

Semiotics and Computational Linguistics. On Semiotic Cognitive Information Processing 93
B.B. Rieger

Words about Uncertainty: Analogies and Contexts 119
M. J. Smithson

Virtual Meaning: Problems of Interpretation in the Social Sciences 136
V. Dimitrov and B. Hodge

Towards Fixing Some 'Fuzzy' Catchwords: A Terminological Primer 154
H. Toth

3. COMPUTING WITH WORDS AND INFORMATION GRANULARITY

Granular Computing: Fuzzy Logic and Rough Sets 183
T.Y. Lin

Towards an Adaptive Calculus of Granules 201
L. Polkowski and A. Skowron

Semantics and Modelling of Flexible Time Indications 229
R. De Caluwe, F. Devos, P. Maesfranckx, G. De Tré
and B. Van der Cruyssen

4. COMPUTING WITH WORDS: LOGICAL ASPECTS

Towards Fuzzy Logic 259
W. Ostasiewicz

Fuzzy Negation 297
E. Ferri, A. Kandel and G. Langholz

Triangular Operations, Negations, and Scalar Cardinality of a Fuzzy Set 326
M. Wygralak

Fuzzy Implications in Approximate Reasoning 342
E. Czogała and J. Łęski

On the Semantics of Fuzzy Linguistic Quantifiers 358
H. Thiele

Evaluating Linguistic Expressions and Functional Fuzzy Theories in Fuzzy Logic 383
V. Novák and I. Perfilieva

5. COMPUTING WITH WORDS: NUMERICAL ASPECTS

Calculation over Verbal Quantities 409
M. Mareš and R. Mesiar

Aggregation of Linguistic Information Based on a Symbolic Approach 428
M. Delgado, F. Herrera, E. Herrera-Viedma,
J.L. Verdegay and M.A. Vila

6. GENERAL FRAMEWORKS FOR COMPUTING WITH WORDS

Object Networks: A Computational Framework to Compute with Words 443
R.R. Gudwin and F.A.C. Gomide

Study on a Framework for Solving Ill-defined Problems Using Patterns and Symbols 479
Y. Hattori and T. Furuhashi

From Expert Words Directly to Numerical Simulations: Group-Theoretic Approach to Computing with Words in Information/Intelligent Systems 495
V. Kreinovich, B. Penn and S. Starks

1

INTRODUCTORY SECTIONS

Fuzzy Logic = Computing with Words*

Lotfi A. Zadeh

Computer Science Division and Electronics Research Laboratory
Dept. of Electrical and Electronics Engineering and Computer Science
University of California
Berkeley, CA 94720-1776, USA
E-mail: zadeh@cs.berkeley.edu

To Professor Michio Sugeno, who has contributed so much and in so many ways to the development of fuzzy logic and its applications

Abstract. As its name suggests, computing with words, CW, is a methodology in which words are used in place of numbers for computing and reasoning. The point of this note is that fuzzy logic plays a pivotal role in CW and vice-versa. Thus, as an approximation, fuzzy logic may be equated to CW.

There are two major imperatives for computing with words. First, computing with words is a necessity when the available information is too imprecise to justify the use of numbers. And second, when there is a tolerance for imprecision which can be exploited to achieve tractability, robustness, low solution cost and better rapport with reality. Exploitation of the tolerance for imprecision is an issue of central importance in CW.

In CW, a words is viewed as a label of a granule, that is, a fuzzy set of points drawn together by similarity, with the fuzzy set playing the role of a fuzzy constraint on a variable. The premises are assumed to be expressed as propositions in a natural language. For purposes of computation, the propositions are expressed as canonical forms which serve to place in evidence the fuzzy constraints that are implicit in the premises. Then, the rules of inference in fuzzy logic are employed to propagate the constraints from premises to conclusions.

At this juncture, the techniques of computing with words underlie -- in one way or another -- almost all applications of fuzzy logic. In coming years, computing with words is likely to evolve into a basic methodology in its own right

* Research supported in part by NASA Grant NCC 2-275 and the BISC (Berkeley Initiative in Soft Computing) Program. Reprinted from IEEE Transactions on Fuzzy Systems, **4**, pp. 103-111, 1996 by permission of IEEE.

with wide-ranging ramifications on both basic and applied levels.

Introduction

Fuzzy logic has come of age. Its foundations have become firmer, its applications have grown in number and variety; and its influence within the basic sciences -- and especially in mathematical and physical sciences -- has become more visible and more substantive.

And yet, there are two questions that are still frequently raised: (a) What is fuzzy logic?; and (b) What can be done with fuzzy logic that cannot be done equally well with other methodologies, e.g., predicate logic, probability theory, neural network theory, Bayesian networks and classical control.

The title of this note is intended to suggest a succinct answer: The main contribution of fuzzy logic is a methodology for computing with words (CW). No other methodology serves this purpose.

What follows is an elaboration on this suggestion. A fuller exposition of the methodology of CW will appear in a forthcoming paper.

Needless to say, there is more to fuzzy logic than a methodology for CW. Thus, strictly speaking, the equality in the title of this note should be an inclusion; using the equality serves to accentuate the importance of computing with words as a branch of fuzzy logic.

What is Computing with Words?

In its traditional sense, computing involves for the most part manipulation of numbers and symbols. By contrast, humans employ mostly words in computing and reasoning, arriving at conclusions expressed as words from premises expressed in a natural language or having the form of mental perceptions. As used by humans, words have fuzzy denotations. The same applies to the role played by words in computing with words (CW).

The concept of CW is rooted in several papers starting with my 1973 paper "A New Approach to the Analysis of Complex Systems and Decision Processes," in which the concepts of a linguistic variable and granulation were introduced. The concepts of a fuzzy constraint and fuzzy constraint propagation were introduced in "The Calculus of Fuzzy Restrictions," (1974), and developed more fully in "A Theory of Approximate Reasoning," (1979) and "Outline of a Computational Approach to Meaning and Knowledge Representation Based on a Concept of a Generalized Assignment Statement," (1986). Application of fuzzy logic to meaning representation and its role in test-score semantics are discussed in "PRUF - A Meaning Representation Language for Natural Languages," (1978), and "Test-Score Semantics for Natural Languages and Meaning-Representation via PRUF" (1981).

Although the foundations of computing with words were laid some time ago, its evolution into a distinct methodology in its own right reflects many advances in our understanding of fuzzy logic and soft computing -- advances which took place within the past few years. (See References and Related Papers.) A key aspect of CW is that it involves a fusion of natural languages and computation with fuzzy variables. It is this fusion that is likely to result in an evolution of CW into a basic methodology in its own right, with wide ranging ramifications and applications.

We begin our exposition of CW with a few definitions. It should be understood that the definitions are dispositional, that is, admit of exceptions.

The point of departure in CW is the concept of a granule. In essence, a granule is a fuzzy set of points having the form of a clump of elements drawn together by similarity. A word, *w*, is a label of a granule, *g*, and conversely *g* is the denotation of *w*. A word may be atomic, as in *young*, or composite, as in *not very young*. Unless stated to the contrary, a word will be assumed to be composite. The denotation of a word may be a higher order predicate, as in a Montague grammar (Partee 1976).

In CW, a granule, *g*, which is the denotation of a word, *w*, is viewed as a fuzzy constraint on a variable. A pivotal role in CW is played by fuzzy constraint propagation from premises to conclusions. It should be noted that, as a basic technique, constraint propagation plays important roles in many methodologies, especially in mathematical programming, constraint programming and logic programming. (See References and Related Papers.)

As a simple illustration, consider the proposition *Mary is young*. In this case, *young* is the label of a granule *young*. (Note that for simplicity the same symbol is used both for a word and its denotation.) The fuzzy set *young* plays the role of a fuzzy constraint on the age of Mary.

As a further example consider the propositions

p_1 = *Carol lives near Mary*

and

p_2 = *Mary lives near Pat.*

In this case, the words *lives near* in p_1 and p_2 play the role of fuzzy constraints on the distances between the residences of Carol and Mary, and Mary and Pat, respectively. If the query is: How far is Carol from Pat?, an answer yielded by fuzzy constraint propagation might be expressed as p_3, where

p_3 = *Carol lives not far from Pat*

More about fuzzy constraint propagation will be said at a later point.

A basic assumption in CW is that information is conveyed by constraining the values of variables. Furthermore, information is assumed to consist of a collection of propositions expressed in natural or synthetic language.

A basic generic problem in CW is the following:

We are given a collection of propositions expressed in a natural language which constitute the *initial data set*, or IDS for short.

From the initial data set we wish to infer an answer to a query expressed in a natural language. The answer, also expressed in a natural language, is referred to as the *terminal data set*, or TDS for short. The problem is to derive TDS from IDS.

A few problems will serve to illustrate these concepts. At this juncture, the problems will be formulated but not solved:

1. Assume that a function, f, f: $U \rightarrow V$, $X \in U$, $Y \in V$, is described in words by the fuzzy if-then rules:

   f: if X is small then Y is small
   if X is medium then Y is large
   if X is large then Y is small

What this implies is that f is approximated to by the fuzzy graph f^* (Fig. 1), where

$f^* = small \times small + medium \times large + large \times small$

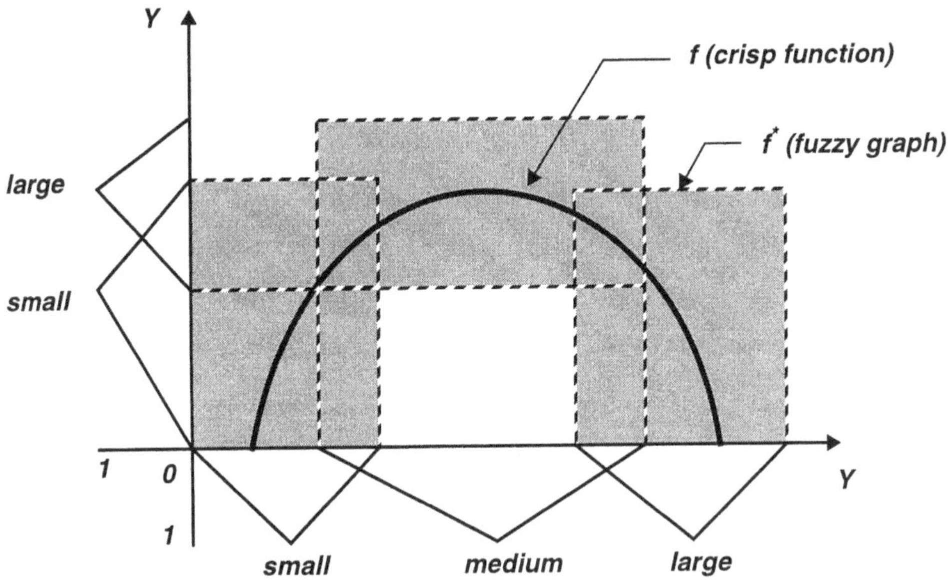

Figure 1. f^* is a fuzzy graph which approximates a function f

In f^*, + and × denote, respectively, the disjunction and cartesian product. An expression of the form $A \times B$, where A and B are words, will be referred to as a *cartesian granule*. In this sense, a fuzzy graph may be viewed as a disjunction of cartesian granules. In essence, a fuzzy graph serves as an approximation to a function or a relation (Zadeh 1974,1994).

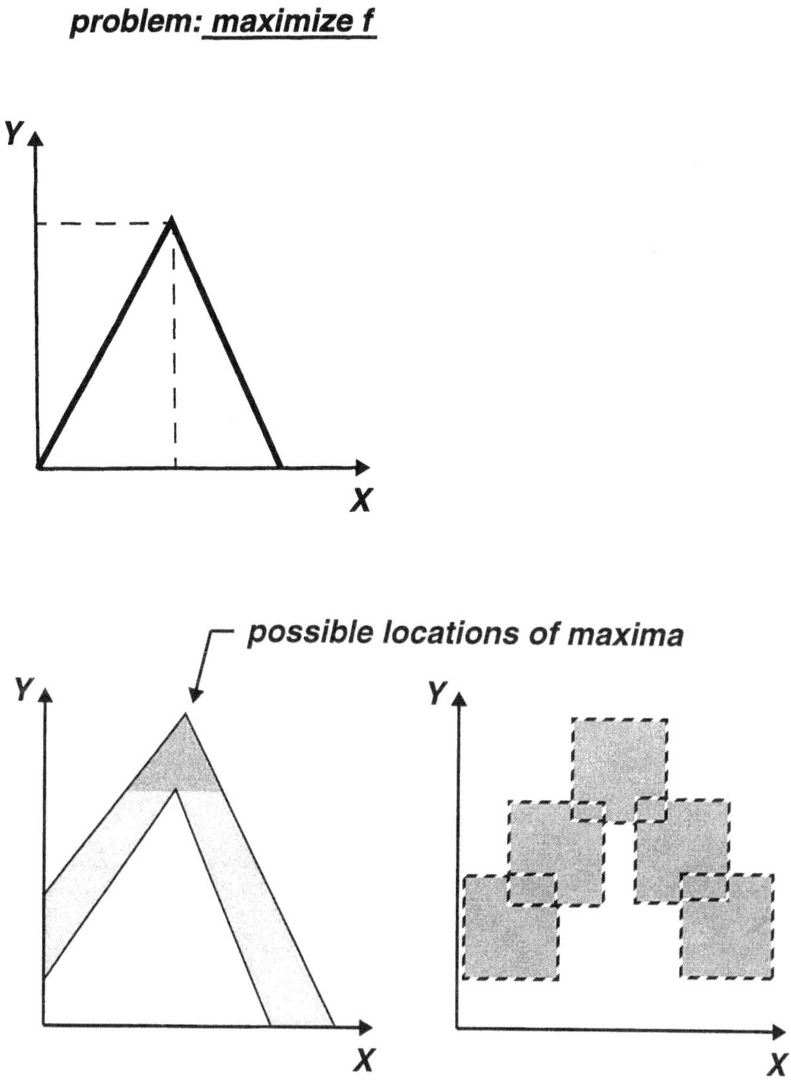

Figure 2. Maximization of a crisp function; an interval-valued function; and a fuzzy graph

In the example under consideration, the IDS consists of the fuzzy rule-set *f*. The query is: What is the maximum value of f^* (cf. Fig. 2)?

More broadly, the problem is: How can one compute an attribute of a function, *f*, e.g., its maximum value or its area or its roots if *f* is described in words as a collection of fuzzy if-then rules?

2. A box contains ten balls of various sizes of which several are large and a few are small. What is the probability that a ball drawn at random is neither large nor small? In this case, the IDS is a verbal description of the contents of the box: The TDS is the desired probability.

3. A less simple example of computing with words is the following.

Let *X* and *Y* be independent random variables taking values in a finite set $V=\{v_1,\ldots,v_n\}$ with probabilities $p_1,\ldots, p_n$ and $q_1,\ldots, q_n$, respectively. For simplicity of notation, the same symbols will be used to denote *X* and *Y* and their generic values, with p and q denoting the probabilities of *X* and *Y*, respectively.

Assume that the probability distributions of *X* and *Y* are described in words through the fuzzy if-then rules:

P: if *X* is small then p is small
if *X* is medium then p is large
if *X* is large then p is small

and

Q: if *Y* is small then q is large
if *Y* is medium then q is small
if *Y* is large then q is large

where the granules small, medium and large are the values of the linguistic variables *X* and *Y* in their respective universes of discourse. In the example under consideration, those rule-sets constitute the IDS. Note that small in *P* need not have the same meaning as small in *Q*, and likewise for medium and large.

The query is: How can we describe in words the joint probability distribution of *X* and *Y*? This probability distribution is the TDS.

For convenience, the probability distributions of *X* and *Y* may be represented as fuzzy graphs:

P: *small* × *small* + *medium* × *large* + *large* × *small*
Q: *small* × *large* + *medium* × *large* + *large* × *large*

with the understanding that the underlying numerical probabilities must add up to unity.

Since *X* and *Y* are independent random variables, their joint probability distribution (P,Q) is the product of P and Q. In words, the product may be expressed as (Zadeh 1994):

$$(P,Q): small \times small \times (small * large) + small \times medium \times (small * small) + \\ + small \times large \times (small * large) + \ldots + large \times large \times (small * large)$$

where * is the arithmetic product in fuzzy arithmetic (Kaufmann and Gupta 1986, Mares 1994). In this example, what we have done, in effect, amounts to a derivation of a linguistic characterization of the joint probability distribution of *X* and *Y* starting with linguistic characterizations of the probability distribution of *X* and the probability distribution of *Y*.

A few comments are in order. In linguistic characterizations of variables and their dependencies, words serve as the values of variables and play the role of fuzzy constraints. In this perspective, the use of words may be viewed as a form of granulation, which in turn may be regarded as a form of fuzzy quantization.

Granulation plays a key role in human cognition. For humans, it serves as a way of achieving data compression. This is one of the pivotal advantages accruing through the use of words in human, machine and man-machine communication.

In the final analysis, the rationale for computing with words rests on two major imperatives. First, computing with words is a necessity when the available information is too imprecise to justify the use of numbers. And second, when there is a tolerance for imprecision which can be exploited to achieve tractability, robustness, low solution cost and better rapport with reality.

The conceptual structure of computing with words is schematized in Fig. 3a and Fig. 3b. Basically, CW may be viewed as a confluence of two related streams: fuzzy logic and test-score semantics, with the latter based on fuzzy logic. The point of contact is the collection of canonical forms of the premises, which are assumed to be propositions expressed in a natural language (NL). The function of canonical forms is to explicitate the implicit fuzzy constraints which are resident in the premises. With canonical forms as the point of departure, fuzzy constraint propagation leads to conclusions in the form of induced fuzzy constraints. Finally, the induced constraints are translated into a natural language through the use of linguistic approximation (Zadeh 1973, Mamdani and Gaines 1981).

In computing with words, there are two core issues that arise. First is the issue of representation of fuzzy constraints. More specifically, the question is: How can the fuzzy constraints which are implicit in propositions expressed in a natural language be made explicit. And second is the issue of fuzzy constraint propagation, that is, the question of how can fuzzy constraints in premises be propagated to conclusions.

These are the issues which are addressed in the following.

Representation of fuzzy constraints and canonical forms

Our approach to the representation of fuzzy constraints is based on test-score semantics (Zadeh 1978, 1981). In outline, in this semantics, a proposition, p, in a natural language is viewed as a network of fuzzy (elastic) constraints. Upon aggregation, the constraints which are embodied in p result in an overall fuzzy constraint which can be represented as an expression of the form

X is R

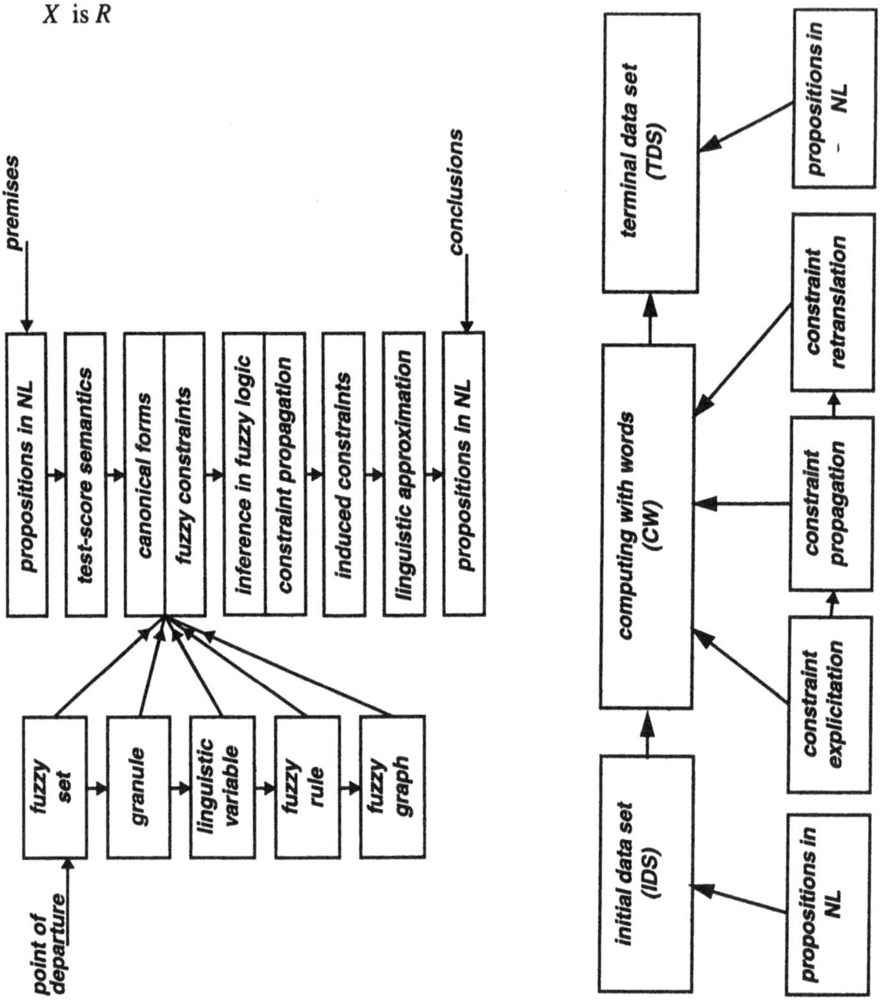

(a) (b)

Figure 3. Conceptual structure of CW. Figure 3b is a more detailed version of Figure 3a where R is a constraining fuzzy relation and X is the constrained variable. The expression in question is called a *canonical form*. The function of a canonical form is to place in evidence the fuzzy constraint which is implicit in p. This is represented schematically as

$$p \rightarrow X \text{ is } R$$

in which the arrow $\rightarrow$ denotes explicitation. The variable X may be vector-valued and/or conditioned.

In this perspective, the meaning of p is defined by two procedures. The first procedure acts on a so-called explanatory database, ED, and returns the constrained variable, X. The second procedure acts on ED and returns the constraining relation, R.

An explanatory database is a collection of relations in terms of which the meaning of p is defined. The relations are empty, that is, they consist of relation names, relations attributes and attribute domains, with no entries in the relations. When there are entries in ED, ED is said to be *instantiated* and is denoted EDI. EDI may be viewed as a description of a possible world in possible world semantics (Cresswell 1973), while ED defines a collection of possible worlds, with each possible world in the collection corresponding to a particular instantiation of ED.

As a simple illustration, consider the proposition

p = *Mary is not young*

Assume that the explanatory database is chosen to be

$$ED = \text{POPULATION[Name; Age]} + \text{YOUNG[Age; } \mu]$$

in which POPULATION is a relation with arguments Name and Age; YOUNG is a relation with arguments Age and μ; and + is the disjunction. In this case, the constrained variable is the age of Mary, which in terms of ED may be expressed as

$$X = \text{Age(Mary)} =_{\text{Age}} \text{POPULATION[Name=Mary]}$$

This expression specifies the procedure which acts on ED and returns X. More specifically, in this procedure, Name is instantiated to Mary and the resulting relation is projected on Age, yielding the age of Mary.

The constraining relation, R, is given by

$$R = ({}^{2}\text{YOUNG})$$

which implies that the intensifier *very* is interpreted as a squaring operation, and the negation *not* as the operation of complementation.

Equivalently, R may be expressed as

R = YOUNG [Age; $1-\mu^2$]

As a further example, consider the proposition

p = *Carol lives in a small city near San Francisco*

and assume that the explanatory database is

ED = POPULATION[Name;Residence]
+SMALL[City; μ] +NEAR[City1; City2; μ]

In this case

X = Residence(Carol) $=_{Residence}$ POPULATION[Name=Carol]

and

R = SMALL[City; μ] $\cap_{City1}$ NEAR[City2=San Francisco]

In R, the first constituent is the fuzzy set of small cities; the second constituent is the fuzzy set of cities which are near San Francisco; and $\cap$ denotes the intersection of these sets.

So far we have confined our attention to constraints of the form

X is R

In fact, constraints can have a variety of forms. In particular, a constraint -- expressed as a canonical form -- can be conditional, that is, of the form

if X is R then Y is S

which may also be written as

Y is S if X is R

The constraints in question will be referred to as *basic*.

For purposes of meaning representation, the richness of natural languages necessitates a wide variety of constraints in relation to which the basic constraints form an important though special class. The so-called generalized constraints (Zadeh 1986) contain the basic constraints as a special case and are defined as follows.

A generalized constraint is represented as

X isr R

where isr, pronounced "ezar," is a variable copula which defines the way in which R constrains X. More specifically, the role of R in relation to X is defined by the value of the discrete variable r. The values of r and their interpretations are defined below:

e:	equal	(abbreviated to =)
d:	disjunctive (possibilistic)	(abbreviated to blank)
c:	conjunctive	
p:	probabilistic	
λ:	probability value	
u:	usuality	
rs:	random set	
rsf:	random fuzzy set	
fg:	fuzzy graph	
ps :	rough set (Pawlak Set)	
.:	...	

As an illustration, when $r=e$, the constraint is an equality constraint and is abbreviated to =. When r takes the value d, the constraint is *disjunctive* (possibilistic) and is abbreviated to is, leading to the expression

X is R

in which R is a fuzzy relation which constrains X by playing the role of the possibility distribution of X. More specifically, if X takes values in a universe of discourse, $U=\{u\}$, then $Poss\{X=u\} = \mu_R(u)$, where μ_R is the membership function of R, and Π_X is the possibility distribution of X, that is, the fuzzy set of its possible values. In schematic form:

$$X \text{ is } R \quad \rightarrow \Pi_X = R$$
$$\rightarrow Poss\{X=u\} = \mu_R(u)$$

Similarly, when R takes the value c, the constraint is *conjunctive*. In the case,

X isc R

means that if the grade of membership of u in R is μ, then $X = u$ has truth value μ. For example, a canonical form of the proposition

p= *John is proficient in English, French and German*

may be expressed as

Proficiency(John) isc (1/English + 0.7/French + 0.6/German)

in which 1.0, 0.7 and 0.6 represent, respectively, the truth values of the propositions *John is proficient in English*, *John is proficient in French* and *John is proficient in German.*

When $r = p$, the constraint is *probabilistic*. In this case,

X isp r

means that R is the probability distribution of X. For example

X isp $N(m,\sigma^2)$

means that X is normally distributed with mean m and variance σ^2. Similarly,

X isp (0.2\a + 0.5\b + 0.3\c)

means that X is a random variable which takes the values, a, b and c with respective probabilities 0.2, 0.5 and 0.3.

The constraint

X isu R

is an abbreviation for

usually(X is R)

which in turn means that

Prob{X is R} is *usually*

In this expression X is R is a fuzzy event and *usually* is its fuzzy probability, that is, the possibility distribution of its crisp probability.

The constraint

X isrs P

is a random set constraint. This constraint is a combination of probabilistic and possibilistic constraints. More specifically, in a schematic form, it is expressed as

$$\frac{\begin{array}{c} X \text{ isp } P \\ (X,Y) \text{ is } Q \end{array}}{Y \text{ isrs } R}$$

where Q is a joint possibilitistic constraint on X and Y, and R is a random set. It is of interest to note that the Dempster-Shafer theory of evidence is, in essence, a theory of random set constraints.

In computing with words, the starting point is a collection of propositions which play the role of premises. In most cases, the canonical forms of these propositions are constraints of the basic, disjunctive type. In a more general setting, the constraints are of the generalized type, implying that the explicitation of a proposition, p, may be represented as

$$p \rightarrow X \text{ isr } R$$

where X isr R is the canonical form of p.

As in the case of basic constraints, the canonical form of a proposition may be derived through the use of *test-score semantics*. In this context, the depth of p is, roughly, a measure of the effort that is needed to explicitate p, that is, to translate p into its canonical form. In this sense, the proposition X isr R is a surface constraint (depth=zero), with the depth of explicitation increasing in the downward direction (Fig. 4). Thus a proposition such as *Mary is young* is shallow, whereas a proposition *it is not very likely that there will be a substantial increase in the price of oil in the near future*, is not.

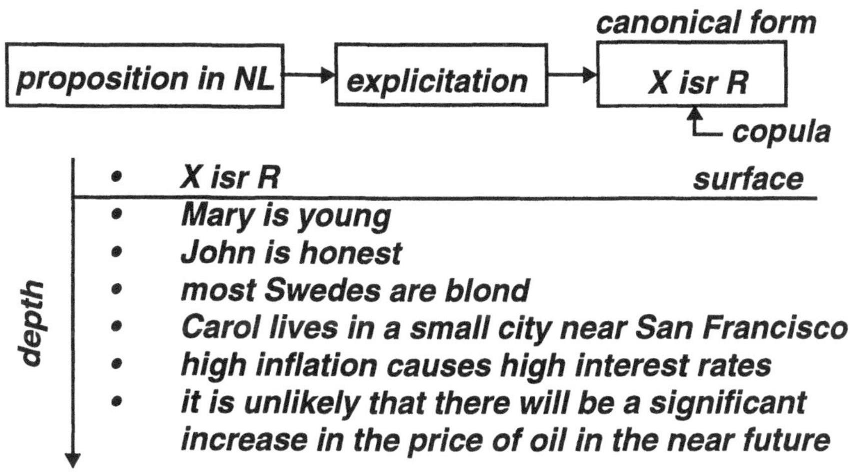

Figure 4. Depth of expliciation

Once the propositions in the initial data set are expressed in their canonical forms, the groundwork is laid for fuzzy constraint propagation. This is a basic part of CW which is discussed in the following section.

Fuzzy constraint propagation and the rules of inference in fuzzy logic

The rules governing fuzzy constraint propagation are, in effect, the rules of inference in fuzzy logic. In addition to these rules, it is helpful to have rules governing fuzzy constraint modification, The latter rules will be discussed at a later point in this section.

In a summarized form, the rules governing fuzzy constraint propagation are the following [A and B are fuzzy relations. Disjunction and conjunction are defined, respectively, as max and min, with the understanding that, more generally, they could be defined via *t*-norms and *s*-norms (Klir and Yuan 1995).]:

- *conjunctive rule 1*

$$\frac{\begin{array}{l} X \text{ is } A \\ X \text{ is } B \end{array}}{X \text{ is } A \cap B}$$

- *conjunctive rule 2* $(X \in U,\ Y \in B,\ A \subset U,\ B \subset V)$

$$\frac{\begin{array}{l} X \text{ is } A \\ Y \text{ is } B \end{array}}{(X, Y) \text{ is } A \times B}$$

- *disjunctive rule 1*

$$\frac{\begin{array}{l} X \text{ is } A \\ X \text{ is } B \end{array}}{X \text{ is } A \cup B}$$

- *disjunctive rule 2* $(A \subset U,\ B \subset V)$

$$\frac{\begin{array}{l} X \text{ is } A \\ Y \text{ is } B \end{array}}{(X, Y) \text{ is } A \times V \cup U \times B}$$

where $A \times V$ and $U \times B$ are cylindrical extensions of A and B, respectively.

- *conjunctive rule for isc*

$$\frac{\begin{array}{l} X \text{ isc } A \\ X \text{ isc } B \end{array}}{X \text{ isc } A \cup B}$$

- *disjunctive rule for isc*

$$\frac{X \text{ isc } A \quad \text{or} \quad X \text{ isc } B}{X \text{ isc } A \cap B}$$

- *projective rule*

$$\frac{(X,Y) \text{ is } A}{Y \text{ is proj}_v A}$$

where $\text{proj}_v = \sup_u A$,

- *surjective rule*

$$\frac{X \text{ is } A}{(X,Y) \text{ is } A \times V}$$

Derived rules

- *compositional rule*

$$\frac{\begin{array}{l} X \text{ is } A \\ (X,Y) \text{ is } B \end{array}}{Y \text{ is } A^\circ B}$$

where $A^\circ B$ denotes the composition of A and B.

- *extension principle* (mapping rule)

$$\frac{X \text{ is } A}{f(X) \text{ is } f(A)}$$

where $f\!: U \rightarrow V$, and $f(A)$ is defined by

$$\mu_{f(A)} = sup_{u \mid v = f(u)}\, \mu_A(u)$$

- *inverse mapping rule*

$$\frac{f(X) \text{ is } A}{X \text{ is } f^{-1}(A)}$$

where $\mu_{f^{-1}(A)}(u) = \mu_A(f(u))$,

- *generalized modus ponens*

$$\frac{\begin{array}{l} X \text{ is } A \\ \text{If } X \text{ is } B \text{ then } Y \text{ is } C \end{array}}{Y \text{ is } A \circ ((\neg B) \oplus C)}$$

where the bounded sum $\neg B \oplus C$ represents Łukasiewicz's definition of implication,

- *generalized extension principle*

$$\frac{f(X) \text{ is } A}{q(X) \text{ is } q(f^{-1}(A))}$$

where $\mu_q(v) = sup_{u \mid v = f(u)}\, \mu_A((q(u))$.

The generalized extension principle plays a pivotal role in fuzzy constraint propagation.

- *syllogistic rule* (Zadeh 1981)

$$\frac{\begin{array}{l} Q_1\ A\text{'s are } B\text{'s} \\ Q_2\ (A \text{ and } B)\text{'s are } C\text{'s} \end{array}}{(Q_1 \otimes Q_2)\ A\text{'s are } (B \text{ and } C)\text{'s}}$$

where Q_1 and Q_2 are fuzzy quantifiers; A, B, and C are fuzzy relations; and $Q_1 \otimes Q_2$ is the product of Q_1 and Q_2 in fuzzy arithmetic,

- *constraint modification rules* (Zadeh 1972,1979)

X is $mA \rightarrow X$ is $f(A)$

where m is a modifier such as *not*, *very*, *more or less*, etc. and $f(A)$ defines the way in which m modifies A. Specifically,

if m = *not* then $f(A) = A'$ (complement)
if m = *very* then $f(A) = {}^2A$ (left square)

where $\mu^2{}_A(u) = [\mu_A(u)]^2$. This rule is a convention and should not be construed as a realistic approximation to the way in which the modifier *very* functions in a natural language.

- *probability qualification rule* (Zadeh 1979)

$(X$ is $A)$ is $\Lambda \rightarrow P$ is Λ

where X is a random variable taking values in U with probability density $p(u)$; Λ is a linguistic probability expressed in words like *likely*, *not very likely*, etc.; and P is the probability of the fuzzy event X is A, expressed as

$$P = \int_U \mu_A(u)p(u)du$$

The primary purpose of this summary is to underscore the coincidence of the principal rules governing fuzzy constraint propagation with the principal values of inference in fuzzy logic. Of necessity, the summary is not complete and there are many specialized rules which are not included. Furthermore, most of the rules in the summary apply to constraints which are of the basic, disjunctive type. Further development of the rules governing fuzzy constraint propagation will require an extension of the rules of inference to generalized constraints.

As was alluded to in the summary, the principal rule governing constraint propagation is the generalized extension principle which in a schematic form may be represented as

$$\frac{f(X_1,\ldots,X_n) \text{ is } A}{q(X_1,\ldots,X_n) \text{ is } q(f^{1}(A))}$$

In this expression, $X_1,\ldots,X_n$ are database variables; the term above the line represents the constraint induced by the IDS; and the term below the line is the TDS expressed as a constraint on the query $q(X_1,\ldots,X_n)$. In the latter constraint, by $f^1(A)$ we denote the preimage of the fuzzy relation A under the mapping f: $U \rightarrow V$,, where A is a fuzzy subset of V and U is the domain of $f(X_1,\ldots,X_n)$.

Expressed in terms of the membership functions of A and $q(f^1(A))$, the generalized extension principle reduces the derivation of the TDS to the solution of the constrained maximization problem

$$\mu_{q(X_1,\ldots,X_n)}(v) = \sup_{(u_1,\ldots,u_n)}(\mu_A(f(u_1,\ldots,u_n)))$$

in which $u_1,\ldots,u_n$ are constrained by

$$v = q(u_1,\ldots,u_n)$$

The generalized extension principle is simpler than it appears. An illustration of its use is provided by the following example.

The IDS is:

most Swedes are tall

The query is:

What is the average height of Swedes?

The explanatory database consists of a population of N Swedes, $Name_1, \ldots, Name_N$. The database variables are $h_1, \ldots, h_N$, where h_i is the height of $Name_i$, and the grade of membership of $Name_i$ in *tall* is $\mu_{tall}(h_i)$, $i = 1, \ldots, n$.

The proportion of Swedes who are tall is given by

$$\tfrac{1}{N}\textstyle\sum_{i=1}^{N}\mu_{tall}(h_i)$$

from which it follows that the constraint on the database variables induced by the IDS is

$$\tfrac{1}{N}\textstyle\sum_{i=1}^{N}\mu_{tall}(h_i) \text{ is } \textit{most}$$

In terms of the database variables, $h_1, \ldots, h_N$, the average height of Swedes is given by

$$h_{ave} = \tfrac{1}{N}\textstyle\sum_{i=1}^{N} h_i$$

Since the IDS is a fuzzy proposition, h_{ave} is a fuzzy set whose determination reduces to the constrained maximization problem

$$\mu_{h_{ave}}(v) = \sup_{h_1,\ldots,h_N}(\mu_{most}(\tfrac{1}{N}\textstyle\sum_{i=1}^{N}\mu_{tall}(h_i)))$$

subject to the constraint

$$v = \tfrac{1}{N}\textstyle\sum_{i=1}^{N} h_i$$

It is possible that approximate solutions to problems of this type might be obtainable through the use of genetic-algorithm-based methods.

A key point which is brought out by this example and the preceding discussion is that explicitation and constraint propagation play pivotal roles in CW. What is important to recognize is that there is a great deal of computing with numbers in CW which takes place behind a curtain, unseen by the user. Thus, what matters is that in CW the IDS is allowed to be expressed in a natural language. No other methodology offers this facility. As an illustration of this point, consider the following problem.

A box contains ten balls of various sizes of which several are large and a few are small. What is the probability that a ball drawn at random is neither large nor small?

To be able to answer this question it is necessary to be able to define the meanings of *large, small, several large balls* and *neither large nor small.* This is a problem in semantics which falls outside of probability theory, neurocomputing and other methodologies.

There are two observations which are in order. First, in using fuzzy constraint propagation rules in computing with words, application of the extension principle reduces, in general, to the solution of a nonlinear program. What we need - and do not have at present - are approximate methods of solving such programs which are capable of exploiting the tolerance for imprecision. Without such methods, the cost of solutions may be excessive in relation to the imprecision which is intrinsic in the use of words. In this connection, an intriguing possibility is to use genetic-algorithms-based methods to arrive at approximate solutions to constrained maximization problems.

Second, given a collection of premises expressed in a natural language, we can in principle express them in their canonical forms and thereby explicitate the implicit fuzzy constraints. For this purpose, we have to employ test-score semantics. However, in test-score semantics we do not have at present effective algorithms for the derivation of canonical forms without human intervention. This is a problem that remains to be addressed.

Concluding remarks

The main purpose of this note is to draw attention to the centrality of the role of fuzzy logic in computing with words and vice-versa.

In coming years, computing with words is likely to emerge as a major field in its own right. In a reversal of long-standing attitudes, the use of words in place of numbers is destined to gain respectability. This is certain to happen because it is becoming abundantly clear that in dealing with real-world problems there is much to be gained by exploiting the tolerance for imprecision. In the final analysis, it is the exploitation of the tolerance for imprecision that is the prime motivation for CW. The role model for CW is the human mind.

References and Related Publications

Berenji, H.R (1994) "Fuzzy Reinforcement Learning and Dynamic Programming," in *Fuzzy Logic in Artificial Intelligence, Proc. IJCAI '93 Workshop*, ed. A.L. Ralescu, Berlin: Springer-Verlag, pp. 1-9.

Black, M. (1963), "Reasoning with Loose Concepts," *Dialog* 2, pp. 1-12.

Bosch, P. (1978), "Vagueness, Ambiguity and All the Rest," in *Sprachstruktur, Individuum und Gesselschaft*, eds. M. Van de Velde and W. Vandeweghe, Tubingen: Niemeyer.

Bowen, J., Lai, R., and Bahler D. (1992), "Fuzzy Semantics and Fuzzy Constraint Networks", *Proc. of the 1st IEEE Conf. on Fuzzy Systems*, San Francisco, pp. 1009-1016.

Bowen, J., Lai, R., and Bahler D. (1992), "Lexical Imprecision in Fuzzy Constraint Networks", *Proc. of the National Conf. on Artificial Intelligence*, pp. 616-620.

Cresswell, M.J. (1973), *Logic and Languages*, London: Methuen.

Dubois, D., Fargier, H., and Prade H. (1994), "Propagation and Satisfaction of Flexible Constraints", in *Fuzzy Sets, Neural Networks, and Soft Computing*, eds. R.R. Yager, L.A. Zadeh, New York: Von Nostrand Reinhold, pp. 166-187.

Dubois, D., Fargier, H., and Prade H. "Possibility Theory in Constraint Satisfaction Problems: Handling Priority, Preference and Uncertainty", to appear in *Applied Intelligence Journal.*

Dubois, D., Fargier, H., and Prade H. (1993), "The Calculus of Fuzzy Restrictions as a Basis for Flexible Constraint Satisfaction," *Proc. of the 2nd IEEE Int. Conf. on Fuzzy Systems*, San Francisco, pp. 1131-1136.

Freuder, E.C. and Snow P. (1990), "Improved Relaxation and Search Methods for Approximate Constraint Satisfaction with a Maximin Criterion", *Proc. of the 8th Biennial Conf. on the Canadian Society for Computational Studies of Intelligence*, Ontario, pp. 227-230.

Goguen, J.A. (1969), "The Logic of Inexact Concepts," *Synthese 19*, pp. 325-373.

Hobbs, J.R. (1978), "Making Computation Sense of Montague's Intensional Logic," *Artificial Intelligence 9*, pp. 287-306.

Katai, O., Matsubara, S., Masuichi, H., Ida, M., et. al. (1992), "Synergetic Computation for Constraint Satisfaction Problems Involving Continuous and Fuzzy Variables by Using Occam," in *Transputer/Occam, Proc. of the 4th Transputer/Occam Int. Conf.*, eds. S. Noguchi and H. Umeo, Amsterdam: IOS Press, pp. 146-160.

Kaufmann, A. and Gupta M.M. (1985), *Introduction to Fuzzy Arithmetic: Theory and Applications*, New York: Von Nostrand.

Klir, G. and Yuan, B. (1995), *Fuzzy Sets and Fuzzy Logic*, New Jersey: Prentice Hall.

Lano, K. (1991), "A Constraint-Based Fuzzy Inference System," in *EPIA 91, 5th Portuguese Conf. on Artificial Intelligence*, eds. P. Barahona, L.M. Pereira, and A. Porto, Berlin: Springer-Verlag, pp. 45-59.

Lodwick, W.A. (1990), "Analysis of Structure in Fuzzy Linear Programs," *Fuzzy Sets and Systems, 38(1)*, pp. 15-26.

Mamdani, E.H. and Gaines, B.R. (1981), Eds., *Fuzzy Reasoning and its Applications*, London.

Mares, M. (1994), *Computation Over Fuzzy Quantities*, Boca Raton: CRC Press.

Novak, V (1991), "Fuzzy Logic, Fuzzy Sets, and Natural Languages," *Int. J. of General Systems 20(1)*, pp. 83-97.

Novak, V., Ramik, M., Cerny, M., and Nekola, J. (1992), Eds., *Fuzzy Approach to Reasoning and Decision-Making*, Boston: Kluwer.

Oshan, M.S., Saad, O.M., and Hassan, A.G. (1995), "On the Solution of Fuzzy Multiobjective Integer Linear Programming Problems with a Parametric Study," *Advances in Modelling & Analysis A, 24(2)*, pp. 49-64.

Partee, B. (1976), *Montague Grammar*, New York: Academic Press.

Qi G. and Friedrich, G. (1992), "Extending Constraint Satisfaction Problem Solving in Structural Design," in *Industrial and Engineering Applications of Artificial Intelligence and Expert Systems, 5th Int. Conf., IEA/AIE-92*, eds. F. Belli and F.J. Radermacher, Berlin: Springer-Verlag, pp. 341-350.

Rosenfeld, A., Hummel, R.A., and Zucker, S.W. (1976), "Scene Labeling by Relaxation Operations," *IEEE Trans. on Systems, Man and Cybernetics, 6*, pp. 420-433.

Sakawa, M., Sawada, K., and Inuiguchi, M. (1995), "A Fuzzy Satisficing Method for Large-Scale Linear Programming Problems with Block Angular Structure," *European Journal of Operational Research, 81(2)*, pp. 399-409.

Tong S.C., (1994), "Interval Number and Fuzzy Number Linear Programming," *Advances in Modelling & Analysis A, 20(2)*, pp. 51-56.

Yager R.R. (1989), "Some extensions of constraint propagation of label sets," *Int. J. of Approximate Reasoning, 3*, pp. 417-435.

Zadeh, L.A. (1972), "A fuzzy-set-theoretic interpretation of linguistic hedges," *J. of Cybernetics 2*, pp. 4-34.

Zadeh, L.A. (1973), "Outline of a New Approach to the Analysis of Complex System and Decision Processes," *IEEE Trans. on Systems, Man, and Cybernetics*, SMC-3, pp.28-44.

Zadeh, L.A. (1974), "On the Analysis of Large Scale Systems," Systems Approaches and Environment Problems, ed. H. Gottinger, Gottingen: Vandenhoeck and Ruprecht, pp. 23-37.

Zadeh, L.A. (1975), "Calculus of Fuzzy Restrictions," in *Fuzzy Sets and Their Applications to Cognitive and Decision Processes*, eds. L.A. Zadeh, K.S. Fu, M. Shimura, New York: Academic Press, pp. 1-39.

Zadeh, L.A. (1978), "PRUF - a Meaning Representation Language for Natural Languages," *Int. J. Man-Machines Studies*, 10, pp. 395-460.

Zadeh, L.A. (1979), "Fuzzy Sets and Information Granularity," in *Advances in Fuzzy Set Theory and Applications*, eds. M. Gupta, R.Ragade and R. Yager, Amsterdam: North-Holland, pp. 3-18.

Zadeh, L.A. (1979), "A Theory of Approximate Reasoning," *Machine Intelligence 9*, eds. J. Hayes, D. Michie, and L.I. Mikulich, New York: Halstead Press, pp. 149-194.

Zadeh, L.A. (1981), "Test-Score Semantics for Natural Languages and Meaning Representation via PRUF," *Empirical Semantics*, ed. B. Rieger, W. Germany: Brockmeyer, pp. 281-349. Also *Technical Report Memorandum 246*, AI Center, SRI International, Menlo Park, CA.

Zadeh, L.A. (1986), "Outline of a Computational Approach to Meaning and Knowledge Representation Based on a Concept of a Generalized Assignment Statement," Proc. of the Int. Seminar on Artificial Intelligence and Man-Machine Systems, eds. M. Thoma and A. Wyner, Heidelberg: Springer-Verlag, pp. 198-211.

Zadeh, L.A. (1994), "Fuzzy Logic, Neural Networks and Soft Computing," *Communications of the ACM*, 37(3), pp. 77-84.

PERFORMING APPROXIMATE REASONING WITH WORDS?

Didier DUBOIS* – Laurent FOULLOY** – Sylvie GALICHET**
Henri PRADE*

* IRIT
Université Paul Sabatier
118 route de Narbonne
31062 Toulouse Cedex 04, France
Email: {dubois@irit.fr
prade@irit.fr

** LAMII – CESALP
Université de Savoie
41 avenue de la Plaine, B.P. 806
74016 Annecy Cedex, France
Email: {foulloy@univ-savoie.fr
galichet@univ-savoie.fr

Abstract: When defining a term set as a finite family of fuzzy sets on a universe of discourse, two description levels are introduced: the level of the referential and the level corresponding to the symbolic term set. Depending on the level which is privileged, two different views of reasoning with fuzzy set labels can be thought of: Zadeh's view of approximate reasoning which takes place at the level of the universe of discourse, and another view where fuzzy sets are manipulated in a more symbolic way at the term set level, which would corresponds to the idea of computing with words recently advocated by Zadeh also. The two views are contrasted in this paper, and their differences are laid bare.

1 - INTRODUCTION

For a long time, fuzzy sets have been advocated by Zadeh (1973) as a methodology for interfacing numerical data about the world (which are often imprecisely perceived), with linguistic categories or classes used in reasoning. In particular, it is the case in fuzzy rules or fuzzy algorithms where words are interpreted as the labels of fuzzy sets. When developing his approach to approximate reasoning, Zadeh (1979) was already separating the combination/projection machinery acting at the levels of the fuzzy set membership functions, from the knowledge representation and linguistic approximation steps which respectively turn the linguistic input information into possibility distributions and restate the obtained conclusions into a prescribed vocabulary understandable by the user. See Figure 1. The fuzzy set framework should supply the right tools for mixing a symbolic treatment to be performed at the level of the linguistic labels with facilities for permanently interfacing them with their fuzzy set semantics along the reasoning process. Indeed, fuzzy sets restore gradual transitions between categories on continuous universes, which would be lost if the interface between labels and data were provided by crisp sets only.

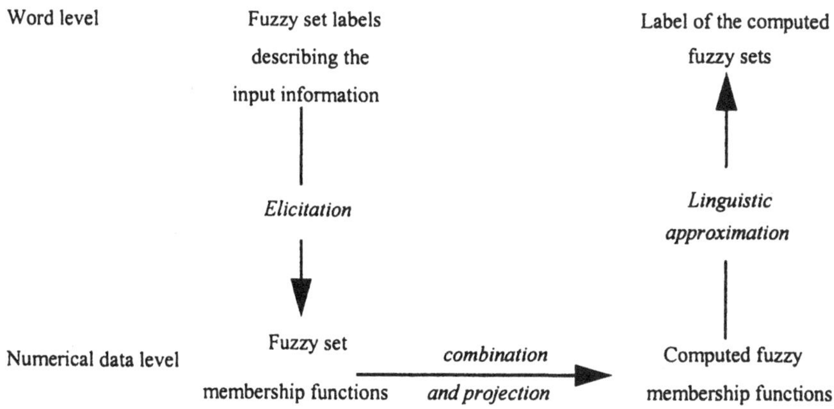

Figure 1 : Approximate Reasoning.

Then symbolic reasoning handled at the level of the fuzzy set labels may be viewed as corresponding to the idea of computing with words recently emphasized by Zadeh (1996). As the expression suggests, 'computing with words' is a methodology in which words are used in place of numbers for computing and reasoning. As pointed out by Zadeh (1996), there are two major imperatives for computing with words:

> «*First, computing with words is a necessity when the available information is too imprecise to justify the use of numbers, and second, when there is a tolerance for imprecision which can be exploited to achieve tractability, robustness, low solution cost, and better report with reality. Exploitation of the tolerance for imprecision is an issue of central importance in computing with words.*»

A key of computing with words is that it involves a fusion of symbolic processing and computation with fuzzy variables. Figure 2 shows an attempt at illustrating the Computer with Words paradigm and contrasting it with the Approximate Reasoning schema of Figure 1. The labelling process of input data may be provided by means of fuzzy sensors (Mauris et al., 1994).

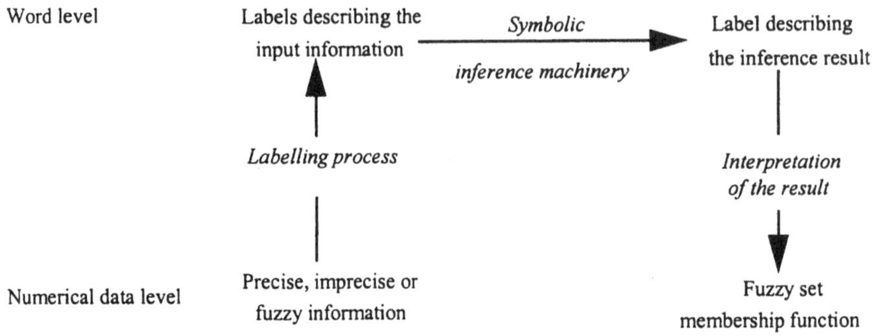

Figure 2 : Computing with Words.

The coexistence of these two views thus suggests two possible approaches to approximate reasoning, one directly performed at the symbolic level (see, e.g., Foulloy and Galichet (1994)) and another at the level of the universe of discourse as in Zadeh (1979)'s approach. This naturally raises the issues of the comparison and the compatibility of the two approaches. This is the topic of the paper, which is organized in the following way. The next section gives the necessary background and also relates the representation of fuzzy sets in terms of a basic vocabulary to the idea of fuzzy rough sets (Dubois and Prade, 1992b). Section 3 discusses the two approaches to reasoning with fuzzy sets. The first one for conjunction-based rules is emphasized in Section 4 while the second one for rules based on Dienes implication is described in Section 5. Chaining of rule-bases is discussed in Section 6. The paper is a revised and expanded version of a previous paper by the authors (Dubois et al., 1997).

2 - APPROXIMATE DESCRIPTORS OF A FUZZY SET

In a paper not often mentioned, Zadeh (1971) has viewed a language L as a fuzzy binary relation from a set of terms T to a universe of discourse U. Namely, a term t is associated with the fuzzy set $M(t)$ of elements in U which represents the meaning of the term t, and conversely, an element u in U is associated with a fuzzy set $D(u)$ of terms in T with which u is compatible. $D(u)$ is called a descriptor by Zadeh (1971). This approach emphasizes a dual view of fuzzy sets both as represented by membership functions on a universe of discourse (which is the most commonly used view), and as inducing a descriptor of each element of the universe of discourse expressed as a weighted set of labels. Following this second interpretation, some authors, e.g., Willaeys and Malvache (1981), have more generally approximated any (fuzzy) set on a universe U by a weighted set of labels belonging to a basic vocabulary covering the universe of discourse.

Let U be a universe of discourse. Let $\mathcal{F}(U)$ denote the set of fuzzy sets in U.

Let $T = \{t_1, \ldots, t_n\}$ be a set of terms or labels whose meaning in U is defined by the membership functions $\mu_{M(t_i)}$ for $i = 1, n$. For instance, U is a universe of sizes and $T = \{\text{very\_small, small, medium, large, very\_large}\}$. Thus, the descriptor of an element $u \in U$, by means of terms in T, can be obtained by the mapping D from U to $\mathcal{F}(T)$, where $\mathcal{F}(T)$ is the set of all fuzzy subsets in T, defined by

$$D(u) = \bigcup_{i=1,\, n} \mu_{M(t_i)}(u) \,/\, t_i \tag{1}$$

where $\mu_{M(t_i)}(u) = \mu_L(u, t_i) = \mu_{D(u)}(t_i)$ and L is the fuzzy relation which relates the element u to the term t_i. In Eq. (1) we are using Zadeh's notation of a fuzzy set as a union of weighted singletons where the weight is before the '/'.

Now, let us consider a fuzzy set A of U defined by a membership function μ_A from U to $[0,1]$. How to approximate A in terms of the labels in T which constitute the basic vocabulary?

An approximate descriptor is a mapping from $\mathcal{F}(U)$ to $\mathcal{F}(T)$. A first approximate description of A, $D^+(A)$, called "upper approximation", can be obtained by computing the consistency of A with each fuzzy set $M(t_i)$ on U, namely

$$\mu_{D^+(A)}(t_i) = \text{cons}(A, M(t_i)) = \sup_{u \in U} \min(\mu_A(u), \mu_{M(t_i)}(u)) \tag{2}$$

i.e.,

$$D^+(A) = \bigcup_{i=1,\, n} \text{cons}(A, M(t_i)) \,/\, t_i. \tag{3}$$

This descriptor, where A and $M(t_i)$ play symmetric roles in Eq. (2), is the one used by Willaeys and Malvache (1981), or more recently by Foulloy and Galichet (1994). $\mu_{D^+(A)}(t_i) = \text{cons}(A, M(t_i))$ is the degree of possibility that an element u of U compatible with A is among the elements of U covered by the term t_i. In other words, Eq. (2) estimates the extent to which A and $M(t_i)$ have a non-empty intersection.

We may also think of computing the degree of necessity, or certainty, of the same event, namely,

$$\text{inc}(A, M(t_i)) = \inf_{u \in U} \max(1 - \mu_A(u), \mu_{M(t_i)}(u)). \tag{4}$$

The quantity $\text{inc}(A, M(t_i))$ is a degree of inclusion of A into $M(t_i)$ such that inc(A, $M(t_i)$) = 1 if and only if support$A$ = $\{u, \mu_A(u) > 0\}$ is included in the core of $M(t_i)$, i.e., core$M(t_i) = \{u, \mu_{M(t_i)}(u) = 1\}$. The quantity inc($A$, $M(t_i)$) estimates our certainty that an ill-known value restricted by A is fully compatible with the term t_i. It induces another descriptor D^- (from $\mathcal{F}(U)$ to $\mathcal{F}(T)$) defined by

$$D^-(A) = \bigcup_{i=1,\, n} \mathrm{inc}(A, M(t_i)) \,/\, t_i, \tag{5}$$

i.e., $\mu_{D^-(A)}(t_i) = \mathrm{inc}(A, M(t_i))$. $D^-(A)$ is the lower image of A by the relation L defined on $U \times T$, while $D^+(A)$ is the upper image of A by L (see, e.g., (Dubois and Prade, 1992a)). $D^-(A)$ is the set of terms each of which is **certainly** an appropriate label for A, while $D^+(A)$ is the set of terms each of which is **possibly** an appropriate label for A. These descriptors have general properties :

i) When A reduces to a singleton $\{u_0\}$, we have inc(A, $M(t_i)$) = $\mu_{M(t_i)}(u_0)$ = cons(A, $M(t_i)$), and therefore:

$$D^-(A) = D(u_0) = D^+(A). \tag{6}$$

ii) If A is a normalized fuzzy set, we have the inequality:

$$\forall t_i,\ \mu_{D^-(A)}(t_i) \le \mu_{D^+(A)}(t_i). \tag{7}$$

Besides, the converse degree of inclusion inc($M(t_i)$, A) is also of interest. It corresponds to the fuzzy set of terms $D_*(A)$ which certainly entail A, namely

$$D_*(A) = \bigcup_{i=1,n} \mathrm{inc}(M(t_i), A) \,/\, t_i, \tag{8}$$

i.e., $\mu_{D_*(A)}(t_i) = \inf_{u \in U} \max(1 - \mu_{M(t_i)}(u), \mu_A(u))$. $D_*(A)$ is the lower inverse image of A by the relation L (Dubois and Prade, 1992a). $D_*(A)$ is called lower approximation of A. Note that, due to the symmetry of $D^+(A)$, the upper image and upper inverse image coincide.

The pair ($D_*(A)$, $D^+(A)$) can be viewed as the fuzzy extension of a rough set (Dubois and Prade, 1992b) where the fuzzy set A of U is approximated by means of terms t_i. $D_*(A)$ is a lower approximation in the sense that it gathers all the t_i's more or less included in A, while $D^+(A)$ is an upper approximation that gathers all the t_i's whose meaning somewhat overlaps with A. Note that $\forall t_i$, $\mu_{D*(A)}(t_i) \leq \mu_{D^+(A)}(t_i)$, i.e., $D*(A) \subseteq D^+(A)$. In classical rough set theory, the family of sets, used for the approximation, form an ordinary partition of U. Here nothing has been assumed on the t_i's, although the $M(t_i)$'s are supposed to cover U in practice, and even to make a fuzzy partition of U in a sense to be defined. It can be easily seen that we have the following inclusions, which express the idea of lower and upper approximation,

$$\forall A, \bigcup_{i:\text{inc}(M(t_i),A)=1} M(t_i) \subseteq \text{core}(A) \subseteq \text{support}(A) \subseteq \bigcup_{i:\text{cons}(M(t_i),A)>0} M(t_i) \quad (9)$$

provided that $\forall\, u \in U, \exists\, t_i \in T, \mu_{M(t_i)}(u) = 1$; this latter requirement, which expresses a strong coverage condition, is necessary in order to have the rightest inclusion. In (Dubois and Prade, 1992b), it has been suggested to use $D*(A)$ and $D^+(A)$, for providing linguistic approximations of a fuzzy set A in terms of a given vocabulary. The idea is:

i) to approximate linguistically the numerical values of inc($M(t_i)$, A) on a scale including levels like "**rather certainly**", "**almost certainly**", "**certainly**", and those of cons($M(t_i)$, A) on a scale with levels such as "**not very possibly**", "**rather possibly**", "**possibly**", and

ii) to describe A by directly interpreting $D^+(A)$ (or $D*(A)$), and thus getting a description like "**not very possibly very_small or possibly small**".

Note that it is impossible to have inc(A, $M(t_i)$) = 1 = inc($M(t_i)$, A) (except if $A = M(t_i)$ is an ordinary set), since it means support(A) $\subseteq$ core($M(t_i)$) and support($M(t_i)$) $\subseteq$ core(A) which leads to an obvious contradiction with genuine fuzzy sets. However, we can have inc(A, $M(t_i)$) > 0 and inc($M(t_i)$, A) > 0, since it only means that core(A) $\subseteq$ support($M(t_i)$) and core($M(t_i)$) $\subseteq$ support(A).

A duality property holds, saying that the lower approximation of a fuzzy set is the complement of the upper approximation of its complement :

$$\text{inc}(M(t_i), A) = 1 - \text{cons}(M(t_i), \overline{A}) \quad (10)$$

inducing the fuzzy set equality:

$$\overline{D*(A)} = D^+(\overline{A}). \quad (11)$$

Remark: When defining inc(A, $M(t_i)$) (and inc($M(t_i)$, A)) we have been using Dienes implication $a \to b = \max(1 - a, b)$. Other inclusion degrees of the form

$$\text{inc}_{\to}(A, M(t_i)) = \inf_{u \in U} \mu_A(u) \to \mu_{M(t_i)}(u) \tag{12}$$

could be used. Using a residuated implication as Gödel implication for instance ($a \to b = 1$ if $a \leq b$ and $a \to b = b$ if $a > b$), we have $\text{inc}_{\to}(A, M(t_i)) = 1$ if and only if $\forall u$, $\mu_A(u) \leq \mu_{M(t_i)}(u)$, which expresses an inclusion weaker than the one induced by Dienes implication, and which agrees with the semantical entailment "X is $A \Rightarrow X$ is $M(t_i)$" (Zadeh, 1979). See also Dubois and Prade (1992b) on the use of residuated implications for defining fuzzy rough sets. Clearly, the advantage of a S-implication, like Dienes', is to have the duality property (11).

3 - THE TWO LEVELS OF REPRESENTATION FOR FUZZY RULES AND THE TWO REASONING VIEWS

Let U and V be two universes of discourse, $S = \{s_1, \ldots, s_m\}$ and $T = \{t_1, \ldots, t_n\}$ be two sets of terms whose meanings are defined on U and V respectively. In the following, since we are dealing with four sets, indices will be added to the fuzzy meanings and descriptors with respect to the universe on which they are defined. Namely $M_U(s_i)$ and $M_V(t_j)$ are fuzzy sets of U and V respectively. Let us assume that we have a set of rules of the form

"if X is s_i then Y is $t_{f(i)}$" for $i = 1, m$.

Note that we assume a "complete" description of the relation between X and Y in terms of the available vocabulary. Namely, we assume that for each $s_i \in S$, we know the associated label $t_{f(i)}$ for Y when 'X is s_i' and we also assume that $t_{f(i)} \in T$. We also assume, without lack of generality, that f is onto, i.e., that $\forall\ t_j \in T$, $\exists i$, $f(i) = j$. Such a situation is common, in particular with fuzzy control rules.

Obviously these rules define a fuzzy relation which can be interpreted in two ways.

i) X and Y pertain to numerical values u and v. In this case, each rule links the meaning of the linguistic term s_i to the meaning of the linguistic term $t_{f(i)}$. Therefore each rule i is represented by a fuzzy relation on $U \times V$ of the form

$$\mu_{R(i)}(u,v) = \mu_{M_U(s_i)}(u) * \mu_{M_V(t_{f(i)})}(v)$$

where * can be a fuzzy conjunction (i.e., a t-norm), or a fuzzy implication. The set of rules defines a fuzzy relation R on the Cartesian product $U \times V$. It is obtained by aggregating the rules by max operation for a conjunctive representation, and by min operation when using a fuzzy implication; see, e.g., Dubois and Prade (1991). Depending on the chosen interpretation for the rules, we may have $R = R_{\mathrm{T}}$ or $R = R_{\rightarrow}$, with

$$R_{\mathrm{T}} = \bigcup_{i=1,m} M_U(s_i) \mathrm{~T~} M_V(t_{f(i)}) \tag{13}$$

$$R_{\rightarrow} = \bigcap_{i=1,m} M_U(s_i) \rightarrow M_V(t_{f(i)}) \tag{14}$$

where T is a conjunction operation, $\rightarrow$ an implication (and $\mu_{F\mathrm{T}G} = \mu_F \mathrm{~T~} \mu_G$, $\mu_{F\rightarrow G} = \mu_F \rightarrow \mu_G$), and where $\bigcup_i$ and $\bigcap_i$ stand for max- and min-based disjunction and conjunction respectively. This will be referred to as the numerical representation of the rules.

ii) X and Y are variables whose possible values are the terms s_i and t_j themselves. It means that a rule links two terms of this kind. In this case, the set of rules defines a relation r on the Cartesian product $S \times T$, as follows

$\mu_r(s,t) = 1$ iff $\exists i$, $s = s_i$, $t = t_{f(i)}$, i.e., "if X is s_i then Y is $t_{f(i)}$" is one of the rules(15)

$\mu_r(s,t) = 0$ otherwise.

Note that r is a crisp relation (but could be a fuzzy one when considering weighted rules). This will be called the symbolic (or linguistic) representation of the rules.

The problem addressed in this paper is the following: "Given a set of fuzzy rules and given an imprecise/fuzzy input, what can be said, using a prescribed set of linguistic terms, about the image of an imprecise input"?

Example: Let S = {**small, normal, big**} and T = {**slow, medium, fast**}. Assume that the set of rules is

if size is **small** then speed is **fast**
if size is **normal** then speed is **medium**
if size is **big** then speed is **slow**

The meanings of the terms $s_i \in S$ and $t_j \in T$ of the example are given in Figure 3.

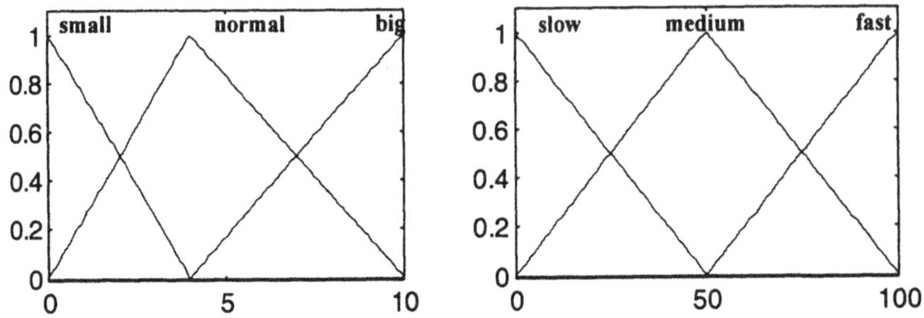

Figure 3 : Fuzzy meanings.

Then, the problem is the following: knowing that the size is about 6m, which is represented by the possibility distribution given in Figure 4, what can be said about the speed using the terms $t_j \in T$?

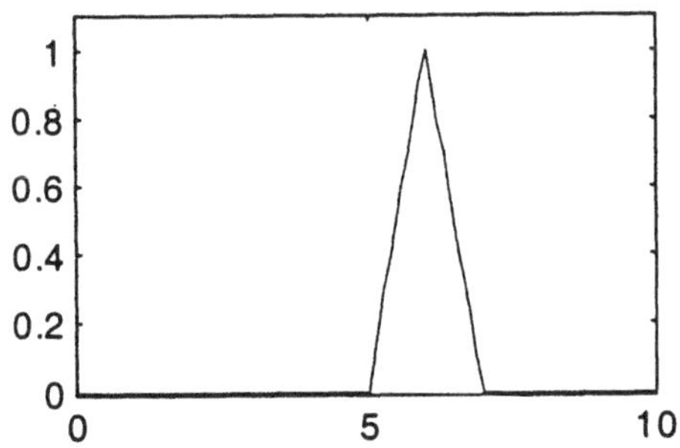

Figure 4 : Fuzzy input.

As we are going to see, such a problem can be approached in two ways, as pointed out by Foulloy and Galichet (1994): one based on the numerical representation of the rules, the other on the symbolic representation. Let A denote the fuzzy input.

i) The first one consists in inferring the image of $A \in \mathcal{F}(U)$ from the numerical representation of the rules. It leads to compute the image $B = A \circ R$ of A via R, where $B \in \mathcal{F}(V)$, where $B = A \circ R$ is the sup-min composition

$$\mu_B(v) = \sup_{u \in U} \min(\mu_A(u), \mu_R(u, v)) \tag{16}$$

and R is a fuzzy relation on $U \times V$ defined from the set of rules. Then, once μ_B is computed, we may try to approximate B linguistically in terms of the labels in T, that is $b' = D_T(B) \in \mathcal{F}(T)$, thus leading to the following inference schema,

$$\mathcal{F}(U) \xrightarrow{B = A \circ R} \mathcal{F}(V) \xrightarrow{b' = D_T(B)} \mathcal{F}(T) \quad . \tag{17}$$

ii) The second solution consists in first approximating A linguistically with the labels in S using some approximator D_S, that is $a = D_S(A) \in \mathcal{F}(S)$. Then, the image of a is computed using the symbolic representation r of the rules, that is $b = r \circ a$, thus leading to the following inference schema

$$\mathcal{F}(U) \xrightarrow{a = D_S(A)} \mathcal{F}(S) \xrightarrow{b = a \circ r} \mathcal{F}(T)$$

$$\text{with } \mu_b(t) = \max_{s \in S} \min(\mu_a(s), \mu_r(s,t)) \tag{18}$$

or $\mu_b(t) = \max_{s \in r^{-1}(t)} \mu_a(s)$, with $r^{-1}(t) = \{s \,/\, \mu_r(s,t) = 1\}$, then

$$\mu_b(t) = \max_{i \mid t_{f(i)}=t} \mu_a(s_i) \tag{19}$$

which directly yields a fuzzy set of labels in T. From a computational point of view, this second approach is simpler.

The problem, see Figure 5, is now to provide some answers about the relationship between b and b' depending on the choice of the type of fuzzy descriptors D_S and D_T among the ones introduced in Section 2, namely D^+, D^-, D_*, and the type of fuzzy connectives used in the numerical representation of the rules. In the following, we first investigate the case where R is based on min (T = min in Eq. (13)) and the fuzzy descriptors are D_S^+ and D_T^+.

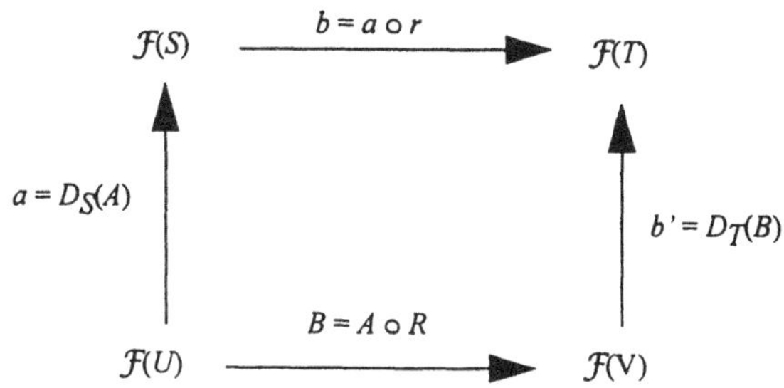

Figure 5 : Obtaining b and b'.

4 - CONJUNCTION-BASED REPRESENTATION OF THE RULES

Let us first consider that the set of rules are represented by Eq. (13) on the universe of discourse, i.e., that each rule is represented by means of a conjunction. Then, the following result holds

Proposition 1: $D_S^+(A) \circ r \subseteq D_T^+(A \circ R)$ for $R = R_{\min}$.

Proof: $B = A \circ R = A \circ \bigcup_{i=1,m} M_U(s_i) \cap M_V(t_{f(i)})$. hence it holds that $\mu_B(v) = \max_{i=1,m} \min(\text{cons}(A, M_U(s_i)), \mu_{M_V(t_{f(i)})}(v))$

Then

$$b' = D_T^+(B) = \bigcup_{j=1,n} \text{cons}(B, M_V(t_j)) / t_j$$

$$\begin{aligned}\text{cons}(B, M_V(t_j)) &= \sup_{v \in V} \min(\mu_{M_V(t_j)}(v), \max_{i=1,m} \min(\text{cons}(A, M_U(s_i)), \\ &\qquad \mu_{M_V(t_{f(i)})}(v))) \\ &= \max_{i=1,m} \min(\text{cons}(A, M_U(s_i)), \sup_{v \in V} \min(\mu_{M_V(t_j)}(v), \mu_{M_V(t_{f(i)})}(v))) \\ &= \max_{i=1,m} \min(\text{cons}(A, M_U(s_i)), \text{cons}(M_V(t_{f(i)}), M_V(t_j)))\end{aligned} \tag{20}$$

Since $\text{cons}(M_V(t_j), M_V(t_j)) = 1$, we obtain $\text{cons}(B, M_V(t_j)) \geq \max_{i \mid f(i)=j} \text{cons}(A, M_U(s_i))$ and therefore:

$$b' \supseteq \bigcup_{j=1,n} \max_{i \mid f(i)=j} \text{cons}(A, M_U(s_i)) / t_j . \tag{21}$$

Now using Eq. (19) we have

$$\begin{aligned} b = a \circ r = D_S^+(A) \circ r &= \bigcup_{j=1,n} \max_{i \mid t_{f(i)}=j} \mu_a(s_i) / t_j \\ &= \bigcup_{j=1,n} \max_{i \mid t_{f(i)}=j} \mu_{D^+(A)}(s_i) / t_j \\ &= \bigcup_{j=1,n} \max_{i \mid t_{f(i)}=j} \text{cons}(A, M_U(s_i)) / t_j. \end{aligned} \tag{22}$$

■

$D_T^+(B)$ is larger than b, since when describing B with the terms in T, we are taking into account the fact that a $M_V(t_j)$ may overlap with another $M_V(t_k)$, which expresses that if the term t_j applies, the term t_k possibly applies also. On the contrary, when working at the symbolic level, the terms t_j and t_k are considered as distinct. Thus, only the term t_j is obtained with a non-zero weight if a rule i such that $f(i) = j$ is fired by A (i.e., if $\text{cons}(A, M_U(s_i)) > 0$), but not the other t_k's, even if support($M_V(t_j)$) $\cap$ support($M_V(t_k)$) $\neq \emptyset$.

However, if we extend the mapping from T to V which associates $M_V(t_i)$ to t_i, to fuzzy sets of terms $\bigcup_j \mu_j / t_j$ by the formula

$$\mu_{M_V(\bigcup_{j=1,n} \mu_j / t_j)}(v) = \max_{j=1,n} \min(\mu_j, \mu_{M_V(t_j)}(v)) \tag{23}$$

we obtain the

Proposition 2: $M_V(b) = B$.

Proof: use (22) and (23), and get the very expression of $B = A \circ R$.

■

This proposition shows that the two inference schemas represented in Fig. 6 are equivalent.

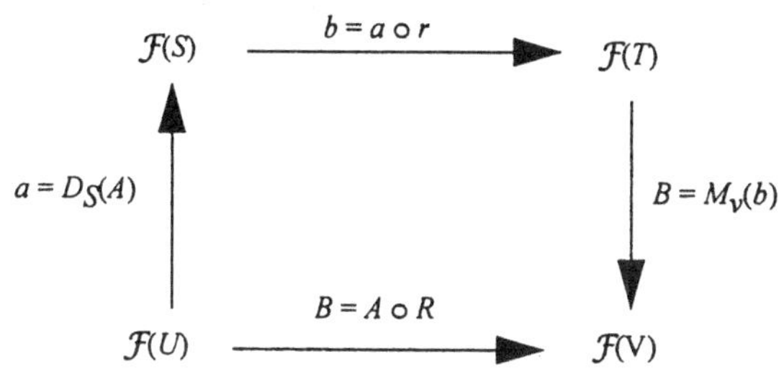

Figure 6 : The two inference schemas

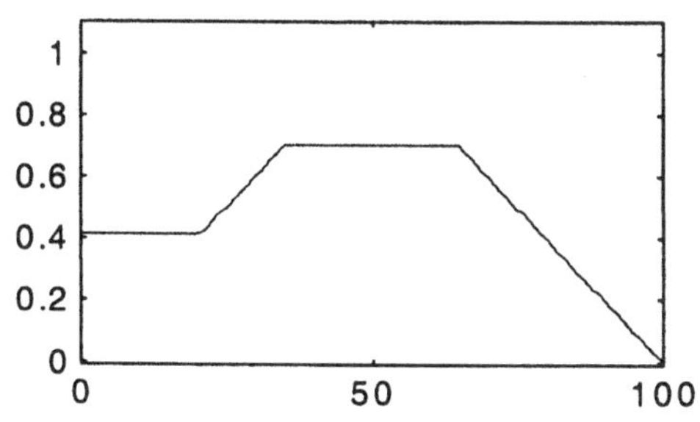

Figure 7 : Fuzzy set resulting from the conjunctive representation.

Example (continued): Using the numerical representation, we get B as pictured in Fig. 7 and then

$$b' = D_T^+(B) = \{0.5/\text{slow}, 0.7/\text{medium}, 0.5/\text{fast}\}. \quad (24)$$

Using the symbolic representation, we first compute

$$D_S^+(A) = \{0/\text{small}, 0.7/\text{normal}, 0.41/\text{big}\} \quad (25)$$

and then we get $b = \{0.41/\text{slow}, 0.7/\text{medium}, 0/\text{fast}\}$.

We can observe that $b \subset D_T^+(B)$.

■

5 - IMPLICATION-BASED REPRESENTATION OF THE RULES

Let us now interpret the rules as certainty rules, namely "the more X is $M_U(s_i)$, the more certain Y is $M_V(t_{f(i)})$", which leads (e.g., Dubois and Prade, 1991, 1996) to

$$\mu_R(u,v) = \min_{i=1,m} \max(1 - \mu_{M_U(s_i)}(u), \mu_{M_V(t_{f(i)})}(v)). \quad (26)$$

Then we have

$$\mu_B(v) = \sup_u \min(\mu_A(u), \min_i \max(1 - \mu_{M_U(s_i)}(u), \mu_{M_V(t_{f(i)})}(v)))$$
$$= \sup_u \min_i \max(\min(\mu_A(u), 1 - \mu_{M_U(s_i)}(u)), \min(\mu_A(u), \mu_{M_V(t_{f(i)})}(v))). \quad (27)$$

However there is no easy simplification of this formula that leads to a simple computation of the fuzzy subset B, in particular it is no longer possible to compute this subset from rule by rule inferences as in the conjunctive case. We present in this section three aproaches to deal with this case. We assume that A is normalized in the following.

5.1 - DISJUNCTIVE NORMAL FORM

One solution to overcome this problem is to transform the initial set of rules, where each rule is interpreted as a certainty rule, into a new set of rules where each rule is interpreted as a conjunctive one, that is to transform the set of rules into its disjunctive normal form.

For the sake of simplicity, let us denote $\overline{\sigma}_i = 1 - \mu_{M_U(s_i)}(u)$ and $\tau_{f(i)} = \mu_{M_V(t_{f(i)})}(v)$. Using the property of mutual distributivity of the operators max and min, Eq. (26) becomes:

$$\mu_R(u,v) = \max_{\substack{c_i \in \{\bar{\sigma}_i, \tau_{f(i)}\} \\ i = 1,m}} \min_{i = 1,m} c_i \tag{28}$$

Eq. (28) means that the original set of m implicative rules is transformed into a new set of 2^m conjonctive rules. The fuzzy relation R is the disjunction of 2^m elementary relations given by the conjunction of the c_i's. Since each c_i is taken in a set of two terms, the elementary relations are easily obtained as the leaves of a binary tree.

Let us apply it to our example where we have : S = {**small, normal, big**} and T = {**slow, medium, fast**}, therefore $m = n = 3$. According to the set of rules, we have the following definition for the mapping f:

$$f(1) = 3, f(2) = 2 \text{ and } f(3) = 1. \tag{29}$$

The binary tree generated by the terms is represented in Fig. 8.

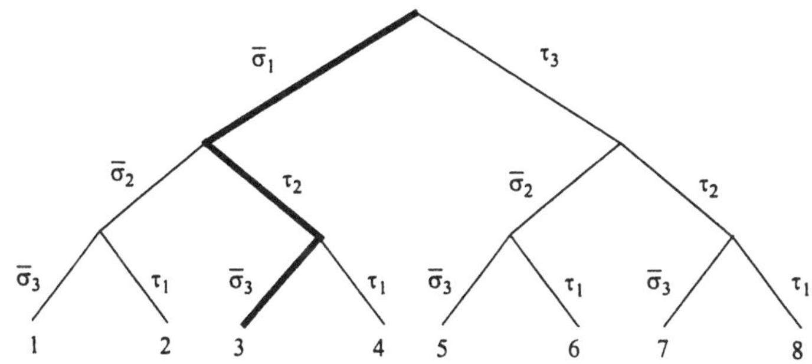

Figure 8 : Binary tree generated by the three rules.

The path in bold gives the elementary fuzzy relation R_3 (here, the index of the relation is the index of the leaf, numbered from left to right) :

$$\mu_{R_3}(u,v) = \min(\bar{\sigma}_1, \tau_2, \bar{\sigma}_3) = \min(1 - \mu_{M_U(\text{small})}(u), \mu_{M_V(\text{medium})}(v), 1 - \mu_{M_U(\text{big})}(u)). \tag{30}$$

Eq. (30) is also the expression of a fuzzy relation which would have been provided by a conjunctive representation of the following rule:

If size is **not small** and size is **not big** then speed is **medium,** (31)

The antecedent part of this rule is given by $\min(1 - \mu_{M_U(\text{small})}(u), 1 - \mu_{M_U(\text{big})}(u))$ which can be interpreted as the fuzzy meaning of the new linguistic term "**not small and not big**" which leads to the final writing of the rule:

If size is **not small and not big** then speed is **medium**. (32)

For the general point of view, the transformation of the initial set of rules into its disjunctive normal form has generated a new set S' of 2^m terms, associated with the antecedent parts of the new rules and a set T' of 2^n terms, associated with the conclusion parts. It should be noted that these two sets contain a specific symbol "**anything**" associated with a membership function always equal to one. In the example of Fig. 8, these terms are generated, respectively in T' and S', when writing the elementary relations R_1 and R_8.

if size is **small** then speed is **fast**
if size is **normal** then speed is **medium**
if size is **big** then speed is **slow**

if size is **not small and not normal and not big** then speed is **anything**
if size is **not small and not normal** then size is **slow**
if size is **not small and not big** then speed is **medium**
if size is **not small** then speed is **slow and medium**
if size is **not normal and not big** than speed is **fast**
if size is **not normal** then speed is **slow and fast**
if size is **not big** then speed is **medium and fast**
if size is **anything** then speed is **slow and medium and fast**

Figure 9 : New set of rules obtained by the transformation into the disjunctive normal form.

The global relation can be written under the following form :

$$R = \bigcup_{i=1,p} M_U(s'_i) \mathrm{T} M_V(t'_{f(i)}) \text{ with } p = 2^m. \tag{33}$$

Then we know (see Proposition 1) that

$$B = A \circ R = A \circ \bigcup_{i=1,p} M_U(s'_i) \mathrm{T} M_V(t'_{f(i)}) \tag{34}$$

Hence

$$\begin{aligned} \mu_B(v) &= \max_{i=1,p} \min(\text{cons}(A, M_U(s'_i)), \mu_{M_V(t'_{f(i)})}(v)) \\ &= \max_{i=1,p} \min(\alpha_i, \mu_{M_V(t'_{f(i)})}(v)). \end{aligned} \tag{35}$$

The transformation into the disjunctive normal form is interesting since we can now apply all the results of Section 4 and thus make the inference rule by rule either at the symbolic level or the numerical one. The result derived from our example is shown in Fig. 10.

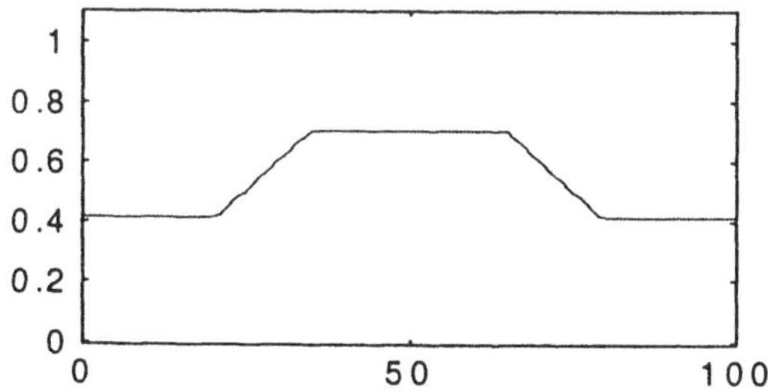

Figure 10 :Fuzzy set resulting of implicative representation.

The main inconvenience of this approach is the exponential growth of the number of rules. In fact, the number of rules can be drastically reduced when considering the number of useful rules. For instance, a rule which is not activated or which provides, for a given symbolic term, a result contained in the result obtained with another rule can be removed. This kind of information can be obtained, when considering the inference at the symbolic level, by the analysis of the fuzzy description of the input on the set of terms *S*'. However, computing the fuzzy description on *S*' still requires the computation of the fuzzy meanings of the new terms in *S*' from the fuzzy meanings of the terms in *S*.

In order to reduce the computation of these 2^m functions which are necessary to obtain an exact result, one can try to find an approximate result based on a simpler computation. As shown previously, all the fuzzy meanings of the terms in the new set *S*' are obtained as conjunctions of negations of the fuzzy meaning of the terms in *S*. Therefore, instead of computing the fuzzy descriptor on *S*', that is $D_{S'}{}^{+}(A) = \bigcup_{i=1,p} \alpha_i / s'_i$, using 2^m membership functions, one can think of computing upper and lower bounds from the fuzzy description on *S* as shown below.

Let us take a term s_i' in *S*' and, for the sake of simplicity and without loss of generality, let us consider that s_i' = **not** s_k **and not** s_l then

$$\alpha_i = \mu_{D_{S'}{}^{+}(A)}(s_i') = \sup_{u \in U} \min(\mu_A(u), \mu_{M_U(s_i')}(u))$$
$$= \sup_{u \in U} \min(\mu_A(u), \min(1-\mu_{M_U(s_k)}(u), 1-\mu_{M_U(s_l)}(u))). \quad (36)$$

We can first define an upper approximation since:

$$\mu_{D_{S'}^{+}(A)}(s_i') \le \min(\sup_{u \in U} \min(\mu_A(u), 1-\mu_{M_U(s_k)}(u)),$$
$$\sup_{u \in U} \min(\mu_A(u), 1-\mu_{M_U(s_l)}(u)))$$
$$= \min(1 - \inf_{u \in U} \max(1-\mu_A(u), \mu_{M_U(s_k)}(u)),$$
$$1 - \inf_{u \in U} \max(1-\mu_A(u), \mu_{M_U(s_l)}(u)))$$
$$= \min(1 - \mu_{D_S^{-}(A)}(s_k), 1 - \mu_{D_S^{-}(A)}(s_l))$$
$$= \min(1 - \mathrm{inc}(A, M_U(s_k)), 1 - \mathrm{inc}(A, M_U(s_l))). \tag{37}$$

Eq. (37) means that the upper fuzzy description of the imprecise input A on the set S' can be approximated by an upper bound obtained using the lower fuzzy description of the input A on the set S. This approximation replaces the computation of the 2^m membership functions by the computation of 2^m grade of membership which is much simpler. Let us notice also that Eq. (37) has an interpretation in terms of possibility measure, since we retrieve that the possibility of the intersection of two fuzzy events is not greater than the minimum of the possibility of each fuzzy event.

Now, a lower approximation can also be defined since:

$$\mu_{D_{S'}^{+}(A)}(s_i') \ge \mu_{D_{S'}^{-}(A)}(s_i') = \inf_{u \in U} \max(1- \mu_A(u),$$
$$\min(1-\mu_{M_U(s_k)}(u), 1-\mu_{M_U(s_l)}(u)))$$
$$= \min(\inf_{u \in U} \max(1- \mu_A(u), 1-\mu_{M_U(s_k)}(u)),$$
$$\inf_{u \in U} \max(1- \mu_A(u), 1-\mu_{M_U(s_l)}(u)))$$
$$= \min(1- \sup_{u \in U} \min(\mu_A(u), \mu_{M_U(s_k)}(u)), 1 - \sup_{u \in U} \min(\mu_A(u), \mu_{M_U(s_l)}(u)))$$
$$= \min(1 - \mu_{D_S^{+}(A)}(s_k), 1 - \mu_{D_S^{+}(A)}(s_l))$$
$$= \min(1 - \mathrm{cons}(A, M_U(s_k)), 1 - \mathrm{cons}(A, M_U(s_l))). \tag{38}$$

Once again, this approximation is obtained by a simple computation with the membership degrees provided by the upper fuzzy descriptor of A on S. This lower bound can be interpreted as the certainty of the intersection of the two fuzzy events defined by the fuzzy meanings of **not s_k and not s_l**. The computing schema is summarized in Fig. 11 where the operation between the grades of membership is represented by the mapping g. According to these approximations we have $B^{-} \subset B \subset B^{+}$.

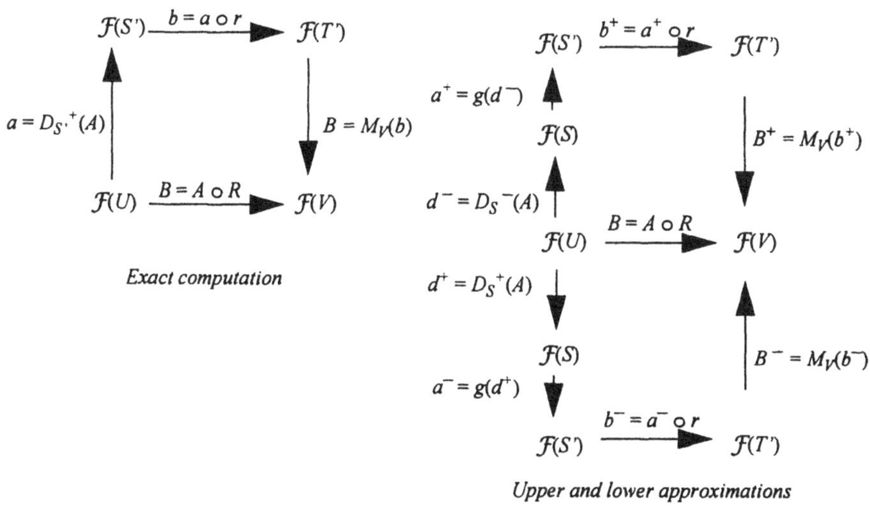

Figure 11 : Exact and approximate computations.

The application of this computation schema provides the result given in Fig. 12.a where the upper approximation is equal to the exact result. However, it is not always the case as shown in Fig. 12.b where the modal value of the fuzzy input has been translated from 6 to 7.

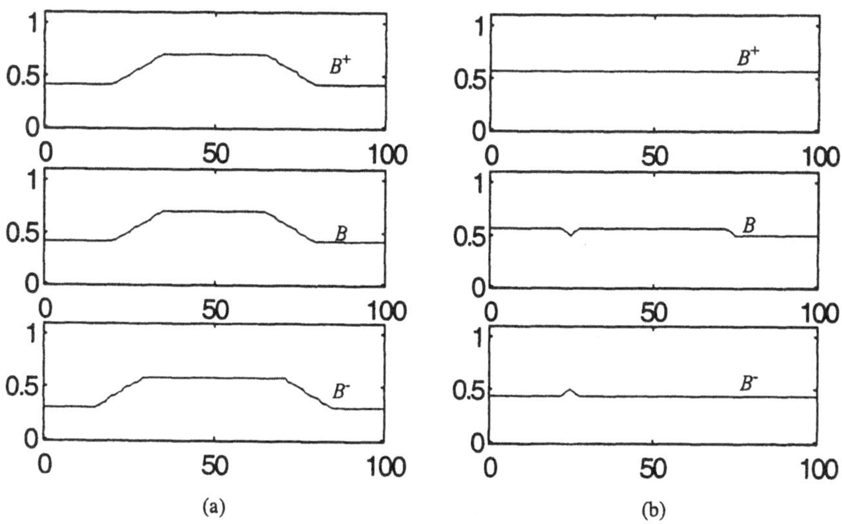

Figure 12 : Approximations of the result.

5.2 - SATURATION OF THE RULE BASE

Another idea, originally proposed by (Dubois, Martin-Clouaire and Prade, 1988) and been developed in (Ughetto et al., 1997) consists in another transformation of the rule-base in order to apply the inference rule by rule but without modifying the interpretation of the rule, that is the interpretation as certainty rules is preserved. Starting from Eq. (34), we can use once again the distributivity of the fuzzy union, that is the max operator, with respect to the min operator. Surprisingly, this operation provides a result of the form (see Ughetto et al., 1997 for the proof) :

$$\mu_B(v) = \min_{i=1,p} \max(\mathrm{cons}(A, \ \overline{M_U(s''_i)}\ ), \mu_{M_V(t''_{f''(i)})}(v)). \tag{39}$$

This equation means that the inference can be performed rule by rule, each rule being represented by the Dienes' implication and the partial result being aggregated conjunctively. The proposed transformation generates new sets S'' and T'' with respectively 2^m and 2^n terms . The elements of these two sets are the terms s''_i and t''_j which are obtained respectively as the or's of the terms in S and T. The new sets S'' and T'' include a new term "**nothing**" whose fuzzy meaning is a membership function always equal to zero. Applying this transformation to the initial set of rules provides the following new rules, each rule is now represented by a Dienes' implication, where obviously the first rule is of no use and could be removed.

if size is **small** then speed is **fast**
if size is **normal** then speed is **medium**
if size is **big** then speed is **slow**

if size is **nothing** then speed is **nothing**
if size is **small** then size is **fast**
if size is **normal** then speed is **medium**
if size is **big** then speed is **slow**
if size is **small or normal** than speed is **fast or medium**
if size is **small or big** then speed is **slow or fast**
if size is **normal or big** then speed is **slow or medium**
if size is **small or normal or big** then speed is **slow or medium or fast**

Figure 13 : New set of rules obtained by the saturation of the rule base.

Now, we can compare Eq. (34) and Eq. (39). It should be noted that the terms s'_i are built as conjunctions of negations of terms in S, while the terms s''_i are disjunctions of terms in S. Therefore, according to Morgan's laws we have:

$$\mathrm{cons}(A, M(s'_i)) = \mathrm{cons}(A, \ \overline{M(s''_i)}\ ) = \alpha_i, \tag{40}$$

and therefore:

$$\mu_B(v) = \min_{i=1,p} \max(\alpha_i, \mu_{M_V(t''_{f''(i)})}(v)). \tag{41}$$

This last result means that the computation cost can be reduced by using the lower and upper approximations given by Eq. (37) and (38), in the same manner as in the disjunctive normal form. However, as a main difference with the conjunctive approach, it should be noted that it is no longer possible to perform the inference at the symbolic level directly on the initial rule base; this leads to search for a logical machinery.

5.3 - TOWARDS A LOGICAL MACHINERY

From the duality between the upper and lower descriptor (duality between the degree of possibility and necessity of a fuzzy event, Eq. (39) gives:

$$\begin{aligned}\mu_B(v) &= \min_{i=1,p} \max(\mathrm{cons}(A, \overline{M_U(s''_i)}), \mu_{M_V(t''_{f''(i)})}(v)) \\ &= \min_{i=1,p} \max(1 - \mathrm{inc}(A, M_U(s''_i)), \mu_{M_V(t''_{f''(i)})}(v)).\end{aligned} \tag{42}$$

Due to the fuzzy intersection operator, each term $\max(1 - \mathrm{inc}(A, M_U(s''_i)), \mu_{M_V(t''_{f''(i)})}(v))$ provides an upper bound of the fuzzy subset B. Moreover, since each s''_i and each $t''_{f''(i)}$ are disjunctions of terms in S and T, we obtain the upper bound given by Eq. (43) where s''_i and $t''_{f''(i)}$ are the disjunctions of two terms:

$$\forall v, \mu_B(v) \leq \max(1 - \mathrm{inc}(A, M_U(s_i) \cup M_U(s_j)), \mu_{M_V(t_{f(i)})}(v), \mu_{M_V(t_{f(j)})}(v)). \tag{43}$$

This suggests that the inference can be processed at the symbolic level, but not as the result of a composition of the form $b = a \circ r$, like the one defined by (18), where the relation r is stated at the label level, even if we choose $a = D_S^-(A)$, i.e., $a = \bigcup_{i=1,m} \mathrm{inc}(A, M_U(s_i)) / s_i$, and we modify the composition appropriately. This is due to the fact that we have to consider new rules, which are obtained from the initial ones by aggregating the condition and the conclusion parts disjunctively, in order to deal with such imprecise inputs A (namely, here the rule "if X is s_i or s_j then Y is $t_{f(i)}$ or $t_{f(j)}$"). See (Ughetto et al., 1997).

One way to get the tightest result (43) for B would be to use a logical machinery at the symbolic level based on resolution principle in order to avoid the limitations of the composition $b' = a \circ r$ which corresponds to a one-by-one processing of the rule. Such a logical machinery should be able to process the weights attached to disjunctions of terms in S, generated by the computation of coefficients inc(A,

$M_U(\bigvee_i s_i))$. The idea is also to benefit from the symbolic level for performing more easily a part of the computation using appropriate logical tools, before rebuilding on V the result of the symbolic inference, as indicated in Figure 14 (where $B' = M_V(b)$ is computed using a formula such as (23)).

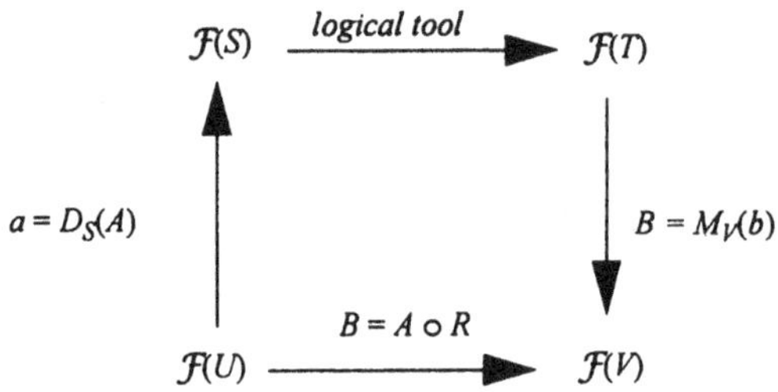

Figure 14 : Using a logical machinery for the inference.

Let us illustrate the idea on an example and let us also show some limitations encountered when using Dienes implication. Let us consider the following fuzzy propositions

$$p_1 \equiv \text{'}X \text{ is } s_1\text{'}, p_2 \equiv \text{'}X \text{ is } s_2\text{'}, q_1 \equiv \text{'}Y_1 \text{ is } t_1\text{'}, q_2 \equiv \text{'}Y_2 \text{ is } t_2\text{'}$$

which are involved in the fuzzy pieces of knowledge

'X is s_1 or s_2'
'if X is s_1 then Y is t_1' (I)
'if X is s_2 then Y is t_2'.

These three premises can be symbolically encoded by the logical clauses

$p_1 \vee p_2$
$\neg p_1 \vee q_1$ (II)
$\neg p_2 \vee q_2$,

from which is it is easy to deduce by resolution[1] that $q_1 \vee q_2$ holds, i.e., that 'Y is t_1 or t_2' (since we have the equivalence between 'Y is t_1 or t_2' and 'Y is t_1' or 'Y is t_2',

1. The resolution rule in the propositional case reduces to the cut rule: from $\neg p \vee q$ and $p \vee r$ deduce $q \vee r$.

in agreement with the fuzzy set semantics).

Using Dienes implication $\alpha \to \beta = \max(1 - \alpha, \beta)$, the combination/projection machinery on the fuzzy set membership representation of (I) yields to 'Y is B^*' with (see (Ughetto et al., 1997), for instance)

$$\mu_{B^*}(v) = \max(\mu_{B_1}(v), \mu_{B_2}(v), 1 - \mathrm{inc}(s_1 \cup s_2, s_1 \cup s_2)) \tag{44}$$

where $\mathrm{inc}(s_1 \cup s_2, s_1 \cup s_2) = 1$ if s_1 and s_2 are crisp sets and $\mathrm{inc}(s_1 \cup s_2, s_1 \cup s_2) = 1/2$ (for fuzzy sets with continuous membership functions), using (12) with Dienes implication. This is because Dienes implication is such that we conclude that 'Y is B' from 'if X is A then Y is B' only if it is shown that X *is in the core of* A, i.e., X takes typical values in A. When the value of X is fuzzily restricted by A, we cannot be completely sure that X is a typical value of A, i.e., that the value of X is an element of A with membership degree 1 (since rules based on Dienes implication express statements such as "the more X is A, the more certain Y is B").

In the general case, when the first premise is 'X is s'_1 or s'_2' (instead of 'X is s_1 or s_2'), (44) is changed by replacing the last term in the max by $1 - \mathrm{inc}(s'_1 \cup s'_2, s_1 \cup s_2)$. Then the first premise can be encoded by the possibilistic formula $(p_1 \vee p_2, \mathrm{inc}(s'_1 \cup s'_2, s_1 \cup s_2))$ and by extended resolution we indeed obtain $(q_1 \vee q_2, \mathrm{inc}(s'_1 \cup s'_2, s_1 \cup s_2))$; see (Dubois, Lang and Prade, 1994) for an introduction to possibilistic logic.[1] However note that the complete agreement between this symbolic machinery and the combination/projection method requires that s_1 and s_2 be ordinary sets, since p_1, p_2, q_1, q_2 should be classical propositions; only input facts 'X is A'' can be fuzzy since they can be translated in certainty-qualified non-fuzzy propositions corresponding to the condition parts of the rules. Otherwise, the combination/projection method yields a result which is larger in the sense of fuzzy set inclusion, as it was the case in (44) where the symbolic processing does not take into account the term $1 - \mathrm{inc}(s_1 \cup s_2, s_1 \cup s_2) = 1/2$.

This problem can be coped with if the proper matching coefficients (for instance 0.5 as above) are sent to the symbolic level. However if fuzzy rules are chained then it is much harder to use possibilistic logic at the symbolic level, because the gap between symbolic and numerical levels cannot be avoided.

---

1. In possibilistic logic, a classical logic formula is weighted by a degree estimating to what extent the formula is certainly true. In our example, rules will be regarded as fully certain and encoded by $(\neg p_i \vee q_i, 1)$. Extended resolution then reads $(\neg p \vee q, \alpha)$ and $(p \vee r, \beta)$ entails $(q \vee r, \min(\alpha, \beta))$.

6 - CHAINING RULE-BASES

In Section 4, it was shown that the conjunctive inference can be performed either at the numerical or symbolic levels. Let R and r be the relations associated with the rule-base for both representations, then we have from Proposition 2:

$$B = A \circ R = M_V(b) = M_V(a \circ r) = M_V(D_S{}^{+}(A) \circ r). \tag{45}$$

Now, we can wonder if this property is preserved when chaining two rule-bases. Let us denote R_1 and r_1 on the one hand, and R_2 and r_2 on the other hand, the relations associated with the two sets of rules. The numerical and symbolic inference schemas are represented in Fig. 15 and a link between C and C' can be obtained which shows that a more precise result, in the sense of the inclusion, is obtained when performing the inference at the symbolic level than at the numerical one.

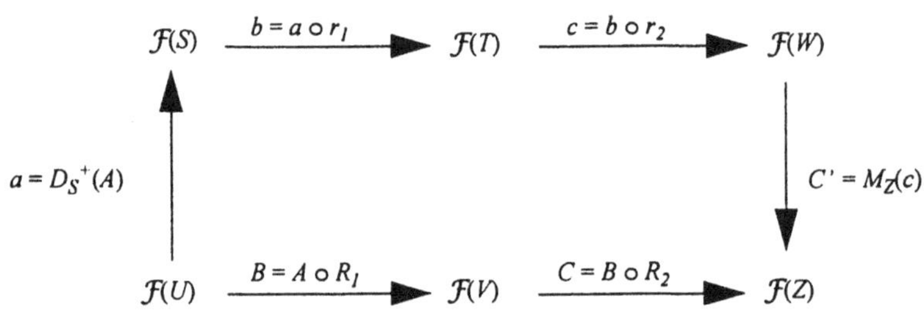

Figure 15 : Inference schemas when chaining two rule-bases.

Proposition 3: $C' = M_Z(c) \subseteq C$.

From Proposition 1, we have $b \subseteq D_T{}^{+}(B)$, therefore

$c = r_2 \circ b \subseteq r_2 \circ D_T{}^{+}(B)$ and

$C' = M_Z(c) \subseteq M_Z(r_2 \circ D_T{}^{+}(B)) = C.$

■

However, to obtain this result we have only used the Proposition 1. However Proposition 2, that is, the equality between the result of the numerical inference and the meaning of the result of the symbolic inference, does not always carry over the case of chained rules. As proved now, we have :

Proposition 4: generally $M_Z(D_S{}^+(A) \circ (r_1 \circ r_2)) \neq A \circ (R_1 \circ R_2)$.

Suppose two sets of fuzzy rules {if X is s_i then Y is $t_{f(i)}\}_{i=1,m}$ and {if Y is t_j then Z is $q_{g(j)}\}_{j=1,n}$. At the symbolic level, denoting r_1 and r_2 the two crip relations on term sets SxT and TxW as in Fig. 15, we have $c = a \circ (r_1 \circ r_2)$ and $r_1 \circ r_2$ corresponds to function $g \circ f$, and the set of rules {if X is s_i then Y is $q_{g \circ f(i)}\}_{i=1,m}$. Then, from Proposition 2 we know that $C' = M_Z(c)$ calculated as:

$$\mu_{C'}(z) = \max_{i=1,m} \min(\text{cons}(A, M_U(s_i)), \mu_{M_Z(q_{g \circ f(i)})}(z)) \tag{46}$$

is exactly what is computed at the numerical level from relation R_3 on XxZ where $R_3 = \bigcup_{i=1,m} (M_U(s_i) \cap M_Z(q_{g \circ f(i)}))$, due to Proposition 2.

However computing $R_1 \circ R_2$, the reader can check that:

$$R_1 \circ R_2 = \bigcup_{i=1,m\,;\,j=1,n} \min((M_U(s_i) \cap M_Z(q_{g(j)})), \text{cons}(M_V(t_{f(i)}), M_V(t_j))). \tag{47}$$

■

Hence $R_1 \circ R_2 \supset R_3$, where the inclusion is generallly strict, therefore $C = A \circ (R_1 \circ R_2)$ contains C' but generally differs from it.

Chaining conjunctive rules at the numerical level leads to more imprecise results than performing inference at the symbolic level. This result is related to the fact pointed out by Di Nola et al. (1990) that while for a single rule $A_1 \circ (A_1 \cap B_1) = B_1$ holds (modus ponens), this result no longer holds for a set of conjunctive rules whose condition parts overlap.

A similar result holds for certainty rules, simply because they do not chain nicely at the numerical level : $(A \to B) \circ (B \to C)$ generally strictly contains $A \to C$ because (in the continuous case) $(A \to B) \circ (B \to C) = \max(0.5, A \to C)$ (see Dubois and Prade, 1991). On the contrary at the symbolic level $\{s_i \to t_j, t_j \to w_k\}$ implies $s_i \to w_k$, in classical as in possibilic logic.

This lack of coherence between syntactic and semantic inference levels is due to the fact that despite the fuzzy nature of the rules, the syntactic level handles them as if they were propositions in classical logic. This symbolic representation works for simple sets of parallel rules, where possibilistic logic accounts for weight propogation. However, possibilistic logic handles binary propositions not fuzzy ones. For fuzzy proposition, $p \wedge \neg p$ is not a contradiction which makes problem for chaining certainty rules for instance. Hence if chaining rule-based systems is needed in fuzzy controllers, genuine many-valued logics must be used at the syntactic level (see Hajek, 1995).

Besides, fuzzy rules based on residuated implications (such as Gödel implication) perform better for chaining, but other difficulties might arise pertaining to the interpolative behavior of such fuzzy rules. A general study of the full compatibility between symbolic and numerical inference for complex fuzzy rule-based systems and residuated implications is left for further research.

7 - CONCLUDING REMARKS

Zadeh (1996) has recently advocated a view of fuzzy logic as a scheme for computing with words. In such a perspective, it seems natural to be concerned with the two levels of representation, the numerical and the symbolic ones. This paper provides a preliminary comparative discussion of the fuzzy set approximate reasoning machinery with a more symbolic treatment of the inference. It can be seen that what was obtained by performing the inference directly at the symbolic level may be more accurate than when computing the representation of the result of the inference on the numerical scale first, before approximating it. Only two types of representation have been considered for rules. The symbolic processing of gradual rules (Dubois and Prade, 1996), based on another type of implication, should be also investigated, but raises new difficulties in relation with the interpolative nature of these rules. Indeed the vocabulary at the label level should be sufficiently flexible and accurate for expressing the result of interpolations between other fuzzy set labels.

8 - REFERENCES

Di Nola A., Pedrycz W., Sessa S. (1989) An aspect of discrepancy in the implementation of modus ponens in the presebce of fuzzy quantities. Int. J. of Approximate Reasoning 3, 259-265.

Dubois D., Foulloy L., Galichet S., Prade H. (1997) Two different views of approximate reasoning. Proc. of the 7th Inter. Fuzzy Systems Assoc. World Congress (IFSA'97), Prague, Czech Republic, June 25-29, 1997, Academia, Prague, 238-242.

Dubois D., Martin-Clouaire R., Prade H. (1988) Practical computing in fuzzy logic. In : Fuzzy Computing (M. M. Gupta, T. Yamakawa; Eds), North-Holland, Amsterdam, 11-34.

Dubois D., Prade H. (1991) Fuzzy sets in approximate reasoning — Part 1: Inference with possibility distributions. Fuzzy Sets and Systems, 40, 143-202.

Dubois D., Prade H. (1992a) Upper and lower images of a fuzzy set induced by a fuzzy relation: Applications to fuzzy inference and diagnosis. Information Sciences, 64, 203-232.

Dubois D., Prade H. (1992b) Putting rough sets and fuzzy sets together. In: Intelligent Decision Support — Handbook of Applications and Advances of the Rough Sets Theory (R. Slowinski, ed.), Kluwer Academic Publ., Dordrecht, 203-231.

Dubois D., Lang J., Prade H. (1994) Automated reasoning using possibilistic logic: semantics, belief revision and variable certainty weights. IEEE Trans. on Data and Knowledge Engineering, 6(1), 64-71.

Dubois D., Prade H. (1996) What are fuzzy rules and how to use them. Fuzzy Sets and Systems, 84, 169-185.

Foulloy L., Galichet S. (1994) Typology of fuzzy controllers. In: Theorical Aspects of Fuzzy Control (H.T. Nguyen, M. Sugeno, R. Tong, R.R. Yager, eds.), Wiley, New-York, 65-90.

Hajek D. (1995) Fuzzy logic as logic. In Mathematical Models for Handling Partial Knowledge in Artificial Intelligence (G. Coletti, D. Dubois, R. Scozzafava Eds.) Plenum Press, New York, 21 - 30.

Mauris G., Benoit E., Foulloy L. (1994) Fuzzy symbolic sensors: From concept to applications. Int. J. of Measurement, 12, 357-384.

Ughetto L., Dubois D., Prade H. (1997) Efficient inference procedures with fuzzy inputs. Proc. of the 6th IEEE Inter. Conf. on Fuzzy Systems (FUZZ-IEEE'97), Barcelona, Spain, July 1-5, 567-572.

Willaeys D., Malvache N. (1981) The use of fuzzy sets for the treatment of fuzzy information by computer. Fuzzy Sets and Systems, 5, 323-328.

Zadeh L.A. (1971) Quantitative fuzzy semantics. Information Sciences, 3 159-176.

Zadeh L.A. (1973) Outline of a new approach to the analysis of complex systems and decision processes. IEEE Trans. Systems, Man and Cybernetics, 3, 28-44.

Zadeh L.A. (1979) A theory of approximate reasoning. In: Machine Intelligence, Vol. 9 (J.E. Hayes, D. Michie, L.I. Mikulich, eds.), Elsevier, New York, 149-194.

Zadeh L.A. (1996) Fuzzy logic = computing the words. IEEE Trans. on Fuzzy Systems, 4(2), 103-111.

Approximate Reasoning as a Basis for Computing with Words

Ronald R. Yager
Machine Intelligence Institute
Iona College
New Rochelle, NY 10801
E-Mail: yager@panix.com

ABSTRACT. In order to be able to carry out the agenda of computing with words we need a formal knowledge representation and manipulation systems, approximate reasoning provides such a tool. In this work we introduce the basic ideas of approximate reasoning. We show the generality of this framework by indicating how some classical reasoning systems, such as binary propositional logic can be formulated within this framework

1. Introduction

In [1] Zadeh discusses his concept of computing with words and indicates the central role of fuzzy sets in this methodology. The use of fuzzy sets to help develop a methodology for computing with words is pervasive throughout Zadeh's work on fuzzy sets [2]. The current state of Zadeh's idea of computing with words should not be misunderstood as a attempt to construct a full blown natural language understanding system but involves a much more structured use of words. Here the focus is on the use of words as the value of variables and other formal objects. With the idea of computing with words one is trying to move the information interchange (or interface) between computers and humans more towards grounds that are easier for humans to function within. By allowing information, such as values for variables, to be provided in linguistic terms one is taking the strenuous burden of precision off the human. Also by allowing the output of computers to be expressed in words, it provides information to the "customer," the human user, in a way that they can most easily process. As an additional benefit, by allowing words to be used at the human/machine interface we can reduce the loss of information, which is a necessary result of the use a less expressive mode of knowledge transfer. Also, the use of words allows us to maintain the uncertainties we may in our knowledge and doesn't require us to impose a unjustified precision.

In figure #1 we show the basic structure of this paradigm of computing with words.

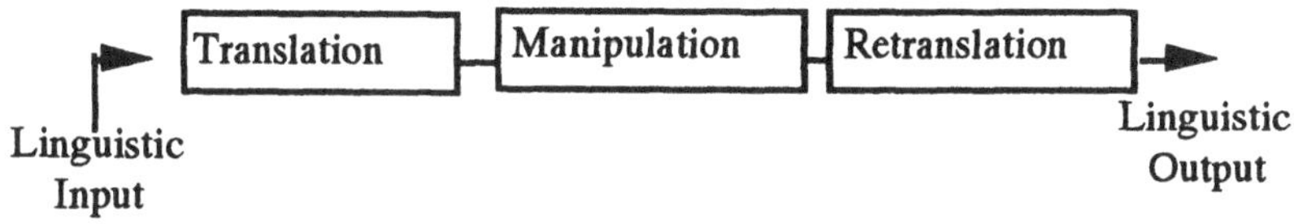

Figure #1: Computing with words paradigm

We see that the process of computing with words consists of a translation of information containing linguistic components into a formal representation, a manipulation of this formal representation to attain the required result and then a retranslation into an output which can contain linguistic components. The manipulation step is carried out using the methodology of Approximate Reasoning (AR). [3-6] A fundamental aspect of AR is the view of knowledge as constraints on the allowable values associated with variables. Different kinds of knowledge induce different types of constraints. In [7] Zadeh provides a comprehensive discussion of the different kinds of constraints induced by various types of natural language statements. The reasoning mechanism, AR, can be seen as a manipulation of these constraints. The constraints represent the knowledge available to the system. Thus the knowledge that John is a teenager puts some constraint on the allowable values that John's age can assume. Essentially the constraints are expressed as subsets of the domains of the variables. Since much of the knowledge provided by human beings involves concepts and words which have a degree of imprecision, fuzzy sets provide a natural mechanism for representing the constraints induced by humans in providing knowledge.

One characteristic of the approximate reasoning (AR) framework is that it allows for a unified representation of many different knowledge modeling technologies. Binary logic and functional modeling are two examples of methodologies representable in AR. It is noted that the ability to represent complex functional relationships in AR forms the basis of fuzzy systems modeling which is used in fuzzy logic controllers [8] and many other applications.

In this work we provide a basic overview of the approximate reasoning machinery and look at its connections to binary logic as well as the possibilistic logic introduced by Dubois and Prade [9-12].

2. Approximate Reasoning: Basic Concepts

The primary elements of an AR representation of a knowledge base are a collection of variables, V_j for j = 1 to n, called the atomic variables. These variables are the objects of interest in the current context. It is information about the value of these variables and relationships between the values of these variables that constitute the knowledge of interest. Associated with each variable V_j is a set X_j, indicating the allowable values for the variable. The terms base set, domain and universe of discourse are used to indicate the set X_j. It is implicitly assumed, unless otherwise stated, that a variable can attain only one value in its base set. A joint variable is any tuple of one or more distinct atomic variables; V_3, (V_2, V_5) and (V_1, V_2, V_6) are examples of joint variables. Associated with any joint variable is a set consisting of the Cartesian product of the domains of the variables making up the joint variable. Thus if a joint variable has q components its domain is a set of q-tuples.

A proposition (or statement) in theory of approximate reasoning is an object of the form

V *is* A,

here V is a joint variable and A is a fuzzy subset of the domain of V, the Cartesian product of the base sets of the atomic variables which make up the joint variable V. In an approximate reasoning system knowledge is represented by propositions of the above form. A proposition which involves only one variable is called a canonical proposition while those involving two or variables are sometimes called relational or joint proposition.

The fuzzy subsets appearing in the propositions in an AR representation take their membership grade in some set L, called the membership set. The default assumption for this set is the unit interval I = [0,1]. However it should be noted that other possibilities exist for L, for example L = {0,1}. In this case we get crisp sets instead of fuzzy sets. More generally L can be any negated lattice having a maximal and minimal elements [13].

The propositions in AR can be seen as imposing restrictions on the possible values of the variables involved. For example if A is a crisp subset then the meaning of the proposition V_1 *is* A is to indicate that the value for the variable V_1 is restricted to be a member of the set A, that is element in A are the possible+ values for V_1. The use of fuzzy subsets provides for a grading of this idea. Thus one meaning of the canonical proposition V_1 *is* B, where B is a fuzzy subset, is that for any $x \in X_1$, B(x) indicates the possibility that $V_1 = x$. [14] If $V = (V_1, V_2, V_3)$ is a joint variable then the meaning of the proposition V *is* M is that for any $(x_1, x_2, x_3) \in X_1 \times X_2 \times X_3$, $M(x_1, x_2, x_3)$ is the possibility that simultaneous $V_1 = x_1$, $V_2 = x_2$ and $V_3 = x_3$. Thus we see that the knowledge represented in the propositions used in AR is contained in the fuzzy subsets associated with the propositions.

We shall say a proposition, V *is* M, is **normal** (consistent) if $Max_x[M(x)] = 1$, there exists at least one element in the base set of V that has possibility one. We shall call a proposition **subnormal** if $Max_x[M(x)] < 1$. We call a proposition V *is* M a tautology if M(x) = 1 for all x in the domain of V. It should be noted that a tautology existentially provides no restriction of the value of a variable and thus induces no new information other than that the variable must be in its base set.

When using the approximate reasoning framework we are generally involved in one of three tasks. The first task, translation or knowledge representation is the process of taking knowledge normally expressed in knowledge is language and converting into an appropriate representation within the framework of AR. That is this task takes natural language statements and then expresses them as propositions in AR. We essentially construct our knowledge base via this translation process. The second task is extracting knowledge from the knowledge base. This task which is called the inference process. It involves the manipulation of AR, proposition to obtain other AR propositions. Within the spirit of Zadeh's idea of computing with words we can consider a third task, that of retranslation. Here we are interested in the process of converting propositions of AR into statements of natural language. Here we shall mainly focus on the second task, inference, and to a lesser extent on the translation task and to an even lesser extent on the retranslation.

3. Basic Operations in AR

Manipulation within the framework of AR can be seen to be based, for the most part, on three basic operations [4]; conjoin, containment and negation.

The operation of conjoin [4], provides the system with the facility for combining or fusing information. In the translation process it allows us to represent knowledge involving multiple variables and allows us to construct joint variables from atomic variables. In the inference process it will allow us to combine individual pieces of knowledge. The operation of conjoin, as we shall see, is a generalization and unification of the set operations of conjunction and cartesian product. It is also closely related to the join operation used in databases [15].

Definition: Assume V_a and V_b are two joint variables on the universes X and Y respectively. Let V_a *is* D and V_b *is* E be two propositions. Their conjoin (conjunction) denoted V_a *is* D × V_b *is* E is the proposition V *is* F where V is a joint variable consisting of the union of the atomic variables making up V_a and V_b. F is a fuzzy subset of the domain of V, Z, such that for each $z \in Z$

$$F(z) = D(x) \wedge E(y)$$

where x is the portion of z corresponding to the domain X and y is the portion of corresponding to the domain Y. The operation $\wedge$ is most generally a t-norm [16] however unless otherwise specified we shall assume it is the min operator.

In the case when the two variables being conjoined are the same the conjoin operation reduces to the usual intersection of fuzzy sets [4]:

$$V_a \textit{ is } D \times V_a \textit{ is } E = V_a \textit{ is } D \cap E.$$

We shall find it convenient to sometimes use $\cap$ in place of ×.

In the case when the two joint variables being conjoined have no common variables this operation reduces to the cartesian product.

$$V_a \textit{ is } D \times V_b \textit{ is } E = (V_a, V_b) \textit{ is } D \times E.$$

A few observations are worth making. If V_a *is* D and V_b *is* E are both normal propositions and if V_a and V_b are disjoint then V *is* F = V_a *is* D × V_b *is* E is also a normal proposition. We see this as follows, let D(x) = 1 and E(y) = 1 the for z = (x,y) we have $F(z) = D(x) \wedge E(y) = 1 \wedge 1 = 1$.

Again let V_a *is* D and V_b *is* F be normal propositions but assume there are not disjoint, V_c is common to both. Let us denote the tuples associated with V_a as (q, w) where w is the portion corresponding to V_c. Similarly let us denote the tuples associated with V_b as (p, w). Then the tuples associated V can be expressed as (q, p, w). Since we see that F is normal only if there exists a w such that D(q, w) = 1 and D(p,w) = 1 for some q and p.

We now define a special conjoin operation, as we shall see this operation plays a role in making propositions which are not necessarily about the same variable be about the same variable.

Definition: Assume V_a and V_b are two joint variables such that V_b contains all the variables that are in V_a. The **cylindrical extension** of the proposition V_a *is* *F* to the proposition V_b *is* F° is defined by

$$V_b \text{ is } F^\circ = V_a \text{ is } F \times V_1 \text{ is } X \times V_2 \text{ is } X_2 \ldots\ldots \times V_q \text{ is } X_q$$

where V_1, V_2. Vq are the atomic variables in V_b that are not in V_a and the X_i's are the respective base sets of these variables.

Note: We can equivalently express this cylindrical extension of V_a *is* F to V_b by

$$V_b \text{ is } F^\circ = V_a \text{ is } M \times V_b \text{ is } X$$

where X is the domain of the variable V_b.

The membership function F° can be obtained from the membership function of F by setting $F^\circ(y) = F(x)$ where x is the tuple in the base set of V_a that corresponds to the portion of y in this subspace.

We now turn to the second basic operation used in approximate reasoning, containment. At a very fundamental level this operation provides us with a facility for ordering propositions in approximate reasoning.

Definition: Assume V_a *is* D and V_b *is* E are two propositions, we say that V_a *is* D contains V_b *is* F denoted V_b *is* $E \subseteq V_a$ *is* D if

$$F^\circ(z) \geq D^\circ(z) \text{ for all } z$$

where F° and D° are the cylindrical extensions of F and D to the base set of variable V, the union of the atomic variables in V_a and V_b.

We note that if V_a and V_b are the same joint variables then this is the definition of fuzzy containment suggested by Zadeh [17].

It can be shown that if P_1 and P_2 are two propositions and $P = P_1 \times P_2$ then

$P_3 \subseteq P_1$ and $P_3 \subseteq P_2$.

Containment allows us to define equivalence of propositions.

Definition: Two propositions P_1 and P_2 are equivalent if $P_1 \subseteq P_2$ and $P_2 \subseteq P_1$, we shall denote this as $P_1 = P_2$

Equivalent propositions are interchangeable under conjoin, assume P_1 and P_2 are equivalent, $P_1 = P_2$, and let P_3 be any other proposition then $P_1 \times P_3 = P_2 \times P_3$

The third basic operation in AR is negation. While the other two operations involve more than one proposition, the operation of negation essentially provides a facility for complimenting propositions.

Definition: Assume V *is* A is a proposition in AR in which the domain of V is X. The negation of V *is* A, denoted **not**(V *is* A) is the proposition V *is* $\overline{A}$ where $\overline{A}(x) = 1 - A(x)$ for each x.

An important relationship exists between negation and containment

Theorem: If V_a *is* $A \subseteq V_b$ *is* B then V_b *is* $\overline{B} \subseteq V_a$ *is* $\overline{A}$

Proof: If V_a *is* $A \subseteq V_b$ *is* B then for all z in the extensions $A^\circ(z) \leq B^\circ(z)$, this implies $\bar{A}^\circ(z) \leq \bar{B}^\circ(z)$ and the result follows.

We shall here introduce an operation which is based upon a combination of conjoin and negation. Assume V_a *is* A and V_b *is* B are two propositions in AR. We define the operation ⊥ as

$$V_a \textit{ is } A \perp V_b \textit{ is } B \equiv \text{not}(V_a \textit{ is } \bar{A} \times V_b \textit{ is } \bar{B}) \equiv \overline{(V_a \textit{ is } \bar{A} \times V_b \textit{ is } B)}.$$

It can be shown that this can be expressed as V *is* D where V is the union of the atomic variables in the joint variables V_a and V_b and D is a fuzzy subset on the universe of V such that

$$D(z) = A(x) \vee B(y),$$

where x is the component of the tuple z associated with the domain of V_a and y is a component of the tuple z corresponding to the domain of V_b. Furthermore, if $\wedge$ is implemented using Min then $\vee$ = Max, more generally if $\wedge$ is any t-norm then $\vee$ is the associated De Morgan t-conorm. [18] Again here Max will be the default operator. It should be noted that if V_a and V_b are the same this operator is the union. With this in mind we shall use ∪ synonymously with ⊥.

4. Some Translation Rules

An important task in the use of the approximate reasoning framework in computing with words is the translation of statements from natural language into propositions in approximate reasoning. The rules for going from natural language to representation in AR are called translation rules. A study of Zadeh's work as found in [2] as well as in [19] will provide the reader with a large collection of translation rules useful for the representation of knowledge in AR. Since our main purpose here is not the investigation of translation rules, but the study of inference, we shall just briefly introduce a few of these rules.

The most basic translation rule is the assignment of a value to an atomic variable. Assume V_1 is an atomic variable and let A be some linguistic expression providing a value for V_1. If V_1 is the height of John then an example of A could be tall. The natural language statement V_1 is A gets translated in the AR proposition V_1 *is* A where A is a fuzzy subset representing the concept A. In this representation we are essentially saying for any x is the domain of V_1, A(x) is the possibility that $V_1 = x$.

Assume P is a statement that has representation in AR V_a *is* A and Q is a statement that has representation V_b *is* B then the following are some translation rules:

- **not**(P) is represented as V *is* $\bar{A}$.
- For $\alpha \in [0, 1]$, P *is* α *certain* is represented as V *is* B where $B(x) = A(x) \vee (1 - \alpha)$.
- *P and Q* is represented as V_a *is* A × V_b *is* B
- *P or Q* is represented as V_a *is* A ⊥ V_b *is* B
- *If P then Q*, is represented as V_a *is* $\bar{A}$ ⊥ V_b *is* B

The implication, *If P then Q*, requires additional comment. Rather then always using the default t-conorm, Max, to implement the operation $\perp$ we sometimes use other t-conorms. More specifically with $D = \bar{A} \perp B$ we have $D(z) = S(\bar{A}(x), B(y))$, with S being a t-conorm. Some examples are $D(z) = \text{Max}\ [\bar{A}(x), B(z)]$ and $D(z) = \text{Min}\ [1, \bar{A}(x) + B(y)]$

In the preceding we have described the translation of some types of natural language statements into propositions in AR. These types of statements have been very close in structure to those appearing in logic. Rules are available for translating information about functional relationships into propositions in AR. Functional relationships and their representation play a crucial role in the application of fuzzy logic to control [8, 20]. Assume V_a and V_b are two joint variables, a functional relationship between these variables is denoted $V_a = F(V_b)$, indicating that for a given value of V_b there is a corresponding value for V_a. A fuzzy point in this functional relationship consists of a pair $<p_i, q_i>$ where $p_i \equiv V_a$ *is* A_i and $q_i \equiv V_b$ *is* B_i. More specifically a solution point of the functional relationship F consists of the conjunction of the components of the pair, thus $<p_i, q_i> = p_i$ ***and*** $q_i = V_a$ *is* $A_i \times V_b$ *is* B_i. Typical our knowledge about the functional relationship F consists of a collection of fuzzy solution points, $<p_i, q_i>$ i = 1 to n. Since the organization between these fuzzy solution points is disjunctive, only one of them can be valid at a time, then the overall functional relationship F is expressed as

$$F = <p_1, q_i> \textit{ or } <p_2, q_2> \textit{ or } \dots\dots\dots \textit{ or } <p_n, q_n>$$

thus

$$F = (V_a \textit{ is } A_1 \times V_b \textit{ is } B_1) \perp (V_a \textit{ is } A_2 \times V_b \textit{ is } B_2) \dots\dots \perp (V_a \textit{ is } A_n \times V_b \textit{ is } B_n)$$

As shown in [8] this is the formal model used in fuzzy logic control.

5. Information and AR

Once having a representation of our knowledge, a knowledge base, in terms of propositions in the language of approximate reasoning, the next step is to use this knowledge. One use made of this knowledge is the deduction of other knowledge. Before we investigate this we must look more carefully at the knowledge contained in the propositions of AR.

Consider the statement V *is* A where V is an atomic variable. For ease of explanation we shall initially assume A is a crisp subset of the domain X of V. Effectively this statement is saying that our knowledge of the value of the variable V is that it is an element in the set A. Thus all the elements in A are possible values for V. We note that if we know that V lies in the set A then if $A \subseteq B$ we also know that the value of V lies in B. This ability can be seen as a kind of inference, for example, if we know that John is in his twenties then we can infer that he is over fifteen years old. While we are able to go from smaller subsets to larger subsets with surety we can't go the other way around, from larger subsets to smaller subsets. For example, knowing John is in his twenties doesn't allow us to conclude that John is between 21 and 23.

In statements such as V *is* A it should be noted that the smaller the subset A the more information we have about the value of the variable V. For example knowing that John is between 20 and 25 is more informative then knowing that John is in his twenties, we have less possible values. One important proviso should be noted with respect to the observation that the smaller the set A the more knowledge we have about the value of V. This proviso is with respect to the case in which A is the empty set. For as we mentioned the statement V *is* A indicates that the value of V is an element in the set of A. If A is the null set, there exists no elements in A. In this case we are faced with a conflict, there are no elements which can be the value of V. Confusion exists, we don't know what to do. This is clearly a very uninformative situation. We may have to question the validity of our knowledge. On the other hand, if A is a normal fuzzy subset the normality of A insures us that there exists at least one element that is completely possible as the value of V.

Consider now that we have two pieces of knowledge about the same variable; V *is* A and V *is* B. Again for simplicity of discussion we shall assume A and B are crisp subsets. The first statement indicates that the possible value for V lies in the set A, the second statement indicates that the possible value for V lies in the set B. Consider the situation where one statement says John is between 10 and 20 and the other says that he is over 15. In this case we can conclude that he is between 15 and 20. More generally in the case of multiple pieces of information we take the intersection; that is we conclude V *is* D where $D = A \cap B$. However, if $A \cap B = \varnothing$ we must be careful in using the intersection for in this case the two pieces of information are conflicting.

While we have restricted the preceding discussion to the situation in which the sets involved were considered as crisp subsets the basic observations made in the preceding hold in the case when the subsets are allowed to be fuzzy. As noted in the crisp environment the statement V *is* A indicates that A are the set of possible values for the variable V. More formally A(x), the membership grade of x in A, indicates the **possibility** that x is the value for V. In the case when A is crisp $A(x) \in \{0, 1\}$, x is fully possible or full impossible as a value for V. When we allow the subsets to be fuzzy we still can interpret A(x) as the possibility that x is the value for V, however here we get a grading on these possibilities. Thus in the case of fuzzy subsets the possibility that x is the value of V becomes a number in the unit interval.

What should be clear, is the use of sets, whether crisp or fuzzy, to convey information about the value of a variable allows for a representation which can capture uncertainty in our knowledge. A number of measures have been introduced into to help evaluate different aspects of uncertainty associated with AR propositions. In the following we shall discuss some of these measures as they will prove to be useful in the subsequent investigation.

In [21-23] Yager discusses the concept of **specificity** of a fuzzy subset. Assume A is a fuzzy subset of the space X. The measure of specificity of A, denoted Sp(A), is a number in the unit interval such that

1. Sp(A) = 1 if A is a crisp subset consisting of exactly one element, A =

{x} for some $x \in X$

2 $Sp(\varnothing) = Sp(X) = 0$

3. If A and B are two normal fuzzy subsets of X, then $Sp(A) \geq Sp(B)$ if $A \subset B$

In [23] we provide an alternative axiomatization. A number of different manifestations of this measure have been discussed in the literature. One manifestation that we shall find useful, because of its simplicity is the following. Assume x* is an element with maximal membership grade in A, $A(x^*) = Max_X[A(x)]$, and if $Aver_{x^* \notin X}[A(x)]$ is the average of all the elements in X excluding x* then

$$Sp(A) = A(x^*) - Aver_{x^* \notin X}[A(x)]$$

Here we see that Sp(A) is the maximal membership grade in A minus the average of the membership grades of the other elements.

As discussed by Yager [22] one application of the measure of specificity is that it provides a measure of the amount of information contained in a proposition in AR. Thus if *P* is a proposition expressible in AR as V *is* A then the amount of information contained in P, Inf(P) = Sp(A).

The connection between specificity and the information is based upon the idea that specificity measures the degree to which a fuzzy subset contains one and only one element. We can see that sets containing one and only one element are the most informative, we know exactly the value of the variable, no uncertainty exists. As a set moves away from having one element either by having many elements or by having no elements, the information it provides about its associated variable becomes less. In the case when we have many possible values for a variable we lack information because we don't know which is the correct one. On the other hand when the set assigned to a variable becomes empty we have no information as to the value associated with the variable.

We know turn to another measure of uncertainty. Assume V_a *is* A and V_b *is* B are two propositions in AR. We define the possibility of V_a *is* A given V_b *is* A, denoted Poss[V_a *is* A | V_b *is* B] as $Max_X[F(x)]$ where V *is* F = V_a *is* A × V_b *is* B.

Thus the possibility is measure of the maximal membership grade in the conjoin of the two propositions involved. We note that if V_a and V_b are the same joint variable, then F is the pure intersection, $F = A \cap B$. Here then we are measuring the largest membership grade in the intersection, the degree of intersection. Possibility essentially measures the degree to which two propositions have some solution in common.

It is interesting to consider the special case when A = {x}, we shall denote this as $V_a = x$. With Poss[$V_a = x$ | V_b *is* B] we are measuring the possibility that $V_a = x$ given that V_b *is* B. Formally here we are in finding $Max_z F(z)$ where $F = A \times B$
We see that $F(z) = A(x) \wedge B(y)$
where x and y compose z. Let us consider three cases

(i) $V_a = V_b$. Here $F(x) = A(x) \wedge B(x)$ and Poss[x | B] = B(x), the membership grade of x in B.

(ii) $V_a \cap V_b = \emptyset$, they have no elements in common. Here F(z) = A(x) ∧ B(y) = B(y), thus Poss[x | B] = Max_y B(y), the maximal membership grade is B. If B is normal this is one.

(iii) Assume V_a and V_b have some variables in common. Let us denote these as V_c. Assume we express any tuple in Y as (u, w) where u is the portion in common with V_b and w is the remainder. Let us indicate Y_x is the subset of elements of Y which have the same value of the element of x for the common element. Then Poss[x | B] = $Max_{y \in Y_x}$ B(y)].

A closely related measure is the certainty measure. The certainty of V_a *is* A given V_b *is* B, is denoted Cert[V_a *is* A|V_b *is* B] and defined as defined as

$$\text{Cert}[V_a \textit{ is } A \mid V_b \textit{ is } B] = 1 - \text{Poss}\,[V_a \textit{ is } \bar{A} \mid V_b \textit{ is } B]$$

(Dubois and Prade refer to this as the necessity measure)

Theorem: If B is normal then Poss[V_a *is* A|V_b *is* B] ≥ Cert[V_a *is* A | V_b *is* B]

Proof: Let D(z) = A(x) ∧ B(y) and let y* be an element for which B(y*) = 1. Let x* be the element in domain V_a which agrees with y* on their common variables and which has the maximum membership in A, then Poss[V_a *is* A|V_b *is* B] ≥ A (x*). We shall denote this element z*. Denoting F = $\bar{A}$ × B, we have F(z) = $\bar{A}$(x) ∧ B(y) and hence F(z*) = (1 - A(x*)). Since Cert[V_a *is* A | V_b *is* B] = 1 - Max_z[F(z)] then Cert[V_a *is* A | V_b *is* B] ≤ 1 - F(z*) ≤ A (x*)

The following theorem is worth noting

Theorem: If B is a singleton, B(x*) = 1 and B(x) = 0 for x ≠ x*, then

$$\text{Poss}[V_a \textit{ is } A|V_b \textit{ is } B] = \text{Cert}[V_a \textit{ is } A \mid V_b \textit{ is } B] = A(x^*)$$

We note that Poss[V_a *is* A|V_b *is* B] is a measure of the degree of intersection of A and B and Cert[V_a *is* A | V_b *is* B] is a measure of the degree to which B is contained in A. To understand this it is easiest to consider the case when $V_a = V_b = V_1$, an atom variable. Here Poss[V_1 *is* A | V_1 *is* B] = Max_x[A(x) ∧ B(x)], the maximal intersection and Cert[V_1 *is* A | V_1 *is* B] = 1 - Poss[V_1 *is* $\bar{A}$ | V_1 *is* B]= 1 - Max[$\bar{A}$(x) ∧ B(x)] = Min_x[$\bar{A}$(x) ∨ $\bar{B}$(x)]. Since A(x) ∨ $\bar{B}$(x) is essentially if B(x) then A(x) we see that this is a measure of the degree to which B is contained in A.

An important interpretation of the measures of possibility and certainty are respectively as the upper and lower bounds of the truth of the statement. V_a *is* A given the knowledge that V_b *is* B. To see an intuitive indication of this we shall consider the situation again in which $V_a = V_b = V_1$ and A and B are crisp sets. Here then we address the problem "given that V_1 lies in the set B is it true that V_1 lies in A", we denote this as Truth[V_1 *is* A | V_1 *is* B].

We see that if B is a singleton, x*, the answer is quite clear; if x* ∈ A then it answer is yes otherwise it is no. This can be formally represented as $A(x^*)$. Consider now the case in which B is a subset. Three distinct cases can be indicated: i) $A \cap B = \emptyset$, ii) $B \subseteq A$ and iii) $A \cap B \neq \emptyset$ but $B \not\subset A$.

In case i the answer is no, Truth[V_1 *is* A | V_1 *is* B] = 0. It is noted in this case Poss[V_1 *is* A | V_1 *is* B] = Cert[V_1 *is* A | V_1 *is* B] = 0

In case ii) the answer is yes, Truth[V_1 *is* A | V_1 *is* B] = 0. It is noted in this case Poss[V_1 *is* A | V_1 *is* B] = Cert[V_1 *is* A | V_1 *is* B] = 1

In case iii) the answer is unknown. It is noted in this case Poss[V_1 *is* A | V_1 *is* B] = 1 and Cert[V_1 *is* A | V_1 *is* B] = 0.

It should be emphasized that the measure of specificity provides a measure "about" a given approximate reasoning system while the measures of possibility provides measures "within" the system.

6. Basic Inference in Approximate Reasoning

We now turn to the question of reasoning or deduction in approximate reasoning. Essentially a proposition, in AR places some constraint on the allowable values for the associated variables. Thus the simple atomic statement V_1 *is* A_1 says that the values for the variable V_1 must be in the set A_1, it eliminates elements not in A_1 as possible solutions. More generally, a statement V_a *is* A places restrictions on the tuple of variables making up the joint variable V_a. Assume we have a knowledge base consisting of a set of propositions, P_i, for i = 1 to n. Since each proposition P_i induces a restriction the totality of our knowledge can be seen to be the conjunction (conjoin) of these individual restrictions Thus the set of propositions $\{P_1, P_2, , ..., P_n\}$, our knowledge base, induces a combined restriction

$$KB = P_1 \text{ and } P_2 \text{ and ...... and } P_n$$

hence $KB = P_1 \times P_2 \times .... \times P_n$. Thus our knowledge KB is also a proposition in AR, V *is* A, which is the conjoin of all pieces of knowledge we have.

Let us comment on the above. Each proposition puts some restriction on the possible values that V can assume. The result of conjuncting all the knowledge, combining all restrictions, leads to a set A within which the value of V should be. In the spirit of binary modal logic the set A provides the set of values that make all the premises true it is the set of possible worlds. In the fuzzy framework, A(x) can be seen as the degree to which x satisfies all the premises, it is that possibility that x is the unique value the variable V.

What should be observed is that if the value of V is constraint to lie in the set A then it must also lie in any set containing A. In [3] Zadeh suggested a basic rule for inference in approximate reasoning, called the entailment principle, which is a formalization of the preceding observation.

Entailment Principle: From the knowledge V_a *is* A we can infer V_b *is* B if

$$V_a \; is \; A \subseteq V_b \; is \; B$$

The use of the entailment principle, along with the process of conjuncting individual pieces of knowledge, premises, leads to a very powerful reasoning mechanism. We shall say that proposition P is inferable from a collection of propositions $P_1, P_2, , ..., P_n$ denoted

$$(P_1, P_2, , ..., P_n) \quad P$$

if

$$P_1 \times P_2 \times .... \times P_n \subseteq P,$$

Thus P is inferable from the premises $P_1, P_2, , ..., P_n$ if the conjunction of the premises entails P. Essentially we see that the premises provide constraints on the allowable values for the variables, the conjunction of these provide a set within which the actual state must exist.

A number of important and useful properties are inherent in this reasoning mechanism. In the following we note some of them, more details can be found in [8].

An important property that this system has is ***monotonicity***. Monotonicity requires that if $(P_1, P_2, , ..., P_n) \quad P$ then for any P_{n+1}, $(P_1, P_2, , ..., P_n, P_{n+1}) \quad P$. The implications of monotonicity are very interesting and useful. First it implies that if we add any information to our knowledge base everything that was valid before is still valid.

Monotonicity also allows us to simplify the process of determining whether a proposition P^* can be inferred from our knowledge base. Because of monotonicity we don't need to consider all the propositions in our knowledge base to decide whether P^* is inferable. In particular, if our knowledge base is the set $\{P_1, P_2, , ..., P_n\}$ and $\{\hat{P}_1, \hat{P}_2, ..., \hat{P}_q\}$ is some subset of these then if $(\hat{P}_1, \hat{P}_2, ..., \hat{P}_q) \quad P^*$.we can conclude that $(P_1, P_2, , ..., P_n) \quad P^*$

Because of its satisfying monotonicity AR allows for a very simple deductive mechanism based upon two rules of inference. We denote these rules of inference IR-1 and IR-2 and we define as follows:

IR-1: $(P_1) \quad P_2$ if $P_1 \subseteq P_2$ **Entailment**

IR-2: $(P_1, P_2) \quad P_1 \times P_2$ **Conjunction**

Definition: A deduction from a set of AR propositions $\{P_1, P_2, , ..., P_n\}$, called the premises or knowledge base, is a sequence of AR propositions $B_1, B_2, ...$ B_m where each B_k is one of the following:

1. A premise, $B_k \in \{P_1, P_2, , ..., P_n\}$
2. A tautology
3. For some $i < k$, B_k come from B_i as a result of using IR-1
4. For some $i, j < k$, B_k comes from B_i and B_j as a result of using inference rule (IR-2). The following theorem [4] from the bases of deductive reasoning in AR.

Theorem: If there exists from the set of premises $\{P_1, P_2, , ..., P_n\}$ a deduction terminating in B then $(P_1, P_2, , ..., P_n) \quad B$, B is inferable from the premises.

This result greatly simplifies the process of reasoning. For with this result we need only consider the propositions directly needed to prove what we desire. While obvious, its worth noting that all premises are inferable from the knowledge base; $(P_1, P_2, , ..., P_n)$ P_j for all $P_j \in \{P_1, P_2, , ..., P_n\}$.

In the following we introduce an operation which we shall find useful.

Definition: Let V_a and V_b be two joint variables with domains X and Z respectively. The **projection** of the proposition V_a *is* A onto V_b, denoted $Proj_{V_b}[V_a$ *is* A] is the proposition V_b *is* B in which

$$B(z) = Max_Q[A(x)].$$

Here Q is the subset of elements in X which have the same value as z for the atomic variables which V_a and V_b have in common. (If V_a and V_b are disjoint then B(z) = 1 for all z).

The process of projection is closely related to the projection operation used in relational database theory. One important use of projection is in the case when the variable we project onto, V_b, is an an atomic variable in the joint variable, V_a, we project from. In this situation obtaining information about a variable from information about its relationship with other variables. This case of projection is closely related to the process of marginalization used in probability theory

The following theorem about the projection operation is proven in [4]

Theorem: For any V_b, V_a *is* A $\subseteq Proj_{V_b}[V_a$ *is* A].

This theorem says that any statement in AR is contained in its projection onto any joint variable, essentially projection is a special case of entailment. The implication of this for inference is following:

Corollary: If $(P_1, P_2, , ..., P_n)$ P then $(P_1, P_2, , ..., P_n)$ $Proj_{V_a}(P)$.

The significance of this is that the projection of anything inferable is also inferable.

An important related idea that can be introduced at this time is the idea of a minimal solution associated with an atomic variable. Assume $\{P_1, P_2, , ..., P_n\}$ is a knowledge base, and V_i is an atomic variable. If $P = P_1 \times P_2 \times .... \times P_n$, then the proposition V_i *is* A_i ■ $Proj_{V_i}(P)$ is called the minimal proposition associated with V_i. The importance of this minimal proposition is that any proposition about the V_i inferable from our knowledge base is contained, inferable, from the minimal solution. In particular if $(P_1, P_2, , ..., P_n)$ V_i *is* B then V_i *is* $A_i \subseteq V_i$ *is* B. In many cases when using AR we are interested in the most informed value of a variable, the minimal solution can be seen as this value for the variable.

7. Propositional Logic in AR

Since classic Binary Proposition Logic (BPL) provides a very pervasive and useful reasoning system, one in which our intuition is well developed, it is worth looking at its representation within the framework of the theory of approximate reasoning, for more details see [8, 24]. In BPL the basic objects are atomic propositions. We shall indicate the set propositions of concern in a particular environment as x_j for j = 1 to n. In BPL our concern is with the truth value of these propositions. In the representation of BPL within AR we associate with each proposition x_j an atomic variable V_j. The variable V_j is used to indicate the truth value of the proposition x_j, and thus has as its base set X_j = B ={T, F}. In this representation the space L in which we draw our membership grades from is {1, 0}, the sets involved are crisp sets. Atomic statements in this representation of BPL which are of the from V_i *is* A are used to indicate that the truth value of the proposition x_i lies in the set A. Since X_j and L each have only two values there are only four possible values for A, each of which can be given a unique linguistic designation.

$$A = \{T\} = \{\frac{1}{T}, \frac{0}{F}\} \equiv \text{TRUE}$$

$$A = \{F\} = \{\frac{0}{T}, \frac{1}{F}\} \equiv \text{FALSE}$$

$$A = \{T, F\} = \{\frac{1}{T}, \frac{1}{F}\} \equiv \text{UNKNOWN}$$

$$A = \varnothing = \{\frac{0}{T}, \frac{0}{F}\} \equiv \text{INCONSISTENT}$$

The representation of propositions from BPL as statements in AR is rather straight forward. In the following we use x_j to indicate atomic items in BPL and V_j to indicate atomic variables in AR, the truth value of x_j.

BPL	**AR**
x_j	V_j *is* TRUE
not x_j	V_j *is* FALSE
x_j and x_i	V_j *is* TRUE × V_i *is* TRUE
x_j or x	V_j *is* TRUE ⊥ V_i *is* TRUE
$x_j \rightarrow x_i$	V_j *is* FALSE ⊥ V_i *is* TRUE

More generally if G and H are statements in BPL having representation V_a *is* P and V_b *is* Q in AR then: not(G) translates to V_a *is* $\overline{P}$, G and H translates to V_a *is* P × V_b *is* Q; G or H translates to V_a *is* P ⊥ V *is* Q; G → H translates to V_a *is* $\overline{P}$ ⊥ V *is* Q.

Using these translation rules we can represent complex propositions in BPL in AR. For example (x_1 and $\overline{x_2}$) or (x_1 and x_3) gets translated as

(V_1 *is* TRUE × V_2 *is* FALSE) ⊥ (V_1 *is* TRUE × V_3 *is* TRUE).

We then can express this as a proposition involving the joint variable (V_1, V_2, V_3) defined on the space $X = X_1 \times X_2 \times X_2$ where $X_j = \{T, F\}$. In particular V_1 *is* TRUE $\times$ V_2 *is* FALSE = (V_1, V_2) *is* TRUE $\times$ FALSE = (V_1, V_2) *is* A_1 where $A_1 = \{(T, F)\} = \{\frac{1}{(T, F)}, \frac{0}{(T,T)}, \frac{0}{(F, T)}, \frac{0}{(F, F)}\}$. The component V_1 *is* TRUE $\times$ V_3 *is* TRUE = (V_1, V_3) *is* A_2
where $A_2 = \{(T, T)\} = \{\frac{1}{(T, F)}, \frac{0}{(T,T)}, \frac{0}{(F, T)}, \frac{0}{(F, F)}\}$. Finally we get (V_1, V_2, V_3) *is* $A_1 \perp A_2$. In expressing this care must be taken with respect to the underlying base sets. If we take the cylindrical extension of (V_1, V_2) *is* A, we get (V_1, V_2, V_3) *is* $\mathring{A}_1$ where

$$\mathring{A}_1 = \{(T, F, T), (T, F, F)\}$$

and if we take the cylindrical extension of (V_1, V_3) *is* A_2 we get (V_1, V_2, V_3) *is* $\mathring{A}_2$ where $\mathring{A}_2 = \{(T, T, T), (T, F, T)\}$. Finally taking the disjunction of $\mathring{A}_1$ and $\mathring{A}_2$ we get as our final representation (V_1, V_2, V_3) *is* A where

$$A = \{(T, T, T), (T, F, T)\ (T, F, F)\}.$$

It is interesting to note that if we made a truth table of $(x_1$ and $\bar{x}_2)$ or $(x_1$ and $x_3)$ then the elements in A are those that make the statement true.

Let us look at an example of reasoning in this environment. Consider the simple modus ponens

P_1: If x_1 then x_2

P_2: x_1

P_2 is represented as V_1 *is* TRUE, hence its cylindrical extension is (V_1, V_2) *is* A_1 where $A = \{(T,T), (T, F)\}$. P_2 is represented as V_1 *is* FALSE or V_2 *is* TRUE, this becomes (V_1, V_2) *is* A_2 where $A_2 = \{(T,T), (F, T)\ (F, F)\}$. Taking the conjunction of these we get (V_1, V_2) *is* A where $A = A_1 \cap A_2 = \{(T, T)\}$. Taking the projection of this onto V_2 we get V_2 *is* TRUE.

It should be strongly emphasized that we are not advocating the use of AR to replace the very effective reasoning mechanism of BPL but just indicating that AR provides an equivalent representation which may be of use in some situations.

Let us now consider the issue of the measurement of information contained in BPL statements, using the representation of AR will help. Here considerable use be made of the measure of specificity introduced earlier. We recall that if V is variable with domain Y having cardinality n then the AR proposition V *is* A has information content Inf(V *is* A) = Sp(A), where $Sp(A) = A(y^*) - \frac{1}{n-1} \sum_{\substack{y \in Y \\ y \neq y^*}} A(y)$ and y^* is an element with largest membership grade in A.

Let us first consider atomic propositions in binary logic, V_1 *is* A. We recall that there are four possible values for A, TRUE, FALSE, UNKNOWN and INCONSISTENT. It is easy to see that

$$\text{Inf}(V_1 \textit{ is } \text{TRUE}) = \text{Sp}(\{\tfrac{1}{T}, \tfrac{0}{F}\}) = 1 - 0 = 1$$

$$\text{Inf}(V_1 \textit{ is } \text{FALSE}) = \text{Sp}(\{\tfrac{0}{T}, \tfrac{1}{F}\}) = 1 - 0 = 1$$

$$\text{Inf}(V_1 \textit{ is } \text{UNKNOWN}) = \text{Sp}(\tfrac{1}{T}, \tfrac{1}{F}\}) = 1 - 1 = 0$$

$$\text{Inf}(V_1 \textit{ is } \text{INCONSISTENT}) = \text{Sp}(\{\tfrac{0}{T}, \tfrac{0}{F}\}) = 0 - 0 = 0$$

Thus we see that the knowledge that an atomic proposition is either True or False provides the same maximal information. On the other hand propositions whose truth values is either unknown or inconsistent provide zero information.

Consider now a knowledge base, KB, comprised of n atomic propositions, x_i for i = 1 to n and their associated AR variables V_i, i = 1 to n. This knowledge base is expressible as a proposition involving a joint variable, $(V_1, \quad V_n)$ *is* P where P is a subset of B^n. Since B = {T, F}we see that the cardinality of B^n is 2^n. Let us look at the measure of information. First we note that if P = Ø, the null set, then since Sp(Ø) = 0 we have zero information. In addition if P = B^n, the whole domain, then we have a tautology and again we have no information, $\text{Sp}(B^n) = 0$.

Let us indicate $B^n = \{y_1, \ldots, y_{2^n}\}$. Assume that at least one element in B^n has non-zero. Without loss of generality we shall assume $P(y_1) = 1$, because L = {0, 1} all non-zero membership grades must be one. In this case

$$\text{Sp}(P) = P(y_1) - \frac{1}{2^n - 1} \sum_{j=2}^{2^n} P(y_1)$$

Letting #yes be the number elements having membership grade one in P we get

$$\text{Sp}(P) = 1 - \frac{1}{2^n - 1}(\#\text{yes} - 1) = \frac{\#\text{NO}}{2^n - 1}$$

where #NO is the number of elements not in P, the number of impossible solutions. Thus when P is not the null set the quantity of information contained in V *is* P is equal to the number of impossible elements divided by the total number of possible states minus one. This measure can be seen as being very much in the spirit of viewing knowledge as constraints. For we initially start with 2^n possible values for our variable V and our goal is to find one of these as the appropriate value. In obtaining information we are essentially eliminating elements as being possible values for V, thus we reach maximal information when we have eliminated all but one as the possible value for V, hence we have maximal information when we have eliminated $2^n - 1$ possible values. Thus the measurement of the amount of information in a proposition as the proportion of those we have eliminated, #NO, divided by the amount we have to eliminate, $2^n - 1$, appears extremely reasonable.

Let us look at this measure for some special cases. Consider the proposition (V_1, V_2) *is* $\{\frac{1}{(T, T)}, \frac{1}{(T, F)}, \frac{0}{(F, T)}, \frac{0}{F, F}\}$. We observe that the amount of information available about this joint variable is $Inf(V_1, V_2) = \frac{2}{3}$. Implicit in the preceding proposition is information about both V_1 and V_2. If we take projections of this proposition onto V_1 and V_2 we get V_1 *is* $\{\frac{1}{T}, \frac{0}{F}\}$ and V_2 *is* $\{\frac{1}{T}, \frac{1}{F}\}$ here we see that $Inf(V_1) = 1$ and $Inf(V_2) = 0$. Thus we have complete information about V_1 and zero information about V_2.

Consider now the proposition (V_1, V_2) *is* $\{\frac{1}{(T, T)}, \frac{0}{(T, F)}, \frac{0}{(F, T)}, \frac{1}{(F, F)}\}$. We note that this is essentially the bi-implication, $x_i \leftrightarrow x_2$, x_i if and only if x_2, which is $x_1 \rightarrow x_1$ and $x_2 \rightarrow x_1$. Here again the information about $(V_1, V_2) = \frac{2}{3}$. However since the projections are V_1 *is* $\{\frac{1}{T}, \frac{1}{F}\}$ and V_2 *is* $\{\frac{1}{T}, \frac{1}{F}\}$ we get $Inf(V_1) = Inf(V_2) = 0$.

What we see here is that there is no general fixed relationship between the information in a joint proposition and the information in its projections. However there exists a number of special exceptions. Assume we have the knowledge P: V *is* A and let P1: V_1 *is* A_1 be a projection onto the atomic variable V_1. Three special cases worth noting. If A is a singleton, consists of exactly one element, then A_1 is a singleton and Inf(P) = Inf(P1) = 1. If A is whole space, A = X, then A_1 is also the whole domain of V_1 and here Inf(P) = Inf(P1) = 0. Finally if $A = \varnothing$, the null space then $A_1 = \varnothing$ and here again Inf(P) = Inf(P1) = 0.

It should also be apparent that except for some very special cases no general rule can be expressed for calculating the amount information resulting from the conjunction of propositions from the amount of information contained in the individual conjuncts. We can easily show that the amount of information resulting from a conjunction strongly depends on the relationship of the propositions being conjuncted. Among the special cases are the following. If P_1 and P_2 are two propositions expressed as V *is* A_1 and V *is* A_2 and P = P_1 *and* P_2 then Inf(P) = 0 if P_1 and P_2 are conflicting, $A_1 \cap A_2 = \varnothing$, and $Inf(P) = Inf(P_1)$ if $P_1 \subseteq P_2$. For all other relationships the best we can say is that $Inf(P) \geq Max[Inf(P_1), Inf(P_2)]$ if $A_1 \cap A_2 \neq \varnothing$.

The binary and discrete nature of this environment means that the values assumed by this measure of information, $\frac{\#NO}{2^n - 1}$ will also be discrete. For a system consisting two propositions the information states are $0, \frac{1}{3}, \frac{2}{3}, 1$. For a system consisting of three atomic propositions the information states are $0, \frac{1}{7}, \frac{2}{7}, \frac{3}{7}, \frac{4}{7}, \frac{5}{7}, \frac{6}{7}, 1$.

8. Possibilistic Logic

Dubois and Prade have introduced an extension of binary propositional logic (BPL) which they call possibilistic logic [9, 10, 11, 12]. Possibilistic logic (PL) extends binary propositional logic by allowing the association of some degree of belief with statements from the binary proposition logic; This degree of belief is called the degree necessity by Dubois and Prade, we shall also use the term degree of certainty which is somewhat closer to the intuitive idea being captured. Thus if P is any statement in BPL possibilistic logic allows statements such as

$$P: \alpha,$$

this statement indicating that P is believed to degree α. Thus we can have statements like (John is a man): α. Here α indicates how much we believe the proposition John is a man. Complex propositions can also be qualified by a degree of belief in this logic, thus we can have $((P \vee \bar{Q}) \rightarrow R): \alpha$.

Normally α is a number in the unit interval, where the larger α the more the belief. Statements without qualification are assumed to have $\alpha = 1$, thus BPL can be seen as special case of possibilistic logic where $\alpha = 1$ for all statements.

In this possibilistic logic the form of sentences involve two portions, the first being a statement from BPL and the second being the belief or certainty associated with these statements. It should be emphasized that in possibilistic logic the truth value associated with a proposition is still restricted to being either T or F, but our belief about are knowledge is graded.

Possibilistic logic can be seen to be a special case of the approximate reasoning. We can represent statements from possibilistic logic in the language of approximate reasoning and then use the reasoning mechanism of AR to deduce other statements. The representation of possibilistic logic in AR takes advantage of the two part structure of possibilistic logic statements, which is one in which we have a component that is a BPL statement and a component indicating the associated belief. Consider a statement P: α we can represent the BPL component P in AR just as we have done in the preceding by using linguistic variables taking their values in the space $B = \{T, F\}$. However, in addition to usual logical operations available in BPL, the possibilistic logic of Dubois and Prade make considerable and creative use of the operation of certainty (necessity) qualification. Assume P is BPL statement representable in AR as V_a *is* A. Then the possibilistic statement P: α where $\alpha \in [0,1]$ is equivalent to the AR statement V_a *is* A *is* α certain. As we have previously indicated this can be translated into V_a *is* B where the membership grade of x in B is

$$B(x) = A(x) \vee (1 - \alpha).$$

We note that if $\alpha = 1$ then $B(x) = A(x)$ and thus P: α is effectively P. If $\alpha = 0$ then $B(x) = 1$ for all x and thus P is 0-certain becomes the tautology, unknown, B = X the inverse of V_a.

Thus in possibilistic logic we still have as our basic elements atomic propositions, x_j for j = 1 to n and in the AR representation we associate with each of these an atomic variable V_j which denotes the truth value of the proposition x_j. As in the case of the binary propositional logic the domain of V_j is the space B = {T, F}. However, in the AR representation of possibilistic logic the space L from which the membership grades are drawn is extended from {0, 1}, which is used in the representation of BPL, to the unit interval I = [0. 1]

We shall not pursue here in detail the reasoning mechanism used in possibilistic logic as this done in considerable detail by Dubois and Prade [9-12]. We note that in [24, 25] Yager looked at the reasoning mechanism of possibilistic logic in the framework of AR. We shall, however, make some comments regarding the information content of propositions in possibilistic logic.

Consider the proposition x_1, its representation in AR is V_1 *is* TRUE. We recall that $Inf(x_1) = Sp(TRUE) = 1$. Consider now the possibilistic logic statement x_1 *is* α certain, here the AR is representation is V_1 *is* B where $B = \{\frac{1}{T}, \frac{1-\alpha}{F}\}$. The amount of information contained in this proposition $Inf(x_1{:}\alpha) = Sp(B) = \alpha$. Thus we see the qualification with respect our certainty, as we would expect, reduces the information conveyed. More generally we have the following result.

Theorem: Assume P is any proposition from binary logic then $Inf(P{:}\ \alpha) \le \alpha$.

Proof: Let P be representable as V_a *is* A where the domain of V_a is $B^n = Y = \{y_1, \ldots, y_{2^n}\}$. Without loss of generality we assume the maximal membership of A occurs at y_1. The proposition P: α is representable as V_a *is* B where $B(y) = A(y) \vee (1-\alpha)$. In this case $Inf(P{:}\ \alpha) = Sp(B) = B(y_1) - \frac{1}{2^n - 1}\sum_{j=2}^{2^n} B(y_j)$ Since for all y_j, $B(y_j) \ge 1 - \alpha$ then $Sp(B) \le B(y_1) - (1-\alpha)$ and since $B(y_1) \le 1$ then

$$Sp(B) \le 1 - (1 - \alpha) \le \alpha.$$

It can be shown seen that $Inf(A{:}\ \alpha) = \alpha$ if A is normal and $A(y) \le 1 - \alpha$ for all elements except the one that is normal. This corresponds to a case in which we have V is {y*} *is* α certain.

The following theorem provides a very useful relationship between the measure of information of BPL propositions and possibilistic logic statements.

Theorem: If P is a proposition in BPL then $Inf(P{:}\ \alpha) = \alpha\ Inf(P)$.

Proof: P can be represented as V *is* A where A is a crisp subset of B^n and P: α is represented as V *is* B where $B(y) = A(y) \vee (1-\alpha)$. Two cases will be considered

i. $A = \varnothing$. Here $B(y) = (1-\alpha)$ for all y and $Inf(P) = Sp(A) = 0$ and $Inf(P{:}\ \alpha) = Sp(B) = 0$, From this it follows that $Inf(P{:}\ \alpha) = \alpha\ Inf(P)$.

ii. $A \ne \varnothing$. In this case $Sp(A) = \frac{\#NO}{2^n - 1}$, where #NO is the number of elements in A having zero membership grade. We see that $B(y) = 1$ if $A(y) = 1$ and $B(y) = (1-\alpha)$ if $A(y) = 0$. Since A is non-null at least one element in A has membership grade 1, let us denote this as y_1. Since $Inf((P{:}\ \alpha) = Sp(B)$ we have

$$Sp(B) = B(y_1) - \frac{1}{2^n - 1}\sum_{j=2}^{2^n} B(y_j) = 1 - \frac{1}{2^n - 1}((\#YES - 1) + (1 - \alpha)\ \#NO)$$

$$Sp(B) = \frac{1}{2^n - 1}(\#NO - (1 - \alpha)\#NO) = \frac{1}{2^n - 1}\alpha\ \#NO = \alpha\ Sp(A)$$

Consider an atomic proposition in possibilistic logic V_i *is* A. Since the domain of V_i *is* {T, F} then most generally in possibilistic logic $A = \{\frac{A(T)}{T}, \frac{A(F)}{F}\}$ for some A(T), A(F) $\in$ [0, 1].

The amount of information here is

$$Sp(A) = Max[A(T), A(F)] - Min[A(T), A(F)]$$

Since $Max\ [a, b] = \frac{a + b + (a + b)}{2}$ and $Min\ [a, b] = \frac{a + b - (a + b)}{2}$ we get

$$Sp(A) = |A(T) - A(F)|.$$

Thus the amount of information is the absolute difference between the membership grades of true and false. We see Sp(A) = 0 whenever A(T) = A(F). The amount of information is maximal when Max(A(T), A(F)) = 1 and Min(A(T), A(F) = 0. In this case we know with certainty whether x_1 or $\bar{x}_1$ is true.

Consider two propositions about the same atomic variable $x_1: \alpha$ and $x_1: \beta$ here we get

$$V_1\ is\ \{\frac{1}{T}, \frac{1 - \alpha}{F}\} \text{ and } V_2\ is\ \{\frac{1}{T}, \frac{1 - \beta}{F}\}.$$

In this case the conjunction of these two pieces knowledge gives V_1 *is* $\{\frac{1}{T}, \frac{(1 - \alpha) \wedge (1 - \beta)}{F}\}$, this can be seen to be the possibilistic proposition x_1: Max[α, β]. In this case the total amount of information in our knowledge is equal to Max[α, β].

Consider now the two propositions $x_1: \alpha$ and $\bar{x}_1: \beta$. Here we get in terms of AR V_1 *is* $\{\frac{1}{T}, \frac{1 - \alpha}{F}\}$ and V_1 *is* $\{\frac{1 - \beta}{T}, \frac{1}{F}\}$. Conjuncting these two pieces of knowledge we get V_1 *is* $\{\frac{1 - \beta}{T}, \frac{1 - \alpha}{F}\}$. The total amount of information conveyed here is $|\alpha - \beta|$. We note here the closer α and β the more conflicting our knowledge and hence the less informative.

In the the classic modus ponens from $x_1 \rightarrow x_2$ and x_1 we are able to infer x_2. Let us look at this in possibilistic logic. Assume we have two statements S1 and S2

S1: $x_1 \rightarrow x_2: \alpha$

S2: $x_1: \beta$

From S1 we get (V_1, V_2) *is* A where $A = \{\frac{1}{(T, T)}, \frac{1 - \alpha}{(T, F)}, \frac{1}{(F, T)}, \frac{1}{(F, F)}\}$. From S2 we get (V_1, V_2) *is* B where $B = \{\frac{1}{(T, T)}, \frac{1}{(T, F)}, \frac{1 - \beta}{(F, T)}, \frac{1 - \beta}{(F, F)}\}$. Combing these we get (V_1, V_2) *is* F, where $F = \{\frac{1}{(T, T)}, \frac{1 - \alpha}{(T, F)}, \frac{1 - \beta}{(F, T)}, \frac{1 - \beta}{(F, F)}\}$. Projecting onto V_2 we get V_2 *is* E where $E = \{\frac{1}{T}, \frac{\text{Max}[(1 - \beta), (1 - \alpha)]}{F}\}$. Thus we get x_2: $\text{Min}[\alpha, \beta]$. In this case the amount of information conveyed about V_2 is $\text{Min}[\alpha, \beta]$.

In possibilistic logic an important step is retranslation. Assume V_a *is* B is a proposition of possibilistic logic may have resulted from some manipulation and combination of knowledge. Because of the manipulations the membership grades of the elements in B can be any value in the unit interval. The process of retranslation consists of converting this into a statement P: α where P is a BPL proposition. This step essentially requires obtaining a proposition V_a *is* A: α where A has membership grades in $\{0, 1\}$, is V_a *is* A is a binary logic proposition, and also where V_a *is* A: α inferable from V_a *is* B, .V_a *is* B $\subseteq$ V_a *is* A: α

An interesting question is what is the proposition, V_a *is* A: α satisfying these requirements that conveys the most information. First we recall that the entailment principle tells us that from the proposition V_a *is* B we can infer V_a *is* E where $E(y) \geq B(y)$. Any proposition V_a *is* A: α in which A is binary, $A(y) \in \{0, 1\}$, is effectively V_a *is* F where $F(y) \in \{1, (1 - \alpha)\}$ for all y. Thus our problem is to find V_a *is* F such that:

1. $F(y) \in \{1, (1 - \alpha)\}$ for some $\alpha \in [0, 1]$
2. $F(y) \geq B(y)$
3. Sp(F) is maximal

For simplicity we shall initially assume B is normal. Consider first the case of one variable V_1 *is* B where $B = \{\frac{1}{T}, \frac{a}{F}\}$. Here we can infer any $F = \{\frac{1}{T}, \frac{b}{F}\}$ where $b \geq a$. In this case the specificity is $Sp(F) = 1 - b$. Thus specificity is maximal if $b = a$. Thus in this case we make $\alpha = 1 - a$. Hence our inference is

$$V_a \; is \; \{\frac{1}{T}, \frac{0}{F}\}: 1 - \alpha$$

Consider now the nonnormal case V_a *is* B where $B = \{\frac{u}{T}, \frac{v}{F}\}$ and $u \geq v$. Here we can infer V_a *is* $\{\frac{a}{T}, \frac{b}{F}\}$ with $a \geq u$, $b \geq v$. Here the information is $Sp = |a - b|$. The maximal specificity is obtained if $a = 1$ and $b = v$. Thus the most informative inference is V_a *is* TRUE *is* 1 - v certain.

Let us now look at a more general normal case, assume we have obtained V_a *is* B where B is a fuzzy subset of $y = \{y_1, y_2, \quad, y_n\}$. Without loss of generality assume $B(y_i) \geq B(y_j)$ if $i < j$. Normality means $B(y_1) = 1$ In this case

$$\text{Inf}(V_a \textit{ is } B) = \text{Sp}(B) = 1 - \frac{1}{n-1}\sum_{j=2}^{n} B(y_j)$$

Consider now the proposition V_a *is* A: α where A is crisp. Here we note that

$$\text{Inf}(V_a \textit{ is } A: \alpha) = 1 - \frac{1}{n-1}(\#YES + (1-\alpha)\#NO) = 1 - \frac{1}{n-1}n + \alpha\ \#NO$$

here #YES are the number of elements having membership grade one and #NO is the number of elements have zero membership grade in A. In order to maximize Inf(V_a *is* A: α) we want to make the product α #NO as big as possible. What is clear we can't make any element no if B(x) = 1. As we shall see there exists some conflict between trying to make both α and #NO. Assume we to make #NO as big as possible that is we make all elements with $B(x) \neq 1$ have A(x) = 0. This means that $1 - \alpha$ equals the maximal non one membership grade, this could be a very low value for α. Assume now we try to make α as big as possible, $\alpha = 1$. In this case to satisfy the condition that $A(x) \vee (1 - \alpha) \geq B(x)$ we must have $A(x) \geq B(x)$ this means we only can make elements with B(x) = 0 have A(x) = 0. The following lemma will help us obtain a direct method for finding the best A.

Lemma: Assume A is crisp, $A(y) \vee (1 - \alpha) \geq B(y)$ for y. Let $A(y_j) = 1$ and $A(y_i) = 0$ and $B(y_i) \geq B(y_j)$. If $\hat{A}$ is such that $\hat{A}(y) = \hat{A}(y)$ for all $y \neq y_j$ and $\hat{A}(y_j) = 0$ then $\hat{A}(y) \vee (1 - \alpha) \geq B(y)$ for y.and $\text{Inf}(\hat{A}: \alpha) \geq \text{Inf}(A: \alpha)$.

Proof: 1. Since $\hat{A}(y) \geq A(y)$ for all $y \neq y_j$ then from the assumptions about A we get that $\hat{A}(y) \vee (1 - \alpha) \geq B(y)$. We must consider the case of y_j. First we note that $A(y_i) \vee (1 - \alpha) \geq B(y_i)$. However since $A(y_i) = 0$ we have $(1 - \alpha) \geq B(y_i) \geq B(y_j)$. Consider now $\hat{A}(y_j) \vee (1 - \alpha) = (1 - \alpha) \geq B(y_j)$. Thus $\hat{A}(y) \vee (1 - \alpha) \geq B(y)$ for y

2. $\text{Inf}(\hat{A}: \alpha) - \text{Inf}(A: \alpha) .= \alpha\,(\#NO(\hat{A}) - \#NO(A)) = \alpha \geq 0$

Essentially this theorem shows that if A* is the optimal translating proposition then if the membership grades of B are such that $B(y_i) \geq B(y_j)$ for $i < j$ then $A^*(y_i) \geq A(y_j)$ for $i < j$. What this means is that in the optimal A* there is some index q such that for all $B(y) \geq B(y_q)$ $A^*(y) = 1$ and $A^*(y) = 0$ for all y such that $B(y) < B(y_q)$. Any crisp subset A having the property just indicated, for all $B(y) \geq B(y_q)$ $A(y) = 1$ and A(y) = 0 for all other y, will be said to ***oblige*** B.

The following lemma is also useful in finding the most informative translation.

Lemma: Assume B is appropriately indexed, $B(y_i) \geq B(y_j)$ for $i < j$ and assume A is a crisp subset that obliges B and let y_q be the crossover point in A. Then for the proposition V_a *is* A: α the largest value of α that satisfies V_a *is* $B \subseteq V_a$ *is* A: α is $\alpha = 1 - B(y_{q-1})$.

Proof: Let $F(y) = A(y) \vee (1 - \alpha) = A(y) \vee B(y_{q-1})$. We see that for any $j \geq q$ $F(y_j) = 1$ since $A(y_j) = 1$ and hence $F(y_j) \geq B(y_j)$. For $j \leq q - 1$, $F(y_j) = B(y_{q-1}) \geq B(y_j)$. Having showed that $\alpha = 1 - B(y_{q-1})$ satisfies the condition we must show that $\alpha > 1 - B(y_{q-1})$ doesn't satisfy the condition. Assume $\alpha^* > 1 - B(y_{q-1})$, then $\alpha^* = 1 - u$

where u < $B(y_{q-1})$. In this case $A(y_{q-1}) \vee (1 - \alpha^*) = 0 \vee u = u < B(y_{q-1})$, hence the condition is note satisfied.

Let us now recapitulate the implications of these lemmas with regard to the task of obtaining the most informative retranslation of V_a *is* B, V_a *is* A: α. The first lemma says that A obliges B. This means that assuming the B is appropriately indexed, $B(y_i) \geq B(y_j)$ for $i < j$, selecting the optimal A means deciding on some index $p = q - 1$, corresponding to the first zero, such $A(y_j) = 0$ for $j \geq p$ and $A(y_j) = 1$ for $j < p$. The second lemma tells us associated with each selection of p there is an optimal choice of α, $1 - B(y_p)$. Thus the problem reduces to selecting the best value for p Since we have previously shown that criteria useful for comparing retranslations is α #NO we are essentially faced with a discrete optimization problem: Find the integer $1 \leq p \leq n$ which satisfies this problem

Maximizes $(1 - B(y_p))\,(n + 1 - p)$

where n is the number of elements in the universe. This problem can be easily solved by enumeration. The following example illustrates the process

Example: Assume $B = \{\frac{1}{(T, T)}, \frac{0.6}{(T, F)}, \frac{0.5}{(F, T)}, \frac{0.3}{(F, F)}\}$

P	$B(y_p)$	$(1 - B(y_p))\,(n + 1 - p)$
1	1	0
2	0.6	(0.4) 3 = 1.2
3	0.5	(0.5) 2 = 1.0
4	0.3	(0.7) 1 = 0.7

In this case the optimal solution occurs with p = 2 and $\alpha = 1 - B(y_2) = 0.4$ and

$$A = \{\frac{1}{(T, T)}, \frac{0}{(T, F)}, \frac{0}{(F, T)}, \frac{0}{(F, F)}\}.$$

Consider now the case where $B = \{\frac{1}{(T, T)}, \frac{0.9}{(T, F)}, \frac{0.5}{(F, T)}, \frac{0.3}{(F, F)}\}$, here we increased the support for (T, F)

P	$B(y_p)$	$(1 - B(y_p))\,(n + 1 - p)$
1	1	0
2	0.9	(0.1) 3 = 0.3
3	0.5	(0.5) 2 = 1.0
4	0.3	(0.7) 1 = 0.7

In this case the optimal solution occurs with p = 3 and $\alpha = 1 - B(y_3) = 0.5$ and

$$A = \{\frac{1}{(T, T)}, \frac{1}{(T, F)}, \frac{0}{(F, T)}, \frac{0}{(F, F)}\}.$$

Some care should be taken in the case in which $B(y_1) < 1$.

9. Quantifiers and Predicates in Approximate Reasoning

Thus far we have considered the representation of binary propositional logic and its extension to possibilistic logic in the framework of approximate reasoning. Let us now briefly consider the introduction of predicates. A predicate can be seen as a kind of *pre*-proposition. A single valued predicate Pred(x) defined on a domain Y is an object, that when x is instantiated to some element $y \in Y$, becomes a proposition, a statement which has a truth value of either true or false. Consider the predicate Even, we see that Even(7) has a truth value, False, while Even(24) has a truth value, True, while Even(x) is not a proposition, its truth value depends upon x which is unspecified. Thus an instantiated predicate is in reality a proposition, if $y_i \in Y$ then $Pred(y_i)$ is a proposition. We can represent the truth of this proposition in AR by a variable $V_{Pred(y_i)}$ which takes its value in the space {T, F}.

We have indicated that a predicate, Pred(x), can be used to generate a proposition by instantiating x with some element from the domain Y of Pred. There exists another way of generating a propositional statement from a predicate, this involves making some *global* statement about the predicate. In predicate logic, the two common ways of making global statements about predicates are quantified statements involving the universal and existential quantifiers. These statements are

all Y are Pred $\equiv \forall\, y \in Y\ Pred(y)$

there exists Y that is Pred $\equiv \exists\, y \in Y\ Pred(y)$.

Let us investigate the representation of these statements in approximate reasoning. Assume Pred is a predicate whose domain $Y = \{y_1, y_2, \ \ , y_n\}$. For notational simplicity we shall let U_i indicate the truth value of the proposition, $Pred(y_i)$, that is what we previously denoted $V_{Pred(y_i)}$. As we have indicated quantified statements are global statements about the predicate, that is they say something about the truth of all instantiations of the predicate. In particular if U is the joint variable $(U_1, U_2, \ \ , U_n)$ then these quantified statements are interpretable in AR as U *is* Q where Q is a subset of B^n, $B = \{T, F\}$.

More specifically consider the universal quantified *All Y are Pred*, this says that for all $y_i \in Y$, $Pred(y_i)$ is true. Let $q^* \in B^n$ be the tuple (T, T, , T), all components are true, then the proposition *All Y are Pred* translates into U *is* Q* where

$$Q^*(q^*) = 1$$
$$Q^*(q) = 0 \quad \text{for all } q \neq q^*$$

From U *is* Q* we can, by projection, obtain U_j *is* $\{\frac{1}{T}, \frac{0}{F}\}$ for all U_j.

Let $q_* \in B^n$ be the tuple (F, F, ..., F), all components are false. The proposition *there exists Y that is Pred* translates into U *is* Q_* where

$$Q_*(q_*) = 0$$
$$Q_*(q) = 1 \quad \text{for all } q \neq q_*$$

From U *is* Q_* all we can infer is U_j *is* $\{\frac{1}{T}, \frac{1}{F}\}$ =UNKNOWN.

We can translate *No Y are Pred* into AR, this translates into U *is* Q° where

$$Q°(q_*) = 1$$
$$Q°(q) = 0 \quad \text{for all } q \neq q_*$$

From U *is* Q° it is easy to infer, using projection, that for any j

$$U_j \ is \ \{\frac{0}{T}, \frac{1}{F}\} = \text{FALSE}.$$

It should be noted that these quantified statements are very closely related to the number of T's in any of the tuples. Let $q \in B^n$, its a tuple of n components. We shall define ***T-Count(q)*** as the number of terms in the tuple q that are T, thus T-Count(q^*) = n and T-Count(q_*) = 0. Let Q be any crisp non-null subset of the space N = {0, 1, 2, 3, ..., n}, here n is the cardinality of Y, the domain of Pred. We can provide a general formulation for translation into AR of quantified statements of the form

Q Y's *are* Pred.

We shall represent these propositions in AR as U *is* Q where Q is a crisp subset of B^n such that

$$Q(q) = 1 \ \text{ if T-Count}(q) \in Q$$
$$Q(q) = 0 \ \text{ if T-Count}(q) \notin Q$$

In this approach we are essentially expressing our quantifier as a subset Q of N. In this framework we see that for the *universal quantifier* we have Q = {n}, for the existential quantifier we have Q = N - {0} and for the quantifier none we have Q = {0}. We note that if Q is not null than Q is not null.

We can calculate the amount of information contained in a proposition Q Y's *are* Pred, since it is represented in AR as U *is* Q. Since Q is not null let us denote, without loss of generality, that $Q(q_1) = 1$. In this case

$$\text{Inf}(Q) = Q(q_1) - \frac{1}{2^n - 1}\sum_{j=2}^{2^n} Q(q_j),$$

however this can be expressed as

$$\text{Inf}(Q) = Q(q_1) + \frac{Q(q_j)}{2^n - 1} - \frac{1}{2^n - 1}\sum_{j=1}^{2^n} Q(q_j)$$

$$\text{Inf}(Q) = \frac{2^n}{2^n - 1} Q(q_1) - \frac{1}{2^n - 1}\sum_{j=1}^{2^n} Q(q_j)$$

$$\text{Inf}(Q) = \frac{1}{2^n - 1}(2^n - \sum_{j=1}^{2^n} Q(q_j))$$

We see that $\sum_{j=1}^{2^n} Q(q_j)$ is the cardinality of Q, the number of elements in Q. Thus

$$\text{Inf}(Q) = \frac{1}{2^n - 1}(2^n - \text{Card}(Q))$$

For the universal quantifier, Q*, only one element is in it, q* = (T, T, , T) here

$Inf(Q^*) = \frac{1}{2^n - 1}(2^n - 1) = 1$, perfect information. Similarly for Q° there is only one element, $q_* = (F, F, ..., F)$ here again we have perfect information. For the existential quantifier Q_* all elements except q_* are in Q_* and here then $Card(Q_*) = 2^n - 1$. Hence in this case $Inf(Q_*) = \frac{1}{2^n - 1}$, which is very little information.

More generally the cardinality of Q can be related to the generating quantifier Q. We first note that if $r \in Q$ then there are $\binom{n}{r} = \frac{n!}{r!\,(n-r)!}$ tuples q in B^n such that T–Count(q) = r. From this we see that we can obtain the cardinal of Q as

$$Card(Q) = \sum_{j=0}^{n} \binom{n}{r} Q(j)$$

here $Q(j) = 1$ if $j \in Q$" and zero otherwise. Using this we get as the information in Q

$$Inf(Q) = \frac{1}{2^n - 1}(2^n - \sum_{j=0}^{n} \binom{n}{r} Q(j))$$

We have formally generalized the idea of quantified propositions by introducing a subset Q of the space N = {0, 1, , n} indicating the number of true instantiation of the quantified predicate. Using this from the statement Q *Y are Pred* we get U *is* Q where Q is a subset of B^n and where U is the joint variable $\{U_1, ..., U_n)$, U_j being the variable corresponding to the truth value of the proposition $Pred(y_j)$.

From the point of view of computing with words people usually specify the quantifier Q in terms of some linguistic concepts rather than in terms of a subset of N. This linguistic concept must then be represented as a subset of N. Some examples of this are

at least 50 % of Y are Pred,

here $Q = \{z / z \in N \text{ and } \frac{z}{n} \geq 0.5\}$

an odd number of Y are predicate

here Q = {1, 3, 5, 7, ...},

Concepts like a few and many can also be expressed in this manner.

Predicates and associated quantified statements can also be introduced into the possibilistic logic of Dubois and Prade. Here again if Pred is a predicate defined on the domain $Y = \{y_1, , y_n\}$ we can represent the proposition $Pred(y_j)$ by a linguistic variable U_j indicating the truth value of the predicate and taking its value in the space B = {T, F}. We can also consider quantified propositions Q *Y are Pred* as generating approximate reasoning propositions of the form U *is* Q where $U = \{U_1, ..., U_n\}$.

A number of extensions can be introduced into the possibilistic logic because we allow membership grades drawn from the unit interval rather than {0, 1}. First we can associate with any quantified proposition a degree of certainty or belief α, thus we can have statements.

Q *Y are Pred* : α

With the the component $\mathcal{Q}$ *Y are Pred* represented in AR as U *is* Q this certainty qualified quantified proposition gets represented as U *is* D where D is a fuzzy subset of B^n in which $B(q) = Q(q) \vee (1 - \alpha)$.

An additional extension available to us in possibilistic logic is that we can allow $\mathcal{Q}$ to be what Zadeh [26] calls a linguistic quantifier. In the case of a linguistic quantifier $\mathcal{Q}$ is a fuzzy subset of the space $N = \{0, 1, 2, \quad , n\}$. As Zadeh discusses in [26] linguistic quantifiers allow us to represent in a very natural way quantifiers such as about 7, few and most

For the statement

$\mathcal{Q}$ *Y are Pred*

when $\mathcal{Q}$ is a fuzzy subset of N the associated set Q appearing in its AR representation U *is* Q has membership grade such that for any $q \in B^n$

$$Q(q) = \mathcal{Q}(\text{T-Count}(q))$$

Thus the membership grade of the tuple q in Q is equal to the membership grade of the T-Count of q in $\mathcal{Q}$.

Linguistic quantifiers $\mathcal{Q}$ defined on the set N are called by Zadeh [26] absolute quantifiers. In [26] Zadeh considered another class of quantifiers which he called "proportional" quantifiers. These proportional quantifiers are also fuzzy subsets, however their domain is the unit interval rather than N. Examples of these are linguistic terms such as "most" "few" and "about half". If $\mathcal{Q}$ is a proportional quantifier we can obtain the associated fuzzy subset Q used in the AR representation U *is* Q in a manner similar to the case where $\mathcal{Q}$ is absolute. In this case

$$Q(q) = \mathcal{Q}\left(\frac{\text{T-Count}(q)}{n}\right)$$

Within the framework of possibilistic logic we can now combine these linguistically quantifiers proposition with certainty qualification and are able to represented statements such as

We are ***α certain*** that ***Most Y's are Pred***

Such a statement gets translated into U *is* E where E is a fuzzy subset of B^n.

10. References

[1]. Zadeh, L. A., "Fuzzy logic = computing with words," IEEE Transactions on Fuzzy Systems 4, 103-111, 1996.

[2]. Yager, R. R., Ovchinnikov, S., Tong, R. and Nguyen, H., Fuzzy Sets and Applications: Selected Papers by L. A. Zadeh, John Wiley & Sons: New York, 1987.

[3]. Zadeh, L. A., "A theory of approximate reasoning," in Machine Intelligence, Vol. 9, edited by Hayes, J., Michie, D. and Mikulich, L. I., Halstead Press: New York, 149-194, 1979.

[4]. Yager, R. R., "Deductive approximate reasoning systems," IEEE Transactions on Knowledge and Data Engineering 3, 399-414, 1991.

[5]. Dubois, D. and Prade, H., "Fuzzy sets in approximate reasoning Part I: Inference

with possibility distributions," Fuzzy Sets and Systems 40, 143-202, 1991.
[6]. Dubois, D. and Prade, H., "Fuzzy sets in approximate reasoning Part 2: logical approaches," Fuzzy Sets 40, 203-244, 1991.
[7]. Zadeh, L. A., "Toward a theory of fuzzy information granulation and its centrality in human reasoning and fuzzy logic," Fuzzy Sets and Systems 90, 111-127, 1997.
[8]. Yager, R. R. and Filev, D. P., Essentials of Fuzzy Modeling and Control, John Wiley: New York, 1994.
[9]. Dubois, D. and Prade, H., "Necessity measures and the resolution principle," IEEE Trnasactions on Systems, Man and Cybernetics 17, 474 - 478, 1987.
[10].Dubois, D., Lang, J. and Prade, H., "Automated reasoning using possibilistic logic: semantics, belief revision and variable certainty weights," IEEE Transactions on Knowledge and Data Engineering 6, 65-70, 1994.
[11].Dubois, D., Lang, J. and Prade, H., "Possibilistic Logic," in Handbook of Logic in Artificial Intelligence and Logic Programmling : Volume 3, edited by Gabbay, D. M., Hogger, C. J. and Robinson, J. A., Clarendon Press: Oxford, 439-513, 1994.
[12].Benferhat, S., Dubois, D. and Prade, H., "Nonmonotonic reasoning, conditional objects and possibility theory," Artificial Intelligence 92, 259-276, 1997.
[13]. Goguen, J. A., "L-fuzzy sets," J. of Math. Analysis & Applications 18, 145-174, 1967.
[14]. Zadeh, L. A., "Fuzzy sets as a basis for a theory of possibility," Fuzzy Sets and Systems 1, 3-28, 1978.
[15]. Date, C. J., An Introduction to Database Systems, Addison Wesley: Reading, MA, 1986.
[16]. Hohle, U., "Probabilistic uniformization of fuzzy topologies," Fuzzy Sets and Systems 1, 1978, 1978.
[17]. Zadeh, L. A., "Fuzzy sets," Information and Control 8, 338-353, 1965.
[18]. Alsina, C., Trillas, E. and Valverde, L., "On some logical connectives for fuzzy set theory," J. Math Anal. & Appl. 93, 15-26, 1983.
[19]. Klir, G. J. and Yuan, B., Fuzzy Sets, Fuzzy Logic and Fuzzy Systems: Selected Papers by Lotfi A. Zadeh, World Scientific: Singapore, 1996.
[20]. Kosko, B., Fuzzy Engineering, Prentice Hall: Upper Saddle River, NJ, 1997.
[21]. Yager, R. R., "Measuring tranquility and anxiety in decision making: An application of fuzzy sets," Int. J. of General Systems 8, 139-146, 1982.
[22]. Yager, R. R., "On the specificity of a possibility distribution," Fuzzy Sets and Systems 50, 279-292, 1992.
[23]. Yager, R. R., "On measures of specificity," in Computational Intelligence: Soft Computing and Fuzzy-Neuro Integration with Applications, edited by Kaynak, O., Zadeh, L. A., Turksen, B. and Rudas, I. J., Springer-Verlag: Berlin, 94-113, 1998.
[24]. Yager, R. R., "Fuzzy set methods for representing commonsense knowledge," Journal of Intelligent and Fuzzy Systems, (To Appear).
[25]. Yager, R. R., "Fuzzy logics and artificial intelligence," Fuzzy Sets and Systems 90, 193-198, 1997.
[26]. Zadeh, L. A., "A computational approach to fuzzy quantifiers in natural languages," Computing and Mathematics with Applications 9, 149-184, 1983.

What is Intelligent Measurement?

Leonid Reznik
Department of Electrical and Electronic Engineering
Victoria University of Technology
P.O. Box 14428 MCMC
Melbourne, VIC 8001
Australia
Email: leonreznik@vut.edu.au

Abstract

This paper attempts to look at intelligent measurement as a process of transforming an initial *a priori* information into a final measurement result. This point of view allows to consider all sorts of information available including quantitative and qualitative (expressed in a linguistic format) and to address measurements applied in rather distant areas like engineering and social sciences. In this case the measurement can be considered as a fuzzy granulation process. The classification of all information commonly utilised in measurements is given. The paper reviews some ways of the current fuzzy logic applications in metrology and measurement technology and proposes new ways based on the development of expert system and their inclusion into measuring instruments.

1. What Measurement is Intelligent?

We do not know an exact answer or may be we know too many. Different people have different understanding and their understanding changes in time. Giving definitions is especially difficult in such an area as electronics and computing where the words are often out of date almost as soon as they hit the magnetic oxide, let alone the printed page. For example C.V.Collett and A.D.Hope [1] in 1974 stated that „all measuring systems include three basic elements: (a) a detecting and measuring element (transducer) which detects the physical variable to be measured, (b) an intermediate stage which modifies the signal from the transducer so that a desirable output is available, (c) an indicating or recording stage. No computer even was mentioned in this definition, leaving aside any intelligence. According to [2] at that time measurement science was dominated by high priests of the discipline, the keepers of the mysteries, who, by their own account, could obtain phenomenal accuracy by true observance of the rites. To these practitioners the computer was a frivolous intrusion. Talk of subjectivity in human measurement was a heresy to be suppressed.

By 1985 the situation had changed. G.C.Barney [3] determines intelligent instrumentation as „a term which has come to mean the use of a measurement system to evaluate a physical variable employing usually a digital computer to perform all (or nearly all) the signal/information processing". Initially an intelligent measurement was considered as a process performed by any measuring instrument incorporating a digital processor. Later when the presence of this feature only stopped selling instruments other considerations started being taken into account. Japanese literature seems to overtake the western one that probably is the reflection of their scientific and technological advancement. As a result, in many cases sensor systems have been implemented, that substitute for some or all of the intellectual actions of human beings [4], i.e. intelligent sensor systems. According to the dictionary [5] intelligent means „having or showing (high degree of) understanding; clever, quick of mind". Is the presence of the digital processor enough to name an instrument intelligent?

And another question, which should be answered before further consideration is made. Should the instrument be intelligent? Beyond any doubt a measurement result is associated with some uncertainty. Different methods how to characterise this uncertainty have been proposed. The new international standard was developed recently[6]. It is a common point of view that the best way of dealing with uncertainty is through an intelligence application. This approach requires an inclusion of artificial intelligence methods and tools into measuring systems and instruments.

Because in the areas of artificial and computational intelligence biology is often applied as a main reference point to draw general conclusions and a way to look for an inspiration in research, we can follow [2] in investigating a sensor development and its role in nature. The progress of a sensor in nature was a major factor in the advancement to the higher species. Yet a man, whose organs of sense are very modest in comparison to the eye of an eagle or the nose of a bloodhound, became the dominant species. Why? The possible reason is that in addition to his modest organs of sense, man developed his great brain to process the information they supplied.

Before leaving the biological analogies, let us consider one other factor. Man is more likely than other creatures to be mislead by optical illusions. There are analogous mistakes which can be made by the designer of intelligent sensor systems. One can be tempted to build a tower of deduction on weak foundations of information, with the inevitable result. Hence, one has to try to make this foundation as wide as possible by getting as much different information as available. Of the enormous range of potential physical mechanisms for sensing most had to be rejected because of drawbacks that could be overcome now. All these observations call for a new way of thinking by the designers, the manufacturers and the users of sensors.

Let us have a look at a measuring instrument (MI) as an information system. Although the definition of intelligence is a controversial problem receiving different opinions, basically an intelligent system is commonly considered as an information system and an intelligence as a product of the information system evolution [7]. As a property of advanced information systems, an intelligence can be ascertained only by observing the system dynamical behaviour, or system responses to some events.

In this paper we will consider an intelligent measurement as a process of the result development based on all sorts of information which can be used with an application of intelligent technologies and methodologies. In real life systems, applied for control or testing, the measurement results compose only a part of information which is actually available and used for control purposes [8]. The attempt to classify all the information, which is present, is given below (see section 3). We want to underline that in order to improve the quality of control, test, and measurement systems, it is particularly important not to limit the information applied just within measurement result boundaries but to develop methodologies allowing to incorporate information from all possible sources. So this information definitely may take a qualitative as well as quantitative form, may include numerical results and results expressed in a linguistic format, or in other words, written with words.

2. Is Measurement a Fuzzy Granulation Process?

If one considers the final goal of a measurement system operation, one may conclude that it can be formulated as not receiving a numerical result only but rather providing a user with some recommendations which can be expressed in a linguistic form as well. Thus, from the information point of view an intelligent measurement can be determined as the transformation of an initial a priori information into the final measurement result estimate. Both an initial and final estimates can be linguistic as well as numerical. Such an approach allows to consider both technical measurements applied in engineering systems and qualitative measurements, traditional in social system analysis. From the methodological point of view an intelligent measurement is supposed to realise artificial intelligence methodologies such as expert systems, fuzzy logic and control, neural networks and control. An application of expert systems in measurement instruments is considered in section 5.

Measurement process consists of associating with the measured properties of the objects or events some estimates, which are called the measurement results. Traditionally in technical measurements these measurement results are supposed to be crisp numbers. The technological process of receiving a measurement result is isolated from the mathematical process of the measurement result characteristics evaluation. The probability theory and statistics have been traditionally applied in measurement results processing. In this methodology the technical measurement result is considered as a numerical one and is separated from its metrological characteristics. These characteristics may include some information about the measurement result and errors: the average error, the error distribution, the correlation between different measurement errors, dynamical characteristics, etc. All this information characterises actually the measurement uncertainty and should be considered as a part of the measurement result.

If one crosses the artificial boundaries, one may conclude that a measurement system should be viewed as a part of the whole operational system which may include different control, information, and management systems. In those systems implementation, various technologies are applied, ranging from automatic control engineering to expert systems. A measurement system realises the first step of information processing producing the measurement result.

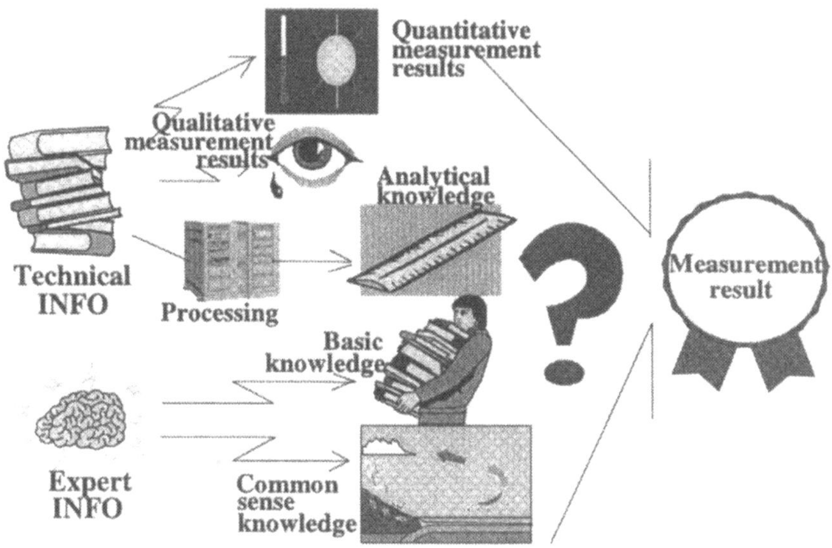

Figure 1. Intelligent measurement result basic components

In the theory of fuzzy information granulation Lotfi Zadeh [9] proposes three basic modes of generalisation:

a) fuzzification, in which one or more crisp sets are replaced by fuzzy sets,
b) granulation, in which an object is partitioned into a collection of granules, with a granule being a clump of points (objects) drawn together by indistinguishability, similarity or functionality,
c) fuzzy granulation , in which a crisp or fuzzy object is partitioned into fuzzy granules.

As any measurement result incorporates some error, it can be considered as a fuzzy granule and a measurement process can be looked at as a fuzzy granulation process. In this approach the information, which usually in measurement is referred to as a priori information, including some data about the possible ranges of the measured values, their relationship and connections, etc. can be reflected as an initial fuzzy granule as well. As this sort of information is commonly supplied by an expert one can see that methodologically there is no difference between the expert information and the measurement result. In this sense an intelligent measurement process can be considered as the processing of fuzzy granules or fuzzy granulation process.

3. Classification of Information

The whole set of information commonly applied in measurement and control systems can be roughly classified as follows (see also Table 1):

1. Special knowledge information which is collected during the control or test sessions

   1.1. quantitative measurement results obtained from sensors,
   1.2. qualitative measurement results obtained from operator's (expert's) observations: e.g. things like the colour of slag during tapping, coke combustion conditions at the tuyeres, strength of the noise,
   1.3. expert's suppositions and guesses.

2. Basic knowledge information, available a priori to the experiment or control:

   2.1. theoretical knowledge of the process or object under measurement and control, e.g. information how the object operates, relationships between different parameters of the object, etc.
   2.2. operational knowledge of the measurement and control equipment, e.g. information about the sensor operational ranges, calibrations, etc.
   2.3. statistical knowledge of the previous experiments and control obtained by processing of the data banks information.

3. Analytical knowledge - a posteriori information which becomes available after some time from the beginning (finish) of the experiment and control:

   3.1. statistical information obtained after statistical processing of all measurement results or at least a part of the results, time when this sort of information becomes available depends on the volume of processing work and computational power applied,
   3.2. technical information - obtained after some special analysis made in the laboratory conditions, e.g. chemical or physical tests of the metallurgical or chemical products, mechanical tests, etc.

4. Common sense knowledge - may be available and utilised at any stage of the measurement and control process - can be generated by the application experts and include facts like the mollification temperature for the ore, or the fact that

hanging is a temporary stagnation in the descent of the raw materials within the furnace [10].

All sorts of information are produced either by measuring instruments or experts. Unlike measuring instruments, expert's estimates are usually not calibrated. Of course, experts can be simply wrong, in which case, if we use their (wrong) estimates, we spoil the results of statistical processing. But suppose that the experts are right (and they mainly are, otherwise they would not be called upon as experts). Can we then guarantee that the use of expert estimates improves statistical estimates?

A natural way to formalise expert knowledge is to use fuzzy sets theory. The question can be reformulated as follows: how to combine fuzzy and statistical (measurement) estimates so as not to make things worse? The answer to this question could be the development of the synergetic fuzzy expert systems combining computational and artificial intelligence techniques and these systems inclusion into intelligent measuring instruments (MI).

4. How is Fuzzy Logic Applied in Metrology Now?

First attempts to apply fuzzy logic in measurement theory appeared quite a long time ago [11]. Since then fuzzy methodology has been tested in solving a number of the problems such as multisensor applications and data fusion [12] and measurement reliability increase due to the use of an extra information available [11,13]. Nowadays new approaches are intensified, especially after the concept of fuzzy granulation is put forward by L.Zadeh [9]. An example of such approaches is a virtual measurement [14] that is computer based measurement of user defined, system specific variables, typically variables of some operational significance such as performance. In virtual measurement system states are evaluated with fuzzy numbers not crisp ones as traditionally. According to Zadeh's classification a virtual measurement can be considered as fuzzification of the measurement results.

The example of a granulation process in measurement is presented in [15]. Here a fuzzy system is introduced for fusing multiple input sensor signals. The further step is made in [16,17] which explores the concept of measuring fuzzy set membership functions directly with receiving a multidimensional membership function in the second case. This can be considered as a process of fuzzy granulation. As the author states this approach has both speed and accuracy advantages over a conventional crisp metrology. The similar way is reported in [18] where fuzzy sensors compute and report linguistic assessments of numerically acquired values.

Main reported advantages of fuzzy approach to measurement can be formulated as:

- - possibility of introducing a unified approach to measurement and processing the measurement results received from all sorts of sources,

- - possibility of improving both the speed and the reliability of measurement, especially in secondary measurements,
- - an ability to expand the measurement process and consider it as a fuzzy granulation that allows not only to measure some attributes of the objects under measurement but to classify those objects as well.

However, another advantage could be the possibility of getting the measured information in linguistic form. It will allow to apply this information in expert systems and design a synergistic measurement, control and management system combining automatic control and management information systems.

Table 1

Type of information	Time of acquisition	Source of information	Actions (or knowledge) necessary to get this information	Expression of information	Addit-ional pro-cess-ing
Quantitative measurement results	during the experiment or control	Sensors and measuring instruments	measurement	Quantitative in measurement scale with known accuracy	no
Qualitative measurement results	during the experiment or control	Expert's (operator's) estimate in linguistic scale	knowledge acquisition procedures (diaries, programs, questionaries)	qualitative in linguistic scale with unevaluated accuracy	no
Expert's Suppositions	during the experiment or control or before	Expert's (operator's) intuition and professional knowledge	expert's questionary	Evaluations and predictions in linguistic scale	no
Theoretical knowledge of the object or process under control	a priori (before) the experiment or control	Physical and chemical laws and their mathematical models	theoretical sciences knowledge and learning	Mathematical expressions and equations	no

Operational knowledge of the measurement and control equipment	a priori (before) the experiment or control	Operation and control manuals, design reports	engineering knowledge and learning	technical data, standards, regulations	no
Statistical knowledge from the previous experience	a priori (before) the experiment or control	Data bases and banks from the previous experience	organisation of the information storing, processing, and retrieving	Statistical characteristics: distributions, mean and variation evaluations, etc.	Statistical processing
Statistical information	a posteriori (after) the experiment or control or partly during it	Sensors and measuring instruments	measurement and processing	Quantitative in measurement scale with known accuracy	Statistical processing
Technical information	a posteriori (after) the experiment or control or partly during it	Laboratory test results, special equipment results	Special tests	Quantitative results or characteristics	no
Common sense knowledge	at any stage	Expert's opinion	expert's questionnaire	usually qualitative but may be categorical in regard to some special events	

5. How Does an Intelligent Instrument Look Like?

5.1. Which features should an intelligent instrument possess?

Breckenridge and Husson of NASA [19] adopt the following Japanese definition of an intelligent or smart sensor [20]. „The sensor itself has a data processing function and automatic calibration/ automatic compensation function, in which the sensor itself detects and eliminates abnormal values or exceptional values. It incorporates an algorithm, which is capable of being altered, and has a certain degree of memory function. Further desirable characteristics are that the sensor is coupled to other sensors, adapts to changes in environment conditions, and has a discrimination function." So this way supposes the definition of an intelligent sensor based on the functions performed.

It is desirable for an intelligent equipment to have the following features:

- - competence, i.e. decisions made by it must be of a very high level, as ones by a professional expert,
- - capability for reasoning based on symbol transformations,
- - capability to use both general and particular procedures of reasoning,
- - capability to solve problems from complex real data domains,
- - capability to reformulate requests and problems,
- - capability for metareasoning.

Such requirements result in the necessity to include expert systems as components of an intelligent instrument, that is an intellectualisation of an instrument.

5.2. Which expert systems can be applied in an intelligent measuring instrument?

Let us present some examples of possible applications. The proposed list in no way covers an extremely wide range and does not pretend to be complete.

Expert Systems for testing and diagnostics of MI. Testing and diagnostics is a classical field of artificial intelligence applications especially for computing systems. If a test execution does not require any considerable intellectual consumption, the task of diagnostics (i.e. fault localisation) supposes a substantial joint man-machine operation. An expert system development for this application could be caused also by the fact that the necessity for solving diagnostics problems is originated by a user, whereas it is a designer who possesses basic knowledge in this field. Therefore, it would be quite reasonable to include an expert system as a part of a measuring instrument. It should be also noted that MI testing (unlike computing systems) is not a simple problem, since even an instrument fault definition is not trivial in the case of measurement. The solution to this problem is related to a MI verification.

Expert Systems for MI verification can be constructed from two interdependent parts: ES for a verification preparation and ES for a verification execution. ES for a verification preparation must ensure the solution of a number of problems, among them are:

- calculation of verification intervals,
- choice of reference MI's and auxiliary facilities for constructing the verification system,
- construction of verification charts and plans,
- choice of verification algorithms.

Any action of these expert systems ideally should result not only in providing recommendations but also in an automatic synthesis of the program, controlling the verification of a particular MI. ES for a verification action should result in a definition of MI metrological characteristics. ES for performing a MI maintenance and repair are related to these ES. The knowledge of the similar systems should contain an information on calendar terms of carrying out preventive and repair work, its contents, schedule, tools to be needed, resources, economical factors of operation.

ESs for a measurement preparation must assist a user in making a choice of the method and algorithm to realise measurements. The ES application here is important because MI users lack the necessary knowledge of computer systems and sciences. This ES can include an automatic synthesis of an algorithm and a program controlling MI operation. The synthesis can be based on measurement optimisation in regard to different criteria. ES for result processing have an extremely wide base of various algorithms and programs for statistical and nonstatistical measurement result processing, the results of direct and joint measurements and a calculation of their metrological characteristics. MI should give the user an opportunity to choose an algorithm and a program as well as to synthesise it from the available ones, including an opportunity of the correction and development.

ESs for the measurement result analysis cover a sufficiently new at the present time field of investigations. It can include the system of previous measurement results of this MI applications, as well as the results of applications of the similar MI and experiments with various models of real objects in order to collect a priori information and recommendations of very various kinds.

6. An Application Example

As a main application example let us consider the system for a blast furnace control [10]. Although usually the control of a such complicated equipment is performed by an operator(s) the automatic control systems are gradually being introduced into practice or at least are being used to assist an operator. In furnace control the operational knowledge about furnace conditions which mainly characterises temperature and moisture in different points of the furnace is very important.

One of the main area where the expert's information and fuzzy control can be utilised is the cohesive zone operation control. The cohesive zone is where the transition from solid to liquid occurs in a blast furnace. The shape of the zone is important. It can collapse and ruin the blast furnace. The shape and location of a cohesive zone is determined somewhat by the temperature profile which can be measured by thermocouples on the surface.

Another reason why fuzzy information can be applied in this area is that of missing data [11]. Sensors and transducers frequently fail under the rigorous high temperature conditions in a blast furnace. A zero signal may be due to failure upstream which should require action, or it may be because of a broken sensor. Decisions must be made with the available sensor output and missing data. Some methods, proposed in [11], can be applied for the determination of the sensor failed and under some conditions even for the sensor signal restoration.

The structure of the measuring information system for the metallurgical furnace control is given in Fig.2. Diagnostic knowledge of the temperature and moisture conditions includes some information which comes from operators (e.g. coke combustion conditions at the tuyeres of the colour of slag during tapping) and sensor information, as well as the information originated from suppositions. Operators instantly bring together all kinds of information, make judgements, and based on these results as well as their knowledge of furnace control, the use of operational manuals decide which actions to take. At this stage actually the joint processing of the information from the sensors and the expert's information takes place. The goal of this processing can be the improvement (of accuracy, reliability) of the information available as well as the generation of the „new" information (creation rules, membership functions, their modification).

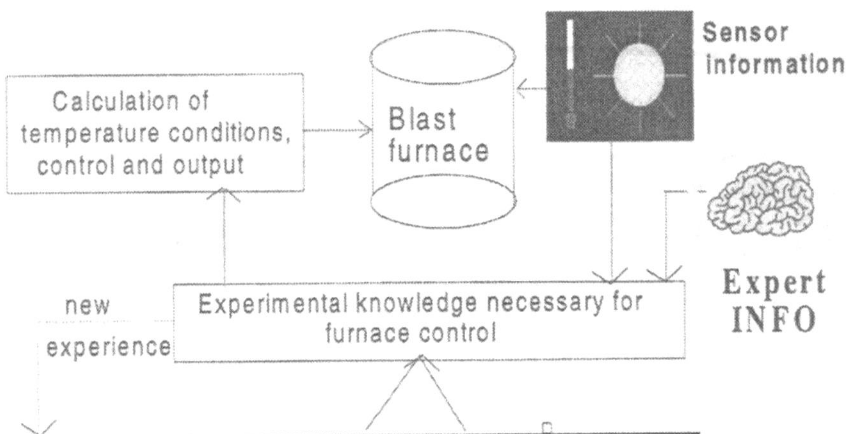

Specialised knowledge of blast furnaces		
Temperature conditions diagnostic knowledge	Basic knowledge	Common sense knowledge
sensor information	scrap analysis	the cohesive zone
intuition	theoretical analysis	central flow, outer flow
information from special actions	change distribution	slipping, channeling

Figure 2. The structure of the intelligent measuring information system

References

[1] Collett C.V. and Hope A.D. *Engineering Measurements* Pitman Publishing, London, 1974

[2] Brignell J. and White N. *Intelligent Sensor Systems* IOP Publlishing 1994

[3] Barney G.C. *Intelligent Instrumentation. Microprocessor Applications in Measurement and Control* Prentice Hall Englewood Cliffs 1985

[4] Yoshifumi Amemiya *Sensa nyumon (Introduction to sensors)*, Ohmu-sha, 1983

[5] *The Australian Pocket Oxford Dictionary*/Ed. G.W.Turner, Oxford University Press, Melbourne, 1984

[6] *Guide to the Expresiion of Uncertainty in Measurement*, International Standard Organisation, 1995

[7] Stonier T. *Beyond Information. The Natural History of Intelligence.* Springer-Verlag, London 1992

[8] Reznik L. *Fuzzy Controllers* Newnes-Butterworth-Heinemann, Oxford, 1997

[9] Zadeh L. *Towards a Theory of Fuzzy Information Granulation and its Centrality in Human Reasoning and Fuzzy Logic*, Fuzzy Sets and Systems, 1997, vol.90, No. 2, p. 111-128

[10] *Applied Fuzzy Systems* /ed. T. Terano,et al. AP Professional 1994

[11] Reznik L. and Solopchenko G.N. *Use of a priori Information on Functional Relations between Measured Quantities for Improving Accuracy of Measurement*, Measurement, 1985, Vol. 3, No. 3, pp. 98--106.

[12] Russo F. and Ramponi G. *Fuzzy Methods for Multisensor Data Fusion* IEEE Transactions on Instrumentation and Measurement Vol: 43 Iss: 2, 1994, p. 288-94

[13] Mourot G., Bousghiri, S. and Kratz, F. *Sensor Fault Detection Using Fuzzy Logic and Neural Network* Conference Proceedings. 1993 International Conference on Systems, Man and Cybernetics. Systems Engineering in the Service of Humans, IEEE, NY, 1993, vol.2, p. 369-374

[14] Tsoukalas L.H. *Virtual Measurement and Prediction in Human-Centered Automation* Proceedings of the Topical Meeting on Computer-Based Human Support Systems: Technology, Methods, and Future, La Grange, IL, USA, 1995, p.235-241

[15] Brockmann W. *Fuzzy System for Optical Position Sensing* In: Integrating Intelligent instrumentation and Control. 1995 IEEE Instrumentation/Measurement technology Conference. IMTC Proceedings, NY, 1995, p.747-751

[16] Caulfield H.J. *Fuzzy Optical Metrology* IEEE Transactions on Fuzzy Systems, vol. 4, No. 2, 1996, p.206-208

[17] Tanaka F. *Fuzzy Data Smoothing* Conference Proceedings. 10th Anniversary. IMTC/94. Advanced Technologies in I & M. 1994 IEEE Instrumentation and Measurement Technology Conference vol.1, IEEE, 1994 p. 90-93

[18] Mauris G., Benoit E. and Foulloy L. *The Aggregation of Complementary Information via Fuzzy Sensors* Measurement, vol. 17, No. 4, 1996, p.235-249

[19] *Intelligent Sensor Technology* / Ed. Ryoji Ohba John Wiley and Sons, Chichester 1992

[20] Toyoaki Omori *Sensa Jitsuyo Benran (Sensor Application Manual)* Fuji Technosystems, 1978

2

COMPUTING WITH WORDS: LINGUISTIC ASPECTS

Semiotics and Computational Linguistics

On Semiotic Cognitive Information Processing*

Burghard B. Rieger**
FB II: Department of Computational Linguistics
University of Trier, Germany

Abstract

Signs, which are the domain of inquiry in *semiotics*, have a complex ontology. Apart from being used—adequate knowledge provided—by communicators, and recognized as being decomposable into smaller elements and aggregatable to larger structures, they are also meant to be understood. This is a consequence of their manifold identity as compound physical *objects* with real world extensions in space-time-locations a n d as activators for complex mental *processes* which tend to be identified with some mind and/or brain activities responsible for their *understanding*. In the *cognitive sciences* all processes of perception, identification, and interpretation of (external) structures are considered *information processing* which (natural or artificial) systems—due to their own (internal) structuredness or knowledge—are able (or unable) to perform. Combining the *semiotic* with the *cognitive* paradigm in *computational linguistics*, the processes believed to constitute natural language sign structures and their understanding is modeled by way of procedural, i.e. computational (re-)constructions of such processes that produce structures comparable to those that the understanding of (very large) samples of situated natural language discourse would imply. Thus, *computational semiotic* models in cognitive linguistics aim at simulating the constitution of meanings and the interpretation of signs without their predicative and propositional representations which dominate traditional research formats in syntax and semantics so far. This is achieved by analyzing the linear or *syntagmatic* and selective or *paradigmatic* constraints which natural languages impose recursively on the formation and structure of (strings of) linguistic entities on different levels of systemic distinction. It will be argued (and illustrated) that *fuzzy* modeling allows to derive more adequate representational means whose (numerical) specificity and (procedural) definiteness may complement formats of categorial type *precision* (which would appear phenomenologically incompatible) and processual *determinateness* (which would seem cognitively inadequate). Several examples from *fuzzy linguistic* research will be given to illustrate these points.

---

*Revised version of a paper presented at the Pre-ISAS Tutorials of the *Intelligent Systems and Semiotics* conference, National Institute of Standards and Technology (NIST), Gaithersburg, Ma. USA, on September 22–25, 1997

**E-Mail: `rieger@ldv.Uni-Trier.deown.`

Although we plainly can say nothing about matters that lie beyond our current understanding, it is difficult to say why one should retain the faith that traditional conceptions will somehow be applicable there, even though we find them generally useless to the extent that we come to understand some aspects of the nature of organisms, in particular, the mental life of humans.[1]

1 Introduction

Anything we know or believe about the world can—more or less precisely—be communicated verbally. We do so by language means, employing words, forming sentences, producing texts whose meanings are understood to convey, stand for, designate, refer to or deal with topics and subjects, entities and domains, structures and processes in the real world. Natural language texts (still) are the most flexible and as that highly efficient means to represent knowledge for and convey learning to others. What appears to be conditional for this kind of text understanding is humans' language faculty, i.e. the (*performative*) ability to identify, recognize, produce, and structure some fragments of real world stimuli according to some internal—though externally conditioned—principles (*competence*). Traditional approaches in linguistics proper (LP), computational linguistics (CL) and artificial intelligence research (AI) have developed structural and procedural conceptions for (parts of) the process of language understanding. Their notational systems employed allow for the distinction of *linguistic knowledge* formally represented in rule based formats, and of *world knowledge* whose structuredness is mediated by symbol representational formats which are combined to model language processing by machine. However, important features characteristic of natural language understanding processes, like e.g. vagueness, robustness, adaptivity, dynamism, etc. had to be overlooked or intentionally put aside because of the representational formats chosen and their processing possible.

Computational Semiotics (CS) neither depends on rule-based or symbolic formats for (linguistic) knowledge representations, nor does it subscribe to the notion of (world) knowledge as some static structures that may be abstracted from and represented independently of the way they are processed. Instead, knowledge structures and the processes operating on them are modeled as procedures that can be implemented as algorithms. *Semiotic Cognitive Information Processing* (SCIP) systems are defined as collections of cognitive information processing devices whose semiotics consists in their multi-level representational performance of (working) structures emerging from and being modified by such

[1]Chomsky: The Managua Lectures, 1986, p. 48

processing. The emergence of sign structures as a self-organizing process may in particular be studied on the basis of combinatorial and selective constraints universal to all natural languages. Both, (linguistic) entity formation and (semiotic) function acquisition may thus be reconstructed from *syntagmatic* constraints observed in linear agglomeration, and *paradigmatic* constraints on selectional choice of elements of natural language sign structures in discourse. Their regularities are exploited by text analyzing algorithms operating on and defining levels of *morpho-phonemic, lexico-semantic, phraseo-syntactic* and *situational* or *pragma-semantic* representation. Initially, the algorithms accept natural language discourse as input and produce vector space structures as output. These may be interpreted as intermediate (internal) representations on different levels of a semiotic system's states of adaptation to the (external) structures of its environment as signaled and mediated by the natural language discourse processed.

2 Modeling Cognition

The alliance of logics and linguistics, mediated mainly by (language) philosophy in the past and by (discrete) mathematics since the first half of this century, has long been (and partly still is) dominating the way in what terms natural languages expressions should be explicated and how their processing could be modeled. It is ironic that the dramatic increase of computational power and symbol manipulation means has changed the fundamentals of many scientific disciplines, creating even new ones, but has left linguistically oriented disciplines, even new ones, adhere to the lore of seemingly well grounded and traditionally dignified concepts (like *phrase* and *sentence, predicate* and *proposition, grammatical correctness* and *formal truth*, etc.) in describing natural language structures and their processing. Considering our as yet very limited understanding of natural language understanding which explicatory cognitive models as well as implemented operational systems of computational natural language processing demonstrate, it may well be suspected that some of the problems encountered by these model constructions are due to the representational formats they employ in depicting and manipulating entities (elements, structures, processes, and procedures) considered to be of interest or even essential to the understanding of the communicative use of natural languages by humans.

2.1 Information Systems View

Following a systems theoretical paradigm of information processing and accepting the cognitive point-of-view according to which information processing is knowledge based, humans appear to be far from being just another species of natural information processing systems with some higher cognitive abilities.

Instead, they have to be considered very particular cognitive systems whose outstanding plasticity and capability to adapt their behavior more rapidly to changing environmental conditions than others, is essentially tied to their use and understanding of natural languages in communicative discourse. It seems that the language faculty expands their learning potential well beyond experimental experience into realms of virtual reality (*Gedankenexperimente*) which allows for the recognition of consequences inferred from *potentially real* instead of *factually existing* conditions for survival[2]. The basic idea of model construction in terms of such an ecological theory of information systems [39] is that the processing structure of an information system is a correlate of those structures which that system is able to process in order to survive. For cognitive models of natural language processing the systems theoretical view suggests to accept natural language discourse in situations of communicative interaction as analyzable and empirically accessible evidence for tracing such processes. Thus, situated natural language communication might reveal essential parts of the particularly structured, multi-layered information representation and processing *potential* to a system analyzer and model constructor in rather the same way as this potential is accessible to an information processing system. The difference here, however, between the system and its analyzer is that they are active in and part of different information processing situations of which only the former—and not the latter—can be said to be properly attuned. It is this lack of attunement to the *semiotics* underlying situational natural language understanding which prompts cognitive linguists as system analyzers to fall back on their attunement to *situations* of language understanding [2]. But whereas in language understanding one can, and even has to take the semiotic dimension of sign and meaning constitution for granted (and beyond questioning) in order to let any particular sign or meaning be understood, the purpose of modeling that very process must not in aiming at the conditions for the possibility of such processes of understanding. Hence, a system analyzer and model constructor in semiotics should not rely (solely) on linguistic categories in describing and modeling semiotic entities. She/he has to make any provision that her/his ideas about the modeling of both, the representation a n d the processing are not unduly pre-defined by long established, but possibly inadequate concepts and related formats. Rule-based models of syntactic processing as well as truth-functional models of (sentence) meaning appear to be as inadequate as predicative and propositional formats of semiotic entity representation and processing.

[2]This expansion—however *genotypically* advantageous—has *phenotypical* drawbacks for individual semiotic systems whose *virtual* realities may become *vicious* to the extend they might replace instead of complement the systems' factual situatedness. Illustrating the case is a tendency to blur the distinction of *reality* from *fiction* due to the (semiotic) media's increasing degree of experiential (situational) density: print literature < theatre < film < television < VR environments.

2.2 Semiotic Attunement

In a systems theoretic approach, *attunement* obviously replaces the notion of *static* knowledge structures as realized in cognitive information processing models so far, by a *dynamic* conception of structuredness which defines knowledge as an open, modifiable, and adaptive system whose organization can be conceived as a function of the system's own processing results (*knowledge acquisition*). This, however, can only be achieved by allowing *semiotic entities* to have their own[3] (perhaps yet unknown) ontology which is not (or not fully) accounted for by predicative and propositional representations or rule-based and truth-functional formats which tacitly make believe that semiotic entities can be characterized and their functions be modeled exclusively by these categorial structures and associated processing of symbol manipulation. Instead, *semiotic modeling* is to find and employ representational formats and processing algorithms which do not prematurely decide and delimit the range of semiotically relevant entities, their representational formats and procedural modes of processing. One of the advantages of semiotic models would be that the entities considered relevant would not need to be defined prior to model construction but should emerge from the very processing which the model simulates or is able to enact. It appears that—if any—this property of models does account for the intrinsic (co- and contextual) constraining of the meaning potential characteristic of natural language discourse which renders them *semiotic* in a (meaning or function) constituting sense which is the core of *understanding*. Representing a system's environment (or fragments thereof) in a way, that such representations not only take part in that system's direct (*immediate*) environment (via language texts) but may moreover be understood as virtual in the sense that new (*mediate*) environments (via textual meanings) can also be processed, has been explicitly introduced elsewhere [41] [37] [38]. It is again dependent on a system's attunement to these kinds of discourse situations.

2.3 Discourse Situations

These situations (comprising *system*, *environment*, and *processing*) are considered *cognitive* inasmuch as the system's internal (formal and procedural) knowledge has to be applied to identify and to recognize structures external to the system (allowing *meaning interpretation*). These situations become *semiotic* whenever the internal knowledge applied to identify and interpret environmental structures is derived from former processes of structure identification and interpretation as the result of self-organizing feedback through different levels of (inter-)mediate representation and organization. This process (of *meaning* constitution or structure *understanding*) has its procedural analogue in the mul-

[3] i.e. with reference to *intrinsic* interdependencies within the *system-environment-processing* situation (see Peirce's *tri-relative influence* below).

tiple enactment of the threefold relation which is called—following PEIRCE—*semiosis*[4]. The triadic relation allows for the different ontological abstractions of *language*

▷ as a component (*sign*) in a system's external environment, i.e. material *discourse* as a physical space-time location;
▷ as a constituent of virtuality which systems properly attuned experience as their environment (*object*), i.e. structured *text* as an interpretable potential of meanings, and
▷ as a process of actualization (*interpretant*) in a particular system-environment situation, i.e. *understanding* as the constitution of meaning.

Under these preliminary abstractions, the distinction between (the formats of) the representation and (the properties of) the represented is not a prerequisite but an outcome of *semiosis*, i.e. the semiotic process of sign *constitution* and *understanding*. Hence, it should not be a presupposition or input to, but a result or output of the processes which are to be modeled procedurally and called *semiotic*.

2.4 Cognitive Models

An earlier attempt [46] to classify model constructions as forwarded in the cognitive sciences had distinguished three types of modeling approaches:

▷ the *cognitive* approach presupposes the existence of the external world, structured by given objects and properties, and the existence of representations of (fragments of) that world internal to the system, so that the cognitive systems' (observable) behavior of action and reaction may be modeled by processes operating on these structures;
▷ the *associative* approach is described as a dynamic structuring based on the model concept of self-organization which cognitive systems constantly apply to adapt to changing environmental conditions and to modify their internal representations of them;
▷ the *enactive* approach may be characterized as being based upon the notion of *structural coupling*. Instead of assuming an external world and the systems' internal representations of it, some unity of structural relatedness is considered to be fundamental of—and the (only) condition for—any abstracted or acquired duality in notions of the external and the internal, object and subject, reality and its experience.

Whereas the first two approaches apparently draw on the traditional rationalistic paradigm of mind-matter-duality—*static* the former, *dynamic* the latter—by assuming the existence of *external* world structures and *internal* representations of them, the third type does not. Considering the importance that the notions

[4]By *semiosis* I mean [...] an action, or influence, which is, or involves, a coöperation of *three* subjects, such as *sign*, its *object*, and its *interpretant*, this tri-relative influence not being in any way resolvable into actions between pairs. ([21], p.282)

of formatting and representation (both internal and external to an information processing system) have gained in tracing processes on the grounds of their observable or resulting structures, it appears to be justified to add the fourth type: [40]:

▷ the *semiotic* approaches focus on the notion of *semiosis* and may be characterized by the process of *enactment* too, complemented, however, by the representational impact. It is considered fundamental to the distinction of e.g. *cognitive processes* from their *structural results* which—due to the traces these processes leave behind—may emerge in some form of *knowledge* whose different representational modes comply with the distinction of *internal* or *tacit* knowledge (i.e. *memory*) on the one hand and of *external* or *declarative* knowledge (i.e. *language* expressions) on the other.

According to these types of cognitive modeling, *computational semiotics* can be characterized as aiming at the dynamics of meaning constitution by simulating processes of multi-resolutional representation [19] within the frame of an ecological information processing paradigm [39]. When we take human beings to be *systems* whose knowledge based *processing* of represented *information* makes them *cognitive*, and whose sign and symbol generation, manipulation, and understanding capabilities render them *semiotic*, we will do so due to our own daily experience of these systems' outstanding ability for representing results of cognitive processes, organize these representations, and modify them according to changing conditions and states of system-environment adaptedness.

3 Natural Language Processing

Computational systems for natural language processing which are based upon relevant CL and AI research are presently undergoing some fundamental scrutiny. It may broadly be characterized by challenges concerning some of the founding assumptions and basal hypotheses implied in the research *goals* (*Erkenntnisinteresse*), the critical evaluation of methodological standards and their possible completion by new research *methods* (*Untersuchungsmethoden*), and a re-definition of the linguistic domain of language research *objects* in general (*Forschungsgegenstände*).

3.1 Challenging Representational Formats

As is well known, computational systems for natural language analysis and generation are based upon correct structural descriptions of input strings and their semantic interpretations. This is made possible by rule based representations of (syntactic and lexical) knowledge of a language and of (referential and situative) world knowledge concerned in formats which grammar formalisms and deductive inferential mechanisms can operate on. Notwithstanding the considerable advances in the development and theoretical testing of increasingly more complex systems, this kind of *cognitive* (or *knowledge-based*) language processing (based on monotone logics, symbolic representations, rule-based operations, serial processing, etc.) and the essential statics of their representational structures were challenged—although for differing reasons—by connectionistic and empirical approaches. These were particularly successful in simulating dynamic properties of processes of cognitive natural language processing (based on the theory of dynamic systems, sub-symbolic or distributed representation, numerically continuous operations, parallel processing, etc.) in ANN models [20], [22], [7]. And there were new insights gained into the wealth of structural patterns and functional relations which could be observed in large corpora of communicative natural language performance and specified by results from models of quantitative and statistical analyses (based on probability and possibility theory, stochastic and fuzzy modeling, numerical mathematics and non-monotone logics, strict hypothesizing and rigorous testing, etc.) [1] [17].

3.2 Common Grounds

Discussing connectionistic vs. rule-based approaches and models of natural language processing [44] [13] [45] [42], differences have in the majority of contributions been characterized from an epistemological position common for both directions in *cognitive linguistics*. Proponents of both sides seem to accept that the study of language *competence*, its principles, components, and their organization is the primary concern and basal objective for computational linguistics proper. Following the discussion so far, there is a predominant interest in the theoretical aspects of what the different, even *hybrid* model constructions would claim and may justifiably be said to explain [22] [6] [16] although the empirical and quantitative approaches in language research have hardly been involved yet. The reasons are manifold as the availability of masses of performative language data not only require the methodological mastery of a whole spectrum of tools and methods, new to most linguists, but also tend to imply some compensating shift from language competence towards language performance studies corresponding to a wider domain of research objects for linguistics proper [12] which many computational linguists would refrain from. However, in view of the formal complexity and applicational limitations which rule based cognitive models show on the one hand, and considering the surprisingly efficient practicability of stochastic parsers [10] [3] and statistical machine translation systems [5] [4] on the other, there is good reason to expect some revision of assumptions and basal hypotheses defining cognitive linguistics.

3.3 Language Reality

According to Chomsky [8] the cognitive study of natural language phenomena has to be concerned primarily with the principles underlying observable language phenomena, i.e. the structure and the organization of the human language faculty (*competence*) which may (theoretically) be analyzed and (formally) be characterized well without empirical exploration of observable language data as produced in situations of communicative interaction by real speakers/hearers (*performance*). Nowadays [9] the speaker's language knowledge or *competence* is named *internalized* (or I-) language whose set of entities (lexicon) aggregatable according to a set of rules (computational system) constitutes the proper domain (mental grammar) of linguistic inquiry; accordingly, the speakers' *performative* language use named *externalized* (or E-) language may be considered cognitively uninteresting. One of the results which the ongoing discussion may produce is the understanding [43] that the grounding of cognitive linguistic research so far might turn out to be based on a too principled abstraction of language reality as experienced in communicative interaction.

Taking into account some language regularities and structures which are empirically traceable but may not be identified within the categorial framework of established linguistic concepts[5], and in view also of tendencies in cognitive linguistics, computational linguistics, and AI research to come up with increasingly complex systems and/or narrowing scopes dealing with natural language structures and functions [24], the empirical study of performative language phenomena may provide valuable insights and explanations because of the domain's new research objects and methods complementary to those of competence centered linguistics. Moreover, it appears that empirical approaches allow for quantitative-statistical as well as fuzzy-theoretical model constructions which may allow for a more *semiotic* understanding of the functioning of language signs as used by interlocutors in communicative interaction.

3.4 Research Situation

The availability (and still increasing number) of very large text corpora[6], will facilitate to investigate a type of natural language properties whose categorial

[5]Phenomena like linear short-distance orderings (*Nah-Ordnung*) of performative language entities (e.g. co-occurences) whose regularities are deprived of rule-based notations but can easily be represented and processed as numerical expressions of correlation values with any precision, are an example in point here, as they appear to be the observable results of structuring principles which have been overlooked by competence theoretical investigations only because they do not comply with linear long-distance orderings (*Fern-Ordnung*) that are constitutive of linguistic categories as represented and processed by familiar grammar formalisms[14], [11], [15].

[6]The Trier *dpa*-Corpus comprises the complete textual material from the *basic news real service* of 1990–1993 (720.000 documents) which the Deutschen Presseagentur (*dpa*), Hamburg, deserves thanks to have the author provided with for research purposes. After cleaning of editing commands the *dpa*-Corpus consists of approx. 180 million ($18 \cdot 10^7$) running words (*tokens*) for which an automatic tagging and lemmatizing tool is under development. It is this corpus which provides the performative data of written language use for the current (and planned) *fuzzy*-linguistic projects at our department.

vagueness (uncertain, under-determined, fuzzily delimited, etc.) or whose limited to dubious observability (sparse data, uncertain information, etc.) had left them inaccessible and hence irrelevant to language research.

As the processing of very large language corpora (VLLC) has shown, categorial type concepts common in traditional linguistics have to be considered highly problematic when applied to classify finer grained structures which quantitative-numerical computations will easily identify operationally. Categorial type, symbol processing encounters increasing numbers of borderline cases, variations, and ambiguities which cannot be dealt with consistently. Such problems ought to—and can infact—be avoided from the very start as they emerge from mappings of structurally related data sets to inadequate categories. Therefore, classical categorial conceptions in linguistics have begun to be scrutinized and may possibly be substituted by *soft categories* [38] [27] before there is substantial hope to improve chances to understand and to explain *knowledge* as some form of (*world*) and/or *language*) structures emerging from rather than fed into information processing models that can truly be called *semiotic*.

3.5 SCIP Systems

Other than value attributing procedures that reorganize input data computationally according to predefined structures of intermediate representations (as hypothesized by *competence* theoretical linguistics and realized in cognitive CL models) *semiotic cognitive information processing* (SCIP) systems [37] may have to, and will indeed, be distinguished sharply as sets of procedures whose computations will transform structured input data according to its immanent regularities to yield new, structural representations emerging from that computation (as hypothesized by *performative* linguistics and realized in procedural models of computational semiotics). The elements of these new structures are value distributions or vectors of input entities that depict properties of their structural relatedness in a *granular* and multi-layered fashion, constituting multi-dimensional (metric) space structures (*semiotic spaces*). Their elements may also be interpreted as *fuzzy sets* allowing set theoretical operations be executed on these representations that do not require categorial type (*crisp*) definitions of symbol or concept formation. Computation of letter (*morphic*) vectors in *word space*, derived from n-grams of letters *graphemes*, as well as of word (*semic*) vectors in *semantic space*, derived from correlations of words [29], [25], [36] will serve to illustrate the operational flexibility and varying granularity of vector representations to identify regularities of language performance which traditional linguistic categories fail to represent.

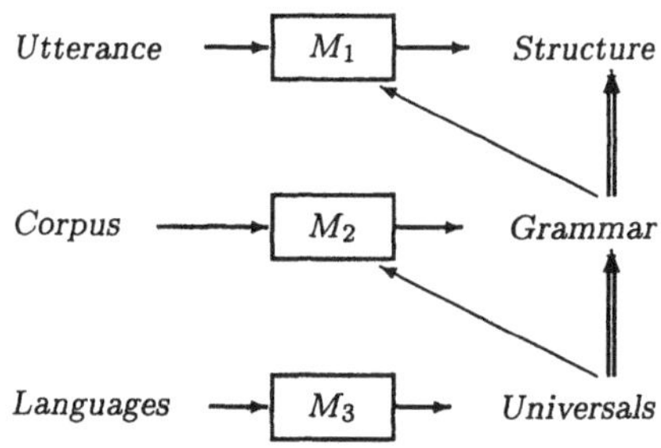

Figure 1

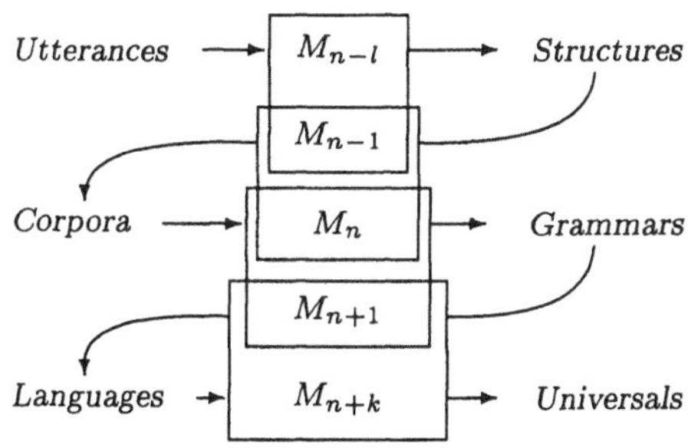

Figure 2

Schemata of model hierarchy of *cognitive linguistic* strata of mechanisms (BIERWISCH) as compared to model tiling of *computational semiotic* coverage of procedures (RIEGER) for the analysis and representation of (abstracted and observable) language phenomena.

3.6 Visualizing Vector Representations

Returning to the ecological systems theoretical view applied to information processing, we will focus on the problem of visualizing results of computational procedures developed to model and simulate semiotic processes whose numerical representations—by definition—do not have an immediate interpretation. Various techniques have been applied to analyze, scrutinize, and visualize the structuredness of vectoral representations and their results reported elsewhere [30] [31] [32] [33] [34]. As these have been able to demonstrate the definite non-contingency of *meaning points* z in the *semantic space*, a short introduction to its conception will suffice here. We will concentrate on the level of *semantic* meaning constitution as based upon the measurement of differences of usage regularities in VLLC of situated or *pragmatically homogeneous* texts.

For a vocabulary $V = \{x_n\}, n = 1, \ldots, i.j. \ldots, N$ of lexical items, their meanings $z_n \in \langle S, \zeta \rangle$ are re-constructed as a composite function $\tilde{\delta} \mid y_n \circ \tilde{\alpha} \mid x_n$ of the difference distributions

$$\tilde{\delta} \mid y_n : C \to S; \{z_n\} =: S \tag{1}$$

and the grounding usage regularity distributions

$$\tilde{\alpha} \mid x_n : V \to C; \{y_n\} =: C \tag{2}$$

The empirical measures employed to specify intensities of co-occurring lexical items are centered around a modified correlational coefficient

$$\alpha(x_i, x_j) = \frac{\sum_{t=1}^{T}(h_{it} - e_{it})(h_{jt} - e_{jt})}{\left(\sum_{t=1}^{T}(h_{it} - e_{it})^2 \sum_{t=1}^{T}(h_{jt} - e_{jt})^2\right)^{\frac{1}{2}}}; \tag{3}$$
$$-1 \leq \alpha(x_i, x_j) \leq +1$$

where $e_{it} = \frac{H_i}{L} l_t$ and $e_{jt} = \frac{H_j}{L} l_t$ denote (theoretical) estimate values, computed over a corpus $K = \{k_t\}; t = 1, \ldots, T$ of texts whose lengths summed up will define the overall length of the corpus $L = \sum_{t=1}^{T} l_t; 1 \leq l_t \leq L$ The length l_t of each text t in the corpus K is measured by the number of occurring word-tokens which form the basis of the vocabulary V of word-types whose frequencies are denoted by $H_i = \sum_{t=1}^{T} h_{it}; 0 \leq h_{it} \leq H_i$.
A second measure of similarity (or rather, dissimilarity) is applied to specify the α-value distributions' differences

$$\delta(y_i, y_j) = \left(\sum_{n=1}^{N}(\alpha(x_i, x_n) - \alpha(x_j, x_n))^2\right)^{\frac{1}{2}}; \tag{4}$$
$$0 \leq \delta(y_i, y_j) \leq 2\sqrt{n}$$

The consecutive application of (*Eqns.* 2) on input texts and (*Eqns.* 1) on its output data allows to derive for each word-type $x_n \in V$ an entity $z_n \in S$ which denotes a structural representation of differences of usage regularities detected and numerically specified by these coefficients. They allow to model the meanings of words as a two-level function of δ-values of *paradigmatic* selections (measured as differences of usage regularities) and of α-values of *syntagmatic* aggregations (computed as correlations of word-type pairs in texts of the corpus), as schematized in *Tab.* 1.

As a result of this two-stage *consecutive* mapping any meaning point's position in the *semantic space* $\langle S, \zeta \rangle$ is determined by all the differences (δ- or distance-values) of all regularities of usage (α- or correlation-values) each lexical item shows against all others in the discourse analyzed. Without recurring to any investigator's or his test-persons' word or world knowledge (*semantic*

$$
\begin{array}{ccccc}
\alpha = V \times V & \alpha\text{-abstraction} & \delta = C \times C & \delta\text{-abstraction} & \zeta = S \times S \\
\begin{array}{c|c}
\tilde{\alpha} & x_1 \ldots x_N \\ \hline
x_1 & \alpha_{11} \ldots \alpha_{1N} \\
\vdots & \vdots \ \ddots \ \vdots \\
x_N & \alpha_{N1} \ldots \alpha_{NN}
\end{array}
& \begin{array}{c} \Downarrow \\ \xrightarrow{\tilde{\alpha} \mid x_i} \\ \Uparrow \\ \textit{Syntagmatic} \end{array} &
\begin{array}{c|c}
\tilde{\delta} & y_1 \ldots y_N \\ \hline
y_1 & \delta_{11} \ldots \delta_{1N} \\
\vdots & \vdots \ \ddots \ \vdots \\
y_N & \delta_{N1} \ldots \delta_{NN}
\end{array}
& \begin{array}{c} \Downarrow \\ \xrightarrow{\tilde{\delta} \mid y_j} \\ \Uparrow \\ \textit{Paradigmatic} \end{array} &
\begin{array}{c|c}
\zeta & z_1 \ldots z_N \\ \hline
z_1 & \zeta_{11} \ldots \zeta_{1N} \\
\vdots & \vdots \ \ddots \ \vdots \\
z_N & \zeta_{N1} \ldots \zeta_{NN}
\end{array}
\end{array}
$$

C o n s t r a i n t s

Table 1: Formalizing (*syntagmatic/paradigmatic*) constraints by consecutive (α and δ) abstractions over usage regularities of items x_i, y_j respectively.

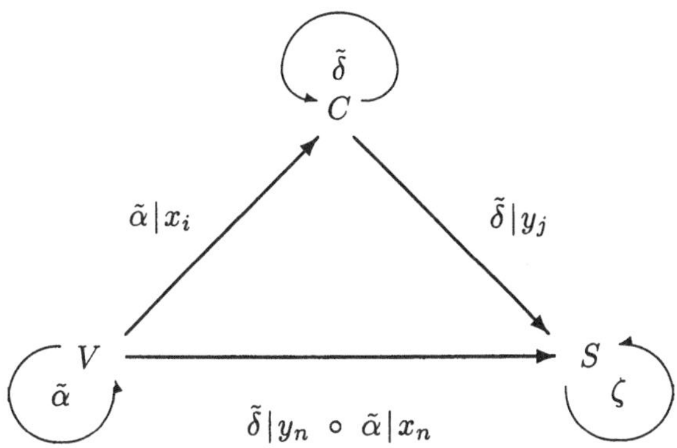

Figure 3: Fuzzy mapping relations $\tilde{\alpha}$ and $\tilde{\delta}$ between the structured sets of vocabulary items $x_n \in V$, of corpus points $y_n \in C$, and of meaning points $z_n \in S$.

competence), but solely on the basis of usage regularities of lexical items in discourse (*communicative performance*), some natural language understanding is modeled procedurally by computational processes which construct and identify emergent topological positions of any meaning point $z_i \in \langle S, \zeta \rangle$ corresponding to the vocabulary item's $x_i \in V$ meaning representation.

Thus, the application of *Eqns.* 2 and *Eqns.* 1 is tantamount to a double (α- and δ-) abstraction of identical elements in the ordered pairs as computed by the α-coefficient *Eqn.* 3 and the δ-coefficient *Eqn.* 4 respectively. This mapping may be considered a *semiotic* one due to the different ontological status which the α- and δ-representations of identical labels x_n acquire via this mapping process. Therefore, this *semiotic mapping* can formally also be stated as a fuzzy set theoretical *composition* of two restricted (fuzzy) relations $\tilde{\delta} \mid y$ and $\tilde{\alpha} \mid x$, or as a category of *semiotic morphisms* as in *Fig.* 3.

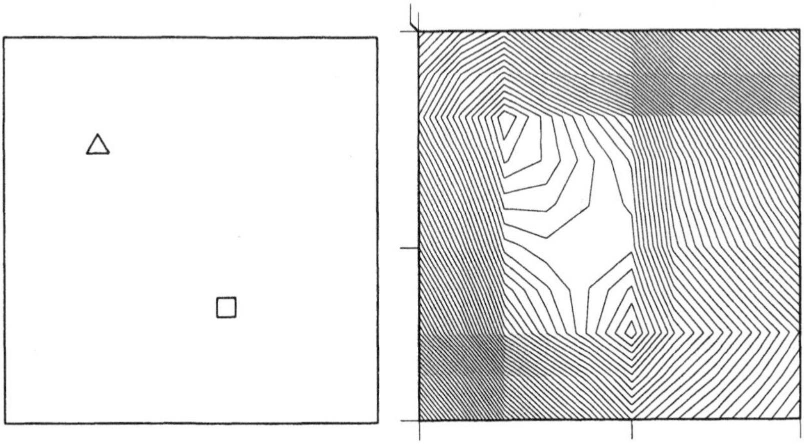

Figure 4: Reference plane with location of objects (△ and □) propositionally described by texts in the training corpus and 2-dim-image of SCIP system's *endo*-view showing regions of potential object locations (*isoreferentials*) under crisp hedge interpretation.

3.7 Reconstructing Reference

The *semantic space* structure $\langle S, \zeta \rangle$ may be viewed as the information processing system's internal representation (IR) of its external reality (ER). To be more precise: as an IR it depicts some of those ER structures which (firstly) are presented in the natural language discourse as its *meaning* a n d which (secondly) the system is able to detect according to its own structuredness and processing capabilities, constituting this *meaning* without knowing the i*semantics* underlying it. In order to let the internal (*endo*) picture which the system computes from discourse and represents in the form of the *semantic space* be evaluated against the external (*exo*) reality, this reality has to be mediated to the system as its environment in an intersubjectively controlled way a n d via those very propositional language structures whose non-propositional understanding by the system is to be tested. To facilitate this, the system is placed in an experimental environment which both are heavily restricted compared to our real world. The *immediate* environment consist solely of a text corpus of situated natural language discourse—aggregated from correct sentence expressions of true propositions—describing as *mediate* environment fixed object locations in a plane from changing system positions. The sentences were generated according to a (very simple) phrase structure grammar and a formal fuzzy referential semantics both unknown to the system. These formalisms (grammar and semantics) allowed to specify and interpret composite predicates of *cores* (like: *on the* *left, on the right — in front, behind*) and *hedges* (like: *extremely, very, rather — nearby, faraway*) in a consistent way as employed in sentences automatically generated to describe the object location and system position relations as the system's/environment's *structural coupling* in an intersubjectively controlled way. Submitted to the system's non-propositional, non-symbolic, numerical language processing capabilities, the generated corpus would reveal hidden structural informational constraints which the system's own structuredness (*attunement*) and internal processing or meaning constitution (*understanding*) would have to reflect in its representational structure (*knowledge*). The experimental setting and implemented tests which where reported in detail elsewhere [37] [38] [39] allowed to compare the external (*exo*) reality (*Fig.* 4 left)—as described by the texts and formally specified by the underlying syntax and semantics—with its two-dimensional transform of the system's internal multi-dimensional (*endo*) view of its discourse environment, demonstrating quite convincingly the computed structure's (at least partial) adequacy (*Fig.* 4 right).

Considering the structural properties, locational preferences, and adjacency relations of objects in the system's environment, the tests have produced under varying fuzzy interpretations of hedges very promising results which illustrate the *SCIP* system's miniature (cognitive) language understanding and meaning acquisition capacity w i t h o u t having any syntactic and/or semantic knowledge in whatever format made available to it prior to processing [39]. This is a case in point showing that the formats of syntax and semantics as employed in traditional linguistic and logic analysis and representation of natural language expressions is clearly one [but not the only) *façon de parler* or rather, way of submitting language structure to a representational framework which models prevailing constituents and dependencies.

3.8 Dispositional Dependencies

Following the semiotic understanding of meaning more as a constitutional process rather than an entity of invariable constancy or static representation, the present *semantic space* may be considered part of a word meaning/world knowledge representation system of a new kind. It is characterized by its two-stage representational process which separates the format of basic (stereotyped) meaning components (*meaning points*) from their latent (dependency) relational organization as meaning potential (*semantic dispositions*). Whereas the former is a static, topologically organized multi-dimensional memory structure, the latter can be characterized as a dynamic and flexible structuring process which reorganizes and thereby transforms the basic relatedness of the elements it operates on.

This is achieved by a recursively defined procedure that produces hierarchies of meaning points, reorganized under given aspects according to and in dependence of their co- and contextual relevancy. Taking up ideas from cognitive

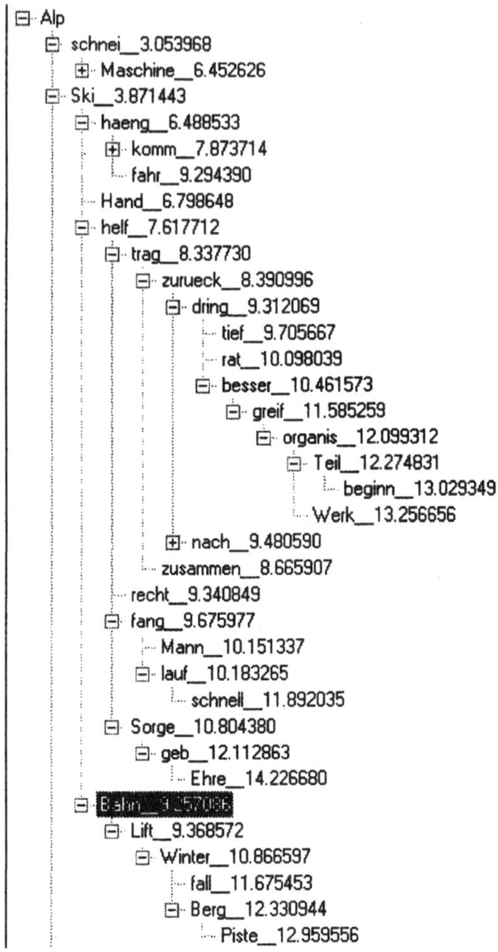

Figure 5: Fragment of DDS-tree of `Alpen` (root) as generated from *semantic space* data ($V = 345$ types, $H_i \geq 10$) of a German newspaper sample (DIE WELT, 1964 Berlin edition).

theories of semantic memory, *priming*, and *spreading activation* [18], the *DDS*-algorithm was devised to operate on the semantic space data and to generate *dispositional dependency structures* (DDS) in the format of n-ary trees. Given one meaning point's position, the algorithm will

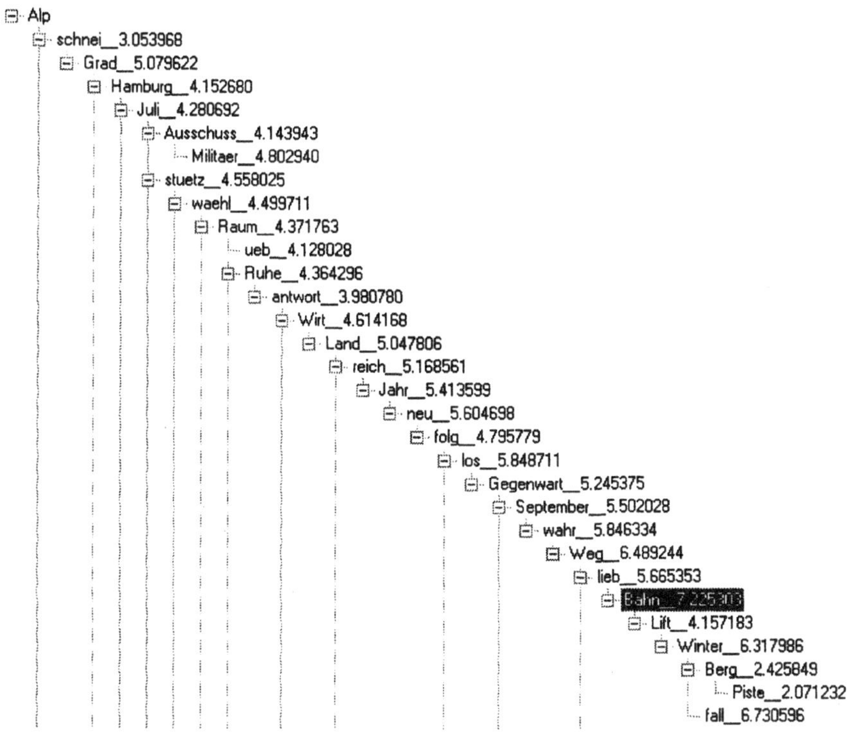

Figure 6: Fragment of MST-graph of `Alpen` (root) as generated from the same *semantic space* data.

1. take that meaning point's label as a start,
2. stack labels of all its neighboring points by decreasing distances,
3. open DDS-tree with starting point's label as primed head or root node. Then it will
4. take label on top of stack as daughter node,
   4.1 list labels of all its neighbors,
   4.2 intersect it with nodes in tree,
   4.3 determine from intersection the least distant one as mother node,
5. link it as daughter to identified mother node
6. and repeat 4. either
   6.1 until 2. is empty
   6.2 or other stop condition (given number of nodes, maximum distance, etc.) is reached
7. to end.

The tree structured graphs[7] may serve as a visualization of the dependencies that any labeled meaning point $z_n \in \langle S, \zeta \rangle$ chosen as root node will produce ac-

[7]The figures present subtrees of a semantic space which was computed from a sample of

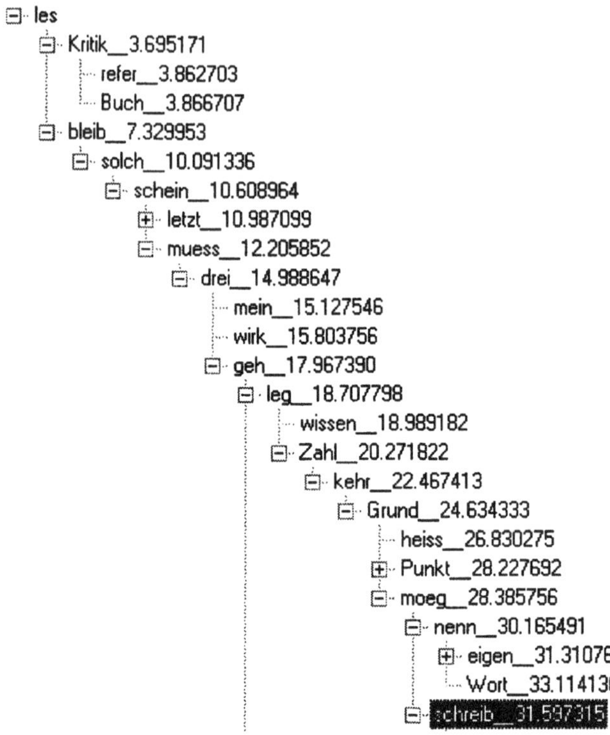

Figure 7: *Dependency path* of `lesen`/*to read* $\Longrightarrow$ `schreiben`/*to write* as traced in DDS-tree of `les`.

cording to the adjacencies of other points in the *semantic space* (*Fig.* 5). Their positions—being determined by and reconstructed operationally from the differences of usage regularities of word distributions in the texts analyzed—will thus guarantee that semantically related meanings will also be related in that tree structure, and that the direction of that relation (*dependency*) will vary contextually according to the semantic *aspect* (or starting node chosen) under which the system of structurally derived *meaning* representations is algorithmically reorganized. The tree has been named *dispositional* because of the potentiality of possible meaning relations and dependencies which it represents.

In order to illustrate the contextual sensitivity which distinguishes the DDS-algorithm from e.g. *minimal spanning trees* (MST) [23], the latter (*Fig.* 6) has been generated from the same data with the same starting node. Note, that the Bahn-node (*track, course, trail*) with identical subtrees is to be found on

texts from the German daily newspaper (DIE WELT, 1964, Berlin edition); $\oplus$ marked nodes hide subtrees not expanded; the numerical values stated are direct ζ-distances from the root node.

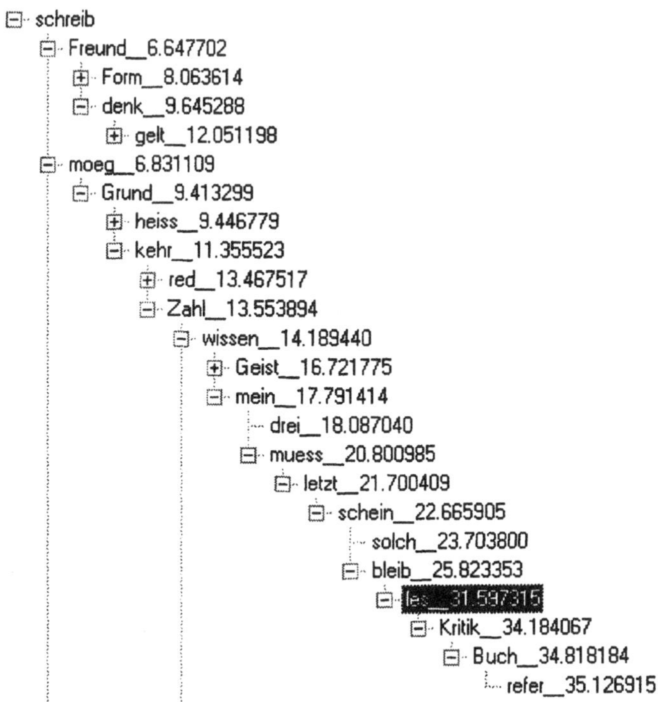

Figure 8: *Dependency path* of `schreiben`/*to write* $\Longrightarrow$ `lesen`/*to read* as traced in DDS-tree of `schreib`.

extremely different levels comparing DDS (level 3) and MST (level 23)[8].

Apparently, although the DDS-algorithm can simply be characterized as an encapsulated MST-procedure, this encapsulation serves a meaning constituting purpose. Where the MST is searching for shortest possible distance relations between points qualifying for tree node relatedness, the DDS is looking for highest *meaning similarities*, i.e. for shortest possible distance relations between points which are interpretable as *semiotically* derived representations. It is this property that allows the algorithm's search space to be *semantically* constrained as the starting point's or root node's topological environment (capsule), rendering it *aspect*-dependent and structurally *context sensitive*.

This has a number of consequences of which the following seem interesting enough to be listed:

▷ The procedural (semiotic) approach replaces the storage of fixed and ready set relations of (semantic) networks in AI by source- or aspect-oriented induction of relations among meaning points by the DDS algorithm;

▷ DDSs dependencies may be identified with an algorithmically induced *rele-*

[8]The numerical MST values given are direct ζ-distances between (mother and daughter) nodes.

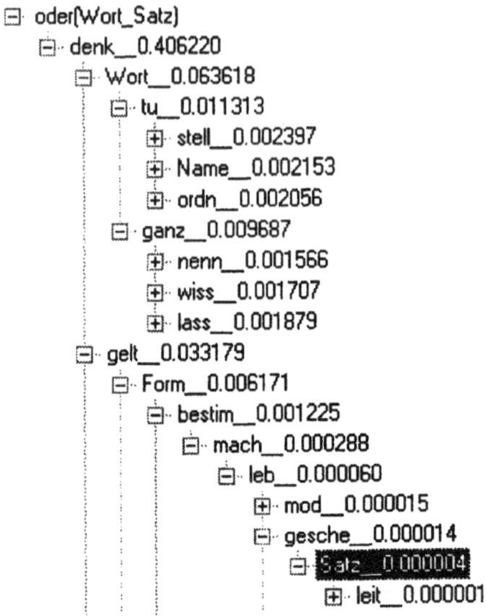

Figure 9: Fragment of DDS of `Wort`/*word* ∨ `Satz`/*sentence* (with *criteriality*-values) as generated from the new meaning point derived by the *fuzzy* `OR` operation.

vance relation which is reflexive, non-symmetric, and (weakly) transitive as illustrated by the *dependency paths*' listings of node transitions **`les`** (*to read*) ⟹ **`schreib`** (*to write*) and its (partial) inverse **`schreib`** ⟹ **`les`** (*Figs.* 7 and 8);

▷ the relevance relation gives rise to the notion of *criteriality* which allows to specify to what degree a meaning compound contributes to the *meaning potential* a root node's DDS is to represent. It may numerically be specified as a function of any node's level and ζ-distance by

$$Cr_i(d)_{\kappa+1} = Cr_i(m)_\kappa \cdot e^{-\frac{\zeta(d,i)}{\lambda+\zeta(d,m)}} \tag{5}$$

with i, m, d for root, mother, and daughter nodes respectively, and the counters κ for (left to right) nodes, and λ for (top down) levels in the tree;

▷ as the criteriality values are decreasing monotonously from 1.0 (root) they may be interpreted as membership values which reflect the relevance related *soft* structure of components (nodes) in the DDS as *fuzzy meaning potential*. Applying the fuzzy set theoretical extensions for logical operators (*and*, *or*, *non*, etc.) opens new possibilities to generate composite meaning points (`Wort`/*word* ∧ `Satz`/*sentence*) and `Wort`/*word* ∨ `Satz`/*sentence*)) without assuming a propositional structure a n d to get these composites' structural *meanings* determined by their DDSs as computed from the semantic space data (*Figs.* 9 and 10)[9];

[9]The numerical values given here are Cr-criterialities of daughter nodes as defined by *Eqn.*

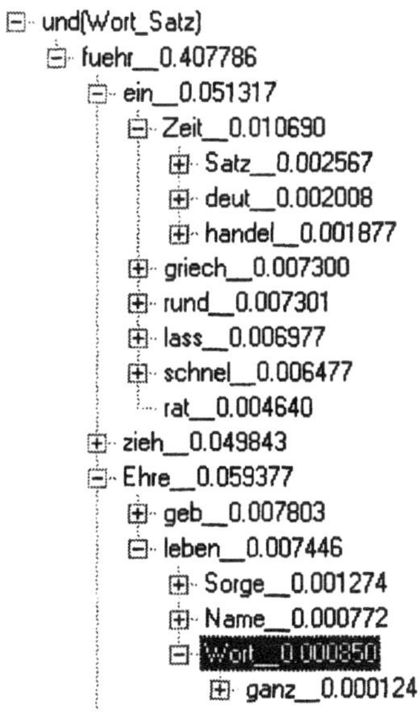

Figure 10: Fragment of DDS of `Wort`/*word* ∧ `Satz`/*sentence* (with *criteriality*-values) as generated from the new meaning point derived by the *fuzzy* `AND` operation.

▷ experiments are underway to employ DDSs as structural frame for semantic inferencing without the need to have the premises be stated in a predicative or propositional form prior to the concluding process. The DDS algorithm lends itself easily to the modeling of *analogical* reasoning processes by a procedure which takes two (or more) root nodes (as semantic premises), initiates two (or more) DDS processes each of which—in selecting their respective daughter nodes—will tag the corresponding meaning points in the semantic space. Stop condition for this process which may proceed *highest criteriality breadth first* through the respective DDSs could be the first meaning point found to be tagged when met by either (or any) of the processes active. This point would be considered the (first) candidate to be semantically inferred or concluded from the premises (with the option to extend the number candidates).

4 Conclusion

It is hoped that devising representational structures which result from procedures of systematic exploration of *syntagmatic* and *paradigmatic* constraints on different levels of natural language discourse will allow to come up some day with a new understanding of how entities and structures are formed which are *semiotic*, i.e. do not only emerge from processes as their results which have an objective (material) extension in space-time, but can above that and due to their (recursively defined) co- and context dependency be understood as having interpretable meaning.

In order to be able to interpret, we need to have structures, but we are about to experience that the model structures available so far do not serve the purpose we are looking for. When we have to deal with problems which might result from the lack of concepts, of structures, and of formats to describe or represent them adequately, we should not be too surprised to find these problems unsolvable. Procedural models and their computational enactment generating structures sensitive to situational embeddings appear to be good candidates for progress.

References

[1] S. Armstrong-Warwick (ed): *Using Large Corpora I & II.* Special Issues: *Computational Linguistics*, 19:1 & 2. MIT Press for ACL, Boston, MA, 1993.

[2] J. Barwise/ J. Perry: *Situations and Attitudes.* MIT Press, Cambridge, MA, 1983.

[3] T. Briscoe/ J. Carroll: Generalized Probabilstic LR Parsing of Natural Language (Corpora) with Unification-Based Grammars. *Computational Linguistics*, 1993(1):25–59, 1993.

[4] P. Brown/ S. DellaPietra/ V. DellaPietra/ R. Mercer: The Mathematics of Statistical Machine Translation: Parameter Eestimation. *Computational Linguistics*, 1993(2):263–311.

[5] P. E. Brown: A statistical approach to language translation. In: D. Vargha (ed): *COLING-88 Budapest*, ICCL, J.v.Neumann Society of Computing Science. Budapest 1988, pp. 71–76.

[6] H. Bunke (ed): *Advances in Structural and Syntactic Pattern Recognition.* World Scientific, Singapore, 1992.

[7] G. A. Carpenter/ S. Grossberg (eds): *Pattern Recognition by Self-Organizing Neural Networks.* MIT Press, Cambridge, MA, 1991.

[8] N. Chomsky: *Language and Problems of Knowledge. The Managua Lectures.* (Current Studies in Linguistics 16). MIT Press, Cambridge, MA, 1988.

[9] N. Chomsky: *The Minimalist Program.* (Current Studies in Linguistics 28). MIT Press, Cambridge, MA, 1995.

[10] K. Church: A stochastic parts program and noun phrase parser for unrestricted text. In: *Second Conference on Applied Natural Language Processing*, ACL, Austin, TX, 1988, pp. 136–143.

[11] K. W. Church/ P. Hanks: Word association norms, mutual information, and lexicography. *Computational Linguistics*, 1990(1):22–29.

[12] K. W. Church/ R. L. Mercer: Introduction to the Special Issue on Computational Linguistics Using Large Corpora. *Computational Linguistics*, 1993(1):1–24.

[13] J. Fodor/ Z. Pylyshyn: Connectionism and cognitive architecture: A critical analysis. *Cognition*, 1988(28):3–71.

[14] W. Fucks: On Nahordnung and Fernordnung in samples of literary texts. *Biometrica*, 1954(2):116–132.

[15] D. Hindle/ M. Rooth: Structural Ambiguity and Lexical Relations. *Computational Linguistics*, 1993(1):103–120.

[16] G. Hinton (ed): *Connectionist Symbol Processing.* MIT Press, Cambridge, MA, 1992.

[17] R. Köhler/ B. Rieger (eds): *Contributions to Quantitative Linguistics. Proceedings 1st Quantitative Linguistics Conference – QUALICO-91.* Kluwer Academic Publishers, Dordrecht, 1993.

[18] R. Lorch: Priming and search processes in semantic memory: a test of three models of spreading activation. *Journal of Verbal Learning and Verbal Behavior*, 1982(21):468–492.

[19] A. Meystel: *Semiotic Modeling and Situation Analysis: an Introduction.* AdRem Inc, Bala Cynwyd, PA, 1995.

[20] L. Nadel/ L. Cooper/ P. Culicover/ R. Harnish (eds): *Neural Connections, Mental Computation.* MIT Press, Cambridge, MA, 1989.

[21] C. S. Peirce: Pragmatism in Retrospect: A Last Formulation. In: J. Buchler (ed): *The Philosophical Writings of Peirce*, Dover, New York, 1906, pp. 269–289.

[22] R. Pfeiffer/ Z. Schreter/ F. Fogelman-Soulié/ L. Steels (eds): *Connectionism in Perspective.* North Holland, Amsterdam, 1989.

[23] C. Prim: Shortest connection networks and some generalizations. *Bell Systems Technical Journal*, 1957(36):1389–1401.

[24] B. Rieger: Theoretische Grundlagen der Computerlinguistik: eine Paneldiskussion mit M. Bierwisch, C. Habel, B. Rieger, H. Uszkoreit und W. Wahlster. In: I. Bátori/ U. Hahn/ M. Pinkal/ W. Wahlster (eds): *Computerlinguistik und ihre theoretischen Grundlagen*, (KI–Informatik-Fachberichte Bd.195). Springer, Berlin/ Heidelberg/ NewYork, 1988, pp. 192–218.

[25] B. Rieger: Unscharfe Semantik: zur numerischen Modellierung vager Bedeutungen von Wörtern als fuzzy Mengen. In: H. Friemel/ G. Müller-Schönberger/ A. Schütt (eds): *Forum-90: Wissenschaft und Technik.*

Neue Anwendungen mit Hilfe aktueller Computertechnologien, (Informatik-Fachberichte Bd. 259). Springer, Berlin/ Heidelberg/ NewYork, 1990, pp. 80–104.

[26] B. Rieger: Fuzzy Modellierung linguistischer Kategorien. In: W. Feldmann/ H. Hinrichs (eds): *Text und Lexikon*, (Lexicographica Series Maior 73). Niemeyer, Tübingen, 1996, pp. 155-169.

[27] B. Rieger: Warum Fuzzy Linguistik? Überlegungen und Ansätze einer computerlinguistischen Neuorientierung. In: D. Krallmann/ W. Schmitz (eds): *Internationales Gerold-Ungeheuer-Symposium*, Nodus Verlag, Münster, 1998, pp. 153–18.

[28] B. B. Rieger: Feasible Fuzzy Semantics. On some problems of how to handle word meaning empirically. In: H. Eikmeyer/ H. Rieser (eds): *Words, Worlds, and Contexts. New Approaches in Word Semantics*, (Research in Text Theory 6). de Gruyter, Berlin/ NewYork, 1981, pp. 193–209.

[29] B. B. Rieger: Fuzzy Representation Systems in Linguistic Semantics. In: R. Trappl/ N. Findler/ W. Horn (eds): *Progress in Cybernetics and Systems Research*, Vol. XI. McGraw-Hill Intern., Washington/NewYork/London, 1982, pp. 249–256

[30] B. B. Rieger: Clusters in Semantic Space. In: L. Delatte (ed): *Actes du Congrès International Informatique et Science Humaines.* Laboratoire d'Analyse Statistique des Langues Anciennes, LASLA, Liège, 1983, pp. 805–814.

[31] B. B. Rieger: Generating Dependency Structures of Fuzzy Word Meanings in Semantic Space. In: S. Hattori/ K. Iounu /eds): *Proceedings of the XIIIth International Congress of Linguists.* Comité International Permanent des Linguistes, CIPL.Tokyo, 1983, pp. 543–548.

[32] B. B. Rieger: Semantic Relevance and Aspect Dependancy in a Given Subject Domain. In: D. Walker (ed): *COLING-84 10th International Conference on Computational Linguistics*, International Committee of Computational Linguistics, ACL-ICCL. Stanford, 1984, pp. 298–301.

[33] B. B. Rieger: Inducing a Relevance Relation in a Distance-like Data Structure of Fuzzy Word Meaning Representations. In: R. Allen (ed): *Data Bases in the Humanities and Social Sciences. 4th International Conference on Data Bases in the Humanities and Social Sciences*, Paradigm Press, Osprey, FL, 1985, pp. 374–386.

[34] B. B. Rieger: Lexical Relevance and Semantic Disposition. On stereotype word meaning representation in procedural semantics. In: G. Hoppenbrouwes/ P. Seuren/ T. Weijters (eds): *Meaning and the Lexicon.* Foris Publications, Dordrecht, 1985, pp. 387–400.

[35] B. B. Rieger: Distributed Semantic Representation of Word Meanings. In: J. D. Becker/ I. Eisele/ F. W. Mündemann (eds): *Parallelism, Learning, Evolution. Evolutionary Models and Strategies, WOPPLOT-89*, (Lecture Notes in Artificial Intelligence 565). Springer, Berlin/ Heidelberg/ New York, 1991, pp. 243–273.

[36] B. B. Rieger: On Distributed Representation in Word Semantics. (ICSI-Technical Report TR-91-012), International Computer Science Institute. Berkeley, CA, 1991.

[37] B. B. Rieger: Meaning Acquisition by SCIPS. In: B. M. Ayyub (ed): *ISUMA-NAFIPS-95*, IEEE-Transactions: Joint Intern. Conf. on Uncertainty Modeling and Analysis, North American Fuzzy Information Processing Society. IEEE Computer Society Press, Los Alamitos, CA, 1995, pp. 390–395.

[38] B. B. Rieger: Situations, Language Games, and SCIPS. Modeling semiotic cognitive information processing systems. In: A. Meystel/ N. Nerode (eds): *Architectures for Semiotic Modeling and Situation Analysis in Large Complex Systems*, 10th IEEE Symposium on Intelligent Control. AdRem, Bala Cynwyd, PA, 1995, pp. 130–138.

[39] B. B. Rieger: Situation Semantics and Computational Linguistics: towards Informational Ecology. A semiotic perspective for cognitive information processing systems. In: K. Kornwachs/ K. Jacoby (eds): *Information. New Questions to a Multidisciplinary Concept.* Akademie Verlag, Berlin, 1996, pp. 285–315.

[40] B. B. Rieger: Computational Semiotics and Fuzzy Linguistics. On meaning constitution and soft categories. In: A. Meystel (ed): *A Learning Perspective: Proceedings of the 1997 International Conference on Intelligent Systems and Semiotics (ISAS-97)*, (NIST Special Publ. 918). US Gov. Printing Office, Washington, DC, 1997, pp. 541–551.

[41] B. B. Rieger/ C. Thiopoulos: Semiotic Dynamics: a self-organizing lexical system in hypertext. In: R. Köhler/ B. B. Rieger (eds): *Contributions to Quantitative Linguistics. Proceedings of the 1st Quantitative Linguistics Conference – QUALICO-91.* Kluwer Academic Publishers, Dordrecht, 1993, pp. 67–78.

[42] H. Schnelle: Die Herausforderung des Konnektionismus in der kognitiven Linguistik. In: H. Friemel/ G. Müller-Schönberger/ A. Schütt (eds): *Forum-90: Wissenschaft und Technik*, (Informatik-Fachberichte 259). Springer, Berlin/ Heidelberg/ NewYork, 1990, pp. 42–58.

[43] H. Schnelle: Welcher Sprachwissenschaft auf der Spur? Plädoyer für größere Klarheit und Toleranz. *Zeitschr.f.Sprachwissenschaft*, 1994(1):110–120.

[44] P. Smolensky: On the proper treatment of connectionism. *Behavioral and Brain Sciences*, 1988(11):1–74.

[45] P. Smolensky: Connectionism and Constituent Structure. In: R. E. Pfeiffer (ed): *Connectionism in Perspective.* North Holland & Elsevier, Amsterdam/ NewYork, 1989, pp. 3–24.

[46] F. Varela/ E. Thompson/ E. Rosch: *The Embodied Mind. Cognitive Science and Human Experience.* MIT Press, Cambridge, MA, 1991.

Words about Uncertainty: Analogies and Contexts

Michael J. Smithson

Division of Psychology
Australian National University
Canberra, A.C.T. 0200
Australia
Email: `Michael.Smithson@anu.edu.au`

Introduction

The study of uncertainty in many fields has been beset by debate and even confusion over the meaning(s) of uncertainty and the words that are used to describe it. Normative debates address questions such as whether there is more than one kind of uncertainty and how verbal descriptions of uncertainty ought to be used. Descriptive research, which we shall deal with in this paper, concerns how people actually use words to describe uncertainty and the distinct meanings they apply to those words. The main reason for what might seem an obvious statement is to clarify the somewhat odd context in which most studies of decision making take place.

Until recently almost all descriptive research on judgment and decision making under uncertainty has been guided (some would even say, constrained) by a Bayesian normative framework. That influence is most visible in work whose object has been translating verbal probability expressions into numerical form (and vice-versa), but it is evident in other areas too. The past decade has seen a tentative movement away from exclusive reliance on a Bayesian and SEU (Subjective Expected Utility) benchmark, possibly for three reasons. First, some researchers have become convinced that there is more than one kind of uncertainty, and that probability may not adequately describe all types. Second, increasingly many researchers have undertaken studies under conditions where Bayesian approaches may not be applicable. And third, a host of new normative frameworks have been developed, along with others that might best be described as normative-descriptive hybrids.

The relevant empirical research itself falls into four groups. Perhaps the most 'mainstream' group is research on words-to-numbers translations of verbal probability expressions. The oldest comprises what are called "framing effects", such as the impact of expressing a possible outcome in positive or negative terms on its perceived likelihood. A more recent but closely related research stream is one I refer to as "naming effects", and these concern the effect of naming a possible outcome on its perceived likelihood. Finally, there is a loose-knit group of studies that investigate whether people make basic distinctions among different uncertainty-related words (e.g., "probability" and "ambiguity"), or on the other hand the nature of the analogies people draw between related words (e.g., "ambiguity" and "conflict"). This paper addresses these four types of research, each in a separate section.

Words versus Numbers in Human Judgment

Early research on verbal probability expressions followed closely related research on verbal quantifiers in general. Just as the latter research asked people to answer questions such as "how often is 'often'?', students of verbal probability asked subjects to make pointwise numerical estimates of probabilities that best represented verbal probability phrases (e.g., 'likely' vs. 'unlikely'). On the positive side, these investigations yielded reports of reasonably high intra-subjective reliability (e.g., Lichtenstein and Newman 1967, Beyth-Marom 1982, Budescu and Wallsten 1985, and Wallsten, Budescu, and Erev 1988) and reliable aggregate means (Simpson 1944, 1963, and Regan et al. 1990). Some of these findings highlighted relevant differences between meanings or usages in natural vs. formal language. For instance, negation was found to be asymmetric in its effects, so that „unlikely" is not subjectively equivalent to 1 - „likely".

However, the same research also revealed considerable inter-subjective variability and overlap among phrases (Stone and Johnson 1959, Lichtenstein and Newman 1967, Hakel 1968, Beyth-Marom 1982, and Boettcher 1995). Budescu and Wallsten (1985) argued that the variability among individuals may be partly due to individual differences in language use, and Budescu, Weinberg and Wallsten 1988 provided evidence that people vary widely in the probability phrases they regularly use.

Worse still, several researchers demonstrated context effects that seemed to eliminate the possibility of finding stable consensual numerical translations of verbal probability expressions (e.g., Cohen, Dearnaley, and Hansel 1958, Pepper and Prytulak 1974, Pepper 1981, and Wallsten, Fillenbaum, and Cox 1986). Brun and Teigen (1988) claimed that to some extent inter-subjective variability may be due to context effects, but other researchers found that specifying context does not seem to reduce that variability (e.g., Beyth-Marom 1982). Early investigations of context effects emphasized the impact of perceived base-rates on the interpretation of probability phrases. Base-rates seem to affect medium and high probability phrases most (Newstead 1988).

Other specific contextual influences have been identified since. Teigen (1988) demonstrated that interpretations of probability phrases can be drastically affected by the number of possible events, especially if they are believed to be equally likely. Kohler and Tversky (1994) have based their „Support Theory" on this insight and on arguments by writers such as Zimmer (1983) that people assess the likelihood of alternative hypotheses on the basis of accumulations of arguments and counter-arguments, i.e., weight of evidence. Fillenbaum et al. (1991) found that interpretations of probability phrases differed depending on whether the person was conveying or receiving them in a message. It is obvious in this connection that people's interpretations of such phrases might be influenced by their beliefs and perceptions about source credibility, trustworthiness, and/or intentions.

Nevertheless, we need not conclude from these findings that context effects are ineffable. Indeed, several of the studies cited here point to law-like regularities in specific effects. However, the current state of knowledge about context effects is sketchy, and the question of whether these also vary widely across individuals remains unanswered. As for the possibility of a universal words-to-numbers translation of verbal probability expressions, little has been added to Bass et al.'s (1974) suggestion that a subset of phrases be selected whose meanings exhibit the greatest agreement and the least sensitivity to context effects. Hamm (1991) has provided evidence that an ordered list of such phrases works better than an unordered one.

As previously mentioned, the large bulk of research in this area assumed that verbal probability phrases could be translated effectively into a pointwise 'best' probability value. Zimmer (1984) and Wallsten et al. (1986) were the first to use fuzzy set membership functions to model numerical translations of verbal probability phrases. The main argument for doing so is that the phrases themselves are vague and flexible, so that a range of probabilities might be considered acceptable referents by users, just as a quantifier such as „several" may refer to integers from about 4 to about 10 (Smithson 1987). This idea seems to have been adopted fairly widely by researchers in the past decade. Its importance lies in the fact that vagueness (or ambiguity) elicits responses in people that have decisional consequences, a point to which we shall return shortly.

Aside from the obvious cautionary lessons about using verbal probability phrases to communicate risks (e.g., Boettcher 1995), what else have researchers learned about using words or numbers to communicate probabilities? Are words more or less effective in communnication than numbers? Which do people prefer to use, and why? Do the same kinds of effects on judgment occur for verbal expressions as for numerical ones, and if so, to the same extent? How does the quality of decision making compare between the two modes?

At first glance, it might seem that when it comes to quality of judgment or decision making, numbers would be undeniably superior. However, there are at least two reasons for investigating this matter carefully. One is that people are better at 'qualitative' judgment tasks such as sorting, categorizing, and comparing than they are at quantitative estimation; and much that is important about judgment and decision making under uncertainty is encompassed by those qualitative aspects. Indeed, there is a large literature on symbolic and logical methods for dealing with uncertainty in AI (see Krause and Clark 1993 for a balanced review of quantitative and qualitative AI approaches). The second reason is that a large empirical literature in psychology has revealed that people regularly deviate from standard probability theories in various systematic ways when they use numerical information and estimates; and it is possible that such tendencies might not be as pronounced were they to use verbal expressions instead.

Let us begin with issues in communication. People are divided on whether they prefer words or numbers for both communicating and receiving information, but if they differ on the two tasks they prefer to express with verbal phrases but receive numerical estimates (Erev and Cohen 1990 and Wallsten, et al. 1993). People generally believe that the numerical mode is more precise, but the verbal mode is more natural, personal, and easier to use.

The purposes and intentions behind communications are likely to influence preferences for numbers or words. Two candidate explanations presented by Erev and Cohen (1990) are the "spontaneous vs controlled behavior" explanation and the "cover" explanation. The first holds that people are more likely to behave spontaneously when communicating than when receiving information, so they are shaped by previous experiences to convey probabilistic information with verbal phrases but consciously decide in favor of the more 'accurate' numerical mode when eliciting information from others. The second explanation simply appeals to a preference for being vague rather than wrong. People are more likely to prefer the vagueness of verbal phrases for expressive purposes than for understanding someone else's message; so they are more likely to demand numerical precision from others than from themselves. Erev and Cohen found some support for the first explanation but not for the second, although they acknowledged that their studies did not provide a definitive test of either. The effect of accountability has not been systematically investigated in this connection, although it has been suggested as an important factor in the study by Curley et al. (1986).

A third possible explanation is one that stems from studies of people's responses to vague (or "ambiguous") probabilities (e.g., Ellsberg 1961, Einhorn and Hogarth 1985). Those studies indicate that people tend to be "ambiguity averse" in the sense that they will prefer gambles based on precise probabilities over gambles whose probabilities are imprecise. Given the consistent findings by Wallsten and his colleagues that verbal probability expressions are vague, according to this literature we should find that people prefer to make decisions on the basis of pointwise (precise) numerical probabilities instead of verbally expressed probabilities. Arrayed against this prediction are Zimmer's (1983, 1984) claims that people operate naturally in a verbal mode and therefore forcing them to use numbers will require greater mental effort, retard decision making, and introduce biases.

Do verbal and numerical representations of probability differentially affect the quality of judgments or decisions? Thus far, the research literature has produced intriguing findings but no over-arching framework for addressing this question. Starting with the question of judgmental biases, Teigen and Brun (1995) found that many verbally expressed probabilities are directionally unambiguous to a greater extent than are numerical estimates, in the sense that they focus the perceiver's attention on one or the other end of the [0,1] interval. Moreover, affirmative phrases are more vague insofar as they apply to a wider range of probabilities than do negative phrases.

More recently, Dusenbury and Fennema (1996) examined preferences between lotteries with probabilities presented either numerically or linguistically. They hypothesized that presentation mode effects are due to the perception of linguistic chance as skewed distributions, and therefore would be detectable in very small and large risks. Their results suggested that theories of the effects of second order uncertainty (i.e., imprecise probabilities) on risky choice may be used to model decisions involving linguistic risk, along the lines of Einhorn and Hogarth (1985) and subsequent work stimulated by their paper.

Gonzalez-Vallejo and Wallsten (1992) explored whether the usual reversal of preference between choice and bidding procedures (see the next section on framing effects) would be found as frequently when probabilities were expressed verbally as when they were expressed numerically. Their results indicated that the frequency of preference reversals was significantly reduced in the verbal condition, apparently because risk aversion was reduced in choice when verbal estimates were given whereas expressive mode had no effect on bidding. Budescu, Weinberg, and Wallsten (1988) found that subjects preferred verbal probabilities for gambles with a prospect of gain but preferred numerical or graphical representations when the gambles involved a prospect of loss.

As for actual quality of decision making, the evidence thus far is inconclusive. Budescu, Weinberg, and Wallsten (1988) and Budescu and Wallsten (1990) found greater variability in bidding when probabilities were expressed verbally, and that subjects' payoffs were somewhat worse in the verbal mode even though decisions were made more quickly and easily. On the other hand, Gonzalez-Vallejo, Erev, and Wallsten (1994) produced evidence that subjects' preference rankings for gambles correlated more closely with payoffs when probabilities were expressed verbally rather than numerically. Finally, Erev and Cohen (1990) failed to find any differences between the numerical and verbal modes in decision making quality, efficiency, or judgmental bias.

Overall, the research on verbal probability expressions raises some important issues while leaving them only partly resolved. For purposes of computing with words, verbal probability phrases have limitations. Their meanings are inherently imprecise, vary substantially from one person to another, and are context-sensitive. These limitations may be problematic for communication, comparisons across contexts, and group decision making; but not necessarily so for individuals making decisions in unique or very specific situations. In the latter kind of setting, people seem to make choices with much the same efficacy using words as they do when using numbers. Moreover, even where the limitations introduce difficulties, they may be overcome for the most part by explicit translations and the use of phrases whose meanings enjoy the greatest consensus.

Finally, there are cognitive and expressive advantages in verbal probability phrases that go largely unremarked in this literature. Such phrases are cognitively efficient (i.e., they require little calculation or pre-processing), and in situations where probabilities are not precisely known they may provide a more faithful representation of the real state of knowledge than falsely precise pointwise numerical estimates. Under imprecision, the overlap between 'neighboring' phrases may highlight a realistic inability to discern which option has greater likelihood, whereas a precise numbers may create the illusion of a reliable difference in likelihood.

Naming Effects

Merely naming a possible outcome or option can influence people's assessment of its likelihood. This matter seems of no concern when all possible outcomes and options are known and explicitly represented. However, in many real-world decisions we do not know all of the possibilities. Even when possible outcomes are known, they may be 'unpacked' into sub-cases or 'repacked' into a summary category that hides particular cases. Choices about how fine-grained the representations of various possible outcomes should be may influence perceptions of how likely and/or desirable those outcomes are. Naming effects were noted in early studies of survey question construction. In a classic study, Payne (1951) demonstrated that explicitly mentioning only the 'affirmative' option in a question's wording substantially increased respondent agreement with that option in comparison with a version of the question in which both the affirmative and negative options were expressed. In a similar vein, a review of the literature by Molenaar (1982) reported that a question of the form "Is P better than Q?" results in greater endorsement of P than one of the form "Which is better: P or Q?".

The earliest line of research on human judgment under uncertainty to investigate these phenomena concerned the "Catch-All Underestimation Bias" (CAUB), first studied by Fischhoff, Slovic, and Lichtenstein (1978). They conducted experiments concerning people's assignments of probabilities to possible causes of a given outcome (e.g., an automobile that will not start), and found that those possible causes that were explicitly listed received higher probabilities than those that were implicitly incorporated into a "Catch-All" category of additional causes. At least three explanations have since been proposed for this effect:

1. Unlisted causes are not as available to a person's mental representation of the situation, and therefore not rated as highly likely;
2. People may perceive ambiguity in a list that is incomplete and mentally redefine some of the items on the list by adding other unlisted causes to them (Hirt and Castellan 1988); and
3. A list that is incomplete may be perceived as lacking credibility, so people inflate the probabilities of the explicitly listed causes (Dube-Rioux and Russo 1988).

Russo and Kozlow (1994) conducted further studies and found the most evidence for the unavailability explanation and the least for the credibility explanation. However, Bonini and Caverni (1995) provided evidence from the literature and their own experiments that casts doubt on all three explanations. For instance, they found that making the unlisted causes more available to people did not decrease the CAUB.

In a similar vein, Support Theory (Tversky and Koehler 1994 and Rottenstreich and Tversky 1997) is a framework that begins with the claim that people do not follow the extensional logic of conventional probability theory. Instead, unpacking a compound event into disjoint components tends to increase the perceived likelihood of that event. An immediate implication is that unpacking an hypothesis and/or repacking its complement will increase the judged likelihood of that hypothesis. Moreover, while the sum of the subjective probabilities of an hypothesis and its complement might sum to 1, finer-grained partitions of either will result in 'probabilities' whose sum exceeds 1. Support Theory revives the Keynesian (1921) distinction between the balance of evidence in favoring a given proposition and the weight or strength of evidence for that proposition.

Both the CAUB and Support Theory are important because they suggest that people are sensitive to the sample space in which events are embedded, and how that sample space is partitioned. If true, then people may violate principles in formal frameworks such as Walley's (1991, 1996) imprecise probability theory. They may also exhibit judgments and decisions that differ markedly from any AI system that does not differentiate between implicit and explicit representations of alternatives.

Moreover, such 'naming effects' could have important consequences for people's preferences when making choices under ignorance about possible outcomes (i.e., sample-space ignorance). Smithson and Bartos (1997) performed a simple experiment, in which 46 subjects were asked to make two choices, each involving two gambles.

Gamble 1: Suppose you were offered a choice between two urns, with a bet on each.

Urn 1 has 1000 marbles whose colors may be either Red or various other colors, but you don't know how many are Red or what any of the other colors are. You will receive $100 if the next marble drawn from this urn is Red, otherwise you pay $5.

Urn 2 has 1000 marbles whose colors are unknown. You will receive $100 if the next marble drawn from this urn is Red, otherwise you pay $5.

Gamble 2: Suppose you were offered a choice between two urns, with a bet on each.

Urn 1 has 1000 marbles whose colors may be either Green or various other colors, but you don't know how many are Green or what any of the other colors are. You will receive $100 if the next marble drawn from this urn is Black, otherwise you pay $5.

Urn 2 has 1000 marbles whose colors are unknown. You will receive $100 if the next marble drawn from this urn is Black, otherwise you pay $5.

About 72% of the 46 subjects chose Urn 1 in the first gamble and Urn 2 in the second. Clearly, simply naming one of the possible colors influenced subjects' choices. One reasonable interpretation of those results is that they reflect the propensity to think a named alternative is more likely than one that has not been named. Thus, merely naming one possible color of marble in a bag (Red, say) makes it seem more likely than any other (unnamed) color. If we are betting on Red then we prefer the bag for which Red has been named as a possible color to one where it has not; but if we are betting on Black then we prefer the bag where no color has been named to one for which Green has been named.

Smithson and Bartos (1997) also conducted experiments in which subjects were asked to estimate lower and upper probabilities of events that they had not (yet) seen after observing a sample of events generated by a process whose possible outcomes were not known to the subjects beforehand. Under sample space ignorance, three 'naming effects' were reliably observed.

First, many people gave nonzero lower probabilities to unobserved events. The percentages of such people ranged from 39% to 65%, with the percentage increasing with the number of events they had already witnessed. Second, the difference between people's upper and lower estimates (i.e., their imprecision) was greater for observed than for unobserved events. This was the case not only when they were asked to make estimations for specific unobserved events, but even when asked to do so for "any new event", thereby corroborating the CAUB in a sense. The implication is that people may be inclined to underestimate the likelihood of events they have not yet observed, relative to the estimates they provide for events that they have already seen.

Third, however, people also gave higher lower and upper probability estimates for "any new event" than for a specific unobserved event. In other words, they clearly regarded "any new event" as more encompassing and thence more likely than a specific unobserved event. It is noteworthy in this connection that some frameworks for imprecise probabilities such as Walley's (1991, 1996) stipulate that people should give identical lower and upper probabilities for any conceivable unobserved event, whether that event is compound or simple.

Framing Effects

It has been widely established that logically equivalent wordings of survey questions can affect people's responses in different ways. Research on judgment and decision making under uncertainty has extended and systematized these findings in relation to the impact of 'framing' on people's perceptions of likelihood or risk and their preferences for decisions under risk. The main idea here is that just as simply naming or omitting to name an alternative can influence perceptions of its likelihood, people respond as if the valuation attached to an alternative can also affect its perceived likelihood. We will review this literature only briefly here, since it is well-reviewed in several other places.

The most famous framing effect is one incorporated in Kahneman and Tversky's (1979) Prospect Theory, wherein people are found to be risk-averse if faced with the prospect of gain and risk-seeking if faced with the prospect of loss. That is, people prefer a sure gain over a gain with a probability attached to it, even when the expectated payoff is larger for the probabilistic option. Conversely, they prefer loss with a probability attached to it over a sure loss, even when the expected payoff is worse for the probabilistic option.

A good example of this kind of framing effect is from Tversky and Kahneman (1981), in which they ask subjects to choose between two public health programs to combat a "rare plague" endangering a village of 600 people. In one condition, the programs's outcomes are framed in terms of lives saved:

- Program A: Exactly 200 lives will be saved.
- Program B: There is a 1/3 chance of saving all 600 lives, and a 2/3 chance of saving none.

In the other condition, outcomes are framed in terms of lives lost:

- Program A: Exactly 400 lives will be lost.
- Program B: There is a 1/3 chance that nobody will die, and a 2/3 chance that all 600 lives will be lost.

While 72% of the subjects selected the sure alternative in the first condition, only 22% did in the second.

These framing effects seem to apply to imprecise probabilities and even nonprobabilistic kinds of uncertainty. In Smithson's (1989) revision of the disease scenario, outcomes were framed in terms that cross-linked success and failure with lower and upper bounds on the probabilities concerned. The version for the first condition was as follows:

- Program A: The treatment is known to fail at least 1/3 of the time.
- Program B: The treatment is known to succeed at least 2/3 of the time.

The second condition reversed the framing but otherwise posed equivalent alternatives:

- Program A: The treatment is known to succeed at most 2/3 of the time.
- Program B: The treatment is known to fail at most 2/3 of the time.

Subjects were asked to rate A and B on s subjective scale of effectiveness. Although B should be rated as superior to A, in the second condition 39% of the subjects rated A as superior to B and only 7% rated B better than A. In the first condition, 45% rated B as superior to A and 2% did the opposite.

In another experiment, Smithson (1989) found that framing effects apply to possibilistic uncertainty. Subjects rated restrictions expressed in terms of what is possible or available to people as having greater freedom than equivalent restrictions expressed in terms of what is impossible or unavailable to people.

Kuhn (1997) has recently investigated the impact of framing on how people respond to vagueness in probability estimates. She used both verbal qualifiers and numerical intervals to represent vagueness. Although people generally demonstrate vagueness aversion, gain/loss framing influences how people respond in a way that is analogous to Prospect Theory's predictions, with one qualification. Negative framing elicits greater preference for vague prospects, unless vagueness is described by a numerical range with the higher value presented first.

A related but distinct framing effect has been widely documented that arises from selective attention to probabilities or outcomes in decision tasks. If people are asked to choose between two gambles, for instance, they tend to focus on which has the higher probability of winning. However, if asked to nominate a minimum selling-price for the same gambles, they usually focus on the amounts in their respective payoffs. The result is that people may exhibit preference reversals, whereby they choose one gamble but nominate a higher selling-price for the other. This effect, first established in laboratory studies by Lichtenstein and Slovic (1971), was replicated in numerous studies and found to hold in real-world settings. Tversky, Slovic, and Kahneman (1990) concluded that the explanation for this robust effect is that response tasks (e.g., choosing between two gambles vs nominating selling-prices) induce people to give greater emphasis to those informative aspects of alternatives that are compatible with the response mode. An implication is that the verbal framing of the decisional task itself may affect how people treat quantitative dimensions.

In contrast to Prospect Theory, rank-dependent expected utility (RDEU) theory (Quiggin 1982) is based on the claim that people's subjective probability assessments for outcomes may be influenced by the rank-order of the utility of those outcomes. In particular, RDEU researchers hypothesize that people overweight probabilities of outcomes that are extremely good or bad.

Recently some researchers have argued that Prospect Theory conflicts with commonly held notions of risk taking for opportunities and risk aversion for threats. Highhouse and Yuce (1996) were able to empirically separate threat and opportunity perceptions from loss and gain perspectives. They found that decision makers, faced with a traditional framing problem, perceived the risky alternative as an opportunity when they were in the loss domain, but perceived it as a threat when they were in the gain domain. Moreover, they were more risk taking for opportunity-framed problems and risk averse for threat-framed problems.

Finally, a substantial body of work (e.g., Loomes and Sugden 1982, Bell 1985) has concentrated on the role of anticipations and regret in decision making under uncertainty. The tendency of people to honor sunk costs is an example of anticipated regret driving a decision (i.e., forseeing the regret of abandoning something already invested in). An important framing effect in this connection hinges on the distinction between regrets over things done (comissions) and things undone (omissions). Gilovich and Medvec (1995) have ascertained that while regrets over comissions are more sharply felt in the short term, in the long run omissions loom larger. The implication here is that when people are anticipating possible regrets for decision making, if they are focused on the here-and-now they are likely to perceive regrets as greater if they arise from comissions than if they arise from omissions. However, if people are basing their decision on something in the distant past, the reverse may be the case.

At first glance, framing effects might seem to be mere 'verbal trickery'. If that were so, then once the 'trick' is explained to people they should reralize their inconsistency and cease to behave inconsistently. However, although people can be induced to agree that their choices are inconsistent, many will not change even when framing effects are pointed out to them. There may be deep psychological or even evolutionary reasons for such phenomena. For instance, the fact that people weigh losses more heavily than seemingly equivalent gains may have had adaptive advantages for homo sapiens in the past. Likewise, many framing effects can be understood via one of the tenets of Prospect Theory, which holds that people frame judgments and choices in terms of changes from the status quo rather than in terms of absolute magnitudes of final consequences. Finally, most people seem to behave as if any quantitative gain or loss has a diminishing returns characteristic. Thus, 200 lives saved is subjectively more than 1/3 as valuable as 600 saved; and conversely 400 lives lost is subjective more than 2/3 as bad as 600 lost.

Tversky, Slovic, and Kahneman (1990) state that framing effects alone demonstrate the impossibility of constructing a decision-making framework that is both normatively and descriptively valid. If they are correct, then any enterprise that involves computing with words to handle uncertainty will necessarily be compromised to some extent on one or the other criterion. The chief stumbling-blocks are naming, framing, and context effects, and possibly individual differences among human decision makers.

Analogies, Synonyms, and Preferences

Where do our concepts of uncertainty come from? Do particular uncertainty-related words refer to fundamentally different kinds of uncertainty? Do other words (or their referents) cause or induce different representations of uncertainty? In this concluding section, we will examine some metaphorical and causal connections between uncertainty-words and cognitive schema and behavioral dispositions.

Despite the fairly long-running normative debates over issues such as whether "fuzziness" is different from "probability", relatively little systematic investigation has been conducted in the descriptive mode other than the attempts to model the meanings of verbal quantifiers and probability phrases that were reviewed in the first section of this paper. Yet it would seem investigations along those lines could lend insights into the variety and sources of human heuristics regarding uncertainty. A number of such heuristics have been identified and studied concerning subjective probability, but not often in relation to other kinds of uncertainty.

A simplified model of an expanded research program along these lines is shown below:

Antecedent triggers→
Categorization into uncertainty type→
Judgmental heuristics and mental models→
Preferred coping strategies and heuristics.

Thus, for instance, Einhorn and Hogarth (1985) claimed that conflicting information "causes" people to view that information as uncertain, "ambiguous" in particular. Along with Ellsberg (1961) and others, they would say that people decide on the basis of the conflict that the information is of an uncertain nature, and that the kind of uncertainty is describable in terms of ambiguity. They would also say that by characterizing information as "ambiguous", people then set in motion (whether consciously or not) judgmental heuristics, strategies, and mental models that pertain to ambiguity rather than to, say, probability.

Smithson (1989) proposed a typology of uncertainty and speculated that various kinds might be linked to distinct coping strategies. Teigen (1994) proposed distinctions even within probabilistic uncertainty that are verbally-based, and which in turn may trigger different mental models or heuristics. In a recent study, Lipshitz and Strauss (1997) took up this idea and found that decision makers distinguished among three types of uncertainty: inadequate understanding, incomplete information, and undifferentiated alternatives. Moreover, they found that the methods decision makers chose for dealing with uncertainty varied according to these three types. Inadequate understanding was primarily managed by reduction of uncertainty (e.g., obtaining more information), incomplete information primarily by assumption-based reasoning, and conflict among alternatives primarily by weighing pros and cons.

Not all distinctions among types of uncertainty imply different responses or coping strategies, however. There are a number of instances in which seemingly different kinds of triggers lead to different representations and verbal labels for uncertainty, which nevertheless seem to call forth the same responses and strategies. Two or more words that call forth precisely the same responses under all conditions are synonyms; here we shall use a weaker term and speak of concepts or words that are analogous to one another. One of the most well-established analogies is between delay and probability (see Rachlin 1989 for an interesting overview, but the idea goes at least as far back as the 19th century). People (and other organisms) respond to delay and probability in strikingly similar ways. Immediate rewards or punishments are treated as if they are certainties, and deferred ones as if they are low-probability events. Moreover, the analogy may be strengthened and parameterized by equating probabilities to delays in a reward or punishment schedule over time (e.g., in repeated gambles). Rachlin (1989) builds an argument from this equivalence for the claim that many heuristics and strategies for coping with probabilistic uncertainty originated from the ways organisms have learned to cope with delays. One implication from all this is that the vocabularies of delay and time may be mined for meanings that are analogous to probability phrases. It is also possible that similar kinds of spatial analogues might exist, but to my knowledge they have not been investigated.

Another intriguing analogy, suggested by the notion of arguments and counter-arguments engendering uncertainty, is between conflict and ambiguity. Both refer to discrete possible states, and in a special case ambiguity can refer to incompatible possible states which is very similar to conflict. Smithson (1997) has found that people respond in rather similar ways to conflicting information and ambiguous information. However, conflict and ambiguity are not subjectively equivalent. Instead, people treat conflicting but precise information as if it is riskier than objectively equivalent consensual but ambiguous information. Thus, while they are analogous, conflict and ambiguity have a preference-ordering.

Moreover, the analogy between the two concepts is not perfectly supported by the evidence. Overall, most of the choice preference findings in Smithson (1997) suggested only weak framing effects which also were asymmetric, indicating a tendency towards conflict aversion that is only partly mollified by framing. Likewise, a large majority of subjects regarded human information sources as more knowledgeable when they were consensual and ambiguous than when they were precise but conflictory, regardless of frame. Thus, conflict aversion may be distinct from either ambiguity or probability aversions.

As a final example, the aforementioned 'naming effect' results reported by Smithson and Bartos (1997) may be interpreted in terms of the relationship between sample-space ignorance and mere vagueness concerning the probability of an outcome that is already known to be possible. Most people regard sample-space ignorance as riskier than vague probabilities of known outcomes, even when those probabilities are vacuous. Likewise, the findings also suggest that people tend to under-estimate the likelihood of an event when they have never seen it before or when they do not know whether it is possible. However, that tendency diminishes to some extent when people are asked to consider any conceivable new event. What remains unclear from all of this is whether sample-space ignorance is analogous to probability, vagueness, or any other uncertainty-related concept.

Conclusion

The current mood in intelligent systems seems fairly democratic and eclectic with regard to the issue of whether (or when) to use quantitative or qualitative representations of uncertainty. There seems little doubt that human languages comprise a complex variety of words for expressing uncertainty. As Teigen (1994: 234) avers, people may well be sophisticated about uncertainty in most respects other than quantification. The object of this paper has been to survey the extant research on how uncertainty-related words are used and with what consequences for human judgment and decision making.

The earliest attempts to decipher the meanings of verbal probability expressions such as „rather likely" were guided by what Evans (1993) has called „Rationality 2", namely the comparison of what people do with a normative theory of what is logically or mathematically justifiable. „Rationality 1", which amounts to a pragmatist stance that human (or any other) intelligence is to be judged according to whether it 'works', has been applied only recently to research on human judgment under uncertainty. This distinction is important both because it suggests alternatives to the so-called 'biases-and-heuristics' approach to explaining human judgment and decision making, and because it might shed light on the kinds of talk used when people communicate or even think about uncertainty. Insofar as soft computing systems are intended for compatibility with human intelligence, such considerations are worthwhile. If humans are predisposed to distinguish among different kinds of uncertainty then they may respond differently to each kind, and any intelligent system will need to take these distinctions into account even if its own normative framework disagrees with them.

Likewise, the literature on numerical translations of verbal probability expressions highlights the need for intelligent systems to take account of individual differences among decision makers, the vagueness inherent in such expressions, and context effects. The material on framing and naming effects provides a partial guide to context, but we are far from a complete or thorough understanding of such effects. Perhaps the largest gap in our knowledge concerns social context. Words are seldom employed outside of some social context, and it is arguable that some coping strategies for dealing with uncertainty have their basis in sociability. Conflict aversion, for instance, may originate from the function it performs in enabling groups to reach a workable consensus and thus mobilize for collective action or cooperation. Substituting vagueness or ambiguity in place of precision under conflict is an effective way to attain consensus.

References

Bass, B.M., Cascio, W.F., and O'Connor, E.J. (1974). "Magnitude estimation of expression of frequency and amount." *Journal of Applied Psychology*, 59, 313-320.

Bell, D. E. (1985). Disappointment in decision making under uncertainty. *Operations Research*, 33, 1-27.

Beyth-Marom, R. (1982). How probable is probable? A numerical translation of verbal probability expressions. *Journal of Forecasting*, 1, 257-269.

Boettcher, W.A. (1995). Context, methods, numbers, and words: Prospect theory in international relations. *Journal of Conflict Resolution*. 39, 561-583.

Bonini, N. and Caverni, J.-P. (1995). The "catch-all underestimation bias": Availability hypothesis vs. category redefinition hypothesis. *Current Psychology of Cognition*. 14, 301-322.

Brun, W. and Teigen, K.H. (1988) Verbal probabilities: ambiguous, context-dependent, or both? *Organizational Behavior and Human Decision Processes*. 41, 390-404.

Budescu, D.V., Weinberg, S. and Wallsten, T.S. (1988). Decisions based on numerically and verbally expressed uncertainties. *Journal of Experimental Psychology: Human Perception and Performance*. 14, 281-294.

Budescu, D.V. and Wallsten, T.S. (1985). Consistency in interpretation of probabilistic phrases. *Organizational Behavior and Human Decision Processes*, 36, 391-405.

Cohen, J., Dearnaley, E.J., and Hansel, C.E.M. (1958). Skill and chance: Variations in estimates of skill with an increasing element of chance. *British Journal of Psychology*, 49, 319-323.

Curley, S.P., Yates, J.F., and Abrams, R.A. (1986). Psychological sources of ambiguity avoidance. *Organizational Behavior and Human Decision Processes*, 38, 230-256.

Dube-Rioux, L. and Russo, J.E. (1988). An availability bias in professional judgment. *Journal of Behavioral Decision Making*. 1, 223-237.

Dusenbury, R. and M. G. Fennema, M.G. (1996). Linguistic-Numeric Presentation Mode Effects on Risky Option Preferences. *Organizational Behavior and Human Decision Processes*. 68, 109-122.

Einhorn, H. J. and Hogarth, R. M. (1985). Ambiguity and uncertainty in probabilistic inference. *Psychological Review*. 92, 433-461.

Ellsberg, D. (1961). Risk, ambiguity, and the Savage axioms. *Quarterly Journal of Economics*. 75, 643-669.

Erev, I. and Cohen, B.L. (1990). Verbal versus numerical probabilities: Efficiency, biases, and the preference paradox. *Organizational Behavior and Human Decision Processes*. 45, 1-18.

Evans, J.St.B.T. (1993) The mental model theory of conditional reasoning: Critical appraisal and revision. *Cognition*. 48, 1-20.

Fillenbaum, S., Wallsten, T.S., Cohen, B.L. and Cox, J.A. (1991). Some effects of vocabulary and communication task on the understanding and use of vague probability expressions. *American Journal of Psychology*. 104, 35-60.

Fischhoff, B., Slovic, P, and Lichtenstein, S. (1978). Fault trees: Sensibility of estimated failure probabilities to problem representation. *Journal of Experimental Psychology: Human Perception and Performance*. 4, 330-344.

Gilovich. T. and Medvec, V.H. (1995). The experience of regret: What, when, and why. *Psychological Review*. 102, 379-395.

Gonzalez-Vallejo, C.C., Erev, I. and Wallsten, T.S. (1994). Do decision quality and preference order depend on whether probabilities are verbal or numerical? *American Journal of Psychology*. 107, 157-172.

Gonzalez-Vallejo, C.C. and Wallsten, T.S. (1992). Effects of probability mode on preference reversal. *Journal of Experimental Psychology: Learning, Memory, and Cognition*. 18, 855-864.

Hakel, M. (1968). How often is often? *American Psychologist*, 23, 533-534.

Hamm, R.M. (1991). Selection of verbal probabilities: A solution for some problems of verbal probability expressions. *Organizational Behavior and Human Decision Processes*. 48, 193-223.

Highhouse, S. and Yüce, P. (1996) Perspectives, Perceptions, and Risk-Taking Behavior. *Organizational Behavior and Human Decision Processes*, 65, 159-167.

Hirt, E.R. and Castellan, N.J. Jr. (1988). Probability and category redefinition in the fault tree paradigm. *Journal of Experimental Psychology: Human Perception and Performance*. 20, 17-32.

Kahneman, D. and Tversky, A. (1979). Prospect theory: An analysis of decision under risk. *Econometrica*, 47, 263-291.

Keynes, J. M. (1921). *A Treatise on Probability*. London: Macmillan.

Krause, P. and Clark, D. (1993). *Representing Uncertain Knowledge: An Artificial Intelligence Approach*. Oxford: Intellect.

Kuhn, K.M. (1997) Communicating Uncertainty: Framing Effects on Responses to Vague Probabilities. *Organizational Behavior and Human Decision Processes*, 71, 55-83.

Lichtenstein, S. and Newman, J.R. (1967). Empirical scaling of common verbal phrases associated with numerical probabilities. *Psychonomic Sciences*, 9, 563-564.

Lichtenstein, S. and Slovic, P. (1971). "Reversal of preference between bids and choices in gambling decisions." *Journal of Experimental Psychology*, 89, 46-55.

Lipshitz, R. and Strauss, O. (1997). Coping with Uncertainty: A Naturalistic Decision-Making Analysis. *Organizational Behavior and Human Decision Processes*, 69, 149-163.

Loomes, G. and Sugden, R. (1982). Regret theory: An alternative theory of rational choice under uncertainty. *Economic Journal*. 92, 805-824.

Molenaar, N.J. (1982). Response effects of 'formal' characteristics of questions. In W. Dijkstra and J. van der Zouwen (eds.), *Response Behavior and the Survey Interview*. N.Y.: Academic Press.

Newstead, S.E. (1988). Quantifiers as fuzzy concepts. In T. Zetenyi (ed.) *Fuzzy Sets in Psychology*. Amsterdam: North-Holland, 51-72.

Payne, S.L. (1951). *The Art of Asking Questions*. Princeton: Princeton University Press.

Pepper, S. (1981). Problems in the quantification of frequency expressions. In D. Fiske (ed.) *New Directions for Methodology of Social and Behavioral Sciences: Problems with Language Imprecision*. San Francisco: Jossey-Bass.

Pepper, S. and Prytulak, L.S. (1974). Sometimes frequently means seldom: Context effects in the interpretations of quantitative expressions. *Journal of Research in Personality*, 8, 95-101.

Quiggin, J. (1982). A theory of anticipated utility. *Journal of Economic Behavior and Organization*. 3, 323-343.

Rachlin, H. (1989). *Judgment, Decision, and Choice*. N.Y.: Freeman.

Regan, R.T., Mosteller, F. and Youtz, C. (1990). Quantitative meanings of verbal probability expressions. *Journal of Applied Psychology*. 74, 433-442.

Rottenstreich, Y. and Tversky, A. (1997). Unpacking, repacking, and anchoring: Advances in support theory. *Psychological Review*. 104, 406-415.

Russo, J.E. and Kozlow, K. (1994). Where is the fault in fault trees? *Journal of Experimental Psychology: Human Perception and Performance*. 20, 17-32.

Simpson, R.H. (1944). The specific meanings of certain terms indicating differing degrees of frequency. *Quarterly Journal of Speech*, 30, 328-330.

Simpson, R.H. (1963). Stability in meanings for quantitative terms: A comparison over 20 years. *Quarterly Journal of Speech*, 49, 146-151.

Smithson, M. (1987). Fuzzy Set Analysis for Behavioral and Social Sciences. New York: Springer Verlag.

Smithson, M. (1989). *Ignorance and Uncertainty: Emerging Paradigms*. New York: Springer-Verlag.

Smithson, M. (1997). *Conflict Aversion*. Working paper, Division of Psychology, The Australian National University.

Smithson, M. and Bartos, T. (1997). *Judgment under Outcome Ignorance*. Working paper, Division of Psychology, The Australian National University.

Stone, D.R. and Johnson, R.J. (1959). A study of words indicating frequency. *Journal of Educational Psychology*, 50, 224-227.

Teigen, K.H. (1988). When are low-probability events judged to be 'probable'? Effects of outcome-set characteristics on verbal probability judgments. *Acta Psychologica*. 67, 157-174.

Teigen, K.H. (1994). Variants of subjective probabilities: Concepts, norms, and biases. In G. Wright and P. Ayton (eds.) *Subjective Probability*. Chichester: Wiley, 211-238.

Teigen, K.H. and Brun, W. (1995). Yes, but it is uncertain: Direction and communicative intention of verbal probabalistic terms. *Acta-Psychologica*. 88, 233-258.

Tversky, A. and Kahneman, D. (1981). The framing of decisions and the rationality of choice. *Science*, 221, 453-458.

Tversky, A. and Koehler, D. J. (1994). Support theory: a nonextensional representation of subjective probability. *Psychological Review*. 101, 547-567.

Tversky, A., Slovic, P. and Kahneman, D. (1990). The causes of preference reversal. *The American Economic Review*. 80, 204-217.

Walley, P. (1991). *Statistical Reasoning with Imprecise Probabilities*. London: Chapman and Hall.

Walley, P. (1996). Inferences from multinomial data: Learning about a bag of marbles. (with discussion) *Journal of the Royal Statistical Society, Series B*. 58, 3-57.

Wallsten, T.S., Budescu, D.V. and Erev, I. (1988). Understanding and using linguistic uncertainties. *Acta Psychologica*. 68, 39-52.

Wallsten, T.S., Fillenbaum, S. and Cox, J.A. (1986). Base-rate effects on the interpretation of probability and frequency expressions. *Journal of Memory and Language*, 25, 571-581.

Wallsten, T.S., Budescu, D.V., Zwick, R. and Kemp, S.M. (1993). Preferences and reasons for communicating probabilistic information in verbal or numerical terms. *Bulletin of the Psychonomic Society*. 31, 135-138.

Wallsten, T.S., Budescu, D., Rappoport, A., Zwick, R., and Forsyth, B. (1986). Measuring the vague meanings of probability terms. *Journal of Experimental Psychology: General*, 115, 348-365.

Zimmer, A.C. (1983). Verbal vs. numerical processing of subjective probabilities. In R.W. Scholz (ed.) *Decision Making Under Uncertainty*. Amsterdam: North-Holland.

Zimmer, A.C. (1984). A model for the interpretation of verbal predictions. *International Journal of Man-Machine Studies*, 20, 121-134.

Virtual Meaning: Problems of Interpretation in the Social Sciences

Vladimir Dimitrov and Bob Hodge

University of Western Sydney - Hawkesbury
Richmond, NSW2753
Australia
Email: {V.Dimitrov, B.Hodge}@uws.edu.au

Abstract

An original *fuzzy* approach to meaning and interpretation in the social sciences is developed. It leads to the concept of virtual meaning emerging at the overlap of fuzzy set theory and semiotics. Its relations both to classic and postmodern social theories are discussed. A case study is described to illustrate how the theory of virtual meaning helps to explore 'real' dynamics of social complexity. Practical examples of dealing and 'computing' with virtual meanings are considered in such fields of social activity as management, consensus seeking and politics.

1 Introduction

Our starting point is Zadeh's proposition that for computing, a 'paradigm shift' is needed in approaches to data from a traditional valuation of numbers over words, to one in which words are recognised as important tools for thinking, able to solve problems which are 'intractable when merely numerical solutions are sought' (Zadeh 1996).

In the social sciences, this shift has taken place in two phases. One is the 'qualitative' (or 'linguistic') turn, which corresponds to Zadeh's proposed paradigm shift, from the previously dominant 'positivist' empiricist tradition to a form of social analysis that draws on qualitative data, meanings, discourse, text, words and other signs. The second is the 'postmodern turn', which recognises indeterminacy, instability, approximation as endemic in contemporary social life and intrinsic to systems of meaning and interpretation. 'Qualitative' approaches have been decentred, and qualities that correspond to 'fuzzy' are part of the basis for these new approaches to the social sciences which can be grouped together under the label of Postmodern Social Theory.

The result of these parallel developments, in social theory and in theories of information and intelligence systems, is that there are exciting new possibilities for fruitful collaboration that can integrate these two areas of knowledge. Where classical ('modernist') sociology rested on assumptions about society and meanings that severely limited the scope of possible strategies of analysis and uses of computers, the newer ('postmodern') forms of social theory are highly compatible with the principles of fuzzy logic, and with ideas from chaos theory and complexity science.

In this chapter we will outline a fuzzy approach to meaning and interpretation in the social sciences, and explore how such an approach could hope to find compatible possibilities for computing with words.

2 Observations on Social Process and the Theory of Virtual Meaning

2.1 Social Analysis and its Objects

Social processes and actions (development and deployment of concepts, opinions, judgements and expectations, the unfolding of events) change and evolve in the dynamics of real-life complexity, with outcomes that can be paradoxical and chaotic, because its dynamics are unpredictable and sensitive to changes in the magnitude and location of the relevant forces.

Many social situations and processes typically pass into a situation of criticality, an out-of-equilibrium condition where the phenomena of bifurcation, phase transition and rapid system change or system collapse occur.

The relationship between higher levels of phenomena ('macro-social') and lower levels ('micro-social', 'individual/personal') is fractal and not 'part-whole', so that 'micro-social' lower level phenomena are as complex and socially significant as 'macro-social' phenomena.

Social forces act through processes of meaning, (discourse, language, significant contexts and behaviours) and social processes can only take place through the medium of semiotic activity.

Social action always involves in some way the management of emerging complexity through ongoing systems of interpretation and intermittent systems of control. These systems of control and the systems of interpretation on which they rest normally follow one of two broad strategies:

(i) *Containment strategies*, where complexity is reduced by identifying linear processes, eliminating fuzziness, contradiction, ambiguity, and targeting individual elements in simple causal chains, and

(ii) *Fuzzy strategies*, where contradiction, indeterminacy and ambiguity is tolerated and managed.

2.2 Virtual Meaning

The Theory of Virtual Meaning can be built on the overlap of Fuzzy Set Theory and Semiotics (or the Theory of Semiosphere).

Fuzzy set theory, as introduced by Zadeh (1965), has its roots in the social nature of human understanding. Our abilities to understand (up to a degree) have been developed through our 'being-in-common', that is, through an inevitable process of fuzzification of meaning, so that to make it understandable, acceptable and operational for a multitude of people with different mental, emotional or spiritul worldviews.

According to fuzzy set theory, meanings of words can never be precisely defined - each linguistic construct in use can be described by a set of 'degrees of freedom', i.e. ways to be understood (interpreted or transformed into action) by individuals or groups. The larger the power of this set, the richer in meaning the linguistic construct related to it.

The semiosphere penetrates all dimensions of life and consists in complexity of communication: sounds, odour, movements, colours, electro-magnetic fields, waves of any kind, chemical signals, touch, speech, etc. The semiosphere poses both constraints to the *umwelt* of populations (since these are forced to occupy specific semiotic niches, i.e. they will have to master a set of signs of visual, acoustic, olfactory, tactile, bio-chemical and social origin in order to survive in the semiosphere) and opportunities for their further evolution (growth, adaptation and transformation).

Main Postulates of the Theory of Virtual Meaning:

(1) *The character of life is fundamentally semiotic*: since living systems are mortal their survival has to be secured through semiotic rather than physical means (genetic communication through generations, communication throughout all ecological and social space).
(2) *Meaning cannot be precisely defined*: it is always fuzzy - it leads to more than one way of understanding.
(3) *Meaning in the social sciences* (meaning in action as the primary object of the social sciences) *is open:* it always includes virtual meaning as a potential open set of meanings arising from the different relations it may form, in different contexts, through different transformations or metaphors, at different levels and in different semiotic media.

Main Propositions in the Theory of Virtual Meaning:

(1) *Virtual Meanings exert a force on a core meanings* as well as being the sites where core meanings are extended, elaborated, and negotiated.
(2) *Virtual Meanings act as catalysts of human creativity* by activating, propelling and helping 'materialize' people's search for understanding their world.
(3) Due to the fractal structure of the semiosphere, *Virtual Meanings are both 'microcosmic' expressions of larger semiotic systems and 'macrocosmic' expressions of smaller semiotic systems.*

3 Vortices of Communication as Generators of Virtual Meanings

Communication is a complex dynamic process, in which physical, emotional and mental characteristics of communicators are inseparably tangled together.

The notion of the ***vortex of communication*** is introduced (Dimitrov 1997) in order to emphasize both this unique inseparability and the emergence of new meanings in communication process.

The study of fluid dynamics shows that the sucking 'self-organizing' force at the centre of a vortex cannot appear, unless the participating streams (e.g., masses of running water, turbulent airs, etc.) are: (1) permanently in motion, that is, in an *out-of-equilibrium* state, and (2) intensively interacting with each other through various *feedback loops*.

The streams of thoughts and feelings, expectation and hope, intentions and aspirations, expressed in verbal or non-verbal ways, are involved in the dynamics of human communication. In analogy with the sucking force of a maelstrom or tornado, the *self-organising force of meaning-creation* arises from the vortex of communication.

The meanings emerging from the vortex of communication are virtual - they are unknown before the act of emergence and once emerged, they open a new space for interpretation and understanding by communicators. They are meanings in dynamics - not settled beforehand, not imposed from outside the vortex, but born from within the vortex and impregnated by its whirling 'energies'.

One can find examples of so called 'trivial communication', deprived of virtual meanings. In those examples, the thoughts and feelings, expressed in communication process, seem to be in a kind of 'standstill' - without intellectual or emotional drive or zeal. As usual, any once-for-ever adopted conceptual stanza, habit and stereotype, as well as any 'borrowed' from outside the communication vortex viewpoints and arguments, intent to impose frozen patterns in the space of mutual exchange of thoughts and feelings. Examples of such frozen patterns are the 'groupthink' (strongly manifested in former East-European communist societies) and the exhaustive competition (manifested in the present Western democracies).

The unknown, felt and experienced in different ways by different individuals, serves as an activator of communication vortices and as a catalyst for emergence of virtual meanings.

It is the unknown, reflected in existential uncertainty of human life, that

- pulls people towards creative discussions, debates, negotiation
- makes people's thoughts and feelings to flow and move out of the frozen zones of equilibrium (no matter how desirable, suitable and comfortable these zones might appear at first sight), and not to be trapped into the standstill of any pre-selected, 'scientifically' proved or simply taken for granted mental or emotional patterns
- interconnects different and even entirely opposite opinions and beliefs - either through various feedback interactions or through complementarity

In this way the unknown exerts a force for transforming communication from a mere information exchange into a creative search for virtual meanings.

4 The Reality of Social Complexity: A Case Study

We will begin to illustrate these concepts by reference first of all to a particular case, one which is 'unimportant' in the sense that it is not out of the ordinary and has no obvious wider consequences or effects on larger social structures. Our aim in doing this is to show how the concept of virtual meaning allows us to examine complex and representative instances of social action under a powerful microscope that throws light on the constitutive elements of society itself, in the sociological equivalent of the close analysis of processes at the level of cells or chemical reactions.

4.1 Phases

Phase 1 was largely a private matter. It involved a male academic in his mid fifties who had migrated to Australia, where he lived in a small provincial town which hosts a university. The man had developed a habit of walking in the evenings, along some of the streets in this semi-rural town, and along pathways designed by the town council for precisely this purpose. One of his preferred routes took him along a road which was a cul-de-sac for cars but had a pathway for walkers opening out into a larger green area. One of the houses in this cul-de-sac was occupied by a young woman, an unemployed single parent with two children.

Over a period of six months, this woman became very agitated about the activity of this man. On a number of occasions at night she heard noises which she attributed to an intruder, and summoned the police. She became convinced that the man whose habit of walking disturbed her was also responsible for the noises at night.

Phase 2 moved into the public sphere, when this woman made accusations to the police. The man was duly charged with the offences of 'stalking' and 'trespass', and the matter was heard by a magistrate. Some features of the case caught the attention of a court reporter from a national newspaper, so it entered into the next phase.

In Phase 3, details of the first day of the hearing appeared in a prominent place in the next day's issue of a paper with millions readers in Australia ("Daily Telegraph", Sydney).

In this case there is sufficient data even regarding phase 1, which often occurs outside the gaze of social theorists and public administrators. From this data it is possible to recreate the main stages and processes in phase 1. The young woman's anxieties about noises she heard at night connected with her sense of unease at the behaviour of the walker, which did not fit in with the cultural expectations of her group, who did not have the custom of walking in this way. These anxieties fed into a system of positive feedback in the small cul-de-sac community and exploded into paranoia and hysteria, creating the conviction in the woman that the walker was a threat to her safety. The anxieties of this woman as potential victim were taken up and acted on by a number of legitimate or self-appointed protectors - her mother and brother, her 'boarder' or lover and four other people. The actions they took on her behalf contributed to the sense of solidarity and community in the cul-de-sac, and gave everyone, including the young woman, a role and status.

The process from the point of view of the walker would have been an extraordinary example of dangerous paranoia if he had known about it, which for a long while he did not. But from the point of view of the cul-de-sac community it was very productive and socially bonding.

4.2 Key-features

(1) *Criticality* - the situation reaches a situation where meaning follows non-rational trajectories in an increasingly turbulent space.

(2) *Butterfly effect* - within this kind of situation very small changes in the initial conditions produce dramatic effects of meaning, interpretation and action. So the walker, for reasons that seem unimportant at the time, follows one route rather than another. As a person from a different cultural background, there are some minor differences in his habits, perhaps his way of walking, that initially seem 'odd' but as they are inspected again and again come to seem dangerously perverse.

(3) *Bifurcation* - at a certain point, two separate anxieties in the mind of the woman converge, and she has a sudden certainty that the walker is a stalker, the cause of all her night-time fears. For eight other persons there is a transition point, when they too are co-opted into an experience that is not theirs (or anyone else's) but which they act on as though it were.

(4) *System Collapse* and the loss of reality. The cul-de-sac community closed around an agreed interpretation of reality in which there is no distinction made between what is said (by members of the community) and what anyone has seen or experienced. This dominant reality, which determines as well as arising out of their ongoing roles and relationships, is a pure discursive construct.

4.3 Generation of Virtual Meanings

The above features are of fundamental social importance, because they occur at all levels of social life. This single situation is a microcosm of processes which on a larger scale produce social prejudice and discrimination in pathologically bonded communities, where paranoia overdetermines the processes of social judgement and action, and where 'truth' ceases to be available in the constitutive public discourse.

In the second phase, this private process intersected with the legal and policing process which has the typical qualities of a normal system of control over social actions, such as this one, where 'things have got out of hand' - where either the actions of one party are declared to be intolerable and prevented, or the complaints of the other are declared to be without substance.

Police and legal action that occurred in this case contained a number of devices deliberately designed to act as negative feedback to contain the processes of discursive explosions that are well-known to activate sets of virtual meaning, which in this system are always seen as negative and undesirable.

The police used their 'professional judgement' not to respond to every complaint made by the woman. They collected statements by the various witnesses from which hearsay evidence was carefully removed by the rules of evidence, and they cleaned up the fuzzy everyday language of the complainants and replaced it with the seemingly more neutral and precise language of the police statement. In the court room, further checks continued to operate, all designed to replace the disorderly and fuzzy discursive processes of phase 1 with an idealised non-fuzzy form of discourse, in which rational (linear, objective, non-emotive) 'truth' would prevail.

However, as meanings pass from phase 1 to phase 2 they enter a situation where the discursive stakes are raised, producing its own kind of effects on virtual meanings. For instance, the terms 'stalking' and 'entering a property without lawful excuse' are not used in everyday language, and they are supposedly carefully defined in their legal sense. However, they are also situated in a conflictual context in which innumerable disputes have once again activated a whole set of virtual meanings. To 'stalk' in this context no longer means simply to follow a person. It now signifies a serious but vaguely defined criminal offence, with significant penalties. In the situation of phase 2, then, the energy contained in the virtual meanings of phase 1 is damped down and neutralised, but such elements that survive the process acquire an expanded scope in the force of their virtual meaning.

This is the sequence that precedes the third stage, the entry into media discourse. The third stage shows a similar pattern: the entry of meanings from one phase to another is carefully controlled by specific rules that aim to prevent a paper publishing anything that might prejudice a fair trial. So the newspaper account gives evidence on both sides, implying both innocence and guilt. In contrast to the requirements of legal discourse, media discourse is 'fuzzy' - it allows contradictory meanings to co-exist and its descriptions are loose and often inaccurate summaries of what was said in the court. Yet this is also a condition where virtual meaning grows and flourishes, with significant effects on all parties.

The evidence of both the man and the woman is severely reduced, but this version now reaches a million readers. Photographs of the man and the woman are included, able to be inserted into a highly active set of virtual meanings (is he really a weirdo or a decent man?, is she hysterical or an unfortunate victim?) which are expanded, by the normal creative processes of interpretation of countless readers, into a set of narratives in which the truth of the matter is decided in summary ways that will often be deeply prejudicial to the reputations of one or both the key participants. Whatever the outcome of the trial, both are certain losers.

4.4 Virtual 'Resolution' of the Conflict

A genuinely 'fuzzy' alternative to this linear process would seek reconciliation and consensus, instead of pursuing the aim of legalism, to end the matter by determining who was right and therefore who was wrong, and distributing rewards and punishments accordingly. The legal method achieves an enforceable outcome, but the two sets of meanings of the two sets of participants are equally negated - the pleasure of the walker in his walking, and the anxiety and fear of the woman, leading her to an excessive dependence on a range of authority figures. In a fuzzy solution in this instance, as in the use of fuzzy logic in any turbulent social or socio-ecological situation, it is essential to introduce the two principles of non-exclusion (of options, interpretations, values) and non-isolation (of a supposed reconciled outcome).

Virtual meanings and their networks inevitably proliferate through the semiotic space of all participants. They can be controlled in some contexts but they can never be eliminated or contained. The only reliable way of managing social conflict is to work at the level of seeking integration of the virtual.

5 Classic Sociology: The Case of Durkheim

For most of this century the dominant approach in sociology has been 'classic' ('positivist', 'modernist') sociology as represented by the work of the French sociologist Emile Durkheim, its methodological assumptions developed in Rules of Sociological Method (1964) and exemplified in his major study: Suicide (1951). This approach aspired to the status of a science of society, drawing on modernist (linear, non-fuzzy) concepts of science as the articulation of causal laws, based on inductive generalisations drawn from a large set of carefully collected empirical facts.

There are three aspects of this tradition that we need to address, in order to explore how it relates to a postmodern fuzzy set of approaches. First is its analytic method, which prioritises macro over micro levels and attempts to establish correlations among social variables. Second is its attitude to language and meaning, which is modernist and non-fuzzy. Third is its attitude to crisis and order, where disorder is seen as the greatest enemy of any social form.

5.1 Method

For Durkheim, in this tradition the primary object of sociology was the 'social fact', a pattern in social life that was above the level of the individual, a set of forces and factors conditioning behaviour, often in ways the individual was unaware of. The case of suicide was an exemplary instance. His study took what appears the most individual and asocial of acts and demonstrated regularities which connect with and express basic features of the overall social order. The theory established links between macro and micro, but it was the state of society as a whole which conditioned the individual instance.

Social analysis in the classic tradition following Durkheim sought clues about these underlying and invisible 'social facts' through correlations between observable factors. Some of these factors might be items of meaning, particular words or sentiments that could be reliably encoded and correlated with other variables, but in order to treat them in this way all fuzziness had to be removed, so that they could be treated by a standard set of statistical procedures, which can now be powerfully assisted by computers. That is, non-fuzziness in the elements of meaning under analysis was essential to the operation of this paradigm.

There is a scope here within the modernist paradigm for introducing some elements of fuzzy logic. For instance, Smithson has developed a computer program called FUZZYSTAT[1] which extends the use of statistical techniques

[1] * FUZZYSTAT is available through its author: Michael Smithson, Faculty of Science, Australian National University, Canbera 0200, E-mail: Michael.Smithson@anu.edu.au

when dealing with linguistic variables, i.e. variables which instead of numbers are characterised by words, such as 'large', 'medium', 'small', etc. described as fuzzy sets (Zadeh 1975).

Anderson's computer program FUZZYGRID (Anderson 1998) uses fuzzy sets to incorporate the 'natural' fuzziness of human ability to discriminate between observed items into Kelly's Repertory Grid technique based on his Personal Construct Psychology (Kelly, 1955).

5.2 Meaning

The meaning in its fullest most fuzzy form as virtual meaning has a paradoxical status in Durkheim's sociology. While his rules of method attempted to control fuzziness, its goal was precisely to understand the fuzzy meanings that for him were at the heart of social life. For instance his study of suicide enabled him to identify a crisis in the condition of meaning in contemporary capitalism which he labelled 'anomie', a condition of loss of order, lack of rules, a social pathology expressed through particular types of suicide. In this process, the term 'suicide' is treated as an important index, dealt with in a way that eliminates fuzziness as far as possible, avoiding the differences introduced by fuzziness in methods of reporting (since different people might classify the particular event, the death of someone, in different ways that significantly affected the objective picture that resulted). But in contrast, the key term 'anomie' itself is a fuzzy term, bringing together a whole set of factors and meanings into a complex and undecidable whole. In this sense, we can say that 'anomie' has operated in sociology for a hundred years as a term with a powerful and extensive virtual meaning.

This is equally true of most of the important concepts in sociology, such as 'alienation', 'ideology', 'legitimacy', 'class', and of course 'society' itself, all of which are continually and extensively debated in the literature, never with any stable outcome. In a framework based on fuzzy sets, then, it would be possible to investigate these primary fuzzy categories directly, instead of leaving them to be inferred from a set of individual linear empirical studies of their supposed component variables. The goal would be to set up search techniques for the core fuzzy word, in which the scope and dynamism of its field virtual meanings would be central to the study.

5.3 Criticality

For classic sociology in the Durkheimian mould 'crisis' is typically given a negative value, opposed to order which is seen as typically good. So 'anomie' is seen as a social pathology in Durkheim's work. But in terms of chaos theory, a state of criticality will always be characterised by turbulence, through which there are many different critical paths, with possible bifurcations that in some cases may lead to the transition to a different and perhaps more comprehensive state. Criticality is the precondition for creativity as well as the system-death that a sociologist like Durkheim so feared.

Criticality is also the condition under which the scope of virtual meanings is massively extended. Paradoxically, Durkheim's own work illustrates this, since the unlimited plenitude of meaning of his famous and durable term anomie owes much to the double point of transition in which he worked, at the boundary of modern capitalism, and at the founding moment of the discipline of sociology.

6 Discourse Analysis and the New Social Theory

As we have said, classic sociology in the Durkheimian tradition has insuperable problems in using empirical methods to account systematically for the role of meaning in social processes, which are however indispensable in their account of society. Meaning has a more central role in the various forms of the 'verstehen' tradition in sociology, stemming from the work of Max Weber, represented by the 'Symbolic Interactionist' tradition influenced by Mead (1964), and the 'ethnomethodology' of Schutz (1972). From this view point, social reality is ongoingly constructed by the social processes of the construction of meaning. A social act is only social insofar as all of its elements are understood in particular ways by social actors.

This emphasis on meaning in the 'new' social science approach has been developed in influential ways by Foucault, whose core concept is the notion of 'discourse' as the primary site through which social relations, processes and identities are activated. Foucault understands discourse not simply as a form of communication but as a force whose chaotic potential (in our terms, its power of virtual meaning) is in constant need of control: „I am supposing that in every society the production of discourse is at once controlled, selected, organised and redistributed according to a certain number of procedures, whose role is to avert its powers and its dangers, to cope with chance events, to evade its ponderous, awesome materiality." (Foucault 1976:216)

Foucault has a conception of power that has proved influential and productive for the new (postmodern) social sciences. Foucault emphasises the study of the micro-politics of power in a set of relationships mediated through discourse and operating like a diffuse network. In this vein he writes (1978:92-3): „Power must be understood in the first instance as the multiplicity of force relations immanent in the sphere in which they operate and which constitute their own organisation; as the process which, through ceaseless struggles and confrontations, transforms, strengthens, or reverses them; as the support which these force relations find in one another, thus forming a chain or system or on the contrary, the disjunctions and contradictions which isolate them from one another; and lastly, as a strategies in which they take effect, whose general design or institutional crystallization is embodied in the state apparatus, in the formulation of the law, in the various social hegemonies."

In this conception society and the operations of power which constitute it are a complex and diffuse set of relationships at many levels, not simply a force from above which determines everything beneath it. We believe that it will prove fruitful to see this set of relationships in terms of fractals (Mandelbrot 1982) in which self-similar structures at different levels are linked by a vortex trajectory.

7 Postmodernism and the Crisis of Meaning

Foucault's concept of 'discourse' is a generic one which applies to all forms of communication and the production of meaning in all forms of society. But in postmodern social science there has recently been a productive concern with new technologies and forms of communication and with the new social relationships and forms of meaning and consciousness that these forms have allowed or produced. Influential here has been the provocative work of Baudrillard on the implications of the new rules of 'virtual reality' and the conditions of a society which produces and is affected by the vertiginous possibilities of cyberspace. Baudrillard is as negative about these possibilities as Durkheim was about anomie. He projects a cataclysmic collapse of the possibility of meaning itself, moving from the 'soft inferno of simulation' of 1980s communication technologies to a cancerous invasion of every part of the socio-semiotic fabric of contemporary life, which he sees organised in terms of fractals, all characterised by a self-similar vacuity in which „there is no point of reference at all, and value radiates in all directions, occupying all interstices, without reference to anything whatever, by virtue of pure contiguity" (Baudrillard 1993: 5).

With Baudrillard's apocalyptic prediction as with Durkheim's it is not essential for him to be right for his work to still be important. In his picture of the exponential expansion of 'virtual space' and its dangers his greatest value for postmodern social theory is that he is identifying a rapidly emerging and important condition of criticality of the kind that can be and has been achieved by many other technologies of communication, including verbal language and the print media. In this space of criticality, divergences and convergences, collapses and system deaths and explosions of creativity and phase transitions are equally possible paths and trajectories. It is precisely this far greater set of possibilities that needs analysis in terms of the kind of theory of virtual meaning that we propose.

For Baudrillard this point is reached only in the semiotic end-game of postmodern communications technologies, when meaning passes through a cascading set of fractal levels like a virus or cancer causing everything to implode and become indistinguishable from everything else. But in the particular case study we looked at there is a similar outcome, even though only the simplest communication technology is involved - the human voice. So it is important to note that in both instances, at the two extremes in level (a new global condition versus an everyday incident in a small community) and in technologies (latest and future technologies versus the timeless language resources of everyday life) there is an important outcome in common: total fusion of what is said and what is seen and what happened. Mediated reality constructed in language under conditions in which the processes of virtual meaning have ample scope is not only indistinguishable from 'reality', it actually takes its place. Baudrillard's 'virtual space' meets the virtual meanings of everyday discourse, and they turn out to be the same.

8 Virtual Meaning: Applied Aspects

8.1 Fuzzy Management

In the theory of Fuzzy Management (Dimitrov 1975, 1976), the process of understanding a fuzzy instruction by an individual is described as a generation of a fuzzy set by this individual - the support of the fuzzy set (i.e. its non-zero elements) includes a number of alternative ways of interpretation of the instruction. Each alternative way is presented by a weight (rank, priority) assigned by the individual to express up to what degree this alternative way relates to the meaning of the instruction as understood by him/her. In the case when the fuzzy instruction is presented to a group of individuals, a group choice rule can be applied to map the individual meanings of the instruction (i.e. the individual ways of understanding it) into a virtual (or fuzzy) meaning that is satisfactory for the group as a whole.

According to the Incoherence Principle (Dimitrov 1983), the more certain (non-fuzzy, determine) individuals, the more uncertain (fuzzy, indeterminate) the group, and on the contrary: the more fuzzy are individuals in their ways of interpreting (understanding, executing) the meaning of an instruction, the greater is the chance for the group to negotiate a concrete (categorical, non-fuzzy) way(s) for practical execution of this instruction. Thus, the Incoherence Principle helps overcome the Arrow Impossibility Theorem establishing the impossibility of generating a 'socially satisfactory' choice function from the choice functions of individuals making up a group (society). Under fuzzy management, i.e. in the context of the virtual meanings, there is a socially satisfactory choice function mapping fuzzy individual choices into a non-fuzzy choice of the group (Dimitrov 1976).

The above result provides a sound theoretical basis for the use of innovative participatory approaches in the contemporary management practice. It serves also as a theoretical basis for seeking consensus between stakeholders with different positions (this is discussed in the next section).

Unfortunately, in Western democracies, the Incoherence Principle is often misused by the politicians: the fuzzy charisma in their speeches serves as a tool for deceptive 'selling' of policies and decisions based on hidden agenda of ideology and power. By keeping majority of people ignorant (uncertain, fuzzy) about these agenda, they try to impose (with the help of their most influential supporters) non-fuzzy 'group' decisions which work only for a privileged part of the society.

8.2 Virtual Consensus

In the turbidity of human interactions, consensus ceases to be a peaceful long-term commonality of stakeholders' interests. Such commonality grows on 'determinacy' and stability. Unfortunately, neither determinacy nor stability are features of social complexity. The more we reach for commonality in human interactions, the farther away it seems to be. „Consensus is a horizon that is never reached" (Lyotard 1984).

An irreducible indeterminacy constantly emerges when we explore more deeply both variety and uncertainty of group decision-making. Paradoxically, instead of consensus being the power house of common social action, it is 'dissensus' which operates in consensus seeking enterprise, permanently implanting chaotic vibrations in the process of communication. However, in this case chaos does not cause the communication network to dissipate. Rather, it eventually gives birth to an emerging order in the form of a new type of dynamic consensus between stakeholders: consensus for seeking a consensus.

This can be defined as a 'second order consensus' or *virtual consensus* - people try to seek consensus by exploring different virtual meanings of the issues of common concern that might lead to mutual understanding and preparedness to move together - to make the next step into the fuzziness of common expectations.

It does not matter that actually achieved consensus in to-day's dynamics is 'condemned' to be momentary and transient - what can endure in time is human anticipation and aspiration, the impulse to act together, the natural desire to interact and communicate, to share with and care for others. These are factors that bring forth virtual consensus.

Virtual consensus is a search process entirely open for emergence of new features and unpredictable situations - spontaneity is an important characteristic of this process. Any pre-imposed goals, constraints or requirements inevitably narrow the scope of the stakeholders' search.

The search for consensus by itself is a powerful generator for virtual meaning - the propelling force of this generator is stakeholders' drive to be mutually complementary in their efforts to more fully understand complexity of the issues of their concern and to find out how to act together in order to benefit from the differences in their knowledge. While conducting their inquiry, the stakeholders are aware of the irreducible fuzziness and uncertainty of this knowledge, yet they agree to explore it together and construct it anew.

Virtual consensus is inherently dynamical - not a static overlap of stakeholders' views, but interplay between their interests, motives, values, goals, positions. Virtual consensus assumes a shared acknowledgement that stakeholders' knowledge abounds in zones of ignorance in which neither the causes nor the effects of what occurs is clear or even can be known. Also, there must be a kind of tacit agreement between the stakeholders to explore social complexity together in order to arrive at a better understanding of it, by using not only your own but each other's experience, expertise and ideas. Virtual consensus assumes an improved *preparedness to act together*; that is, to engage in a joint, collaborative action to work with complexity.

Dimitrov and Kopra (1998) express group preparedness to act together (PAT) as a fuzzy composition of the following three fuzzy characteristics of the stakeholders: willingness to engage in dialogue (W), trustworthiness (T) and creativity (C).

Fuzzy Logic based rules of the form "if W and T and C then PAT" have been generated and used to map the fuzzy characteristics (W, T and C) of the stakeholders into the fuzzy class of their preparedness to take actions together (PAT).

All fuzzy classes have been described using three linguistic variables: 'low', 'moderate' and 'high'. An assumption has been made that in the consensus-seeking practice, the values of the membership function to the above fuzzy classes could be assigned by a facilitator who participates (observes, facilitates, helps) in the process of search for virtual meanings as realised by participating stakeholders. A software prototype called FLOCK (Fuzzy Logic-based Consensus Knowledge)[2] has been specially designed to help facilitators in practical realisation of this search. The program computes the degrees of (virtual) consensus between the stakeholders in any stage of negotiation and maps them into a comprehensive picture of the overall dynamics of the facilitation process.

8.3 Political Discourse

Virtual meanings are at the very basis of politics. The fuzziness of political statements and narratives is constructed to be endlessly reproduced. The expressions politicians use are chosen with a view to persuasion and pleasing.

---

[2] FLOCK is available through the Cooperative Research Centre for Waste Management and Pollution Control Ltd (High Street, POBox 1, Kensington 2033, Australia; fax: +61(2)96621971)

They project an image of the politician as someone 'good' - likeable and close to the people, dedicated to the great principles of democracy. The fuzzy umbrella of words is used to generate virtual meanings which cover the inevitable struggle for power and compulsory deceptions inherent in it. A deliberate linguistic fuzzification is used as a tool for deceptive 'selling' of policies and decisions based on hidden agendas of ideology and power.

The treatment of this false face of representative politics requires a continued *public disclosure* of the ambiguity and deception in policy narratives and decisions as well as in the charisma and behaviour of politicians and political parties; it requires a permanent exposure and denouncement of political actions in conflict with the public interest (Dimitrov and Kopra 1998).

The butterfly effect (or sensitive dependence on initial conditions), characteristic for chaotic dynamics, clearly manifests itself in the socio-political contexts of virtual meaning and can serve as a signal for organised community actions aimed at urgent socio-political changes.

People living in Western democracies know well that slight changes in the ideological platform of a political party or a politician, expressed by means of seemingly insignificant fuzzy hedges (that is, words used in the statements to intensify or dilute their degree of fuzziness, such as: 'more or less', 'very', 'quite', 'somewhat', 'slightly', 'extremely', 'positively', 'generally', 'around', 'about', 'near', etc.) can bring forth enormous changes in the way these statements are interpreted as a basis for action.

For example, during an election campaign, politicians can promise 'to pay an increased attention to the defence potential of the state', but once in power, they can use the virtual meaning imbedded in this statement as justification of quite a large program for testing new nuclear weapons with enormous negative consequences for the life on the planet. This was the case with the French nuclear experiments in 1996. People in France and in the rest of the world energetically protested against the experiments.

There are situations where the butterfly effect manifested in the virtual meanings of the political discourse can bring forth gigantic social transformations. The world still remember the initial 'tiny little' changes in the virtual meanings of the political statements used by the ruling politburo of the former Soviet Union in the mid-eighties (after the appointment of M. Gorbachev as a secretary-general of the Soviet communist part). The effects of those initial changes were shocking.

Both Fuzzy Logic, with its tools for computing with fuzzy hedges (Zadeh 1975, 1991), and Chaos Theory, with its analysis of sensitivity of social dynamics (Dimitrov *et al* 1996), provide opportunity to grasp the virtual meanings imbedded in the political discourse and withstand its antisocial connotations.

9 Conclusion

Social systems function in a virtual reality of meanings constantly emerging from the vortices of human communication. The dynamics of this reality is chaotic and yet subject to human action. Virtual meanings are of crucial significance in such 'real' and complex fields of social activity as management, consensus seeking and politics. By providing unique tools for computing with words as well as describing and analysing their virtual meanings, fuzzy logic expands human understanding of social complexity and thus helps humanity deal with it in a better way.

References

Anderson, A 1998 A model for fuzzy personal construct psychology In *Fuzzy System Design: Social and Engineering Applications* Eds. L. Reznik, V.Dimitrov and J. Kacprzyk, Heidelberg and New York: Physica-Verlag

Baudrillard, J 1993 *The transparency of evil: essays on extreme phenomena* trans James Benedict, New York: Verso

Dimitrov, V 1975 Optimal fuzzy control of humanistic systems In *Proceedings of the Sixth World Congress of IFAC*, Pittsburgh, PA: Instrument Society of America

Dimitrov, V 1976 Social choice and self-organisation under fuzzy management, *Kybernetes*, 6: 153-156

Dimitrov, V 1983 Group choice under fuzzy information, *Fuzzy Sets and Systems*, 9: 25-39

Dimitrov, V., Woog, R., Kuhn-White, L. 1996 The divergence syndrome in social systems In *Complex Systems 96*, eds R.Stocker, H.Jelinek, B. Durnota and T. Bossomaier, Amsterdam: IOS Press
URL. http://www.csu.edu.au/ci/vol3/dimitro/dimitro.html

Dimitrov, V 1997 Communication as interaction with uncertainty (Personal communication)
URL. http://bart.northnet.com.au/~pfell/vladimir.html

Dimitrov, V 1997 Use of fuzzy logic when dealing with social complexity, *Complexity International*, 4
URL. http://www.csu.edu.au/ci/vol4/dimitrov1/dimitrov.htm

Dimitrov, V., Kopra, K. 1998 Fuzzy logic and the management of social complexity In *Fuzzy System Design: Social and Engineering Applications* Eds. L. Reznik, V.Dimitrov and J. Kacprzyk, Heidelberg and New York: Physica-Verlag

Durkheim, E 1951 *Suicide: a study in sociology* trans J Spaulding and G Simpson, New York: Free Press

Durkheim, E 1964 *Rules of sociological method* trans S A Solovay and J H Mueller New York: Free Press

Foucault, M 1976 The discourse on language. In *The Archaeology of Knowledge* NY: Colophon Books.

Foucault, M 1978 *History of Sexuality* Volume 1 trans Robert Hurley Harmondsworth: Penguin

Kelly, G 1955 The psychology of personal constructs Volumes 1&2, NY: Norton

Lyotard, J. *1984 The postmodern conditions: a report of knowledge* Manchester: Manchester University Press

Mandelbrot, B 1982 *The fractal gemetry of nature* NY: Freeman and Co.

Mead, G.H. 1964 *On social psychology: selected papers.* Ed A. Strauss, Chicago: Chicago University press.

Schutz, A 1972 *The phenomenology of the social world* London: Heinemann.

Zadeh, L 1965 Fuzzy sets, *Information and Control*, 8: 338-359

Zadeh, L. 1975 The concept of a linguistic variable and its application to approximate reasoning, *Information Science*, 8: 199-249

Zadeh, L 1996 Computing with words - a paradigh shift In *Fuzzy Logic and the Management of Complexity: Proceedings of the First Discourse on Fuzzy Logic and the Management of Complexity*, Eds. J. &V.Dimitrov, Richmond: FLAMOC'96

TOWARDS FIXING SOME 'FUZZY' CATCHWORDS: A TERMINOLOGICAL PRIMER

HERBERT TOTH

Riedstraße 17a, A-1140 Wien, Austria

Resorting to some semantical considerations and results from basic philosophy and to some basic mathematical concepts we try to fix suitable explanations for some fundamental notions of and around fuzzy set theory on a semiformal level. For some of them this will – to the author's knowledge for the first time at all – lead us to proposals for definitions of what is to be understood by these terms, simultaneously clarifying their epistemic rôle.

Keywords: Generality, ambiguity, fuzziness, vagueness; imprecision, indeterminism, specificity, uncertainty, possibility.

1. The motivation: a short look at history

The huge wave of both enthusiasm and marketing on fuzzy set theory (FST) beginning in the late eighties has become possible only by the success of fuzzy control in various industrial applications. This success demands for a commonly intelligible explanation and justification in order to increase the understanding of FST and to establish it as a well accepted method and technology on a par with probability theory, thus freeing it from being considered as something mysterious, dubious or ridiculous.

Despite of this success there has always been a considerable amount of criticism. It thus seems that there must still be some lack of intuitively plausible, correct, and well founded information on the concepts of *fuzziness* and *fuzzy set*. Otherwise, it would be inexplicable to me that such a natural, straightforward and obvious paradigm as the one intiated by Lotfi Zadeh is not even now fully accepted by the scientific and engineering community. (See the recent discussions in [1] and [12].)

The area mainly dealt with in this paper is that of the relationships between the conceptual foundations and the basic formal notions of FST. But why is this area of interest at all? The reason for the above mentioned unsatisfactory situation with regard to the understanding and acceptance of FST, in my opinion, is that over all the years the technical or syntactical development was much faster than the foundational and semantical progress. As a consequence, the relations between the conceptual and the formal framework should have but usually have not been a central subject of fuzzy set research.

If, however, we claim that we are not doing useless but amusing things on only a mathematical playground, then we should be able to explain all the sceptical and astonished people outside the fuzzy community, why we are so convinced of the paradigms of FST, and why they mark one of the most important revolutions in scientific approaches to understand men's modeling the world by his and her methods of knowledge representation and manipulation. In short, the paradigm of fuzziness must no longer remain in the unclear shape it usually presents itself to the scientific community and the application engineers.

A fundamental presupposition for achieving this goal is to have at hand clear and intelligible characterizations of the most important core notions of and around FST. The following sections aim to be a contribution to this undertaking. Some of the considerations are presented in more detail in [34].

2. Epistemic and formal preliminaries

2.1. *Linguistic aspects*

Languages of one kind or the other are the only means by which living beings organize and communicate their knowledge and experience. As this is the more true for human beings, any serious and eventually successful investigation of fuzziness must include an analysis of human natural language. This is in full accordance with [41, p. 302] who stated the most important (but usually neglected) fact about fuzziness as follows:

> Any notion of fuzziness can be meaningful only in dependency on human systems, human observers, and human tools and strategies for describing reality: That is, *human beings are the only and exclusive source of fuzziness in linguistic labeling* - there are no other sources.

Even if it may be an incomplete point of departure, the following is certainly a correct and plausible assertion to begin with ([26, p. 2]):

> Our claim is that knowledge is deep-seated in the classificatory abilities of human beings and other species. For example, knowledge about the environment is primarily manifested as an ability to classify a variety of situations from the point of view of survival in the real world. Complex classification patterns of sensor signals probably form fundamental mechanisms of every living being. ...
> We simply assume here that knowledge is based on the ability to classify objects, and by object we mean anything we can think of, for example, real things, states, abstract concepts, processes, moments of time, etc.

As already pointed out in e.g [32, Section 1.3] and [33, Section1] it is at least plausible, if not reasonable, to assume a two-stage decision process underlying every classificational act. With the first step (in both ontogenetical and phylogenetical respect) we make a yes-no decision about whether objects under consideration do or do not have a certain property P by assigning them a corresponding predicate, name, or linguistic label l_P. The underlying universe, thus, is partitioned into two crisp sets: $M_P \cap M_{\neg P} = \emptyset$ and $M_P \cup M_{\neg P} = U$ (see also Section 2.2.2 below). Only those objects, which have been classified to have the property P may, in a second step refining the first one, eventually be ordered according to the degree to which they exhibit property P.

It is again plausible to suspect that the emergence of the first predicators and their use for classificational and communication purposes is strongly connected to properties that can easily be recognized, are important in some way, and are occurring often and together with relevant objects and processes. Thus, it is absolutely no surprise that the typical examples for fuzzy sets like e.g. TALL, LOUD, OLD, HIGH, COOL, FAST etc. are all connected to men's perceptual equipment.*

In later periods of phylogenetical evolution it must then have become an advantage or even a necessity for survival to make finer discriminations. In other words this means: to have at hand not only (binary) qualitative and classificatory linguistic labels, but to proceed to qualitative linguistic scales like COLD, COOL, WARM, HOT or to comparative notions, i.e. to enrich the pool of basic primary classificators of the form *"x is* P*"* with predicators like *"x is* P*-er than y"*, *"x is most* P*"*, or *"low* P*"* etc. in order to differentiate real phenomena more accurately. The situation, however, is probably not thus simple as outlined above, as can be seen from the following quotation from [37, p. 323] (with the author's italics, but our numbering of references):

> As early as 1944, Sapir proposed the idea that although *wide, young,* and *big* linguistically precede *wider, younger,* and *bigger,* respectively, the comparative forms precede the simple forms *logically.* The simple forms are *implicitly graded antonyms.* They can only be understood in terms of the comparative forms, with respect to some *norm* set by the object being described [27]. This opinion has been accepted by many other linguistics [6], [25].

However, the above mentioned ability to make finer and finer discriminations, finally resulting in the real numbers, and to fix them by linguistic labels, is only one side on the way from perceiving to conceiving and communication. The other one is the capability for generalization and abstraction as basic presuppositions for the evolution of language. It is on the basis of these two processes that the emergence of fuzziness can be explained in a natural way as follows:

1. One of the main assumptions of hypothetical realism – as well as of common sense and natural science – is the existence of a real world that is structured and is at least partially knowable by perception and experience. This is described by G. Vollmer as follows [36, p. 188, p. 191] (For a detailed discussion see also [35, pp. 28-40]):

*Furtheron I will use different fonts do distinguish between CONCEPTS and the linguistic labels designating them, if this seems appropriate.

> All knowledge is hypothetical, i.e., conjectural, fallible, preliminary. There exists a real world, independent of our consciousness; it is structured, coherent, and quasi-continuous; it is at least partially knowable and explainable by perception, experience, and intersubjective science. ... Our forms of intuition and our categories of experience, the qualities of our perceptions, and the basic elements of inference, of classification, of abstraction, are, according to evolutionary epistemology, innate, ontogenetically *a priori* and constitutive for mesocosmic knowledge.

2. Structure means a certain kind of order, i.e. a temporal or spatial coincidence of states or events.
3. So there exists the possibility for, and also the capability of *re*-cognizing objects and events: Only this makes the emergence of predicators both plausible and reasonable at all.
4. *Re*-cognition in turn requires for comparisons, the result of which can be either 'discriminate' or 'make equal' (i.e. regard as equivalent).
5. Fuzziness, finally, arises by the possibility of regarding as equal some attribute values (that are discriminable in principle and, hence, if necessary) in certain situations, but in general, without having to fear any bad consequences or serious problems for the individual doing so and, consequently, for the species too.

   (If you want e.g. to cross a road and you see a car coming along, you will neither be interested in its exact distance nor its exact speed; the only thing which is relevant for you is whether the distance is large enough and the speed is sufficiently low. Take as a second the following example: For hundreds of years various kinds of watches (sundial, hourglass, clockwork) have been of satisfactory granularity without giving us accurate information on a numerical scale. As the other extreme, I think approximately fifteen years ago, there has been a trend towards the digital watch; however, as far as I know, they have not generally been accepted in common everyday usage. Guess why!)

2.2. *Formal prerequisites*

2.2.1. *Basic notions*

Closely following Section 2.1 of [24] we introduce the notion of refinement, an important concept for the considerations to follow, with

Definition 2.1. Let A and B be two disjoint non-empty sets.

(a) B is called *refinement of* A if there is a mapping $\hat{\Pi} : A \longrightarrow \mathbf{2}^B$, the *refinement mapping*, such that

(1) $\hat{\Pi}(a) \neq \emptyset$ for all $a \in A$,

(2) $\bigcup\{\hat{\Pi}(a) | a \in A\} = B$, and

(3) $\hat{\Pi}(C) = \bigcup\{\hat{\Pi}(c) | c \in C\}$, for $C \subset A$.

(b) A refinement mapping $\hat{\Pi}$ is called *class preserving* if $a \neq a' \rightarrow \hat{\Pi}(a) \cap \hat{\Pi}(a') = \emptyset$.

(c) A refinement mapping $\hat{\Pi}$ is called *proper* if $\exists a \in A : |\hat{\Pi}(a)| \geq 2$.

For sake of convenience we introduce the following notations:

Definition 2.2. For given sets A, B let R be a crisp binary relation from A to B.

(a) The *afterset* of $a \in A$ w.r.t. R is $aR :\Leftrightarrow \{b \in B | aRb\}$ (also written as $R(a)$).

(b) The *foreset* of $b \in B$ w.r.t. R is $Rb :\Leftrightarrow \{a \in A | aRb\}$ (also written as $R^{-1}(b)$) .

2.2.2. *Classificational systems*

It is a common and characteristic feature of both empirical science and common sense reasoning that their assertions can be regarded as being confirmed or refuted solely in terms of evidence based upon the execution of a physical operation. In both cases, if we want to document our findings or to communicate them to others, we have to use a certain set of classificators, marks, or linguistic labels as the pool of symbolic items we are allowed to use for recording the outcomes of our systematic or everyday experiments. This situation is in no way different from the one used in the meanwhile classical, well known and commonly accepted framework of probability theory; so we take a short glance at it.

By the term *physical operation*, introduced above, we shall mean an instruction sequence in the widest possible sense that describes a well-defined, physically realizable, and reproducible procedure and that, furthermore, specifies which one out of a given set of symbols $\mathcal{R_P}$ – the *result set* of the physical operation $\mathcal{P}$ – has to be recorded as the unique outcome of an arbitrary realization (i.e. execution) of that procedure. The above mentioned pool of symbolic items clearly corresponds to the result set $\mathcal{R_P}$ of a physical operation (or to a union of such sets), also referred to in probability theory as *sample space* ([13, pp. 9 and 14]):

The concept introduced under the name 'sample space' can be found either as corresponding concept or as part of such under a lot of well-known other names too, as e.g.: *universe of discourse, frame of discernment, states of the world, frame of reference, behaviour system, admissible data space, representation structure* etc. All of these can obviously be seen to refer, in one way or the other, to the basic epistemic situation of classificational acts. And all of them have in common the aspect of providing the possible data to be recorded, implying both the grid and granularity in which models of the real world have to be embedded. In the following we will use the neutral term 'classificational system'. A minimal formal setup for this concept is provided by

Definition 2.3.
(a) A *classificational system* is an ordered pair $\mathbf{C} := \langle L, \perp \rangle$, where
(1) L denotes a set of linguistic labels, classificators, symbolic items etc. at hand for expressing the result of a classificational act;
(2) $\perp$ is a relation on L, where $l_1 \perp l_2$ intuitively means that l_1 and l_2 *classificationally reject* each other in the sense that they are mutually exclusive outcomes of a classificational act.
(b) Let $\mathbf{C} = \langle L, \perp \rangle$ and $\mathbf{C}' = \langle L', \perp' \rangle$ be two classificational systems. $\mathbf{C}'$ is called a *refinement* of $\mathbf{C}$ if L' is a refinement of L.

Definition 2.4. $\mathbf{V} := \langle V, \preceq \rangle$ is called a *valuation space.* For reasons given in [31, p.294], $\mathbf{V}$ is assumed to be a finite chain: $\mathbf{V}_n := \langle V_n, \preceq \rangle$, $n \geq 1$, with $V_n := \{0 := v_0, v_1, ..., v_n =: 1\}$ and $\preceq := \{\langle v_i, v_j \rangle | i \leq j\}$.

Obviously, the minimal cardinality for a valuation chain V_n is 2, since we want at least to be able to symbolize the presence or absence of properties of objects. This, however, gives us the coarsest mechanism only for stating differences: it corresponds to a qualitative, binary, all-or-nothing, or simple yes-no decision possibility. Thus the most simple valuation space which makes sense for classification purposes is of course the one used in the classical symbolizations, viz. $\mathbf{V}_2 := \mathbf{2} := \langle \{0, 1\}, < \rangle$.

Within this framework of classification and valuation spaces, fuzzy sets obviously arise from triples $\langle \mathbf{C}, \mathbf{C}', \mathbf{V}_n \rangle$, such that $\mathbf{C}'$ is a refinement of $\mathbf{C}$, in the following way: If $\mathbf{C} = \langle L, \perp \rangle$ and $\mathbf{C}' = \langle L', \perp' \rangle$ then the classical case of a fuzzy set is given by $\mu_l(l') \in V_n$, with $l \in L, l' \in L'$ and is usually called "l is a V_n-fuzzy set on L'".It is characteristic for such fuzzy sets that $L' \subseteq \mathbb{R}$. As an example take $L = \{$COLD, COOL, PLEASANT, WARM, HOT$\}$, $L' = \{10, 11, \ldots, 35\}$ with dimension $^\circ$C, and let $V_{11} = \{0, \frac{1}{10}, \ldots, \frac{9}{10}, 1\}$; then WARM is an V_{11}-fuzzy set on $L' \subset \mathbb{N}$, with $\mu_{\text{WARM}}(28^\circ \text{C}) = 0.8$.

Now, what about the semantics of 0 and 1 in this formal model for describing human discriminative abilities? Their main aim is to distinguish, and not to order; syntactically this means: to emphasize $0 \neq 1$, and not $0 < 1$, in order to assert a *qualitative* difference between "to be" and "to be not", between "to have" and "to have not" etc. This binary classification is, but only implicitly, already present in traditional fuzzy set theory via the notion of the *support* of a fuzzy set, defined as $\text{supp}_A := \{x \in U | A(x) > 0\}$, commonly related to the interpretation of $A(x) = 0$ as "x is not member of A (at all)", or "x does not have property P_A" etc., whence $A(x) > 0$ must have the meaning "x has property P_A". Thus, $A(x) = v > 0$ means "x exhibits property P_A to the degree v", and we get (see also [29, p. 230])

$$\mathrm{supp}_A := \{x \in U | A(x) > 0\} = \{x \in U | P_A(x)\} \qquad \text{(ED)}$$

as the set of objects possessing property P_A, according to which they can be ordered. This, in fact, corresponds to the two-stage classification process mentioned above: Only after the yes-no problem has been decided, i.e. after certain objects have been classified as having a property P_A or not, those which have (i.e. $x \in \mathrm{supp}_A$) may, in a further step refining the first one, be ordered according to the degree to which they exhibit the property under consideration.

3. Basic epistemic and semantic structures

As a sufficiently detailed ontological structure for our further considerations we take from [3, p. 58] the following one, consisting of three interconnected layers:

$$\textit{linguistic level} \xrightarrow{\mathcal{D}} \textit{conceptual level} \xrightarrow{\mathcal{R}} \textit{physical level}$$

$\mathcal{D}$ is called the *designation* (or *naming*) relation; $\mathcal{R}$ is the relation of *reference*, which gives information about what things a given construct is talking about at all. The most obvious interrelationship in everyday situations of communication and information is the one from the linguistic to the physical level, called *denotation*, arising from the composition of designation and reference: $\Delta \mathrel{\widehat{=}} \mathcal{R} \circ \mathcal{D}$.

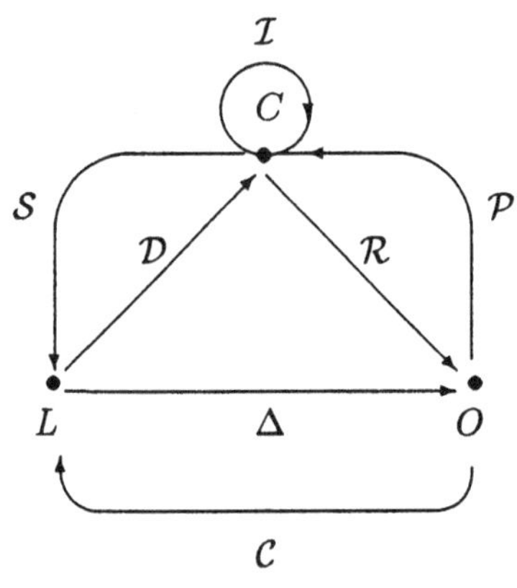

Fig. 1. The basic semantic and epistemic relations

The logical structure induced by these three levels and their interconnections has, of course, correlates in the basic assumptions of both EE and hypothetical realism, as well as in common sense reasoning and also in the ontological assumptions of every branch of natural science. Illustrating this logical and epistemic structure in a slightly changed and enriched version results in Fig. 1. We have

1. the linguistic level, which usually appears as a set L of signs, words, symbols, linguistic labels, marks etc.;
2. the conceptual level C of concepts, ideas, sense, intension;
3. the object level: From our current point of view (i.e. without much more sophisticated and deep philosophical considerations) we regard it to be enough to take as an object anything we can think about; thus, especially, $C \subset O$ and $L \subset O$.

Furthermore, besides the already mentioned relations

$\mathcal{D} \subset L \times C$ of *designation*,
$\mathcal{R} \subset C \times O$ of *reference*, and
$\Delta \subset L \times O$ of *denotation*

we have to take into account some more, viz. the relations

$\mathcal{P} \subset O \times C$ of *perception*, relating (extensional) objects to (intensional) concepts,
$\mathcal{S} \subset C \times L$ of *speech*, mapping concepts to words,
$\mathcal{C} \subset O \times L$ of *classification*, associating words to objects, and
$\mathcal{I} \subset C \times C$ of *intension*, relating concepts to other concepts.

Together with Def. 2.2 we get the following examples:

- $l\Delta$ is the set of objects denoted by l;
- Δo is the set of labels denoting o;
- $l\mathcal{D}$ is the set of concepts designated by l;
- $c\mathcal{R}$ is the set of objects referred to by c;
- $c\mathcal{S}$ is the set of labels naming c;
- $\mathcal{S}l$ is the set of concepts labelled as l;
- if $|\mathcal{D}c| > 1$, then $\mathcal{D}c$ is the set of synonyms for c.

4. Some fuzzy flowers

Probably, one of the most confusing things – perhaps not only for fuzzy beginners – is the great number of different *names* (I do, but only here and deliberately, not use the words *notion* or *concepts*) surrounding the central term in the area, viz. *fuzziness*. To give you an impression of what I mean, let me start with the meanwhile classical triple of notions from Black [2] (vagueness, generality and ambiguity), which – to the best of my knowledge – has been introduced to FST as early as 1968 in [15, p. 344], and has been echoed in some prominent textbooks on FST as e.g. in [8, p.1], or in [21, p. 3/4] (where, however, they are regarded as three "kinds of inexactness" which, certainly, is a wrong and indefensible viewpoint on basis of our natural presuppositions).

Practically, the information transmitted on Black's paper is the same in all cases, since either of them presents us the same passages and, hence, leaves away the same important parts (italicized by me in the subsequent quotation), perhaps because it is not quite clear how the second half of it can be understood. Black [2, p.430] makes us acquainted with the terms *generality, ambiguity* and *vagueness* in the following way:

> Vagueness is distinguished from generality and from ambiguity. The former is constituted by the application of a symbol to a multiplicity of objects in the fields of reference, the latter by the association of a finite number of alternative meanings having the same phonetic form; *but it is characteristic of the vague symbol that there are no alternative symbols in the language, and its vagueness is a feature of the boundary of its extension, and is not constituted by the extension itself.*

But this is only a modest starting point, as the following enumeration does show us. In the literature of FST and its neighbouring areas you can find discussions on the meaning and interrelationships of at least the following (twenty-five) additional notions (in alphabetical order): *(degree of) belief, confusion, credibility, dissonance, error, fuzziness, ignorance, imperfectness, imprecision, inaccuracy, incompleteness, indeterminism, indistinguishability, inexactness, necessity, non-specificity, plausibility, possibility, probability, similarity, specificity, (degree of) truth, uncertainty, underdetermination, underspecification.*

4.1. *Black's classical concepts*

From the above quotation from Black's 1937 paper [2] we have the following characteristics for (see Fig. 1):

- GENERALITY: $|l\Delta| > 1$, i.e. $\Delta(l) = \{o_1, \ldots, o_n\}, n > 1$: denotation Δ is not a function.
- AMBIGUITY (homonymy): $|l\mathcal{D}| > 1$, i.e.$\mathcal{D}(l) = \{c_1, \ldots, c_n\}, n > 1$: designation $\mathcal{D}$ is not a function.

Ambiguous labels are – of course by $\Delta \mathrel{\widehat{=}} \mathcal{R} \circ \mathcal{D}$ – but only a small part of the general labels. Thus, it seems that GENERALITY in Black's sense is a concept far too unspecific to be of great value in our analysis. Ambiguity is just another word for homonymy; thus, one will, usually, not be uncertain about the designated concept due to the context dependent constraints imposed by the situation of communication.

Some typical properties of ambiguous labels l are the following: Let $l\mathcal{D} = \{c_1, c_2, \ldots, c_n\}, n \geq 2$; then

- $c_i\mathcal{I} \cap c_j\mathcal{I} = \emptyset$, for all $i \neq j$;
- $c_i\mathcal{R} \cap c_j\mathcal{R} = \emptyset$, for all $i \neq j$.

Following Dubois and Prade [8, p. 1], we take VAGUENESS and FUZZINESS to be the same concept. Let us start by looking to which kind of objects this concept applies. Black attributes all of the properpties of generality, ambiguity and vagueness to 'symbols', which we take to designate concepts like 'linguistic label', 'predicator' etc. And while Black, in case of generality and ambiguity, relates symbols to objects and meanings, respectively, no analogous association of that kind is made by him for the notion of vagueness.

What we learn from Black [2, p.429/30] about vagueness is, that it is different from the other two and

> "that while the vague symbol has a part to play in language which cannot be equally well performed by more accurate symbols from another level (wave lengths as substitute for names of colors) the transition to levels of higher accuracy can always in principle be made."

Furthermore, from the second half of the quotation given above at the begin of Section 4 we learn about the vague symbol that "vagueness is a feature of the boundary of its extension, and is not constituted by the extension itself". Although laid bare now for almost sixty years, this most simple and basic fact has practically gained no influence over the conceptual and formal development of fuzzy set theory, which, contrary to its name, is *not* a theory for manipulating collections, but instead a theory for manipulating valuations over sets and their corresponding vague notions, respectively. (For a detailed discussion of associated epistemic and formal aspects see [30, 33].) Strange enough then, the nearest candidate for a possible interpretation of 'boundary of extension' then seems to be the vague symbol's corresponding concept, i.e. its associated intension that acts as an flexible and variable constraint on (concrete instances of) the extension. And it is in fact not a symbol s that can be vague or fuzzy, but (one of) the concept(s) $c \in s\mathcal{D}$ designated by s: words can be ambiguous or not and can designate vague and/or sharp concepts. (An example from German: leitend designates the two concepts CONDUCTING (heat, electricity) and LEADING (employee), the former one being a sharp and the latter one – be it only out of psychological reasons and among employees – being a vague concept.)

4.2. *Some more epistemics*

When we say that a concept $c \in C$ is vague or fuzzy, then we usually want to express that there is something unclear or left unfixed about what commonly is called its meaning or sense. Therefore, we may be uncertain whether c applies to an object $o \in O$ or not; but if we have to choose or to decide in a concrete situation, we must perform a classificational act that results in assigning a corresponding label $l \in cS$ or not.

The epistemic situation underlying this formal model is, in principle, the same for everyday as well as for scientific discourse: ultimately, we have to resort to single binary yes-no classifications, usually communicated by linguistic labels or by means of some other sign system (universe of discourse, frame of discernment, sample space, evidence space ...). And *naturally* there is then no other possibility than to choose one out of a certain set of discrete and distinct markers to express the result of a classificational act (recall Section 2.2.2).

Thus, no single speech act can be "intrinsically uncertain" or indeterminate, since every classification finally rests upon a yes-no decision between linguistic labels and thus gives a unique result. Hence, only a sample of such classifications can yield us the epistemological categories of probability or traditional (valuational) fuzziness due to one speaker's intrasubjective or many speakers' intersubjective variability of applying predicators to objects or events.

So, fuzziness shares an essential property with other important epistemic categories like continuity, functional dependency, and probability: they all can be conceived, discovered or asserted only by means of repetition or recurrence of activities and events. That means that all of the above mentioned epistemic categories are 'sample properties'! (Besides: I know fore sure that at least my children at least until now did not learn the meaning of any vague predicator by looking at a membership curve, but by again and again applying it, and getting corrected or reaffirmed.)

An important result of recognizing and emphasizing the emergence of the phenomenon called fuzziness out of a multiplicity of analogous (re)actions or results gives natural answers to two old and fundamental problems of FST (see [30, 33]): (i) the epistemic relationship between fuzzy sets and probabilities (i.e. between membership curves and frequency curves), and (ii) how to understand one of the most confusing facets of FST, viz. the lack of the *excluded middle* and *contradiction laws*. For details see Section 4.2 of [34].

4.3. *Towards a formal description of fuzziness*

According to our foregoing considerations, fuzziness is to be analyzed in connection with at least the two mappings $\mathcal{P}$ and $\mathcal{R}$ (remember Zeleny [41, p. 302]: linguistic labeling is the only source of fuzziness). In addition to the ones mentioned in Section 4.1 above, fuzzy concepts have the following properties (where the $\lambda_i, 1 \leq i \leq n$, are assumed to represent wavelengths perceived of the attribute colour of objects $o_j, 1 \leq j \leq m, m > n$):

- $|\mathcal{P}c| > 1$: We have e.g. $\{\lambda_1, \ldots, \lambda_n\} \mapsto$ RED, $n > 1$, i.e. $\mathcal{P}$ is not injective;
- $|c\mathcal{R}| > 1$: We have e.g. RED $\mapsto \{\lambda_1, \ldots, \lambda_m\}, m > 1$, i.e. $\mathcal{R}$ is not a function.

These two properties are at most necessary but not sufficient for the presence of fuzziness as a simple example can show: $|\mathcal{P}\text{CAR}| > 1$ and $|\text{CAR}\mathcal{R}| > 1$, but I never heard someone claiming that CAR is a fuzzy predicate. So there must be something else which is specific for vagueness. Let us continue with

Definition 4.2. A concept $c \in C$ is said to be *coarse* if there is a set $B \subset C$ which is a proper refinement of $\{c\}$, such that the following compatibility relation is satisfied:

$$c\mathcal{R} \cap \bigcup_{b \in B} b\mathcal{R} \neq \emptyset. \qquad (\mathcal{R})$$

This definition also reflects the fact that the notion of refinement is a purely syntactical concept and thus demands for a semantical supplement connecting it with the domain of interest: The condition $(\mathcal{R})$ clearly assures that all the involved concepts pertain to the same domain (of attributes, interest etc.), i.e. that they 'are speaking about the same things'. However, this is only a necessary but not a sufficient property of a concept which usually is said to be fuzzy as will be illustrated by the following

Example 1. (taken from [24, p. 10]): The set $\Gamma :\Leftrightarrow$ {NOT_AT_SEA, AT_SEA} may be considered as a typical example for a frame of discernment. If the granularity of Γ turns out to be too coarse we may instead use the set $\Gamma' :\Leftrightarrow$ {OPEN_SEA, 12_MILE_ZONE, 3_MILE_ZONE, CANAL, REFUELING_DOCK, LOADING_DOCK}. Obviously, Γ and Γ' are compatible, i.e. for each $\gamma \in \Gamma$ we have $\gamma\mathcal{R} \cap \bigcup_{\gamma' \in \Gamma'} \gamma'\mathcal{R} \neq \emptyset$, and the corresponding refinement mapping $\hat{\Pi} : \Gamma \longrightarrow \mathbf{2}^{\Gamma'}$ is given by

$\hat{\Pi}$(AT_SEA) = {OPEN_SEA, 12_MILE_ZONE, 3_MILE_ZONE},
$\hat{\Pi}$(NOT_AT_SEA) = {CANAL, REFUELING_DOCK, LOADING_DOCK}.

The two concepts AT_SEA and NOT_AT_SEA are coarse: we have just provided a proper refinement for them, which is class preserving and obviously fulfills condition $(\mathcal{R})$. But nobody would classify them as fuzzy. So we are still missing a crucial criterion. Let us therefore have a look at some typical examples for fuzzy sets in

Example 2. Some refinement mappings:

$\hat{\Pi}_1$(LONG) = {30 MM, 35 MM, ... , 80 MM}, for e.g. lenght of nails;
$\hat{\Pi}_2$(LONG) = {600 KM, ... , 1500 KM}, for e.g. lenght of a journey;
$\hat{\Pi}_3$(COLD) = {10° C, ... , 16° C}, for e.g. room temperature,
$\hat{\Pi}_3$(COOL) = {14° C, ... , 20° C},
$\hat{\Pi}_3$(PLEASANT) = {18° C, ... , 24° C},
$\hat{\Pi}_3$(WARM) = {22° C, ... , 28° C}.

In examples like the ones given above we can find the crucial components that will help us to deepen our understanding of FUZZINESS. These are two measurement devices for the same attribute domain with different levels of granularity (the term 'different levels of precision' would induce a pejorative and misleading connotation) that allow for a certain way of comparison. The means for doing so are provided by natural and artificial equipments like eyes, ears, nose, centimeter sticks, microscopes, watches etc.

An important consequence we get from this is the following: Fuzziness is not an absolute but a relative phenomenon that is inseparably connected to two different classificational systems, such that one of them is a refinement of the other. Obviously, the recognition of the phenomenon of fuzziness arose out of the confrontation of the two most often used classificational systems, viz. *natural language* which we use in everyday discourse, and the *artificial man-made formal systems* used in the various scientific and engineering disciplines, leading to what has been called the 'eye versus meter-stick' situation by Hisdal.

What more can be learned from the examples above?

1. vague concepts usually are context dependent;
2. the refinements associated to vague concepts usually are not class preserving;
3. in addition to the refinement we have a change of the underlying scale, roughly speaking, from a "qualitative" to a "quantitative" one. i.e. from natural to artificial measurement devices in order to get 'exact' instead of 'inexact' data.

It seems that these three properties are what essentially makes a concept fuzzy. This gives us

Definition 4.3. A concept $c \in C$ is called *fuzzy* if it is coarse and the refinement mapping goes from a qualitative to a quantitative scale and is not class preserving.

Typical properties of fuzzy concepts c are the following: Let $c\mathcal{I} = \{c_1, c_2, \ldots, c_n\}, n \geq 2$; then

- if $c_i, c_j \in c\mathcal{I}$ then $c_i\mathcal{I} \cap c_j\mathcal{I} \neq \emptyset$, for all $i \neq j$;
- only labels l designating vague concepts c, i.e. $l \in \mathcal{D}c$, can be combined with modifiers like very, more or less, rather ...;
- usually, fuzzy concepts have a context dependent meaning: whereas 1 M always means the same, concepts like TALL, HIGH or LONG do not.
- usually, fuzzy concepts can be applied to different universes of discourse, even if they are measured along the same physical scale as LONG and HIGH: we speak e.g. about high mountains, trees, or buildings. But both concepts do not only refer to object attributes measured in units of MM, CM or M etc. LONG e.g. also applies to durations, and HIGH also to income and tones.

- Thus, fuzzy concepts are flexible, universally applicable, and highly economic tools for human communication, due to the above mentioned properties.

Let us finally propose a notion of *crispness* (presumably the expected one) and check whether it fits to intuition and common usage of this term.

Definition 4.4. A concept $c \in C$ is called *crisp* if it is not fuzzy.

It follows that AT_SEA is a crisp, since it fails to fulfill the scale-change requirement, but coarse concept. However, since at_sea$\mathcal{D}$ = {AT_SEA}, the label at_sea is not ambiguous. Note that well known fuzzy labels like high can also designate concepts which are not fuzzy in the sense of Def. 4.3: take HIGH SOCIAL POSITION or HIGH QUALITY. The latter one, however, being more likely to fall under our concept of FUZZINESS than the former one, at least in technical contexts and perhaps via many-dimensional measurements. These two examples clearly demonstrate the obvious fact that not all which can be ordered is so via FUZZINESS in our sense.

4.4. *Uncertainty and indeterminism*

A short examination of classification schemes as e.g. in [22, p. 138], [28, p. 7ff] and [14, p. 162f] or some book titles as e.g. of [16, 17, 22, 24, 40] indicates that focusing ourselves to the term uncertainty as another undefined basic notion in the core of the domain of interest is an unavoidable task.

As whatever uncertainty may be conceived to be, its basic characteristic feature is that, in one way or the other, a one-to-many relation must be involved: If there are no alternatives, no possibility to choose, or only predetermined results, what shall (one) be uncertain (about)? What kind of variability could be expected?

Uncertainty, understood in this way, is a very general concept which is applicable, and actually is applied, to a variety of situations; we can e.g. at once take some examples from the material presented thus far:

- generality: denotational uncertainty;
- ambiguity: designational uncertainty;
- fuzziness: intensional uncertainty.

Uncertainty is – according to one's point of view – either a subjective feeling of a person ("I am not quite sure") or an objective trait of epistemic situations ("It is not quite sure"). If we call the latter one *indeterminism* then the term *uncertainty* becomes free for referring to a mental state, a kind of knowledge or expectation concerning some future (re)action or event which is either unknown (not yet observed, has not yet happened, ...), or a (re)action (e.g. a classificational act) that is known from repetitions to yield varying results. (Note that in the former case the future event may even be deterministic, whereas in the latter case the event need not be a future one.) This usage of terminology then takes UNCERTAINTY as the subjective psychological correlate to INDETERMINISM as an objective trait of some parts of reality, both notions being closely related to a third one, viz. that of *information* in a generic as well as in the special sense of Shannon. But we will not follow these lines here.

Note that before we can conceive INDETERMINISM as an epistemic phenomenon, we must have done some classificational acts which are tied together by a group of situations regarded as equ(iv)al(ent) and data regarded as different. So, again it is a sample of classificational acts that lie at the basis. (Remember Section 4.2)

Here we can, unconditionally, agree with the following assertion in [16, p. ix], where uncertainty is obviously used for designating our concept of INDETERMINISM:

> "Two types of uncertainty arise: The first involves only uncertainties in the outcomes of the experiment, the second involves, in addition, uncertainties in the meaning of the data. Examples of the first situation occur in any well-defined random experiment such as tossing a coin, observing queues, and recording observed signals. Examples of the second type include experiments involving linguistic outcomes, where for information processing purposes, it is necessary to exercise greater care in the modelling of meaning representation."

This is, in fact, the fundamental and correct differentiation, in its most obvious and explicit formulation. We can find it, disguised in one way or the other, elsewhere too:

1. Smithson [28, pp. 7ff], in his taxonomy of ignorance, speaks about distinctions 'in kind' and 'in degree'. (E.g., he calls *absence* the incompleteness in kind, and *uncertainty* the incompleteness in degree.)
2. Kosko [23, p. 213] distinguishes between 'event occurrence' and 'event ambiguity', which are modeled by probability and fuzzy set theory, respectively, answering the underlying basic question of 'whether vs. how much' which fits nicely to the following, since 'how much' presupposes that 'at all'.)
3. Toth [30, p. 105] divides a classificational act into two steps (see also Section 2.1 above): the first is pertaining to a yes-no decision, the second to a refinement of a positive classification. In more technical terms: By the first step we single out the support supp_A of the fuzzy set A corresponding to a linguistic label l_A. In a second step, the objects in the support are ordered according to the degree to which they exhibit (are compatible with) the property under consideration.

Summarizing we can say, that we have found two concepts which are presented under different names in different contexts, but which seem to be used in both a consistent and convergent way.

4.5. *Possibility*

4.5.1. *Epistemic aspects*

Much has been written on the concept of possibility and derived notions as possibility distribution, possibility (and necessity) measures, possibilistic inference, possibilistic logic etc. However, as it has happened with FST itself, also possibility theory has (been) turned away very soon from its intuitive and epistemic to a mainly mathematical background. Therefore, let us look back to the origin. Once again, it was Lotfi Zadeh [39] who introduced the notion of possibility to FST as follows:

> The theory of possibility described in this paper is related to the theory of fuzzy sets by defining the concept of possibility distribution as a fuzzy restriction which acts as an elastic constraint on the values that may be assigned to a variable. More specifically, if F is a fuzzy subset of a universe of discourse $U = \{u\}$ which is characterized by its membership function μ_F, then a proposition of the form "X is F", where X is a variable taking values in U, induces a possibility distribution Π_X which equates the possibility of X taking the value u to $\mu_F(u)$ – the compatibility of u with F. [Abstract, p. 3]

Concerning a further clarification of the relationship between fuzzy sets and possibility distributions we have to take an epistemic viewpoint. Fuzzy sets or membership functions, respectively, are a means that enables us to represent the meaning of vague concepts in a formal way, and thus make them accessible for various transformations and combinations by computer programs.

The classical starting point for FST is the situation where a certain (presumably or actually) exactly known attribute value is ascribed its degree of compatibility with a linguistic label designating a VAGUE concept, thereby classifying this attribute value: a perceptual item gets fixed by a linguistic expression F which in turn can be used later on for various purposes.

One of them arises in just the opposite epistemic constellation if somebody wants to communicate a knowledge item to someone else. Usually, this can only be done with a certain kind of linguistic expressions, namely propositions of the form "X is F" that bear information for both the sender and receiver. (See Fig. 2 which nicely shows that classification and knowledge appear to come as Siamese twins.)

This is explained in full detail in [11, p. 213] as follows:

> $\pi_{\text{height(John)}}$ estimates to what degree it is possible that the proposition "height(John) $= u$" is true knowing the available information (i.e. "John is tall"), while $\mu_{\text{tall}}(u)$ estimates to what extent it is true that somebody, whose height is precisely u, is tall. *Thus, a degree of possibility and degree of truth respectively,* $\pi_{\text{height(John)}}(u)$ *and* $\mu_{\text{tall}}(u)$ *refer neither to the same proposition nor to the same state of knowledge.*

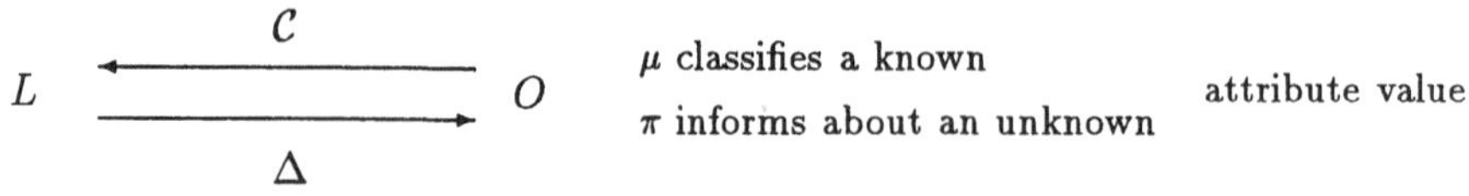

Fig. 2. The epistemic roles of μ and π

Sentences like $p \mathrel{\hat{=}}$ "o is A" represent a vague, incompletely specified, or un(der)determined characterization about a property of $o \in O$. More precisely: about the unknown value of a certain attribute of o. Corresponding to p there is a set of *possible* attribute values, restricted by the fuzzy set μ_A in the sense of the compatibility degrees induced by A.

From the above we then get the following interpretation:

- $\pi_X(u) = 0$ ... $X = u$ is impossible;
- $\pi_X(u) > \pi_X(u')$ ... $X = u$ is "more possible than" $X = u'$;
- $\pi_X(u) = 1$ ... $X = u$ is possible (without any restriction).

Expressions as the one quoted in the second line can be found very often in the literature on possibility theory. However, what can really be understood by the comparison of possibility degrees with one another? What, at all, is POSSIBILITY?

4.5.2. *Semantic aspects*

Trying an answer to the above questions results in philosophical rather than formal considerations. Let us first resort to the origin. Zadeh himself explicitly states that his notion of possibility is different from the one of modal logic in [39, p.4, footnote 2]: The latter one clearly is a binary and not a many-valued concept. So far we only know what possibility has certainly not been intended to designate, namely the alethic modality $\Diamond$. Thus, there must be some other aspects that are essential to POSSIBILITY and also for making its gradedness a reasonable feature.

Zadeh himself, in the above mentioned paper, proposes – via the well-known example of "Hans the egg-eater" – a physical view of possibility in terms of ease of attainment, feasibility etc. This gives us a first hint where to search for further explanation alternatives. We take advice from [5, Ch. 4], where we learn from a thorough analysis that POSSIBILITY is an AMBIGUOUS concept:

(a) The notions of *conceptual possibility* all refer to formulas and propositions. Let K denote a body of knowledge, p an arbitrary formula, and let $A \subseteq K$. Bunge introduces, besides others, the following special case (p. 165, Def. 4.1):

   - p is *logically possible relative to* A $:\Leftrightarrow$ A does not entail $\neg p$;

(b) Contrary to the above the concept of *real* (or *physical*) *possibility* refers to factual items: Statements of the form "It is possible that p" attribute possibility to the factual referent(s) of the proposition p, and not to p itself. Note that facts are possible in an absolute sense in that their being possible does in no way depend on any body of knowledge.

For our purposes it suffices to establish the physical possibility of any circumstance as its property to not contradict to any law of nature. (A much more detailed discussion is provided by Bunge, loc. cit.) Two kinds of real possibility can be distinguished:

1. *Causal propensity* (also: *causal disposition*) is called every capacity or potentiality, that always becomes actualized as soon as certain suitable conditions occur. Examples are e.g. solubility (in water etc.), elasticity (in the sense of physics), fragility (of glass etc.). Since a causal disposition means to always react or behave in the same manner under certain circumstances, it may also well be called *deterministic disposition* in contrast to
2. *Chance propensity* which is to be regarded as a probabilistic disposition, i.e. a potential property that is exhibited only with a certain probability. Whereas suitable circumstances are necessary and sufficient for the realization of a potency in case of causal disposition, in the case of chance propensities the possibilities lie wholly in the thing itself, and the occurrence of an actual property may be spontaneous, uncaused, and independent of the environment.

Applying these considerations to possibility theory we get that its special notion of POSSIBILITY is also AMBIGUOUS since it is used with the following meanings in terms of the general concept analysed above:

- in the sense of (a): p is logically possible relative to a certain knowledge base A, i.e. is consistent with the information contained in A to a certain degree $\pi(p)$.
- in a special sense of (b).2 that can well be characterized with 'pragmatical': Every action the realization of which requires a certain amount of effort may serve as a protopical example. In other words: Only by referring to additional aspects we can make the syntactical concept of possibility a gradeable one in a reasonable way (e.g. degree of ease, of feasibility, of being likely).

4.6. *Specificity*

Closely related to the notion of possibility distributions is the notion of specificity, which is defined according to Yager [38] as follows:

Definition 4.5. Assume π is a possibility distribution over a finite universe $U = \{u_1, \ldots, u_n\}$, i.e. $\pi : U \longrightarrow [0,1]$. The *specificity of* π is the value

$\mathrm{Sp}(\pi) \in [0,1]$ determined by some function Sp with the following properties:

(1) $\mathrm{Sp}(\pi) = 1$ iff $\pi(u) = \begin{cases} 1 & u = u_0 \\ 0 & u \neq u_0; \end{cases}$

(2) if supp $\pi = \emptyset$ then $\mathrm{Sp}(\pi) = 0$;

(3) if π_1, π_2 are normal and $\pi_2 \subseteq \pi_1$, then $\mathrm{Sp}(\pi_1) \leq \mathrm{Sp}(\pi_2)$;

(4) if π_1, π_2 are normal and crisp, and $|\mathrm{supp}\pi_2| \leq |\mathrm{supp}\pi_1|$, then $\mathrm{Sp}(\pi_1) \leq \mathrm{Sp}(\pi_2)$.

From the above definition one can easily see that specificity measures the amount of information contained in a possibility distribution π_X for a variable X:

> The concept of specificity plays a role in possibility theory, comparable to the concept of entropy in probability theory. Both these measure the amount of information contained in the associated distribution by *calculating the degree to which the distribution points to one and only one element as its manifestation ([38, p. 280]).*

To see this, let p be a probability distribution over U; the neg-entropy is given as $NH(p) = -H(p) = -\big(-\sum_{i=1}^{n} p(u_i) \cdot \ln p(u_i)\big)$, i.e. the negative of the well known Shannon entropy. Then we have that $NH(p)$ takes its maximum for $p(u) = 1$ iff $u = u_0$, and $p(u) = 0$, otherwise. Thus, like specificity, neg-entropy is maximal when we are certain as to the outcome. On the other hand, $NH(p)$ takes its minimum when $p(u_i) = \frac{1}{n}$ for all i, that is when we are most uncertain about the result. In case of normal possibility distributions this corresponds to the situation when $\pi(u_i) = 1$ for all i; i.e. all elements in U are held possible, and one does not know any restrictions on what is 'less possible'.

4.7. *Imperfect: Imprecise, inexact or incomplete*

One of the most notable books in FST ([10]) presents us the following explanation in its Section 1.1 (my italics):

> *Imprecision* and *uncertainty* can be considered as two complementary aspects of a single reality, that of *imperfect* information. ... imprecision relates to the content of an item of information ... while uncertainty relates to its truth, understood as its conformity to a reality ....

Let me explicitly state that the above quotation is not given with a contemptuous attitude, but only to demonstrate that explaining and fixing some fundamental notions is not a trivial thing even for leading authorities in the field. And, of course, a consistent usage and a standardized meaning of notions like the above are far from reality. Again, this makes an attempt of analyzing the various concepts within the framework built up in Sections 2 and 3 a reasonable undertaking.

First of all, note that the notions we are going to consider now are all comparative ones: they all relate what we have to what we could possibly have, what we would like to have, what we would need, or what we are expected to have. These notions thus have a normative attitude rather than a descriptive one. Before we can say something about the reference classes of these concepts, we have to introduce two more notions:

Definition 4.6. (a) Let $\langle L, \perp \rangle$ be a classificational system, $\langle V_n, \preceq \rangle$ a valuation space, and $I^L_{V_n} :\Leftrightarrow L \times O^* \times V_n$, where $O^* := \{\emptyset\} \cup O \cup O^2 \cup \ldots$ An element $i \in I^L_{V_n}$ is called an *informational item* or *infon* for short (a term taken from [7], and used in a similar way as there).

(b) An *elementary datum* d is an infon $i \in I^L_{V_n}$, or an infon-aggregate i_1 OR i_2 OR ...OR $i_m, m \geq 2$, such that $i_j \in I^L_{V_n}$ for $1 \leq j \leq m$. d is to be understood as an 'information' in the usual sense, describing some relevant aspects or events of reality.

(c) A *datum* is a set $\hat{d} = \{d_1, \ldots, d_n\}$ of elementary data. From a semantic point of view, a datum d is regarded to be equivalent to the conjunction $d_1 \wedge \ldots \wedge d_n$.

(d) A *state of knowledge* is a set of data $K = \{\hat{d}_1, \ldots, \hat{d}_m\}$ such that all elementary data in $\bigcup_i \hat{d}_i$ are held to be 'true (reliable, ...) to some degree', this degree being evaluated by an element $v \in V_n$.

Let $S = S_1 \times \ldots \times S_n, n \geq 2$, be the Cartesian product of n sets S_i; the *projection mapping* $\text{pr}_i : S \longrightarrow S_i$ is defined as $\text{pr}_i(\langle s_1 \times \ldots \times s_n \rangle) = s_i, 1 \leq i \leq n$.

Definition 4.7. (a) An elementary datum is called IMPRECISE if it is an infon-aggregate $i := i_1$ OR i_2 OR ...OR $i_m, m \geq 2$, (or has i as part of it) such that there exist j, k with $\text{pr}_2(i_j) = \text{pr}_2(i_k), 1 \leq j, k \leq m$, and PRECISE otherwise.

(b) A datum or a state of knowledge are called IMPRECISE if they contain IMPRECISE elementary data, and PRECISE otherwise.

This definition conforms to e.g. Dubois and Prade [9, Section 1.1] and Kruse et al. [24, Section 5.1]. Kruse et al. introduce so-called *observation mappings* $\Gamma : \theta \longrightarrow X$, where θ is thought to belong to a set of sensors or agents, and $\Gamma(\theta)$ are data obtained from θ. If $X = L$ data are called precise, if $X = \mathbf{2}^L$ IMPRECISE, and if $X = [0,1]^L$ VAGUE (or FUZZY in the classical sense of Zadeh). Put informally, by Def. 4.7 an IMPRECISE elementary datum d consists of ORed infons $i_k = \langle l_k, o, 1 \rangle$, so we learn from d about a certain attribute value of an object o that it lies in $\{l_1, \ldots, l_m\} \subseteq L$.

Note that within the terminology proposed so far, the property of being IMPRECISE is ascribed to data, i.e. pieces of information understood in the usual colloquial sense, whereas COARSE and VAGUE / FUZZY refer to concepts $c \in C$ (recall Section 3). We further define

Definition 4.8. (a) An infon $i := \langle l, o, v \rangle$ is called *fuzzy/coarse* if l designates a FUZZY/COARSE concept, and CRISP otherwise.

(b) An datum is called *fuzzy/coarse* if it uses a FUZZY/COARSE infon for its representation, and CRISP otherwise .

Thus, a datum can be both PRECISE and FUZZY at the same time: If $C = \langle\{\mathsf{small}, \mathsf{medium}, \mathsf{high}\}, \perp\rangle$ is a given classification system, then an infon $i = \langle$ small, salary, $1\rangle$ is PRECISE relative to the frame of discernment C, but also VAGUE, because usually small designates a FUZZY concept on e.g. (a suitable subset of) the natural numbers $C' = \langle\{\mathsf{one}, \mathsf{two}, \mathsf{three}, \ldots\}, \neq\rangle$ with C' being a refinement of C.

Note that in the above terminology interval-valued elementary data, i.e. $d = [l, u] \subset U$, where $l < u$ and U is some ordered universe, are IMPRECISE: $d \equiv i_1$ OR $\ldots i_j$ OR $\ldots$OR i_n, with $i_1 = \langle \mathsf{u}_1, o, 1\rangle, \ldots, i_j = \langle \mathsf{u}_j, o, 1\rangle, \ldots, i_n = \langle \mathsf{u}_n, o, 1\rangle$, $\mathsf{u}_l < \mathsf{u}_j < \mathsf{u}_n$.

Let us continue with three other notions and their interrelationships: In a way analogous to UNCERTAINTY, also IMPERFECT is used in a generic rather than definite sense within FST and related literature. We take imperfect as an AMBIGUOUS label designating the three concepts IMPRECISE, INEXACT and INCOMPLETE, formally $\mathcal{D}(\mathsf{imperfect}) = \{$IMPRECISE, INEXACT, INCOMPLETE$\}$. First, let us turn to the concept INCOMPLETE.

Let $\mathcal{O} = \{o_1, \ldots, o_n\} \subset O$ be a finite set of epistemic objects, physical or not, that are to be considered under a certain viewpoint of investigation; thus our starting point is a pair $\langle \mathcal{O}, S\rangle$ consisting of a set of objects $\mathcal{O}$ and an epistemic situation or context S. Assume that from the properties of the objects $o \in \mathcal{O}$ the ones that are relevant in the current epistemic situation S are $A_1, \ldots, A_m$. A formal framework might be set up as follows (recall Section 3):

Definition 4.9. A *frame of discernment* is a triple $\mathcal{F} = \langle \mathcal{V}, \mathcal{A}, s\rangle$ where

(1) $\mathcal{V} = \{V_1, \ldots, V_m\} \subset L$ is a set of variables pertaining to attributes $\mathcal{A}^{\mathcal{V}} = \{A_1^{\mathcal{V}}, \ldots, A_m^{\mathcal{V}}\} \subset C$, such that $A_i^{\mathcal{V}} \in \mathcal{D}(V_i)$;

(2) $\mathcal{A} = \{A_1, \ldots, A_n\} \subset \mathbf{2}^C$ is a family of value sets or state sets for the attributes $A_i^{\mathcal{V}}$; and

(3) s is an onto assignment $s : \mathcal{A}^{\mathcal{V}} \longrightarrow \mathcal{A}$, such that $\mathcal{R}(A_i^{\mathcal{V}}) \cap \bigcup_{j=1}^{n_i} \mathcal{R}(a_{ij}) \neq \emptyset$, where $s(A_i^{\mathcal{V}}) = \{a_{ij} | 1 \leq j \leq n_i\} \in \mathcal{A}$.

Thus, $S_{\mathcal{F}} = \prod_{i=1}^{n} A_i$ is called the *state space induced by* $\mathcal{F}$.

Be aware that Definition 4.9 is of course a simplification in many respects: (i) The epistemic situation S is not incorporated explicitly; instead we assume that it has an implicit impact on the choice of $\mathcal{V}, \mathcal{A}$ and s. (ii) $\mathcal{V}, \mathcal{A}^{\mathcal{V}}$ and $\mathcal{A}$ are assumed to fit together in a plausible and economic way, i.e. they are as 'small and simple' as possible for $\langle \mathcal{O}, S\rangle$. (iii) $\mathcal{O}$ is assumed to have objects that are homogenuous enough for being reasonably modeled with $\mathcal{F} = \langle \mathcal{V}, \mathcal{A}, s\rangle$. Probably, some more restrictions hold for the simple proposal as given in the above definition which, however, seems to be both a suitable as well as a traditional starting point.

Let d be an elementary datum; we set

$$\mathrm{pr}_O(d) = \begin{cases} \{o\} & \text{iff} d = \langle l, o, v\rangle \in I^L_{V_n}; \\ \bigcup_{j=1}^m \mathrm{pr}_O(i_j) & \text{iff} d \equiv i_1 \text{ OR } \dots \text{ OR } i_m, m \geq 2, \end{cases}$$

and

$$\mathrm{pr}_L(d) = \begin{cases} \{l\} & \text{iff} d = \langle l, o, v\rangle \in I^L_{V_n}; \\ \bigcup_{j=1}^m \mathrm{pr}_L(i_j) & \text{iff} d \equiv i_1 \text{ OR } \dots \text{ OR } i_m, m \geq 2. \end{cases}$$

Definition 4.10. (a) An *$\mathcal{F}$-description* of an object $o \in \mathcal{O}$ is given by a datum $\hat{d} = \{d_1, \dots, d_k\}$ such that

(1) $o \in \mathrm{pr}_O(d_i)$, for all $i, 1 \leq i \leq k$;

(2) $\prod_{i=1}^k \mathrm{pr}_L(d_i) \subset A_{\hat{d}} := A_{i_1} \times \dots \times A_{i_k}$, for a suitable subsequence $(i_1, \dots, i_k)$ of $(1, \dots, n)$.

(b) $\hat{d}$ is called COMPLETE iff $A_{\hat{d}} = S_{\mathcal{F}}$, and INCOMPLETE otherwise, i.e. if we lack information in one or more of the attribute dimensions $A_i^{\mathcal{V}}$.

Up to now we have presented formal definitions for the concepts of IMPRECISION and INCOMPLETENESS, but we still lack a counterpart for INEXACTNESS. As we will shortly see, the latter differs from the former two in that it is not of a descriptive but of a purely normative nature and presupposes some definite knowledge about the attributes of the objects under consideration: In order to ascribe the property of being INEXACT, one has to know at least the expected or the 'true' value of the measured attribute (they need not be identical!) at the time of measurement, and eventually in addition to that what is the usually achieved or what is, in principle, the achievable specificity of (the data symbolizing) the measured value. One can easily imagine from this that INEXACT is also a highly context sensitive concept.

In the following let l_0 symbolize the true value and l the measured value. $A^{\mathcal{V}}_{(0)} \in \mathcal{A}^{\mathcal{V}}$ is the concept such that both attribute values l and l_0 pertain to. Formally we have (at least)

(i) $\mathcal{R}(A^{\mathcal{V}}_{(0)}) \cap \bigcup_{j=1}^{n_{(0)}} \mathcal{R}(a_{ij}) \neq \emptyset$, where $s(A^{\mathcal{V}}_{(0)}) = \{a_{ij} | 1 \leq j \leq n_{(0)}\} \in \mathcal{V}$.

(ii) $l_0 \in s(A^{\mathcal{V}}_{(0)})$.

Furthermore, $|. \bowtie .|$ symbolizes some suitably chosen – qualitative or quantitative – semantical distance measure on L. Explained in a totally informal way, this serves to discriminate INEXACT from simply wrong measurement results. This topic, however, is not part of our considerations.

Definition 4.11. An infon $i = \langle l, o, v\rangle$ is called INEXACT with respect to $\mathcal{F} = \langle \mathcal{V}, \mathcal{A}, s\rangle$ if one of the following holds:

(1) In case i is CRISP, the true value of $A^{\mathcal{V}}_{(0)}$ is l_0 and $l \in s(A^{\mathcal{V}}_{(0)})$: if $l \neq l_0$

and $|l \bowtie l_0| \leq \epsilon$.

(2) In case i is FUZZY, the true value of $A^{\nu}_{(0)}$ is l_0 with a possibility distribution $\pi_{(0)}$ as formal representation, and $l \in s(A^{\nu}_{(0)})$ with a possibility distribution π_l as formal representation: if $\pi_l \neq \pi_{(0)}$, $|\pi_l \bowtie \pi_{(0)}| \leq \epsilon$ and $\mathrm{supp}\pi_{(0)} \cap \mathrm{supp}\pi_l \neq \emptyset$.

Let the above, on the occasion of this paper, be a sufficiently detailed formalization of our intuitive idea of INEXACTNESS. Note that the main characteristic of INEXACT infons is to be 'distinct from, but near enough to the true value'. Do also note that case (2) of the above definition covers both situations illustrated in Fig. 3 and Fig. 4, respectively: i.e. $l \neq l_0$ as well as, loosely speaking, $l = l_0$ but $\mathrm{Sp}(\pi_l) < \mathrm{Sp}(\pi_{(0)})$.

The way we have defined INEXACTNESS clearly shows what should be obvious: being INEXACT has, in general, nothing to do with being FUZZY: Consider a fuzzy partition of an attribute dimension as commonly used in fuzzy control (with values around zero constituting a critical region): negative big (NB), negative medium (NM), negative small (NS), negative zero (NZ), zero (Z), positive zero (PZ), positive small (PS), positive medium (PM), positive big (PB). Assume the true value is NZ; then both NS and Z are plausible candidates for INEXACT infons, whereas the others would probably be classified as being simply wrong. Note that both NS and Z, though INEXACT, are also PRECISE and usually FUZZY within our terminology. Furthermore, (NZ OR Z) would be an example for an IMPRECISE elementary datum.

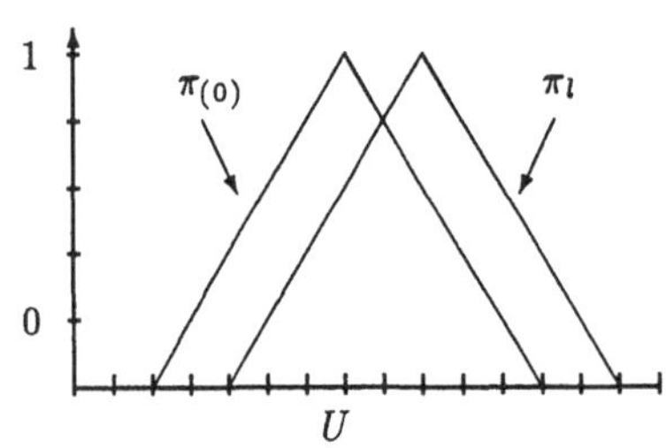

Fig. 3. INEXACT by distinct values

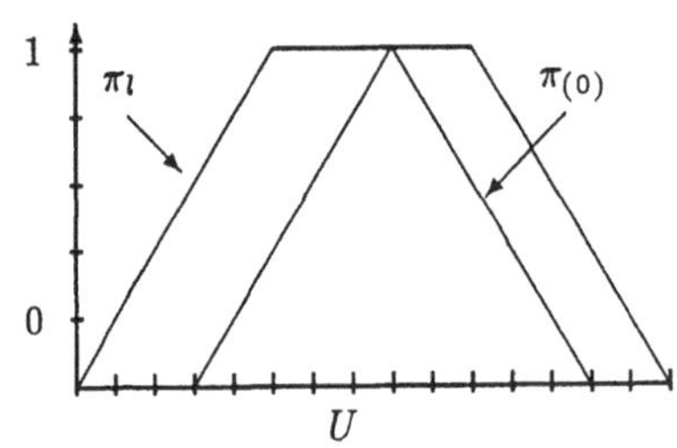

Fig. 4. INEXACT by distinct specificity

5. Conclusions

As has occasionally been discussed in other papers too (see e.g. [1, 12, 18, 19, 20, 29, 33, 41, 42]) from different points of view, what can be stated as a simple generalization from $\{0, 1\}$ to $[0, 1]$ or any other suitable poset on a formal level is, on the conceptual and semantical level, of a much more complex nature. This paper, hopefully, can not only be helpful to the newcomer as a first terminological orientation in and around the area of FST, but can also serve as a platform for further discussions by the experienced fuzzyist as well. Let me finally summarize what I hold to be the major contributions:

- An emphasis of the neglected area of the relationships between the conceptual foundations and the formal framework of FST. This is achieved by discussing the most relevant notions of FST and neighbouring fields in a semiformal way based on only a few simple concepts (introduced in Section 2.2), but founded on a natural and epistemic viewpoint (described in Sections 2.1 and 3).
- Explaining the emergence of the phenomenon of FUZZINESS, or VAGUENESS respectively, by viewing it, in a way, as a summary of the results of a multiplicity of classificational acts, these results being divergent due to both the intraindividual and interindividual variability over persons and times (Section 4.2).
- We recapitulate our proposal from [34] for a semi-formal definition of what may be understood by the terms *crisp, coarse,* and *fuzzy*, simultaneously clarifying to which epistemic objects these properties may be attributed (Section 4.3).
- In Section 4.5 a more complete discussion of the concept of POSSIBILITY with respect to both epistemic and semantic aspects is provided than is usually done.
- Section 4.6 is a short refresher on the concept of SPECIFICITY of a possibility distribution, which is subsequently used to propose a definitions of INEXACTNESS, Besides, a formal framework for embedding also the notions of IMPRECISION, INCOMPLETENESS and IMPERFECTNESS is introduced in Section 4.7.

References

1. J. Bezdek et al., Fuzziness vs. Probability – Again (! ?), *IEEE Trans. on Fuzzy Systems* **2** (1994) 1-42.
2. M. Black, Vagueness: An exercise in logical analysis, *Philos. Sci.* **4** (1937), 427-455. (Recently reprinted in *Int. J. General Systems* **17**(1990), 107-128.)
3. M. Bunge, *Scientific Research I: The Search for System* (Springer, Berlin/Heidelberg/New York, 1967).
4. M. Bunge, *Semantics I: Sense and Reference.* Vol. 1 of *Treatise on Basic Philosophy* (Reidel, Dordrecht/Boston, 1974).
5. M. Bunge, *Ontology I: The furniture of the world.* Vol. 3 of *Treatise on Basic Philosophy* (Reidel, Dordrecht/Boston, 1977).
6. D. Cruse, *Lexical Semantics*, (Cambridge Univ. Press, Cambridge, 1986).
7. K. Devlin, *Logic and information* (Cambridge University Press, 1991).
8. D. Dubois and H. Prade, *Fuzzy Sets and Systems: Theory and Applications* (Academic Press, New York, 1980).
9. D. Dubois and H. Prade, An introduction to possibilistic and fuzzy logics, in: P. Smets, E.H. Mamdani, D.Dubois and H. Prade, Eds., *Non-Standard Logics for Automated Reasoning* (Academic Press, New York, 1988) 288-326.

10. D. Dubois and H. Prade, *Possibility Theory. An Approach to Computerized Processing of Uncertainty* (Plenum Press, New York, 1988).
11. D. Dubois and H. Prade, Fuzzy sets in approximate reasoning, Part 2: Logical approaches, *Fuzzy Sets and Systems* **40** (1991) 203-244.
12. C. Elkan, The paradoxical success of fuzzy logic (with responses), *IEEE Expert* **9** (1994), 1-49.
13. W. Feller, *An Introduction to Probability Theory and its Applications* , Vol. 1 (J. Wiley, New York, 1970).
14. C. Freksa, Fuzzy Systems in AI: An Overview, in: R. Kruse, J. Gebhardt and R. Palm, Eds., *Fuzzy Systems in Computer Science* (Vieweg, Braunschweig/Wiesbaden, 1994) 155-169.
15. J. Goguen, The logic of inexact concepts, *Synthese* **19** (1968/69) 325-373.
16. I.R. Goodman and H.T. Nguyen, *Uncertainty Models for Knowledge-Based Systems* (North-Holland, Amsterdam, 1985).
17. J.W. Grzymala-Busse, *Managing Uncertainty in Expert Systems* (Kluwer, Boston/ Dordrecht/London, 1991).
18. E. Hisdal, Infinite valued logic based on two-valued logic and probability. Part 1.1. Difficulties with present-day fuzzy set theory and their resolution in the TEE model, *Int. J. Man. Machine Studies* **25** (1986) 89-111.
19. E. Hisdal, Infinite valued logic based on two-valued logic and probability. Part 1.2. Different sources of fuzziness, *Int. J. Man. Machine Studies* **25** (1986) 113-138.
20. E. Hisdal, Are grades of membership probabilities ?, *Fuzzy Sets and Systems* **25** (1988), 325-348.
21. A. Kandel, *Fuzzy mathematical techniques with applications*, (Addison-Wesley, Reading, Mass. 1986).
22. G. Klir and T.A. Folger, *Fuzzy sets, uncertainty, and information* (Prentice-Hall, Englewood Cliffs, 1988).
23. B. Kosko, Fuzziness vs. Probability, *Internat. J. General Systems* **17** (1990) 211-240.
24. R. Kruse, E. Schwecke and J. Heinsohn, *Uncertainty and Vagueness in Knowledge Based Systems* (Springer, Berlin-Heidelberg-New York, 1991).
25. F. Palmer, *Semantics* 2nd ed., (Cambridge Univ. Press, New York, 1981).
26. Z. Pawlak, *Rough Sets* (Kluwer, Boston/Dordrecht/London, 1991).
27. E. Sapir, Grading: A study in semantics, *Philosophy Sci.* **11** (1944) 93-116.
28. M. Smithson, *Ignorance and Uncertainty* (Springer, Berlin, 1989).
29. H. Toth, From fuzzy-set theory to fuzzy set-theory: some critical remarks on existing concepts, *Fuzzy Sets and Systems* **23** (1987) 219-237.
30. H. Toth, Categorial properties of *f*-set theory, *Fuzzy Sets and Systems* **33** (1989) 99-109.
31. H. Toth, On algebraic properties of *f*-spaces , *Fuzzy Sets and Systems* **36** (1990) 293-303.
32. H. Toth, Probabilities and fuzzy events: An operational approach, *Fuzzy Sets and Systems* **48** (1992) 113-127.
33. H. Toth, Reconstruction possibilities for fuzzy sets: Towards a new level of understanding ?, *Fuzzy Sets and Systems* **52** (1992) 283-304.
34. H. Toth, Fuzziness: From epistemic considerations to terminological clarification, *Int. J. of Uncertainty, Fuzziness and Knowledge-Based Systems* **5** (1997)

481-503.
35. G. Vollmer, *Evolutionäre Erkenntnistheorie* (Hirzel, Stuttgart, 1983).
36. G. Vollmer, On supposed circularities in an empirically oriented epistemology, in: G. Radnitzky and W.W. Bartley, III, Eds., *Evolutionary Epistemology, Theory of Rationality, and the Sociology of Knowledge* (Open Court, La Salle, Illinois, 1987), 163-200.
37. P. Wang, The Interpretation of Fuzziness, *IEEE Trans. on Systems, Man and Cybernetics – PartB: Cybernetics* **26** (1996) 321-326.
38. R.R. Yager, On the specificity of a possibiity distribution, *Fuzzy Sets and Systems* **50** (1992) 279-292.
39. L.A. Zadeh, Fuzzy sets as a basis for a theory of possibility, *Fuzzy Sets and Systems* **1** (1978) 3-28.
40. L.A. Zadeh/K.S. Kacprzyk, Eds., *Fuzzy Logic for the Management of Uncertainty* (John Wiley, New York, 1992)
41. M. Zeleny, On the (ir)relevancy of fuzzy set theory. *Human Systems Management* **4**(1984), 301-306.
42. M. Zeleny, Cognitive equilibrium: A knowledge-based theory of fuzziness and fuzzy sets. *Int. J. General Systems* **19** (1991) 359-384.

3

COMPUTING WITH WORDS AND INFORMATION GRANULARITY

Granular Computing: Fuzzy Logic and Rough Sets

T.Y. Lin

Department of Mathematics and Computer Science
San Jose State University
San Jose, California 95192-0103
and
Department of Electric Engineering and Computer Science
University of California
Berkeley, California 94720
E-mail:tylin@cs.sjsu.edu or tylin@cs.berkeley.edu

Abstract

The primary goal of granular computing is to elevate the lower level data processing to a high level knowledge processing. Such an elevation is achieved by granulating the data space into a concept space. Each granule represents certain primitive concept, and the granulation as a whole represents a knowledge. In this paper, such an intuitive idea is formalized into a mathematical theory: Zadeh's informal words are taken literally as a formal definition of granulation. Such a mathematical notion is a mild generalization of the "old" notion of crisp/fuzzy neighborhood systems of (pre-)topological spaces. A crisp/fuzzy neighborhood is a granule and is assigned a meaningful name to represent certain primitive concept or to summarize the information content. The set of all linear combinations of these names, called formal words, mathematically forms a vector space over real numbers. Each vector is intuitively an advanced concept represented by some "weighted averaged" of primitive concepts. In terms of these concepts, the universe can be represented by a formal word table; this is one form of Zadeh's veristic constraints. Such a representation is useful; fuzzy logic designs can be formulated as series of table transformations. So table processing techniques of rough set theory may be used to simplify these tables and their transformations. Therefore the complexity of large scaled fuzzy systems may be reduced; details will be reported in future papers.

1 Introduction

This paper continues our study of the notion of granular computing [9, 10]. Earlier the focus was on the single level granulation, namely, the granulation is a crisp/fuzzy binary neighborhood system which can also be defined by a crisp/fuzzy binary relation and vice versa. In the present paper, we generalize the idea to any fuzzy granulation. For convenience of readers, we re-iterate some "old" messages. The notion of information granulation can be traced back to [17]; it is an essential ingredient in fuzzy logic. For more recent idea we refer readers to Lofti Zadeh's latest article [19]. Let us quote a few words from [9].

"Granulation ... appears ... in different names, such as chunking, clustering, data compression, divide and conquer, information hiding, interval computations, and rough set theory, just to name a few." " the computing theory on information granulation has not been fully explored in its own right." "... in mathematics, the notion of partitions is well explored."

As Lotfi Zadeh pointed out information processing is fuzzy. For example, neck, head, and body have no precise and exact regions. In this paper we explore the formal structures of fuzzy granulation. The results are somewhat surprising: We find very nice single valued table representations for fuzzy coverings or more generally fuzzy neighborhood systems; while the crisp analogous can only be established for multi-valued tables. Such single valued representations turn out to be very useful; we use it formalize the fuzzy logic design. With such representations, we believe, we can use table processing technique of rough set theory to simplify the processing of linguistic/fuzzy rules of a large scaled fuzzy control systems; the study will be reported in future papers.

Acknowledgements: This research is partially supported by Electric Power Research Institute, Palo Alto, California, San Jose State University, NASA Grant NCC2-275, ONR Grant N00014-96-1-0556, LLNL Grant 442427-26449, ARO Grant DAAH04-961-0341, and BISC Program of UC Berkeley.

2 Formalizing Granulation

In this section, we literally take Zadeh's informal notion and paraphrase it into a formal definition of granulation.

Let us recall Lotfi Zadeh's informal definition and our paraphrasing from [9],

- *"information granulation involves partitioning a class of objects(points) into granules, with a granule being a clump of objects (points) which are drawn together by indistinguishability, similarity or functionality."*

Implicitly the phrase "drawn together" implies certain level of symmetry in the clumps. Namely, if P is drawn towards Q, then Q is also drawn towards P. Such a symmetry, we believe, is imposed by imprecise-ness of natural languages. To avoid that we will use the phrase "drawn toward the object P," so that it is clear the reverse may or may not be true. Further, we observe that there are no constraints on how many clumps an object may be associated. So the notion of fuzzy granulation can be rephrase as

- fuzzy information granulation is a collection of fuzzy granules, with a granule being a clump of objects which are drawn *towards an object.* In other words, each objects is associated a family of fuzzy clumps. In general, a fuzzy clump is more than a fuzzy set; it has certain "information structure." For this paper, we will consider the simplest case, namely, fuzzy clumps are fuzzy sets.

To avoid any pre-conception, let us examine the procedure closely

1. Take an object p, we form a fuzzy clump by certain semantics; let us name it $CLUMP_1(p)$. For example, let the universe be a set of balls. To each ball we associate the fuzzy set of all those balls that have brighter colors (in terms of degrees).
2. We shall make a few more clumps $CLUMP_j(p)$, $j = 1, 2, \ldots$ for the same object p, but based on different semantics. For example, the fuzzy clump fuzzily consists of all the ball that are much heavier than p.
3. Repeat the same procedures for next object q until we exhaust all objects. In other words, to each object p, we associate a collection (empty, finite, or infinite) of fuzzy clumps $CLUMP_j(p), j = 1, 2, \ldots$.
4. We assume that an object and the associated fuzzy clumps may or may not be in the same universe; objects are in V and fuzzy clumps are fuzzy subsets of U.
5. In general fuzzy clumps are fuzzy sets equipped with some "information structure." For simplicity, in this paper, we will assume fuzzy clumps are fuzzy sets.

Do such "arbitrary" clump systems constitute some formal mathematics? Surprisingly in crisp world, they are! They are the neighborhood system of (pre-)topological spaced. This subject, including its fuzzification, is the topic of Section 3.

Intuitively a fuzzy clump at p is a group of data clinging to a common object p. Each data in the fuzzy clump has some common characteristics that are "related" or "near to" the object p. These common characteristics may formally form an "information structure" on the fuzzy clump. The underlying fuzzy set of these clump is a neighborhood of a (pre-)topological space. Of course original notion of neighborhoods is in the crisp world, now we need its extension to the fuzzy world.

- Fuzzy neighborhood systems: To each object $p \in V$, we associate a family of fuzzy subsets of U, $\{G_{p,h(p)}\}$, where $h(p)$ is an index. Each,

  $$G_{p,h(p)} : U \longrightarrow [0,\ 1]$$

  is the membership function of a fuzzy *fundamental* neighborhood of p; it is called an *elementary* neighborhood if the neighborhood system is binary; see Section 3.1. The association,

  $$p \longrightarrow \{G_{p,h(p)}\},\ \forall\, p,$$

is called a fuzzy neighborhood system [7].

If we impose some additional "information structure" on $G_{p,h(p)}$, then it is called a fuzzy clump, and the association a fuzzy clump system. To simplify notations, we use $G_{p,h(p)}$ instead of $CLUMP_{h(p)}(p)$. In this paper, we are not considering information structure, so we may use clump or neighborhood interchangeably. Each fuzzy neighborhood (or fuzzy clump) contains certain information. So we will give each fuzzy neighborhood (or fuzzy clump) a meaningful name to summarize its information content; the name is a primitive concept. After such a naming, the processing of fuzzy neighborhoods (or fuzzy clumps) becomes processing of meaningful names (words). In other words, some computing of data is elevated into computing with words(names).

The best example to illustrate such an elevation may be the "word processing" of relational databases and rough set theory. Relations and information tables are closely related [8]. They are, however, different in their respective "word processing." In rough set theory, all word processing is referred back to partitions, while in databases, they are processed by the semantics of words. For examples, attribute dependencies (called functional dependency) are checked via partitions in rough set theory, while in databases, the dependencies are determined by the semantics of the attribute names. Briefly data processing in relational databases is "word processing" of rough set theory.

A simple granular computing may consist of, at least,

1. granulation: forming a neighborhood system or clump system
2. representation: naming the granules to represent the knowledge by words
3. word computing.

3 Fuzzy Granular Structures

3.1 Single Level Granulation and Fuzzy Binary Relations

Let U and V be crisp sets, and [0, 1] the unit interval; V is called an object space, U a data space. All results are good for both crisp and fuzzy worlds. We collect few definitions and simple facts in the following:

1. Single level granulation: For each object $p \in V$, we associate a fuzzy subset, called a *fuzzy elementary neighborhood* at p

   $$B_p : U \longrightarrow [0,1]$$

   The map $B : p \longrightarrow B_p$ or the collection $\{B_p\}$ is referred to as a *fuzzy binary neighborhood system.*
2. Fuzzy binary relations: B is a fuzzy binary relation on $U \times V$ if

   $$B : V \times U \longrightarrow [0,1]$$

is a membership function.

3. A fuzzy binary relation induces a single level granulation and vice versa. This is clear from the equation $B_p(u) = B(p, u)$.
4. Fuzzy classifier: Given a fuzzy binary neighborhood system, we consider the following composition map, a knowledge representation of the universe:

$$p \longrightarrow B_p \longrightarrow NAME(B_p).$$

The set of complete inverse images

$$(B \bullet NAME)^{-1}(c) = B^{-1}(NAME^{-1}(c)), \forall\, c \in C.$$

forms a partition on V. This new partition classifies the objects in V. So a fuzzy binary relation is a fuzzy classifier. This is a potentially useful fact [21, 9]; we will come to the details in future reports.

5. Perhaps, we should note a counter intuitive point: Even if $q \in N_p$, the elementary neighborhood of q may or may not be the N_p. Intuitively N_p is a neighborhood of q, if q is one of the "centers" of N_p.
6. If the binary relation B is an equivalence relation, then elementary set $[p]$ (equivalence class) is the elementary binary neighborhood of p. In this case $[p]$ is the elementary neighborhood of q, $\forall\, q \in [p]$, i.e., every point is a "center" of $[p]$.
7. A subset X is a definable neighborhood/set, if X is a union of elementary neighborhoods/sets; equivalence classes are called elementary sets by rough setters. If a definable neighborhood/set X contains an elementary neighborhood/set B_p, it is a definable neighborhood of p.

3.2 Multilevel Granulation and Fuzzy Neighborhood Systems

The goal of this section is to establish the necessary terminology and some fundamental properties of neighborhood systems.

1. Let $G(U)$ be either the family, $FUZ(U)$, of all fuzzy sets or the family, $POW(U)$, of all crispy subsets, and $POW(G(U))$ is the family of all subset of $G(U)$. Next, let us consider the mapping

$$GS : V \longrightarrow POW(G(U));\ p \longrightarrow \{G_{p,h(p)}\}.$$

that is, $GS(p) = \{G_{p,h(p)} \mid h(p) \textit{ is an index}\}$. GS will be called *a neighborhood system of V on U*, or *a clump system of V on U*. We should point out here that that the term neighborhood or clump covers both crisp and fuzzy cases.

2. We will identify the single level granulation as a special form of multilevel granulation. The map

$$G : V \longrightarrow G(U);\ p \longrightarrow G_p,$$

is identified with the map

$$GS: p \longrightarrow \{G_p\},$$

where $\{G_p\}$ is a singleton for every p.

3. So an empty set (when $G_p = \emptyset$) will be identified with empty family (when $\{G_{p,h(p)} \mid h(p) \text{ is an index}\} = \emptyset$).

In single level granulation, a binary relation corresponds uniquely to a binary neighborhood system and vice versa; see Section 3.1. In multilevel granulation, the correspondence is many to one.

Proposition A set of fuzzy binary relations induces uniquely a fuzzy neighborhood system. The converse is not unique.

By the obvious correspondence between binary relations and binary neighborhood systems, the set of binary relations

$$B^i : V \times U \longrightarrow [0,1], \quad i = 1, 2, \ldots$$

induces a neighborhood system:

$$p \longrightarrow \{B^i_p(\bullet) = B^i(p, \bullet) : U \to [0,1] \mid i = 1, 2, \ldots\}.$$

The converse is somewhat chaotic. Assume we are given a neighborhood system:

$$p \to \{B^i_p : U \to [0,1] \mid i = 1, 2, \ldots\}.$$

Then, for any selection h of a neighborhood $B_p^{h(p)}$ at each point p, it defines a binary relation(h maps each point p to an index):

$$B^h : V \times U \longrightarrow [0,1] \text{ defined by } B^h(p,u) = B_p^{h(p)}$$

So there are as many binary relations as the number of all possible mappings that map each point to an index. We should, however, note that all selections define the same "lower and upper" approximations. So even though algebraically the selection is not unique, topologically the selection is unique. Hence we would like to use the geometric notion, neighborhood systems, instead of the algebraic notion, binary relations.

The notion of neighborhood systems is a mild generalization of the very old notion of neighborhood systems of (pre-)topological spaces [15]. It is an "instance" of a topological space [5]. Such a notion is so natural, it has been independently used by many authors, for examples, in databases [1, 2, 3, 4, 5, 6, 13], and in logic [3, 11, 12]. If neighborhoods are taken from topological spaces, then they are a very common notion: For example, the nearest neighborhood at each point (used in pattern recognition) defines a binary neighborhood system (binary relation) in the feature space. If we restrict binary relations to equivalence relations, then neighborhoods are elementary sets in rough set theory. The lower and upper approximations of rough set theory are the interior and closure of (pre-)topological spaces: Let X be a subset of U.

$$I[X] = \{p \mid \exists\, N(p) \subseteq X\} = \text{the interior of } X,$$

that is, $I[X]$ is the largest open set contained in X,

$$C[X] = \{p \mid \forall\, N(p)\ X \cap N(p) \neq \emptyset\} = \text{the closure of } X$$

that is, $C[X]$ is the smallest closed set contains X.

3.3 Granular Structures

We shall slightly modify the formal definition of granular structure [10].

A *fuzzy granular structure* consists of 4-tuple

$$(V, U, B, C)$$

where V is called the object space, U is the data space (V and U could be the same set), B is a fuzzy clump or fuzzy neighborhood system, and C is the concept space which consists of all the names of the fundamental fuzzy clump or fuzzy neighborhoods of B; recall that a fuzzy neighborhood with information structure is called a fuzzy clump. B is a multilevel granulation; see Section 3.2.

If B is a fuzzy/crisp binary relation (see Section 3.1), then the 4-tuple (V, U, B, C) is a single level granulation, called a *fuzzy binary granular structure*, in which at most one fuzzy fundamental neighborhood is assigned to each object. In this case, the fundamental neighborhood is called the elementary neighborhood.

4 Knowledge Representations Using Words

In rough set theory, the universe is partitioned by equivalence relation. So we consider the following composition map:

$$p \longrightarrow [p] \longrightarrow NAME([p]).$$

We map each object p to the equivalence class $[p]$ (called elementary set), then to its name, $NAME([p])$. If the universe has several partitions in U $(= V)$ and hence several such maps, then the Cartesian product of such maps form the information table, a representation of the universe using words, of rough set theory [9, 10].

In this section, we apply the idea to general neighborhood systems. To each object, there are several neighborhoods, so we get a multi-valued representation. However, in fuzzy world, we can form a "weighted average representation," hence the multi-valued table becomes a single-valued table. We will illustrate the idea by a simple example. First, we observe that each fuzzy set is uniquely determined by its membership function, so we will *identify the membership function with its fuzzy set*(see [20], pp. 12). Let

$$U = \{0.0, 0.1, 0.2, 0.3, 0.4, 0.5, 0.6, 0.7, 0.8, 0.9\}$$

be the universe. Let $A_i, i = 1, 2, 3$ *and* 4, be fuzzy sets (membership functions) defined in Table 1. A (i+1)-th column represents the grades of a fuzzy set A_i. These fuzzy sets form a fuzzy covering on U, hence, a fuzzy neighborhood system; see Section 4.2.

Objects	$A_1(p)$	$A_2(p)$	$A_3(p)$	$A_4(p)$
0.0	1.0	0.0	0.0	0.0
0.1	0.67	0.33	0.0	0.0
0.2	0.33	0.67	0.0	0.0
0.3	0.0	1.0	0.0	0.0
0.4	0.0	0.67	0.33	0.0
0.5	0.0	0.33	0.67	0.0
0.6	0.0	0.0	1.0	0.0
0.7	0.0	0.0	0.67	0.33
0.8	0.0	0.0	0.33	0.67
0.9	0.0	0.0	0.0	1.0

Table 1. Grades of Membership Functions of the Fuzzy Covering

4.1 A Rough Set Representation

Let us modify the rough set example in [10]. Assume U has two partitions. We name the elementary sets by Light, Average, and Heavy in one partition, and the other by *Group_1*, *Group_2*, *Group_3*, and *Group_4*; see Table 2 and 3. In terms of these names, we have an information table to represents the universe; see Table 4. This is how rough set theory represents equivalence relations into an information table. In next section, we generalize the idea to fuzzy coverings.

4.2 Multi-valued Representations

It is clear that $COV = \{A_1, A_2, A_3, A_4\}$ forms a fuzzy covering of U. Each A_i is called a cover and COV the covering. COV is, in fact, a fuzzy neigh-

Elementary Concept	Elementary Set
Light	0.0, 0.1, 0.2, 0.3
Average	0.4, 0.5
Heavy	0.6, 0.7, 0.8, 0.9

Table 2. Class-Partition and Their Names

Elementary Concept	Elementary Set
Group_1	0.0, 0.1, 0.2
Group_2	0.3
Group_3	0.4, 0.5
Group_4	0.6, 0.7, 0.8, 0.9

Table 3. Group-Partition and Their Names

borhood system. Each cover is a fuzzy neighborhood of each object (point) in the cover; every point is a "center;" see Section 3.1. A_i is a fundamental fuzzy neighborhood of p, if p has a positive grade. Let $FNS(U)$ denote the fuzzy neighborhood system defined by the covering COV. Let $FNS(p)$ be the fuzzy neighborhood system at point p; it is the collection of covers that cover p. The fundamental fuzzy neighborhoods (or fuzzy covers) $FNS(p)$, $p = 0.0, 0.1, ...$, are listed below:

$FNS(0.0) = \{A_1\}$, $FNS(0.1) = \{A_1, A_2\}$, $FNS(0.2) = \{A_1, A_2\}$
$FNS(0.3) = \{A_2\}$, $FNS(0.4) = \{A_2, A_3\}$, $FNS(0.5) = \{A_2, A_3\}$
$FNS(0.6) = \{A_3\}$, $FNS(0.7) = \{A_3, A_4\}$, $FNS(0.8) = \{A_3, A_4\}$
$FNS(0.9) = \{A_4\}$

Each object fuzzily belongs to several fundamental neighborhoods(covers). Foillowing the idea in Section 4.1, we can associate each object to the names of those neighborhoods which fuzzily contains the object(have positive grades). These names are called fundamental concepts. The association

$$p \longrightarrow \{NAME(A_i(p)) \mid A_i(p) > 0\}$$

a multi-valued table representation of the universe (single attribute).

In Table 5, the first column is the object, the second column is the collection of fundamental neighborhoods (covers) that contain the object, and the third column is the fundamental concepts.

Balls	Classes	Group
0.0	Light	*Group_1*
0.1	Light	*Group_1*
0.2	Light	*Group_1*
0.3	Light	*Group_2*
0.4	Average	*Group_3*
0.5	Average	*Group_3*
0.6	Heavy	*Group_4*
0.7	Heavy	*Group_4*
0.8	Heavy	*Group_4*
0.9	Heavy	*Group_4*

Table 4. A Representation by Classes and Groups

Objects	Fundamental Neighborhood	Fundamental Concepts NAME(Fundamental Neighborhood)
0.0	$\{A_1\}$	$Low = NAME(A_1)$
0.1	$\{A_1\}$	$Low = NAME(A_1)$ $Median\_Low = NAME(A_2)$
0.2	$\{A_1, A_2\}$	$Low = NAME(A_1)$ $Median\_Low = NAME(A_2)$
0.3	$\{A_2\}$	$Median\_Low = NAME(A_2)$
0.4	$\{A_2, A_3\}$	$Median\_Low = NAME(A_2)$ $Median\_high = NAME(A_3)$
0.5	$\{A_2, A_3\}$	$Median\_Low = NAME(A_2)$ $Median\_high = NAME(A_3)$
0.6	$\{A_3\}$	$Median\_high = NAME(A_3)$
0.7	$\{A_3, A_4\}$	$Median\_high = NAME(A_3)$ $High = NAME(A_4)$
0.8	$\{A_3, A_4\}$	$Median\_high = NAME(A_3)$ $High = NAME(A_4)$
0.9	$\{A_4\}$	$High = NAME(A_4)$

Table 5. Multi-valued Representations

4.3 Vector Valued Representations - Formal Word Tables

Using the scheme of Section 4.1, we get a multi-valued representation for a multilevel granulation (a general neighborhood system, such as a covering). However, if the granulation is fuzzy, we can use "weighted average" to make it single valued. Let us consider the following formal expressions:

$$r_1 * Low + r_2 * Median\_Low + r_3 * Median\_high + r_4 * High$$

where r_1, r_2, r_3, r_4 are real numbers. Mathematically the collection of all such expressions forms an abstract vector space over real numbers; see Appendix. We will denote the vector space by $FW(U)$. Each vector is called a formal word.

Let $w_i(p)$ represents the grade of A_i at p, i.e., $A_i(p) = w_i(p)$. We will call $w_i(p)$ the weight of p in A_i. Based on the weight $w_i(p)$ and multi-valued table representation (Table 5, 1), we will form a FW-representation, a formal word representation, as follows:

$$W : V \longrightarrow FW;\ p \longrightarrow W(p)$$

defined by

$$W(p) = \sum_i (w_i(p) * NAME(A_i(p))$$

In terms of the current example, we have

$$W(p) =$$
$$w_1(p) * Low + w_2(p) * Median\_Low + w_3(p) * Median\_high + w_4(p) * High$$

The expression is called *the formal word representation of p*; it is Zadeh's veristic constraint [19].

Table 6 consists of all such formal expressions; it is a vector-valued representation of the universe. Each expression represents a certain weighted sum of fundamental concepts; it succinctly expresses the overlapping semantics of fundamental neighborhoods.

Objects	Weighted Fundamental concepts (veristic constraints)
0.0	$W(0.0) = w_1(0.0) * Low$
0.1	$W(0.1) = (w_1(0.1) * Low) + (w_2(0.1) * Median\_Low)$
0.2	$W(0.2) = (w_1(0.2) * Low) + (w_2(0.2) * Median\_Low)$
0.3	$W(0.3) = (w_3(0.3) * Median\_high)$
0.4	$W(0.4) = (w_1(p) * Low) + (w_2(p) * Median\_Low) +$ $(w_3(p) * Median\_high) + (w_4(p) * High)$
0.5	$W(0.5) = (w_1(p) * Low) + (w_2(p) * Median\_Low) +$ $(w_3(p) * Median\_high) + (w_4(p) * High)$
0.6	$W(0.6) = (w_1(p) * Low) + (w_2(p) * Median\_Low) +$ $(w_3(p) * Median\_high) + (w_4(p) * High)$
0.7	$W(0.7) = (w_1(p) * Low) + (w_2(p) * Median\_Low) +$ $(w_3(p) * Median\_high) + (w_4(p) * High)$
0.8	$W(0.8) = (w_1(p) * Low) + (w_2(p) * Median\_Low) +$ $(w_3(p) * Median\_high) + (w_4(p) * High)$
0.9	$W(0.9) = (w_1(p) * Low) + (w_2(p) * Median\_Low) +$ $(w_3(p) * Median\_high) + (w_4(p) * High)$

Table 6. A Single Attribute Representation using Formal Words

5 Fuzzy Logic

In this section, we reformulate the "standard" fuzzy logic by formal word tables, so we may use table processing techniques of rough set theory to reduce the size and complexity of the fuzzy logic; the reduction details will be in forth coming papers.

5.1 The Decision Table and Set of Linguistic Rules

We will use simple example to illustrate the idea. Suppose we are given the following four linguistic rules:

1. If s_x is s_Low and t_x is t_Low, then y is $Weak$;
2. If s_x is s_Med_Low and t_x is t_Low, then y is $Moderate$;
3. If s_x is s_Med_high and t_x is t_Med_high, then y is $Strong$;
4. If s_x is s_High and t_x is t_Med_high, then y is $Extreme$;

We have two sets of input variables, s_x and t_x; say s stand for speed, and t stand for temperature. The output variable is y; the output linguistic constants represent the level of control actions. The four linguistic rules is expressible by a decision table (Table 7); it is clear one can reduce the size and complexity of this table by its reduct [14]. However, we need to consider whither such a reduction will yield an equivalent fuzzy logic control system; this will be reported in future work.

s_x	t_x	y
s_Low	t_Low	$Weak$
s_Med_low	t_Low	$Moderate$
s_Med_high	t_Med_high	$Strong$
s_High	t_Med_high	$Extreme$

Table 7. Decision Table of the Linguistic Rules

5.2 Linear Inferences

There are many inferences in fuzzy logic. We will use the simplest one. Let us call it linear influence, a variant of Sugeno and Tarkagi inference [20]. First we need to consider formal word representations for s-input, t-input and output variables; see Section 4.3. For simplicity, we will assume we have scaled s-input and t-input properly, so that the membership functions that represent, say s_LOW, and t_Low, are the same. In other words, as numerical functions

$$A\_s_i(p) = A\_t_i(p),\ i\ =\ 1,\ 2,\ \ldots$$

The grades of these membership functions are defined by A_i; see Table 1. So we will use the same $w_i(p)$ to denote the numerical value for both grades, $A\_s_i(p) = A\_t_i(p)$. ¿From Table 7, we know the output formal words are of the following form of expressions:

$$r_1 * Weak + r_2 * Moderate + r_3 * Strong + r_4 * Extreme$$

Such a collection is called the output space and denoted by $FW(Y)$.

Linear inference uses Table 7 to transforms the formal expressions of s- and t- input spaces :

$W(p) = (W_s(p), W_t(p))$

$W_s(p) =$
$w_1(p) * s\_Low + w_2(p) * s\_Med\_low + w_3(p) * s\_Med\_high + w_4(p) * s\_High$

$W_t(p) = w_1(p) * t\_Low + w_2(p) * t\_Low + w_3(p) * t\_Med\_high + w_4(p) *$
t_Med_high

into the following formal expression of output space.

$$V(p) = v_1(p) * Weak + v_2(p) * Moderate + v_3(p) * Strong + v_4(p) * Extreme$$

where $v_i(p) = a * A\_s_i(p) + b * A\_t_i(p)$; in this expression a and b are given constants defined by the linear influence.

For this particular example, we will choose a=1 and b=0; in other words, $v_i(p) = w_i(p)$. In Table 6, the first column is the objects(points), the second and the third column are their representations in s- and t-input spaces respectively, the fourth column is the result of linear inference.

5.3 Defuzzification

For simplicity, we choose a constant membership function for each output. For example, $Weak = 0.2$, $Moderate = 0.4$, $Strong = 0.6$, and $Extreme = 0.8$, so the defuzzified value is

$$y\ =\ V(p)\ =\ (v_1(p) * 0.2)\ +\ (v_2(p) * 0.4)\ +\ (v_3(p) * 0.6)\ +\ (v_4(p) * 0.8)$$

$y = V(p)$ is the desirable control function. Recall that in this particular example, we have choose a=1 and b=0, or equivalently, $v_i(p) = w_i(p)$. The control function is expressed in Table 9; the first column is the object p, the second column is the output expression, and the third column is the output values y for the input p. The first column and the last column define the control function.

Objects	Formal expression in s-input space $W_s(p)$	Formal expression in t-input space $W_t(p)$	Formal expression in output space $V(p)$
0.0	$W_s(0.0) =$ $w_1(0.0) * s\_Low$	$W_t(0.0) =$ $w_1(0.0) * t\_Low$	$V0.0) =$ $v_1(0.0) * Weak$
0.1	$W_s(0.1) =$ $(w_1(0.1) * s\_Low)+$ $(w_2(0.1) * s\_Med\_low)$	$W_t(0.1) =$ $(w_1(0.1) * t\_Low)+$ $(w_2(0.1) * t\_Low)$	$V(0.1) =$ $(v_1(0.1) * Weak)$ $+(v_2(0.1) * Moderate)$
0.2	$W_s(0.2) =$ $(w_1(0.2) * s\_Low)$ $+(w_2(0.2) * s\_Med\_low)$	$W_t(0.2) =$ $(w_1(0.2) * t\_Low)$ $+(w_2(0.2) * t_{Low})$	$V(0.2) =$ $(v_1(0.2) * Weak)$ $+(v_2(0.2) * Moderate)$
0.3	$W_s(0.3) =$ $(w_3(0.3) * s\_Med\_high)$	$W_t(0.3) =$ $(w_3(0.3) * t\_Med\_high)$	$V(0.3) =$ $(v_3(0.3) * Strong)$
0.4	$W_s(0.4) =$ $(w_1(p) * s\_Low)$ $+(w_2(p) * s\_Med\_Low)+$ $(w_3(p) * s\_Med\_high)$ $(w_4(p) * s\_High)$	$W_s(0.4) =$ $(w_1(p) * t\_Low)$ $+(w_2(p) * t\_Low)+$ $(w_3(p) * t\_Med\_high)+$ $(w_4(p) * t\_Med\_high)$	$V(0.4) =$ $(v_1(p) * Weak)+$ $(v_2(p)Moderate)+$ $(v_3(p) * Strong)+$ $(v_4(p) * Extreme)$
0.5	$W_s(0.5) =$ $(w_1(p) * s\_Low)$ $+(w_2(p) * s\_Med\_low)+$ $(w_3(p) * s\_Med\_high)+$ $(w_4(p) * s\_High)$	$W_t(0.5) =$ $(w_1(p) * t\_Low)$ $+(w_2(p) * t\_Med\_Low)+$ $(w_3(p) * t\_Med\_high)+$ $(w_4(p) * t\_Med\_high)$	$V(0.5) =$ $(v_1(p) * Weak)+$ $(v_2(p) * Moderate)+$ $(v_3(p) * Strong)+$ $(v_4(p) * Extreme)$
0.6	$W_s(0.6) =$ $(w_1(p) * s\_Low)+$ $(w_2(p) * s\_Med\_low)+$ $(w_3(p) * s\_Med\_high)+$ $(w_4(p) * s\_High)$	$W_t(0.6) =$ $(w_1(p) * t\_Low)+$ $(w_2(p) * t\_Low)+$ $(w_3(p) * t\_Med\_high)+$ $(w_4(p) * t\_Med\_high)$	$V(0.6)+$ $(v_1(p) * Weak)+$ $(v_2(p) * Moderate)+$ $(v_3(p) * Strong)+$ $(v_4(p) * Extreme)$
0.7	$W_s(0.7) =$ $(w_1(p) * s\_Low)+$ $(w_2(p) * s\_Med\_low)+$ $(w_3(p) * s\_Med\_high)+$ $(w_4(p) * s\_High)$	$W_t(0.7) =$ $(w_1(p) * t\_Low)+$ $(w_2(p) * t\_Low)+$ $(w_3(p) * t\_Med\_high)+$ $(w_4(p) * t\_Med\_high)$	$V(0.7) =$ $(v_1(p) * Weak)+$ $(v_2(p) * Moderate)+$ $(v_3(p) * Strong)+$ $(v_4(p) * Extreme)$
0.8	$W_s(0.8) =$ $(w_1(p) * s\_Low)+$ $(w_2(p) * s\_Med\_low)+$ $(w_3(p) * s\_Med\_high)+$ $(w_4(p) * s\_High)$	$W_t(0.8) =$ $(w_1(p) * t\_Low)+$ $(w_2(p) * t\_Low)+$ $(w_3(p) * t\_Med\_high)+$ $(w_4(p) * t\_Med\_high)$	$V(0.8) =$ $(v_1(p) * Weak)+$ $(v_2(p) * Moderate)+$ $(v_3(p) * Strong)+$ $(v_4(p) * Extreme)$
0.9	$W_s(0.9) =$ $(w_1(p) * s\_Low)+$ $(w_2(p) * s\_Med\_low)+$ $(w_3(p) * s\_Med\_high)+$ $(w_4(p) * s\_High)$	$W_t(0.9) =$ $(w_1(p) * t\_Low)+$ $(w_2(p) * t\_Low)+$ $(w_3(p) * t\_Med\_high)+$ $(w_4(p) * t\_Med\_high)$	$V(0.9) =$ $(v_1(p) * Weak)+$ $(v_2(p) * Moderate)+$ $(v_3(p) * Strong)+$ $(v_4(p) * Extreme)$

Table 8. A Linear Inference

Objects	Formal expression in output space	Inference value
0.0	$V0.0) = v_1(0.0) * Weak$	1.0*0.2
0.1	$V(0.1) = (v_1(0.1) * Weak)$ $+(v_2(0.1) * Moderate)$	0.67*0.2+0.33*0.4
0.2	$V(0.2) = (v_1(0.2) * Weak)$ $+(v_2(0.2) * Moderate)$	0.33*0.2+0.67*0.4
0.3	$V(0.3) = (v_3(0.3) * Strong)$	1.0*0.4
0.4	$V(0.4) = (v_1(p) * Weak)+$ $(v_2(p) * Moderate) + (v_3(p) * Strong)+$ $(v_4(p) * Extreme)$	0.67*0.4+0.33*0.6
0.5	$V(0.5) = (v_1(p) * Weak)+$ $(v_2(p) * Moderate) + (v_3(p) * Strong)+$ $(v_4(p) * Extreme)$	0.33*0.4+0.67*0.6
0.6	$V(0.6) = (v_1(p) * Weak)+$ $(v_2(p) * Moderate) + (v_3(p) * Strong)+$ $(v_4(p) * Extreme)$	1.0*0.6
0.7	$V(0.7) = (v_1(p) * Weak)+$ $(v_2(p) * Moderate) + v_3(p) * Strong)+$ $(v_4(p) * Extreme)$	0.67*0.6+0.33*0.8
0.8	$V(0.8) = (v_1(p) * Weak)+$ $(v_2(p) * Moderate) + (v_3(p) * 0.6)+$ $(v_4(p) * 0.8)$	0.33*0.6+0.67*0.8
0.9	$V(0.9) = (v_1(p) * Weak)+$ $(v_2(p) * Moderate) + (v_3(p) * Strong)+$ $(v_4(p) * Extreme)$	1.0*1.0

Table 9. A Defuzzification

5.4 Reducts of Rough Set Theory

The notion of reducts is in the heart of rough set theory [14]. It allows us to reduce a table to a smaller one; even to the smallest one, if we are willing to tackle an NP-hard problem [16]. Using formal word tables, fuzzy logic can be expressed succinctly as a series of table transformations; Table 7, Table 8, and Table 9. To each table, we can apply the notion of reduct to simplify it. Such simplification will be most useful in large scaled fuzzy systems. Case studies will be reported in fourth coming works.

6 Conclusions

In this conclusion, we will reflect on our over all approach. In this series of papers, we literally take Zadeh's intuitive description of clumps as a formal mathematical notion of granulation. It turns out that the notion of clumps is not new, it is essentially a mild generalization of the notion of neighborhood systems in (pre-)topological spaces [15, 4, 5, 9]. If clumps are equivalence classes, then the granulation is a partition. Next important question is: How do we process such a granulation? The answer seems lie in the computing with words [18]. We explore a very simple case, namely, computing with names of granules (neighborhoods or clumps). In stead of study the objects (or data), we study the names of these granules (called fundamental concepts). By giving a meaningful name to each granule, we represent each object by the names of granules that contain the object. In crisp words, such an association is multi-valued. In fuzzy words, we can use grades to combine these names linearly (a weighted average) and form a formal word; this gives a single-valued representation, namely, a formal word table; see Section 4.3. Using Zadeh's terminology, such formal word representations are veristic constraints [19]. A formal word table is a generalization of information table. So by employing table processing techniques of rough set methodology to formal word tables, we can reduce the set of linguistic rules to a smaller set; we will report case studies in future papers.

Our study seems saying that granular computing is a reasonable notion. At this point, its essential ingredients are (1) a granular structure (data space is granulated by fuzzy neighborhood systems), (2) a word-representation (using names to summarize the information contents of granules), and (3) word processing (table processing of rough set methodology).

7 Appendix - Vector Spaces of Formal Words

Let R be the set of real number and G_i a granule (a fuzzy neighborhood). Let FW be the set of all linear combination of names. i.e.,

$$FW = \{x_1 * NAME(G_1) + x_2 * NAME(G_2) + \ldots + x_m * NAME(G_m) : \\ x_j \in R, j = 1, 2, \ldots m\}$$

It is easy to verify that the collection forms an abstract vector space over the real number R:

Addition:

$$r_1 * NAME(G_1) + r_2 * NAME(G_2) + \ldots + r_m * NAME(G_m)$$

$+$

$$s_1 * NAME(G_1) + s_2 * NAME(G_2) + \ldots + s_m * NAME(G_m)$$

$=$

$$t_1 * NAME(G_1) + t_2 * NAME(G_2) + \ldots + t_m * NAME(G_m)$$

where$t_j = r_j + s_j, j = 1, 2, \ldots, m$.

Scalar product:

$$r * (s_1 * NAME(G_1) + s_2 * NAME(G_2) + \ldots + s_m * NAME(G_m))$$

$$=$$

$$r * s_1 * NAME(G_1) + r * s_2 * NAME(G_2) + \ldots + r * s_m * NAME(G_m)$$

It is clear *FW* form a vector space and is called an abstract vector space of formal words or simply formal words

References

1. S. Bairamian, *Goal Search in Relational Databases*, Thesis, California State niversity at Northridge, 1989.
2. W. Chu, Neighborhood and associative query answering, *Journal of Intelligent Information Systems*, 1(1992), 355-382.
3. K. Engesser, Some connections between topological and Modal Logic, *Mathematical Logic Quarterly*, 41(1995), 49-64.
4. T. Y. Lin, Neighborhood Systems and Relational Database. In: *Proceedings of 1988 ACM Sixteen Annual Computer Science Conference*, February 23-25, 1988, 725
5. T. Y. Lin, Neighborhood Systems and Approximation in Database and Knowledge Base Systems. In; *Proceedings of the Fourth International Symposium on Methodologies of Intelligent Systems*, Poster Session, October 12- 15, 1989, pp. 75-86.
6. T. Y. Lin, Topological and Fuzzy Rough Sets. In: *Decision Support by Experience - Application of the Rough Sets Theory*, R. Slowinski (ed.), Kluwer Academic Publishers, 1992, 287-304.
7. T. Y. Lin, Neighborhood Systems-A Qualitative Theory for Fuzzy and Rough Sets. In: *Advances in Machine Intelligence and Soft Computing*, Volume IV. Paul Wang (ed), 1997, 132-155. Also in *Proceedings of Second Annual Joint Conference on Information Science*, Wrightsville Beach, North Carolina, Sept. 28-Oct. 1, 1995, 257-260.
8. T. Y. Lin, An Overview of Rough Set Theory from the Point of View of Relational Databases, *Bulletin of International Rough Set Society*, Vol I, No1, March ,1993, 30-34.
9. T. Y. Lin, Granular Computing of Binary relations I: Data Mining and Neighborhood Systems. In:*Rough Sets and Knowledge Discovery* Polkowski and Skowron (eds), Springer-Verlag, 1998 (to appear).
10. T. Y. Lin, Granular Computing of Binary relations II: Rough Set Representation and Belief Functions. In:*Rough Sets and Knowledge Discovery* Polkowski and Skowron (eds), Springer-Verlag, 1998 (to appear).
11. T. Y. Lin, Q. Liu and Y. Y. Yao A Logic System for Approximate Reasoning via Rough Sets and Topology. In: *Methodologies of Intelligent Systems, Lecture notes in Artificial Intelligence*, Z. Ras, and M. Zemankova (eds), 1994, 65-74.

12. T. Y. Lin and Q. Liu First Order Rough Logic I: Approximate Reasoning via Rough Sets, *Fundamenta Informaticae.* Volume 27, Number 2,3, 1996, 137-153
13. B. Michael and T. Y. Lin Neighborhoods, Rough sets, and Query Relaxation. In: *Rough Sets and Data Mining: Analysis of Imprecise Data* (Lin and Cercone eds), Kluwer Academic Publisher, 1997, 229 -238. (Final version of paper presented in CSC'95 Workshop on Rough Sets and Database Mining , March 2, 1995
14. Z. Pawlak, *Rough sets. Theoretical Aspects of Reasoning about Data*, Kluwer Academic Publishers, 1991
15. W. Sierpenski and C. Krieger, *General Topology*, University of Torranto Press,1956.
16. A. Skowron and C. Rauszer, The discernibility matrices and functions in information systems. In : *Decision Support by Experience - Application of the Rough Sets Theory* R. Slowinski (ed.), Kluwer Academic Publishers, 1992, 331-362.
17. Lotfi Zadeh, Fuzzy Sets and Information Granularity. In: *Advances in Fuzzy Sets and Information Granularity* M. Gupta, R. Ragade, R. Yager (eds), North-Holland, Amsterdam, 1979, 3-18
18. Lotfi Zadeh, Fuzzy logic = computing with words, *IEEE Transaction on Fuzzy Systems* 4(1996), 103-111.
19. Lotfi Zadeh, Towards a theory of fuzzy information granulation and its centrality in human reasoning and fuzzy logic, *Fuzzy Sets and Systems* 90(1997), 111-127.
20. Zimmermann, H., *Fuzzy Set Theory –and its Applications*, 2nd ed., Kluwer Academic Publisher, 1991.
21. M. Viveros, *Extraction of Knowledge from databases*, California State University, thesis, 1989.

Towards an Adaptive Calculus of Granules

Lech Polkowski[3,1] *and Andrzej Skowron*[2,3]

[1] Institute of Mathematics, Warsaw University of Technology
Pl. Politechniki 1, 00-665 Warsaw, Poland
e-mail: polk@mimuw.edu.pl
[2] Institute of Mathematics, Warsaw University
Banacha 2, 02-097 Warsaw, Poland
e-mail: skowron@mimuw.edu.pl
[3] Polish–Japanese Institute of Computer Techniques
Koszykowa 86
02-008 Warsaw, Poland

Abstract. We propose a notion of a granule of knowledge as an atom in the mereological algebra generated locally in time from the actual state of the triple ⟨ input_interface, logic_of_ knowledge, output_interface ⟩. We illustrate our approach with examples of rough set as well as fuzzy set approach. A calculus of granules over distributed systems is presented which generalizes both rough and fuzzy approaches.

1 Introduction

The metafor "granule of knowledge" has appeared recently [61, 62], in the research literature devoted to the problems of approximate reasoning and soft computing and the importance of granulation of knowledge for these problems has been stressed therein. The meaning of the phrase "knowledge granulation" is related to the phenomenon that reasoning under incomplete or uncertain knowledge is carried out by means of knowledge about objects decomposed into indivisible units i.e. "granules".

The changing character of our knowledge due to influx of a new information causes currently existing granules to divide or merge into new granules. Dynamic processes of granule of knowledge formation are very important for problems related to synthesis of approximate solutions to specifications formulated in an uncertain or incomplete way e.g. in the problems of synthesis of adaptive decision algorithms.

The problem of synthesis of adaptive decision algorithms has been studied within paradigms of soft computing such as fuzzy sets, evolutionary computation, neural networks as well as rough sets (see e.g. [12], [17, 3, 15], [59], [40]). The problem can be presented as the problem of synthesis of approximate descriptions of concepts from the available dynamically changing knowledge e.g. by means of decision systems in rough set approach, respectively, knowledge based fuzzy controllers in fuzzy set approach.

In this introduction, we first present the rough set approach [26], then we outline the fuzzy set approach. Next we introduce elements of rough mereological theory by means of which we will define in the sequel the notion of a granule of knowledge in a unified way.

We begin with rough set approach. In this approach, knowledge is represented by means of either an *information system* or a *decision system*; the former is formalized as a pair $\mathcal{A} = (U, A)$ where U is a (current) set of objects, A is a (current) set of (conditional) attributes and the latter is a triple $\mathcal{A} = (U, A, d)$ where d is a *decision attribute*, d does not belong to A. Each attribute $a \in A \cup \{d\}$ is formalized as a mapping on the set U i.e. $a : U \to V_a$ where V_a is the set of values of a. The decision system $\mathcal{A}$ can be perceived as a translation table between the language of conditional attributes accessible to the experimenter and the oracle language of the decision attribute belonging to an expert.

The basic assumption about objects described by means of the decision or information system $\mathcal{A}$ is the following: objects with identical descriptions behave identically and are not discernible to the user of the system. This assumption leads on a formal level to quotient structures on which one operates to generate decision rules.We first introduce a formal way of object denotation: for each object $u \in U$, and a set $B \subseteq A$ of attributes, the *information set (vector)* $Inf_B(u)$ of the object u over the set B of attributes is defined via the following

(Inf) $Inf_B(u) = \{(c, c(u)) : c \in B\}$.

We introduce the set INF_B of information sets over B as follows:

(INF) $INF_B = \{Inf_B(u) : u \in U\}$.

The set $PARTINF_B$ is defined as the set $\{Inf_C(u) : C \subseteq B, u \in U\}$.

The indiscernibility of objects can be expressed now as the identity of their information sets:

(IND) $IND_A(u, w)$ *is TRUE* iff $Inf_A(u) = Inf_A(w)$ for any pair u, w of objects in U.

The indiscernibility relation IND_A is clearly an equivalence relation and it partitions the set U into classes $[u]_{IND_A}$ of its objects; we let $U/IND_A = \{[u]_A : u \in U\}$. It is obvious that we could have a relativized version as well: given a set $B \subseteq A$ of attributes, we could define a restriction $\mathcal{A}_B$ of the decision (information) system $\mathcal{A}$ over the set B by letting $\mathcal{A}_B = (U, B, d)$ (respectively, $\mathcal{A}_B = (U, B)$). The restriction operator induces a projection operator on the space INF_A of information sets: $proj(A, B) : INF_A \to INF_B = \{Inf_B(u) : u \in U\}$ acting coordinate-wise i.e. $proj(A, B)(Inf_A(u)) = Inf_B(u)$. $proj(A, B)$ induces a projection operator $\mathtt{proj}(A, B)$ from the equivalence space U/IND_A onto the equivalence space U/IND_B.

We have therefore a variety of indiscernibility spaces $\{U/IND_B : B \subseteq A\}$. The boolean algebra generated over the set of atoms U/IND_B by means of set–theoretical operations of union, intersection and complement is said to be the *B-algebra $CG(B)$ of conditional pre–granules.*

We have an alternative logical language in which we can formalize the notion of a pre–granule; for a set of attributes $B \subseteq A$, we recall [48] the definition of B-logic L_B: elementary formulae of L_B are of the form (a, v) where $a \in B$ and $v \in V_a$. Formulae of L_B are built from elementary formulae by means of logical connectives $\vee, \wedge$; thus, each formula in DNF is represented as $\vee_{j \in J} \wedge_{i \in I_j} (a_i, v_i)$. The formulae of L_B are interpreted in the set of objects U : the denotation $[(a, v)]$ of an elementary formula (a, v) is the set of objects satisfying the equation $a(x) = v$ i.e. $[(a, v)] = \{u \in U : a(u) = v\}$ and this is extended by structural induction viz. $[\alpha \vee \beta] = [\alpha] \cup [\beta]$, $[\alpha \wedge \beta] = [\alpha] \cap [\beta]$ for $\alpha, \beta \in L_B$.

Clearly, given a pre-granule $G \in CG(B)$, there exists a formula (unique in DNF) α_G of L_B such that $[\alpha_G] = G$; we may regard α_G as the logical representation of the pre - granule G.

In the same way as above we can treat the decision attribute d as well as the whole set $A' = A \cup \{d\}$ of attributes which would lead to algebras $CG(A'), CG(d), CG(B)$ where $B \subset A'$ and logics, respectively, $L_{A'}, L_d, L_B$.

An atom of the boolean algebra $CG(B)$ will be called a $B-$ *elementary pre - granule;* clearly, for any atom G of $CG(B)$ there exists a unique DNF α_G of the form $\wedge_{a \in B} (a, v_a)$.

For given non - empty sets $B, C \subseteq A$, a pair (G_B, G_C) where $G_B \in CG(B)$ and $G_C \in CG(C)$ is called a $(B, C)-$ *granule of knowledge.* There exist formulae $\alpha_{G_B} \in L_B$, $\alpha_{G_C} \in L_C$ such that $[\alpha_{G_B}] = G_B$ and $[\alpha_{G_C}] = G_C$. In the case when G_B, G_C are atoms of, respectively $CG(B), CG(C)$, the pair (G_B, G_C) is called a *(B, C) - elementary granule of knowledge.*

With any $(B, C)-$ *granule of knowledge* (G_B, G_C) we may associate a rule $\alpha_{G_B} \Longrightarrow \alpha_{G_C}$.

The set of elementary granules generates the algebra of granules in the standard way.

The notion of a granule corresponds to the *logic of knowledge content* of the decision system; however, there is more to the notion of a granule of knowledge: we have to take into account the restrictions which on the choice of *good granules* are imposed by the structure and demands of two interfaces: *input - interface* which controls the input objects (signals) and *output - interface* which controls the output objects (actions, signals). We put here two kinds of restrictions on granules of knowledge; it is enough to consider elementary granules only.

Consider a granule (G, G'); let $G = [\alpha_G]$, $G' = [\alpha_{G'}]$. There are two characteristics of the granule (G, G') important in applications to decision algorithms (see e.g. [37], [56]) viz. the characteristic whose values measure what part of $[G']$ is in $[G]$ (the *'strength'* of the rule $\alpha_G \Longrightarrow \alpha_{G'}$) and the characteristic whose values measure what part of $[G]$ is in $[G']$ (the *'strength of the support'* for the rule $\alpha_G \Longrightarrow \alpha_{G'}$).

A "standard" choice of an appropriate measure is based on frequency count; the formal rendering is the *standard rough inclusion* function (see e.g. [37] and compare [23]) defined for two sets $X, Y \subseteq U$ by the formula $\mu(X, Y) = \frac{card(X \cap Y)}{card(X)}$ when X is non - empty and $\mu(X, Y) = 1$, otherwise.

To select sufficiently strong rules, we would set thresholds: tr, tr'. We define, by analogy with machine learning or data mining techniques (see e.g. , [14], [16], [56]), two characteristics:

(ρ) $\rho(G, G') = \mu([G], [G'])$;

(η) $\eta(G, G') = \mu([G'], [G])$

for any granule (G, G'), and we call an (η, ρ, tr, tr') – *elementary granule of knowledge* any elementary granule (G, G') such that

(i) $\rho(G, G') \geq tr$ and

(ii) $\eta(G, G') \geq tr'$.

Let us observe that given sets $B, C \subseteq A, u \in Inf_B$ and $v \in Inf_C$, we may define the value $Gr(B, C, \eta, \rho, tr, tr', u, v)$ to be $TRUE$ in the case when the pair (G, G') where $[G] = [u]_{IND_B}$ and $[G'] = [v]_{IND_C}$ is an (η, ρ, tr, tr')– elementary granule of knowledge. In this way we define the relation Gr which we call the *granulation relation* induced by the triple ⟨*input_interface, logic of knowledge, output_interface*⟩ related to the information system $\mathcal{A}$.

The functions η and ρ are particular realizations of the interface between input object information and inner knowledge of the system. One could consider another measures of inexactness in communication among distinct sources of information. A proper choice of a measure according to a context is an important factor in approximate reasoning; we would not discuss this aspect here.

Consider now a fuzzy decision system presented as a *knowledge based fuzzy controller* [24]. It consists of a set A *of attributes* split into the two sets: the set A' of *input attributes* and the set A'' of *output attributes.* Each of the attributes is expressed as a linguistic label e.g. *temperature, pressure* with values labelled by linguistics denominators e.g. *big, medium, small.* For each attribute a and its value v, the denotation of (a, v) is given as a pair $(D_a, \mu_{v,a})$ where the set D_a is the *domain* of a and $\mu_{v,a} : D_a \to [0, 1]$ is the fuzzy membership function giving the meaning of v.

Elementary decision rules are given in the form of implications:

$$\textbf{if } a \text{ is } v \textbf{ then } b \text{ is } w$$

where $a \in A'$, $b \in A''$.

The meaning of this rule is a fuzzy relation $R(a, v; b, w)$ on the set $D_a \times D_b$. Let $R = \{R(a, ., b, .))\}_{a \in A', b \in A''}$

The *input - interface* is defined by the choice of the fuzzification strategy F [24] and the *output - interface* is defined by the choice of the defuzzification strategy D [24]; given F, R, D, we obtain, as in the rough case, a relation $Gr(F, R, D, u, v)$ where u is the vector of input values, v is the vector of output values, and $Gr(F, R, D, u, v)$ is $TRUE$ in the case when v is among the values resulting from first applying F to the input u, next fuzzy logic using R have to be applied to the results of F and finally applying D to the result of the previous stage. The relation $Gr(F, R, D, u, v)$ is the granularity relation in the fuzzy case.

Clearly, from now on, we may in the fuzzy case consider $Gr(F, R, D, u, v)$ only and we could represent this relation as a decision system in the rough set sense. Hence from now on we will consider only the case of information systems in the rough sense regardless of the way in which they were originally represented i.e. as rough decision systems or fuzzy decision systems.

Now we will introduce a scheme of rough mereology which formalizes our intuitions about the notion of a part to a degree and permits us to discuss this notion with greater flexibility.

2 Rough mereology

The scheme of rough mereology stems from the mereological theory) ($\mu\varepsilon\rho\omega\sigma$ (*greek*) = *a part*) proposed first by St. Leśniewski [21] and later developed in few alternative systems e.g. Tarski [54, 55], Leonard and Goodman [20], Clark [6, 7]. We adhere here to the original system of Leśniewski which we extend to the system of rough mereology in which we could formalize the intuitive notion of being a part to a certain degree. For the completeness of exposition, we first include a brief account of the Leśniewski mereological system.

2.1 Mereology of St. Leśniewski

The first modern mathematical system based on the notion of the relation of *being a (proper) part* was proposed by Stanislaw Leśniewski [21]. We recall here the basic notions of the mereological system of Leśniewski; in the next section the mereological system of Leśniewski will be extended to the system of approximate mereological calculus called *approximate (rough) mereology.*

We consider a finite non - empty set U of objects. A binary relation *part* on the set U will be called the *relation of being a (proper) part* in the case when the following conditions are fulfilled

(P1) (*irreflexivity*) for any $x \in U$, it is not true that x *part* x;

(P2) (*transitivity*) for any triple $x, y, z \in U$, **if** x *part* y and y *part* z, **then** x *part* z.

It follows obviously from (P1) and (P2) that the following property holds

(P3) for any pair $x, y \in U$, **if** x *part* y **then** it is not true that y *part* x.

In the case when x *part* y we say that the object x is a (*proper*) *part* of the object y. The notion of being (possibly) an improper part is rendered by the notion of an ingredient [21]; for objects $x, y \in U$, we say that the object x is a *part-ingredient* of the object y when either x *part* y or $x = y$. We denote the relation of being a *part*-ingredient by the symbol *ingr*(*part*); hence we have

(I1) for $x, y \in U$, x *ingr*(*part*) y iff x *part* y or $x = y$.

It follows immediately from the definition that the relation of being an ingredient has the following properties:

(I2) (*reflexivity*) for any $x \in U$, we have x *ingr*(*part*) x;

(I3) (*weak antisymmetry*) for any pair $x, y \in U$, **if** x *ingr*(*part*) y and y *ingr*(*part*) x **then** $x = y$;

(I4) (*transitivity*) for any triple $x, y, z \in U$, **if** x *ingr*(*part*) y and y *ingr*(*part*) z **then** x *ingr*(*part*) z;

i.e. the relation *ingr*(*part*) is a partial order on the universe U.

We will call any pair (U,*part*), where U is a finite set and *part* a binary relation on the set U, which satisfies the conditions (P1) and (P2), a *pre-model of mereology.*

We now recall the notions of a set of objects and of a class of objects [21]. For a given pre-model (U,*part*) of mereology and a property m which can be attributed to objects in U, we say that an object x is an object m (x *object* m, for short) when the object x has the property m. The property m is said to be *non-void* when there exists an object $x \in U$ such that x *object* m. Consider a non-void property m of objects in a set U where $(U, part)$ is a pre-model of mereology.

An object $x \in U$ is said to be a *set of objects with the property* m when the following condition is fulfilled:

(SETm) for any $y \in U$, **if** y *ingr(part)* x **then** there exist $z, t \in U$ with the properties: z *ingr(part)* y, z *ingr(part)* t, t *ingr(part)* x and t *object* m.

We will use the symbol x *set* m to denote the fact that an object x is a set of objects with the property m.

Assume that x *set* m; if, in addition, the object x satisfies the condition

(CLm) for any $y \in U$, if y *object* m then y *ingr(part)* x

then we say that the object x is *a class of objects with the property* m and we denote this fact by the symbol x *class* m.

We will say that a pair $(U, part)$ is a model of mereology when the pair $(U, part)$ is a pre - model of mereology and the condition

(EUC) for any non-void property m of objects in the set U, there exists a unique object x such that x *class* m holds.

The following Proposition 2.1 recapitulates the fundamental metamathematical properties of mereology of Leśniewski; observe that in mereology there is no hierarchy of objects contrary to the Cantorian naïve set theory. We denote for an object $x \in U$ by the symbol $ingr(x)$ the property of being an ingredient of x (non-void in virtue of (I2)) and for a property m, we denote by the symbol $s(m)$ the property of being a set of objects with the property m.

Proposition 2.1

(i) x *class*$(s(m))$ if and only if x *class* m;

(ii) x *class*$(ingr(x))$;

(iii) x *set*$(s(m))$ if and only if x *set* m.

We recall the notions of an element and of a subset in mereology of Leśniewski. For $x, y \in U$, we will say that

(SUB) the object x is a *subset* of the object y (x *sub* y, for short) when for any $z \in U$,

$$\textbf{if } \ z \ ingr(part) \ x \ \textbf{then} \ z \ ingr(part) \ y$$

and

(EL) the object x is an *element* of the object y (x *el* y, for short) when there exists a non-void property m such that x *object* m and y *class* m.

The following proposition is a direct consequence of (I4) and Proposition 2.1(ii).

Proposition 2.2

The following conditions are equivalent for any pair x, y of objects

(i) x *ingr* y;

(ii) x *sub* y;

(iii) x *el* y.

2.2 Approximate (rough) mereology

An approximate mereological calculus called *approximate (rough) mereology* has been proposed (see e.g. [30, 35, 37, 38, 45]), as a formal treatment of the hierarchy of relations of being a part to a degree. We begin with an exposition of rough mereological calculus in the form of a rough mereological logic L_{rm}. This abstract exposition will be in the next section made more comprehensible by interpreting this logic in a model; it will then turn out that the main object of approximate mereology is a rough inclusion μ^M which denotes in the model M the functional symbol μ and for any pair x, y of objects in the model returns the degree $\mu^M(x, y)$ to which x is a part of y.

We begin with the syntactical part of the logic L_{rm}.

2.3 Syntax of L_{rm}

We have the following basic ingredients of the syntactic part of the logic L_{rm}.

Variables: $x, x_1, x_2, \ldots,\ y, y_1, y_2, \ldots,\ z, z_1, z_2, \ldots$ of type *set_element* and r, $r_1, r_2, \ldots,\ s, s_1, s_2, \ldots$ of type *lattice_element*;

Constants: ω of type *lattice_element*;

Predicate symbols, function symbols: $\leq$ of type (*lattice_element, lattice_element*) and μ of type (*set_element, set_element, lattice_element*);

Auxiliary symbols: propositional connectives: $\vee$, $\wedge$, $\Longrightarrow$, $\neg$, quantifier symbols: $\forall$, $\exists$ and commas, parentheses.

Formulae: atomic formulae are of the form $\mu(x, y, r)$, $s \leq r$ and formulae are built from atomic formulae as in the predicate calculus.

Thus, approximate mereological calculus is formalized within predicate calculus. The following formulae are axioms of L_{rm}. We assume axioms of the classical predicate calculus and axioms of partial order and equality for $\leq$ and $=$.

AXIOMS:

(A1) $\forall x.\mu(x, x, \omega)$;
this axiom does express the fact that any object x is an improper part (ingredient) of itself.

(A2) $\forall x.\forall y.\{\mu(x, y, \omega) \Longrightarrow \forall s.\forall r.\forall z.[\mu(z, x, s) \wedge \mu(z, y, r) \Longrightarrow (s \leq r)]\}$;
this axiom does express the (left) monotonicity of the degree of being a part.

(A3) $\forall x.\forall y.\{\mu(x, y, \omega) \wedge \mu(y, x, \omega) \Longrightarrow$

$$\forall s.\forall r.\forall z.[\mu(x, z, s) \wedge \mu(y, z, r) \Longrightarrow (s \leq r)]\}$$

this axiom does express the (right) monotonicity in a weak form.

(A4) $\exists x.\forall y.\mu(x, y, \omega)$;
this axiom asures the existence of a null object which is a part of every object. In mereology of Leśniewski such objects are excluded unless the theory is trivial [54, 55].

(A5) $\forall x.\forall y.\{[\forall z.[[\exists u.\neg(\mu(z,u,\omega)) \wedge \mu(z,x,\omega)] \Longrightarrow$

$$\exists t.(\exists w.(\neg\mu(t,w,\omega)) \wedge \mu(t,z,\omega) \wedge \mu(t,y,\omega)] \Longrightarrow \mu(x,y,\omega)\};$$

this axiom is an inference rule: x is an ingredient of y in case the antecedent of the rule holds.

The axiom schemata $(\text{A6})_n$ for n = 2,3,... where

$\textbf{(A6)}_n$

$$\forall x_1,...,x_n \exists y\, [\alpha_n(x_1,...,x_n,y) \wedge \beta_n(x_1,...,x_n,y) \wedge \gamma_n(x_1,...,x_n,y)]$$

where

$$\begin{aligned} \alpha_n(x_1,...,x_n,y) &: \forall z.\{[\exists t.(\neg\mu(z,t,\omega)) \wedge \mu(z,y,\omega)] \Longrightarrow \\ &\quad \exists x_i.\exists w.[(\exists u.(\neg\mu(w,u,\omega))) \wedge \mu(w,z,\omega) \wedge \mu(w,x_i,\omega)]\} \\ \beta_n(x_1,...,x_n,y) &: \mu(x_1,y,\omega) \wedge ... \wedge \mu(x_n,y,\omega) \\ \gamma_n(x_1,...,x_n,y) &: \forall z.\{[\alpha_n(x_1,...,x_n,z) \wedge \beta_n(x_1,...,x_n,z)] \\ &\quad \Longrightarrow \mu(y,z,\omega)\}. \end{aligned}$$

The condition $\alpha_n(x_1,...,x_n,y)$ states that y is a set of objects over $x_1, ... \, x_n$; the conjunction

$$\alpha_n(x_1,...,x_n,y) \wedge \beta_n(x_1,...,x_n,y) \wedge \gamma_n(x_1,...,x_n,y))$$

does express the fact that y is the class of objects $x_1,...,x_n$.

2.4 Semantics of L_{rm}

We will call an *interpretation* of L_{rm} a triple $M = (U^M, L^M, F^M)$ where U^M is a finite set, L^M is a (complete) lattice with the lattice partial order $\leq^M$and with the greatest element Ω^M and F^M is a mapping which assigns to constants and predicate symbols of L_{rm} their denotations in M in the following manner: $F^M(\omega) = \Omega^M$, $F^M(\leq) = \leq^M$and $F^M(\mu) = \mu^M \subseteq U^M \times U^M \times L^M$, where the relation $\mu^M \subseteq U^M \times U^M \times L^M$ is a function i.e. $\mu^M : U^M \times U^M \longrightarrow L^M$. We will call μ^M an *approximate (rough) inclusion.*

An M-value assignment g is a mapping which assigns to any variable x of L_{rm} of type *set - element* the element $g(x) \in U^M$ and to any variable r of L_{rm} of type *lattice - element* the element $g(r) \in L^M$. For an M-value assignment g, a variable x of L_{rm} of type *set - element* and an element $u \in U^M$, we denote by the symbol $g[u/x]$ the M-value assignment defined by the conditions: $g[u/x](v) = g(v)$ in case $v \neq x$ and $g[u/x](x) = u$; the same convention will define $g[p/r]$ in case of a variable r of type *lattice - element* and $p \in L^M$.

For a formula α of L_{rm}, we denote by the symbol $[\alpha]^{M,g}$ the meaning of the formula α in the interpretation M relative to an M-value assignment g by the following conditions

(M1) $[\mu(x,y,r)]^{M,g} = true$ iff $\mu^M(g(x),g(y),g(r)) = true$

(M2) $[s \leq r]^{M,g} = true$ iff $g(s) \leq^M g(r)$;

(M3) $[\alpha \vee \beta]^{M,g} = true$ iff $[\alpha]^{M,g} = true$ or $[\beta]^{M,g} = true$;

(M4) $[\neg\alpha]^{M,g} = true$ iff $[\alpha]^{M,g} = false$;
(M5) $[\exists x.\alpha]^{M,g} = true$ iff there exists $u \in U^M$ such that $[\alpha]^{M,g[u/x]} = true$;
(M6) $[\exists r.\alpha]^{M,g} = true$ iff there exists $p \in L^M$ such that $[\alpha]^{M,g[p/r]} = true$.

We will also write $\mu(x,y) = r$ and $\mu(x,y) \geq r$ instead of $\mu(x,y,r)$ and $\exists p(\mu(x,y,p) \wedge p \geq r)$, respectively. Hence, $\mu(x,y) \geq r$ has the intended meaning that "the object x is a part of the object y to degree at least r".

A formula α is *true in an interpretation* M iff α is M,g - true (i.e. $[\alpha]^{M,g} = true$) for any M-value assignment g.

An interpretation M is a *model* of L_{rm} iff all axioms (A1)-(A6) are true in M.

We will give the basic deduction rules for L_{rm}; recall that a deduction rule in the form

$$\frac{\alpha, \beta, ...}{\psi}$$

is said to be *valid in a model* M iff for any M-value assignment g if the premises $\alpha, \beta, ...$ are M,g - true then the conclusion ψ is M,g-true. The deduction rule is *valid* when it is valid in any model M of L_{rm}. We have the following valid deduction rules

$$\text{(D1)}\ \frac{\mu(x,y,\omega), \mu(y,z,\omega)}{\mu(x,z,\omega)}$$

$$\text{(D2)}\ \frac{\mu(y,z,\omega), \neg\mu(y,x,\omega)}{\neg\mu(z,x,\omega)};$$

$$\text{(D3)}\ \frac{\mu(x,y,\omega), \neg\mu(z,y,\omega)}{\neg\mu(z,x,\omega)}.$$

We show the consistency of the axiom system (A1)-(A6) by revealing a class of models of L_{rm}. We denote by *Stand* the class consisting of pairs (U, μ_U) where U is a finite set and μ_U is the standard rough inclusion on the power set $\exp(U)$. For a pair $M = (U, \mu_U)$, we let L^M to be the unit interval $[0,1]$, $\leq^M$ to be the natural linear ordering on $[0,1]$, $\mu^M = \mu_U$ and $U^M = \exp(U)$. Then we denote by *Stand_Mod* the class of triples $M^* = (U^M, L^M, F^M)$ where $M = (U, \mu_U)$ and $F^M(\omega) = 1$, $F^M(\leq) = \leq^M$ and $F^M(\mu) = \mu_U$. We have the following statement whose proof is straightforward.

Proposition 2.3
Any $M^* = (U^M, L^M, F^M)$ in *Stand_Mod* is a model of L_{rm}.

2.5 Rough inclusions

In this section we are concerned with the structure in models of L_{rm} induced by rough inclusions. We show that in any model of L_{rm} we have a canonical model of mereology of Leśniewski introduced by means of the rough inclusion of this model. One can then apply the Tarski idea of fusion of sets [55] in order to define in a model of L_{rm} the structure of a (complete) Boolean algebra which contains isomorphically the quasi-boolean structure (without the least (zero) element) corresponding to the model of mereology of Leśniewski. The rough inclusion satisfies with respect to boolean operations of join and meet the same formal conditions which the rough membership function satisfies with respect to the set-theoretic operations of union and intersection.

We study relations of rough inclusions with many-valued logic and fuzzy logic; in particular, we show that when the rough inclusion is regarded as a fuzzy membership function then any fuzzy containment induced by a residual implication [12] is again a rough inclusion and, moreover, the hierarchy of objects set by the induced model of mereology of Leśniewski is invariant under these fuzzy containment operators.

We are concerned also with the problem of consistency of deduction rules of the form

$$(D_f)\frac{\mu(x,y,r),\mu(y,z,s)}{\mu(x,z,f(r,s))}$$

where f is a functional symbol of type (*lattice_element*, *lattice_element*, *lattice_element*).

The consistency of (A1)-(A6)+(D_f) can be obtained by revealing a class of models in which the deduction rule (D_f) is valid under an appropriate interpretation of f.

Given a model M of L_{rm}, $M = (U^M, L^M, F^M)$, we will call the function $\mu^M : U^M \times U^M \longrightarrow L^M$ the M-rough inclusion. We define a relation $congr(\mu^M)$ on the set U^M by letting for $u, w \in U^M$: u $congr(\mu^M)$ w iff $\mu^M(u,w) = \Omega^M = \mu^M(w,u)$. The following proposition, whose proof follows immediately by (A2) and (A3) and is therefore omitted, establishes the basic properties of the relation $congr(\mu^M)$ and demonstrates it to be a μ^M-congruence.

Proposition 2.4

The relation $congr(\mu^M)$ is a μ - congruence on U i.e.
(i) if u $congr(\mu^M)$ w then $\mu^M(u,v) = \mu^M(w,v)$ for any $u, v, w \in U$;
(ii) if u $congr(\mu^M)$ w then $\mu^M(v,u) = \mu^M(v,w)$ for any $u, v, w \in U$;
(iii) $congr(\mu^M)$ is an equivalence relation on U.

It follows from this proposition that the rough inclusion can be factored throughout the relation $congr(\mu^M)$ i.e. we define the quotient set

$$U^M_\mu = U^M / congr(\mu^M)$$

and the quotient function

$$\mu^M_\sim : U^M_\mu \times U^M_\mu \longrightarrow L^M$$

by letting $\mu^M_\mu(u_\mu, w_\mu) = \mu^M(u,w)$; clearly, the pair $(U^M_\mu, \mu^M_\sim)$ introduces a model $M_\sim$ of L_{rm}. In the sequel we will always work with a fixed reduced model $M_\sim$. We denote by the symbol n_μ the *null object* i.e. the object existing in virtue of (A4) and such that $\mu^M_\sim(n_\mu, w_\mu) = \Omega^M$ for any $w_\mu \in U^M_\mu$. We will write

$u_\mu \neq_\mu n_\mu$ to denote the fact that the object u_μ is not the null object. Let us recall that the existence of a null object in a model of mereology of Leśniewski reduces the model to a singleton, as observed in Tarski [55]. In the sequel, for simplicity of notation, we will write μ in place of $\mu^M_\sim$, U in place of U^M_μ, u in place of u_μ etc.

We now show how the rough inclusion μ introduces in U a model of mereology of Leśniewski. To this end, we define a binary relation $part(\mu)$ on the set U by letting

$u\ part(\mu)\ w$ iff $\mu(u,w) = \Omega^M$ and it is not true that $\mu(w,u) = \Omega^M$.

Then we have the following proposition whose straightforward proof is omitted:

Proposition 2.5

The relation $part(\mu)$ satisfies the conditions (P1) and (P2) i.e. it is a relation of being a (proper) part in the sense of Leśniewski.

We now define in the model $M_\sim$ for any collection Ψ of objects in U, the notions of a set of objects in Ψ and of a class of objects in Ψ. We will say then that $u \in U$ is a *set of objects in* Ψ, *u set* Ψ for short, when

(S1) for any $w \neq_\mu n$ such that $w\ ingr(part(\mu))\ u$ there exist $v \neq_\mu n$ and $t \in \Psi$ such that $v\ ingr(part(\mu))\ w$, $v\ ingr(part(\mu))\ t$, $t\ ingr(part(\mu))\ u$;

if in addition, we have

(S2) $t\ ingr(part(\mu))\ u$ for any $t \in \Psi$;

(S3) for any t, if t satisfies (S1) and (S2) with Ψ then $u\ ingr(part(\mu))\ t$

then we say that u is a *class of objects in* Ψ, *u class* Ψ, for short. It follows from (A6) that for any collection Ψ there exists a unique object u such that *u class* Ψ and there exists objects of the form *set* Ψ.

We sum up the last few observations.

Proposition 2.6

For any model $M = (U^M, L^M, F^M)$ of L_{rm}, the pair $(U - \{n\}, part(\mu))$ is a model of mereology of Leśniewski.

2.6 Rough inclusion vs. fuzzy containment

In this section we will reveal some of the basic connections between rough mereology and many-valued logic [12], announced above. We recall that a *t-norm* $\top$ is a mapping $\top : [0,1] \times [0,1] \longrightarrow [0,1]$ which satisfies the conditions $\top(r,1) = r$, $\top(r,s) = \top(s,r)$, if $r \leq s$ then $\top(r,t) \leq \top(s,t)$ and $\top(r,\top(s,t)) = \top(\top(r,s),t)$. A *residual implication* $\vec{\top}$ induced by a t-norm $\top$ is a mapping $\vec{\top} : [0,1] \times [0,1] \longrightarrow [0,1]$ which satisfies the condition

$$\top(r,s) \leq t \text{ iff } r \leq \vec{\top}(s,t).$$

Clearly, when a t-norm $\top$ is a continuous mapping then we have a unique residual implication

$$\vec{\top}(s,t) = \sup\{r : \top(r,s) \leq t\}.$$

We consider a model $M_{\sim}$ of L_{rm}. As the induced model of mereology has the property that the notions of a set and of a subset are equivalent, we can interpret the value $\mu(u,w)$ as the value of a fuzzy membership function $\mu_w(u)$ in the sense of fuzzy set theory [12]. The partial containment can be expressed in this theory [12] by means of a many-valued implication viz. for a given many-valued implication $I : [0,1] \times [0,1] \longrightarrow [0,1]$, the induced partial containment function $\sigma_I(u,w)$ is defined by the formula: $\sigma_I(u,w) = \inf\{I(\mu_u(z), \mu_w(z)) : z \in U\}$. We show that when the implication I is a residual implication $\vec{\top}$ induced by a continuous t-norm $\top$ then the resulting function $\sigma_\top$ is a rough inclusion and, moreover, the function $\sigma_\top$ preserves the relation $ingr(part(\mu))$.

Our next proposition reads as follows.

Proposition 2.7

For a model $M_{\sim}$ of L_{rm}, a strict rough inclusion $\mu^{M^{\sim}}$ (meaning that $\mu^{M^{\sim}}(x,n)$ $= 0$ for any object x) and a continuous t-norm $\top$, the function

$$\sigma_\top(u,w) = \inf\{\vec{\top}(\mu_u(z), \mu_w(z)) : z \in U\}$$

is a rough inclusion and moreover $\sigma_\top(u,w) = 1$ if and only if $\mu(u,w) = 1$.

We denote by $M_\top$ the model which is produced from a model $M_{\sim}$ with a strict rough inclusion μ by replacing μ with $\sigma_\top$. By the symbol *Stand_Mod*$(\top)$ we denote the class of models of the form $M_\top$ where M is a standard model of L_{rm}.

We now observe the consistency of the deduction rule of the form (D_f) [37]; the symbol Con((A1)-(A6)+(D_f)) denotes the consistency of (D_f) i.e. the existence of the model of L_{rm} in which (D_f) is valid under a plausible interpretation of the function symbol f. We extend the syntax of L_{rm} by adding a functional constant symbol f of type

$$(lattice\text{ - }element,\ lattice\text{ - }element,\ lattice\text{ - }element).$$

We extend accordingly the domain of F^M. Then we have

Proposition 2.8

Con((A1)-(A6)+(D_f))

2.7 Rough inclusions from information systems

In this section we address the question which poses itself: how to define rough inclusions in models induced by information/decision systems (data tables). To this end, we introduce a weaker notion of a pre - rough inclusion.

A *pre-rough inclusion* μ_o on a set U is any function

$$\mu_o : U \times U \to [0,1]$$

which satisfies the following conditions
(i) $\mu_o(x,x) = 1$;
(ii) if $\mu_o(x,y) = 1$ then $\mu_o(z,y) \geq \mu_o(z,x)$ for any $z \in U$;
(iii) $\mu_o(x,y) = \mu_o(y,x)$.

We recall that a *t-conorm* $\perp$ [12] is a function $\perp : [0,1] \times [0,1] \to [0,1]$ such that $\perp$ is increasing coordinate-wise, commutative, associative and satisfies the condition $\perp(r,0) = r$. We extend the operators $\top, \perp$ over the empty set of arguments and over singletons by adopting the following convention : $\top(\emptyset) = 1, \perp(\emptyset) = 1, \top(r) = r = \perp(r)$. We observe that by the associativity and commutativity of $\top$ and $\perp$, the values $\top(x_1, ..., x_k)$ and $\perp(x_1, ..., x_k)$ are defined uniquely for any finite set of arguments. We have the following proposition, whose straightforward proof is omitted.

Proposition 2.9
For any *pre-rough inclusion* μ_o on the set U, the function

$$\mu(A,B) = \top\{\perp\{\mu_0(a,b) : b \in B\} : a \in A\}$$

defined for any pair A, B of finite subsets of U, is a rough inclusion on the universe $U^{<\omega}$ of finite subsets of U.

We will work from now on rather with pre - rough inclusions which may be used to introduce a closeness (similarity) measure directly on the universe of an information/decision system. Formulae of type as in Proposition 2.9 above permit us to extend this similarity measure to a rough inclusion on concepts (i.e. subsets of the universe). Any interpretation of L_{rm} in which requirements for μ_0 are satisfied is called a *pre - model* of L_{rm}.

Pre–rough inclusions can be generated from an information/decision system **A** in a variety of ways; for instance, for a given partition $P = \{A_1, \ldots, A_k\}$ of the set A of attributes into non-empty sets $A_1, \ldots, A_k$, and a given set $W = \{w_1, \ldots, w_k\}$ of weights, $w_i \in [0,1]$ for $i = 1, 2, \ldots, k$ and $\sum_{i=1}^{k} w_i = 1$ we let

$$\mu_{o,P,W}(x,y) = \sum_{i=1}^{k} w_i \cdot \frac{| IND_i(x,y) |}{| A_i |}$$

where $IND_i(x,y) = \{a \in A_i : a(x) = a(y)\}$. It is easy to check that $\mu_{o,P,W}$ is a pre-rough inclusion. This approach is especially useful as it allows for applying neural networks or evolutionary computations (like genetic algorithms) in order to define an optimal set of weights. We give an example illustrating this procedure.

Example 2.1
Consider an information system H

The table below shows values of the initial rough inclusion $\mu_{o,P,W}(x,y) = \sum_{i=1}^{3} \frac{|IND(x,y)|}{3}$ i.e. we consider the simplest case when $k = 1$, $w_1 = 1$.

	hat	ker	pig
x_1	1	0	0
x_2	0	0	1
x_3	0	1	0
x_4	1	1	0

Table 1. The information system H

	x_1	x_2	x_3	x_4
x_1	1	0.33	0.33	0.66
x_2	0.33	1	0.33	0.00
x_3	0.33	0.33	1	0.66
x_4	0.66	0.00	0.66	1

Table 2. Initial rough inclusion for H

Example 2.2

In addition to the information system (agent) (H) from Example 2.1, we consider agents (B) and (HB). Together with H they form the string $\mathbf{ag} = (H)(B)(HB)$ in *Link* i.e. (HB) takes objects: x sent by (H) and y sent by (B) and assembles a complex object xy. The information systems of (B) and (HB) are shown below. The standards are taken as: x_1, x_2 at (H) and y_1, y_3 at (B) and in the table for (HB) we have only standards x_1y_1, x_1y_3, x_2y_1 and x_2y_3. The attributes at (HB) are related to those of (H) and (B) by formulas: $har = pis \wedge cut \wedge kni$, $lar = pis \wedge \neg cut \wedge \neg kni \vee \neg pis \wedge cut \wedge \neg kni \vee \neg pis \wedge \neg cut \wedge kni$, $off = hat \wedge pis$, $tar = kni \wedge pig \wedge \neg cr$ hence one can easily complete the table for (HB).

	pis	*cut*	*kni*	*cr*
y_1	1	1	1	1
y_2	1	0	0	0
y_3	0	0	1	0
y_4	1	1	1	0

Table 3. The information system B

	har	*lar*	*off*	*tar*
x_1y_1	1	0	1	0
x_1y_3	0	1	0	0
x_2y_1	1	0	0	0
x_2y_3	0	1	0	1

Table 4. The information system HB

The values of the initial rough inclusion $\mu = \mu_{o,P,W}$ are calculated for (B) and (BH) by the same procedure as in Example 2.1.

2.8 Approximate mereological connectives

An important ingredient in our scheme is related to the problem of rough mereological connectives: given information systems $\mathbf{A}, \mathbf{B}, \mathbf{C}, ...$ we will say that $\mathbf{A}$ *results from* $\mathbf{B}, \mathbf{C}, ...$ if there exists a (partial) mapping (an *operation*) $o_{\mathbf{A}} : U_{\mathbf{B}} \times U_{\mathbf{C}} \times ... \rightarrow U_{\mathbf{A}}$ with $rng\ o_A = U_{\mathbf{A}}$ i.e. any $x \in U_{\mathbf{A}}$ is of the form $o_{\mathbf{A}}(y, z, ...)$ where $y \in U_{\mathbf{B}}$ and $z \in U_{\mathbf{C}}, ...$. In the case when pre - rough inclusions $\mu_A, \mu_B, \mu_C, ...$ are defined in respective universes $U_{\mathbf{A}}, U_{\mathbf{B}}, U_{\mathbf{C}}, ...$ there arises the problem of *uncertainty propagation* i.e. we have to decide in what way is the measure μ_A related to measures $\mu_B, \mu_C, ...$ Formally, we have to find an (approximation) to a function f satisfying the following property:

---

for any $\epsilon_1, \epsilon_2, \epsilon_3, ... \in [0, 1]$:
for any $x, x_1 \in U_{\mathbf{B}}, y, y_1 \in U_{\mathbf{C}}, ...$:
  if $\mu_{\mathbf{B}}(x, x_1) \geq \epsilon_1$, $\mu_{\mathbf{C}}(y, y_1) \geq \epsilon_2$ and ...
  then $\mu_{\mathbf{A}}(o_A(x, y, ...), o_A(x_1, y_1, ...)) \geq f(\epsilon_1, \epsilon_2, ...)$

In practice, it is unrealistic to expect the existence of a function f satisfying the above condition globally; therefore, we localize this notion. To this end, let us select a subset $S_A \subseteq U_A$ of objects which we will call *standard objects*; we will use the symbol $xyz...$ to denote the object $o_A(x, y, ...) \in U_A$. Given a standard $s = xyz...$, we will call a function f an (approximation to) *rough mereological connective relative to* o_A and s in case it satisfies the condition:

---

for any $\epsilon_1, \epsilon_2, \epsilon_3, ... \in [0, 1]$:
for any $x_1 \in U_{\mathbf{B}}, y_1 \in U_{\mathbf{C}}, ...$:
  if $\mu_{\mathbf{B}}(x_1, x) \geq \epsilon_1$, $\mu_{\mathbf{C}}(y_1, y) \geq \epsilon_2$ and ...
  then $\mu_{\mathbf{A}}(o_A(x_1, y_1, ...), s) \geq f(\epsilon_1, \epsilon_2, ...)$

We outline an algorithm which may be used to extract from information systems approximations to uncertainty functions (rough mereological connectives).

Example 2.2 We will determine an approximation to the mereological connective at the standard x_1y_1 in Table 4 of Example 2.1 i.e. a function f such that (for simplicity of notation we omit subscripts of μ):

$$\textbf{if } \mu(x, x_1) \geq \epsilon_1 \text{ and } \mu(y, y_1) \geq \epsilon_2$$
$$\textbf{then } \mu(xy, x_1y_1) \geq f(\epsilon_1, \epsilon_2), \text{ for any pair } \epsilon_1, \epsilon_2.$$

Tables 5 and 6 show conditions which f is to fulfill.

This full set T_0 of conditions can be reduced: we can find a minimal set T of vectors of the form $(\varepsilon_1', \varepsilon_2', \varepsilon)$ such that if f satisfies the condition $f(\varepsilon_1', \varepsilon_2') = \varepsilon$ for each $(\varepsilon_1', \varepsilon_2', \varepsilon) \in T$ then f extends by the formula (1), below.

x	$\mu(x,x_1)$	y	$\mu(y,y_1)$	$\mu(xy,x_1y_1)$
x_1	1	y_1	1	1
x_1	1	y_2	0.25	0.5
x_1	1	y_3	0.25	0.25
x_1	1	y_4	0.75	1
x_2	0.33	y_1	1	0.75
x_2	0.33	y_2	0.25	0.25
x_2	0.33	y_3	0.25	0.00
x_2	0.33	y_4	0.75	0.5

Table 5. The conditions for f (first part)

x	$\mu(x,x_1)$	y	$\mu(y,y_1)$	$\mu(xy,x_1y_1)$
x_3	0.33	y_1	1	0.75
x_3	0.33	y_2	0.25	0.25
x_3	0.33	y_3	0.25	0.25
x_3	0.33	y_4	0.75	0.75
x_4	0.66	y_1	1	1
x_4	0.66	y_2	0.25	0.5
x_4	0.66	y_3	0.25	0.25
x_4	0.66	y_4	0.75	1

Table 6. The conditions for f (second part)

The following algorithm produces a minimal set T of conditions.

Algorithm
Input : table T_0 of vectors

$$(\mu(x,x_1),\mu(y,y_1),\mu(xy,x_1y_1));$$

Step 1. For each pair $(\mu(x,x_1)=\varepsilon_1,\mu(y,y_1)=\varepsilon_2)$, find $\varepsilon(\varepsilon_1,\varepsilon_2)=\min\{\varepsilon:\varepsilon_1'\geq\varepsilon_1,\varepsilon_2'\geq\varepsilon_2,(\varepsilon_1',\varepsilon_2',\varepsilon)\in T_0\}$. Let T_1 be the table of vectors $(\varepsilon_1,\varepsilon_2,\varepsilon(\varepsilon_1,\varepsilon_2))$.
Step 2. For each ε^* such that $(\varepsilon_1,\varepsilon_2,\varepsilon(\varepsilon_1,\varepsilon_2)=\varepsilon^*)\in T_1$, find: $row(\varepsilon^*)=(\varepsilon_1^*,\varepsilon_2^*,\varepsilon^*)$ where $(\varepsilon_1^*,\varepsilon_2^*,\varepsilon^*)\in T_1$ and if $(\varepsilon_1',\varepsilon_2',\varepsilon^*)\in T_1$ then $\varepsilon_1'\geq\varepsilon_1^*,\varepsilon_2'\geq\varepsilon_2^*$.
Output: table T of vectors of the form $row(\varepsilon)$.

One can check that Table 7 shows a minimal set T of vectors for the case of Tables 5 and 6.

One can extract from the algorithm the synthesis formula of f from conditions T_0 :

$$f(\varepsilon_1,\varepsilon_2)=\min\{\varepsilon':(\varepsilon_1',\varepsilon_2',\varepsilon')\in T_0\wedge(\varepsilon_1'\geq\varepsilon_1)\wedge(\varepsilon_2'\geq\varepsilon_2)\} \quad (1)$$

ε_1	ε_2	ε
0.66	0.75	1
0.33	0.75	0.5
0.66	0.25	0.25
0.33	0.25	0.00

Table 7. A minimal set T of vectors

2.9 Rough mereological component of granulation

We now introduce explicitly the mereological component into our analysis and a fortiori we modify the definition of the notion of a granule.

Rough inclusion μ_o may enter our discussion of a granule and of the relation Gr in each of the following ways:

1. Concerning the definitions $(\eta), (\rho)$ of functions η, ρ, we may replace in them the rough membership function μ with a function μ_o possibly better suited to a given context.

2. The function μ_o can be extended to a rough inclusion $\overline{\mu}$ by means of a formula in Proposition 2.9, relative to $\perp$ and $\top$ suitably chosen. Elementary granules (G, G') can be defined more generally by considering any pair (G, G'), $G = [\alpha_G]$, $G' = [\alpha_{G'}]$, such that

$$\rho(G, G') \geq tr,$$

$$\eta(G, G') \geq tr',$$

where

$$\rho(G, G') = \overline{\mu}([G], [G']),$$

$$\eta(G, G') = \overline{\mu}([G'], [G]).$$

To stress the role of parameters $\mu_0, \perp$ and $\top$, we will use the symbol

$$Gr(B, C, \eta, \rho, \mu_0, tr, tr' \perp, \top, u, v)$$

to denote the granulation predicate.

3 Adaptive Calculus of Granules in Distributed Systems

We now present a conceptual scheme for adaptive calculus of granules aimed at synthesizing solutions to problems posed under uncertainty. This exposition is based on our earlier analyses presented in [30, 32, 34, 35, 37, 38, 40, 41]. We construct a scheme of agents which communicate by relating their respective granules of knowledge by means of transfer functions induced by rough mereological connectives extracted from their respective information systems.

We now define formally the ingredients of our scheme of agents.

3.1 Distributed Systems of Agents

We assume that a pair (Inv, Ag) is given where Inv is an *inventory of elementary objects* and Ag is a set of inteligent computing units called shortly *agents.*

We consider an agent $ag \in Ag$. The agent ag is endowed with tools for reasoning about objects in its scope; these tools are defined by components of the agent label. The *label of the agent ag* is the tuple

$$lab(ag) = (\mathcal{A}(ag), M(ag), L(ag), Link(ag), O(ag), St(ag),$$

$$Unc\_rel(ag), H(ag), Unc\_rule(ag), Dec\_rule(ag))$$

where

1. $\mathcal{A}(ag) = (U(ag), A(ag))$ is an information system of the agent ag;

2. $M(ag) = (U(ag), [0,1], \mu_o(ag))$ is a pre - model of L_{rm} with a pre - rough inclusion $\mu_o(ag)$ on the universe $U(ag)$;

3. $L(ag)$ is a set of unary predicates (properties of objects) in a predicate calculus interpreted in the set $U(ag)$; we may assume that formulae of $L(ag)$ are constructed as conditional formulae of logics L_B where $B \subseteq A(ag)$.

4. $St(ag) = \{st(ag)_1, ..., st(ag)_n\} \subset U(ag)$ is the set of *standard objects* at ag;

5. $Link(ag)$ is a collection of strings of the form $ag_1ag_2...ag_kag$; the intended meaning of a string $ag_1ag_2...ag_kag$ is that $ag_1, ag_2, .., ag_k$ are children of ag in the sense that ag can assemble complex objects (constructs) from simpler objects sent by $ag_1, ag_2, ..., ag_k$. In general, we may assume that for some agents ag we may have more than one element in $Link(ag)$ which represents the possibility of re - negotiating the synthesis scheme.

We denote by the symbol $Link$ the union of the family $\{Link(ag) : ag \in Ag\}$.

6. $O(ag)$ is the set of operations at ag; any $o \in O(ag)$ is a mapping of the Cartesian product $U(ag_1) \times U(ag_2) \times ... \times U(ag_k)$ into the universe $U(ag)$ where $ag_1ag_2...ag_kag \in Link(ag)$; the meaning of $o(ag)$ is that of an operation by means of which the agent ag is able to assemble from objects $x_1 \in U(ag_1), x_2 \in U(ag_2), ..., x_k \in U(ag_k)$ the object $o(ag)(x_1, x_2, ..., x_k) \in U(ag)$.

7. $Unc\_rel(ag)$ is the set of uncertainty relations unc_rel_i of type

$$(o_i(ag), \rho_i(ag), ag_1, ag_2, ..., ag_k, ag, \mu_o(ag_1), ..., \mu_o(ag_k), \mu_o(ag),$$
$$st(ag_1)_i, st(ag_2)_i, ..., st(ag_k)_i, st(ag)_i)$$

where $ag_1ag_2...ag_kag \in Link(ag)$, $o_i(ag) \in O(ag)$ and ρ_i is such that

$$\rho_i((x_1, \varepsilon_1), (x_2, \varepsilon_2), .., (x_k, \varepsilon_k), (x, \varepsilon))$$

holds for $x_1 \in U(ag_1), x_2 \in U(ag_2), .., x_k \in U(ag_k)$ and $\varepsilon, \varepsilon_1, \varepsilon_2, .., \varepsilon_k \in [0,1]$ iff $\mu_o(x_j, st(ag_j)_i) = \varepsilon_j$ for $j = 1, 2, .., k$ and $\mu_o(x, st(ag)_i) = \varepsilon$ for the collection of standards $st(ag_1)_i, st(ag_2)_i, .. ., st(ag_k)_i, st(ag)_i$ such that

$$o_i(st(ag_1)_i, st(ag_2)_i, .., st(ag_k)_i) = st(ag)_i.$$

Uncertainty relations express the agents knowledge about relationships among uncertainty coefficients of the agent ag and uncertainty coefficients of its children. The relational character of these dependencies expresses their intensionality.

8. $Unc\_rule(ag)$ is the set of uncertainty rules unc_rule_j of type
$(o_j, f_j, ag_1, ag_2, \ldots, ag_k, ag, st(ag_1), st(ag_2), \ldots, st(ag_k), st(ag),$
$\mu_o(ag_1), \ldots, \mu_o(ag_k), \mu_o(ag))$
of the agent ag where $ag_1 ag_2 \ldots ag_k ag \in Link(ag)$ and $f_j : [0,1]^k \longrightarrow [0,1]$ is a function which has the property that
if $o_j(st(ag_1), st(ag_2), \ldots, st(ag_k)) = st(ag)$ **and**
$x_1 \in U(ag_1), x_2 \in U(ag_2), \ldots, x_k \in U(ag_k)$
satisfy the conditions $\mu_o(x_i, st(ag_i)) \geq \varepsilon(ag_i)$ for $i = 1, 2, .., k$

then $\mu_o(o_j(x_1, x_2, \ldots, x_k), st(ag)) \geq f_j(\varepsilon(ag_1), \varepsilon(ag_2), .., \varepsilon(ag_k))$.

Uncertainty rules provide functional operators (approximate mereological connectives) for propagating uncertainty measure values from the children of an agent to the agent; their application is in negotiation processes where they inform agents about plausible uncertainty bounds.

9. $H(ag)$ is a strategy which produces uncertainty rules from uncertainty relations; to this end, various rigorous formulas as well as various heuristics can be applied among them the algorithm presented in Section 2.8.

10. $Dec\_rule(ag)$ is a set of decomposition rules dec_rule_i of type

$$(o_i, ag_1, ag_2, \ldots, ag_k, ag)$$

such that $(\Phi(ag_1), \Phi(ag_2), .., \Phi(ag_k), \Phi(ag)) \in dec\_rule_i$ (where $\Phi(ag_1) \in L(ag_1)$, $\Phi(ag_2) \in L(ag_2)$, ..., $\Phi(ag_k) \in L(ag_k)$, $\Phi(ag) \in L(ag)$ and $ag_1 ag_2 \ldots ag_k ag \in Link(ag)$) and there exists a collection of standards $st(ag_1)$, $st(ag_2)$,..., $st(ag_k)$, $st(ag)$ with the properties that

$$o_j(st(ag_1), st(ag_2), .., st(ag_k)) = st(ag),$$

$st(ag_i)$ satisfies $\Phi(ag_i)$ for $i = 1, 2, .., k$ and $st(ag)$ satisfies $\Phi(ag)$.

Decomposition rules are decomposition schemes in the sense that they describe the standard $st(ag)$ and the standards $st(ag_1), \ldots, st(ag_k)$ from which the standard $st(ag)$ is assembled under o_i in terms of predicates which these standards satisfy.

We may sum up the content of 1 - 10 above by saying that for any agent ag the possible sets of children of this agent are specified and, relative to each team of children, decompositions of standard objects at ag into sets of standard objects at the children, uncertainty relations as well as uncertainty rules, which relate similarity degrees of objects at the children to their respective standards and similarity degree of the object built by ag to the corresponding standard object at ag, are given.

We take rough inclusions of agents as measures of uncertainty in their respective universes. We would like to observe that the mereological relation of being a part is not transitive globally over the whole synthesis scheme because distinct agents use distinct mereological languages.

3.2 Approximate synthesis of complex objects

The process of synthesis of a complex object (signal, action) by the above defined scheme of agents consists in our approach of the two communication stages viz. the top - down communication/negotiation process and the bottom - up communication/assembling process. We outline the two stages here in the language of approximate formulae.

Approximate logic of synthesis For simplicity of exposition and to avoid unnecessarily tedious notation, we assume that the relation $ag' \leq ag$, which holds for agents $ag', ag \in Ag$ iff there exists a string $ag_1 ag_2 ... ag_k ag \in Link(ag)$ with $ag' = ag_i$ for some $i \leq k$, orders the set Ag into a tree. We also assume that $O(ag) = \{o(ag)\}$ for $ag \in Ag$ i.e. each agent has a unique assembling operation.

The process of synthesis of a complex object (signal, action) by the above defined scheme of agents consists in our approach of the two communication stages viz. the top - down communication/negotiation process and the bottom - up communication process. We outline the two stages here in the language of approximate formulae. To this end we build a logic $L(Ag)$ (cf. [37]) in which we can express global properties of the synthesis process. We recall our assumption that the set Ag is ordered into a tree by the relation $ag' \leq ag$.

Elementary formulae of $L(Ag)$ are of the form

$$\langle st(ag), \Phi(ag), \varepsilon(ag) \rangle$$

where $st(ag) \in St(ag), \Phi(ag) \in L(ag), \varepsilon(ag) \in [0,1]$ for any $ag \in Ag$. Formulae of $L(ag)$ form the smallest extension of the set of elementary formulae closed under propositional connectives $\vee$, $\wedge$, $\neg$ and under the modal operators $\Box$, $\Diamond$.

To introduce a semantics for the logic $L(ag)$, we first specify the meaning of satisfaction for elementary formulae. The meaning of a formula $\Phi(ag)$ is defined classically as the set $[\Phi(ag)] = \{u \in U(ag) : u \text{ has the property } \Phi(ag)\}$; we will denote the fact that $u \in [\Phi(ag)]$ by the symbol $u \models \Phi(ag)$. We extend now the satisfiability predicate $\models$ to approximate formulae: for $x \in U(ag)$, we say that x *satifies* an elementary formula $\langle st(ag), \Phi(ag), \varepsilon(ag) \rangle$, in symbols: $x \models < st(ag), \Phi(ag), \varepsilon(ag) >$, iff

(i) $st(ag) \models \Phi(ag)$;

(ii) $\mu_o(ag)(x, st(ag)) \geq \varepsilon(ag)$.

We let

(iii) $x \models \neg \langle st(ag), \Phi(ag), \varepsilon(ag) \rangle$ iff it is not true that

$$x \models \langle st(ag), \Phi(ag), \varepsilon(ag) \rangle;$$

(iv) $x \models \langle st(ag)_1, \Phi(ag)_1, \varepsilon(ag)_1 \rangle \vee \langle st(ag)_2, \Phi(ag)_2, \varepsilon(ag)_2 \rangle$ iff
$x \models \langle st(ag)_1, \Phi(ag)_1, \varepsilon(ag)_1 \rangle$ or $x \models \langle st(ag)_2, \Phi(ag)_2, \varepsilon(ag)_2 \rangle$.

In order to extend the semantics over modalities, we first introduce the notion of a selection: by a *selection* over Ag we mean a function sel which assigns to each agent ag an object $sel(ag) \in U(ag)$.

For two selections sel, sel' we say that *sel induces sel'*, in symbols $sel \rightarrow_{Ag} sel'$ when $sel(ag) = sel'(ag)$ for any $ag \in Leaf(Ag)$ and

$$sel'(ag) = o(ag)(sel'(ag_1), sel'(ag_2), ..., sel'(ag_k))$$

for any $ag_1 ag_2 ... ag_k ag \in Link$.

We extend the satisfiability predicate $\models$ to selections: for an elementary formula $\langle st(ag), \Phi(ag), \varepsilon(ag)\rangle$, we let $sel \models \langle st(ag), \Phi(ag), \varepsilon(ag)\rangle$ iff $sel(ag) \models \langle st(ag), \Phi(ag), \varepsilon(ag)\rangle$.

We now let $sel \models \Diamond < st(ag), \Phi(ag), \varepsilon(ag) >$ when there exists a selection sel' satisfying the conditions:

(i) $sel \rightarrow_{Ag} sel'$;

(ii) $sel' \models \langle st(ag), \Phi(ag), \varepsilon(ag)\rangle$.

In terms of logic $L(Ag)$ it is posible to express the problem of synthesis of an approximate solution to the problem posed to the team Ag. We denote by $head(Ag)$ the root of the tree $(Ag, \leq)$.

In the process of top - down communication, a requirement Ψ received by the scheme from an external source (which may be called a *customer*) is decomposed into approximate specifications of the form

$$\langle st(ag), \Phi(ag), \varepsilon(ag)\rangle$$

for any agent ag of the scheme. The decomposition process is initiated at the agent $head(Ag)$ and propagated down the tree.

We are able now to formulate the synthesis problem.

Synthesis problem

Given a formula

$$\alpha : \langle st(head(Ag)), \Phi(head(Ag)), \varepsilon(head(Ag))\rangle$$

find a selection sel over the tree $(Ag, \leq)$ *with the property* $sel \models \Diamond\alpha$.

A solution to the synthesis problem with a given formula

$$\langle st(head(Ag)), \Phi(head(Ag)), \varepsilon(head(Ag))\rangle$$

is found by negotiations among the agents; negotiations are based on uncertainty rules of agents and their succesful result can be expressed by a top-down recursion in the tree $(Ag, \leq)$ as follows: given a local team $ag_1 ag_2 ... ag_k ag$ with the formula $\langle st(ag), \Phi(ag), \varepsilon(ag)\rangle$ already chosen in negotiations on a higher tree level, it is sufficient that each agent ag_i choose a standard $st(ag_i) \in U(ag_i)$, a formula $\Phi(ag_i) \in L(ag_i)$ and a coefficient $\varepsilon(ag_i) \in [0, 1]$ such that

(v) $(\Phi(ag_1), \Phi(ag_2), .., \Phi(ag_k), \Phi(ag)) \in Dec\_rule(ag)$ with standards $st(ag)$, $st(ag_1), .. ., st(ag_k)$;

(vi) $f(\varepsilon(ag_1), .., \varepsilon(ag_k)) \geq \varepsilon(ag)$ where f satisfies $unc\_rule(ag)$ with $st(ag)$, $st(ag_1), ..., st(ag_k)$ and $\varepsilon(ag_1), .., \varepsilon(ag_k), \varepsilon(ag)$.

For a formula $\alpha : \langle st(head(Ag)), \Phi(head(Ag)), \varepsilon(head(Ag))\rangle$, we call an α - *scheme* an assignment of a formula $\alpha(ag) : \langle st(ag), \Phi(ag), \varepsilon(ag)\rangle$ to each $ag \in Ag$ in such manner that (v), (vi) above are satisfied and $\alpha(head(Ag))$ is $\langle st(head(Ag)), \Phi(head(Ag)), \varepsilon(head(Ag))\rangle$; we denote this scheme with the symbol

$$sch(\langle st(head(Ag)), \Phi(head(Ag)), \varepsilon(head(Ag))\rangle).$$

We say that a selection sel is *compatible* with a scheme

$$sch(\langle st(head(Ag)), \Phi(head(Ag)), \varepsilon(head(Ag))\rangle)$$

when $\mu_o(ag)(sel(ag), st(ag)) \geq \varepsilon(ag)$ for each leaf agent $ag \in Ag$ where $\langle st(ag), \Phi(ag), \varepsilon(ag)\rangle$ is the value of the scheme at ag for any leaf $ag \in Ag$.

Any leaf agent realizes its approximate specification by choosing in the subset $Inv \cap U(ag)$ of the inventory of primitive constructs a construct satisfying the specification.

The goal of negotiations can be summarized now as follows.

Proposition 3.1
For a given a requirement $\langle st(head(Ag)), \Phi(head(Ag)), \varepsilon(head(Ag))\rangle$ we have:
if a selection sel is compatible with a scheme

$$sch(\langle st(head(Ag)), \Phi(head(Ag)), \varepsilon(head(Ag))\rangle)$$

then $sel \models \Diamond\langle st(head(Ag)), \Phi(head(Ag)), \varepsilon(head(Ag))\rangle$.

The bottom-up communication consists of agents sending to their parents the chosen constructs. The root agent $root(Ag)$ assembles the final construct.

3.3 Algebras of granules over the agent system (Inv, Ag)

We construct here for a given tree $(Ag, \leq)$ of agents a granulation relation $Gr(ag)$ for any agent $ag \in Ag$. These relations will be generally constructed along the lines pointed to in Introduction.

For any agent ag, we denote by $syst(ag)$ the subtree of the tree $(Ag, \leq)$ which consists of all agents ag' such that $ag' \leq ag$.

For a formula $\alpha : < st_o(ag), \Phi_o(ag), \varepsilon_o(ag) >$, we call an α – *scheme* an assignment of a formula $\alpha(ag') : < st(ag'), \Phi(ag'), \varepsilon(ag') >$ to each ag' from $syst(ag)$ in such manner that (v), (vi) above are satisfied and $\alpha(ag)$ is α; we denote this scheme with the symbol $sch(\alpha)$.

We denote by the symbol $[[< st(ag), \Phi(ag), \varepsilon(ag) >]]$ the collection of all $< st(ag), \Phi(ag), \varepsilon(ag) >$ - schemes.

We thus collect in $[[< st(ag), \Phi(ag), \varepsilon(ag) >]]$ all assignments of approximate formulae at agents of $syst(ag)$ which satisfy (v) and (vi) above.

For a selection *sel*, we will say that *sel* satisfies a formula

$$\langle st(ag), \Phi(ag), \varepsilon(ag)\rangle$$

in a strong sense, in symbols:

$$sel \models^* \langle st(ag), \Phi(ag), \varepsilon(ag)\rangle,$$

iff there exists a selection sel' and a $< st(ag), \Phi(ag), \varepsilon(ag) >$ - scheme S in

$$[[\langle st(ag), \Phi(ag), \varepsilon(ag)\rangle]]$$

such that

(vii) sel' is compatible with the scheme S;

(viii) $sel' \models \Diamond\langle st(ag), \Phi(ag), \varepsilon(ag)\rangle$ which is witnessed by a selection sel'' in the sense of (i), (ii) above and $sel''(ag) = sel(ag)$.

Thus, $sel \models^* \langle st(ag), \Phi(ag), \varepsilon(ag)\rangle$ means that the object $sel(ag) \in U(ag)$ can be constructed by means of a scheme from $[[\langle st(ag), \Phi(ag), \varepsilon(ag)\rangle]]$.

We now make each information system $\mathcal{A}(ag)$ where $ag \in Ag$ into a decision system $\mathcal{A}^d(ag)$.

To this end, we define the decision attribute $d(ag)$ on the universe $U(ag)$ by letting $d(ag)(x) =$

$$\{\langle st(ag), \Phi(ag), \varepsilon(ag)\rangle : \exists sel.x = sel(ag) \text{ and } sel \models^* \langle st(ag), \Phi(ag), \varepsilon(ag)\rangle\}.$$

From each decision system $\mathcal{A}^d(ag)$, we generate the granulation relation

$$Gr(ag)(B, d, \eta, \rho, \mu_0, tr, tr', \bot, \top, u, v)$$

depending on parameters

$$B \subseteq A(ag), \eta, \rho, \mu_0, tr, tr', \bot, \top$$

chosen e.g. in the learning stage of the synthesis process.

Elementary granules of knowledge $(G, G')(ag)$ represent therefore pairs of the form $([x]_{IND(B)}, [d(ag)(y)]_{IND(d(ag))})$ such that sufficiently many schemes from the class $[d(ag)(y)]_{IND(d(ag))}$ synthesize satisfactorily many objects from the class $[x]_{IND(B)}$ (which is measured by the functions $\eta(ag), \rho(ag)$).

It will be convenient to introduce the vector notation: $\overline{\eta} = \langle \eta(ag) : ag \in Ag\rangle$, $\overline{\rho} = \langle \rho(ag) : ag \in Ag\rangle$ and $\overline{B} = \{B(ag) \subseteq A(ag) : ag \in Ag\}$.

Let us now observe that by (v) and (vi) above approximate mereological connectives $f(ag)$ induce mappings $F(ag)$ on decision classes of agents: for $ag_1 ag_2 ... ag_k ag \in Link(ag)$ and elementary granules $(G_i, G_i')(ag_i)$ representing pairs $([x_i]_{IND(B_i)}, [d(ag_i)(y_i)]_{IND(d(ag_i))})$ where $i = 1, 2, ..., k$, the mapping $F(ag)$ maps the product $\times_i [d(ag_i)(y_i)]_{IND(d(ag_i))}$ into the class

$$[d(ag)(o_{ag}(y_1, y_2, ..., y_k))]_{IND(d(ag))}$$

according to the formula:

$F(ag)(\times_i [d(ag_i)(y_i)]_{IND(d(ag_i))}) =$

$$\{\langle st(ag), \Phi(ag), f(ag)(\varepsilon(ag_1), ..., \varepsilon(ag_k))\rangle : \\ \langle st(ag_i), \Phi(ag_i), \varepsilon(ag_i)\rangle \in [d(ag_i)(y_i))] \text{ for } i = 1, ..., k\}$$

where $f(ag)$ are chosen such that (v) and (vi) are satisfied for $\Phi(ag)$, $\Phi(ag_1)$, ... $\Phi(ag_k)$ and $\varepsilon(ag)$, $\varepsilon(ag_1)$, ... $\varepsilon(ag_k)$.

We denote by $\overline{F}$ the mapping assignment which assigns to any non–leaf agent ag the above mapping $F(ag)$. We say that the mapping $\overline{F}$ induces the $(\overline{B}, \overline{\eta}, \overline{\rho})$–*granule transfer* in case when for any $ag_1ag_2...ag_kag \in Link$ and elementary $(\rho(ag_i), \eta(ag_i)), tr(ag), tr'(ag)$ - granules $(G_i, G_i')(ag_i)$ representing pairs

$$([x_i]_{IND(B_i)}, [d(ag_i)(y_i)]_{IND(d(ag_i))})$$

for $i = 1, 2, ..., k$, we have

(ix) $\rho(ag)(o(ag)(\times_i[x_i]_{IND(B_i)}), F(ag)(\times_i[d(ag_i)(y_i)]_{IND(d(ag_i))}) \geq tr(ag)$,

(x) $\eta(ag)(F(ag)(\times_i[d(ag_i)(y_i)]_{IND(d(ag_i))}), o(ag)(\times_i[x_i]_{IND(B_i)})) \geq tr'(ag)$,

where

$$\rho(ag)(G, G') = \overline{\mu}(ag)([G], [G']),$$

$$\eta(ag)(G, G') = \overline{\mu}(ag)([G'], [G]).$$

Granules defined above may be conveniently aggregated over elementary teams of agents of the form $ag_1ag_2...ag_kag \in Link$

We may now present the synthesis scheme in terms of granules of knowledge defined above.

3.4 Synthesis in terms of granules

The process of synthesis described above in the language of approximate formulae, can be now described concisely in terms of granules of knowledge of agents. The process of synthesis of an object satisfying the approximate specification Ψ may be presented as follows. We will say that an object x *satisfies a granule of knowledge* (G, G'), symbolically $x \models (G, G')$, in case $x \in [G]$.

Step 1. The root agent $root(Ag)$ selects an elementary granule of knowledge $(G, G')(root(Ag))$.

Step 2. The children $ag_1, ag_2, ..., ag_k$ of $root(Ag)$ select elementary granules of knowledge $(G_i, G_i')(ag_i)$ where $i = 1, 2, .., k$ such that the mapping $F(ag)$ maps the product $\times_i(G_i, G_i')(ag_i)$ into the granule $(G, G')(root(Ag))$.

Steps 2...m. The process in Step 2 is repeated until in the step m leaf agents are reached.

Step m+1. Any leaf agent ag chooses an object $x \in Inv \cap U(ag)$ such that $x \models (G, G')(ag)$ where $(G, G')(ag)$ is the granule selected for ag in step m and sends it to its parent agent.

Steps (m+2)...2m. Any non - root non - leaf agent ag accepts objects $x(ag_i)$ sent by its children $ag_i, i = 1, 2, .., k$, and applies its operation $o(ag)$ to compose from the sent objects the object $x = o(ag)(x_1, x_2, ..., x_k)$ satisfying its granule of knowledge. Then ag sends $x(ag)$ to its parent.

Step 2m+1. The root agent $root(Ag)$ synthesizes the final object $x(root(Ag))$ and sends it to Cs.

We denote by *comp* the mapping which assigns to leaf objects $x(ag), ag \in Leaf(Ag)$ the object $x(root(Ag))$ synthesized over the scheme as described in steps $(m+2)...2m+1$.

The correctness of this scheme is subject to the condition described by the following

Proposition 3.2

Assume that $\{(G,G')(ag) : ag \in Ag\}$ is a set of elementary granules of knowledge over the scheme (Inv, Ag) of agents such that for any $ag \in Ag$ and any $ag_1 ag_2 ... ag_k ag \in Link$ the mapping $F(ag)$ maps the product $\times_i (G,G')(ag_i)$ into $(G,G')(ag)$.Then the following is true: **if** $x(ag) \models (G,G')(ag)$ for any leaf agent ag **then** $comp(< x(ag) : ag \in Leaf(Ag) >) \models (G,G')(root(Ag))$.

3.5 Adaptivity of calculus of granules

The adaptivity of our scheme is due to the following factors.

1. The possibility of changing the parameters $\eta, \rho, \mu_0, \perp, \top$ in the granulation predicate $Gr(ag)(B, \eta, \rho, \mu_0, tr, tr', \perp, \top, u, v)$ for any agent $ag \in Ag$.
2. The possibility of new granule formation at any agent $ag \in Ag$.
3. The possibility of forming new standards at any agent $ag \in Ag$.

Acknowledgments

This research has been supported by the ESPRIT-CRIT 2 project #20288, and by the Polish National Research Committee (KBN) grant #8T11C01011.

References

1. S.Amarel (1991), *PANEL on AI and Design.* In: J. Mylopoulos and R. Reiter, (Eds.), Proceedings Twelfth International Conference on Artificial Intelligence, Sydney, Australia, pp. 563–565.
2. R. Axelrod (1984), *The Evolution of Cooperation.* Basic Books.
3. T. Bäck (1998), *An overview of parameter control methods by self-adaptation in evolutionary algorithms.* Fundamenta Informaticae **35** (in print).
4. E.M. Brown (1990), *Boolean Reasoning.* Kluwer Academic Publishers, Dordrecht.
5. M. Burns (1993), *Resources: Automated Fabrication. Improving Productivity in Manufacturing.* Prentice Hall, Englewood Cliffs, NJ.
6. B.L. Clarke (1981), *A calculus of individuals based on "Connection".* Notre Dame Journal of Formal Logic **22**, pp. 204–218.
7. B.L. Clarke (1985), *Individuals and points.* Notre Dame Journal of Formal Logic **26**, pp. 61–75.
8. S.H. Clearwater, B.A. Huberman, T. Hogg (1992), *Cooperative problem solving.* In: B.A. Huberman (Ed.), Computation: The Micro and Macro View, (World Scientific, Singapore, pp. 33–70.

9. J.H. Connolly, E.A. Edmunds (1994), *CSCW and Artificial Intelligence.* Springer-Verlag, Berlin.
10. R. Davis, R.G. Smith (1989), *Negotiations as a metaphor for distributed problem solving.* Artificial Intelligence **20**, pp. 63–109.
11. K. Decker, V. Lesser (1993), *Quantitative modelling of complex computational task environments.* In: Proceedings AAAI-93, Washington, DC, pp. 217–224.
12. D. Dubois, H. Prade and R.R. Yager (1993), *Readings in Fuzzy Sets for Intelligent Systems.* Morgan Kaufmann, San Mateo.
13. E.H. Durfee (1988), *Coordination of Distributed Problem Solvers* (Kluwer Academic Publishers, Boston, 1988).
14. U. Fayyad, G. Piatetsky-Shapiro, G. (Eds.) (1996), *Advances in knowledge discovery and data mining,* MIT/AAAI Press.
15. D.B. Fogel (1998), *Unearthing a fossil from the history of evolutionary computation.* Fundamenta Informaticae **35** (in print).
16. J.W. Grzymała–Busse (1998), *Applications of the rule induction system LERS.* In: L. Polkowski, A. Skowron (Eds.), Rough Sets in Knowledge Discovery 1: Methodology and Applications, Physica-Verlag, Heidelberg, pp. 366–375.
17. J.H. Holland (1992), *Adaptation in Natural and Artificial Systems.* (MIT Press, Cambridge, MA.
18. T. Ishida (1994), *Parallel, Distributed and Multiagent Production Systems.* Lecture Notes in Computer Science **878**, Springer–Verlag, Berlin.
19. J. Komorowski, L. Polkowski and A. Skowron (1997), *Towards a rough mereology-based logic for approximate solution synthesis, Part 1.* Studia Logica **58**, pp. 143-184.
20. H.S. Leonard, N. Goodman (1940), *The calculus of individuals and its uses.* Journal of Symbolic Logic **5**, pp. 45–55.
21. S. Leśniewski (1916), *Foundations of the general theory of sets (in Polish),* Polish Scientific Circle, Moscow (1916); also in: S.J. Surma, J.T. Srzednicki, D.I. Barnett and V.F. Rickey (Eds.), Stanislaw Leśniewski, Collected Works, Kluwer Academic Publishers, Dordrecht (1992). 128–173.
22. B.T. Low (1993), *Neural-logic belief networks - a tool for knowledge representation and reasoning.* Procedings the 5-th IEEE International Conference on Tools with Artificial Intelligence, Boston, MA, pp. 34–37.
23. J. Łukasiewicz (1913), *Die logishen Grundlagen der Wahrscheinilchkeitsrechnung.* Kraków.
24. E.H. Mamdani, S. Assilian (1975), *An experiment in linguistic synthesis with a fuzzy logic controller.* International Journal of Man– Machine Studies **7**, pp. 1–13.
25. E. Mendelson (1964), *Introduction to Mathematical Logic.* Van Nostrand - Reinhold, New York.
26. Z. Pawlak (1991), *Rough sets: Theoretical Aspects of Reasoning about Data.* Kluwer Academic Publishers, Dordrecht.
27. Z. Pawlak, A. Skowron (1994), *Rough membership functions,* In: R.R. Yager, M. Fedrizzi and J. Kacprzyk (Eds.), Advances in The Dempster–Shafer Theory of Evidence, Wiley, New York, pp. 251–271.
28. J.W. Payne, J.R. Bettman, E.J. Johnson (1993), *The Adaptive Decision Maker.* Cambridge University Press, Cambridge.
29. J. Pearl (1988), *Probabilistic Reasoning in Intelligent Systems: Networks of Plausible Beliefs.* Morgan Kaufmann, San Mateo.

30. L. Polkowski, A. Skowron (1994), *Rough mereology.* In: Proceedings of the Symposium on Methodologies for Intelligent Systems, Charlotte, NC, October 16–19, Lecture Notes in Artificial Intelligence **869**, Springer–Verlag, Berlin, pp. 85–94.
31. L. Polkowski, A. Skowron (1994), *Logic of rough inclusion, Rough mereological functions, Rough functions.* ICS Research Report **12/94**, Institute of Computer Science, Warsaw University of Technology.
32. L. Polkowski, A. Skowron (1995), *Introducing rough mereological controllers: Rough quality control.*, In: T.Y. Lin and A.M. Wildberger (Eds.), Soft Computing, Simulation Councils, Inc., San Diego, pp. 240–243.
33. L. Polkowski, A. Skowron (1995), *Rough mereology analytical mereology, New developments in rough set theory.* In: M. De Glas, Z. Pawlak (Eds.), Proceedings of the Second World Conference on Fundamentals of Artificial Intelligence (WOCFAI'95), July 13–17, Angkor, Paris, pp. 343–354.
34. L. Polkowski, A. Skowron (1996), *Rough mereological approach to knowledge – based distributed AI.* In: J.K. Lee, J. Liebowitz, and J.M. Chae (Eds.), Critical Technology, Proceedings of the Third World Congress on Expert Systems, February 5–9, Seoul, Korea, Cognizant Communication Corporation, New York, pp. 774–781.
35. L. Polkowski, A. Skowron (1996), *Implementing fuzzy containment via rough inclusions: Rough mereological approach to distributed problem solving.* In: F.E. Petry, D.H. Kraft (Eds.), Proceedings of the Fifth IEEE International Conference on Fuzzy Systems (FUZZ-IEEE'96). September 8–11, New Orleans, Louisiana, pp. 1147–1153.
36. L. Polkowski, A. Skowron (1996), *Learning synthesis schemes in intelligent systems.* In: R.S. Michalski, J. Wnek (Eds.), Proceedings of the Third International Workshop on Multistrategy Learning (MSL'96), Harpers Ferry, West Virginia, May 23–25, George Mason University and AAAI Press, pp. 57–68.
37. L. Polkowski, A. Skowron (1996), *Rough mereology: A new paradigm for approximate reasoning.* International Journal of Approximate Reasoning **15/4**, pp. 333–365.
38. L. Polkowski, A. Skowron (1996), *Adaptive decision-making by systems of cooperative intelligent agents organized on rough mereological principles.* Journal of the Intelligent Automation and Soft Computing **2/2**, pp. 121-132.
39. L. Polkowski, A. Skowron (1998), *Rough mereology analytical morphology.* In: E. Orłowska (Ed.), Incomplete Information, Rough Set Analysis, Physica–Verlag, Heidelberg, pp. 399–437.
40. L. Polkowski, A. Skowron (1998), *Towards adaptive calculus of granules.* In: Proceedings of the FUZZ-IEEE'98 International Conference, Anchorage, Alaska, USA, May 5–9, pp. 111–116.
41. L. Polkowski, A. Skowron (1998), *Rough sets: A perspective.* In: L. Polkowski, A. Skowron (Eds.), Rough Sets in Knowledge Discovery 1: Methodology and Applications, Physica-Verlag, Heidelberg, pp. 31–58.
42. L. Polkowski, A. Skowron (Eds.) (1998), *Rough Sets in Knowledge Discovery 1: Methodology and Applications.* Physica-Verlag, Heidelberg.
43. L. Polkowski, A. Skowron (Eds.) (1998), *Rough Sets in Knowledge Discovery 2: Applications, Case Studies and Software Systems.* Physica-Verlag, Heidelberg.
44. L. Polkowski, A. Skowron (Eds.) (1998), *Proc. First International Conference on Rough Sets and Current Trends in Computing (RSCTC'98.* Warszawa, Poland, June 22–27, Springer-Verlag, LNAI **1424**.

45. L. Polkowski, A. Skowron, J. Komorowski (1997), *Towards a rough mereology-based logic for approximate solution synthesis, Part 1. Studia Logica* **58/1**, pp. 143-184.
46. R.B. Rao, S.C.-Y. Lu (1993), *Building models to support synthesis in early stage product design.* In: Proceedings of AAAI-93; Eleventh National Conference on Artificial Intelligence, AAAI Press/MIT Press, Menlo Park, pp. 277–282.
47. G. Shafer, J. Pearl (1990), *Readings in Uncertainty Reasoning.* Morgan Kaufmann, San Mateo, CA.
48. A. Skowron (1995), *Synthesis of adaptive decision systems from experimental data.* In: A. Aamodt and J. Komorowski (Eds.), Proceedings of the Fifth Scandinavian Conference on Artificial Intelligence (SCAI'95), IOS Press, Amsterdam, pp. 220–238.
49. A. Skowron, J.W. Grzymała-Busse (1994), *From rough set theory to evidence theory.*, In: R.R. Yager, M. Fedrizzi and J. Kacprzyk (Eds.), Advances in The Dempster - Shafer Theory of Evidence, Wiley, New York, pp. 193–236.
50. A. Skowron, L. Polkowski (1995), *Adaptive decision algorithms.* In: Proceedings Intelligent Information Systems III, The International Workshop, Institute of Foundations of Computer Science PAS, Warsaw, pp. 103–120.
51. A. Skowron, L. Polkowski (1998), *Rough mereological foundations for design, analysis, synthesis, and control in distributive systems.* Information Sciences **104/1-2**, pp. 129–156.
52. A. Skowron, C. Rauszer (1992), *The discernibility matrices and functions in information systems.* In: R. Słowiński (Ed.), Intelligent Decision Support, Handbook of Applications and Advances of the Rough Sets Theory, Kluwer Academic Publishers, Dordrecht, pp. 331–362.
53. D. Sriram, R. Logcher, S. Fukuda (1991), *Computer– Aided Cooperative Product Development.* Lecture Notes in Computer Science **492**, Springer–Verlag, Berlin.
54. A. Tarski (1935), *Zur Grundlegung der Booleschen Algebra I.* Fundamenta Mathematicae **24**, pp. 177–198.
55. A. Tarski (1937), *Appendix E.* In: J.H. Woodger, The Axiomatic Method in Biology, Cambridge University Press, Cambridge.
56. S. Tsumoto (1998), *Induction of expert decision rules using rough sets and set–inclusion.*, In: S.K. Pal, A. Skowron (Eds.),Rough–Fuzzy Hybridization: A New Trend in Decision Making, Springer-Verlag, Singapore (in print).
57. I. Wegener (1987), *The Complexity of Boolean Functions.* Wiley, New York.
58. A.N. Whitehead (1919), *An Enquiry Concerning the Principles of Natural Knowledge.* Cambridge University Press, Cambridge.
59. B. Widrow, M.A. Lehr (1990), *30 years of adaptive neural networks: Perceptron, madaline, and backpropagation.* In: Proc. of the IEEE 78, pp. 1415–1442.
60. L.A. Zadeh (1965). *Fuzzy sets.* Information and Control, **8**, pp. 338–353.
61. L.A. Zadeh (1996), *Fuzzy logic = computing with words.* IEEE Trans. on Fuzzy Systems **4**, pp. 103-111.
62. L.A. Zadeh (1997), *Toward a theory of fuzzy information granulation and its certainty in human reasoning and fuzzy logic.* Fuzzy Sets and Systems **90**, pp. 111-127.
63. G. Zlotkin, J. Rosenshein (1993), *Negotiations and conflict resolutions in non-cooperative domains.* In: Proceedings of AAAI-90; Eight National Conference on Artificial Intelligence, Boston, MA, pp. 100–105.
64. G. Zlotkin, J. Rosenshein (1991), *Incomplete information and deception in multi-agent negotiations.* In: Proceedings IJCAI-91, Sydney, Australia, pp. 225–231.

Semantics and Modelling of Flexible Time Indications

R. De Caluwe[1], F. Devos[2], P. Maesfranckx[2*], G. De Tré[1] and B. Van der Cruyssen[1]

[1] Computer Science Laboratory - University of Ghent (Belgium)
[2] Department of Dutch Linguistics - University of Ghent (Belgium)
[*] Scientific Associate of the Fund for Scientific Research (Flanders)

Abstract

This chapter presents an in-depth discussion of the semantics of time indications and proposes a formal time model suited to a variety of computer applications in which temporal databases play a role. The main characteristics of the model are the flexibility inherent to the ability of expressing approximate time indications in a way very close to natural language and the setting of a hierarchical framework, which allows to take into account the most appropriate level of granularity when expressing time indications.

1 Introduction

There is a big discrepancy between the scientific notion of time, the common perception of time and the way time is traditionally modelled for purposes of computer applications.

As a physical notion, time has been thoroughly studied and its definition given and gradually refined according to the limits of the actual level of human knowledge of physics and astronomy.

The common perception of time is at the same time simple and sophisticated. It is simple as time indications tend to inscribe themselves in an elementary way in a hierarchical system of directly related magnitudes. It is sophisticated, as in natural language the time indications are most of the time only approximate, implicitly carrying extra semantics, and as the relationships between the magnitudes in the hierarchical reference frame are in fact also very roughly defined.

Moreover, it has been observed that the semantics of time indications are context-bound.

The modelling of time for the purpose of computer applications has been addressed in the context of knowledge representation and handling for AI, for database programming, for retrieval etc. However, only very few authors have taken into account the approximativeness of the indications and of the reference frame. The proposed models are mainly based on the introduction of time points and of time intervals.

Trying to bridge the gap, fuzzy set theory has been used for modelling purposes [Dub89] [Dub91]. This is not as straightforward as it might look. Nevertheless, it is worth the effort, as this way much more information can be preserved.

In this chapter, the semantics of the linguistic time indications, the semantics of the natural reference frame and the modelling issues are addressed by means of fuzzy set theory and the related possibility theory.

It is indicated how this leads to the definition of a formal granular system which is able to take into account the imperfections of the natural hierarchical time system. Within this framework the practical issues concerning relative and absolute time indications are also discussed.

2 Notions of time

2.1 The physical notion of time

In scientific work, time is treated in a formal way. A numerical time scale is used to describe the order of events and phenomena.

Such a time scale is determined by the choice of an origin and a time unit. It is customary to assign the numerical value zero to the origin, negative values to anterior times and positive values to posterior times.

The definition of a time unit is usually based on the observation of a physical periodic phenomenon. Further, other units can be defined as multiples or subdivisions of this unit.

As scientific time observations are always limited by a finite precision, a characterisation by discrete values is sufficient.

The most important scientific and astronomic time scales are:

- *Astronomical time*: the definition of astronomical time is based on the apparent diurnal movement of the spring equinoctial point.
- *Universal time*: the definition of this time is based on the apparent diurnal movement of the sun.
- *Dynamic time*: this time was introduced in 1984 and is a uniform time scale which is independent of any irregularities (dynamic time is used amongst others in the drawing up of astronomic ephemerides).
- *Atomic time*: the definition of atomic time relies on the radiation frequency that corresponds with the transition between two hyper-fine levels of the base state of Caesium 133.
- In 1991 the IAU (International Astronomic Union) decided to take Einstein's *theory of general relativity* as the theoretical background of the definition of

time. Hereby, the measurement of time is no longer independent of the movement of the observer.

Almost every scientific time scale defines a unit "*second*" as its basic unit of time. Since 1967 the second is theoretically defined according to the atomic standards as the duration of 9.192.631.770 periods of the radiation corresponding to the transition between the two hyperfine levels of the ground state of the cesium-133 atom.

Apart from physical factors the choice of units has also been influenced by historical conventions. For instance the unit "*minute*" is defined as 60 seconds, "hour" as 60 minutes and "*day*" as 24 hours. Additionally this has led to several calendar systems that are used to denominate the consecutive days. The most commonly used calendars are: the Julian calendar and the Gregorian calendar.

2.2 The notion of time in natural language

The physical notion mentioned in § 2.1 is reflected in lexical items which refer to natural phenomena on the one hand (e.g. year, season, day, night, noon) or to an artificial time unit system on the other hand (e.g. century, week, hour, quarter, minute). In fact, time can be rendered very precisely by means of unique proper names or numbers (e.g. on Wednesday December 31st 1997 at 23h 59min and 59sec).

Apart from the physical notion, there is an experiential notion of time which expresses the way humans experience time. These "experiential" facts are either individually determined (e.g. often, soon, now and then cf. § 4.2) or culturally (e.g. week in our tradition of the five-day working week; either Sunday or Monday as the first day of the week).

These different concepts are all reflected in linguistic time and often combined in linguistic time expressions. This makes linguistic time an extremely complex notion. For instance, in natural language the notion of "year" seems clearly defined: it refers to a period of 12 months or 365 days (and under specific conditions 366 days), starting on 1st January. However, when one considers the examples below, things seem not as uncomplicated as they look:

(a) When do people buy most presents? *At the end of the year.*
(b) When do we have exams? *At the end of the year.*

Applying the above-mentioned definition will render a correct, though fuzzy interpretation of "year" in example (a). For example (b), uttered in a university context, it will not work, even though the time indications are identical in both sentences. In (b) an "academic year" is meant, which (in Belgium) starts on 1st October. "Year" is thus ambiguous in the sense that an academic or a civil year may be meant, without explicit mentioning in the text. Further interpretation problems may arise because of cultural differences: the academic year in Sweden starts on 1st September and the Jewish or Chinese civil years do not start on 1st January.

Natural language users are normally aware of the context of the utterance and they automatically derive the correct interpretation. However, it is not easy for them to make explicit what exactly is meant by "at the end of the year", as this is a vague time indication, which is cognitively understood as a fuzzy interval (cf. their representation in § 6). In inquiries carried out by our research group, informants were asked to indicate the interval which the given time indications definitely did refer to as well as the interval the time indications definitely did not refer to. The individual responses showed that those two intervals were mostly not adjacent. Some space was left in between, which means that these vague lexical time indications are cognitively represented as fuzzy rather than crisp intervals:

(c) I lived in London *last year*.
(d) *Last year* we spent our holidays in Austria.
(e) *Last year* my marks for English were very bad, but after two months with the new teacher they have improved a lot.

These examples all contain the same time indication "last year". Still they get three different interpretations. Suppose these three sentences are all uttered on 1st November 1997. In (c) the time indication refers to 1996 but it is ambiguous in the sense that it is not clear whether the whole year is referred to or just part of it. Only the speaker, and not the hearer, will know what exactly is meant: a time point or a time interval (cf. § 5.2). In (d), the hearer can rely on his real world knowledge to resolve the ambiguity: holidays normally do not last a whole year. How long they actually did last and when exactly they did take place is not relevant here. The new, relevant information in this sentence, which is placed in focus-position by the speaker, is "in Austria". Finally, in (e) "last year" most probably refers to the whole year, but this time a school year is meant. In Belgium this would mean from 1st September 1996 until 30th June 1997.

(f) *Every year* I spend New Year's Eve with some friends.
(g) In Finland it snows *every year*.
(h) *Every year* some 20.000 people visit the museum.

These three examples all contain the same frequency indication: "every year". Apart from the repetitive element their semantics have very little in common, however. In (f), it can be derived from the rest of the sentence that the repetition refers to a time point, namely one specific day in the year, 31st December. In (g), our real world knowledge helps us to interpret this time indication as a repetition of a time period (or several time periods), which however not always starts on the same day nor always has the same duration. Finally, in (h), the duration is more important than the starting point. It does not matter when the year starts, the calculation will always result in "some 20.000 people". In other words, the repetition refers to a span (cf. § 6.2).

3 The modelling of time

The examples (a)-(h) show that a time model, based on natural language, should distinguish the concepts of time position, duration and repetition (cf. § 6.1). It should take into account the context-sensitiveness of time indications and the possibility offered by natural language to express time at different levels of precision (cf. § 4). Moreover, it should be able to handle the uncertainty which may arise when switching from one level to another and the vagueness which is inherent to some time indications (cf. § 5.2).

The central role of temporality in many computer applications makes the representation and manipulation of temporal information highly relevant. This is especially the case for information systems, planning and scheduling systems, real time systems and databases.

Up to now several time models have been proposed [Tso96] originating from three research areas [Mai92]: conceptual modelling focusing on time representation, database systems concerned with the management of temporal information, and artificial intelligence addressing time reasoning. Important contributions to the research field of data modelling has been the independently specified time model of Bubenko [Bub80], the modelling approach based on first order logic of Bolour and Dekeyzer [Bol83] and the extensions of the entity-relationship model proposed by Chen [Che86] and by Kloprogge and Lockemann [Klo83]. An overview of some results in the database system domain is given in [Kim95] whereas Knight and Ma [Kni92] summarise some of the most important contributions in the domain of artificial intelligence.

Almost all these contributions deal with time in a crisp way, hereby approaching the scientific notion of time. Linguistic research has shown however that vagueness is an integrated part of natural language [Dev95] [Mae97]. The same idea has also been put forward by Zadeh [Zad96] [Zad97]. Today even the traditional database community is beginning to recognise the importance of dealing with incomplete data in database systems [Kor97]. A cognitively adequate linguistic description of the meaning of vague lexical time indications, as they are interpreted by natural language users, constitutes the necessary basis for this modelling. This chapter is the result of a theoretical study concerning the modelling of vague lexical time indications, supported by research on vagueness in general and empirical research on lexical time indications in particular.

4 Granularity

In recent publications it has been recognised that information granulation is one of the basic concepts of human cognition (e.g. [Zad96] [Zad97]). Information granulation refers to the way information is provided and manipulated based on a decomposition of objects, entities, units, etc. into parts. Probably the most eminent and most familiar example is the granulation of time into years, months, days, hours, minutes, ... Depending on the availability, relevance or preference, the appropriate level of accuracy is used for expressing and reasoning with time. For instance, the age of an infant is typically expressed in terms of months (e.g. 'Our daughter is 14 months old now.'), though the age of older children and adults is referred to by years only.

Most generally, a granule is defined as a clump of points (objects) drawn together by indistinguishability, similarity, proximity or functionality [Zad97]. A time granule is defined as a unit constituted by the time points which are observed as indistinguishable with respect to a given precision. A time granularity is defined as the division of the time axis in one kind of time granules. (In the following, the terms granule and granularity will be used instead of time granule and time granularity.)

In general, a granulation is hierarchical in nature. Maiocchi et al. [Mai92] have proposed a five-level granularity structure, with year as an "absolute" datum and month, day, hour and minute as cyclical data, as illustrated in figure 1.

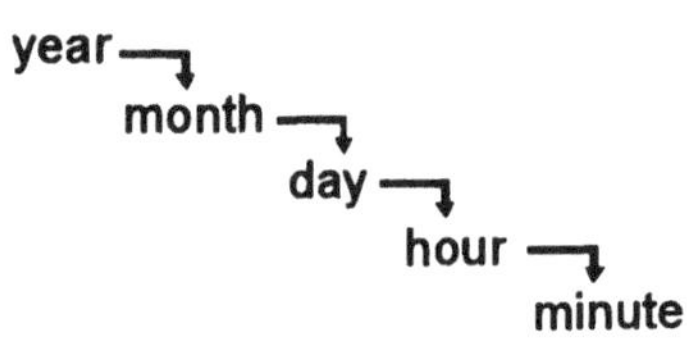

Figure 1. The five-level time model (Maiocchi et al.)

Several objections can be made to this quite self-evident unit system. First, this time model only supports crisp indications (1-12 for month, 1-31 for day, 0-23 for hour, 0-59 for minute). Secondly, many other granularities can be needed or desirable in different contexts, like second, week, quarter, trimester, semester, academic year, decade, and so on. Further, it is rather awkward to build the time unit system by descending to greater detail, since the connection with the absolute time cannot be brought into the model. In fact it is impossible to define some years or months to be one or more days longer (in absolute time) than others, unless their definition is based on the definition of day. Therefore, it is better to organise the granularity system from the smallest level (absolute time) towards larger units. The term organisation is used as in [Zad97], i.e. as the dual concept of granulation: the integration of parts into a whole.

An alternative approach is given in [Wan97] where the notion of a temporal type is introduced to formalise time granularity. A temporal type is defined as a mapping from the set of positive integers (time ticks) to the set of absolute time sets. In other words, every time granularity is defined by a mapping from its time granules to the absolute time. This can be visualised as in figure 2.

This model is still limited to crisp time, but in contrast to the previous model, it allows the addition of other than the mentioned temporal types, like for instance week, academic year or decade.

However, the interrelationships between the different granularities does not appear in the latter granularity structure. In order to let the system benefit of this additional information, we propose a granularity structure that is hierarchical by definition. An example of such a granularity hierarchy is shown in figure 3. The availability of the interrelationships between granularity is very important for allowing explicit or implicit conversions between the different granularities. This will be discussed further in § 6.

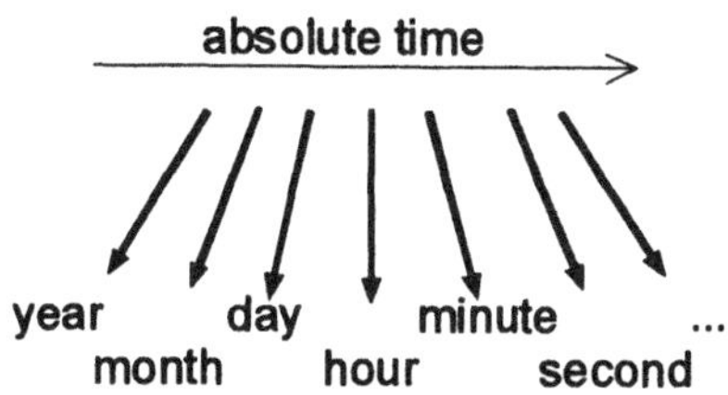

Figure 2. Temporal types (Wang et al.)

Figure 3. A hierarchical granularity structure

The basic granularity is determined by the highest precision supported by the model. The definition of the basic granularity can be seen as a discretisation of the continuous absolute time T. By way of illustration, suppose a crisp, uniform discretisation based on a given origin $t_0 \in T$ and a precision Δ. Then, a possible choice for the basic granularity G_0 could be the set of granules $\gamma_{0,k}$:

$$G_0 = \{\gamma_{0,k} | k \in \{0,\ 1,\ -1,\ 2,\ -2,\ \ldots\}\}$$

Each granule $\gamma_{0,k}$ can be defined as:

$$\gamma_{0,k} = [t_0 + k\mathrm{D}\ ,\ t_0 + (k+1)\mathrm{D}\ [$$

or, alternatively :

$$\gamma_{0,k} = \left[t_0 + (2k-1)\frac{\mathrm{D}}{2},\ t_0 + (2k+1)\frac{\mathrm{D}}{2}\right[$$

and is said to be the k-th granule G_0 of the granularity .

The definition of the basic granularity G_0 can be formally represented by a mapping g_0 :

$$g_0 : T \to G_0$$
$$t \to g_0(t) = \gamma_{0,k}\ ,\ \text{if } t \in \gamma_k$$

Other granularities are derived from an existing granularity by taking granules together into new coherent units. The definition of a new granularity G_n derived from its parent granularity G_p is again given by a mapping g_n (see also Figures 4a and 4b):

$$g_n : G_p \to G_n$$
$$\gamma_{p,k} \to g_n(\gamma_{p,k}) = \gamma_{n,l}\ ,\ \text{if } \gamma_{p,k} \subset \gamma_{n,l}$$

Note that several granularities can be derived from the same parent, and all granularities are either directly or indirectly derived from the basic granularity. As a result a granularity hierarchy is formed, in which each granularity is linked to its parent granularity by its mapping function, except the basic granularity (as root) which is linked to the absolute time by the discretisation mapping.

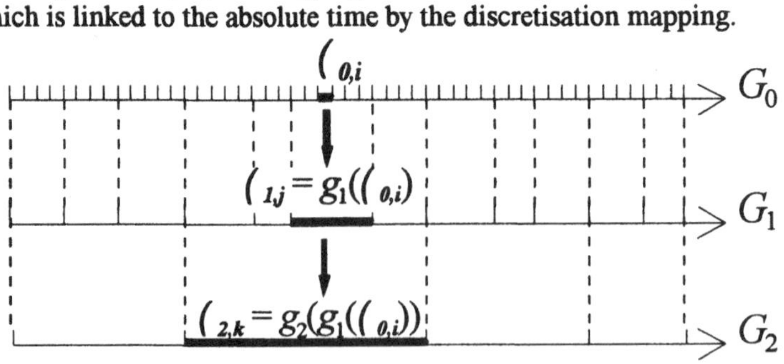

Figure 4a. Definition of granularities

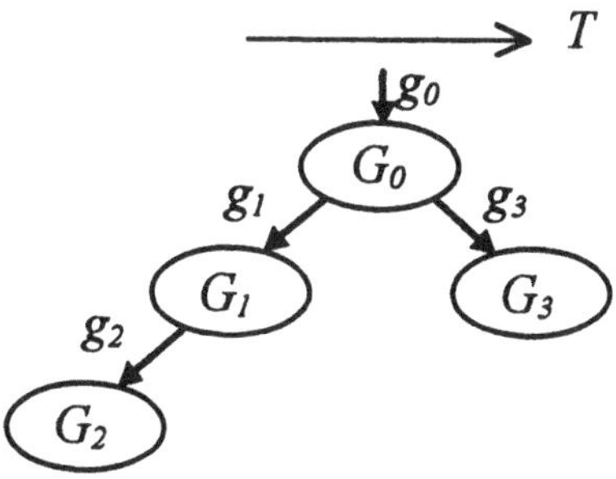

Figure 4b. Definition of granularities

A crisp and total granulation corresponds to a partition of the parent granularity and therefore can be modelled by an equivalence relationship R_{pn}:

$$R_{pn} = \left\{ (x,y) \in G_p \times G_p \,\middle|\, g_n(x) = g_n(y) \right\}$$

And, since all granules have to be convex:

$$\forall\, x,y,z \in G_p : x \leq y \leq z \;\wedge\; (x,z) \in R_{pn} \;\Rightarrow\; (x,y) \in R_{pn}$$

More generally, considering partial granularities like weekend or fuzzy granularities like season, implies that the definitions can not longer be based on an equivalence relationship.

5 Lexical time indications (LTI's) in natural language

Before presenting a formal time model, it is necessary to clearly describe the phenomenon which is going to be modelled. As this is also a natural language phenomenon (lexical time indications), a linguistic description is the starting point.

The next paragraphs discuss:

- What is meant by *lexical time indications* (LTI's) and how can they be classified.
- What is meant by *vague lexical time indications* (VLTI's) and what is the difference with uncertain and ambiguous ones.
- The need for the use of VLTI's in natural language and consequently the relevance of modelling them.

Finally a case study of three sorts of VLTI's is presented. The results of this linguistic investigation shed a light on the way human beings cognitively interpret VLTI's.

5.1 LTI's: description and classification

In natural language time is expressed in many different ways [Kle94]. Not only tense, which has received most attention in the literature, but also aspect, temporal adverbials, word order, temporal particles (e.g. Chinese le) and compound expressions (e.g. to finish crying), amongst others, determine temporal reference. Our research focuses on what is traditionally called 'temporal adverbials': lexical time indications (LTI's), where the time indication lies in the meaning of the words (lexemes) that are used, not in their grammatical features, as with verb tenses. [Kle94] points out that there are languages which lack grammatical categories to express time but there is no language without lexical time indications. The meaning of LTI's is to a large extent independent of other temporal categories like tense marking and aspect marking, but some types of LTI's can only be disambiguated by the tense of the utterance they are part of (cf. § 7). The use of LTI's makes it possible to express time at different levels of granularity. Language users will chose the most appropriate level of granularity, according to their communicative purposes (cf. §5.3).

LTI's may indicate time **position** (e.g. yesterday, in 1994, two days after his first birthday), **duration** (e.g. three hours, a whole month, half a century) or **repetition** (e.g. every week, twice a year, every other day). These different categories can also be combined, e.g. on Sundays is a combination of position and repetition, from 25th November 1996 until 5th January 1997 is a combination of position and duration. Positional LTI's can further be subdivided according to the following parameters:

(1) Deictic-independent

Deictic LTI's refer to times relative to the deictic centre of orientation, which is usually the moment of speaking (cf. "relative time" in § 6.1). Examples are: now, three days ago, this week, next year. **Independent LTI's** refer to times directly, their meaning is independent from the moment of speaking (cf. "absolute time" in § 6.1). Examples are: in 1994, when Napoleon died, in the night, on Sundays). Derived from these two main categories, anaphoric LTI's can be distinguished, which refer to times previously established in the context. In other words, their meaning depends on time indications previously mentioned during the conversation (deictic or independent ones). Examples are: the day before, three minutes later, after two months. Indirectly they are thus also connected with either relative or absolute time.

(2) Situational-relational

Situational LTI's point to a time fact itself (e.g. yesterday, on 21st July 1995 at 10h26). **Relational LTI's** refer to a relation with a time point or interval and this relation is an anterior (e.g. shortly before 20h), a posterior (e.g. three years after the Second World War) or an approximative one (e.g. around half past ten). For the interpretation of relational LTI's first an operation must be carried out to resolve the indirectness (e.g. three years after the Second World War: 1945 + 3 = 1948).

(3) Bound-unbound

Unbound LTI's do not refer to past, present or future on their own (e.g. at half past ten, shortly before 20h). Their interpretation depends on the verb tense, as explained in §7). **Bound LTI's**, on the other hand, do refer to past, present or future (e.g. yesterday, on 21st July 1995).

These classifications show that LTI's constitute a class full of variation, which makes the description of their meaning a complex matter. Especially problematic is the interpretation of vague LTI's, which is discussed in the next paragraphs.

5.2 Vague lexical time indications (VLTI's)

In most of the examples given in § 5.1 time is indicated in a precise way. Very often, however, this precision is irrelevant or unnecessary within the context (cf. § 5.3). Therefore language users often use imprecise time indications. Examples can be found for each of the categories mentioned above:

(i) The show lasted for *about two hours*. (duration)
(j) I play tennis *about 3 times a week*. (repetition)
(k) I received this letter *about a month ago*. (position - deictic)
(l) The accident happened *around 21st July 1995*. (position - independent)
(m) *In the beginning of the 20th century* Norway became independent. (position - situational)
(n) *Shortly before 20h* there was an electricity breakdown. (position - relational)
(o) I'll call you *around 9 a.m.*. (position - unbound)
(p) I'll call you *tomorrow after 10 a.m.*. (position - bound)

All of these examples contain vague LTI's. The meaning of expressions such as "shortly before 20h" is not sharply delimited, as one may wonder whether 7h45 still falls within its range.

Vagueness should be distinguished from other forms of "lexical polyvalence", such as ambiguity and incompleteness, with which it is often confused. Semantic **vagueness** refers to an intrinsic uncertainty as to the application of a word to a denotatum [Dev95]. With **ambiguity** the uncertainty is not intrinsic, as it is situated only on the side of the hearer. If a speaker says: "I'll call you at 9 o'clock" and it is not obvious from the context whether "a.m." or "p.m." is meant, the hearer has the choice between a limited range of possible interpretations. The speaker however, knows exactly which one is meant. This is not the case for vague expressions. LTI's can be vague without being ambiguous (e.g. I'll phone you tomorrow around 9 a.m.) or the other way around (e.g. I'll phone you tomorrow at 9 o'clock). Being ambiguous means that one is referring to one specific moment or period without specifying which one, like in the second example where it is not specified whether "a.m." or "p.m." is meant, even though the hearer most probably knows which of the two is meant, as in most cases, the context disambiguates the utterance. Incomplete information or "**incompleteness**", on the other hand, is found especially in situational and unbound expressions. A typical case is when the information is expected at a finer level of granularity than the level which is actually used. In "My birthday is in May", where day-granularity is expected, the information is underdetermined, though the boundaries of the period are fixed (i.e. between 1st and 31st May), as opposed to vague expressions. The formal time model, presented in § 6 accounts for both the vagueness and the incompleteness of LTI's.

As mentioned above, semantic vagueness refers to an intrinsic uncertainty as to the application of a word to a denotatum. Basically, two types of vagueness can be distinguished: vagueness in degree and vagueness in criteria [Dev95]. The first kind of vagueness resides in the fact that one and only one well-determined criterion is being scaled (e.g. the criterion of "age" in "an old man", or the criterion of "length" in "a tall man"). Vagueness in criteria, on the other hand, can be found in expressions like "a big house" or "an intelligent man": most often different criteria are called upon in naming a building a "big" house (e.g. the surface area, the number of floors, the number of (bed)rooms, etc.), just as different criteria can be called upon in naming someone "intelligent". Hence, this kind of vagueness is multidimensional. It should be noted that many lexemes are vague in both senses (e.g. "a big house" (vague in criteria) → "a big house, i.e. with many bedrooms" (vague in degree)).

Vagueness in degree can easily be modelled by means of fuzzy set theory using membership degrees. Modelling vagueness in criteria is less straightforward as the different criteria add an additional dimension. However, time is a one-dimensional fact, and only vagueness in degree and not vagueness in criteria is involved. Moreover, time can be expressed numerically (which makes time objectifiable). All this should facilitate a formal representation of vague time expressions by means of fuzzy set theory. For instance, around 18h can be modelled as in figure 5. The membership function indicates to which degree the time points belong to the extension of around 18h. The value 0 (e.g. for 17h30) means that it does not belong to it, the value 1 (e.g. for 17h55) means that it fully belongs to it. A value in between (e.g. 0,4 for 17h40) specifies the degree to which the point belongs to it.

From a linguistic point of view, it is not difficult to describe the meaning of ambiguous or incomplete LTI's. It is simply a matter of listing the different possibilities. For example:

- His birthday is *in May* → His birthday is on one of the 31 days of the month 'May'
- He called her *yesterday at 9 o'clock* → He called her yesterday either at 9 a.m. or at 9 p.m.

Describing the meaning of vague LTI's (VLTI's) is much more problematic. It is surprising that people rarely have difficulties to interpret them. As will be shown in § 5.3 VLTI's are very frequently used and still do not seem to cause major communication problems or misunderstandings. However, it is very hard for language users to make explicit how they interpret VLTI's. What exactly is meant by e.g. shortly before 20h or in the beginning of the 20th century? As a linguistic description of the meaning of VLTI's is not available, the linguistic part of our research has concentrated on VLTI's.

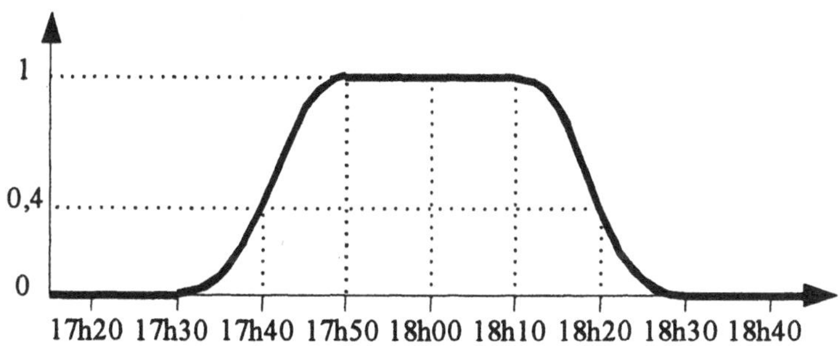

Figure 5. Around 18h00

5.3 The need for VLTI's

One could wonder why people use VLTI's in natural language. There is a system that allows them to give precise time indications, so why do they not use it all the time? This question can be answered within the linguistic subdiscipline called "pragmatics" which studies language as it is used in communication, taking into account the context-dependency of linguistic expressions. As the examples will show, some basic pragmatic rules, especially Grice's maxims [Lev83], impel us to be vague in certain contexts (these maxims should be seen as basic communication rules):

- the maxim of quality states: "try to make your contribution one that is true (do not say what you believe to be false and do not say that for which you lack adequate evidence)". Applied to time indications, this means that we should not use precise time indications unless we know the exact time. As this is rarely the case for instance when telling things about the past or making predictions about the future, VLTI's are a necessity for adequate conversation.
- the maxim of quantity states: "make your contribution as informative as is required for the current purposes of the exchange and do not make your contribution more informative than is required". Even if one knows the exact time, it is not always appropriate to mention it, as utterances may become stuffed with unnecessary details.
- the maxim of relevance states: "make your contributions relevant". In the case of VLTI's, this maxim often coincides with the maxim of quantity. For instance, in the context of telling a friend about something that happened to you, being too informative means you are telling irrelevant details. In the case of providing yourself with an alibi in a police station, on the other hand, these precise time indications are relevant.
- the maxim of manner states: "be perspicuous, and specifically: a) avoid obscurity, b) avoid ambiguity, c) be brief and d) be orderly". (a) actually pleads against using VLTI's, but (c) impels us to use them in contexts where everybody knows what we are talking about. If one is discussing a meeting which took place two days before with ones colleagues, it is more appropriate to refer to it as "the meeting the other day" instead of saying "the meeting on 25th April at 2 p.m.". The latter will probably be more obscure to the listeners in this case (they will have to start thinking "Which day is today?" and will finally infer that the speaker is actually referring to the meeting two days ago.) and moreover it is not brief. Ambiguity is a different matter, which does not really have anything to do with vagueness (cf. § 5.2).

These maxims are not always followed, but even for this there is a pragmatic reason. Together with the maxims Grice defined an underlying general co-operative principle [Lev83]: "make your contribution such as is required, at the stage at which it occurs, by the accepted purpose or direction of the talk exchange in which you are engaged". If the speaker obviously flouts one of the maxims, the listener still believes him to be co-operative, at some deeper level. Suppose John makes an appointment with his friend Woody at 4 p.m. and John is 45 minutes late. Upon arrival, Woody might exclaim: "Where have you been? I've been waiting here for hours!". Taken literally, this is clearly a breach of the maxim of quality. As John supposes Woody to be co-operative, however, John infers that Woody must be trying to communicate something else than the "amount of time he has been waiting". This something else is probably "the impression Woody got of the time he has been waiting: it seemed like hours". In other words, he is referring to experiential time rather than to scientific time (cf.

§ 2). This sort of inferences, following from the maxims or the breach of the maxims are called "conversational implicatures" [Lev83]. The main difference with logical or semantic inferences is that conversational implicatures are cancellable. In our example the implicature is "Woody has not really been waiting for hours, it just seemed to him like hours" but this will be cancelled if the next utterance is: "You did say you would come at 2 p.m., didn't you?", indicating that Woody thought the appointment was two hours earlier and thus has really been waiting there for hours.

Given these principles of conversation, which are the situations in which the use of VLTI's is appropriate? In other words, which communicative purposes make us choose a vague instead of a precise lexical time indication? [Cha94] gives a list of ten communicative situations in which the use of vague language is appropriate. [Mae97] gives specific examples of VLTI's for these ten situations. To summarise we may say that VLTI's are appropriate in the following situations:

(a) in informal situations;
(b) in formal situations if
  (1) the speaker lacks specific information,
  (2) the speaker wants to make a polite request to a more powerful hearer,
  (3) the speaker is uncertain about time or if he wants to protect himself against being proved wrong (especially when talking about the past or making predictions about the future),
  (4) the speaker has reasons to withhold information,
  (5) the speaker wants to be persuasive,
  (6) specific time reference is irrelevant for the purposes of the conversation.

[Cha94] also discusses three main strategies to make an utterance (or part of it) vague. These can be applied to time indications as well [Mae97]:

(1) *using vague additives*: a word or a phrase is added to what would otherwise be a precise time indication (e.g. *around* 10h30, *approximately* 2 hours, *more or less* 5 months). Vague additives in LTI's can be called "approximators", and the words or phrases they determine are called "approximata". Usually these approximata are numerical (e.g. around *10h30*) but they can also be lexical (e.g. about *a week*) or both (e.g. approximately *7 hours*).

(2) *choosing vague expressions*: these expressions are always vague, vagueness is inherent to their meaning (e.g. briefly, sometimes, for a while, recently, soon, regularly). Instead of using exact numbers one can use vague quantifiers, like a few, some, several, many. They are combined with countable nouns (for instance, years, days, hours or minutes in the case of lexical time indications). Most adverbs of frequency display this sort of inherent vagueness (e.g. sometimes, seldom, rarely, often).

(3) *vagueness by implicature*: an apparently precise utterance can be used and understood to have a vague meaning (e.g. I'll meet you there at 10 o'clock; The sunny weather only lasted a fortnight; I met her two years ago). We often use precise time indications with a vague meaning. Especially "round" numbers are used in this way and the hearer seems to successfully decode them as vague. This is a matter of pragmatics and more exactly of conversational implicatures (cf. § 7). Which numbers function as round numbers has partly been investigated by Rosch [Ros75], Johansson [Joh80] and Sigurd [Sig88]. These numbers serve as reference points in the natural category of numbers.

(4) *using "semi-infinite" intervals* (i.e. intervals which are infinite on one side): a possibility which Channell does not mention is the use of "semi-infinite" intervals, which does not completely fit into one of the above mentioned strategies. This strategy is partly a matter of "vagueness by implicature", as "semi-infinite" intervals are not vague from a logical-semantic point of view (e.g. Before 1830 Belgium did not exist as an independent state). Pragmatically however, infinity will often be limited by a fuzzy border which is relevant in the given context (e.g. in the example "Before 1865 slavery existed in the USA" the lower border is not interpreted as stretching into infinity, as it can be derived from common world knowledge that there have not always been slaves in the USA). On the other hand this strategy is also a matter of using vague additives, as in *shortly* before the accident, *immediately* after 24th December or *long* before 1800. These additives are different from the ones mentioned earlier. Here, the vague additives are added not to something precise, but to something which is (pragmatically) vague, a "semi-infinite" interval. Instead of making things more vague, they actually help us locate the unspecified border of the interval. This border will still be fuzzy if the additives are vague. A precise additive (e.g. *two days* before Christmas) would result in a lexical time indication with crisp borders.

In this section it has been argued that VLTI's are an integrated part of natural language. As they are necessary for efficient communication, a system which aims at computing with words cannot simply ignore them. The possibility to use VLTI's in e.g. database systems would certainly make those more user-friendly, even though it means just a little step towards human-like communication with a computer.

5.4 A case study: three types of VLTI's

It has been argued in § 5.2 that semantic vagueness can be found in all subclasses of LTI's. However there are three subclasses of LTI's which prototypically display vagueness:

(1) lexical, non-numerical indications of frequency (e.g. often, seldom, sometimes)

(2) approximate lexical time indications (e.g. around 6 p.m., around 1972)
(3) indications of "semi-infinite" intervals, i.e. indications of posterior and anterior relations (e.g. shortly before 6 p.m., some time after the holidays)

These three types have been investigated by our research group by means of inquiries. Language users were asked what was meant by a number of VLTI's. The results of these inquiries shed a light on some (cognitive) principles which determine the interpretation of VLTI's by average language users.

The results show that the second group mentioned above, approximative lexical time indications (henceforth ALTI's) is interpreted as denoting symmetrical intervals around the reference point given. For instance, around 18h is interpreted as an interval from about 17h45 until about 18h15. Moreover, the answers seem to be quite consistent among informants, unlike the answers given for the other two types. Especially non-numerical indications of frequency get a whole range of different interpretations. This can be explained by experiential factors. For example, the values given for now and then in the sentence "He only drinks alcohol now and then" range from 0-2 times a month till 8-12 times a month, most probably due to the informants' own experience with alcohol. The meaning of ALTI's seems to be very little influenced by such factors. A second inquiry was carried out specifically on ALTI's. The results are presented below.

5.4.1 A more detailed study of approximative LTI's (ALTI's)

As outlined above (§ 3.3) ALTI's consist of "approximators" (e.g. around) and "approximata" (lexical or numerical). ALTI's are always vague and their gradual vagueness is to be found in the modifying expression (e.g. *around* 6 p.m.) or in both the modifying and the modified expression (e.g. *around* noon). ALTI's refer to a mostly symmetrical interval stretching between two fuzzy limits. A detailed inquiry was carried out in order to find out which factors determine the interpretation of around in ALTI's having numerical elements as approximate. Lexical items as approximata are often experientially determined (e.g. evening as "period between day and night" or "period between work and sleep" or "period of rest after work")(cf. § 2.2).

The informants were asked two questions about each ALTI: what does the given time expression definitely refer to and what does it definitely not refer to? In other words they gave a yes- and a no-indication for each ALTI. In most of the individual answers these two indications were not complementary (e.g. around 1974: yes-indication = 1972 - 1976; no-indication = before 1970 and after 1978). The fact that some space is left in between shows that people do not interpret these time indications as having crisp borders, but rather fuzzy ones. The results of this inquiry confirm that in most cases symmetrical, fuzzy intervals are a cognitively adequate representation of the meaning of ALTI's. How large these intervals should be depends mainly on the level of granularity (cf. § 5.4.2). Some other factors which may influence the symmetry or the length of the interval are discussed in § 5.4.3-5.4.5.

5.4.2 Granularity

Granularity refers to the (abstract) time levels people use. As outlined in § 4, these levels constitute a rather precise hierarchical system of subordinate and superordinate categories in which different shifts may occur (e.g. second → minute → hour → day → ...). From the inquiry the hypothesis can be derived that ALTI's prototypically can be given the following intervals (Table 1) for each granularity level [Dev97].

It is not sufficient to simply postulate a granularity scheme, one should also look at the functionality of such a scheme, and see if, for instance, the existence of one granularity level acts as a brake on the given value for a sublevel. In other words, does the place of the approximatum relative to a higher or lower level in the hierarchy have any influence on the interpretation of the ALTI? And if so, when does a level shift occur, i.e. when does the interpretation shift to the superordinate of the approximatum?

Our inquiry shows that level shifts are avoided if possible. There is, for instance, no shift of level in around April 28th, around 10h57 (with May 1st and 11h as end point) or around February 3rd, around 14h 10min 05s (with February 1st and 14h 10min as starting point). This implies that some intervals may be asymmetrical: around 10h57 is predominantly valued as [10h55, 11h], around 1979 as [1977, 1980] and around 18h22 as [18h15, 18h30]. In around 4000 BC, however, the shift necessarily does take place (most common value: [4500, 3500 BC]) as it is a "round number" (a number expressed in terms of magnitude), situated on the border of two granularity levels. From this we must conclude that there is a correlation of factors. Not only granularity itself but also the "roundness" of the reference points and the position within this granularity determine the interpretation (cf. § 5.4.5).

5.4.3 Speech time and reference time

Reichenbach [Rei47] subdivides linguistic (tense-related) time into speech time (ST), reference time (RT) and event time (ET). ST is the time at which an expression or sentence is uttered, RT the moment which is referred to and ET the time at which what is reported on takes place. Important for the interpretation of ALTI's is the distance between RT and ST. In general, a small distance (e.g. RT = around 2000; ST = 1997), diminishes the value of the interval, while a big distance (e.g. RT = around 2500; ST = 1997) enlarges this value. However, this rule does not seem to apply (to the same extent) to smaller granularities, like second, minute or hour (e.g. RT = around 19h30; ST = 18h). In some cases ST acts as the limit of the interval, as can be seen in around 2000, which, in 1997, is valued as [1997, 2005].

Table 1: Typical approximation values for ALTI's

Granularity	Example	Typical approximation
Second	around 14h10min05s	5 seconds
Minute	around 18h22	5 minutes
Hour - full hour and half hour	around 19h30	15 minutes
- hour + n × 5 min (multiple of 5 minutes)	around 20h10	5 or 10 minutes
- hour + n × 1 min	around 18h22	5 minutes
Day	around March 15th	7 days
Month	around September 1993	a fortnight
Year	around 4000 BC	50 to 500 years
	around 2500	50 years
	around 350 AD around 1670 around 2070	10 years (decade)
	around 1974 around 1979	2 years
	around 2000	2 to 5 years

5.4.4 The size of the approximatum

A factor correlating with the previously mentioned distance between RT and ST, is the size of the approximatum. The larger level the approximatum refers to, the larger the interval is valued. Undoubtedly, around 4000 BC has a bigger interval than around 350 AD.

5.4.5 Roundness

Round numbers function as cognitive reference points in the numerical system [Cha94] and they seem to play an important part in the interpretation of ALTI's. As our inquiries show, approximations are mostly given in terms of round numbers. An approximation of 10 years is more likely to appear than an approximation of 9 or 11 years. Roundness can also explain the asymmetry in some answers. For instance, for around Easter (= 11th April), there were answers like: [1 April, 30 April], [1 April, 20 April] and [1 April, 15 April]. This is often connected with the avoidance of granularity shifts, as outlined in § 3.4.2. Indeed, the numbers which function as round numbers in our time system are those which coincide with a granularity shift and their multiples (talking about days 7 and 14 are round, because 7 days is the point where there is a shift to a higher level, i.e. "week").

Round numbers are also important in another sense. If the reference point of the ALTI is a round number, the interval is larger than if it is not. This explains why around 4000 BC gets a larger interval ([4500, 3500 BC]) than around 2500 ([2450, 2550]), which again gets a larger interval than around 1670 and around 2070 ([1660, 1680] and [2060, 2080] respectively). In fact round numbers are the ones which are prototypically used in vague expressions, for instance with around [Sig88]. If a language user chooses to insert a non-round number in such a vague expression (e.g. around 6h22), he signals that he is aiming at a higher level of precision, in other words the fuzzy borders should be kept closer to the reference point. This is the cognitive explanation of why lower levels of granularity get smaller intervals (cf. § 3.4.2).

6 The formal modelling of time indications

From the linguistic description in §5, it follows that there exists a gap between the traditional crisp representation and manipulation of temporal information and the use of LTI's and VLTI's in natural language. In the following subsections we propose a model that helps to bridge this gap. This model uses the granularity structure of §4 and results in a general theoretical framework for the modelling of time.

6.1 Basic time elements

We propose basic time elements as the building blocks of the model [VdC97] [VdC97b]. There are two types of basic time elements: the basic time indications and the (simple) time intervals.

A **basic time indication** is a structure $[v, G]$ with two components: a value part v and a granularity indication G (as defined in §4). The value part can take on a fuzzy set value. The granularity indication can be represented by an integer. A basic time indication is interpreted as either:

- a *duration* or *(time) span*:

  $[d, G]$

with d the amount of granules of granularity G. Note that a span is not fixed on the time axis.

Examples:
4 days, represented by [{1/4}, day];
about 4 days, represented by [{.8/3, 1/4, .8/5}, day];

- a *(fixed) time point*:

[p, G]

with p an ordinal number indicating the position in the order of granules of granularity G with respect to a given reference point. The reference point can be some granule considered as the origin of the given granularity o_G (*absolute* time) or can be the granule corresponding to the current point in time: now_G (*relative* time). This distinction will be indicated by adding a subscript *rel* to the value p in the case of a relative time indication.

Examples:
the year 1997, represented by [{1/1997}, year];
around the year 1997, represented by
[{.8/1996, 1/1997, .8/1998}, year];
today, represented by [$\{1/0\}_{rel}$, day];
around today, represented by [$\{.8/\text{-}1, 1/0, .8/1\}_{rel}$, day];

- a *time distance*:
[l, G]
with l the number of granules of granularity G between two time points or between two iterations of a periodic time element (see §6.2).

Examples:
2 weeks later, represented by [{1/2}, week];
about 14 days earlier, represented by
[{.6/-12, .9/-13, 1/-14, .9/-15, .6/-16}, day];

A **time interval** is defined by a fixed time point and a duration. However, it is formally represented in our model by a triple

[p, l, G]

with [p, G] a time point, [l, G] the distance from p to the other point and G the granularity.

In general, an interval is determined by two of the three basic time indications starting point, length and end point. However, a fixed choice can lead to a loss of information, as is outlined in [Vgy94] [VdC97] [Dca97]. As a matter of fact, when an interval is specified by its starting and end point, the most accurate point among them has to be the time point [*p*, *G*] and the distance [*l*, *G*] is calculated subsequently. An interval given by an absolute and a relative time point will be considered as an absolute interval, i.e. the relative time point will be interpreted as an absolute time point with respect to the current time.

Examples:

- from 6 to 8 a.m. / starting at 6 a.m. and lasting 2 hours can both be modelled by [{1/6}, {1/2}, hour];
- at the end of January 1998, represented by [{1/31-12-1998}, {.7/-4, 1/-5, 1/-6, 1/-7, .7/-8}, day];

The definitions of a time point, a duration and a time interval constitute the basis for the modelling of all LTI's (and VLTI's) that indicate a single time **position**, a single time **duration** or the combination of a single time position and a single time duration. The definition of a time distance is used for the handling of repetition indications, which will be one of the subjects of the following subsection.

6.2 Time elements

A *time element* can consist of either time indications or time intervals, or a combination of both. Time elements are provided for the different types of temporal information as described in Section 2.3. We distinguish:

- A *composite span*:

  $$\bigcup_{i=1}^{n} [d_i, G_i]$$

  A composite span is a union of simple spans [di, Gi]. As simple spans are not fixed on the time axis, the elements of a composite span are not necessarily adjacent.
  Example:
  The total amount of time assigned to a software project is e.g. about 60 days (for analysis), about 25 days (for development) and 2 weeks (for testing). This can be represented by:

$$\left[\left\{\mu_1(x)/x \mid x \in \square\right\}, \text{day}\right] \cup \left[\left\{\mu_2(x)/x \mid x \in \square\right\}, \text{day}\right] \cup \left[\{1/2\}, \text{week}\right]$$

$$\text{with } \mu_1(x) = \begin{cases} 0 & ; \text{ if } x \le 30 \\ 0.1\,(x-30) & ; \text{ if } 30 < x < 40 \\ 1 & ; \text{ if } 40 \le x \le 80 \\ 0.05\,(100-x) & ; \text{ if } 80 < x < 100 \\ 0 & ; \text{ if } x \ge 100 \end{cases}$$

$$\text{and } \mu_2(x) = \begin{cases} 0 & ; \text{ if } x < 20 \\ 1 & ; \text{ if } 20 \le x \le 30 \\ 0.2\,(35-x) & ; \text{ if } 30 < x < 35 \\ 0 & ; \text{ if } x \ge 35 \end{cases}$$

- An *aperiodic time element*:

  $$\bigcup_{i=1}^{n} [p_i, l_i, G_i]$$

  An aperiodic time element is a union of intervals $[p_i, l_i, G_i]$.

  Example:
  The time during which person x was employed by company y can be given as e.g.:
  . from 1-9-1992 until 1-11-1992 and from 1-1-1995 until 1-1-1996, which can be represented by:
  $$\left[\{1/1-9-1992\},\ \{1/61\},\ \text{day}\right] \cup \left[\{1/1-1-1995\},\ 365,\ \text{day}\right];$$
  . starting around 1-9-1992 for about 2 months and from 1-1-1995 for one year, which can be represented by:
  $$\left[\{1/1-9-1992\},\ \{.8/58,\ .9/59,\ 1/60,\ 1/61,\ 1/62,\ .9/63,\ .9/64\},\ \text{day}\right]$$
  $$\cup \left[\{1/1-1-1995\},\ 365,\ \text{day}\right];$$

- A *periodic time element* is defined by an aperiodic time element and a time distance $[l_P, G_P]$, specifying the length of the period:

  $$\left(\bigcup_{i=1}^{n} [p_i, l_i, G_i],\ [l_P, G_P]\right)$$

The aperiodic time element describes the relevant part of the recurrent section in the definition (called the *pattern support*). The total length of the aperiodic time element may not exceed the length of one period (otherwise the rest is ignored). A periodic time element is constructed as semi-infinite, which means that l_P is either positive or negative, indicating whether the recurrence is directed towards the future ($+\infty$) or the past ($-\infty$). The singular case $l_P = 0$ must be treated as an aperiodic time element. A periodic time element covering $-\infty$ to $+\infty$ can be constructed as the combination of two periodical time elements resulting in a general time element as defined further.

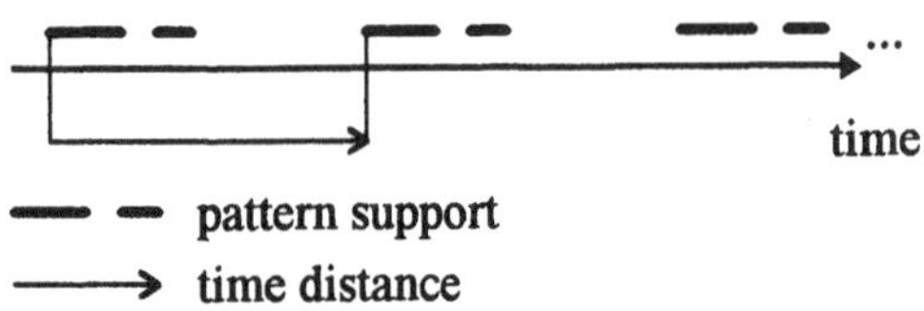

Figure 6. A periodic time element with a positive length

Example:

- from 1997 on, every year in August can be represented by [[{1/31-8-1997}, 31, day], [{1/1}, year]];

- A *general time element* has three components: a periodic time element directed towards the past ($l_{P1} < 0$), an aperiodic time element and a periodic time element directed towards the future ($l_{P3} > 0$):

$$\left(\bigcup_{i=1}^{n1} [p_i, l_i, G_i], [l_{P1}, G_{P1}] \right); \left(\bigcup_{j=1}^{n2} [p_j, l_j, G_j] \right);$$

$$\left(\bigcup_{k=1}^{n3} [p_k, l_k, G_k], [l_{P3}, G_{P3}] \right)$$

Examples:

- summer can be represented by ([{1/22-6-1997}, 93, day], [{1/-1}, year]);([{1/22-6-1997}, 93, day], [{1/1}, year])

From these definitions it is clear that periodic and aperiodic time elements are special cases of general time elements.

Periodic time elements have been introduced to model LTI's (and VLTI's) that indicate a **repetition**. Together with the aperiodic time elements and composite spans they contribute to the modelling of other combinations of position, duration and repetition.

The proposed framework fits the LTI-classifications given in §5.1, as it is able to cope with:

- **Deictic** and **independent** LTI's. Deictic LTI's are handled by choosing the special time point **now** as the origin of the discretisation that is used for the measurement of the value parts of the basic time indications. Independent LTI's are modelled with respect to a fixed origin.

- **Situational** and **relational** LTI's. Since situational LTI's always directly refer to a time fact, they can easily be modelled by using time elements. A relational LTI on its turn can always be converted into a situational LTI by resolving the indirectness (§ 5.1).
- **Bound** and **unbound** LTI's. Bound and unbound LTI's can both be modelled within the proposed framework. Here, allowing a fuzzy set for the value parts of basic time elements plays an important role. Whereas bound LTI's possibly have to deal with fuzzy information (e.g. before 20h today), uncertainty is always inherent to unbound LTI's (e.g. before 20h. Every day? Today? Yesterday? Tomorrow?).

The proposed framework is also well suited to model VLTI's. As stated in [Dub97], fuzzy sets can be used to deal with similarity, preference and uncertainty. Since each basic time element value can be assigned a fuzzy set, it is possible to cope with similarity and uncertainty in the time model.

The linguistic notions of semantic vagueness (vagueness in degree and vagueness in criteria), ambiguity and incompleteness can all be reduced in terms of similarity and uncertainty [Kli88] [Oft94].

7 Some challenging phenomena

Unlike human beings, a computer is not able to use contextual information when interpreting VLTI's. Moreover it is often hard to make explicit the semantic inferences which humans make unconsciously. Therefore some phenomena remain challenging for a time system which aims at cognitively adequate representations of time expressions. As an illustration, three examples are given:

- as explained in § 3.3, LTI's containing round numbers can be used with an approximative meaning, without being overtly marked as vague by additives like around. Having both an exact and a vague reading, these time indications are ambiguous. Humans can disambiguate them by the context, but a computer is unable to do so without extra information.
- we sometimes use LTI's (vague or not) denoting an interval, when we actually mean part of that interval. Consequently an utterance like "They went to Italy in August" is ambiguous, as it is not clear whether the whole month or just part of it is meant (cf. also § 2.2). Often the context has a disambiguating function. "The University is closed during the Christmas holidays" is interpreted as being a precise indication, meaning the whole period. It is very hard for a computer to make a correct choice between these different readings. Of course there is no problem as long as one works on a high level of granularity. "In August" at month-granularity does not need to be further specified, but it should somehow be indicated that at lower levels of granularity the information becomes uncertain.

- unbound lexical time indications (cf. § 3.1) do not refer to past, present or future on their own and they can be interpreted in different ways (e.g. on Tuesday, in April). If they are used in a sentence, however, they are disambiguated by the verb tense. "He'll bring back my bicycle on Tuesday" clearly refers to the Tuesday following the moment of speaking because of the future tense. "He brought back my bicycle on Tuesday" refers to the Tuesday before the moment of speaking, because of the past tense. The time model as it is being developed cannot be expected to analyze verb tenses, however. For the time being this will be a task for the user of the database during the input.

8 Conclusion

Our research aimed at the definition of a formal time model, which can be used as a suitable framework for handling time indications, in a way as close as possible to natural language. This brought us to the conception of a granular time model. The ability to incorporate vagueness and uncertainty is thereby achieved by the use of fuzzy set theory and possibility theory.

Although primarily intended for use in the context of databases, the time model is not confined to this use, nor is it bound to any particular database model. In [DTr97] [DTr97b] it has been explained how it can be used in an object oriented database model.

Before deciding upon the structure of the proposed time model, we heavily invested in research on the semantics of time indications in natural language. As a side effect of this research, it became clear how close the modelling of time and of space can be. Hence, the proposed formal framework of our time model can also be used in a straightforward way for the modelling of space.

References

[Bol83] A. Bolour, L. J. Dekeyser, *Abstractions in Temporal Information*, Information Systems, Vol. 8, No. 1, 1983, pp. 41-49.

[Bub80] J. A. Bubenko, *Information modeling in the context of system development*, Proceedings of the IFIP Information Processing '80, Noord-Holland, Amsterdam, 1980, pp. 395-411.

[Cha94] J. Channell, *Vague Language*, Oxford University Press, Oxford, 1994.

[Che86] P. P. S. Chen, *The time dimension in the entity-relationship model*, Proceedings of the IFIP Information Processing '86, North-Holland, Amsterdam, 1986, pp. 387-390.

[Dca97] R. De Caluwe, B. Van der Cruyssen, G. De Tré, F. Devos, P. Maesfranckx, *Fuzzy Time Indications in Natural Language Interfaces*, T.

Andreasen, H. Christiansen, H. L.Larsen (eds.), Flexible Query -Answering Systems, Kluwer Academic Publishers, Norwell, MA, 1997, pp.163-186.

[Dev95] F. Devos, *Still Fuzzy after All These Years. A Linguistic Evaluation of the Fuzzy Set Approach to Semantic Vagueness*, Quaderni di Semantica, Vol. 16, No. 1, 1995, pp. 47-82.

[Dev97] F. Devos, P. Maesfranckx, G. De Tré, *On granularity in the interpretation of around in approximative lexical time indications,* In: P. Saukkonen, H. Suni (eds.), Proceedings of the Third International Conference on Quantitative Linguistics (Qualico '97), August 26-30, Research Institute for the Languages of Finland, Helsinki, Finland, 1997, pp. 203-209.

[DTr97] G. De Tré, R. De Caluwe, B. Van der Cruyssen, N. Van Gyseghem, *Towards Temporal Fuzzy and Uncertain Object-Oriented Database Management Systems,* C. Isik, V. Cross (eds.), Proceedings of NAFIPS'97, September 21-24, Syracuse, N.Y., 1997, pp.68-72.

[DTr97b] G. De Tré, R. De Caluwe, B. Van der Cruyssen, Dealing with Time in Fuzzy and Uncertain Object-Oriented Database Models Proceedings of EUFIT'97, Aachen, September 9-11 1997, pp. 1157-1161.

[Dub89] D. Dubois, H. Prade, *Processing Fuzzy Temporal Knowledge*, Transactions on Systems, Man, and Cybernetics, Vol. 19, No. 4, July/August 1989, pp. 729-744.

[Dub91] D. Dubois, J. Lang, H. Prade, *Timed Possibilistic Logic*, Fundamenta Informaticae, Vol. XV, No. 3-4, November-December 1991, pp. 211-234.

[Dub97] D. Dubois, H. Prade, *The three semantics of fuzzy sets*, Fuzzy Sets and Systems, Vol. 90, 1997, pp. 141-150.

[Gai81] B. R. Gaines, R. Brian, *Logical foundations for database systems*, In: E. H. Mamdani, B. R. Gaines (eds.), Fuzzy Reasoning and its Applications, Academic Press (Computers and People Series), London, 1981, pp. 289-308.

[Joh80] S. Johansson, *Word Frequencies in British and American English: some preliminary observations,* In: J. Allwood, M.L. Jung (eds.) ALVAR: Stockholm Papers in Language and Literature, Stockholm, 1980.

[Kim95] W. Kim (editor), *Modern Database Systems: The Object Model, Interoperability, and Beyond,* Addison-Wesley Publishing Company, New York, NY, USA, 1995.

[Klei94] W. Klein, *Time in Language*, Routledge, London, 1994.

[Kli88] G. J. Klir, T. A. Folger, *Fuzzy Sets, Uncertainty, and information,* Prentice-Hall International, Inc., Englewood Cliffs, New Jersey, USA, 1988.

[Klo83] M. R. Kloprogge, P. C. Lockemann, *Modeling information preserving databases: Consequences of the concept of time*, Proceedings of the VLDB '83, Florence, November 1983, pp. 399-416.

[Kni92] B. Knight, J. Ma, *A General Temporal Model Supporting Duration Reasoning,* AI Communication Journal, Vol. 5, 1992, pp. 75-84.

[Kor97] H. F. Korth, A. Silberschatz, *Database Research Faces the Information Explosion*, Communications of the ACM, Vol. 40, No. 2, 1997, pp. 139-142.

[Lev83] S. C. Levinson, *Pragmatics*, Cambridge University Press, 1983.

[Mae97] P. Maesfranckx, *Vague lexical time indications: their use in natural language and attempts to model them in computer databases*, Second Chronos Conference, Brussels, January 9-11, 1997, pp 54.

[Mai92] R. Maiocchi, B. Pernici, F. Barbic, *Automatic Deduction of Temporal Information*, ACM Transactions on Database Systems, Vol. 17, No. 4, December 1992, pp. 647-688.

[Oft94] Observatoire Français des techniques avancées, *Logique Floue*, Arago 14, Masson, Paris, France, 1994.

[Rei47] H. Reichenbach, *Elements of Symbolic Logic*, New York, 1947.

[Ros75] E. Rosch, *Cognitive Reference Points*, Cognitive Psychology, Vol. 7, 1975, pp. 532-547.

[Sig88] B. Sigurd, *Round Numbers*, Language in Society, Vol. 17, 1988, pp. 243-252.

[Tso96] V. J. Tsotras, A. Kumar, *Temporal Database Bibliography Update*, ACM SIGMOD Record, Vol. 25, No. 1, March 1996, pp. 41-51.

[VdC97] B. Van der Cruyssen, R. De Caluwe, G. De Tré, D. Vandycke, *A theoretical time model for dealing with crisp and fuzzy time*, C. Isik, V. Cross (eds.), Proceedings of NAFIPS'97, September 21-24, Syracuse, N.Y., 1997, pp.63-67.

[VdC97b] B. Van der Cruyssen, R. De Caluwe, G. De Tré, *A theoretical fuzzy time model based on granularities*, Proceedings of EUFIT'97, September 8-12, Aachen, Germany, 1997, pp. 1127-1131.

[VGy94] N. Van Gyseghem, R. Vandenberghe, F. Devos, R. De Caluwe, *Fuzzy Time Expressions in Natural Language Queries*, Proceedings of the 1994 workshop on Flexible Query-Answering Systems (FQAS'94), Roskilde, Denmark, November 14-16, 1994, pp. 81-86.

[Wan97] X. S. Wang, C. Bettini, A. Brodsky, S. Jajodia, *Logical Design for Temporal Databases with Multiple Granularities*, ACM Transactions on Database Systems, Vol. 22, No. 2, June 1997, pp. 115-170.

[Zad72] L. A. Zadeh, *Fuzzy Languages and their Relation to Human Intelligence*, Proceedings of the International Conference on Man and Computer, Karger, Basel, 1972, pp. 130-165.

[Zad96] L. A. Zadeh, *Fuzzy Logic = Computing with words*, IEEE Transactions on Fuzzy System, Vol. 4, No. 2, May 1996, pp.103-111.

[Zad97] L. A. Zadeh, *Toward a theory of fuzzy information granulation and its centrality in human reasoning and fuzzy logic*, Fuzzy Sets and Systems, Vol. 90, 1997, pp. 111-127.

4

COMPUTING WITH WORDS: LOGICAL ASPECTS

Towards Fuzzy Logic

Walenty Ostasiewicz
Wrocław University of Economics
Komandorska 118/120, 53-345 Wroclaw, Poland
E-mail: ostasiew@manager.ae.wroc.pl

1. INTRODUCTION

The mental activity of people (concerning mainly information handling) for a long time has been divided into two groups: calculating and reasoning. The former deals with numbers and occasionally is called *computing with numbers* and the latter deals with words and is called *computing with words.*

Already in the ancient times there were undertaken attempts to facilitate this kind of mental human job which is essentially algorithmic and which may be performed automatically by the so-called "thinking machines".

It was probably the Catalan poet Rajmunduns Lullus (1232-1316) who for the first time constructed thinking machine for logical reasoning. This machine was subsequently called as *Lull's hand-mill.*

There exist however a common belief that it was Rene Descartes (1540 – 1650) who initiated the proper era of automated reasoning. The analytic geometry is a machine for deciding the truth of statements automatically.

Gottfried Wilhelm Leibniz (1646-1716) was probably inspired by the both ideas of Lull and Descartes, and he devoted a lot of his life to create a calculus of reason (*calculus ratiocinator*) and a universal language (*lingua characterica*). The aim of these two enormously ambitious projects was a development of a universal method whereby all human problems, whether of science, law, or politics, could be worked out rationally, systematically, by simple logical computation.

A rational calculus in Leibniz' sense was partially constructed by George Boole (1815-1864). Next, in 1869 the economist and logician, Boole's pupil, Stanley Jevons (1835-1882), constructed a working machine for verifying Boolean identities.

The further significant step towards automated reasoning has been done by Gottlob Frege (1848-1925) who created the famous *Begriffschrift*- an universal logic language.

It was however J. A. Robinson who have really revolutionised the subject of automatic theorem-proving. His method of resolution invented in the 1960s is now the widely applied in most of expert systems.

The different path towards an automated reasoning has its roots in striving to imitate the human brain.

In 1930s Nicolas Rashevsky started to construct the first real theory of the brain. In 1943 Walter Pitts, Rashevsky's student, together with Warren McCulloch paraphrased Rashevsky's ideas in the form of digital machine. They proposed to simulate neurones by Boolean forms. This idea has been subsequently realised technically in 1957 by F. Rosenblatt in the form of well known perceptron.

Recently, mainly due to the proponents of the so called strong AI, there is persuaded idea that mental activity is simply the carrying out of some well-defined sequence of operations. This sequence is usually called an algorithm. Moreover, all mental qualities like feeling, understanding, thinking etc. considered to be the features merely of the algorithm being carried out by the brain. Maybe it is true that the minds of some are really "computers made of meat", as M. Minsky says, but it seems that for a majority of usual people there are an essentially non-algorithmic ingredients in the action of the brain (for more details see [88]) .

Recent years seem to show a significant shift from the existence-oriented mathematics to the algorithmic-oriented mathematics, conceived mainly as a tool for solving problems.

This tool demands for a new foundations. About a half a century ago Leon Chwistek wrote that "exact thinking based upon the principle of consistency is the sacrificial goat to which all the disasters of our times have been imputed... exact thinking is blamed for drying up the sources of the sacred enthusiasm... the demand for a *new logic*, for new laws of thought more suitable to the needs of spiritual life, has become a hobby - horse for a whole *galaxy* of obscure and false doctrines" (italic is added).

Among many kinds of logics, such as logic of love, logic of religion, logic of decision, etc. there is also the so-called fuzzy logic. It seems to be quite correct to consider it as a logic of fuzzy sets or fuzzy sets logic.

Does it belong to this galaxy of obscure and false doctrines?
The answer to this question might be the philosophical *Est et Non*!
Est, if one places it within the *episteme*; *Non*, if one treats it as *techne*.

The doctrine of fuzzy-ism has been perfectly formulated by M. M.Gupta as follows:

"Fuzzy-ism is a body of concepts and techniques aimed at providing a systematic framework for dealing with vagueness and imprecision inherent in human thought processes"

More particularly, following J.A.Goguen, one can say that this is a method of constructing and studying models of the way we use words.

This means that the main motivation of fuzzy logic is "the urge to do" rather than "the urge to know".

Fuzzy sets (or fuzzy logic in its wide sense, as some would prefer), are considered here as a formal tool for copying with vagueness. Likewise as probability theories are devised for copying with uncertainty.

The core of any probability theory is a degree of belief that an event will occur, this degree should be warranted by some evidence. Likewise in fuzzy logic, the basic notion is a degree of applicability of a term to an object. This degree might be warranted by a convention (or consensus).

About the fuzzy logic one can say the same as Bunge said about the general systems theory, that it is still immature and its reputation is jeopardized by a fringe of charlatans:

"How else can you explain that very large segments of the business, AI vendor, and academic communities still regard fuzzy logic with emotions ranging from a brief chuckle to an outright sneer?"(see[21]).

2. World and words

It seems to be very useful, at least for the methodological reasons, to distinguish between language and the rest of the world, which will be shortly refer to as the world or real world.

The world has been given for us. It is *perfect,* beautiful, without any contradiction, and above all it is the best one of all possible worlds.

In 1710 G.W. Leibniz had written that "there is an infinitude of possible worlds, among which God must needs have chosen the best", almost in the same time L. Euler also asserted that the fabric of the world is the most perfect and was established by the wisest Creator" (see [4]).

Philosophers have defined three different ontological points of view on this world:

- holistic,
- individualistic, and
- systematic.

According to a systematic point of view, known also as discrete ontology ([38]) the world is considered as a collection of *objects* (elements, things, entities), which have some *properties*, and between which some *relations* hold. In their turn all properties of objects are usually divided into two general groups:

- *classificatory* properties, called also sortal concepts,
- *measurable* properties.

Measurable properties are divided into two further groups:

- comparative, or *intensive* properties, which are also called ordinal,
- metrical, or *extensive* properties, which are also called cardinal.

The world of words, on the contrary to the real world, is *imperfect,* and moreover this man-made fabric “impinges on experience only along the edges’ (see [92]) .

It was the Biblical Adam who for the first time "gave names to all cattle, and to the flow of the air, and to every beast of the field". And, at this time, the whole earth was of one language, and of one speech.

But next, when the men have decided to build a tower whose top should reach unto heaven, their language has been confounded. The people could not understood one another, even if they are using the same language. Any language is now defective, vague, and above all is prone to misunderstanding. Any type of expression, that is capable of meaning something, is also capable of being vague.

Language, among other functions, serves to represent an external world. Objects of this world are represented by proper *names,* properties are represented by *adjectives* and common *nouns*, whereas *prepositions* and *verbs* tend to express relations between two or more things (see[107]).

The imperfect world of words can be also considered from the point of view of discrete ontology. Objects of this world are referred to as *expressions.* All expressions are divided according to S. Leśniewski, into three semantic categories:

- names
- sentences, and
- functors.

Functors are of two kinds:

- name-forming, and
- sentence-forming.

For example words "Paul" and "Slave" are the names, expression "Paul is Slave" is the sentence. In the expression: “Paul and Mary are Slaves and Klaus is German” the first entry of "and" is name forming functor, and the second entry of "and" is sentence forming functor.

The main properties of expressions, as objects of a language, are the following: *ambiguity* and *imprecision.*

Summarising , it is possible to confront the basic “ingredients” of these two worlds as follows:

world	words
objects	names(nouns)
properties of objects	predicates (adjectives)
relationships between objects	relations (prepositions, verbs)
lack of knowledge of how world works	lack of precise definitions of a meaning of words
uncertainty	vagueness

3. Uncertainty and Vagueness

Already ancient Greek scientists have distinguished certain knowledge (named *episteme*) from uncertain knowledge i.e. opinion and beliefs (named *doxa*).

This means that the notion of uncertainty stems exclusively from a lack of knowledge. It pertains therefore *facts* i.e. situations or states of affairs about systems or occurring in systems under consideration.

The notion of "fact" is very general term, and in order to give some illustrative examples, the all systems are classified into two groups: real (or concrete) systems and abstract (or formal) systems. In certain sense this division corresponds to the Greek distinction between *phisi* and *thesi.*

Some examples of concrete systems are such systems as celestial mechanics, classical mechanics, quantum mechanics, national economy, firm, factory, family etc.

Just from these examples follows that systems of this kind can be further divided into *mechanistic* systems and *humanistic* systems. This latter distinction is very important because of the mathematical apparatus used for their description differs substantially.

Behaviour of humanistic systems is much too complex to be described by means for example of differential equations or by other traditional tools.

Conceptual systems are mainly various theories. Certain human community could be an example of concrete system, and a theory about it would be a conceptual system.

If a theory is constructed as a deductive theory, then the most important relation connecting elements of this system is the deductibility relation.

Let us take for example a formal theory of numbers, then one knows certainly that $2 + 2 = 4$, and that there exists such an x, that $x + 2 = 8$; one could be however uncertain whether or not holds equality $x^m + y^m = z^m$ for some x, y, and z when m is fixed and is greater than 2. These propositions are some facts (certain or uncertain) occurring within a formal system. Apart from that, one can be interested also about global characteristics of such conceptual systems like their consistency, generality, axiomatibility etc.

The facts occurring in concrete systems are usually changeable, unpredictable and unstable this is they are much more uncertain than facts of conceptual systems. Concrete systems function according to much more complex *laws* than simple deductive systems created artificially by scientists. Uncertainty means a lack of knowledge about these laws. This shortage seems to be inevitable: *ignoramus et ignorabimus*!. The problem is therefore to learn to live with uncertainty and with risk.

Quite different problem, is the problem connected with the second world i.e. word world considered as a man-made fabric. This problem concerns the ambiguity and the vagueness of terms.

There is a very long tradition of philosophical interest in vagueness, and particularly in ambiguity and imprecision. These notions, likewise some others as inexactness or uncertainty are conceived very differently. There is however quite general agreement in attributing the all of them to representational systems, of which a language is a typical example.

Any notion is said to be vague when its *meaning* is not fixed by sharp boundaries but spreads over a range of possibilities, so that applicability in particular case may be *dubious* (see [100]).

It is very important to emphasise once more that an essential characteristic of concept of vagueness is *doubtfulness* which differs from uncertainty.

Any language, or more generally any representational system is obviously *discrete*, but on the contrary, the external world seems to be *continuous*. Already Leibniz observed that *natura non facit saltus*.

This gap between discreteness and continuity explains, according to Aristotle, the prevalence of ambiguity in languages.

"Since we cannot introduce the realities themselves into our discussion, but have to use words as symbols for them, we suppose that what follows in the words will follow in the realities too, like people reckoning with counters. But it is not the same. For whereas words and the quantity of sentences are limited, realities are unlimited in number. It is therefore inevitable for the same sentence and the one word to mean more than one thing" (see[101]).

Among the three possible sources of vagueness:

- ambiguity necessarily stems from the nature of reality,
- it pertains our thinking,
- the necessity of ambiguity lies in symbols (of language),

the third one seems to be the most justified.

This point of view requires however further examination of relationships between *language, thinking* and *perception* of the real world. As it is well known there are two different kinds of theories of perception and thought (see[105]):

- representative theories, and
- identity theories.

The former assumes that the content of perception is never identical with the perceived entity. The latter however asserts that this content is identical with the object perceived, provided that perception is veridical.

Identity theories were strongly criticised by B. Russell, who clearly distinguished the *properties of words* from the *properties of things*. In his famous now paper [106] he writes that vagueness and precision are characteristics which can only belong to a language and that "apart from representation there can be *no such thing as vagueness or precision*" (italic is added).

Essential feature of vagueness, which is to be underline, is that it concerns the *meaning* of sings of a language.

There are two doctrine of meanings: the extensionalist doctrine, according to which the meaning of concept is identical with its *extension*, and the internationalist doctrine asserting that the meaning is identical with its *intention*.

More correctly one can argue that every concept has *both* an intention (or connotation) and an extension (or denotation). *Denotation* is also called a *domain of applicability* of a concept.

With accordance to these two aspects of meaning , one distinguishes also two kind of vagueness: the extensional vagueness denoted by V_e and Intensional vagueness, denoted by V_i.

Let E(C) stands for the extension of a concept C and E($\overline{C}$) for the complementary concept $\overline{C}$, then the extensional vagueness is defined by M. Bunge as follows:

$$V_e = m(E(C) \cap E(\overline{C}) / m(E(C) \cup m(E(\overline{C}))$$

where $m(A)$ is a measure of set A.

Intensional vagueness is defined as follows:

$$V_i(C) = I(C) - K(C)$$

where $I(C)$ is a set of all (known and unknown) properties connoted by C, and $K(C)$ is the set of known properties belonging to intention of C.

Imprecision as a kind of vagueness, is also a characteristic of a language, and more precisely, imprecision pertains the so-called *measurable* concepts, and particularly *metric* properties.

Because such concepts are represented by numbers, one often uses the term of numerical imprecision (see[67,68]). This imprecision stems from a fact that any measurement yields results of limited accuracy. It is possible to speak only of a one-many correspondence between the results of measurement and a real numbers (see [17]).

An attempt to develop a formal theory enabling manipulations with imprecise or indeterminate quantities has been undertaken by R. Young as early as in 1931. This precursory work is continued in present days in the form of the so-called interval mathematics. The idea of a variable which assumes individually considered values, has been replaced by R. Young by a concept of *many-valuedness*. This concept was conceived as a *set* of values considered *collectively*. The theory of such sets has been developed by S. Leśniewski, and it is briefly presented in this chapter.

In all the cases the doubt or indeterminacy can be accounted for by attaching to any element a *grade of applicability of a given concept.*

4. Truthness and like-truthness

Already Aristotle divided all propositions into two basic classes. To one class belong those propositions which can be demonstrated with scientific certainty. These propositions are assigned one of the two of truth values: true and false. The notion "truth value" has been introduced by G. Frege in 1891. (in German *Wahrheitswert)*

The second class of propositions which can be only argued for a grater or lesser *degree of certainty.*

With propositions which can be only argued are associated numerical quantities which resembles truth values.

These values are called very differently:

- approximate truth,
- degree of truth,
- partially truth,
- truthlikeness, etc.

The classic notion of truth forms the foundation of the basic principle of classical logic. This principle is known as the *Principle of bivalence,* and it asserts the following:

every proposition is either true or false.

This principle has been formulated and strongly defended by Chrisippus and his school. It was however contested by Epicureans, and even rejected by them in the case of propositions referring to future contingencies. Like the proposition "there will be a sea battle tomorrow" which is neither true nor false.

Introducing this principle, Aristotle characterised all logical propositions, as opposed to any other kinds of sentences like questions, orders, etc., as follows:

proposition is any sentence which can be true or false.

The notion of the *truth* of a proposition has been defined by Aristotle in his Metaphisic as follows (see [11]):

"To say of what is that is not or of what is not that it is, is false,
while to say of what is that it is, and of what is not that it is not, is true".

The Latin version of this definition (due to St. Thomaso) is:

Veritas est adequatio intellectus et rei, secundum quod intellectus dicit esse quod est vel non esse quod non est.

which is used in a simple form: *adecquatio intellectus et rei.*

Classically, the truth is defined therefore as a correspondence to the facts.

This concept of truth has been formally developed in 1920 by Alfred Tarski (Leśniewski's disciple), in the form of the so-called semantic theory of truth (see [111]).

Jan Łukasiewicz criticising the Principle of Bivalence, called it as an *Aristotelian prejudice*, and decided to put the end to it once and for all (see [62]), and has introduced more general *Principle of Valence.* By this principle, which says the following:

every proposition has a truth value

Łukasiewicz had characterised propositions, contrary to Aristotle, as follows:

propositions are those sentences which predicate something about something.

In other words, propositions are such sentences that assert something. They can have a *truth value* expressed by a number from the unit interval. The first logic of this type has been developed for the three values.

The earliest reference to the three-valued logic is "the farewell lecture" delivered by Łukasiewicz on March 7, 1918 at Warsaw University on the occasion of taking duties in Polish government. In this lecture he announced the following:

"that system, which I worked out in detail last summer, is a coherent and self-consistent as Aristotle logic, and is much richer in laws and formulae. That new logic, by introducing the concept of objective possibilities destroys the former concept of science, based on necessity" (see [62]).

This new system has been published for the first time in Polish in 1920 (see [61]), the English version is given for example in [62], for the motivations see [59,60]. This system has been axiomatized by Wajsberg in 1931 (see [116]).

Independently of Łukasiewicz and starting from different premises the other system of multi-valued logic has been discovered by Emil Post who was born in Poland in 1897, and in 1904 emigrated to New York , where he died in 1954. In his work [90], E. Post has proved , among other things, that every sentence of m-valued logic can be interpreted as an ordered set of m-1 sentences of usual logic. In modern theory of fuzzy sets the analog of this theorem exists under the name of representation of fuzzy sets by a family of usual sets.

Since these works by Łukasiewicz and Post, there were discovered and studied many kinds of multivalued logics (see for example [23,99,109]).

Neither of these systems is non-Aristotelian logic in the sense in which the contrary of one of the Aristotelian principles, for example contradiction or excluded middle, is assumed to be true, and solid inferences are drawn from it. As a matter of fact, it is probably impossible to develop at all any non-Aristotelian logic in this sense.

On the other hand all these logics are argued to "follow the quite serviceable two-valued logic, by defining, for instance, the truth value of the compound proposition 'p or q' wholly in terms of the truth values of p and q" (see [15]).

There are two other approaches to the problem of the assignment of more than two truth values to propositions. One of them has been developed as *modal logics,* and the second one as *probability logics.*

Besides the classical or alethic modalities like possible, and necessary, discussed already by Aristotle, there are considered many other modalities. The most important of them are following[15]:

- epistemic (known, believed, etc.),
- bulimic (feared, hoped, etc.),
- deontic (ought, should, etc.),
- evaluative (is good, bad, etc.).

In 1786 J. J. Ebert has defined the modality as an explicate determination of the *grade* to which extent the intensity of some property is affirmed or negated.

Originally it sounds as follows [28]:

wenn in einem Satze der Grad in welchen man ein gewisses Verhältnis der Begriffe bejahet oder verneinet ausdrücklich angezeigt wird, so nennt man diese Bestimmung die Modalität).

The first significant work on modal logic has been published in 1897 by H. MacColl (see [63,64]), who introduced different modal sentences like known to be true, known to be false, doubtful and neither known to be true nor known to be false.

In his work from 1906 MacColl discussed the following modalities: true, false, certain, impossible and variable i.e. not certain and not impossible (see [3])

Trying to develop calculus for modalities, H. Weyl suggested in the thirties the following approach.

First of all he adopted multi-valued logic with connectives *not, and, or*, and *implies* defined as follows:

$$not\,\alpha = 1-\alpha$$
$$\alpha\ and\ \beta = \min(\alpha,\beta),$$
$$\alpha\ or\ \beta = \max(\alpha,\beta),$$
$$\alpha \rightarrow \beta = \min(1, 1-\alpha+\beta).$$

Within this calculus there were introduced two modal operations: possibility, denoted as p, and necessity, denoted as N. These operations are not to allowed to be graded, and they are defined as follows:

$$P\alpha = 1, \text{if } \alpha > 0, \text{ and} = 0, \text{if } \alpha = 0$$
$$N\alpha = 1, \text{if } \alpha = 1, \text{ and} = 0, \text{if } \alpha < 1.$$

The most developed part of the logic which deals with truthlikness is called a probability theory.

Originally "probability" had nothing to do with numbers and even with mathematics. Some opinion or doctrine had been called probable if came on reliable authority to be worthy of belief. It derives from Latin word "*probablis*" and it did mean, among other things, something like "worthy of approbation", and therefore "probability" chiefly meant the approvability of an opinion.

In some languages probability means literally *truth-like*, for example in Latin *veri-simile*, in Polish *prawdo-podobne*, in German *wahr-scheinlich*.

The probability as a number denoting numerical measurement for the first time has been mentioned at the end of the Port Royal Logic. Two Jansenists A. Arnauld (1612-1694) and P. Nicole (1625-1695) have written in 1662 the book under the title:

"*La logique ou l'art de penser, contenant, outre les regles communes, plusieurs observations nouvelles, propres a former le jugement*"

which is better known under shorter title: "*L'art de penser*" (the art of thinking), or under the Latin title as *Ars cogitandi,* which is also often referred to as Port Royal Logic (from the name of monastery near to Paris where it was written). At the end of this book was summarised the famous Pascal's wager (see [37]).

As a continuation of this book it was the other book published fifty years later by J. Bernoulli. The title of it was *Ars conjectandi* i.e. the art of conjecturing (see [37]). The author by himself connects these two kinds of arts as follows:

we are said *to know* or to understand those things that are certain and beyond doubt, but only *to conjecture* or to have opinions about all other things. To conjecture about something is to measure its probability. Therefore, we define the art of conjecture, or stochastics, as the art of measuring the probabilities of things as exactly as possible (see [30]).

Generally there are distinguished two kinds of probabilities: epistemic probability and aleatory probability. T. L. Fine distinguished yet a third kind, namely, pragmatic probabilities, and in his work [29] he discussed in great details almost all approaches to the problem of probabilities.

There were undertaken many attempts to relate somehow these two theories, some were trying to import probability theory into realm of logic, the others were trying to reconstruct the whole logic in accordance with the probabilistic laws.

B. Bolzano, for instance, has introduced in 1837 a new logical concept, which he called "the validity of proposition". In order to explain this concept let us consider propositions of the type "x is A", where one variable is declared to be changeable and the other not. For example in the proposition "the entity Caius is mortal", the idea "Caius" is treated as one that can be changed at will and replaced by new ideas. By changing this idea we obtain propositions some of which are true, and some false. The quantity of the true and the false propositions in certain circumstances can be computed. The ratio of the number of the true propositions obtainable from a given proposition by exchanging certain ideas, to the number of all proposition obtainable in accordance with a given rule is the "validity" of a proposition.

Suppose for example that the whole universe of discourse is the set of six numbers {1,2,...,6}. Furthermore assume that in proposition "5 is divisible by 3" the idea 5 is changeable, then the validity of this proposition is equal to 2/6.

A similar idea has been developed in 1909 by J. Łukasiewicz when he attempted to give the logical foundation of probability theory. J. Łukasiewicz has introduced the concept "the truth value of an propositional function". That is in opposite to B. Bolzano he attaches the truth value to predicate instead to proposition. For example the truth value of the propositional sentence "x is divisible by 3" is false.

In 1932 Z. Zawirski distinguished two kinds of multi-valed logics: qualitative and metrical. (for more detail see [122,123]).

The qualitative multi-valud logic has been called by H. Reichenbach the topological logic. In 1934 H. Reichenbach introduces the notion of *probability proposition* to which he assigns the probability interpreted as a grade of truthness.

The probability proposition has the form of implication

$$A \ni_p B$$

which is treated as a relation between two classes: the class A which is called the reference class, and class B, the attribute class.

The expression " $A \ni_p B$ " means "the probability of the attribute B that is concerned with reference to A is equal to p".

Suppose that x denotes the event "the die is thrown", this means that x belongs to a certain class A. Furthermore , let y be the event "the die has come to rest on the table with face 1 up", this means that y is regarded as belong to certain class B.

The probability statement has then the form:

$$x \in A \ni_p y \in B$$

which is written also as $P(A,B) = p$ and is read as "probability from A to B is p" This expression has the same grammatical form as "the distance from A to B" (for more details see [98]).

5. VAGUENESS CALCULI

5.1. Three approaches

Vagueness is a characteristic of language i.e. vagueness is a property which pertains the objects of the word world. Each language is considered from three different aspects:

-syntactic,
-pragmatic, and
-semantic.

There are therefore three possible types of definitions of vague terms: syntactic, pragmatic and semantic.

The **pragmatic** definition is following:

The name "T" of some language L is vague if and only if there is some thing (object) which by a majority of subjects (understanding the language L) is considered neither as the designate of the name "T" nor as a designate of the name "non-T".

This definition for the first time has been explicitly used by E. Borel for the resolution of the heap paradox.

The **semantic** definition involves the concept of fringe or border, and is the following:

> The term "T" is vague if and only if its fringe is not empty. The fringe of a term "T" is defined as a set of such objects which are denoted neither by "T" nor by "non-T".

This definition traditionally is attributed to M. Black, who introduced the concept of "border cases".

The **syntactic** definition was defined by T. Kubiński in the following way:

> A non-individual term "T" is vague if and only if there exists such individual term t that neither the expression:
>
> 1. "t is T", nor the expression
> 2. "t is non-T"

are theses of a formal, deductive system.

This definition is based therefore on the concept of *provability*. It means that if it is impossible to prove in some system that "t is T", or that "t is non-T", then term T is to be considered as a vague term.

Formal systems in which can be used precise as well as vague terms has been developed by T. Kubiński. These systems are called quasi-ontologics, because they are based on Leśniewski's ontology.

Kubiński's system seems to be the only existing as yet syntactical approach to the problem of vagueness. This system is very briefly presented in the next section.

Sematical approach is based on the concept of applicability, and it has been considered by a number of researchers. The most significant of them are presented below.

5.2. Ontology and quasi-ontology

The great Polish logician Stanisław Leśniewski (1886-1939), the most famous disciple of K. Twardowski, and the leading philosopher of that time has developed the original system of foundations of mathematics (see[56,57,58,109]).

This system embraces the following three deductive theories:

1. Protothetic,
2. Ontology,
3. Meorology.

Prothotetic and Ontology are logical theories. The former, very roughly, is the most comprehensive *Logic of Propositions* or a theory of deduction. The latter is the most comprehensive *Logic of Names*, it comprises calculus of predicates, calculus of classes, calculus of relations and the theory of identity (see [109]).

Mereology, contrary to Prothotetic and Ontology, is not a logical theory, its primitive term "is part of" is not a logical constant. Mereology is a deductive theory which inquires into the most general relations that may hold among objects. It is a set theory in a collective sense. This theory will be shortly presented in the next section.

In this section it is briefly characterized Ontology, which will be treated as a general theory of names.

The only primitive term in this theory is the verb "is". From this verb derives also the name of the theory itself. The verb "is" corresponds to the Greek εστι, and the participle of it is the Greek ον (genet. οντος) which means *being*, and Ontology, according to Leśniewski himself, is a theory of "general principles of being". The verb "is" denoted by "ε" appears in the only primitive function of this theory, which in Leśniewski's notation has the following form:

"$\varepsilon\{A\,a\}$",

in which the term "ε" is a constant function sign, while the expressions "A" and "a" appear as two name arguments.

Expression of the type "$\varepsilon\{A\,a\}$" should be considered to be equivalent in meaning to the corresponding Latine sentences about individuals of the type "A est a" (see [58]). Leśniewski has appended himself to the Latin in order to avoid problems connected with definite and indefinite articles.

The Polish language does not have these articles, and therefore Polish "jest" can be treated as an equivalent to Latin "est". On the contrary, English word "is" has at least three different meanings; it could mean the following:

- membership relation
- inclusion relation , or
- identity relation.

This can be demonstrated by means of the following sentences (see [31]):

Socrates is a man	i.e.	Socrates $\in$ men,
the dog is an animal	i.e.	dogs $\subset$ animals,
Socrates is the husband of Xantippe	i.e.	Socrates = husband of Xantippe.

All expressions of any language S. Leśniewski divides into three semantic categories: names, sentences and functors, and the latter are divided into name-forming and sentence-forming functors. For example names "Kate" and "Agate" using the name-forming functor "and" can be combined into the name "Kate and Agate". Similarly, sentences "Kate is diligent" and "Agate is lazy" using sentence-forming functor "and" can be combined into sentence "Kate is diligent and Agate is lazy". In order to avoid any confusion there are used different symbols for the functors which are read equally. For example symbols $\wedge$, $\vee$, -, $\Rightarrow$ are used for statement-forming functors: conjunction, alternative, negation and implication, and the corresponding name-forming functors are symbolised by letters K, A, N and C.

Instead of these symbols there will be used here the words: "or", "and", "not", and "implies". Furthermore the English word "is" will be used instead of Latin "est".

This means that the primitive function of the ontology is the expression of the form:

a is A

where a is a singular name, and A is any name, but both of them are exact terms.

A sentence "a is A" is correct only if to the left of "is" stands non-empty, singular name, and to the right to this particle stands any name.

For example sentences as "Pegasus is big" or "The dog is an animal" are incorrect, because in the first sentence "Pegasus" is an empty name and "dog" in the second sentence is a general (but not singular) name.

Leśniewski was completely successful in providing one single axiom characterising perfectly the term "est" without falling into contradiction.

The only axiom of Leśniewski's ontology is (see [49,58]):

$$\forall A, B{:}\, A \textit{ is } B \Leftrightarrow [(\forall x{:}\, x \textit{ is } A \Rightarrow x \textit{ is } B) \wedge \exists x{:}\, x \textit{ is } A \wedge \exists x, y{:}\, (x \textit{ is } A \wedge y \textit{ is } A \Rightarrow x \textit{ is } y)]$$

This is to be read as follows:

A is B if and only if the following three conditions are satisfied:

1) for all x: if x is A, then x is B
2) exist x such that x is A,
3) for all x and y: if x is A and y is a, then x is y.

This can be illustrated by the following example:

Charles the Great is the great killer of Slaves

this sentence is equivalent to the following assertions (see [49]):

1) about any objects whatsoever it is true, that if it is Charles the Great, it is also true about it that it is the great killer of Slaves,
2) somebody is Charles the Great,
3) if this is Charles the Great and that is Charles the Great, then this is that (therefore, we consider, it is the same individual).

It is well known that exists a perfect analogy between the calculus of propositions and the algebra of sets. Similarly, elementary ontology as a calculus of names constructed over the narrower predicate calculus without identity is equivalent to a system of atomic Boolean algebra (see [43]).

The contemporary Polish logician T. Kubiński made several attempts to develop a formal, deductive theory about the real world phenomena, which would encompasses also vague terms (see [53]).

A theory developed by him is called *quasi-ontology.*

Quasi-ontology S, likewise ontology, is a logic of names, but this time it encompasses the both names: precise and vague. More precisely, all names in this theory should satisfy the following conditions:

1. The set of precise (or exact) names has no common elements with a set of vague names.
2. The union of these two sets forms the all names of language.
3. Set of precise names is closed under the name-forming functors "and", "or", and "non".
4. Any name B from a language of a system S is vague if and only if there is in this language singular name A such that neither the expression "A is B" nor "A is non B" belong to a system S.

Quasi-ontology has been developed axiomatically, and its axioms are divided into two categories: empirical and theoretical.

Empirical axioms are the expressions of the following kind

“a is a”

which are called *axioms of singular existence*, as they simply assert that “exists a”

The second kind of empirical axioms are the so-called *empirical theses*. These theses are the triple of the following form:

<a is b, a is non-b, neither a is b nor a is non-b>

where a is a singular name, and b is any name.

These triples are subject to the following condition:

there exist two names a and b such that only one element of the triple is applicable.

The second part of the System S which has been called here a theoretical one, is a "proper" deductive system.

This system has been called by Kubiński himself as a "system Ω".

The two primitive terms of this system are following:

- sentence forming functor "is",
- name-forming functor "N".

The former axiomatically characterized by the Leśniewski's axiom of ontology, the latter is characterized originally by Kubiński.

The whole system Ω is defined by means of the three axioms and two definitions:

Axiom 1 of this system is the only axiom of Leśniewski's ontology, Kubiński uses the following variant of this axiom:

A1. $\forall x,y:[x \text{ is } y \Leftrightarrow \exists z:(z \text{ is } x \wedge \forall v,w: v \text{ is } x \wedge w \text{ is } x \Rightarrow v \text{ is } w) \wedge \forall u:(u \text{ is } x \Rightarrow u \text{ is } y)]$

Axiom 2 is the most important axiom in the system Ω. Intuitively, it asserts that "if something x is y then that something x in non-y", but the converse is not true. Formally, this axiom has the following form:

A2. $\forall x,y:[x \text{ is } y \Rightarrow \neg(x \text{ is N(y)})]$

where $\neg$ is the usual functor of sentence negation.

The functor N is different from the negation "not" used in Leśniewski's ontology. Very briefly "not" pertains precise terms, and Kubiński's "non" pertains vague terms. Term "N(y)" is to be read therefore as "non y".

The two definitions determine the alternative name and conjunctive name correspondingly:

Definition 1 is:

D1. $\forall x,y,z:[x \text{ is } (y \text{ or } z) \Leftrightarrow x \text{ is } y \vee x \text{ is z}]$

Definition 2 is:

D2 $\forall x,y,z:[x \text{ is } (y \text{ and } z) \Leftrightarrow x \text{ is } y \wedge x \text{ is z}]$

Axiom 3 is an analogue of the De Morgan laws, and the law of double negation applied for names. It sounds as follows:

A3.

$$\forall x, y, z : [x \text{ is } \mathrm{N}(y \text{ or } z) \Leftrightarrow x \text{ is } \mathrm{N}(y) \wedge x \text{ is } \mathrm{N}(z)) \wedge$$
$$(x \text{ is } \mathrm{N}(y \text{ and } z) \Leftrightarrow x \text{ is } \mathrm{N}(y) \vee x \text{ is } \mathrm{N}(z)) \wedge$$
$$(x \text{ is } \mathrm{N}(\mathrm{N}(y)) \Leftrightarrow x \text{ is } y)]$$

Kubiński has proved that this system is consistent, incomplete, and its axioms are independent.

Within this system one can prove for example, that if some object is red, then it is not non-red, but the contrary is not true.

5.3. Classical and empirical classes

Both, semantic and pragmatic definition involve two sets: set of words, say W, and set of objects (things), O. Words refer to things in either two ways: designation and denotation. In the case of pragmatic definition, the reference relation is established by some voting procedure. In the case of semantic definition, the situation is less clear. Avoiding the detailed discussion suppose that the two sets: a set of words and a set of objects are related by means of the following mapping:

$$f : O \times W \to T$$

where T is any set, at least partially ordered , which will be specified later.

In order to obtain any useful calculus of terms one needs some algebraic structures defined on W and T.

Let us consider two extreme classical cases, and next their generalisations proposed by T. Kubiński and by A. Kaplan and H. Schott.

For the both classical cases it is supposed that T = {0 , 1}. The first case concerns the weakest logic, and the second case the strongest logic.

As Peirce has noticed that "there is one primary and fundamental logical relation, that is illation". Suppose that this basic relation of implication (illation) will be denoted $\Rightarrow$, and expression "$A \Rightarrow B$" means that "when the attribute A is present, then the attribute B is also present", or more shortly "A implies B".

Assume that this implication is *the only* operation defined on the set W. Furthermore it is supposed that it fulfils the following conditions, known as the Tarski-Bernays set of axioms:

$1. A \Rightarrow (B \Rightarrow A)$
$2. A \Rightarrow (A \Rightarrow B)) \Rightarrow (A \Rightarrow B)$
$3. (A \Rightarrow B) \Rightarrow ((B \Rightarrow C) \Rightarrow (A \Rightarrow C))$

It would be interesting to note that instead of the three above axioms it can be given only one single axiom.

Using the so-called Polish notation it is expressed only by 13 symbols:

$$\Rightarrow\Rightarrow\Rightarrow ABC \Rightarrow\Rightarrow CA \Rightarrow DA$$

J. Łukasiewicz, who found this axiom, has also proved that it is the shortest axiom.

Suppose that the mapping

$$f : O \times W \to T$$

for any $x \in O$ satisfies the condition:

$$f(x, A \Rightarrow B) = f(x, A) \leq f(x, B)$$

The family of all such functions $f(\cdot, A)$, $f(\cdot, B)$, $f(\cdot, C)$, etc. forms the algebraic structure known as a Hilbert algebra. This algebra coincides with the implication positive logic, which could be considered as a *weakest logic*.

Any ordered set (X, <) with the greatest element 1 is an Hilbert algebra (X, $\Rightarrow$), where $\Rightarrow$ is defined as follows:

$$x \Rightarrow y = \begin{cases} 1, \text{ if} & x<y \\ c, \text{ otherwise} \end{cases}$$

where $c \neq 1$ is a fixed element of X.

As an opposite pole to this weakest logic let us consider now the strongest logic of attributes.

For that reason suppose that having two attributes "*A*" and "*B*" one can form not only the operation "A implies B', but also the negations "not *A*", and "not *B*".

Assume that these two operations fulfil the conditions known as the Frege's system of axioms. This is the oldest deductive logical system, it has been created by Gottlob Frege in 1879.

Frege's axioms are following [42]:

$$1. A \Rightarrow (B \Rightarrow A)$$
$$2. A \Rightarrow (B \Rightarrow C)) \Rightarrow B \Rightarrow (A \Rightarrow C)$$
$$3. A \Rightarrow (B \Rightarrow C)) \Rightarrow ((A \Rightarrow B) \Rightarrow (A \Rightarrow C))$$
$$4. (A \Rightarrow B) \Rightarrow (\overline{B} \Rightarrow \overline{A})$$
$$5. A \Rightarrow \overline{\overline{A}}$$
$$6. \overline{\overline{A}} \Rightarrow A$$

where $\overline{A}$ means "not A".

This is the *strongest* logic, known as the classical logic, strongest in a sense that it is impossible to add more independent properties for connectives "implies" and "not" without falling into contradiction.

This classical logic coincides with an *Boolean algebra.*

It was Gerge Boole who for the first time considered (in 1854) the two classes: a class of all properties and a class of all objects, and has established two fundamental laws connecting properties with objects (see [6]).

First of all, he has defined an algebra on the class of all properties with respect to the words: "and", "or", "non", "implies". The first law asserts that these operations satisfy the conditions of an algebra which is called today an Boolean algebra.

The second law asserts that there exists an isomorphism between an algebra of properties and algebra defined on the family of all sets corresponding to properties. Hence G. Boole assumed that to any property A corresponds a set Â of all objects possessing this property.

Suppose that the expression "*x is A*" means that on object *x* has a property A, than a set Â of all objects having the property A is :

$$\hat{A} = \{x \mid x \text{ is } A\}.$$

If X denotes the universe of all objects, than subset Â can be defined by means of the so-called characteristic function, which has been introduced in 1936 by Ch. de la Vallée Poussin

$$f_{\hat{A}}(x) = \begin{cases} 1, \text{ if } x \in \hat{A} \\ 0, \text{if } x \notin \hat{A} \end{cases}$$

Defining properly algebraic operations on the set of such functions one arrives at the following diagram of isomorphisms:

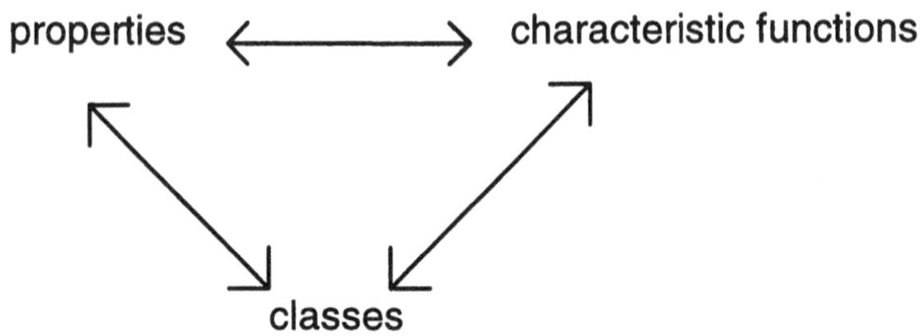

It is interesting to note, that calculus of classes which forms an Boolean algebra is a part of general theory of sets, and namely this part, axioms of which do not contain a primitive term "$\in$".

Let us consider now the two important modification of classical logics and the corresponding algebras. One of them is Kubiński's algebra of vaguely described classes, and the second proposal is due to Kaplan and Schott, who developed an calculus for the so-called empirical classes which are also vaguely described.

Kubiński's proposal is based on the semantic definition of vague properties.

Suppose that W is a set of all terms, which will be denoted this time by lower case letters a, b, c, etc.

Furthermore for the name-forming functions if is assumed the notation used in ontology. For example Aab means the name "a or b".

Assume that the mapping

$$f : O \times W \to \{0,1\}$$

Satisfies the following conditions (for each $x \in O$):

1. $f(x, Aab) = f(x,a) \vee f(x,b)$
2. $f(x, Kab) = f(x,a) \wedge f(x,b)$
3. $f(x, NNa) = f(x,a)$
4. $f(x, NAab) = f(x, Na) \wedge f(x, Nb)$
5. $f(x, NKab) = f(x, Na) \vee f(x, Nb)$
6. $f(x,a) \wedge f(x, Na) = 0$

Term b is vague if and only if the following holds:

$$f(x,b) \vee f(x, Nb) \neq 1 .$$

The formal properties of this system are discussed by Kubiński in [53].

To the contrary to this system, the second calculus described here, known as a Calculus of Empirical Classes (CEC), is based on the idea of graded membership relation, treated as a mapping

$$w_\lambda : O \times W \rightarrow [0,1]$$

As early as in 1946 the philosopher Abraham Kaplan argued the usefulness of classical calculus for practical applications.

The essential novelty with respect to Boolean calculus consists in constructing "entities which have a degree of vagueness characteristic of actual (empirical) classes" (see [45]).

Such calculus has been presented in 1951 jointly by A. Kalplan and H. Schott (see [46]), which has been called the calculus a calculus for empirical classes (CEC).

Instead of a notion "property", Kaplan and Schott prefer to use the term *profile* defined as n-tuple of qualities (such as red, green, etc.).

This means that profile could be a simple property like "red", green", etc or it could be a complex property like "red and 20 cm", "green, 2 years, 25 kg" etc.

Classical characteristic function they have replaced by an **indicator** which take on values in the unit interval. These values are called the weight from a given *profile* to specified *class*..

The notation

$$w_\lambda(x, A) = p$$

states that the weight from the profile λ, characterising object x to the class A is p. Subsequently a simplified notation $w(x, A)$ will be used , and with an accord of modern terminology these weights will be also called grades of membership. According to Kaplan and Schott these degrees are fixed simply by a convention.

The diagram, corresponding to CCC, would have now the following form:

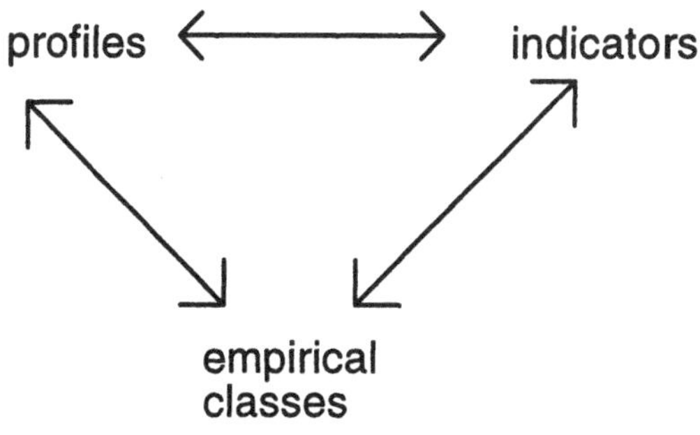

The basic operations for the empirical classes are defined as follows:

1. Class sum

$$w(x, A \cup B) = \max(w(x,A), w(x,B))$$

2. Class product

$$w(x, A \cap B) = \min(w(x,A), w(x,B))$$

3. Class contrary

$$w(x, \overline{A}) = 1 - w(x, A)$$

Without giving a proof in [46] has been stated that these operations fulfil the following conditions: commutativity associativity, De Morgan laws, the laws of tautology, the two distribution laws, the laws of double negation and of transposition.

This means that on the set of all empirical classes they have established the *De Morgan algebra.* This algebra, for the first time has been introduced in 1935 by Romanian logician G. Moisil (see [74]). It is also known as a *quasi-Boolean* algebra. Such algebras are slight generalisation of Boolean algebras, and they have simple representation.

The representation theorem has been proved in 1957 by Białynicki-Birula (see [95]). It simply states that a set lattice of all subsets of $X \neq \emptyset$ is a quasi-Boolean algebra if one defines a quasi-complementation as follows $\overline{Y} = X \setminus g(Y)$, where $g : X \to X$ is any fixed involution on *X*, i.e. $g(g(x)) = x$.

In order to have the analogous to some classical theorems, there were introduced new definitions, particularly concerning the null and universal classes. Their counterexamples in CEC are called *quasi-null class*, denoted by n, and *quasi-universal class*, denoted by u, and they are defined as follows:

1. Null classes $w(x, N) = 0$, for all *x*.
2. Universal classes $w(x, U) = 1$, for all *x*.
3. Quasi- null classes $w(x, n) \leq \frac{1}{2}$, for all *x*.
4. Quasi- universal classes $w(x, u) \geq \frac{1}{2}$ for all *x*.

Using these definitions there were established the following properties:

1. $A \cup N = A$
2. $A \cup \overline{A} = u$
3. $A \cap \overline{A} = n$

4. $A \leq B \Leftrightarrow \overline{A} \cup B = u$
5. $A \leq B \Leftrightarrow A \cap \overline{B} = n$

where the inclusion for empirical classes is defined as follows:

$$A \leq B \Leftrightarrow A = A \cap B$$

this is equivalent to

$$A \leq B \Leftrightarrow w(x, A) \leq w(x, B) \text{ for all } x.$$

In addition to the ordering given by inclusion relation ≤, the different order, called w-sharpening, is defined as follows:

$$A > B \Leftrightarrow \begin{cases} w(x,A) \geq w(x,B) & \text{for } w(x,B) \geq \frac{1}{2} \\ w(x,B) \geq w(x,A), & \text{for } u(x,B) < \frac{1}{2} \end{cases}$$

An idealisation A of a class A is defined as follows:

$$w(x, A) = \begin{cases} 1, \text{ if } & w(x, A) \geq \frac{1}{2} \\ 0, \text{ if } & w(x, A) < \frac{1}{2} \end{cases}$$

Using this notion the sameness of meaning of two terms is defined as follows.

Two terms are said to have the same meaning, if the corresponding classes (i.e. their extensions) are equal, and these terms have substantially the same meaning if the idealisations of corresponding classes are equal.

In order to established the connections with general theory of sets, Kaplan and Schott have modified the principle of extensionality. For this reason they have defined membership of the degree p, symbolised by $\in^p$, as the relation of an object to a class when the weight from the profile characterising this object to the class is p. The principle of extensionality is defined as follows:

$$A = B \Leftrightarrow x \in^p A \Leftrightarrow x \in^p B$$

For the applications of this calculus see [108].

6. SETS

6.1. Kinds of sets

The notion of set is one of the most important notions used frequently in every day life as well as in mathematics. In mathematics this term is particularly important, "every mathematician agrees that every mathematician must know some set theory; the disagreement begins in trying to decide how much is some"[39].

Sets theory in purely mathematical sense is a theory of the whole mathematics sometimes the two notions are even equated

sets theory=mathematics.

Within the traditional theory of sets there are developed some particular theories aimed at the solutions of practical problems. These theories are also called a sets but with some adjectives. The most typical examples are following:

- random sets
- probabilistic sets
- multi sets
- rough sets
- hazy sets
- fuzzy sets.

All of such "sets", strictly speaking are not sets at all, all of them are functions defined *within* the framework of the traditional set theory.

6.2. From Leibniz to Cantor

The notion of set, as the Latin *Totum*, for the first time has been used by Leibniz in 1666 who gave the following definition (see [50,52,65]): "any number of things whatever may be taken simultaneously and yet treated as a whole", originally in Latin it sounds as follows:

"*liceat quotcunque res simul sumere at tanguam unum totum suppouere*" (see [50,52,65])

This definition has been given in Leibniz's famous "Demonstration of the Existence of God".

W. Marciszewski as well as K. Krauze-Blachowicz have discussed in details a set theoretical aspects of Lebniz's *Totum*. Particularly it has been discovered that Leibniz did not made any distinction between the *collective whole* and the *distributive class* (see [50,51,52,65]).

More than two hundreds years later, the same notion of set has been defined by Georg Cantor, one of Kronecker's disciples.

For the first time in 1883, G. Cantor gave the following definition:

"Unter einer Mannigfaltigkeit oder Menge verstehe ich nämlich allgemein jedes Viele, welches sich als Eines denken lässt, d. h. jeden Inbegriff bestimmter Elemente, welcher durch ein Gesets zu definiren, was verwandt ist mit dem Platonischen ετδος oder ιδε'α '.

The above quotation is translated into English as follows (see [89]):

By multitude or set I mean every plurality which can be thought of as one (oneness), i.e., every integral approach to some elements which by law can be bounded in unity, and I think that by the same I define something which is related to Platonic ετδος other ιδε'α '.

After discovering the so-called set-theoretical antinomies, Cantor modified several times his original definition. The evaluation of Cantors idea of the set is presented in [89].

There were undertaken many different attempts to overcome the discovered inconsistency of Cantor's theory. The most important proposals are due to E. Zermelo (1871-1953), B. Russell (1872-1970) and S. Leśniewski.

Russell and Zermelo have introduced some restrictions of different characters to the unlimited freedom in Cantor's Paradise.

Zermelo's method has been improved by A. Fraenkel, and now this system of set theory is known as Zermelo-Fraenkel theory of sets, or shortly as ZF system.

ZF system gained general recognition and deeply influenced the whole mathematics.

There are however very strong reasons for looking for an alternatives to the classical set theory.

First of all, Cantor's theory is not the best possible description of our intuitive comprehension of the real world. Moreover this powerful and beautiful theory, known as sets theory, is a theory of different types of infinities, and not a theory of sets conceived intuitively.

Among the alternative approaches, two proposals are quite well known, one of them is Klaua's many-valued set theory, and the second is Vopenka's semisets theory. Extremely interesting proposal due to S. Leśniewski is much lesser known.

Leśniewski has proposed a system completely different from any other existing systems for the foundations of mathematics, this system is briefly presented in this chapter, for more details see [57,58,89].

6.3. Leśniewski's manifolds

Leśniewski tried to create system which according to his own words will have an exact form as possible and harmonise with the common sense of the representatives of the "esprit laic" who are engaged in investigating a reality not created by them (see [57]).

In 1916 he made a first attempt to give a deductive form of his own conception of classes and collections.

His system called *meorology* is based on the four axioms and the three definitions [58]:

Axiom 1.

If object *P* is a part of object P_1, then object P_1 is not a part of object *P*.

Axiom 2.

If object *P* is a part of object P_1, and object P_1 is a part of object P_2, then object *P* is a part of object P_2.

Definition 1.

"Ingredient of object *P*" is the same object and every part of that object

Definition 2.

"Set of objects m" is every object *P*, which satisfies the following condition:

If *I* is an ingredient of object *P*, then some ingredient of object *I* is an ingredient of some *m*, which is an ingredient of object *P*.

Example: every given nation is a set of people.

Definition 3.

"Set of all objects *m*" or "class of objects *m*" is every object *P*, which satisfies the following conditions:

1. every *m*. is an ingredient of object *P*.
2. if *I* is an ingredient of object *P*, then some ingredient of object *I* is an ingredient of some *m*.

Example: mankind is the class of men

Axiom 3.

If some object is m, then some object is the class of objects m.

Axiom 4.

If P is the class of objects m, and P_1 is the class of objects m, then P is P_1.

To see the essential differences between sets in Cantor's sense and sets in Leśniewski's sense there are given below some short comments.

Cantorian sets as *abstract* entities are conceived distributivelly, this means that an aggregation of things is treated as *one* abstract object, and therefore one says about the concept of sets-as-one. Philosophically, these sets are conceived as Platonic ideas, they exist independently of our thought. For example "whiteness" exists independently of objects. Borrowing from Quine one can say that according of this point of view the collection of seven pairs of shoes is not to be identified with the collection of those fourteen shoes, moreover, the twenty-eight soles and uppers is the third different entity (different set). This is of course intuition-defying.

Essentially different are sets in Leśniewski's theory. These sets are treated collectively as *material* (concrete, physical) objects. In this case one speaks about the sets-as-many. Philosophically, Leśniewski's theory could be considered as a nominalistic theory of sets, according to the basic doctrine of this theory, "whiteness", for example, does not exists at all, exist only white objects [31,119].

In natural language one makes sometimes a distinction between these two approaches, by using different names.

For example the term "soldiers" is conceived as a set in distributive sense. One soldier is an element of a set "soldiers". On the other hand, "army" is conceived as a set in collective sense. Any part of a set "army" is "army" too.

In the case of a "set-as-thing" (set-as-one) the most the most important relation is therefore a relation of *elementhood* or membership, in the case of a "set of" (set-as-many) the fundamental relation in the relation of being *part*.

For sets in distributive sense holds the following:

$x \neq \{x\}$

$x \in X$ and $X \in Y$ but $x \notin Y$; ($\in$, denoting "is member of" is not transitive),

$\varnothing$ is very important set;

on the contrary, for sets in collective sense there holds:

$x = \{x\}$;

$x \mu X$ and $X \mu Y$ then $x \mu Y$; (μ, denoting "is part of" is transitive);

$\varnothing$ does not exist, it has no concrete sense.

6.4. Hazy sets

On many occasions, H. Poincare emphasized the difficulties connected with mathematical description of physical world. Particularly, his famous formulae:

$$A = B \ , \ B = C \ , \ A \neq C$$

are admissible and meaningful as for as they characterise physical continuum. They are however not admissible for description of mathematical continuum. Attempting to overcome the difficulties concerning these formulae, there were suggested various solution. The most significant are those due to H. Weyl, E. Borel and K. Menger.

All the proposed solutions, roughly speaking are based on the same idea:

associating a number from the unit interval with a given term (predicate) and an object.

Formally this association is given by a mapping

$$f(\cdot, A) : O \to [0,1],$$

where A is a term (predicate).

The value $f(x, A)$ for H. Weyl means as

"the grade to which extent object x has a property A"

while, on the other hand, E. Borel and K. Menger treat this value as

"the probability that x belongs to a set A".

E. Borel suggested to determine this probability from pragmatic point of view i.e. as the ratio of "yes" answer to the total number of questions.

Menger's solution was strongly motivated by philosophical trend known as *positivism*, he *suggested* the necessity of developing a theory in which the element-set-relation is replaced by the probability of an element belonging to a set. For that reason he has defined a notion *ensemble flou* (originally in French) which he has translated by himself into English as **hazy set** (see[73]).

Neither E. Borel nor K. Menger have formulated calculi for their proposals.

On the contrary, H. Weyl gave the following calculus:

$$f(x, A \cup B) = f(x, A) \vee f(x, B),$$
$$f(x, A \cap B) = f(x, A) \wedge f(x, B),$$
$$f(x, \overline{A}) = 1 - f(x, A),$$

This calculus satisfies all the conditions of De Morgan algebra.

6.5. Fuzzy Sets

L. A. Zadeh gave the following definition[121]:

A fuzzy set (class) A in X is characterised by a membership (characteristic) function $f_A(x)$ *which associates with each point in X a real number in the interval [0,1], with the value of* $f_A(x)$ *at x representing the 'grade of membership" of x in A.*

The algebraic operations for these sets have been defined exactly in the same way as it has been done by H. Weyl or by Kaplan and Schott.

The two notions: "fuzzy set " and "grade of membership" became very soon the names of a magic power.

Since Goguen's works fuzzy set A is usually identified with a mapping

$$f_A : X \to [0,1],$$

and it is treated as a kind of generalisation of traditional characteristic function of a subset A

$$\chi_A : X \to \{0,1\}.$$

Different ways of generalisation of the notion of characteristic function have been proposed by several authors. Goguen himself defined fuzzy set as a mapping

$$f : X \to L,$$

where L is a lattice.

E. Szpilrajn proposed in 1936 a generalised characteristic function in the following form [99]:

$$S : X \to \{0,1\}^{\infty}.$$

H. Rasiowa used the function (see[95, 96]):

$$f : X \to L,$$

where L is any logical algebra.

The notion *" ensamble flou"*, introduced in 1968 by Y. Gentilhomme as a pair A = (b, s), where s and b are smaller and bigger subsets of X i.e. $s \subseteq b \subseteq X$, can be also defined by means of characteristic function:

$$f : X \to \{0, 1/2, 1\}$$

as follows:

$$f(x) = \begin{cases} 0, & \text{if } x \notin b \\ 1/2 & \text{if } x \in b \setminus s \\ 1 & \text{if } x \in s \end{cases}$$

There are many other generalisations.

7. Concluding Remarks

From the Oxford English Dictionary we read that "fuzzy" means either not firm or sound in substance, or fringed into loose fibres. Fuzzy means also covered by fuzz i.e. with loose volatile matter. Alike any other characteristic, "fuzzy" can be used to form a predicate of the form: "... is fuzzy". For example "this glass is fuzzy". The dockers in Port Sudan are called Fuzzy-Wuzzy probably because of their fuzzy hair.

Vagueness is a *characteristic of words*, and corresponding *property of objects* is called fuzziness (see also [104]).

It is meaningless to say however that "bald is fuzzy", or that "young is fuzzy". The **words** (adjectives in this case) „bald" and „young" are vague (but not fuzzy) because their meanings are not fixed by sharp boundaries. On the other hand **objects** (glass in this example) can be fuzzy, but not vague, their representations by means of words can be vague. This means that the phrase "fuzzy is fuzzy" is to be considered as meaningless. The above distinction is consequently maintained by B. Rolf (see [105]).

There are however different points of view. Quite often, the word "fuzzy" is applied both to words and objects, or alternatively, the word "vague" plays this role.

Since 1965 the word „fuzzy" is used in a completely different sense. It appears in phrases like these: fuzzy set, fuzzy relation, fuzzy number, etc. All such phrases are treated as technical terms denoting abstract entities, and namely *functions* (in mathematical sense) of a particular form taking on value from the unit interval.

The notion of "fuzzy set" is therefore a technical term of some formal theory, known as the theory of fuzzy sets.

Fuzzy sets, in pre-Zadehian terminology they were called empirical classes, or empirical predicates, have been invented as a formal tool enabling the precise (or exact) manipulation of inexact (or imprecise) concepts.

Classically, a concept is represented by a class of objects or by its characteristic function. Vague concepts are represented by a family of classes, or by their generalised characteristic functions which are called fuzzy sets.

Fuzzy sets theories provide the modes for dealing with the two empirical phenomena: *vagueness* and *imprecision.* These two phenomena are very often confused with the other empirical phenomenon called *uncertainty.*

Uncertainty pertains the *knowledge,* which is not complete and not sufficient to formulate exact answers. The problem how to manage this lack of knowledge is treated within the framework of a theory of probabilities.

There are to be distinguished the following three formal calculi:

- the logic of uncertain events, called also probability theory,
- the logic of vague concepts, called fuzzy logic, and
- the arithmetic of imprecise quantities, called fuzzy arithmetic.

Very shortly: fuzzy sets theory provides tools for coping with vagueness and imprecision of words, whereas probability theory provides modes to manage uncertainty pertaining our knowledge about functioning the world.

Term "fuzzy set", as well as any other term of the kind "fuzzy something" is a single name of some abstract object, like "bulldog", or "bus stop" are the names of concrete things. Fuzzy set as a technical term has been defined (or has been identified with) as a function defined on a set of some universe of discourse and taking values from the unit interval or some other set interpreted as truth values (or grades of membership).

Definitions, like this: “fuzzy sets – are sets with boundaries that are not precise”, although they are signed by Big Names, are rather dangerous.

Fuzzy set is neither set nor fuzzy.

It is meaningless to ask whether some set is or isn't fuzzy.

BIBLIOGRAPHY

1. Andreoli, G. (1956). La logica del finito e del concreto, *Giornale di matematiche*, volume LXXXIV, 19-48.
2. Barwise J. and Cooper R. (1981). Generalized quantifiers and natural language, *Linguistics and Philosophy*, vol.4, 159-219.
3. Becker, O. (1930). Zur Logik der Modalitaeten, *Jahrbuch f. Phil. und phaenomenologische Forschung*, 11, 497-548.

4. BeightlerC., Philips D., Wilde D. (1982), Foundations of Optimisation, Prentice-Hall
5. Bell, D. (1979). *Frege's theory of judgement*, Clarendon Press, Oxford.
6. Birkhoff, G. (1967). *Lattice theory*, Providence, Rhode Island.
7. BIRKHOFF, G. (1969). Mathematics and psychology, *SIAM Review*, vol. 11, 429-469.
8. Black, M.(1937). Vagueness, *Phil. of Science*, 4, 427-455.
9. Bolzano, B. (1837). *Wissenschaftslehre* vol. II., Sulzbach.
10. Borel, E. (1956).*Probabilite' et certitude*, Presses Universitaives de France, Paris, (Russin translation by Nauka 1964).
11. Bradley, R. Schwartz, N. (1979), *Possible worlds, Basil Blackwell,* Oxford.
12. Bronowski, J. Neyman J. (1944), The variance of the measure of a two-dimensional random set, *Ann. Math. Stat.* 16 nr.4, 330-341.
13. Bunge, M. (1967). *Scientific research I, The search for systems*, Springer Verlag.
14. Bunge, M. (1967). *Scientific research II, The search for truth,* Springer Verlag.
15. Calabrese P. (1987). An algebraic synthesis of the foundations of logic and probability, Information Sci.,42, 187-237.
16. Checkland P. (1980), Systems Thinking, Systems Practice, John Wiley.
17. Chwistek, L. (1948). *The limits of science*, Routledge and Kegan Paul, London
18. Cohen, M. R. and Nagel, E. (1962). *An introduction to logic*, Harcourt Brace and World.
19. Copi, I. M. (1986). *Introduction to logic*. Macmillan Publishing Company, NY, Collier Macmillan Publishers, London.
20. Copilowish, I. M. (1939). Border-line cases, vagueness, and ambiguity, *Phil. of Science*, 6, 181-195.
21. Cox E. (1992). The great myth of fuzzy logic, *AI Expert*, January, 40-43.
22. Curry, M. B. (1963). *Foundations of mathematical logic*, McGraw-Hill, N.Y.
23. Czezowski, T. (1949). *Logika,* PZWS, Warszawa.
24. Davis M. (1983), The prehistory and early history of automated deduction, in: Siekman J., Whrigston G. (eds.), Automation of Reasoning, Springer Verlag, 1-11.
25. Davis P. J. ((1986). Descartes' dream, Harcourt Brace Jovanovich.
26. Dubois, D., Prade, H., Yager, R. R.(1982). *Readings in Fuzzy Sets for Intelligent Systems.* (eds), Academic Press
27. Dubois, D., Prade, H. (1980). *Fuzzy Sets and Systems. Theory and Applications,* Academic Press.
28. Eisler, R. (1899). *Wörterbuch der Philosophischen Begriffe und Ausdrücke*, Berlin.
29. Fine, T. (1973). *Theories of probability*, Academic Press, New York.
30. von Furstenberg G. M. (1990). *Acting under uncertainty*, Kluwer.

31. Fraenkel, A. A., Bar-Hillel, Y., A. Levy, A. (1973). *Foundations of set theory*, North-Holland.
32. Garret, B. (1991). *Vague identity and vague objects*, Nous,
33. Gentilhomme, Y. (1968). Les ensables flous et linguistquee, *Cahiers de linguistique theoriqueet appliquee*, v.47, Bucarest.
34. Goguen, J.A.. (1968). The logic of inexact concepts, *Synthese*, 19, 325-373.
35. Gottwald, S. (1984). Fuzzy sets theory: some aspects of the early development in: H. J. Skala, S. Termini, E. Trillas (eds.), *Aspects of vaguness*, D. Reidel, 13-29.
36. Gupta, M. M. (1977). Fuzzy-ism, the first decade, in: M.M.Gupta, G.N.Saridis, B.R.Gaines (eds.), *Fuzzy automata and decision processes*, North-Holland, Amsterdam.
37. Hacking, I. (1975). *The emergence of probability*, Cambridge University Press.
38. Hasenjaeger C. (1972). *Introduction to the basic concepts and problems of modern logic*, D. Reidel.
39. Halmos, P. R. (1960). *Naive set theory*. Princeton.
40. Höhle, U. (1991). Foundation of fuzzy sets, *Fuzzy sets and systems*, 40, 257 - 296.
41. Hempel, C. G. (1939). Vagueness and logic, *Phil. of Science*, 6, 163-180
42. Hilbert D, Bernays P. (1968), Grundlagen der Mathematik, Springer.
43. Iwanus, B.(1973). On Lesniewsli's elementary ontology, *Studia logica*, 31, 73-119.
44. Jevons, W.S. (1870). *Elementary lessons in logic*, London; Polish translation: *Logika*, 1886,Warszawa.
45. Kaplan, A.(1946). Definition and specification of meanings, *J. Phil.*, 43, 281-288.
46. Kaplan A., Schott H.F. (1951). A calculus for empirical classes, *Methodos*, vol. III, n. 11, 165-188.
47. Katsoff, (1937). Modality and probability, *Phil. Rev.*, 46, 78-85.
48. Kemeny, J. G. (1963). Analyticity versus fuzziness, *Synthese*, 15, 57-80.
49. Kotarbinski, T. (1985). *Wykłady z dziejów logiki*, PWN, Warszawa.
50. Kruze- Blachowicz, K. (1982). Leibniz's Demonstratio Existentiae Dei ad mathematicam certitudinem exacta. A logical analysis, *Studies in Logic*, Grammar and Rethoric, Białystok, 43-55.
51. Kruze- Blachowicz, K. (1991/92). Ontological import of the logical analysis of Leibniz's Demonstratio Existentiae Dei, *Studia in logic*, Grammar and Rethoric, X/XI, 5-19.
52. Kruze- Blachowicz, K. (1992). *Leibniz, wczesne pojęcie substancji*, Zakład Teorii Poznania, Bialystok.
53. Kubiński, T. (1958). Nazwy nieostre, *Studia logica*, 7, 115-179.
54. Kubiński, T. (1960). An attempt to bring logic nearer to colloquial language, *Studia logica*, 10, 61-75.

55. Kyburg, R. E., Smockler, H.E. (eds.).(1964). *Studies in subjective probability*, J. Wiley.
56. Lejewski, C.(1990). S. Leśniewski, *Wiadomości Mat.*, 28, 153-182.
57. Leśniewski, S. (1916). *Podstawy ogólnej teorii mnogości*, Prace Polskiego Koła Naukowego w Moskwie, Nr. 2, Moscow.
58. Leśniewski, S. (1992). *Collected works*, Polish Scientific Publishers, Warszawa
59. Łukasiewicz, J. (1910). *O zasadzie sprzeczności u Arystotelesa*. Studium Krytyczne (On the principle of contradiction in Aristotle. A critical study) (new edition by PWN 1987).
60. Łukasiewicz, J. (1910). O zasadzie wyłączonego środka, *Przegląd Filozoficzny*, 13, 372-373.
61. Łukasiewicz, J. (1920). O logice trójwartosciowej , *Ruch Filozoficzny*, 5, 170-171.
62. Łukasiewicz, J. (1970). *Selected works*, North-Holland and PWN.
63. MacColl, H. (1897). Symbolic reasoning II, *Mind*, 6, 494-510.
64. MacColl, H. (1900). Symbolic reasoning III, *Mind*, 9,
65. Marciszewski, W. (1981). On Leibniz's anticipation of comprehension axiom in the light of a formalization of "Demonstratio existentiae Dei", *Studies in Logic*, Grammar and Rhetoric II, Warsaw University, Bialystok Branch, 29-41.
66. Matheron G. (1975). *Random sets and integral geometry*, J. Wiley.
67. Mellor, D. H. (1965). Experimental error and deducibility, *Phil. of Science*. vol. 32, Nr.2, 102-122.
68. Mellor, D. H. (1966). Inexactness and explanation, *Phil. of Science*. vol. 33, Nr.4, 345-359.
69. Mellor, D. H. (1967). Imprecision and explanation, *Phil. of Science*. vol. 34, Nr.1, 1-10.
70. Menger, K. (1951). Ensembles flous et fonctions aleatories, *Comptes Rendus de l'Academie de Sciences Paris* 232, 2001-2003.
71. Menger, K. (1951). Probabilistic geometry, *Proc. N.A.S.* vol. 37, 226-229
72. Menger, K. (1951). Probabilistic theories of relations, *Proc. Natl. Acad. Sci.*, vol. 37, 178-180
73. Menger, K. (1979). *Selected papers in logic and foundations, didactics, economics*, D. Reidel.
74. Moisil, Gr.C. (1935). Récherches sur l'algébre de la logique, *Annales Scientifiques de L'université de Jassy*, XXII, 1-118.
75. Mostowski, A. (1957). On a generalization of quantifiers, *Fund. Math.* vol.44,12-36.
76. Murawski, R. (1994), *Filozofia matematyki, antologia tekstow klasycznych*, Wyd. naukowe UAM, Poznań.
77. Narens, L. (1981). A general theory of ratio scalability with remarks about the measurement- theoretic concept of meaningfulness, *Theory and Decision*, 13, 1-70.

78. Nguen, H. T. (1982). On the possibilistic approach to the analysis of evidence in. R. Yager (ed.), *Fuzzy sets and possibility theory*, Pergamon Press, 395-401.
79. Orlov, A. I. (1975). Foundations of fuzzy sets (generalisation of Zadehian concept) in: *Algorithms of multidimensional statistical analysis and their applications*, CEMI AN SSSR, Moscow 1980 pp.287-308 (in Russian).
80. Orlov, A. I. (1980). Random sets with independent elements (Lucyeans) and their applications in: Ayvasian S. A., Enyukov I. C. (eds.), *Algorithms and programms for applied statistical analysis*, Nauka, Moscow 1980 pp. 287-308 (in Russian).
81. Ostasiewicz, W. (1988). Formalisation of quantifier phrases, in Gupta M. M. and Yamawa T. (eds.) *Fuzzy logic in knowledge-based systems*, 271-286, North-Holland.
82. Ostasiewicz, W. (1991). Pioneers of fuzziness, *Busefal*, 46, 4-15
83. Ostasiewicz, W. (1992). Uncertainty and vagueness, in: Tofan I., Gill Aluja J., Costinescu O. and Teodorescu H. N. (eds.). *Advances in fuzzy sets and applications*, Iasi.
84. Ostasiewicz, W. (1992). Half a century of fuzzy sets, *Kybernetika,* 28, 17-20.
85. Ostasiewicz, W. (1994). Remarks on various kinds of sets, *Proc. of EUFIT'94*,
86. Ostasiewicz, W. (1996). Some phylosophical aspects of fuzzy sets, *Fuzzy Economic Review*, 2, 3-33.
87. Pawlak, Z. (1985). Rough sets, and fuzzy sets, *Fuzzy Sets and Systems*, 17, 99-102.
88. Penrose R., (1989). Emperor's New Mind, Oxford University Press.
89. Perzanowski (1973). The development of Cantor's definition of the set, in: Surma S. (ed.) Studies in the history of mathematical logic, Ossolineum, 269-274.
90. Post, E. L. (1921). Introduction to a general theory of elementary propositions, *American J. of Mathematics* 43, 165-185.
91. Przelecki, (1958). W sprawie terminów nieostrych, *Studia Logica*, 8, 313-317.
92. Quine, W. V. (1981). *Theories and things*, The Belknap Press of Harvard University Press, Cambridge.
93. Quine, W. V. (1960). *Word and object*, The MIT Press, Cambridge.
94. Ramirez D. (1990). *G.W. Leibniz, J. Bernuolli i les interpretacions de la probabilitat. De L'ars cogitandi a L'ars conjectandi*, Barcelona, 85-105.
95. Rasiowa , H. (1962). On non -classical calculi of classes, Tihany, 11-15 Sept.
96. Rasiowa, H. (1964). A generalisation of a formalised theory of fields of sets on non-classical logics, *Rozprawy Matematyczne*, 42, 3-29.
97. Rasiowa, H. (1974). *An algebraic approach to non-classical logics*, PWN, Warszawa.
98. Reichenbach, H. (1949). *The theory of probability*, University of California Press.
99. Reichenbach, H. (1966). *Elements of symbolic logic*, The Free Press, New York

100.Rescher, N. (1964). *Introduction to logic*, St. Martins Press, New York.
101.Robinson, R. (1941). III.- Ambiguity, *Mind*, 50, 140-155
102.Robbins, H. E. (1944). On the measure of random set, *Ann. of Math. Stat.* vol. 15, 70-74.
103.Rogers, R. (1971). *Mathematical logic and formalised theories*, North-Holland.
104.Rolf, B. (1980). A theory of vagueness, *Jour. of philosophical logic*, 9, 315-325.
105.Rolf, B. (1981). *Topics on vagueness*, Ph. D. Thesis, University of Lund.
106.Russell, B. (1923). Vagueness, *Austr. J. of Philosophy*, 1, 84-92.
107.Russell, B. (1924).*The problem of philosophy*, Williams & Norgate, London .
108.Schutz, W.C. (1959). Some applications of the logical calculus for empirical classes for social methodology, *Psychometrica,* 24, 69-87.
109.Strzednicki, J.T.J., Rickey, V.F., Czelakowski, J. (eds.) (1984). *Leśniewski's System Ontology and Mereology,* Martinus Nijhoff and Ossolineum.
110.Szpilrajn, E.(1936). Sur l'equvalence des suites d'ensembles of l'equivalence des fonctions, *Fundamenta Mathematicae*, 26, 302-326.
111.Tarski, A. (1933), *Pojęcie prawdy w jezykach nauk dedukcyjnych*, Nakładem Towarzystwa Naukowego Warszawskiego, Warszawa.
112.Tarski, A. (1940). *Introduction to logic,* Oxford University Press.
113.Tatarkiewicz, W. (1982). *Dzieje sześciu pojęć*, PWN, Warszawa.
114.Toth, H. (1987). From fuzzy-set theory to fuzzy set-theory: some critical remarks on existing concepts, *Fuzzy Sets and Systems*, 23, 219-237
115.Vopenka, P., Hajek, P.(1972). *The theory of semisets*, Academia, Prague.
116.Wajsberg, M. (1931). Aksjomatyzacja trówartościowego rachunku zdań, *Comp. Rend. Seanc. Soc. Sci. Lett.* Varsovie, Classe III, 24, 126-148
117.Weyl, H. (1940). The ghost of modality in: *Philosophical essays in memory of Edmund Husserl*, Cambridge (Mass.), 278-303.
118.Weyl, H. (1946). Mathematic and logic, *Amer. Math. Month.* 53, 2-13.
119.Wolenski, J. (1985). *Filozoficzna szkoła lwowsko-warszawska*, PWN, Warszawa.
120.Young, C. (1931). The algebra of many-valued quantities, *Mathematische Annalen,* vol. 104, 260-290.
121.Zadeh, L. H. (1965), Fuzzy sets, *Information Control*, 8, 338-353.
122.Zawirski, Z. (1932). Les logiques nouvelles at le champ de leur application, *Revue de métaphysique et de morale*.
123.Zawirski, Z. (1934). *Stosunek logiki wielowartościowej do rachunku prawdopodobieństwa*, Polskie Towarzystwo Przyjaciół Nauk, Poznań.
124.Zemach, E. M. (1991). Vague objects, *Nous,* 3, 323-340.

Fuzzy Negation

E. Ferri, A. Kandel[1] and G. Langholz
Department of Electrical Engineering-Systems
Tel Aviv University
Tel Aviv 69978, ISRAEL

Abstract

The linguistic terms *negation* and *complementation* are usually used synonymously and often interchangeably in the literature for both crisp and fuzzy notations. In most cases, negation is used where complementation would be in order. We show that, although this collaboration of meanings may be acceptable in the crisp Boolean case, it is generally erroneous in the fuzzy case.

Fuzzy negation is introduced as a fuzzified functional (a fuzzy version) of the fuzzy complement. The properties of this innovative definition are investigated in both the classical and the fuzzy sense.

Keywords: fuzzy negation, fuzzy complement, fuzzy connectives, fuzzy negation of normal forms, fuzzy meaning.

1 Introduction

Communication through natural language is possible without any use of negative forms. However, the negative form is very common in most linguistic and mathematical implementations. In a two-valued world, it is well accepted that the negative form of any one element is the second. In the natural (fuzzy) world, however, the issue of the negative form becomes controversial.

Lotfi Zadeh [61] suggested the use of connectives, referred to as *standard fuzzy set operations*, and defined the *complement* of a fuzzy set A, denoted by A', as:

$$\mu_{A'}(x) = 1 - \mu_A(x) \quad \forall x \in A. \tag{1}$$

where X is the domain space and the set A is characterized by a membership function $\mu_A(x)$ which associates each x in X with a real number in [0,1]. His definition is the most commonly used and is referred to as *Zadeh's complement* or *standard/classical/Lukasiewicz (strong/strict) complement/negation/involution*. Some authors use the original term of *complement* [6,8,27-33,36,43, 44,46,53-54,60,62-63], but many others refer to the same definition as *negation* [2,5,16,19,22-23,34,39,49,51,56] and some even use both terms interchangeably [4,7,20-21,25,38,35,41]. Still, other definitions of both terms exist, but most relate to the same original concept.

---

[1] This work was done while on leave from the Department of Computer Science and Engineering, University of South Florida, Tampa, FL 33620 USA.

We will introduce a variety of such definitions and refer to them as *fuzzy complements*. We will then explore the meaning of *fuzzy negation* and introduce a perspective and definition for understanding and processing it.

The most common shapes of membership functions are triangular (Fig. 1a), trapezoidal (Fig. 1b), "bell-shaped" (Fig. 1c), sigmoid (Fig. 1d), and combinations of triangular with trapezoidal boundaries (Fig. 1e) or "bell-shaped" with sigmoid boundaries (Fig. 1f). For the sake of simplicity and without loss of generality, we will focus our discussion on the triangular with trapezoidal boundaries representation (Fig. 1e), and refer to it for abbreviation as the triangular representation.

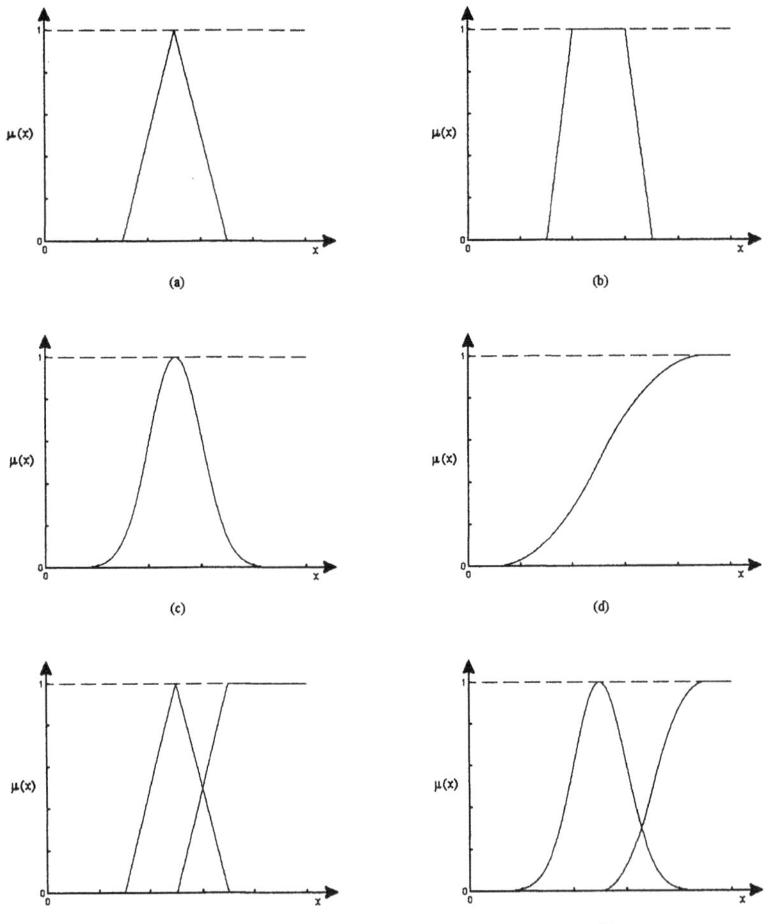

Figure 1 Common membership function shapes

Furthermore, to achieve maximum readability and clarity (and thus maximum reader satisfaction), we will use throughout the following example and some variations of it.

Example 1: Suppose that we want to produce a representation for the fuzzy variable *age* using triangular membership functions. A common representation is depicted in Fig. 2. We assume [0,120] to be the domain of age and will use subsets of this representation throughout the paper. (Note that Fig. 2 includes both the age and the normalized age domains; both will be used throughout the paper.)

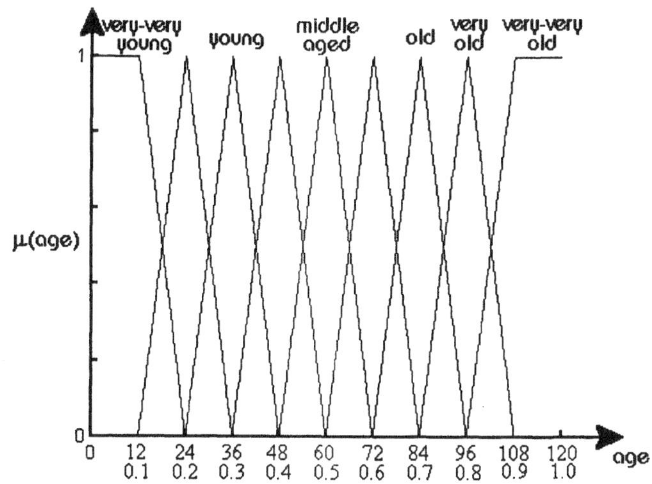

Figure 2 Triangular representation of the fuzzy variable age.

1.1 Complementation versus Negation

We begin the discussion of complementation and negation with their dictionary definitions. Open any dictionary and you will find a variety of definitions for complementation and negation. Each definition corresponds to a different variation of the term, relating to its use in different context or linguistic conditions. A **com•ple•ment** (*noun*) is one of two parts that make up a whole; counterpart; the quantity or amount that completes anything; (*logic*) the class of all the things that are not members of a given class; (*math*) the set of all the elements of a universal set not included in a given set. **Ne•ga•tion** (*noun*) is the opposite or absence of something considered positive or affirmative: Darkness is the negation of light; a negative statement, idea, concept, doctrine, etc.; a contradiction, refutation, or rebuttal; (*logic*) a proposition that is the denial of another proposition and is true only if the original proposition is false [11,12,55,57]. It is very clear that complement deals with parts of a whole, members of a class, elements of a set and, in general, with operands of mathematical nature, whereas negation deals with abstract conditions, statements, propositions and, in general, with natural elements of the world and the language describing it.

Yet, we tend to use negation when we complement Boolean (two-valued) terms because the definition of negation includes opposite concepts such as true versus false and darkness versus light (e.g., a negative in photography). In fuzzy logic, however, abstract elements are frequently represented mathematically as membership functions, and we seldom need to negate such terms in a meaningful way. But when we search for fuzzy negation in the fuzzy logic literature, we often find that, instead of negation, some form of complementation is used when applied to computational problems [1,2,4,5,7,10,14-16,19-24,35,38,39,44,47-51, 56], and that proper negation is used only when applied to theoretical discussions [9,40].

Thus, to put things into perspective, we propose that fuzzy complementation should be viewed basically as an extension of Boolean complementation. In the two-valued setting, we consider opposites to be complementary (e.g., *small/big*, *low/high*, *short/tall*, *thin/fat*, *young/old*, *open/closed*, *narrow/wide*, *empty/full*, *slow/fast*, *front/back*, *forward/backward*, *black/white*, *happy/sad*) and we also consider two parts of a whole as complementary. In the fuzzy setting, the complement of a term is everything but that term. For example, the complement of *old*, which is commonly referred to as *not old*, is everything (in the age domain) but old, including all ages below *old* (e.g., *young*, *middle age*) and above *old* (e.g., *very old*, *very very old*). Hence, using the fuzzy term *old* of Example 1 and applying to it Zadeh's definition of Eqn. (1), we obtain the membership functions of Fig. 3, or the sets of Fig. 4 [26] in which the membership grade of A=*old* is denoted by shades of gray.

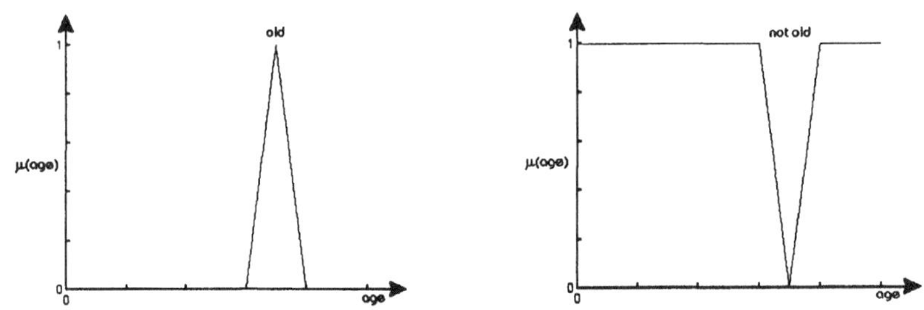

Figure 3 Triangular representations of the fuzzy term *old* and its standard complement *not old*.

We may observe that ages outside the support of *old* receive in *not old* maximum membership grades of 1 as required by Boolean logic. The meaning of such an observation is that every age outside the support is *not old* to the same extent in the complementary sense. This boundary condition property of fuzzy complement (see axiom c1 in section 1.2) is the most basic requirement for upholding Boolean complementation. We assert that this mathematical foundation of the fuzzy complement is either fuzzy or wrong for fuzzy negation and, therefore, using the terms negation and complementation synonymously and interchangeably in the fuzzy setting is incorrect and misleading.

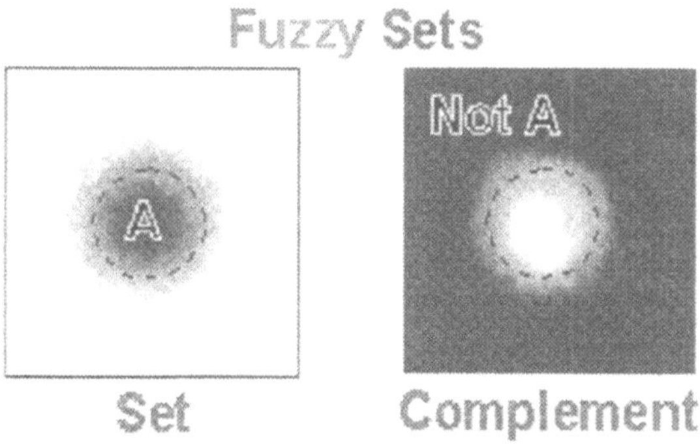

Figure 4 Set representations of the fuzzy term *old* and its standard complement *not old* using shades of gray

It is true that every age except old is *not* old, and that is what the fuzzy complement tells us, however, when we use the phrase *not old* in natural language communication, we do not necessarily relate to a unique age, and we certainly never relate to every other age to the same extent (with the same membership function of 1). In fact, in some context we might mean that the person is *young*, and in another that the person is *middle-aged* or even between the two (the possibility of using *not old* for *very old* or *very-very-old* is much smaller). We are able to make a contextual distinction because in any specific context we generally have some age neighborhood in mind. Similarly, it is clear that, unless we have prior knowledge, a statement like *not middle aged* is difficult to understand and process because we do not know which direction is more plausible: toward younger or older (it is usually a matter of speaker and context). Negating multi-dimensional terms such as colors is even more of a controversy. If we look, for example, for the negation of *white* we may consider *black* a good answer (maybe even the best one), but why cannot the negation of *white* be some other color such as *red* or *blue*?

If we compare the dictionary definitions of complement and negation with their use in the fuzzy logic literature, it seems that fuzzy set theory and fuzzy logic blur even further the two concepts which are very difficult to distinguish to begin with. It does not help, of course, that, the term *not* is used in both the complement and the negation of *old* without any implicit clue to the intended form. We claim that, although fuzzy negation deals with the exact same terms (which guarantees confusion and misconception), the *essence of negation is meaning*. Negation is highly context-based, it may also be highly complex, imprecise, ambiguous, and dynamic in meaning, and furthermore, it is adaptive. While adaptive adjustment is beyond the scope of this paper, it may be achieved using environmental (or user) feedback through a neuro-fuzzy device [13]. Fuzzy negation should be viewed as expanding the meaning of fuzzy complement (without contradicting it), much like fuzzy logic is an expansion of Boolean logic. Hence, in the following sections, we show that we may consider fuzzy negation as a fuzzification (a fuzzy function) of the fuzzy complement. We define the fuzzy meaning of negation in a way that would enable natural language understanding and processing.

1.2 Fuzzy Complementation

In this section we give a brief review of the literature on fuzzy complementation. Because complementation and negation are often used synonymously in the literature, we quote the term negation whenever it is so used. The following definition of complement is based on the one presented in [33] and supported by many others (e.g., [22,24,38,56]).

Let A be a fuzzy set on X and $\mu_A(x)$ be the degree to which x belongs to A (*x*'s *membership grade*). Let *c*(A) denote a function $c\colon[0,1]\rightarrow[0,1]$, called *fuzzy complement* of A of type *c*, then $c(\mu(x))$ is the fuzzy complement of $\mu_A(x)$ (the degree to which *x* belongs to c(A), or the degree to which *x* does not belong to A). To produce meaningful fuzzy complements, *c* must satisfy at least the following two axiomatic requirements (the *axiomatic skeleton of fuzzy complements*):

Axiom c1: $c(0)=1$ and $c(1)=0$ (boundary conditions)

Axiom c2: $\forall x,y\in[0,1]$, if $x\leq y$, then $c(x)\geq c(y)$ (monotonicity)

Axiom c1 requires compatibility with the crisp (Boolean) case and axiom c2 requires non-increasing monotonicity, namely that, when *x* increases, *c*(*x*) should not increase as well (intuitive requirement of a complement).

There are two additional requirements which are desirable in many practical cases and which may be used to break the space of fuzzy complements into classes:

Axiom c3: *c* is a continuous function (continuity)

Axiom c4: *c* is *involutive*, namely $\forall x\in[0,1]$, $c(c(x))=x$ (involutivity)

A decreasing function that satisfies the first three axioms is called *strict complementation* (or strict negation) and one that satisfies all four axioms is called *strong complementation* (or involution, or strict/strong negation) [2,15,17,21,24,38,42,56]. Note that many authors use the term strict complementation or involution for strong complementation. It has been proved [5,24,52] that any strong complementation can be written as:

$$c(x)=t^{-1}(t(1)-t(x))\,. \tag{2}$$

where $t\colon[0,1]\rightarrow[0,\infty)$ is a continuous and strictly increasing function with $t(0)=0$ and $t(1)$ a finite number (also in [1,2,14] but with $t(1)=1$); or as:

$$c(x)=g^{-1}(g(0)-g(x))\,. \tag{3}$$

where $g\colon[0,1]\rightarrow[0,\infty)$ is a continuous and strictly decreasing function with $g(1)=0$ and $g(0)$ a finite number [5, 16].

Examples and common complement functions:

- $c(x) = 1 - x \qquad x \in [0,1]$ (classical/standard complement) satisfies all 4 axioms [33,61] (Fig. 5a). The Lukasiewicz complementation (negation) is defined similarly as $c(x)=p-1-x$, $x \in [0, p-1]$ *or* $x \in \{0, \ldots, p-1\}$ [50].

- $c(x) = \begin{cases} 1 & \text{for } x \le t \\ 0 & \text{for } x > t \end{cases} \qquad x \in [0,1], t \in [0,1)$ (step-threshold function)

  satisfies only the axiomatic skeleton (axioms c1 and c2) [33] (Fig. 5b). For $t=0$, we obtain the *intuitionistic logical complementation* (negation) [47,49] and for $0 \le t < \frac{1}{2}$, we obtain the *intuitionistic complementation* (negation) [48]. A definition of complementation based on the implication $c(x)=x \to 0$ [10] is identical to the step function with $t=0$.

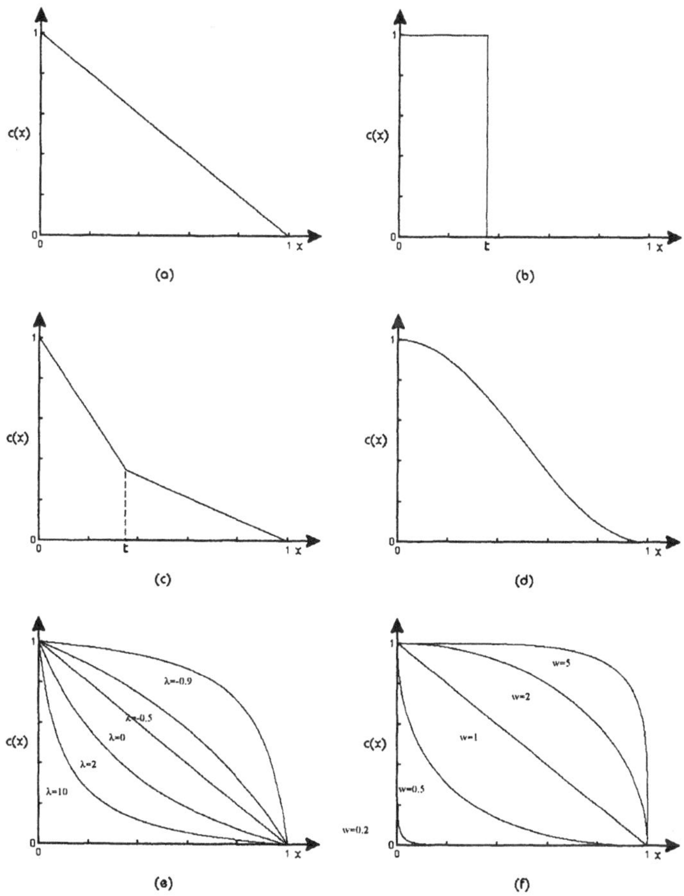

Figure 5 Common complement functions

- $$c(x)=\begin{cases}1-\dfrac{1-t}{t}x & \text{for } x\le t\\ \dfrac{t}{1-t}(1\text{-}x) & \text{for } x>t\end{cases}\qquad x\in[0,1],\ \ t\in(0,1)\qquad \text{(knee-threshold)}$$
  satisfies axioms c1, c2 and c3 (but not c4) [24] (Fig. 5c).

- $c(x)=\frac{1}{2}(1+\cos\pi x)\quad x\in[0,1]$ (raised cosine)
  satisfies axioms c1, c2 and c3 (but not c4) [33] (Fig. 5d).

- $c_\lambda(x)=\dfrac{1-x}{1+\lambda x}\quad x\in[0,1]\,;\ \lambda\in(-1,\infty)$ (Sugeno class [45])
  satisfies all 4 axioms [33] (Fig. 5e).

- $c_w(x)=(1-x^w)^{1/w}\quad x\in[0,1]\,;\ w\in(0,\infty)$ (Yager class [58,59])
  satisfies all 4 axioms [33] (Fig. 5f).

Note that when λ=0 for the Sugeno class, or w=1 for the Yager class, the respective complement functions become Zadeh's complement. Other (less common) examples also exist, such as the "independent" complement [18], complementation on partitions [6], or the two-dimensional "block" complement for image enhancement [3]. An attempt to define fuzzy negation which would be different from the fuzzy complement only devised some different types of fuzzy complement [44].

2 Fuzzy Negation

In this section we introduce a new method for generating meaningful fuzzy negation functions. We begin by focusing on the reasoning behind our approach, followed by a general definition of fuzzy negation and some examples for it. We show that, although complementation has an important part in the construction of fuzzy negation, other types of information must be combined with it to achieve a meaningful definition.

2.1 Reasoning

In section 1.1 we discussed the semantic difference between complementation and negation. Let us now relate to and expand the discussion using Example 1 with the age subsets *old* and *very very old* which are depicted in Fig. 6 and their corresponding standard complements shown in Fig. 7. Recalling that we have set the age domain to [0,120], we have decided in this (subjective) example that *old* is best described by age 84 (a single membership grade of 1) and descends towards both 72 and 96; likewise, *very-very-old* is best described by ages over 108 but is also true for people over 96. It is important to note that the triangular representations of *old* and *very-very-old* also approximate the meaning of the terms and their use in natural language. We probably would not use the term *old* of Fig. 6a for someone under the age of 72 or over the age of 96; for these we might use other terms such as *adult* or *middle-aged* (for ages under 72) and *very-old* or *very-very-old* (for ages over 96). Similarly, we probably would not use the term *very-very-old* of Fig. 6b for someone under 96; instead, we might use other terms such as *old* or *very-old.*

Let us now consider the corresponding standard complements shown in Fig. 7. Although every age except 84 might be considered as *not old* to some extent, and ages outside the region [72,96] might be considered absolutely *not old* (*not old* with a membership-grade of 1), we would hardly refer to a baby as *not old* (although he/she definitely is). In other words, complements are not quite plausible in so far as natural language common sense and meaning are concerned.

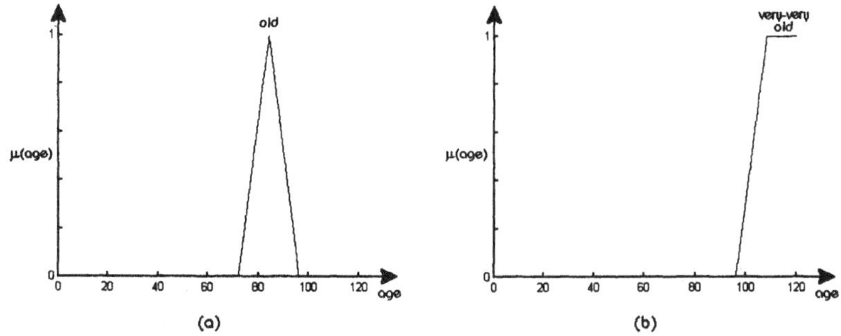

Figure 6 Membership functions of (a) *old* (b) *very-very-old.*

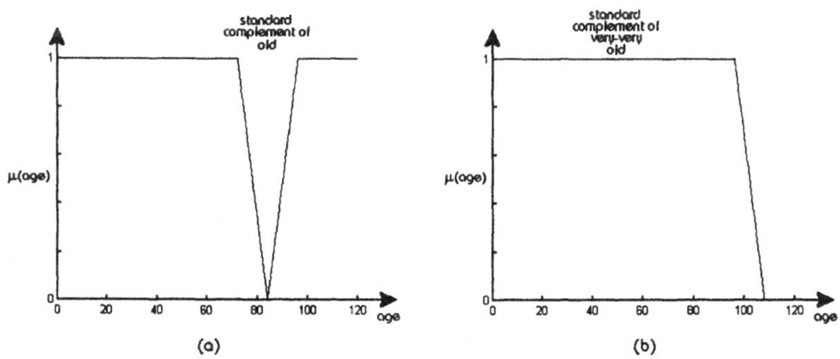

Figure 7 Standard complements of (a) *old* (b) *very-very-old*

We claim that the reason for this is that the complementation function contains limited meaning in the (potentially large) part of the domain in which the membership grade is 1. It is important to notice, however, that the complement does tell us that the membership grade in these regions is *very high* ! (it **is** true that a *baby* is *not old* even if we seldom use it.) Once we remember this important observation, the complement becomes meaningless in these regions. We refer to them as the "non-meaningful regions" of the complementation function and note that these regions are the support of $\mu(x)$. The meaningful regions of the terms *old* and *very-very-old* are outlined in Fig. 8. The size and position of the meaningful regions depend mostly on the fuzzy term and the choice of representation.

The logical conclusion which may be drawn from the discussion thus far is the following: if we want to devise a meaningful negation, we may rely on the complementation function in its meaningful regions but we need another source of information for the remainder of the domain. The choice of the supplementary information source, and the way in which all the information is combined, will determine the general structure of the definition of the negation function.

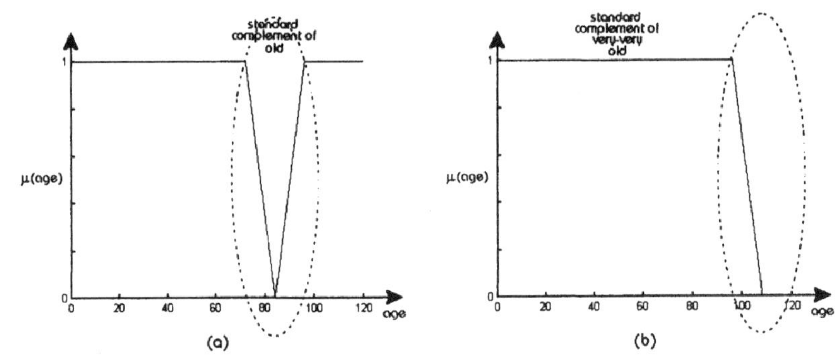

Figure 8 Meaningful regions of complementation functions (a) *old* (b) *very-very-old*

To find a new source of information, recall the dictionary definition of *negation* (section 1.1) as "opposite of something". A common method for formulating an opposite is *reflection*. We have to establish that the reflection is meaningful, and if so in what regions, and then formulate the combination of complementation and reflection. To simplify things, let us assume that the domain is one-dimensional, in which case the reflection may be two-sided in general. Consider the *reflections* of the fuzzy subsets *old* and *very-very-old* of Example 1 (shown in Fig. 6), about the middle of the domain (age=60), depicted in Fig. 9. Note that we have used only single-sided reflection (to the left of the *reflector* at 60) because the other reflection (to the right of the reflector at 60) is outside the domain. Consider further the age subsets of *young* and *very-very-young* of Example 1, which are shown in Fig. 10 for convenience. Observe that the reflections of *old* and *very-very-old* about age=60 are *identical* to the representations of *young* and *very-very-young*, respectively. Now, *young* is not a bad choice for the opposite of *old*, and it probably does more justice to the meaning of *not old* than the complement of *old* in Fig. 7a. In contrast, *very-very-young* may be the opposite of *very-very-old*, but that is seldom what we mean. We would usually use *not very-very-old* to refer to an older person, though not too old, and not use *very-very-young* with that person. Now, note that *old* is a fuzzy term whereas *very-very-old* includes fuzzy predicates. So, how do we produce meaningful reflections in the presence of predicates? As far as natural language is concerned, it stands to reason that negation should operate on the last predicate (the one which is further away from the fuzzy term) with respect to the remainder of the fuzzy expression. We will refer to this predicate as the *leading predicate* and to the remainder of the expression as the *referenced expression.* In our example, this means that we should negate *very-very-old* with respect to *very-old*; in other words, we should choose *very-old* as the reflector rather than age=60 as we did before. Since the reflector is crisp, we can use the defuzzification of the term *very-old*, namely, age 96, to generate the negation of *very-very-old* depicted in Fig. 11.

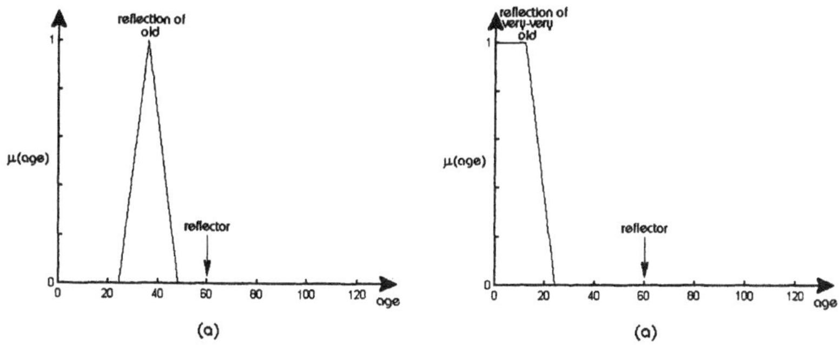

Figure 9 Reflections of membership functions about the reflector age=60 (a) *old* (b) *very-very-old*

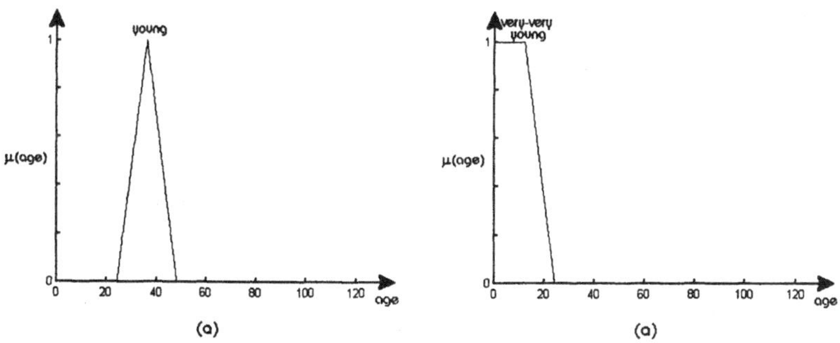

Figure 10 Membership functions of (a) *young* (b) *very-very-young*

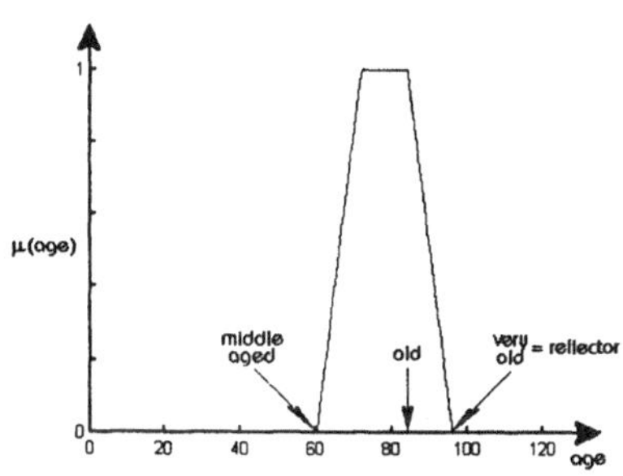

Figure 11 Reflection *very-very-old* about *very-old*

The representation in Fig. 11 seems to make much more sense because when we say *not very-very-old* we probably mean someone who is between *middle-aged* and *very-old*, or, in general, somewhat *old*. Furthermore, it is important to note that *meaning is a function of the chosen reflector* as evidenced by the results in Fig. 9b and Fig. 11 in which the two fuzzy subsets are disjoint.

To compare the results of using complementation (Fig. 8) and reflection (Figs. 10 and 11), we have grouped them in Fig. 12. Note that we use the age=60 reflector for *old* and the age=96 reflector for *very-very-old*. In addition, we have marked the meaningful regions of the reflections as we did for the complementation.

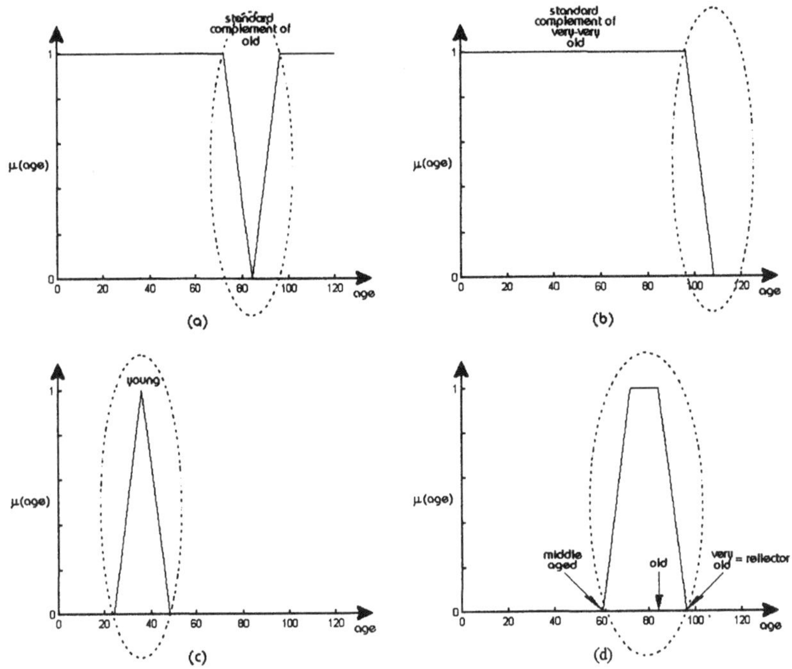

Figure 12 Complementation (a,b) and reflection (c,d) of *old* (a,c) and *very-very-old* (b,d) respectively

We observe that the meaningful regions for complementation and reflection may be different (there may be more than one meaningful region for each). In addition, we may consider each representation as very useful in its meaningful region and less useful in other regions. Therefore, we should combine them in such a way that each will dominate in its meaningful region and contribute less as we draw away from that region. Note that the contribution need not be symmetric because we do expect the negation to be definitely positive (with high membership values) outside the complementation meaningful region (but, remember, that we do not expect it to be all 1).

2.2 Definition

In this section we provide a general definition for a negation function based on the foregoing discussion. To simplify things, we assume in the sequel that all the definitions are on a *normalized domain.*

Let A be a fuzzy set on X and $\mu_A(x)$, for every x, its membership function. Let $c(\mu_A(x))$ denote the fuzzy complement of $\mu_A(x)$, and let $r(\mu_A(x), R)$ (r:$[0,1] \to [0,1]$) denote the two-sided *fuzzy reflection* function of $\mu_A(x)$ with respect to the reflector R. The reflector is designated as $R = \{\vec{R}, \overleftarrow{R}\}$ and the fuzzy reflection function is designated as $r = u(\vec{r}, \overleftarrow{r})$, where u is some t-conorm, $\vec{r}$ is the reflection to the right about $\vec{R}$, and $\overleftarrow{r}$ is the reflection to the left about $\overleftarrow{R}$. Let $n(\mu_A(x))$ (n:$[0,1] \to [0,1]$) denote the *fuzzy negation* of $\mu_A(x)$. We will use $c(x)$ or c, $r(x,R)$ or $r(x)$ or r, and $n(x)$ or n as abbreviations for $c(\mu_A(x))$, $r(\mu_A(x), R)$, and $n(\mu_A(x))$, respectively.

We define fuzzy negation $n(x)$ as a fuzzy function of both fuzzy complementation $c(x)$ and fuzzy reflection $r(x)$:

$$n = u\{\psi(c,r), \phi(r,c)\}\,. \tag{4}$$

where u is some t-conorm (which is usually the same as $u(\vec{r}, \overleftarrow{r})$ but not necessarily so), c(x) is some fuzzy complementation, $r(x,R)$ is a fuzzy reflection of $\mu_A(x)$ with respect to a two-sided reflector R, and ψ and ϕ are some functions. To simplify the discussion, we will use the standard t-conorm and complementation, *max* and *1-x*, respectively.

The choice of R is very important because it determines the position of the reflection. In general, since R may be dynamic and context-dependent, and thus change through some learning method (e.g., [13]), different choices of the reflector will produce different meanings. We restrict our discussion to a constant R, noting however, that it may be used as an initial value in some dynamic process. One example of a two-sided reflector is:

$$R_{\pm} = M \pm (\max(|M - M_{\text{Ref}}|, 0.1) + R_0)\,. \tag{5}$$

where $M \in [0,1]$ is the defuzzification of $\mu_A(x)$ which can be referred to as the *crisp meaning* of the term (note that the choice of defuzzification method is of little importance [37]), M_{Ref} is the crisp meaning of the *referenced expression* or 0.5 if there is no *leading predicate*, and $R_0 \geq 0$ is some delta which is provided to ensure that the reflection is to a region in which $\mu(x) \leq 0.5$ (we do not want the reflection in a region in which the complement is small and dominant) or if none exist, to outside the domain where the reflection would not have any effect. For now, let us assume that R_0 is 0. Note the value 0.1 (or some other rather small value) in Eqn. (5). It is intended to ensure that the reflection would cause some (preferably meaningful) change (i.e., the reflection would not overlay $\mu_A(x)$). Let R_+ designate the right reflector (the reflection to the right with respect to M)

and let R_- designate the left reflector (the reflection point to the left with respect to *M*). A 3D-plot of all possible values of *R* is presented in Fig. 13.

In the simple case of a fuzzy term (i.e., no predicate so that M_{Ref}=0.5), which is not around the middle of the domain, we get from Eqn. (5) the two reflectors: R_-=0.5 and R_+=2·M-0.5. Using them with *old* (Fig. 6a), for which *M*=0.7, yields the reflectors R_-=0.5 and R_+=0.9. (Note that reflecting about R_+=0.9 is outside the domain.) In the more complex case of a fuzzy expression which is not in the middle $(M_{\text{Ref}} \neq 0.5)$, Eqn. (5) produces the two reflectors: $R_- = M_{\text{Ref}}$ and R_+=2·M- M_{Ref}. Using them with *very-very-old* (Fig. 6b) for which *M*>0.9, yields the reflectors R_-=0.8 and R_+>1.0. (Note that reflecting about R_+ is outside the domain). The importance of bi-directional reflection is demonstrated in Example 3.3 for *middle-aged*.

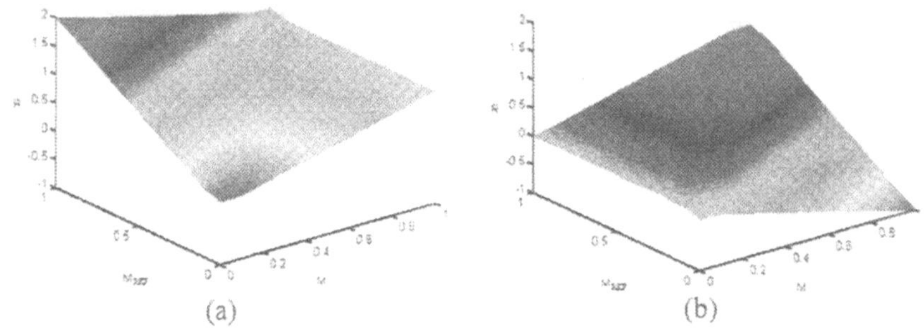

Figure 13 The reflector *R* as a function of M and M_{Ref}: (a) R_+ (b) R_-.

Let $\vec{R} = \max(R_+, R_-)$, $\overleftarrow{R} = \min(R_+, R_-)$, and $\Delta = \vec{R} - M = M - \overleftarrow{R}$. Note that, since *R*≠*M*, $\Delta > 0$. Define:

$$\vec{M} = M + 2 \bullet \Delta = 2 \bullet \vec{R} - M. \tag{6}$$

$$\overleftarrow{M} = M - 2 \bullet \Delta = 2 \bullet \overleftarrow{R} - M. \tag{7}$$

where $\vec{M}$ and $\overleftarrow{M}$ are the crisp meanings of the right ($\vec{r}$) and left ($\overleftarrow{r}$) reflections, respectively. Since $\Delta > 0$, we know that $\overleftarrow{M} < M < \vec{M}$.

The choice of the functions ψ,ϕ: [0,1]→[0,1] determines the composition of complementation and reflection in the negation. The particular choice may change the behavior and properties of the negation function in different domains and thus change the meaning drastically. To simplify things and without any loss of generality, we can change ψ and ϕ to an equivalent multiplicative (product) representation *f* and *g* such that $\psi(c,r)=f(c,r) \cdot c$ and $\phi(r,c)=g(r,c) \cdot r$.

As an example for *f* and g, we will use the following axiomatic structure to illustrate the construction of negation:

Axiom f1: $f(M)=1$ (boundary condition)

Axiom f2: $\forall x, y < \overleftarrow{M}$, if $x \leq y$, then $f(x) \geq f(y)$ (monotonically non-increasing)

$\forall x, y > \overrightarrow{M}$, if $x \leq y$, then $f(x) \leq f(y)$ (monotonically non-decreasing)

Axiom f3: $\forall x \in [0,1]$, if $\mu(x) \leq 0.5$ then $f(x) \geq 0.5/1-\mu(x)$ (minimal influence)

Axiom g1: $g(M)=0$ and $g(\overrightarrow{M})=g(\overleftarrow{M})=1$ (boundary conditions)

Axiom g2: $\forall x, y < \overleftarrow{M}$ or $M < x, y < \overrightarrow{M}$, if $x \leq y$, then $g(x) \geq g(y)$ (monotonically non-increasing)

$\forall x, y > \overrightarrow{M}$ or $\overleftarrow{M} < x, y < M$, if $x \leq y$, then $g(x) \leq g(y)$ (monotonically non-decreasing)

Axiom g3: $\forall x \in [0,1]$, if $\mu(x) \geq 0.5$ then $g(x) \leq 0.5$ (minimal influence)

Axioms f1 and g1 require that each function dominates in its meaningful region; axioms f2 and g2 require non-decreasing/increasing monotonicity for specific regions; and axiom f3 and g3 require that in the non-meaningful regions of $\mu_A(x)$, the complement would have enough effect, whereas in the meaningful regions of $\mu_A(x)$ the reflection should not be too influential. Axioms f3 and g3 also ensure some desirable properties that will be discussed in section 4. The constant 0.5 ensures that the complement would not be suppressed too much and that the reflection would not dominate too much.

There are also additional (optional) requirements which may be used to divide fuzzy negations into subclasses:

Axiom f4: f is a continuous function (continuity)

Axiom f5: f has a minimum at $\overrightarrow{M}$ and/or $\overleftarrow{M}$ (minimum)
<u>or</u>: f has a minimum at the 0 and/or 1

Axiom g4: g is a continuous function (continuity)

Axioms f4 and g4 establish continuity requirements, and axiom f5 establishes the x in which f reaches its minimum (note that f=1 has none).

2.3 Examples for *f* and *g*

This section illustrates several choices of the functions f and g. As was mentioned in the foregoing discussion, these functions determine the composition of complementation and reflection in the negation.

Example 2.1: In this example, we choose $f \equiv 1$ $\forall x \in [0,1]$, $g \equiv 0$ $\forall x \neq \overrightarrow{M}, \overleftarrow{M} \in [0,1]$, and $g(\overrightarrow{M})=g(\overleftarrow{M})=1$ (as required in axiom g1). Note that R is not relevant in this example, and that axioms f5 and g4 do not hold in this case. Namely, in this extreme case, negation specializes into complementation, $n(x)=c(x)$, and the reflection has no effect.

In the following examples, we choose R according to Eqn. (5).

Example 2.2: In this example, we choose:

$$f(x) = 1 - \frac{1-f_0}{M}|x-M|$$

where $\sqrt{0.5} \le f_0 \le 1.0$, and

$$g(x) = \begin{cases} g^u_{1-t/(\overleftarrow{M}-L_b)}\left(\frac{x-L_b}{\overleftarrow{M}-L_b}\right) & L_b \le x \le \overleftarrow{M} \\ g^d_{t/(M-\overleftarrow{M})}\left(\frac{x-\overleftarrow{M}}{M-\overleftarrow{M}}\right) & \overleftarrow{M} < x \le M \\ g^u_{1-t/(\overrightarrow{M}-M)}\left(\frac{x-M}{\overrightarrow{M}-M}\right) & M < x \le \overrightarrow{M} \\ g^d_{t/(R_b-\overrightarrow{M})}\left(\frac{x-\overrightarrow{M}}{R_b-\overrightarrow{M}}\right) & \overrightarrow{M} < x \le R_b \end{cases}$$

where $L_b \le 0$, $R_b \ge 1$ are left and right bounds of the knee-threshold functions (all of them sharing a common threshold t), and

$$g^u_t(x) = \begin{cases} \frac{1-t}{t}x & 0 \le x \le t \\ 1-\frac{t}{1-t}(1-x) & t < x \le 1 \end{cases}$$

$$g^d_t(x) = \begin{cases} 1-\frac{1-t}{t}x & 0 \le x \le t \\ \frac{t}{1-t}(1-x) & t < x \le 1 \end{cases}$$

where $x \in [0,1]$ *and* $t \in (0,1)$.

It can be shown that, unlike Example 2.1, all the axioms hold in this case. The functions f and g with M=0.6, f_0=0.8, $\overleftarrow{M}$=0.4, $\overrightarrow{M}$=0.8, t=0.2 (t is chosen to be such that axiom g3 holds), L_b=0, and R_b=1 are depicted in Fig. 14.

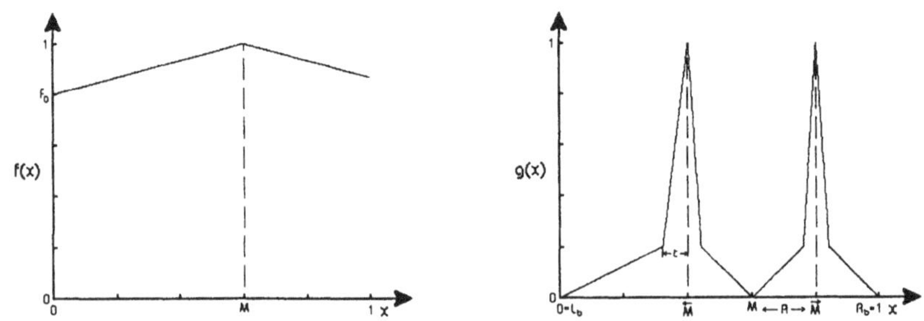

Figure 14 f and g for Example 2.2 (triangular+threshold functions)

Example 2.3: In this example, we choose a different type of functions which are more common with sigmoids and bell-shaped functions. The function f itself is bell-shaped (a normalized normal distribution):

$$f(x) = e^{-(x-M)^2/2\sigma^2}$$

where $f_0 = f(0) = e^{-M^2/2\sigma^2} \geq \sqrt{0.5}$ ($\Rightarrow$ $\sigma \geq \frac{M^2}{2\ln 2} \cong 1.44M^2$). The function g is given by:

$$g(x) = \begin{cases} g^u_{\lambda\, or\, w}(x, L_b, \overleftarrow{M}) & L_b \leq x \leq \overleftarrow{M} \\ g^d_{\lambda\, or\, w}(x, \overleftarrow{M}, M) & \overleftarrow{M} < x \leq M \\ g^u_{\lambda\, or\, w}(x, M, \overrightarrow{M}) & M < x \leq \overrightarrow{M} \\ g^d_{\lambda\, or\, w}(x, \overrightarrow{M}, R_b) & \overrightarrow{M} < x \leq R_b \end{cases}$$

where $L_b \leq 0$, $R_b \geq 1$ are left and right bounds of the Sugeno or Yager functions which share a common parameter λ or w, respectively, and (Sugeno):

$$g^u_\lambda(x,a,b) = \frac{x-a}{(b-a)(1+\lambda(b-x))}$$

$$g^d_\lambda(x) = \frac{b-x}{(b-a)(1+\lambda(x-a))}$$

where $a < b \in [0,1]$, $x \in [a,1b]$, $\lambda \in (-1,\infty)$, or (Yager):

$$g^u_w(x,a,b) = (1-(b-x/b-a)^w)^{1-w}$$

$$g^d_w(x) = (1-(x-a/b-a)^w)^{1/w}$$

where $a < b \in [0,1]$, $x \in [a,b]$, $w \in (0,\infty)$ (Sugeno and Yager respectively).

Similarly to Example 2.2, all the axioms hold in this example too. The functions f and g with M=0.6, f_0=0.8 ($\sigma = \sqrt{-\frac{M^2}{2\ln f_0}} \cong 0.9$), $\overleftarrow{M}$=0.4, $\overrightarrow{M}$=0.8, λ=50 (λ is chosen so that axiom g3 holds), L_b=0, and R_b=1 are shown in Fig. 15.

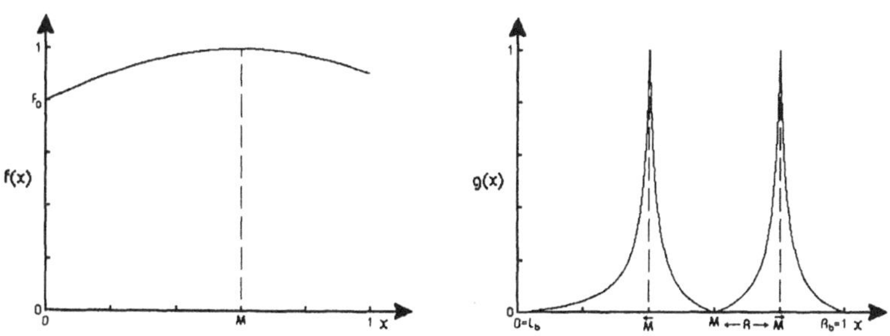

Figure 15 *f* and g for Example 2.3 (normal+Sugeno/Yager functions)

Example 2.4: Here, we choose functions for which the optional axioms f4, f5, and g4 do not hold (Fig. 16). Indeed, both functions are non-continuous (axioms f4, g4 do not hold), and axiom f5 holds but with minimum at { $\overleftarrow{M}$, $\overrightarrow{M}$ } rather than the boundary points.

3 Fuzzy Negation Examples

In this section we examine several examples of the implementation of fuzzy negation.

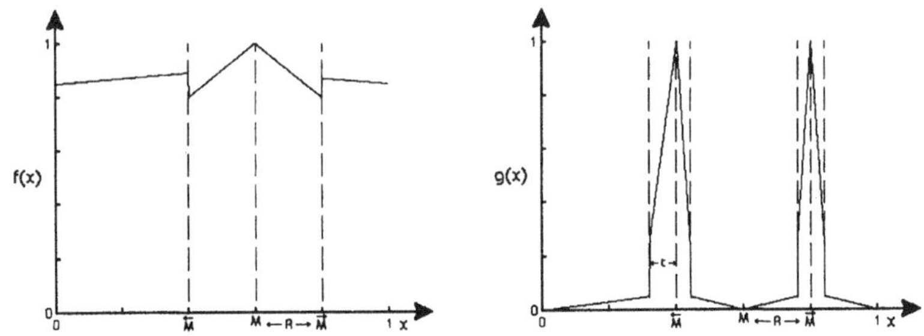

Figure 16 *f* and *g* for Example 2.4 (non-continuous)

Example 3.1: In this example, we negate a common triangular representation of the fuzzy term *old*. We begin with the original function (Fig. 6a) and its standard complement (Fig.7a), shown together in Fig. 17 for convenience.

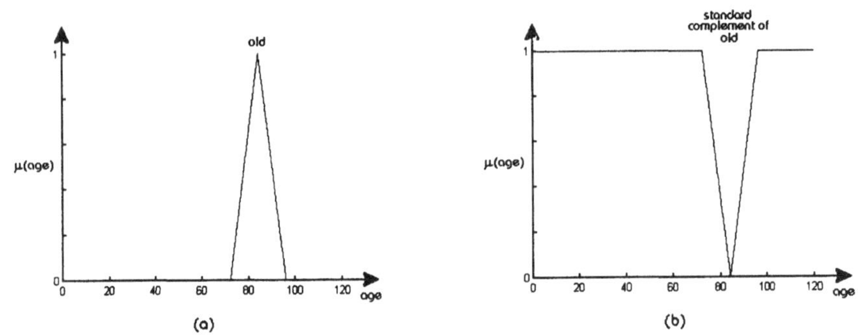

Figure 17 Membership functions of (a) *old* (b) standard complement of *old*

Note that M=0.7 (age=84) and since we do not use a predicate, M_{Ref}=0.5 (default value). Also, assume that R_0 is 0. Hence, using Eqn. (5), we get:

$$R_+ = M + (\max(|M - M_{\text{Ref}}|, 0.1) + R_0 = 0.7 + 0.2 + 0 = 0.9\,.$$

$$R_- = M - (\max(|M - M_{\text{Ref}}|, 0.1) - R_0 = 0.7 - 0.2 - 0 = 0.5\,.$$

Therefore (see section 2.2), $\vec{R} = 0.9$, $\overleftarrow{R} = 0.5$, $\Delta = \vec{R} - M = 0.2$, and (using Eqns. (6) and (7)):

$$\vec{M} = M + 2 \bullet \Delta = 0.7 + 2 \bullet 0.2 = 1.1 \text{ (outside the domain)}$$

$$\overleftarrow{M} = M - 2 \bullet \Delta = 0.7 - 2 \bullet 0.2 = 0.3 \text{ (inside the domain)}$$

Combining these results with the functions f and g of Example 2.2 (with f_0=0.8, t=0.2), we get $\vec{r}$ and $\overleftarrow{r}$ (Fig. 18) and f and g (Fig. 19).

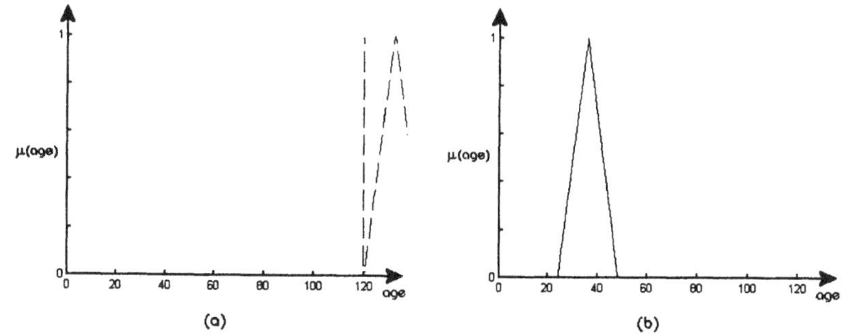

Figure 18 (a) $\vec{r}$ and (b) $\overleftarrow{r}$ for *old* (triangular+threshold functions)

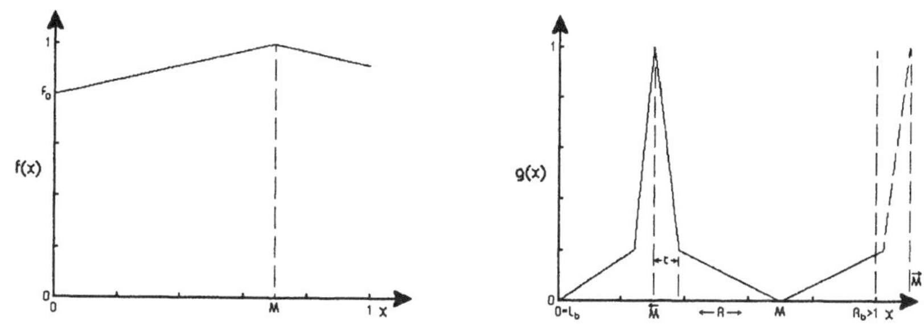

Figure 19 f and g for *old* (triangular+threshold functions)

As we can see, $\vec{r}$ is completely outside the age domain (remember our assumption that the age domain is [0,120]) and is, therefore, meaningless. Still, for completeness, Fig. 20 shows what happens just outside the age domain.

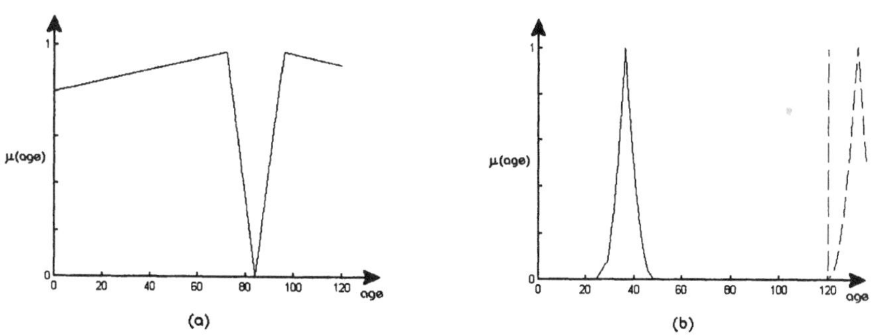

Figure 20 (a) $f{\cdot}c$ and (b) $g{\cdot}u(\vec{r}\,,\overleftarrow{r}\,)$ for *old* (triangular + threshold functions)

We can now combine the complementation and the reflection to generate the negation of *old* - *not old* - shown by the solid line in Fig. 21 (remember that we use the standard t-conorm *max*). Note that the dotted lines in Fig. 21 are not part of *not old*; they are the superposition of Fig. 18 intended to explain the position of the two peaks (spikes) in Fig. 21 (at $\overleftarrow{M} = 0.3 \Rightarrow$ age=36, and $\vec{M} = 1.1 \Rightarrow$ age=132).

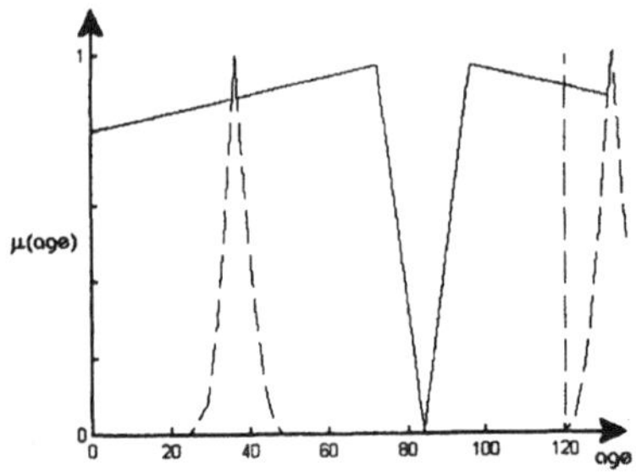

Figure 21 Negation of *old*

Nevertheless, even with these two peaks (see Example 3.4 for "smoother" representations), the result makes sense: Subjectively, *not old* most probably means somewhere in the neighborhood of *young*, or somewhere in between *young* and *old*, although most ages which are not in the neighborhood of *old* are still considered as *not-old* with high possibility. Although superfluous to the meaning of *not old* within the given age domain [0,120], Fig. 21 also shows what happens just outside the domain.

Example 3.2: Consider now the negation of *very-very-old* (Fig. 22)

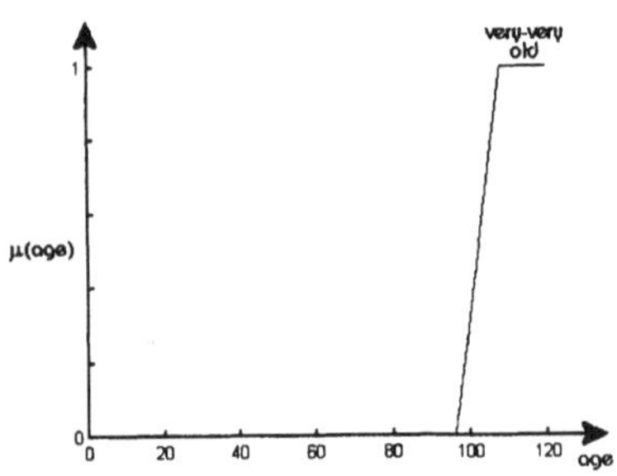

Figure 22 *Very-very-old*

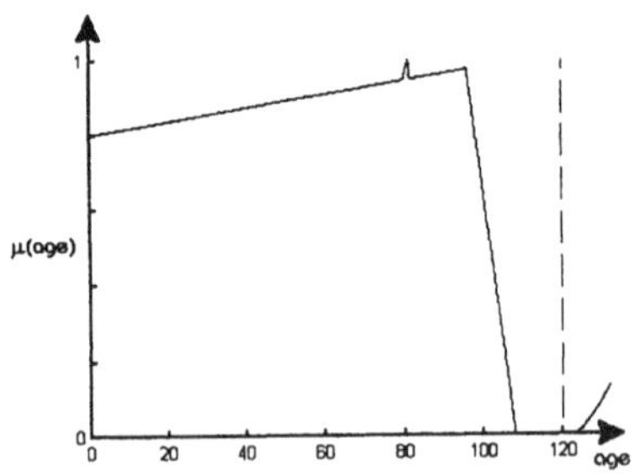

Figure 23 *Not-very-very-old*

We used the *center-of-mass* defuzzification (any defuzzification technique would do) to calculate M=0.925. $M_{\text{Ref}} \neq 0.5$ in this case because we have a predicate *very* that operates on the (referenced) expression *very-old*. Hence, M_{Ref}=0.8 is the crisp meaning of *very-old.* Assuming again R_0=0, we get $R_+ = \vec{R}$=1.05, $R_- = \overleftarrow{R}$=0.8, Δ =0.125, $\vec{M}$=1.175, and $\overleftarrow{M}$=0.675. Finally, using the functions *f* and *g* of Example 3.1, we obtain the negation of *very-very-old, not-very-very-old,* shown in Fig. 23.

Example 3.3: The negation of *middle-aged* (see Fig. 24) means most probably persons "older" than *middle-aged* as well as persons "younger" than *middle-aged.*

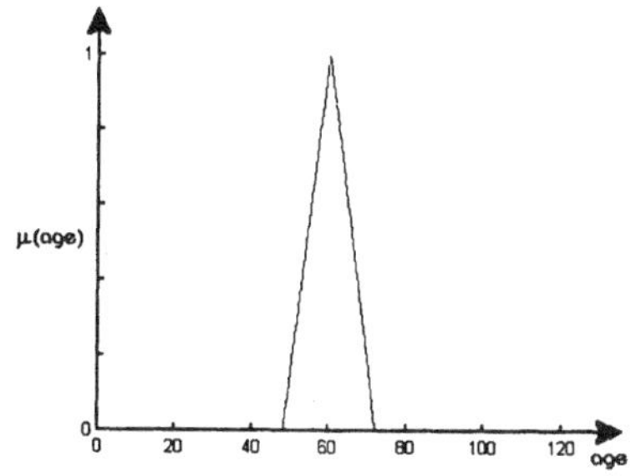

Figure 24 *Middle-aged*

In this case, *M*=0.5 (age=60), and since we do not have a predicate, M_{Ref}=0.5 (default value). Consequently, R_0=0, $R_+ = \vec{R}$=0.6, $R_- = \overleftarrow{R}$=0.4, Δ =0.1, $\vec{M}$=0.7, and $\overleftarrow{M}$=0.3. Reflecting left we get $\overleftarrow{r}$ of Fig. 25a, and reflecting right we get $\vec{r}$ of Fig. 25b.

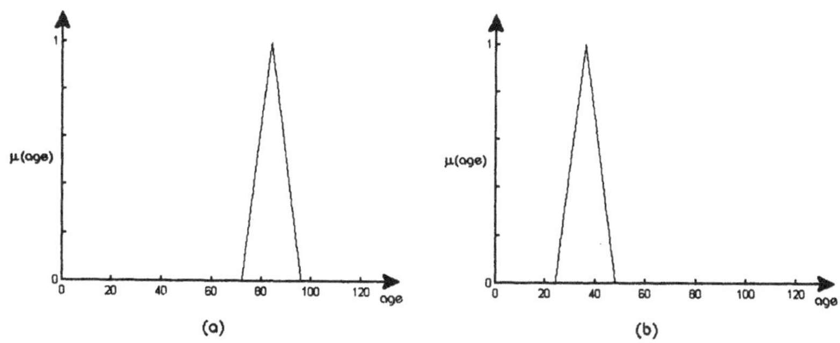

Figure 25 (a) $\overleftarrow{r}$ and (b) $\vec{r}$ for *middle-aged* (triangular + threshold functions)

Using the functions *f* and *g* of Example 3.1, we obtain *not-middle-aged* shown in Fig. 26.

Example 3.4: We repeat Example 3.3, however, here we represent *middle-aged* by the "bell-shaped" representation shown in Fig. 27. We used a raised-cosine for *g* and a smooth sigmoid-t-conorm [13], expecting a much smoother and more logical shape as a result. Here, too, *M*= M_{Ref}=0.5 and, assuming R_0=0 as before, we get the same results as in Example 3.3, namely, $R_+ = \vec{R} = 0.6$, $R_- = \overleftarrow{R} = 0.4$, $\Delta = 0.1$, $\vec{M} = 0.7$, and $\overleftarrow{M} = 0.3$. Using the functions f and g of Example 2.3 (with g based on raised cosine rather than Sugeno which is sharper), we obtain *not-middle-aged* shown in Fig. 28. Note that using sigmoid-addition for a smooth t-conorm [13] is the main reason for the smooth result.

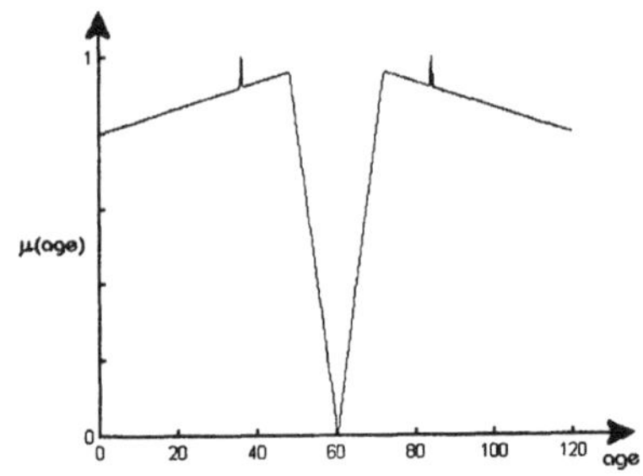

Figure 26 Negation of *Middle-aged*

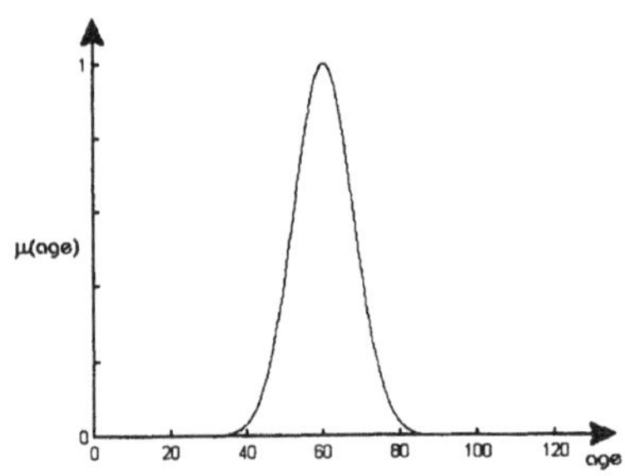

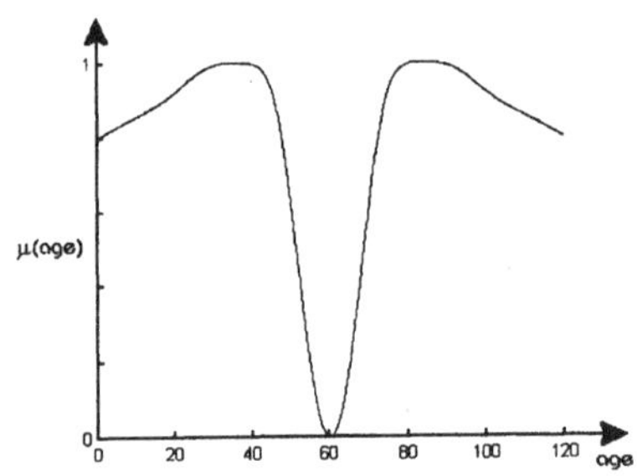

Figure 27 Bell-shaped *middle-aged*

Figure 28 Bell-shaped n*ot-middle-aged*

4 Properties of Fuzzy Negation

In this section we briefly examine several properties of fuzzy negation such as boundary conditions, involution, De-Morgan laws, and fuzzy conjunctive and disjunctive normal forms (FCNF and FDNF) [53].

4.1 Fuzzy Boundary Conditions

The boundary conditions of fuzzy complementation, $c(0)=1$ and $c(1)=0$ (axiom c1) derive directly from the Boolean (crisp) case. However, these *crisp* requirements do not hold for fuzzy negation. Instead, the following *fuzzy* boundary conditions hold for fuzzy negation: For $\mu(x)=0$, axiom f3 guarantees that $n(\mu(x)=0)\geq 0.5$; for $\mu(x)=1$, and with $c(x)=1-x$ ($\Rightarrow c(1)=0$), $g(1)\leq 0.5$ by axiom g3 and, therefore, $n(1)\leq 0.5$. In other words, the crisp boundary conditions required for fuzzy complementation are replaced by fuzzy boundary conditions for fuzzy negation.

4.2 Fuzzy Involution

Involution, $c(c(x))=x$ (axiom c4), holds for Boolean complementation, the standard fuzzy complementation, and for numerous other fuzzy complementation functions. For fuzzy negation, however involution holds *up to a similarity*, namely, the negation of the negation of x does not equal x but is similar to x.

Consider for example the fuzzy term *old* of example 3.1 which is shown again in Fig. 29a. Negating *old* twice results in the representation of *not-not-old* shown in Fig. 29b. Comparing the two, note that the functions are very similar in the meaningful region of *old* and differ mostly in the non-meaningful region of *old*. Note also that *not-not-old* is mostly *old*, it is *not young*, but it may be *very-young* to some small degree.

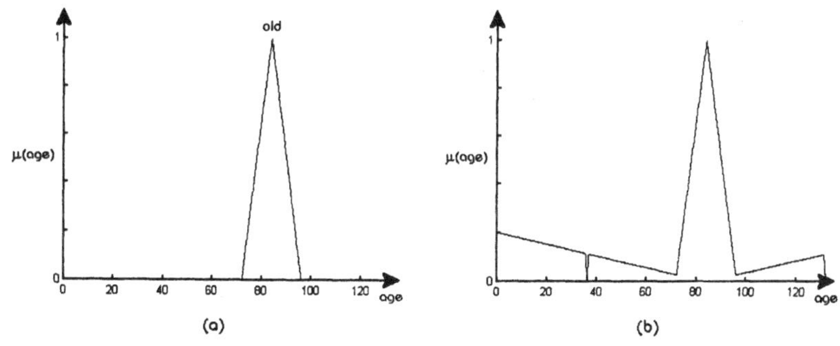

Figure 29 Membership functions of (a) *old* (b) *not-not-old*

Likewise, Figs. 30a and b show the representations of the fuzzy terms *middle-aged* of Example 3.4 and *not-not-middle-aged*, respectively, and a similar analysis can be applied.

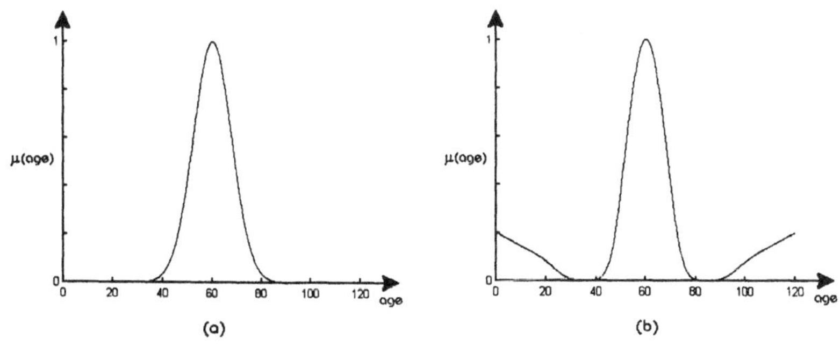

Figure 30 Membership functions of (a) *middle-aged* (b) *not-not-middle-aged*

We can say that the property of involution for fuzzy complementation is replaced by a property of fuzzy involution for fuzzy negation. Negating twice the original function does not produce the *exact* original function but one that is *similar* to it. Note that in most cases (e.g., Example 3.1-3.4) the negation of a function is mostly non-zero (the negation may be zero only when c or f are zero and $u(\vec{r},\vec{r})$ or g are zero). Consequently, in most cases, the reflection would be "thrown" outside the domain and, therefore, only the complement would have effect. Hence, the difference between the original function and its twice-negated replica results from the implementation of f and the use of reflection.

4.3 Fuzzy De-Morgan Laws

De-Morgan's laws are fundamental to crisp set operations. In classical set theory, intersection and union are dual with respect to complementation in the sense that they satisfy De-Morgan laws. In the fuzzy case, however, only some combinations of t-norms, t-conorms, and fuzzy complements satisfy the duality [2,33]:

$$n(i(x, y)) = u(n(x), n(y)) \tag{8}$$

$$n(u(x, y)) = i(n(x), n(y)) \tag{9}$$

where $n \equiv c$. For example, the standard t-norm and t-conorm (*min* and *max*, respectively) are dual with respect to any fuzzy complement [33].

For fuzzy negation, however, even with the standard triplet <*min*, *max*, *1-* >, Eqns. (8) and (9) hold for $n(\,)$ *up to a similarity* (similarly to involution (section 4.2)). In other words, the two sides of Eqns. (8) and (9) are similar rather than equal.

Consider for example the fuzzy terms *old* (Fig. 29a) and *very-very-old* (Fig. 22) with respect to Eqn. (8). As far as the left-hand side is concerned, $i(x, y) \equiv 0$ because the two membership functions do not intersect and, therefore, there is no reflection and the complement $c(x) \equiv 1$. Hence, $n(i(x, y)) = f(x)$. On the right-hand side of Eqn. (8), we have a union of the negations of *old* (Fig. 21) and *very-very-old* (Fig. 23). Applying the standard t-conorm *max* to these negations, we get the function shown in Fig. 31.

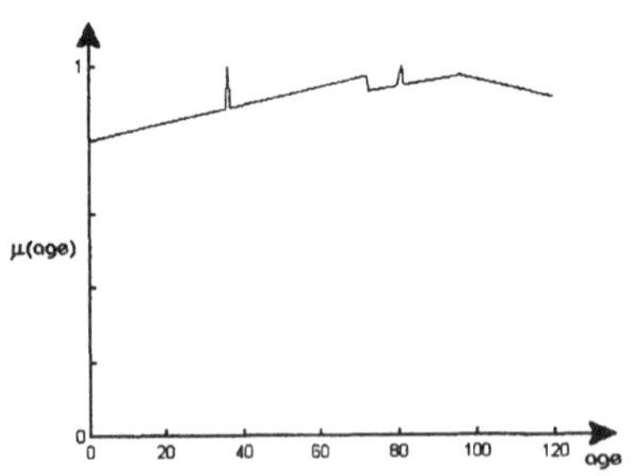

Figure 31 $u(c(old), c(very\text{-}very\text{-}old))$

Note that the function in Fig. 31 is somewhat similar to $f(x)$: $\mu(age)$ is quite high for every index but favors the age *young* and ages somewhat below *very-very-young*.

Let us now repeat the previous example by comparing the two sides of Eqn. (8) for the fuzzy terms *old* (Fig. 29a) and *very-old* (Fig. 32a). The intersection of the two functions using the standard t-norm *min* is depicted in Fig. 32b and the negation of this intersection is shown in Fig. 32c (note that the reflection have no influence on *n*(*i*(*old*, *very-old*)) (Fig. 32c) because the intersection is not normalized). For the right-hand side of Eqn. (8), the union of *not old* and *not-very-old* is shown in Fig. 32d. Comparing Fig. 32c with Fig. 32d, the similarity between the two sides of Eqn. (8) is quite obvious.

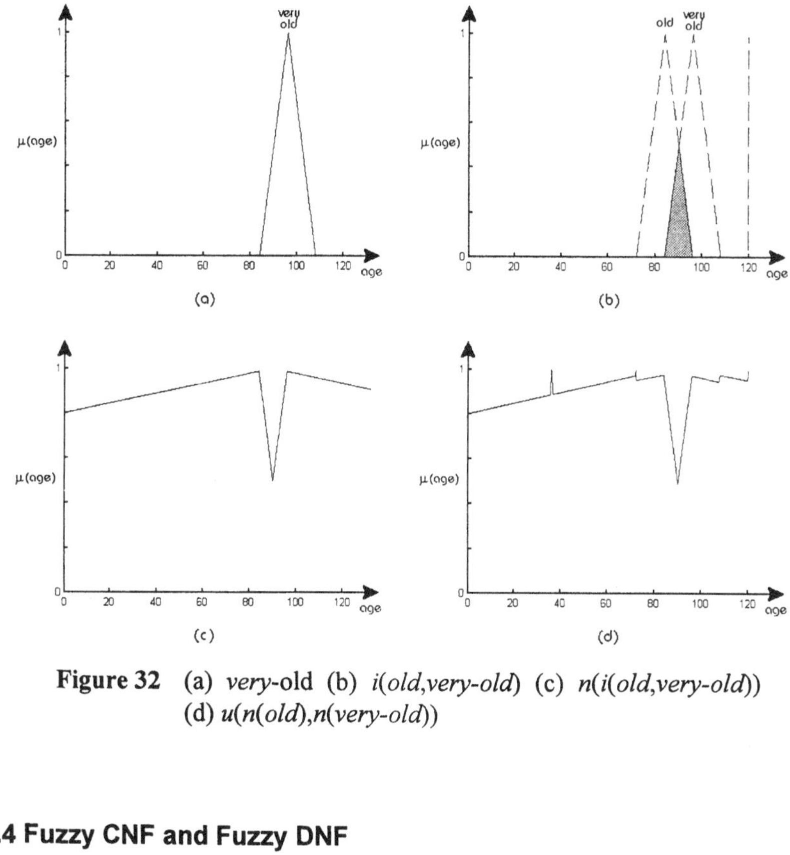

Figure 32 (a) *very*-old (b) *i*(*old*,*very-old*) (c) *n*(*i*(*old*,*very-old*)) (d) *u*(*n*(*old*),*n*(*very-old*))

4.4 Fuzzy CNF and Fuzzy DNF

In classical logic, the law of excluded middle $u(x,c(x))=1$ and the law of contradiction $i(x,c(x))=0$ apply and, therefore, the conjunctive and disjunctive normal forms are equal [53]. In fuzzy logic, however, the laws of excluded middle and contradiction do not apply (and thus a fuzzy "paradox" is created [40]) and therefore, the conjunctive and disjunctive normal forms draw apart and define bounds in the space between them. This space defines possible FCNFs and FDNFs as functions of the triplet $< i, u, c >$. Note that if we use the standard triplet $< min,$

max, *1-* >, the FCNF, FDNF, and the space between them become functions of f and g.

We restrict our brief discussion to the laws of excluded middle and contradiction; the implication to FCNF and FDNF is straightforward. Using the standard triplet <*min*, *max*, *1-*> with our definition of negation, the fuzzy excluded middle satisfies:

$$u(x,n(x))\geq 0.5 \qquad (10)$$

If $\mu(x)\geq 0.5$, Eqn. (10) is immediately true. Therefore, we need only consider the case of $\mu(x)<0.5$. Since $n(x)$ is a t-conorm of the products $f\cdot c$ and $g\cdot r$, it suffices to show that one of the products is greater than or equal to 0.5, e.g., that $f\cdot c\geq 0.5$, $\forall x\in[0,1]$, namely, $f(x)\geq 0.5/c(x)=0.5/(1-\mu(x))$, $\forall x\in[0,1]$. This, however, is guaranteed by axiom f3.

Likewise, for fuzzy contradiction:

$$i(x,n(x))\leq 0.5 \qquad (11)$$

If $\mu(x)\leq 0.5$, Eqn. (11) is immediately true. Therefore, we need only consider the case of $\mu(x)>0.5$. Since $n(x)$ is a t-conorm of the products $f\cdot c$ and $g\cdot r$, it is necessary that each product would be smaller than or equal to 0.5. If $\mu(x)>0.5$, then $c(x)<0.5$ and, since f is bounded in $[0,1]$, $f\cdot c$ is bounded by 0.5. It is enough to show that $g\cdot u\{\vec{r},\overleftarrow{r}\}\leq 0.5$, $\forall x\in[0,1]$; but, since $u\{\vec{r},\overleftarrow{r}\}$ is bounded by $[0,1]$, it enough to show that $g\leq 0.5$, $\forall x\in[0,1]$. This, however, is guaranteed by axiom g3. Note that this is always possible because $\vec{M}$ and $\overleftarrow{M}$ are chosen in such a way that g is 1 only when $\mu(x)\leq 0.5$.

5 Conclusions

Computing with words calls for negation and that is where the problem begins. Complementation is *not* negation but in the fuzzy literature both are used synonymously and interchangeably. Is *not old* the complement of *old*, *c*(*old*), or the negation of *old*, *n*(*old*)?

When we compute with words we must take into account the *meaning* of natural language (fuzzy) expressions. We have argued that complementation is a mathematical artifact of limited meaning in the context of natural language and that to use it when negation is actually called for may be misleading and erroneous. Furthermore, we have claimed that the essence of negation is meaning and, therefore, negation is the proper operator to be used for computing with words.

Nevertheless, fuzzy negation is a complex concept to comprehend, let alone formalize. It may be even argued that a general formalization of fuzzy negation of all linguistic expressions is impossible.

We have asserted that fuzzy negation is a much broader concept than complementation, that *c*(*old*) is definitely not equal to *n*(*old*), that negation and not complementation should be used in natural language understanding and processing, and that fuzzy negation is a fuzzified composition of complementation and reflection of membership functions.

We might have only scratched the surface of the fuzzy negation and negation versus complementation issues. Certainly, there is room for additional research on these issues.

References

[1] Alsina C., Trillas E., "On Splitting Triplets: Beyond Dual Connectives", *Proc. 4th IEEE International Conference on Fuzzy systems,* vol. 3, pp. 1233-1238, 1995.

[2] Alsina C., "As You Like Them: Connectives in Fuzzy Logic", *Proc. 26th International Symposium on Multiple-Valued Logic*, pp. 2-7, 1996.

[3] Bhutani K.R., Battou A., "An Application of Fuzzy Relations to Image Enhancement", *Pattern Recognition Letters*, vol. 16, no. 9, pp. 901-909, 1995.

[4] Bier V.M., "Is Fuzzy Set Theory more General than Probability Theory?", *Proc. 1st International Symposium on Uncertainty, Modeling and Analysis*, pp. 297-301, 1991.

[5] Bilgic T., Turksen I.B., "Interval Valued Fuzzy Sets from Continuous Archimedean Triangular Norms", *Proc. 3rd IEEE Conference on Fuzzy Systems*, vol. 2, pp. 1142-1147, 1994.

[6] Bodjanova S., "Complement of Fuzzy K-Partitions", *Fuzzy Sets and Systems*, vol. 62, no. 2, pp. 175-184, 1994.

[7] Boldrin L., "A Substructural Connective for Possibilistic Logic", *Proc. European Conference (ECSQARU'95) on Symbolic and Quantitative Approaches to Reasoning and Uncertainty*, pp. 60-68, 1995.

[8] Brubaker D.L., "Fuzzy Logic Works with Degrees of Truth", *Computer Design*, vol. 30, no. 5, pp. 98-99, 1991.

[9] Buehrer D.J., "From Interval Probability Theory to Computable Fuzzy First-Order Logic and Beyond", *Proc. 3rd IEEE Conference on Fuzzy Systems*, vol. 2, pp. 1428-1433, 1994.

[10] Cheng L., Hu M., "A General Fuzzy Logical Operator Set", *Proc. 20th International Symposium on Multiple-Valued Logic*, pp. 279-283, 1990.

[11] *Collins Dictionary of the English Language*, Collins, 1983.

[12] *Collins Cobuild English Dictionary*, The University of Birmingham, Harper Collins Publishers, 1995.

[13] Ferri E., Langholz G., "Neuro-Fuzzy Application to Natural Language Understanding", *Proc. International Conference on Intelligent Technologies in Human-Related Sciences*, vol. 1, pp. 31-37, 1996.

[14] Fodor J.C., "Fuzzy Connectives via Matrix Logic", *Fuzzy Sets and Systems*, vol. 56, pp. 67-77, 1993.

[15] Fodor J.C., "A New Look at Fuzzy Connectives", *Fuzzy Sets and Systems*, vol. 57, pp. 141-148, 1993.

[16] Fodor J.C., "Nilpotent Minimum and Related Connectives for Fuzzy Logic", *Proc. 4th IEEE International Conference on Fuzzy Systems*, part 4, pp. 2077-2082, 1995.

[17] Fodor J.C., "Contrapositive Symmetry of Fuzzy Implications", *Fuzzy Sets and Systems*, vol. 69, no. 2, pp. 141-156, 1995.

[18] Gau W.L., Buehrer D.J., "Vague Sets", *IEEE Transactions on Systems, Man and Cybernetics*, vol. 34, no. 2, pp. 610-614, 1993.

[19] Glorennec P.Y., "Neuro-Fuzzy Logic", *Proc. 5th IEEE International Conference on Fuzzy Systems*, vol. 2, pp. 899-904, 1996.

[20] Gottwald S., "Approximate Solutions of Fuzzy Relational Equations and a Characterization of T-Norms that Define Metrics for Fuzzy Sets", *Fuzzy Sets and Systems*, vol. 75, no. 2, pp. 189-201, 1995.

[21] Hirota K., Ozawa K., "The Concept of Fuzzy Flip-Flop", *IEEE Transactions on Systems, Man, and Cybernetics*, vol. 10, no. 5, pp. 980-997, 1989.

[22] Hirota K., "Fundamentals of Fuzzy Logical Circuits", *Proc. IJCAI'91 Workshop on Fuzzy Logic and Fuzzy Control*, pp. 145-157, 1991.

[23] Hirota K., "Fundamentals of Fuzzy Logic and Its Hardware Implementations", *Proc. 13th Brazilian Symposium on Artificial Intelligence (SBIA'96)*, p.231, 1996.

[24] Iancu I., "T-Norms with Threshold", *Fuzzy Sets and Systems*, vol. 85, pp. 83-92, 1997.

[25] Jang J.S.R., Sun C.T., Mizutani E., *Neuro-Fuzzy and Soft Computing*, Prentice Hall, 1997, pp. 21-24.

[26] Jones T.I., "It's a Fuzzy Future: How to Be a Little More Sure About Uncertainties", *1995 Research Forum of the CFM (Centre for Facilities Management)*, University of Strathclyde, 1995.

[27] Jumarie G., "A General Approach to Approximate Reasoning via Probability-Possibility Conversion", *Proc. 1993 International Conference on Systems, Man and Cybernetics*, vol. 4, pp. 656-661, 1993.

[28] Kandel A., "On Minimization of Fuzzy Functions", *IEEE Trans. On Computers*, vol. C-22, no. 9., 1973, pp. 826-832.

[29] Kandel A., "On the Properties of Fuzzy Switching Functions, *J. of Cybernetics*, vol. 4, no. 1, 1974, pp. 119-126.

[30] Kandel A., "Fuzzy Expectation and Energy States in Fuzzy Media, *Intr. J. for Fuzzy Sets and Systems*, vol. 3, 8, no. 3, 1982, 1981, pp. 291-310.

[31] Kandel A., *Fuzzy Mathematical Techniques wuth Applications*, Addison Wesley, 1987, 2nd printing.

[32] Kaufmann A., *Introduction to the Theory of Fuzzy Subsets*, vol. 1, Academic Press, 1975, pp. 10, 335-6.

[33] Klir J.K., Yuan B., *Fuzzy Sets and Fuzzy Logic: Theory and Applications*, Prentice Hall, 1995, pp. 50-96.

[34] Kosko B., *Fuzzy Engineering*, Prentice Hall, 1997, pp. 18-37.

[35] Kovacevic D., "Fuzzy Logic Controller based on Standard Operational Amplifiers", *Fuzzy Logic Conference*, pp. 231-244, 1996.

[36] Liren L., "Fuzzy Solid Sets for Mathematical Morphology and Optical Implementations", *J. of the Optical Society of America A*, vol. 12, no. 12, pp. 2636-2644, 1995.

[37] Ma M., Friedman M., Kandel A., "A New Approach for Defuzzification", *to appear*.

[38] Martin J.A., "Probability and Fuzzy Relational Semantic Systems in Propositional Approximate Reasoning", *Proc. 18th International Symposium on Multiple-Valued Logic*, pp. 205-209, 1988.

[39] Nguyen H.T., Kreinovich V., Lea B., Tolbert D., "How to Control if even Experts are not Sure", *Proc. 2nd International Workshop on Industrial Fuzzy Control and Intelligent Systems*, pp. 153-162, 1992.

[40] Nguyen H.T., Kreinovich V., "Classical-Logic Analogue of a Fuzzy 'Paradox'", *Proc. 5th IEEE International Conference on Fuzzy Systems*, pp. 428-431, 1996.

[41] Pedrycz W., *Fuzzy Sets Engineering*, CRC Press, 1995, pp. 290-297.

[42] Prade H., "Modeles mathematiques de l'imprecis et de l'incertain en vue d'applications en raisonnement natural", *These d'Etat*, University P. Sabatier, 1982.

[43] Ross T.J., *Fuzzy Logic with Engineering Applications*, McGraw-Hill, 1995, pp. 20-27, 50-52, 198.

[44] Schneider M., Shnaider E., Kandel A., "Applications of the Negation Operator in Fuzzy Production Rules", *Fuzzy Sets and Systems*, vol. 34, no. 3, pp. 293-299, 1990.

[45] Sugeno M., Park G.K., "An Approach to Linguistic Instruction Based Learning", *intern. J. of Uncertainty, Fuzziness and Knowledge Systems*, vol. 1, no. 1, pp. 19-56, 1993.

[46] Suzuki H., "A Complementary Fuzzy Logic System", *IEEE Transactions on Systems, Man, and Cybernetics* - Part B: Cybernetics, vol. 27, no. 2, 1997.

[47] Takagi N., Nakashima K., Mukaidono M., "Fundamental Properties of Extended Kleene-Stone Logic Functions", *Proc. 22nd International Symposium on Multiple-Valued Logic*, pp. 243-249, 1992.

[48] Takagi N., Nakashima K., Mukaidono M., "Some Properties of Kleene-Stone Logic Functions and Their Canonical Disjunctive Form", *IEEE Transactions on Information and Systems*, vol. E76-D, no. 2, pp. 163-170, 1993.

[49] Takagi N., Nakashima K., Mukaidono M., "Some Properties and a Necessary and Sufficient Condition for Extended Kleene-Stone Logic Function", *IEEE Transactions on Information and Systems*, vol. E76-D, no. 5, pp. 533-539, 1993.

[50] Takagi N., Nakashima K., Mukaidono M., "A Necessary and Sufficient Condition for Lukasiewicz Logic Functions", *Proc. 26th International Symposium on Multiple-Valued Logic*, pp. 37-42, 1996.

[51] Thiele H., Lehmke S., "On 'Bold' Resolution Theory", *Proc. 3rd IEEE International Conference on Fuzzy Systems*, vol. 3, pp. 1945-1950, 1994.

[52] Trillas E., "Sobre Functions de Negacion en la Teoria de Conjuctos Difusos", *Stochastica*, vol. 1, pp. 47-59, 1979.

[53] Turksen I.B., "Fuzzy Normal Forms", *Fuzzy Sets and Systems*, vol. 69, no. 3, pp. 319-346, 1995.

[54] Wang L.X., *Adaptive Fuzzy Systems and Control*, Prentice Hall, 1994, pp. 9-11.

[55] *Webster's 3rd New International Directory of the English Language Unabridged*, Encyclopedia Britannica Inc., William Benton, 1971.

[56] Weber S., "A General Concept of Fuzzy Connectives, Negations and Implications Based on T-Norms and T-Conorms", *Fuzzy Sets and Systems*, vol. 11, pp.115-134, 1983.

[57] *Webster's College Dictionary*, Random House, 1984.

[58] Yager R.R., "On the Measure of Fuzziness and Negation. Part I: Membership in the Unit Interval", *Intern. J. of General Systems*, vol. 5, no. 4, pp. 221-229, 1979.

[59] Yager R.R., "On the Measure of Fuzziness and Negation. Part II: Lattices", *Information and Control*, vol. 44, no. 3, pp. 236-260, 1980.

[60] Yamakawa T., "Silicon Implementation of a Fuzzy Neuron", *IEEE Transactions on Fuzzy Systems*, vol. 4, no. 4, pp. 488-501, 1996.

[61] Zadeh L.A., "Fuzzy Sets", *Information and Control*, vol. 8, pp. 338-353, 1965.

[62] Zadeh L.A., "PRUF-A Meaning Representation Language for Natural Languages", in E.H. Mamdani and B.R. Gains (eds.): *Fuzzy Reasoning and its Applications*, Academic Press, 1981, pp. 1-66.

[63] Zimmermann H.J., *Fuzzy Set Theory and its Applications*, (2nd edition), Kluwer, 1991, pp. 16-57.

TRIANGULAR OPERATIONS, NEGATIONS, AND SCALAR CARDINALITY OF A FUZZY SET

Maciej Wygralak

Adam Mickiewicz University
Faculty of Mathematics and Computer Science
Matejki 48/49, 60-769 Poznań, Poland
E-mail: wygralak@math.amu.edu.pl

Abstract. Scalar approaches to cardinality of a fuzzy set are very simple and convenient, which justifies their frequent use in many areas of applications instead of more advanced and adequate forms such as fuzzy cardinals. On the other hand, theoretical investigations of scalar cardinalities in the hitherto existing subject literature are rather occasional and fragmentary, and lacking in closer references to triangular norms and conorms. This paper is an attempt at filling that gap by constructing an axiomatized theory of scalar cardinality for fuzzy sets with triangular norms and conorms. It brings together all standard scalar approaches, including the so-called sigma-counts and p-powers, and offers infinitely many new alternative options.

1. Preliminaries

In exactly the same way as cardinality belongs to the most fundamental notions and attributes related to sets, the cardinal aspect of fuzzy sets seems to be difficult to overestimate. The motivations for dealing with it are both theoretical and applicational. We mean a generalization of the ordinary cardinality theory for sets and, on the other hand, multiple applications such as modeling the meaning of imprecise quantifiers and numerical expressions in natural language statements, communication with data bases and information/intelligent systems, decision-making in a fuzzy environment, metrical analysis of grey images, etc. For instance, let us mention the problem of satisfactory answers in data bases to queries of the form

"How many x's are $\boldsymbol{p}$?"

or

"Are there more x's which are $\boldsymbol{p}$ than x's which are $\boldsymbol{q}$?"

which are cardinal queries, i.e. queries about cardinalities or comparisons of cardinalities of fuzzy sets, where $\boldsymbol{p}$ and $\boldsymbol{q}$ denote two properties, generally imprecise ones. A typical example of a query of the first form is "How many individuals in the data base are middle-aged and rather tall?" which requires counting how many elements are in the intersection of two fuzzy sets. If one tries to count the elements in a fuzzy set, the main difficulty and difference in comparison with sets and their cardinalities lies in graduation of membership in that fuzzy set. Counting and cardinal calculus under fuzziness become a task which is much more complicated and advanced from the conceptual viewpoint. Any mathematical formalization is then, in essence, a challenging attempt at adequate modeling of the human perception of numbers which, by its very nature, seems to be flexible, problem-dependent, and having many "resolution levels". Therefore, no wonder that the subject literature offers us a wide spectrum of mathematical approaches to cardinality $|A|$ of a fuzzy set $A: \mathbf{M} \to [0,1]$, where $\mathbf{M}$ denotes throughout the paper a universe (finite or not) of some elements. In the following list, we mention those approaches which are of interest from the viewpoint of the present paper; detailed reviews and further references can be found, for instance, in [4, 11, 19-21, 24]. In each case, $|A|$ is defined as an object which one creates using ordinary numbers from a set NUM.

(1) $|A|$:= a single number from NUM.

(2) $|A|$:= a set of numbers from NUM.

(3) $|A|$:= a multiset of numbers from NUM.

(4) $|A|$:= a convex fuzzy set of numbers from NUM, i.e.

$|A|$:= a function NUM $\to [0,1]$.

As usual, the symbol := stands for "equals by definition". The approaches in (1)-(3) lead to *nonfuzzy* cardinalities of fuzzy sets. In particular, (1) proposes scalar perception of cardinality of fuzzy sets and, then, $|A|$ is called a *scalar* cardinality of A. As yet, (2) and (3) are used occasionally in the practice of fuzzy sets. The dominating options are the extremal forms (1) and (4), which is easy to understand. (4) gives us the possibility of the most complete and adequate description of cardinality of a fuzzy set at the price of relatively high representational and operational complexity. On the other hand, (1) is extremely simple, even naive, but convenient in every respect and, therefore, favoured by many practitioners.

Recall that A is said to be a *finite fuzzy set* if its support supp(A) is a finite set. There is no formal obstacle to use any of the variants (1)-(4) for both finite and infinite fuzzy sets. Nevertheless, (1) and (3) seem to be suitable rather for finite ones. For instance, in the case of infinite fuzzy sets, the use of most types of scalar cardinalities does require additional (inconvenient) preassumptions about convergence of series of (possibly transformed, e.g. raised to a power) membership values.

If A is finite, one uses NUM := $\{0, 1, 2, \ldots\}$; an additional option for (1) is then NUM := $[0, \infty)$. Clearly, if $\mathbf{M}$ is supposed to be finite, too, we put NUM := $\{0, 1, 2, \ldots, |\mathbf{M}|\}$ or NUM := $[0, |\mathbf{M}|)$. If A is infinite, we use as NUM the set of all finite and transfinite cardinal numbers not exceeding $|\mathbf{M}|$.

In this paper, we like to focus the attention on finite fuzzy sets, which play the central role from the viewpoint of applications, allowing however that the universe **M** is possibly infinite. From now on, if not emphasized otherwise, the phrase "fuzzy set" will mean "finite fuzzy set". For the reasons stated above, we like to deal with scalar cardinalities of (finite) fuzzy sets. The subject literature offers us a few candidates for scalar cardinality of A. The most commonly used variant is the so-called *sigma-count* of A

$$\sigma_A := \Sigma_{x\in \mathrm{supp}(A)} A(x),$$

possibly rounded to the nearest integer (see [13, 14, 25-27]), and its modified versions called *p-powers* of A, namely (see [7, 8])

$$\sigma_A^p := \Sigma_{x\in \mathrm{supp}(A)}(A(x))^p \text{ with } p>0.$$

Moreover, let us mention the integer scalar cardinalities

$$|\mathrm{core}(A)|,\ |\mathrm{supp}(A)|,\ |A_{\geq t}|,\ |A_{>t}|$$

with a suitable t, which can be applied to infinite fuzzy sets, too, using no additional assumptions, where

$$A_{\geq t} := \{x\in\mathbf{M}: A(x)\geq t\} \text{ with } t\in(0,1], \qquad (t\text{-cut set of } A)$$

$$A_{>t} := \{x\in\mathbf{M}: A(x)>t\} \text{ with } t\in[0,1), \qquad (\text{sharp } t\text{-cut set})$$

$$\mathrm{core}(A) := A_{\geq 1}, \qquad (\text{core of } A)$$

and thus $\mathrm{supp}(A) = A_{>0}$. Appliations and reviews of scalar cardinalities are presented in [4, 8, 11, 25-27]. Unfortunately, investigations of scalar cardinalities were rather occasional and directed mainly to fuzzy sets with the "classical" max and min operations. A few remarks about p-powers in the context of algebraic and bold operations on fuzzy sets are placed in [4, 11]. In [22, 23], an axiomatic approach to scalar cardinalities of fuzzy sets with max and min operations is constructed and investigated in detail. It brings together all the scalar constructions listed above and, moreover, offers infinitely many new options. In this paper, we like to develop that axiomatic approach by extending it to fuzzy sets with triangular norms and conorms (see Sections 3-5). For the sake of self-containment, in Section 2 we recall those notions and facts from the theory of triangular norms and conorms which are essential from the viewpoint of the main purpose of the paper. An extensive and detailed presentation of that theory can be found, for instance, in [2, 12, 16]; see also [1, 3, 5, 15, 17, 18]. Throughout, in order to avoid any misunderstanding, single capitals in italic ($A, B, C, \dots$) will denote fuzzy sets. Moreover, the following symbols will be used:

$$\mathrm{FFS} := \{D\in[0,1]^{\mathbf{M}}: \mathrm{supp}(D) \text{ is finite}\},$$

$$\mathrm{FCS} := \{D\in\{0,1\}^{\mathbf{M}}: \mathrm{supp}(D) \text{ is finite}\}.$$

So, FFS (FCS, respectively) is the family of all finite fuzzy sets (finite sets, respectively) in $\mathbf{M}$. The characteristic function of a set $\mathbf{D}\subset\mathbf{M}$ will be denoted by $1_\mathbf{D}$. In particular, we define $T:=1_\emptyset$ and $M:=1_\mathbf{M}$. Inclusion and equality between fuzzy sets will be understood in the standard way, i.e. $A\subset B \Leftrightarrow \forall x\in\mathbf{M}$: $A(x)\le B(x)$ and $A=B \Leftrightarrow \forall x\in\mathbf{M}$: $A(x)=B(x)$. Finally, a/x with $a\in[0,1]$ and $x\in\mathbf{M}$ will denote a fuzzy set such that $(a/x)(x):=a$ and $(a/x)(y):=0$ for $y\neq x$; a/x with $a>0$ is thus a singleton supported by x, whereas $0/x=T$.

2. Triangular operations

A binary operation $\mathbf{t}$: $[0,1]\times[0,1]\to[0,1]$ is called a *triangular norm* (*t-norm*, in short) if it is commutative, associative, nondecreasing, and has 1 as unit, i.e. for each $a, b, c, d\in[0,1]$ we have:

(a) $a\,\mathbf{t}\,b=b\,\mathbf{t}\,a$,

(b) $a\,\mathbf{t}(b\,\mathbf{t}\,c)=(a\,\mathbf{t}\,b)\,\mathbf{t}\,c$,

(c) $a\,\mathbf{t}\,b\le c\,\mathbf{t}\,d$ whenever $a\le c$ and $b\le d$,

(d) $a\,\mathbf{t}\,1=a$.

If an operation $\mathbf{s}$: $[0,1]\times[0,1]\to[0,1]$ does satisfy (a)-(c) and has 0 as unit, i.e.

(e) $a\,\mathbf{s}\,0=a$,

it is called a *triangular conorm* (*t-conorm*, in short). Consequently, $a\,\mathbf{t}\,0=0$, $a\,\mathbf{s}\,1=1$, $a\,\mathbf{t}\,a\le a\le a\,\mathbf{s}\,a$, $a\,\mathbf{t}\,b=1 \Leftrightarrow a=b=1$, and $a\,\mathbf{s}\,b=0 \Leftrightarrow a=b=0$. Triangular norms and conorms together will be called *triangular operations* (*t-operations*, in short). The following pairs of t-operations will be useful in further discussion:

(i) $a\,\mathbf{t}_\wedge b := \min(a, b)$, $a\,\mathbf{s}_\vee b := \max(a, b)$,

(ii) $a\,\mathbf{t}_a b := ab$, $a\,\mathbf{s}_a b := a+b-ab$, (*algebraic t-operations*)

(iii) $a\,\mathbf{t}_{S,p} b := (\max(0, a^p+b^p-1))^{1/p}$, (*Schweizer's t-norm*)

$a\,\mathbf{s}_{Y,p} b := \min(1, (a^p+b^p)^{1/p})$, $p>0$, (*Yager's t-conorm*)

(iv) $a\,\mathbf{t}_E b := ab/(2-a-b+ab)$,

$a\,\mathbf{s}_E b := (a+b)/(1+ab)$, (*Einstein t-operations*)

(v) $a\,\mathbf{t}_{F,\lambda} b := \log_\lambda(1+(\lambda^a-1)(\lambda^b-1)/(\lambda-1))$,

$a\,\mathbf{s}_{F,\lambda} b := 1-\log_\lambda(1+(\lambda^{1-a}-1)(\lambda^{1-b}-1)/(\lambda-1))$, $1\neq\lambda>0$,

(*Frank's t-operations*)

(vi) $a\,\mathbf{t}_{W,\lambda} b := \max(0, (a+b-1+\lambda ab)/(1+\lambda))$,

$a\,\mathbf{s}_{W,\lambda} b := \min(1, ((1+\lambda)(a+b)-\lambda ab)/(1+\lambda))$, $\lambda>-1$,

(*Weber's t-operations*)

(vii) $a\,\mathbf{t}_M b := 2/\pi \arccos(\min(1, \cos(\pi/2\, a)+\cos(\pi/2\, b)))$,

$a\,\mathbf{s}_M b := 2/\pi \arcsin(\min(1, \sin(\pi/2\, a)+\sin(\pi/2\, b)))$.

(*Mizumoto's t-operations*)

Although our main interest is in continuous t-operations, worth mentioning are the discontinuous *drastic* t-operations $\mathbf{t}_d$ and $\mathbf{s}_d$ such that

$$a\,\mathbf{t}_d\,b := \min(a, b) \text{ if } \max(a, b) = 1, \text{ else } a\,\mathbf{t}_d\,b := 0,$$
$$a\,\mathbf{s}_d\,b := \max(a, b) \text{ if } \min(a, b) = 0, \text{ else } a\,\mathbf{s}_d\,b := 1.$$

The following chain of inequalities holds true for each $\mathbf{t}$ and $\mathbf{s}$:

$$\mathbf{t}_d \leq \mathbf{t} \leq \mathbf{t}_\wedge \leq \mathbf{s}_\vee \leq \mathbf{s} \leq \mathbf{s}_d,$$

where $\mathbf{u} \leq \mathbf{v}$ iff $a\,\mathbf{u}\,b \leq a\,\mathbf{v}\,b$ for each $a, b \in [0, 1]$. Recall that distributivity is a rare property in the world of t-operations. If $\mathbf{t}$ is distributive with respect to $\mathbf{s}$, then $\mathbf{s} = \mathbf{s}_\vee$; dually, if $\mathbf{s}$ is distributive with respect to $\mathbf{t}$, then $\mathbf{t} = \mathbf{t}_\wedge$. Also, worth recalling are exceptional limit properties of Frank's t-operations:

$$\mathbf{t}_{F,\lambda} \to \mathbf{t}_\wedge \text{ and } \mathbf{s}_{F,\lambda} \to \mathbf{s}_\vee \text{ if } \lambda \to 0,$$
$$\mathbf{t}_{F,\lambda} \to \mathbf{t}_a \text{ and } \mathbf{s}_{F,\lambda} \to \mathbf{s}_a \text{ if } \lambda \to 1,$$
$$\mathbf{t}_{F,\lambda} \to \mathbf{t}_{S,1} \text{ and } \mathbf{s}_{F,\lambda} \to \mathbf{s}_{Y,1} \text{ if } \lambda \to \infty.$$

So, one can define $\mathbf{t}_{F,0} := \mathbf{t}_\wedge$, $\mathbf{t}_{F,1} := \mathbf{t}_a$, $\mathbf{t}_{F,\infty} := \mathbf{t}_{S,1}$, $\mathbf{s}_{F,0} := \mathbf{s}_\vee$, $\mathbf{s}_{F,1} := \mathbf{s}_a$, and $\mathbf{s}_{F,\infty} := \mathbf{s}_{Y,1}$. The extended families $(\mathbf{t}_{F,\lambda})_{\lambda \in [0,\infty]}$ and $(\mathbf{s}_{F,\lambda})_{\lambda \in [0,\infty]}$ are called the *Frank families* of t-norms and t-conorms. The pairs in (i), (ii) and (iv)-(vii) are examples of *associated* t-norms and t-conorms fulfilling the condition $a\,\mathbf{s}\,b = 1-(1-a)\,\mathbf{t}\,(1-b)$; we then write $\mathbf{s} = \mathbf{t}^*$. The operations in (iii) are not associated, unless $p = 1$ (*bold t-operations*). They are *complementary*. The correspondence between $\mathbf{t}$ and $\mathbf{s}$ is then based on the de Morgan law combined with a negation differing from $1-x$ (see Theorem 2.4). There are good reasons for using in some situations complementary t-operations instead of associated ones (see [1, 17]).

The following classes of t-operations will be used in the further discussion.

▸ *Strict t-operations*, i.e. those being strictly increasing functions on $(0, 1) \times (0, 1)$, e.g. (ii), (iv) and (v).

▸ *Archimedean t-operations*

A t-norm $\mathbf{t}$ is said to be Archimedean if $a\,\mathbf{t}\,a < a$ for each $a \in (0, 1)$ (e.g. (ii)-(vii)). A t-conorm $\mathbf{s}$ is called Archimedean if $a\,\mathbf{s}\,a > a$ for each $a \in (0, 1)$.

▸ *t-operations having no zero divisors*

We say that a t-norm $\mathbf{t}$ has no zero divisors if $a\,\mathbf{t}\,b > 0$ whenever $a, b > 0$. The class of all t-norms having no zero divisors will be denoted by $\mathcal{F}$. For instance, $\mathbf{t}_\wedge, \mathbf{t}_a, \mathbf{t}_E, \mathbf{t}_{F,\lambda} \in \mathcal{F}$ with $\lambda < \infty$. Also, the t-conorm associated with a $\mathbf{t} \in \mathcal{F}$ will be called a t-conorm having no zero divisors. $\mathcal{F}^*$ will denote the class of all t-conorms having no zero divisors. So, we have $\mathbf{s} \in \mathcal{F}^*$ iff $a\,\mathbf{s}\,b < 1$ whenever $a, b < 1$.

It is a routine task to observe that a t-norm $\mathbf{t}$ is strict, Archimedean, continuous (respectively) iff $\mathbf{t}^*$ is strict, Archimedean, continuous (respectively). Each strict t-operation is Archimedean and has no zero divisors. $\mathbf{t}_\wedge$ and $\mathbf{s}_\vee$ do exemplify non-Archimedean t-operations having no zero divisors. However, in the universe of Archimedean and continuous t-operations, the notions "strict" and "has no zero divisors" become identical (see Theorem 2.1).

Let us recall the Ling representation theorem for continuous Archimedean t-operations (see [10, 16, 17].

Theorem 2.1. *Let* $\mathbf{t}, \mathbf{s}$: $[0,1]\times[0,1]\to[0,1]$.
(a) $\mathbf{t}$ *is a continuous Archimedean t-norm iff there exists a strictly decreasing and continuous function* g: $[0,1]\to[0,\infty]$ *with* $g(1)=0$ *such that* $a\,\mathbf{t}\,b = g^{(-1)}(g(a)+g(b))$ *for each* $a, b\in[0,1]$, *where* $g^{(-1)}(x) := g^{-1}(\min(g(0),x))$. *Moreover,* $\mathbf{t}$ *is strict iff* $g(0)=\infty$.
(b) $\mathbf{s}$ *is a continuous Archimedean t-conorm iff there exists a strictly increasing and continuous function* h: $[0,1]\to[0,\infty]$ *with* $h(0)=0$ *such that* $a\,\mathbf{s}\,b = h^{(-1)}(h(a)+h(b))$ *for each* $a, b\in[0,1]$, *where* $h^{(-1)}(x) := h^{-1}(\min(h(1),x))$. $\mathbf{s}$ *is strict iff* $h(1)=\infty$.

The function g in (a) is called a *(additive) generator of* $\mathbf{t}$, whereas $g^{(-1)}$ is said to be a *pseudoinverse* of g. If $\mathbf{t}$ is non-strict and $g(0)=1$, g is called a *normed generator*. Analogously, h in (b) is said to be a *(additive) generator of* $\mathbf{s}$, while $h^{(-1)}$ is called a *pseudoinverse* of h. One says that h is normed whenever $\mathbf{s}$ is non-strict and $h(1)=1$. For instance, $g(x)=-\ln x$ for $\mathbf{t}=\mathbf{t}_a$, $g(x)=1-x^p$ for $\mathbf{t}=\mathbf{t}_{S,p}$ and $g(x)=\cos(\pi/2\,x)$ for $\mathbf{t}=\mathbf{t}_M$ (see [12] for a list of generators). If $\mathbf{t}$ and $\mathbf{s}$ are associated, then $h(x)=g(1-x)$ for each $x\in[0,1]$.

Theorem 2.2 ([6]). *A t-norm* $\mathbf{t}$ *and its associated t-conorm* $\mathbf{s}$ *fulfil the equation*

$$a\,\mathbf{t}\,b + a\,\mathbf{s}\,b = a+b \quad \text{for each } a, b\in[0,1]$$

iff the pair $(\mathbf{t}, \mathbf{s})$ *has one of the following forms:*
(i) $(\mathbf{t}_{F,\lambda}, \mathbf{s}_{F,\lambda})$ *with* $\lambda\in[0,\infty]$,
(ii) $\mathbf{t}$ *is the ordinal sum of a family* $\{([a_i, b_i], \mathbf{t}_{F,\lambda(i)})\}$ *of t-norms* $\mathbf{t}_{F,\lambda(i)}$ *assigned to elements of a countable family* $\{[a_i, b_i]\}$ *of pairwise disjoint, closed and nontrivial subintervals of* $[0,1]$, *whereas* $\mathbf{s}$ *is derived from* $\mathbf{t}$ *via the above functional equation.*

Details about ordinal sums can be found e.g. in [5, 6, 12]. The above theorem is a good example of the importance of the Frank families of t-norms and t-conorms which in [2] are called the families of *fundamental* t-norms and t-conorms.

A function ν: $[0,1]\to[0,1]$ is called a *negation* if it is nonincreasing, $\nu(0)=1$ and $\nu(1)=0$. If ν is strictly decreasing and continuous, it is said to be a *strict negation*. An involutive strict negation ($\nu(\nu(a))=a$ for each a) is called a *strong negation*. Clearly, the smallest possible negation is ν_* such that $\nu_*(a) := (1 \text{ if } a=0$, else 0), whereas ν^* such that $\nu^*(a) := (1$ if $a<1$, else 0) is the largest one. Let

$$\nu_{\mathbf{t}}(a) := \sup\{b\in[0,1]\colon a\,\mathbf{t}\,b=0\},$$
$$\nu_{\mathbf{s}}(a) := \inf\{b\in[0,1]\colon a\,\mathbf{s}\,b=1\}$$

for each $a\in[0,1]$, where $\mathbf{t}$ is a t-norm and $\mathbf{s}$ is a t-conorm.

Theorem 2.3 ([17]). *The following holds true for each* $\mathbf{t}$ *and* $\mathbf{s}$.
(a) $\nu_{\mathbf{t}}$ *and* $\nu_{\mathbf{s}}$ *are negations.*
(b) *If* $\mathbf{t}$ *is strict, then* $\nu_{\mathbf{t}} = \nu_{*}$. *If* $\mathbf{s}$ *is strict, then* $\nu_{\mathbf{s}} = \nu^{*}$.
(c) *If* $\mathbf{t}$ *is non-strict, Archimedean and continuous, then* $\nu_{\mathbf{t}}$ *is a strong negation; the same remains true for* $\mathbf{s}$ *and* $\nu_{\mathbf{s}}$.

Let us define additional two binary operations $\mathbf{t}^{\circ}$ and $\mathbf{s}^{\circ}$, where

$$a\,\mathbf{t}^{\circ}\,b := \nu_{\mathbf{t}}(\nu_{\mathbf{t}}(a)\,\mathbf{t}\,\nu_{\mathbf{t}}(b)) \quad \text{and} \quad a\,\mathbf{s}^{\circ}\,b := \nu_{\mathbf{s}}(\nu_{\mathbf{s}}(a)\,\mathbf{s}\,\nu_{\mathbf{s}}(b))$$

for each $a, b \in [0, 1]$.

Theorem 2.4 ([17]). (a) *If* $\mathbf{t}$ *is non-strict, Archimedean and continuous with generator* g, *then* $\mathbf{t}^{\circ}$ *is a non-strict, Archimedean and continuous t-conorm with generator* h *given by the formula* $h(x) = g(0) - g(x) = g(\nu_{\mathbf{t}}(x))$.
(b) *If* $\mathbf{s}$ *is non-strict, Archimedean and continuous with generator* h, *then* $\mathbf{s}^{\circ}$ *is a non-strict, Archimedean and continuous t-norm with generator* g *given by the formula* $g(x) = h(1) - h(x) = h(\nu_{\mathbf{s}}(x))$.
(c) $(\mathbf{t}^{\circ})^{\circ} = \mathbf{t}$ *and* $(\mathbf{s}^{\circ})^{\circ} = \mathbf{s}$ *for non-strict, Archimedean and continuous* $\mathbf{t}$ *and* $\mathbf{s}$.

In the non-strict, Archimedean and continuous case, $\mathbf{t}$ and $\mathbf{t}^{\circ}$ are called *complementary* operations. It is easy to point out that $\nu_{\mathbf{t}} = \nu_{\mathbf{s}}$ whenever $\mathbf{t}$ and $\mathbf{s}$ are complementary. Typical examples of complementary operations are $\mathbf{t}_{S,p}$ and $\mathbf{s}_{Y,p}$, $\mathbf{t}_{W,\lambda}$ and $a\,(\mathbf{t}_{W,\lambda})^{\circ}\,b := \min(1, a + b + \lambda ab)$. It follows from Theorems 2.1 and 2.4 that if $\mathbf{s}$ is a non-strict, Archimedean and continuous t-conorm with generator h and $\mathbf{t} := \mathbf{s}^{\circ}$, then (see [1])

$$(2.1)\qquad \begin{aligned} a\,\mathbf{t}\,b &:= h^{-1}(\max(0, h(a) + h(b) - h(1))), \\ a\,\mathbf{s}\,b &:= h^{-1}(\min(h(1), h(a) + h(b))) \end{aligned}$$

Finally, triangular operations and negations can be transferred to fuzzy sets (finite or not) via pointwise definitions. So, we define
- the *sum* $A \cup_{\mathbf{s}} B$ of $A, B \in \mathrm{FFS}$ induced by a t-conorm $\mathbf{s}$ with $(A \cup_{\mathbf{s}} B)(x) := A(x)\,\mathbf{s}\,B(x)$,
- the *intersection* $A \cap_{\mathbf{t}} B$ and the *Cartesian product* $A \times_{\mathbf{t}} B$ induced by a t-norm $\mathbf{t}$ with $(A \cap_{\mathbf{t}} B)(x) := A(x)\,\mathbf{t}\,B(x)$ and $(A \times_{\mathbf{t}} B)(x, y) := A(x)\,\mathbf{t}\,B(y)$,
- the *complement* A^{ν} of A induced by a negation ν, where $A^{\nu}(x) := \nu(A(x))$.

If $\mathbf{s} = \mathbf{s}_{\vee}$, $\mathbf{t} = \mathbf{t}_{\wedge}$, or $\nu(a) := 1 - a$ (respectively), we simply write $A \cup B$, $A \cap B$, or A' (respectively). Since $a\,\mathbf{s}\,0 = a$ for each a and $\mathbf{s}$, we get

$$(2.2)\qquad A = \textstyle\bigcup^{\mathbf{s}}_{x \in \mathrm{supp}(A)} A(x)/x,$$

where $\bigcup^{\mathbf{s}}_{i \in \mathrm{J}} A_i$ denotes the sum (induced by $\mathbf{s}$) of a finite family $(A_i)_{i \in \mathrm{J}}$ of fuzzy sets which is defined by obvious extension of $A \cup_{\mathbf{s}} B$ to an arbitrary finite number of components; if $\mathbf{s} = \mathbf{s}_{\vee}$, we simply write $\bigcup_{i \in \mathrm{J}} A_i$ ($\mathrm{J} \neq \emptyset$ - a finite set of indices). Clearly,

$$\text{supp}(A \cup_{\mathbf{s}} B) = \text{supp}(A) \cup \text{supp}(B),$$
$$\text{supp}(A *_{\mathbf{t}} B) \subset \text{supp}(A) * \text{supp}(B),$$
$$\text{supp}(A *_{\mathbf{t}} B) = \text{supp}(A) * \text{supp}(B) \quad \text{if} \quad \mathbf{t} \in \mathscr{F},$$

for any t-norm $\mathbf{t}$ and any t-conorm $\mathbf{s}$, where $*$ stands for $\cap$ or $\times$.

3. Axiomatization of scalar cardinalities

At the very beginning of the main part of the paper, we like to propose an axiomatic definition of scalar cardinality of a fuzzy set based on three simple and natural postulates.

Definition 3.1. Let $\mathbf{s}$ denote a t-conorm. A function sc: FFS $\to [0, \infty)$ is called a *scalar cardinality* if

(P1) $sc(1/x) = 1$,

(P2) $a \le b \Rightarrow sc(a/x) \le sc(b/y)$,

(P3) $A \cap B = T \Rightarrow sc(A \cup_{\mathbf{s}} B) = sc(A) + sc(B)$

for each $a, b \in [0,1]$, $x, y \in \mathbf{M}$ and $A, B \in$ FFS. If a function sc does fulfil (P1)-(P3), then $sc(A)$ is said to be a *scalar cardinality of* $A \in$ FFS.

What requires additional comments is (P3) which postulates additivity of scalar cardinalities in the case of fuzzy sets with supports being disjoint in the classical sense (see also Theorem 3.4). Since $A \cup_{\mathbf{s}} B = A \cup B$ for each $\mathbf{s}$ whenever $A \cap B = T$, all the postulates (P1)-(P3) are universal, i.e. their fulfilment does not depend on the choice of t-operations. The t-conorm $\mathbf{t}_{\vee}$ does play the role of a basic t-conorm in this case. Consequently, the family of all possible scalar cardinalities sc is identical with that obtained in [22, 23] for fuzzy sets with max and min operations (see Theorem 3.3). In other words, the use of any sc can be combined with the use of arbitrary t-operations leading to obtain, however, operational features which generally depend on the choice of a t-norm and t-conorm (see Section 4). Let us formulate basic general properties following from (P1)-(P3).

Theorem 3.2. *Let* $A, B \in$ FFS *and* $A_i \in$ FFS *for each* $i \in \mathbf{J}$. *For each scalar cardinality sc and each t-conorm* $\mathbf{s}$, *the following properties are fulfilled*:

(a) $sc(\bigcup^{\mathbf{s}}_{i \in \mathbf{J}} A_i) = \Sigma_{i \in \mathbf{J}}\, sc(A_i)$ *if* $A_i \cap A_j = T$ *for each* $i \ne j$, *(finite additivity)*

(b) $sc(A) = |\text{supp}(A)|$ *if* $A \in$ FCS, *(coincidence)*

(c) $sc(A) = sc(B)$ *whenever there exists a bijection* $\mathbf{b}$: $\text{supp}(A) \to \text{supp}(B)$ *such that* $A(x) = B(\mathbf{b}(x))$ *for each* $x \in \text{supp}(A)$, *(movability)*

(d) $sc(A) \le sc(B)$ *if* $A \subset B$, *(monotonicity)*

(e) $|\text{core}(A)| \le sc(A) \le |\text{supp}(A)|$. *(boundedness)*

Proof. (a) follows from (P3) because $\uplus_{i\in J} A_i = \bigcup_{i\in J} A_i$ whenever $A_i \cap A_j = T$ for each $i \neq j$. (b)-(d) are implied by (a), (P1), (P2) and (2.2). Finally, (e) is a direct consequence of (d) (see also [22, 23]). □

The following theorem presents a simple characterization of scalar cardinalities from Definition 3.1.

Theorem 3.3. *A function sc*: FFS$\to[0,\infty)$ *is a scalar cardinality iff*

$$sc(A) = \Sigma_{x\in \mathrm{supp}(A)} f(A(x)) \text{ for each } A \in \mathrm{FFS}$$

with f: $[0,1]\to[0,1]$ *such that* $f(0)=0$, $f(1)=1$, *and* $f(a)\leq f(b)$ *if* $a \leq b$.

Proof. The thesis follows from the equality $sc(A) = \Sigma_{x\in \mathrm{supp}(A)}\, sc(A(x)/x)$ which is a consequence of Theorem 3.2(a) (see also [22, 23]). □

Each function f satisfying the conditions of Theorem 3.3 will be called a *cardinality pattern* because it expresses our understanding of cardinality of singletons.

Using Theorem 3.3, let us give a few basic examples of possible cardinality patterns and resulting scalar cardinalities. The first two examples do present integer scalar cardinalities which (without any additional preassumption) can be also applied to fuzzy sets with arbitrary supports. The others do describe generally non-integer scalar cardinalities; their limit properties are discussed in [22].

A. $f_{1,t}(a) := (1 \text{ if } a \geq t, \text{ else } 0)$ with $t \in (0,1]$. So, $sc(A) = |A_{\geq t}|$, i.e. $sc(A) = |\mathrm{core}(A)|$ if $t=1$.

B. $f_{2,t}(a) := (1 \text{ if } a > t, \text{ else } 0)$ with $t \in [0,1)$. Thus, $sc(A) = |A_{>t}|$, i.e. $sc(A) = |\mathrm{supp}(A)|$ for $t=0$.

C. $f_{3,p}(a) := a^p$ with $p>0$, i.e. $f_{3,1} = \mathrm{id}$ (the identity function); $sc(A) = \sigma_A^p$.

D. $f_{4,p}(a) := (2^{p-1} a^p \text{ if } a \leq 0.5, \text{ else } 1-2^{p-1}(1-a)^p)$ with $p>0$; $f_{4,2}$ is the classical contrast enhancement operation.

E. $f_{5,\lambda}(a) := (a/\lambda \text{ if } a<0.5,\ (a+\lambda-1)/\lambda \text{ if } a>0.5,\ 0.5 \text{ if } a=0.5)$ with $\lambda \geq 1$.

F. $f_6(a) := (0.5 \text{ if } a \in (0,1),\ 0 \text{ if } a=0,\ 1 \text{ if } a=1)$.

G. By definition, normed generators of non-strict, Archimedean and continuous t-conorms are cardinality patterns. Simple examples are the generators of $(\mathbf{t}_{W,\lambda})^\circ$ and $(\mathbf{t}_M)^\circ$, i.e. the functions $f_{7,\lambda}(a) := \ln(1+\lambda a)/\ln(1+\lambda)$ with $\lambda > -1$ and $f_8(a) := 1-\cos(\pi/2\, a)$. □

Finally, worth mentioning is that (P3) is generally weaker than

(P3)* $\quad A \cap_{\mathbf{t}} B = T \;\Rightarrow\; sc(A \cup_{\mathbf{s}} B) = sc(A) + sc(B)$

with a t-norm **t**. The later form, however, would be too strong. Using it, we are generally unable to prove additivity of scalar cardinalities for arbitrary finite families of pairwise "**t**-disjoint" fuzzy sets ($A_i \cap_{\mathbf{t}} A_j = T$ for $i \neq j$). Clearly, the reason is the lack of distributivity of $\cap_{\mathbf{t}}$ with respect to $\cup_{\mathbf{s}} \neq \cup$. For the sake of completeness, let us note the following.

Theorem 3.4. *If* $\mathbf{s}$ *is a non-strict, Archimedean and continuous t-conorm with normed generator* h, *then* (P3)* *is fulfilled by* $\mathbf{t} = \mathbf{s}^\circ$, $\mathbf{s}$ *and the scalar cardinality* sc *determined by the cardinality pattern* $f = h$.

Proof. The thesis is a consequence of (2.1) and Theorem 3.3. □

So, the stronger system of postulates (P1)-(P2)-(P3)* is satisfied by $sc(A) = \Sigma_{x \in \mathrm{supp}(A)} f(A(x))$ with triplets $(f, \mathbf{t}, \mathbf{s})$ such as $(f_{3,p}, \mathbf{t}_{S,p}, \mathbf{s}_{Y,p})$ with $p > 0$, $(f_{7,\lambda}, \mathbf{t}_{W,\lambda}, (\mathbf{t}_{W,\lambda})^\circ)$ with $\lambda > -1$, and $(f_8, \mathbf{t}_M, (\mathbf{t}_M)^\circ)$. Let us present a simple counterexample showing that (P3)* does not generally lead to finite additivity. Let $f = \mathrm{id}$, $\mathbf{t} = \mathbf{t}_{S,1}$, $\mathbf{s} = \mathbf{s}_{Y,1}$, and $A = B = C = 0.5/x$ with any $x \in \mathbf{M}$. We then have $A \cap_{\mathbf{t}} B = A \cap_{\mathbf{t}} C = B \cap_{\mathbf{t}} C = T$ and $sc(A) = sc(B) = sc(C) = 0.5$. In virtue of Theorem 3.4, we obtain $sc(A \cup_{\mathbf{s}} B) = sc(A) + sc(B)$. But $sc(A \cup_{\mathbf{s}} B \cup_{\mathbf{s}} C) = 1$, i.e. $sc(A \cup_{\mathbf{s}} B \cup_{\mathbf{s}} C) < sc(A) + sc(B) + sc(C)$. Now, we return to (P1)-(P3).

4. On other classical-like properties

With reference to well-known properties of sets and their cardinalities, we like to formulate the following four problems.

▸ *Find a cardinality pattern* f, *a t-norm* $\mathbf{t}$ *and a t-conorm* $\mathbf{s}$ *such that*

(4.1) $\forall A, B \in \mathrm{FFS}$: $sc(A \cap_{\mathbf{t}} B) + sc(A \cup_{\mathbf{s}} B) = sc(A) + sc(B)$.

(*valuation property*)

▸ *Find a cardinality pattern* f *and a t-conorm* $\mathbf{s}$ *such that*

(4.2) $\forall (A_i)_{i \in \mathbf{J}} \subset \mathrm{FFS}$: $sc(\bigcup^{\mathbf{s}}_{i \in \mathbf{J}} A_i) \leq \Sigma_{i \in \mathbf{J}}\, sc(A_i)$.

(*finite subadditivity property*)

▸ *Find a cardinality pattern* f *and a t-norm* $\mathbf{t}$ *such that*

(4.3) $\forall A, B \in \mathrm{FFS}$: $sc(A \times_{\mathbf{t}} B) = sc(A) \cdot sc(B)$.

(*Cartesian product rule*)

▸ *Find a cardinality pattern* f *and a negation* ν *such that* (**M** *finite*)

(4.4) $\forall A \in \mathrm{FFS}$: $sc(A) + sc(A^\nu) = |\mathbf{M}|$.

(*complementarity rule*)

It is easy to construct counterexamples showing that these four laws are really not common in the world of scalar cardinalities. For instance, (4.2) does not hold if $f = f_{1,0.75}$, $\mathbf{s} = \mathbf{s}_{Y,0.5}$ and $A = B = 0.5/x$ with any $x \in \mathbf{M}$.

Theorem 4.1. *The valuation property holds true iff* f, $\mathbf{t}$ *and* $\mathbf{s}$ *are such that*

(4.5) $\forall a, b \in [0,1]$: $f(a\mathbf{t}b) + f(a\mathbf{s}b) = f(a) + f(b)$.

Proof. The sufficiency of (4.5) for (4.1) follows from Theorem 3.3. On the other hand, if (4.5) does not hold, i.e. $f(a\,\mathbf{t}\,b)+f(a\,\mathbf{s}\,b) \neq f(a)+f(b)$ for some $a, b > 0$, then, putting $A := a/x$ and $B := b/x$ with arbitrary x, we get $sc(A \cap_{\mathbf{t}} B) + sc(A \cup_{\mathbf{s}} B) \neq sc(A) + sc(B)$ (see Theorem 3.3). So, (4.5) is necessary for (4.1). □

By the way, in the case $f = \mathrm{id}$, (4.5) is mentioned in [4] as a sufficient condition for (4.1).

Examples. Let us present a few triplets (f, **t**, **s**) satisfying (4.5) and, thus, fulfilling the valuation property. We fix either f or **t** and **s**.
VP1. If $\mathbf{t} = \mathbf{t}_{\wedge}$ and $\mathbf{s} = \mathbf{s}_{\vee}$, then (4.5) is satisfied by each f (see also [22, 23]).
VP2. If $f = \mathrm{id}$, Theorem 2.2 describes the family of all operations **t** and **t*** satisfying (4.5). So, in particular, the valuation property is fulfilled by each (id, $\mathbf{t}_{F,\lambda}$, $\mathbf{s}_{F,\lambda}$) with $\lambda \in [0, \infty]$.
VP3. An immediate consequence of (2.1) is that if **s** is a non-strict, Archimedean and continuous t-conorm with normed generator h, then (h, **s**°, **s**) does satisfy (4.5). The valuation property is thus fulfilled e.g. by $(f_{3,p}, \mathbf{t}_{S,p}, \mathbf{s}_{Y,p})$ with $p > 0$, $(f_{7,\lambda}, \mathbf{t}_{W,\lambda}, (\mathbf{t}_{W,\lambda})^{\circ})$ with $\lambda > -1$, and $(f_8, \mathbf{t}_M, (\mathbf{t}_M)^{\circ})$.
VP4. $(f_{1,1}, \mathbf{t}, \mathbf{s})$ with $\mathbf{s} \in \mathcal{F}^*$ and $(f_{2,0}, \mathbf{t}, \mathbf{s})$ with $\mathbf{t} \in \mathcal{F}$ do satisfy (4.5). □

Our next topic is finite additivity. Although it is not a common property of scalar cardinalities, we understand that finite superadditivity is impossible. Indeed, it suffices to take a family such that $A_i \in \mathrm{FCS}$ for each $i \in \mathbf{J}$ (see Theorem 3.2(b)).

Theorem 4.2. *The finite additivity property is satisfied iff f and* **s** *are such that*

(4.6) $\quad \forall a, b \in [0, 1]\colon f(a\,\mathbf{s}\,b) \leq f(a) + f(b).$

Proof. It is quite analogous to the proof of Theorem 4.1. □

Simple but useful observation is that if (f, **t**, **s**) does satisfy (4.1), then (4.2) is fulfilled by (f, **s**) (see VP1-VP4). Moreover, (4.6) is satisfied e.g. by (id, $\mathbf{s}_E$).

Theorem 4.3. *The Cartesian product rule is preserved iff f and* **t** *are such that*

(4.7) $\quad \forall a, b \in [0, 1]\colon f(a\,\mathbf{t}\,b) = f(a) \cdot f(b).$

Proof. It follows from the equality $sc(A) \cdot sc(B) = \Sigma_{(x,y) \in \mathbf{C}}\, f(A(x)) \cdot f(B(y))$ which is implied by Theorem 3.3, where $\mathbf{C} = \mathrm{supp}(A) \times \mathrm{supp}(B)$ (cf. the proof of Theorem 4.1). □

Examples. In the following, we give examples of pairs (f, **t**) satisfying (4.7) and thus (4.3).
CP1. If $\mathbf{t} = \mathbf{t}_{\wedge}$, then (4.7) holds true iff f is equal to a $f_{1,t}$ or $f_{2,t}$ (see also [22]).
CP2. In consequence of Theorem 2.1, if **t** is strict and continuous with additive generator g, then $g(a\,\mathbf{t}\,b) = g(a) + g(b)$ and, thus, (e^{-g}, **t**) does fulfil (4.7). So, the

Cartesian product rule holds true e.g. for (id, $\mathbf{t}_a$), (f_9, $\mathbf{t}_E$) and ($f_{10,\lambda}$, $\mathbf{t}_{F,\lambda}$) with $1 \neq \lambda > 0$, where $f_9(a) := a/(2-a)$ and $f_{10,\lambda}(a) := ((\lambda^a-1)/(\lambda-1))^{1/\ln\lambda}$.
CP3. If $\mathbf{t} = \mathbf{t}_a$, (4.7) collapses to the Cauchy functional equation with reduced domain. Its unique continuous solutions are the cardinality patterns $f = f_{3,p}$ with $p > 0$ (see e.g. [9]). An instance of discontinuous solution is $f_{1,1}$ and $f_{2,0}$.
CP4. If $f = f_{1,1}$, then (4.7) is satisfied by each t-norm $\mathbf{t}$. If $f = f_{2,0}$, then each $\mathbf{t} \in \mathcal{F}$ does fulfil (4.7).
CP5. If $\mathbf{t}$ is a non-strict, Archimedean and continuous t-norm, then $\mathbf{t} \notin \mathcal{F}$, i.e. $a\,\mathbf{t}\,b = 0$ for some $a, b > 0$. So, no cardinality pattern f such that $f(a) = 0 \Leftrightarrow a = 0$ can satisfy (4.7). In particular, no strictly increasing f and, hence, no normed generator of a non-strict, Archimedean and continuous t-conorm can satisfy (4.7) (cf. VP3). □

In the last part of this section, we like to investigate the question of the complementarity rule. Let $\mathbf{M}$ be finite and let ν denote a negation (see Section 2).

Theorem 4.4. *The complementarity rule is satisfied iff f and ν are such that*

(4.8) $\quad \forall a \in [0,1]\colon f(a) + f(\nu(a)) = 1.$

Proof. ($\Leftarrow$) follows from Theorem 3.3. Suppose $f(a) + f(\nu(a)) \neq 1$ for some $a \in (0,1)$. Taking $A \in \mathrm{FFS}$ such that $A(x) := a$ for each $x \in \mathbf{M}$, we get $sc(A) = |\mathbf{M}|f(a)$ and $sc(A^\nu) = |\mathbf{M}|f(\nu(a))$, i.e. (4.4) does not hold. □

Examples. Again, we present some examples of pairs (f, ν) satisfying (4.8) and, thus, fulfilling the complementarity rule.
CR1. If $\nu(a) = 1 - a$ for each $a \in [0,1]$, then (4.8) holds true whenever the point (0.5, 0.5) is the symmetry middle of the diagram of f. Examples of such cardinality patterns are $f_{4,p}$, $f_{5,\lambda}$ and f_6.
CR2. If $\mathbf{s}$ is a non-strict, Archimedean and continuous t-conorm with normed generator h, then $(h, \nu_\mathbf{s})$ does fulfil (4.8) (see Theorem 2.4(b)). In particular, (4.8) holds true if $f = f_{3,p}$ and $\nu_\mathbf{s}(a) = (1-a^p)^{1/p}$ ($\mathbf{s} = \mathbf{s}_{Y,p}$), $f(a) = 1 - \ln(1+\lambda(1-a))/\ln(1+\lambda)$ and $\nu_\mathbf{s}(a) = 1 - a/(1+\lambda(1-a))$ ($\mathbf{s} = \mathbf{s}_{W,\lambda}$), $f(a) = \sin(\pi/2\, a)$ and $\nu_\mathbf{s}(a) = 2/\pi \arcsin(1 - \sin(\pi/2\, a))$ ($\mathbf{s} = \mathbf{s}_M$).
CR3. If $\nu = \nu_*$, then (4.8) holds true iff $f = f_{2,0}$. If $\nu = \nu^*$, then (4.8) is satisfied iff $f = f_{1,1}$ (see also Theorem 2.3(b)). □

5. On simultaneous fulfilment of more than one property

In the previous section, we investigated three classical-like properties of scalar cardinalities, namely the valuation property (VP), the Cartesian product rule (CP), and the complementarity rule (CR). In each case, we gave a condition which is necessary and sufficient for the fulfilment of the property. Now, we like to formulate a few remarks about possible simultaneous fulfilment of more than one of those properties. Finite subadditivity is implied by VP and, therefore, omitted.

VP and CP

Looking at the examples in Section 4, we see that both the laws under discussion are satisfied, for instance, by the following triplets (f, **t**, **s**):

$(f_{1,t}, \mathbf{t}_\wedge, \mathbf{s}_\vee)$ and $(f_{2,t}, \mathbf{t}_\wedge, \mathbf{s}_\vee)$ with any t allowed,
$(f_{1,1}, \mathbf{t}, \mathbf{s})$ with any **t** and $\mathbf{s} \in \mathcal{F}^*$,
$(f_{2,0}, \mathbf{t}, \mathbf{s})$ with $\mathbf{t} \in \mathcal{F}$ and any **s**,
$(\mathrm{id}, \mathbf{t}_a, \mathbf{s}_a)$.

Combining (4.5) and (4.7), we easily conclude that if both VP and CP are fulfilled and **s** is non-Archimedean, then $f(a) \in \{0, 1\}$ whenever $a \,\mathbf{s}\, a = a$.

CP and CR

The examples CP1-CP5 and CR1-CR3 from Section 4 show that both the rules are fulfilled, for instance, by the following triplets (f, **t**, ν):

$(f_{1,1}, \mathbf{t}, \nu^*)$ with any **t**,
$(f_{2,0}, \mathbf{t}, \nu_*)$ with $\mathbf{t} \in \mathcal{F}$,
$(\mathrm{id}, \mathbf{t}_a, \nu)$ with $\nu(a) = 1 - a$.

On the other hand, CP5 and CR2 do suggest that simultaneous fulfilment of CP and CR by an (f, **t**, ν) with nontrivial f is difficult to expect in the non-strict, Archimedean and continuous case. Finally, suppose **t** is a non-Archimedean t-norm with $a^* \,\mathbf{t}\, a^* = a^*$ for some $a^* \in (0, 1)$, and ν is a negation having a fixed point at the a^*, i.e. $\nu(a^*) = a^*$. Then, no cardinality pattern f can lead to simultaneous fulfilment of CP and CR by (f, **t**, ν). Indeed, if f does satisfy (4.8), we have $f(a^*) = 0.5$, which excludes (4.7). So, in particular, there is no cardinality pattern f such that (4.7) and (4.8) are fulfilled by $(f, \mathbf{t}_\wedge, \nu)$ with $\nu(a) = 1 - a$ or, more generally, with ν being a strict negation (each strict negation has exactly one fixed point as a strictly decreasing and continuous function).

VP and CR

A very interesting class of systems (f, **t**, **s**, ν) fulfilling the valuation property and the complementarity rule is $\{(h, \mathbf{s}^\circ, \mathbf{s}, \nu_\mathbf{s})\}$, where **s** is a non-strict, Archimedean and continuous t-conorm with normed generator h. Other examples of such systems are

$(f, \mathbf{t}_\wedge, \mathbf{s}_\vee, \nu)$ with $\nu(a) = 1 - a$ and $f = f_{4,p}, f_{5,\lambda}$ or f_6,
$(f_{1,1}, \mathbf{t}, \mathbf{s}, \nu^*)$ with any **t** and $\mathbf{s} \in \mathcal{F}^*$,
$(f_{2,0}, \mathbf{t}, \mathbf{s}, \nu_*)$ with $\mathbf{t} \in \mathcal{F}$ and any **s**,
$(\mathrm{id}, \mathbf{t}_a, \mathbf{s}_a, \nu)$ with $\nu(a) = 1 - a$.

VP, CP and CR

Finally, let us point out that the systems

$(f_{1,1}, \mathbf{t}, \mathbf{s}, \nu^*)$ with any $\mathbf{t}$ and $\mathbf{s} \in \mathcal{F}^*$,

$(f_{2,0}, \mathbf{t}, \mathbf{s}, \nu_*)$ with $\mathbf{t} \in \mathcal{F}$ and any $\mathbf{s}$

do satisfy all the three properties. Also, we found a (possibly unique) more advanced system having that feature, namely (id, $\mathbf{t}_a$, $\mathbf{s}_a$, ν) with $\nu(a) = 1 - a$.

6. Final remarks

It seems that the presented axiomatic approach to scalar cardinalities of fuzzy sets with triangular norms and conorms generates a sufficiently rich infinite family of possible scalar cardinalities which covers all standard constructions, including the sigma-counts and p-powers. In Section 3, we gave a characterization theorem for scalar cardinalities and listed their general properties. In the next section, we investigated properties which fulfilment depends on the choice of a cardinality pattern, triangular operations, and negation (valuation and finite subadditivity property, Cartesian product rule, complementarity rule). Simple criteria given in that section are a useful tool for verifying if a specific cardinality pattern, combined with concrete triangular operations and negation, does lead to the fulfilment of a demanded property. Archimedean and continuous triangular operations together with their generators are especially important in this context. The problem of simultaneous fulfilment of a group of properties is discussed in Section 5. It seems that it requires further research.

Each scalar cardinality sc induces a naive cardinality theory for fuzzy sets which is based on the following definitions for $A, B \in \mathrm{FFS}$:

$$|A| := sc(A),$$

$$A \sim B \Leftrightarrow sc(A) = sc(B), \qquad (\textit{equipotency})$$

$$|A| \le |B| \Leftrightarrow sc(A) \le sc(B), \qquad (\textit{inequalities})$$

$$|A| + |B| := sc(A) + sc(B), \qquad (\textit{addition})$$

$$|A| \cdot |B| := sc(A) \cdot sc(B) \qquad (\textit{multiplication})$$

provided that sc satisfies the Cartesian product rule. Without any additional assumptions, the scalar cardinalities from the examples (A) and (B) in Section 3 can be applied to fuzzy sets with quite arbitrary supports, too.

Finally, worth emphasizing is that very different values $sc(A)$ are generally generated for a fixed A by various cardinality patterns f (see Theorem 3.2(e)). Moreover, different operational features of scalar cardinalities are implied by various f's, triangular operations $\mathbf{t}$ and $\mathbf{s}$, and negations ν. The choice of a suitable system $(f, \mathbf{t}, \mathbf{s}, \nu)$ is always problem-dependent. We omit a methodological discussion of this question as it goes beyond the scope of this paper.

References

[1] L. P. Belluce, A. di Nola and S. Sessa, Triangular norms, MV-algebras and bold fuzzy set theory, *Math. Japonica* **36**(1991)481-487.

[2] D. Butnariu and E. P. Klement, *Triangular Norm-Based Measures and Games with Fuzzy Coalitions*, Kluwer Acad. Publ., Dordrecht, 1993.

[3] D. Dubois and H. Prade, A class of fuzzy measures based on tringular norms, *Int. J. General Systems* **8**(1982)43-61.

[4] D. Dubois and H. Prade, Fuzzy cardinality and the modeling of imprecise quantification, *Fuzzy Sets and Systems* **16**(1985)199-230.

[5] J. C. Fodor, Fuzzy connectives via matrix logic, *Fuzzy Sets and Systems* **56**(1993)67-77.

[6] M. J. Frank, On the simultaneous associativity of $F(x, y)$ and $x+y-F(x, y)$, *Aequationes Mathematicae* **19**(1979)194-226.

[7] S. Gottwald, A note on fuzzy cardinals. *Kybernetika*, 16, 156-158, 1980.

[8] A. Kaufmann, *Introduction à la Théorie des Sous-Ensembles Flous*, Vol. IV, Masson, Paris, 1977.

[9] M. Kuczma, *An Introduction to the Theory of Functional Equations and Inequalities*, Polish Scientific Publ. (PWN), Warszawa, 1985.

[10] C. H. Ling, Representation of associative functions, *Publ. Math. Debrecen* **12**(1965)189-212.

[11] Y. Liu and E. E. Kerre, An overview of fuzzy quantifiers. (I). Interpretation, *Fuzzy Sets and Systems* **95**(1998)1-21.

[12] R. Lowen, *Fuzzy Set Theory. Basic Concepts, Techniques and Bibliography*, Kluwer Acad. Publ., Dordrecht, 1996.

[13] A. de Luca and S. Termini, A definition of non-probabilistic entropy in the setting of fuzzy sets theory, *Inform. and Control* **20**(1972)301-312.

[14] A. de Luca and S. Termini, Entropy and energy measures of a fuzzy set, in: M. M. Gupta, R. K. Ragade and R. R. Yager, Eds., *Advances in Fuzzy Set Theory and Applications*, North-Holland, Amsterdam, 1979, 321-338.

[15] M. Mizumoto, Pictorial representations of fuzzy connectives. Part I: Cases of t-norms, t-conorms and averaging operators, *Fuzzy Sets and Systems* **31**(1989)217-242.

[16] H. T. Nguyen and E. A. Walker, *A First Course in Fuzzy Logic*, CRC Press, Boca Raton, 1997.

[17] S. Weber, A general concept of fuzzy connectives, negations and implications based on t-norms and t-conorms, *Fuzzy Sets and Systems* **11**(1983)115-134.

[18] S. Weber, $\perp$-decomposable measures and integrals for Archimedean t-conorms $\perp$, *J. Math. Anal. Appl.* **101**(1984)114-138.

[19] M. Wygralak, Fuzzy cardinals based on the generalized equality of fuzzy subsets, *Fuzzy Sets and Systems* **18**(1986)143-158.

[20] M. Wygralak, Generalized cardinal numbers and operations on them, *Fuzzy Sets and Systems* **53**(1993)49-85 (+Erratum, *ibid.* **62**(1994)375).

[21] M. Wygralak, *Vaguely Defined Objects. Representations, Fuzzy Sets and Nonclassical Cardinality Theory*, Kluwer Acad. Publ., Dordrecht, 1996.

[22] M. Wygralak, From sigma counts to alternative nonfuzzy cardinalities of fuzzy sets, in: *Proc. 7th IPMU Inter. Conf.*, Paris, 1998, 1339-1344.

[23] M. Wygralak, An axiomatic approach to scalar cardinalities of fuzzy sets, *Fuzzy Sets and Systems*, to appear.

[24] M. Wygralak, Questions of cardinality of finite fuzzy sets, *Fuzzy Sets and Systems*, to appear.

[25] L. A. Zadeh, A theory of approximate reasoning, in: J. E. Hayes, D. Michie and L. I. Mikulich, Eds., *Machine Intelligence* 9, Wiley, New York, 1979, 149-184.

[26] L. A. Zadeh, A computational approach to fuzzy quantifiers in natural languages, *Comput. and Math. with Appl.* **9**(1983)149-184.

[27] L. A. Zadeh, Knowledge representation in fuzzy logic, *IEEE Trans. on Knowledge and Data Engineering* **1**(1989)89-99.

FUZZY IMPLICATIONS IN APPROXIMATE REASONING

E. Czogała and J. Łęski
Institute of Electronics, Technical University of Silesia
Akademicka 16, 44-101 Gliwice, Poland
e-mail: jl@biomed.iele.polsl.gliwice.pl

Abstract. At first an axiomatic approach to the definition of fuzzy implication has been recalled in this paper. Based on this definition several important fuzzy implications have been investigated with respect to the results obtained from the inference system. A specific type of equivalence of inference results using logical implication interpretation and conjunctive interpretation of the fuzzy if-then rules has been described. The theoretical considerations are illustrated by means of numerical examples in the field of fuzzy modeling.
KEYWORDS: Fuzzy implication, Approximate reasoning, Defuzzification.

1. Introductory remarks

A study of inference processes when premises in if-then rules are fuzzy is still a subject of many papers in specialized literature [1,2,3,6,8,9,10,12]. In such processes, a sound and proper choice of logical operators plays an essential role. The theoretical (mathematical) and the practical (computational) behavior of logical operators in inference processes has to be known before such a choice is made. Both types of the above mentioned knowledge related to well-known families of triangular norms and implications can also be found in literature (c.f. [2,8,12]).

Some selected logical operators and fuzzy implications were also investigated with respect to their behavior in inference processes. A specific type of equivalence of inference results using on one hand a conjunction interpretation of fuzzy if-then rules and on the other hand the interpretation of such rules in the spirit of classical logical implication was described. Such equivalence is of great importance regarding the inference algorithm construction. The inference algorithms based on logical implication interpretation of the if-then rules may be replaced by the simpler and faster algorithms used for the conjunctive interpretation.

The paper is divided into 6 sections. Some introductory remarks are contained in section 1. Section 2 presents a short review of the study concerning an axiomatic approach to the definition of a fuzzy implication with an ordering of fuzzy implications within the interval [0,1]. Section 3 recalls the main ideas of the inference process and defuzzification methods. In section 4 a specific type of equivalence of inference results using fuzzy conjunction on one hand and fuzzy implication interpretation of fuzzy if-then rules on the other hand has been described. Section 5 contains numerical examples illustrating the theoretical considerations of section 4. In section 6 the most important conclusions are gathered.

2. An approach to axiomatic definition of fuzzy implication

We start our considerations recalling an axiomatic approach (formulated by Fodor c.f. [6,7,8]) to the definition of a fuzzy implication which considers an implication as a connective and seems to possess its most general and characteristic properties.

Definition 1 *A fuzzy implication is a function* I: $[0,1]^2 \to [0,1]$ satisfying the following conditions:

I1. *If* $x \le z$ then $I(x,y) \ge I(z,y)$ for all $x, y, z \in [0,1]$

I2. *If* $y \le z$ then $I(x,y) \le I(x,z)$ for all $x, y, z \in [0,1]$

I3. $I(0,y) = 1$ (falsity implies anything) for all $y \in [0,1]$

I4. $I(x,1) = 1$ (anything implies tautology) for all $x \in [0,1]$

I5. $I(1,0) = 0$ (Booleanity)

Assuming that $^-$is a strong negation (i.e., a strictly decreasing, continuous function $^-$: $[0, 1] \to [0, 1]$ with $\bar{0} = 1$, $\bar{1} = 0$, $\bar{\bar{x}} = x$ for all $x \in [0,1]$), the $^-$*-reciprocal of* I defined by

$$I_{-}(x,y) = I(\bar{y},\bar{x}), \quad x,y \in [0,1] \tag{1}$$

is also considered to be a fuzzy implication.

Now let us recall further properties, in terms of function I, which could also be important in some applications.

I6. $I(1,x) = x$ (tautology cannot justify anything) for all $x \in [0,1]$

I7. $I(x, I(y,z)) = I(y, I(x,z))$ (exchange principle) for all $x, y, z \in [0,1]$

I8. $x \le y$ if and only if $I(x,y) = 1$ (implication defines ordering) for all $x, y \in [0,1]$

I9. $I(x,0) = x$ for all $x \in [0,1]$ is a strong negation

I10. $I(x,y) \ge y$ for all $x, y \in [0,1]$

I11. $I(x,x) = 1$ (identity principle) for all $x \in [0,1]$

I12. $I(x,y) = I(\bar{y},\bar{x})$ with a strong negation $^-$ for all $x, y \in [0,1]$

I13. I is a continuous function.

The two most important families of such implications are related either to the formalism of Boolean logic or to the residuation concept from intuitionistic logic. For the concepts mentioned above, a suitable definition is introduced below [8,11,12]:

Definition 2 An *S-implication* associated with a t-conorm S and a strong negation $^-$ is defined by

$$I_{S,^-}(x,y) = \star_S(\bar{x},y), \quad x,y \in [0,1] \tag{2}$$

An *R-implication* associated with a t-norm T is defined by

$$I_T(x,y) = \sup_z\{z \mid \star_T(x,z) \le y\}, \quad x,y \in [0,1] \tag{3}$$

We can see that both $I_{S,^-}$ and I_T satisfy conditions I1-I5 for any t-norm T, t-conorm S and strong negation $^-$, thus they are fuzzy implications.

For the sake of completeness we mention a third type of implications used in quantum logic and called QL-implication

$$I_{T,S,^-}(x,y) = \star_S(\bar{x}, \star_T(x,y)), \quad x,y \in [0,1] \tag{4}$$

Generally, $I_{T,S,^-}$ violates property I1. However, conditions under which I1 is satisfied by a QL-implication can be found in [6].

Table 1. Selected Fuzzy implication.

Implication Name	Implication Form	Implication Type	Properties
Kleene-Dienes	max(1 - x, y)	S with S = max QL with S=W', T=W	1-7, 9, 10, 12, 13
Reichenbach	1- x + xy	S with S = Π'	1-7, 9, 10, 12, 13
Lukasiewicz	min(1 - x + y, 1)	S with S = W' R with T = W QL with S = W', T = min	1-13
Gödel	$\begin{cases} 1 & if x \leq y \\ y & if x > y \end{cases}$	R with T = min	1-8, 10, 11
Standard Sequence (Sharp)	$\begin{cases} 1 & if x \leq y \\ 0 & if x > y \end{cases}$	R with T = min	1-8, 10, 11
Goguen	min(y / x, 1)	R with T = Π	1-8, 10, 11
Zadeh	max{1 - x, min(x, y)}	QL with S = max, T = min	2, 3, 5, 6, 9, 13
Fodor	$\begin{matrix} 1 & if x \leq \\ max(1-x,y) & if x > \end{matrix}$	R with T = min_0 S with S = max_1 QL with T = min, S = max_1	1-12

Considering a connection between implications and negation we notice that I(·,0) is non-increasing and is continous. However, it is neither strictly decreasing nor continuous in general. Continuity of the implication is sufficient but not necessary to obtain strong negation via residuation. As an example, a particular t-norm (called *nilpotent minimum*) and t-conorm (called *onepotent maximum)* are considered in

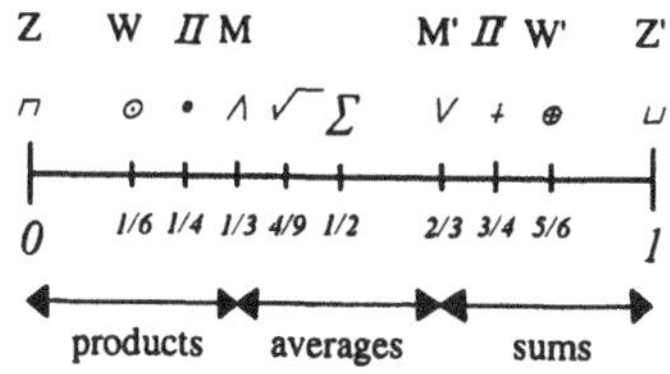

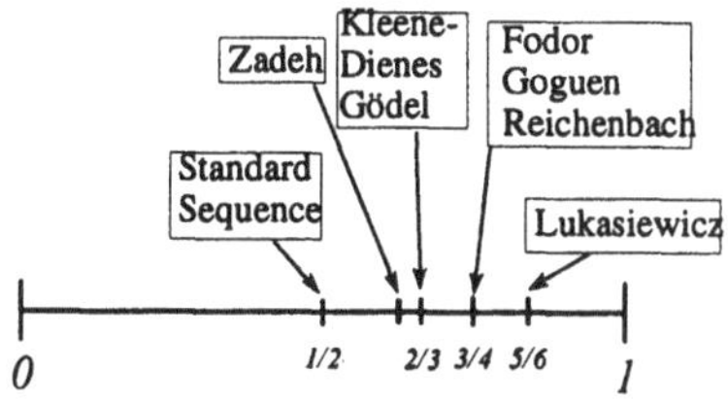

Fig. 1. Relative location of fuzzy operations. Fig. 2. Relative location of fuzzy implication. [6,7]

and recalled below:

$$x \wedge_0 y = \min_0(x,y) := \begin{cases} 0 & \text{if } x + y \le 1 \\ \min(x,y) & \text{if } x + y > 1 \end{cases} \tag{5}$$

and

$$x \vee_1 y = \max_1(x,y) := \begin{cases} 1 & \text{if } x + y \ge 1 \\ \max(x,y) & \text{if } x + y < 1 \end{cases} \tag{6}$$

Then the residuated implication is of the form:

$$I_{\min_0}(x,y) = I_{Fo}(x,y) = \begin{cases} 1 & \text{if } x \le y \\ \max(1-x,y) & \text{if } x > y \end{cases} \tag{7}$$

Although $I_{\min_0}$ is not continuous, $I_{\min_0}(x,0) = 1 - x$, $x \in [0,1]$ is the standard strong negation. Fuzzy implication (7) has been introduced by Fodor c.f. [6,8] and will be taken into account in further considerations.

Since t-norms (e.g. M-, Π-, W-, Z- norms), t-conorms (e.g. M'-, Π'-, W'-, Z'-conorms) and strong negation are well established models for AND, OR, NOT respectively, fuzzy implications should be regarded as closely related to those models. The most important fuzzy implications representing the classes of fuzzy implications discussed above are juxtaposed in Table 1.

We may also classify and order fuzzy implications using an integrated index obtained from the location of fuzzy implications versus fuzzy operations within the interval [0,1].

Let $*_1$, $*_2$: $[0,1] \times [0,1] \rightarrow [0,1]$ be measurable functions treated as two-argument operations in [0,1]. The distance between the operations $*_1$ and $*_2$ with respect to the values of their arguments is calculated as follows [3]:

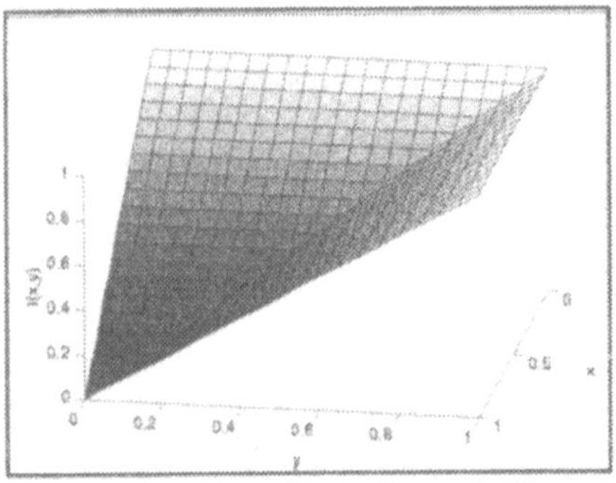

Fig. 3. Graphical illustration of Kleene-Dienes fuzzy implication.

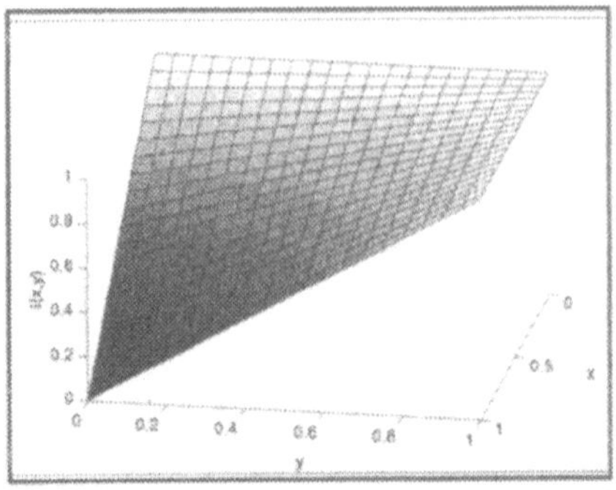

Fig. 4. Graphical illustration of Reichenbach fuzzy implication.

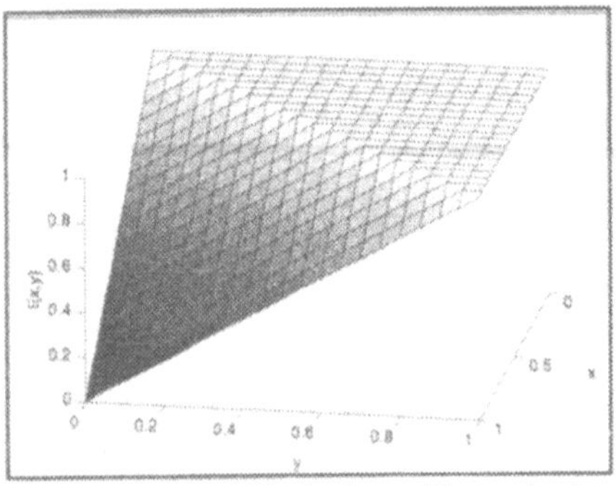

Fig. 5. Graphical illustration of Lukasiewicz fuzzy implication.

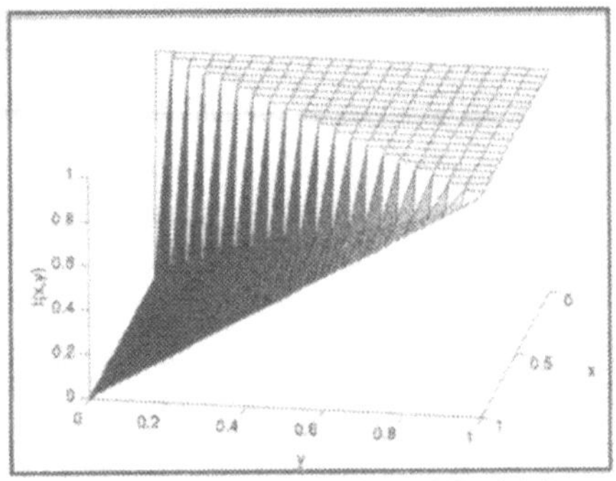

Fig. 6. Graphical illustration of Gödel fuzzy implication.

$$d(*_1, *_2) = \int_0^1\int_0^1 | x *_1 y - x *_2 y | \, dx \, dy \tag{8}$$

where d is here a pseudometric distance.

For constant operations, i.e. for $x *_1 y = 0$, $x *_2 y = 1$, for all $x,y \in [0,1]$ we get $d(*_1, *_2) = 1$. Because constant operations differ from drastic operations only by boundary conditions, we also obtain the distance for drastic operations as follows:

$$d(\sqcap, \sqcup) = 1 \tag{9}$$

where $\sqcap$ and $\sqcup$ denote drastic product (Z-norm) and drastic sum (Z'-conorm), respectively.

Taking into account the min ($\wedge$) (M-norm) and ($\vee$) (M'-conorm) operations, we can divide the [0,1] interval into three basic classes:

- products ($\sqcap \leq *_T \leq \wedge$) $\in$ [1, 1/3],
- averages ($\wedge \leq *_A \leq \vee$) $\in$ [1/3, 2/3],

- sums ($\vee \leq *_S \leq \sqcup$) $\in$ [2/3, 1].

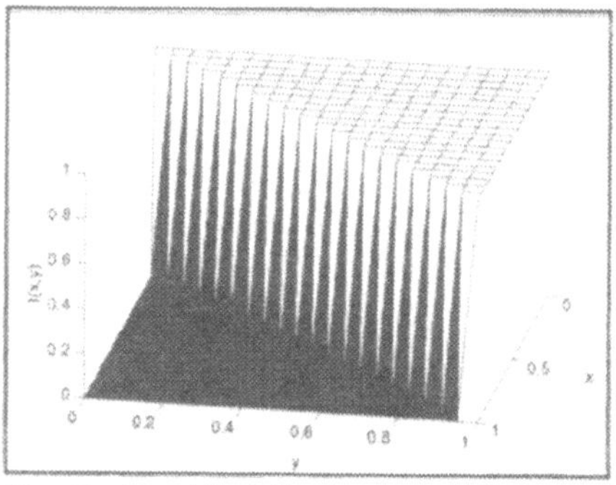

Fig. 7. Graphical illustration of Standard Sequence (Sharp) fuzzy implication.

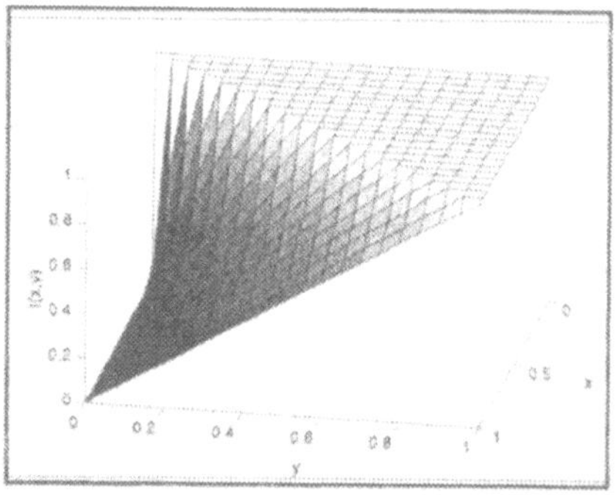

Fig. 8. Graphical illustration of Goguen fuzzy implication.

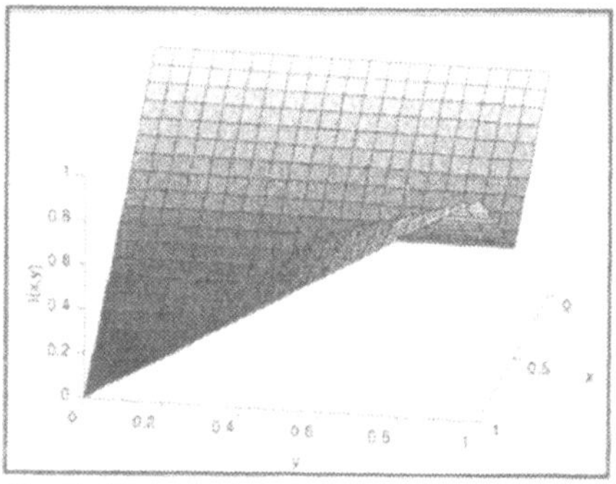

Fig. 9. Graphical illustration of Zadeh fuzzy implication.

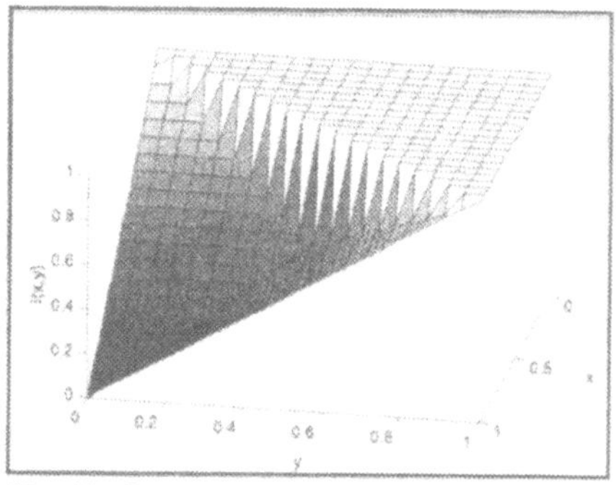

Fig. 10. Graphical illustration of Fodor fuzzy implication.

As an example, let us locate two products (algebraic product $x \bullet y = xy$ and bold product $x \odot y = 0 \vee (x + y - 1)$) within the [0,1] interval according to the pseudometric distance. For the algebraic product the calculated distance is $d(\sqcap,\bullet) = 1/4$ and for the bounded product we get $d(\sqcap,\odot) = 1/6$. Analogically, we get locations for the algebraic sum $x \dotplus y = x + y - xy$ and the bounded sum $x \oplus y = 1 \wedge (x + y)$ which are symmetric to the corresponding products with respect to 1/2 in the [0,1] interval. These and some additional results are illustrated in Fig 1.

We can also classify and order other families of operations which can be obtained using algebraic product and bounded product (e.g. Yager operations, Schweizer and Sklar operations, Frank operations, Hamacher operations and others).

Regarding a fuzzy implication as a two argument function, we can also find its location within the interval [0,1] using the above mentioned pseudometric distance in the same way as for fuzzy operations. In Fig. 2 we illustrate the computed distance $d(\sqcap,I)$ for the above considered fuzzy implications. Such determined distance may be also regarded as the volume under implication functions which are shown in Figs. 3-

10, respectively. Although the above mentioned distance is an integrated index characterizing a fuzzy implication, it also delivers indirectly information for the selection of an aggregation operation.

Below we will recall the idea of approximate reasoning by means of generalized modus ponens using fuzzy implications.

3. Approximate reasoning using generalized modus ponens and fuzzy implications

Fuzzy implications are mostly used as a way of interpretation of the if-then rules with a fuzzy antecedent and/or a fuzzy consequent. Such rules constitute a convenient form of expressing pieces of knowledge and a set of if-then rules forms a fuzzy rule base. Let us consider the canonical form of the fuzzy if-then rule R^k including other types of fuzzy rules and fuzzy propositions as special cases in the (MISO) form

$$R^k\text{: } if\, X_1 \text{ is } A_1^k \text{ and...and} X_n \text{ is } A_n^k \text{ then } Y \text{ is } B^k \tag{10}$$

where X_i and Y stand for linguistic variables of the antecedent and consequent and A_i^k, B^k are fuzzy sets in universes of discourse $_i \subset$, $\subset$ respectively.
Such a linguistic form of fuzzy if-then rule can be also expressed as a fuzzy relation:

$$R^k = (A_1^k \times ... \times A_n^k \rightarrow B^k) = (A^k \rightarrow B^k) \tag{11}$$

where $\underline{A}^k = A_1^k \times ... \times A_n^k$ is a fuzzy relation in $= {}_1 \times ... \times {}_n$ defined by

$$(A_1^k \times ... \times A_n^k)(x_1, ..., x_n) = A_1^k(x_1) \star_T ... \star_T A_n^k(x_n) = A^k(x) \tag{12}$$

where $\star_T$ - denotes any t-norm T.

Fuzzy if-then rules may be interpreted in two ways: as a conjunction of the antecedent and the consequent (Mamdani combination) or in the spirit of the classical logical implication i.e. as a fuzzy implication [5,13]. The second interpretation will be exploited here.

The methods of approximate reasoning are usually executed in a fuzzy inference engine which performs a mapping from an input fuzzy set $\underline{A}'$ in to a fuzzy set B' in via a fuzzy rule base. Two methods of approximate reasoning are mostly used: a composition based inference (first aggregate then inference - FATI) and an individual-rule based inference (first inference then aggregate - FITA).

In a composition based inference, a finite number of rules k= 1,..., K is aggregated via intersection or average operations i.e.

$$R = \bigcap_{T,\Sigma}^{K} R^k \tag{13}$$

or using t-norms or averages (e.g. normalized arithmetic sum) for aggregation of respective membership functions

$$R(\underline{x},y) = R^1(\underline{x},y)\left|\begin{smallmatrix}\star_T\\+\end{smallmatrix}\right|\dots\left|\begin{smallmatrix}\star_T\\+\end{smallmatrix}\right|R^K(\underline{x},y) \tag{14}$$

Taking into account an arbitrary input fuzzy set $\underline{A}'$ in and using the generalized modus ponens we obtain the output of fuzzy inference (FATI):

$$B' = \underline{A}' \circ R = \underline{A}' \circ \bigcap_{T,\Sigma}^{K} R^k = \underline{A}' \circ \bigcap_{T,\Sigma}^{K} (\underline{A}^k \rightarrow B^k) \tag{15}$$

or in terms of membership functions:

$$B'(y) = \sup_{\underline{x}\in X} \star_{T'} [\underline{A}'(\underline{x}), R(\underline{x},y)] = \sup_{\underline{x}\in X} \star_{T'} \left[\underline{A}'(\underline{x}), \left|\begin{smallmatrix}\bigwedge_{T\,k=1}^{K}\\ \sum^{K}\end{smallmatrix}\right| R^k(\underline{x},y)\right] \tag{16}$$

where $\wedge_T$, $\star_{T'}$ denote t-norms (T, T') for aggregation operation and composition respectively.

In the individual - rule based inference (FITA) each rule in the fuzzy rule base determines an output fuzzy set and after that an aggregation via intersection or average operation is perfomed. So the output fuzzy set is expressed by means of the formulas:

$$B'' = \bigcap_{T,\Sigma}^{K} \underline{A}' \circ (\underline{A}^k \rightarrow B^k) \tag{17}$$

or:

$$B''(y) = \left|\begin{smallmatrix}\bigwedge_{T\,k=1}^{K}\\ \sum^{K}\end{smallmatrix}\right| \sup_{\underline{x}\in X} \star_T [\underline{A}'(\underline{x}), R^k(\underline{x},y)] \tag{18}$$

It can be proved that B' is more specified then B" i.e.

$$B' \subseteq B'' \quad or \quad B'(y) \le B''(y) \tag{19}$$

It means that the consequent B' is equal to or contained in the intersection of fuzzy inference results - B". Sometimes for simplicity of calculation the consequent B' is replaced by B", under the assumption that the differences are not so big.

If the input fuzzy sets $A'_1,\dots,A'_n$ or ($\underline{A}'$) are singletons in $x_{10},\dots,x_{n0}$ or ($\underline{x}_0$), the consequence B' is equal to B" (B'(y) = B"(y)).

Sometimes it is not necessary to aggregate the partial inference fuzzy sets $B''^{(i)}$ into one final output fuzzy set B". We only measure their most important characteristics, e.g. center of gravity - COG(B"$^{(i)}$(y)), height τ_i etc., for further processing.

Fuzzy inference engine generates inference results based on fuzzy if-then rules. These results are mainly fuzzy sets. In many applications crisp results are required instead of fuzzy ones. The transformation of fuzzy results into crisp ones is performed by a defuzzification method generally expressed as

$$\delta : \mathscr{F}(Y) \rightarrow Y \tag{20}$$

or equivalently for membership functions

$$\delta_{mf} : \{ B'(y) \mid B' \in \mathscr{F}(Y), y \in Y \} \rightarrow Y \tag{21}$$

where symbols δ, δ_{mf} stand for defuzzification.

It means that defuzzification is defined as a mapping from fuzzy set B' (which is the output of the fuzzy inference) to crisp point $y^* \in$. Thus a defuzzification method should be applied. Although many various defuzzification methods (defuzzifiers) may be proposed, we will recall the most important ones from the class of standard defuzzifiers (SD).

1. The center of gravity (COG) defuzzifier specifying the y* as the center of the area covered by the membership function of B' i.e.

$$y^* = \frac{\int_Y y B\,(y)\,dy}{\int B'(y)\,dy} \tag{22}$$

2. Sometimes it is necessary to eliminate the $y \in$, whose membership values in B' are too small or equal in all (non-informative part of membership function). In this case we use the indexed center of gravity (ICOG) defuzzifier which results in:

$$y^* = \frac{\int_{Y_\alpha} y B\,(y)\,dy}{\int B'(y)\,dy} \tag{23}$$

where Y_α is defined as

$$Y_\alpha = \{ y \in Y \mid B'(y) \geq \alpha \} \tag{24}$$

and α is a constant.

To eliminate the non-informative part under membership function where B'(y) > α the informative part or operative part of the membership function where B'(y) > 0 has to be parallel-shifted downward by the value of α according to the formula

$$B^*(y) = \begin{cases} 0 & if B'(y) \le \alpha \\ B'(y) - \alpha & if B'(y) > \alpha \end{cases} \tag{25}$$

In such a case we may build a modified indexed center of gravity defuzzifier denoted by $MICOG_\alpha$ which may be expressed in the form:

$$y^* = \frac{\int_{Y_\alpha} y B\ (y)\, dy}{\int B^*(y)\, dy} = \frac{\int_{Y_\alpha} y\,(B\ (y) - \alpha)\, dy}{\int (B'(y) - \alpha)\, dy} \tag{26}$$

The last modification can also be obtained considering a COG defuzzifier on bounded difference, i.e.

$$y^* = COG[\max(0, B'(y) - \alpha)] \tag{27}$$

Other modifications are obtained when two cutting levels α_L (left-sided) and β_R (right-sided), ($\alpha_L > \beta_R$) for B'(y) should be taken into account. Denoting the cutting points for constant levels with B'(y) by y_α and y_β respectively, we get:

$$y^* = COG[B'(y) - \beta_R \mathbb{I}(y - y_\beta) - \alpha_L \mathbb{I}(y_\alpha - y)] \tag{28}$$

denoted shortly $MICOG_{\alpha\beta}$, and

$$y^* = COG[B'(y) - \beta_R \mathbb{I}(y - y_\alpha) - \alpha_L \mathbb{I}(y_\alpha - y)] \tag{29}$$

denoted $MICOG_{\alpha\alpha}$, where $\mathbb{I}(\cdot)$ denotes the Heaviside unit step pseudo-function. The interpretation of the above introduced defuzzifiers is obvious.

3. Denoting $y^{(k)}$ as the center of the k-th output fuzzy set and τ_k as its height, the center average defuzzifier (CAD) or height method (HM) determines y* as

$$y^* = \frac{\sum_{k=1}^{K} \tau_k\, y^{(k)}}{\sum_{k=1}^{K} \tau_k} \tag{30}$$

4. The maximum defuzzifier (MD) chooses the y* as the point in at which B'(y) achieves its maximum value i.e. defining the set of all points in at which B'(y) achives its maximum value

$$Y(B') = \{y \in Y \mid B'(y) = \sup_{y \in Y} B'(y)\} \tag{31}$$

the maximum defuzzifier determines y* as an arbitrary element in Y(B').

The mean of a maximum (MOM) defuzzifier is defined as

$$y^{*} = \frac{\int\limits_{Y(B')} y\,dy}{\int\limits_{Y(B')} dy} \tag{32}$$

where the integral denotes the conventional integration for the continuos part of Y(B') (or summation for the discrete part of Y(B')).

The modifications applied to defuzzifier 2, can also be applied to defuzzifiers 3 and 4 denoted shortly as $MISD_{\alpha}$, $MISD_{\alpha\alpha}$, $MISD_{\alpha\beta}$.

4. An equivalence of inference results using fuzzy implication interpretation and conjunctive interpretation of the if-then rules under defuzzification.

An output fuzzy set B'(y) obtained from an inference system based on a fuzzy implication interpretation of the if-then rules is different from the resulting fuzzy set obtained from the inference system based on a conjunctive interpretation of the fuzzy if-then rules. However, in many applications crisp results are required instead of fuzzy ones. Hence, a question arises whether it is possible to get the same or approximately the same crisp results from the inference system when defuzzification is applied. The answer is positive under the respective circumstances. The point of departure of our considerations is the equality expressed in the form:

$$\delta_{mf_L}\left\{ \sup_{\underline{x}\in X} \star_{T'} \left[\underline{A}'(\underline{x}), \left| \begin{matrix} \bigwedge_{T,\, k=1}^{K} \\ \sum_{k=1}^{K} \end{matrix} \right| I(\underline{A}^k(\underline{x}), B^k(y)) \right] \right\} = \delta_{mf_R}\left\{ \sup_{\underline{x}\in X} \star_{T'} \left[\underline{A}'(\underline{x}), \left| \begin{matrix} \bigvee_{S,\, k=1}^{K} \\ \sum^{K} \end{matrix} \right| \underline{A}^k(\underline{x}) *_{T'} B^k(y) \right] \right\} \tag{33}$$

The left-side part of that equality represents the defuzzified output of a fuzzy implication based inference system whereas the right-side part represents an inference system based on Mamdani's composition (a conjunctive interpretation of if-then rules).

The problem is to find such fuzzy implications (for the left-side part of the last equality), conjunctive operators (in the right-side of this equality), aggregation operations and defuzzification methods for both sides of the last equality in order to get the same crisp results. Generally, solving such a problem causes difficulties. One of the most important reasons is the different nature of a fuzzy implication and a conjunction (different truth tables). However, in special cases under some assumptions a pragmatic solution exists. To show such a solution, let us assume for simplicity that the input fuzzy sets $\underline{A}'$ are singletons in $\underline{x}_0$ (in this paricular case FATI is equivalent to FITA). Equality (33) can be rewritten in the simplified form:

$$\delta_{mf_L}\left\{\left[\begin{array}{c}\bigwedge_{T}{}_{k=1}^{K}\\ \sum_{k=1}^{K}\end{array}\right] I(\underline{A}^k(\underline{x}_0), B^k(y))\right\} = \delta_{mf_R}\left\{\left[\begin{array}{c}\bigvee_{S}{}_{k=1}^{K}\\ \sum\end{array}\right] \underline{A}^k(\underline{x}_0) *_{T'} B^k(y)\right\} \tag{34}$$

Because of the differences in aggregation operations, we accept the same for both sides of the equality, aggregation operation i.e. a normalized arithmetic sum. Additionally, we assume different defuzzification methods for both sides of the last equality, e.g. $MISD_\alpha$ (modified indexed standard defuzzifier) for the left-side and SD (standard defuzzifier) for the right-side. For our purposes we will use the method presented in the previous section named $MICOG_\alpha$ as the left-side defuzzification method For many fuzzy implications we have:

$$\alpha = \sum_{k=1}^{K} \overline{\underline{A}^k(\underline{x}_0)} = \sum_{k=1}^{K} (1 - \tau_k) \tag{35}$$

where τ_k stands for firing degree of k-th rule.
However, for some fuzzy implications (e.g. Gödel, Standard Sequence, Goguen and others) α may be taken as zero.

As the right side defuzzification method the well known COG method can be used. Taking into account the above mentioned assumptions and simplifications, the last equality may be written as

$$MICOG_\alpha\left(\sum_{k=1}^{K} I(\underline{A}^k(\underline{x}_o), B^k(y))\right) = COG\left(\sum_{k=1}^{K} \underline{A}^k(\underline{x}_o) *_{T'} B^k(y)\right) \tag{36}$$

It should be pointed out here that the modification in $MICOG_\alpha$ is responsible for elimination of the non-informative part of output membership function B'(y) (if such a part exists). The non-informative part of the membership function (e.g. a constant level of B'(y) in whole) is delivered by many fuzzy implications (e.g. Kleene-Dienes, Lukasiewicz, Reichenbach, Zadeh, Fodor and others).

The specific equivalence of inference results mentioned above can be seen straight on, if we take e.g. Reichenbach fuzzy implication under assumption that α is computed by means of the formula (26), as aggregation operation a normalized arithmetic sum is applied and the defuzzification method $MICOG_\alpha$ is represented by the formula (17) or (18). On the right side of the formula (27) an algebraic product operation is taken in order to get Larsen's inference system with a normalized arithmetic sum as an aggregation operation and COG as a defuzzification method. The above mentioned equivalence can also be described by the chain of identities:

$$
\begin{aligned}
&MICOG_{\alpha}\Big[\sum_{k=1} (\underline{A}^{k}(\underline{x}_0) + \underline{A}^{k}(\underline{x}_0) B^{k}(y))\Big]_{Re} = MICOG_{\alpha}\Big[\sum_{k=1} (1 - \tau_k) + \sum_{k=1} \tau_k B^{k}(y)\Big]_{Re} \\
&= MIHM_{\alpha}\Big[\sum_{k=1}^{K} \alpha_k + \sum_{k=1}^{K} (1 - \alpha_k) B^{k}(y)\Big]_{Re} = COG\Big[\sum_{k=1}^{K} \tau_k B^{k}(y)\Big]_{La} \\
&= HM\Big[\sum_{k=1}^{K} \tau_k B^{k}(y)\Big]_{La} = \left(\frac{\sum_{k=1}^{K} \tau_k y^{(k)}}{\sum_{k=1}^{K} \tau_k}\right)
\end{aligned}
\qquad (37)
$$

where Re stands for Reichenbach and La stands for Larsen.

A similar equivalence can be shown for Lukasiewicz fuzzy implication and Mamdani's minimum under the same conditions as for Reichenbach fuzzy implication and Larsen's product.

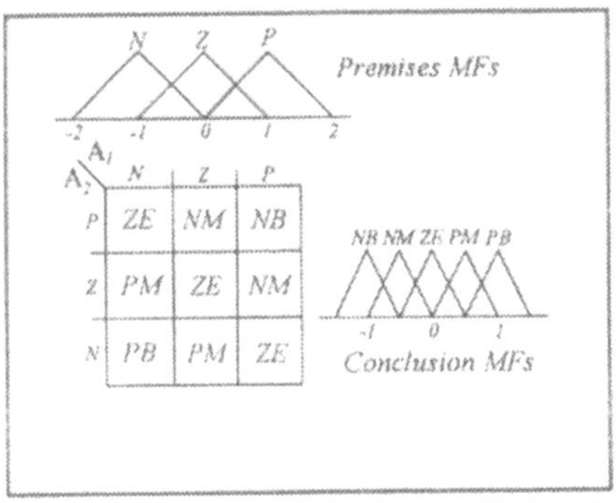

Fig. 11. Fuzzy knowledge base with inputs and output membership functions.

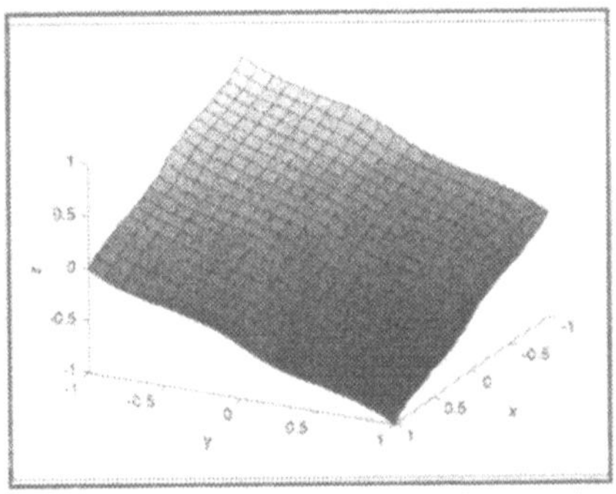

Fig. 12. Graphical illustration of the output surface for Lukasiewicz fuzzy implication.

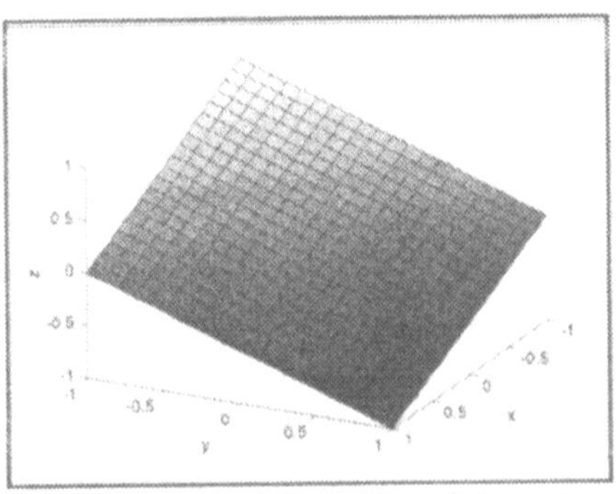

Fig. 13. Graphical illustration of the output surface for Reichenbach fuzzy implication.

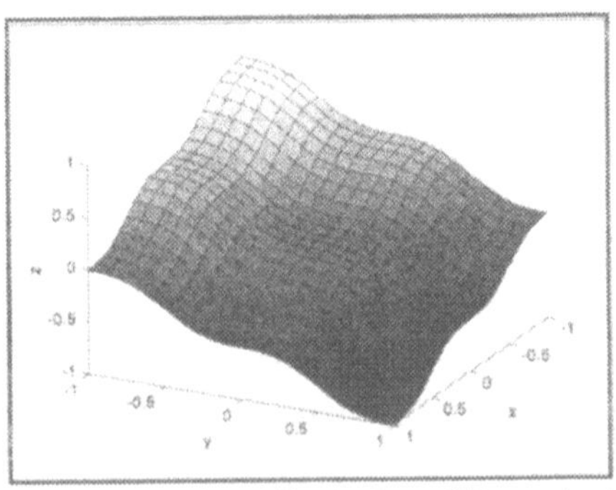

Fig. 14. Graphical illustration of the output surface for Kleene-Dienes fuzzy implication.

Below we present some numerical examples to illustrate the considerations given above.

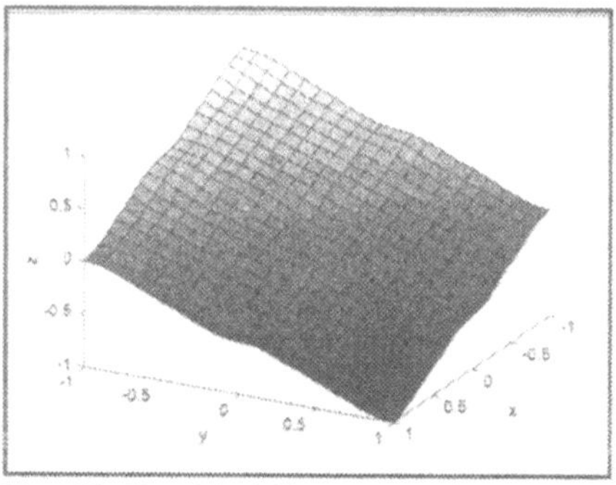

Fig. 15. Graphical illustration of the output surface for Fodor fuzzy implication.

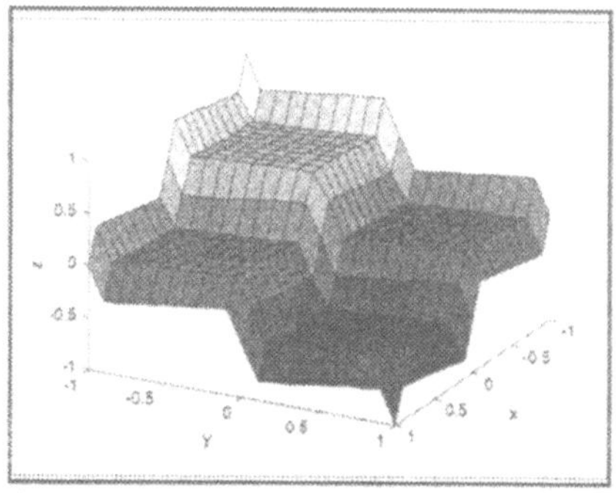

Fig. 16. Graphical illustration of the output surface for Gödel fuzzy implication.

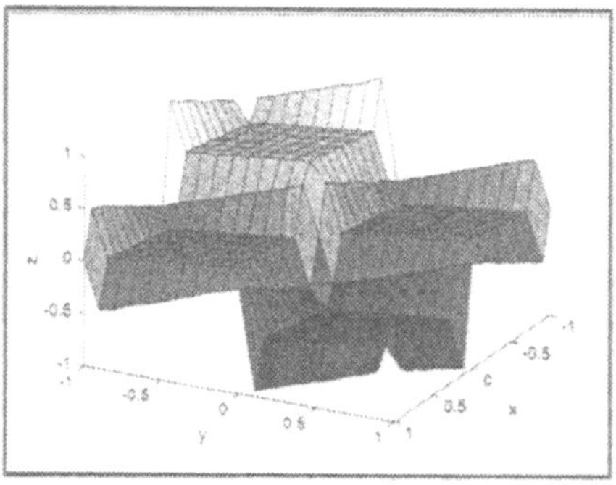

Fig. 17. Graphical illustration of the output surface for Standard Sequence (Sharp) fuzzy implication.

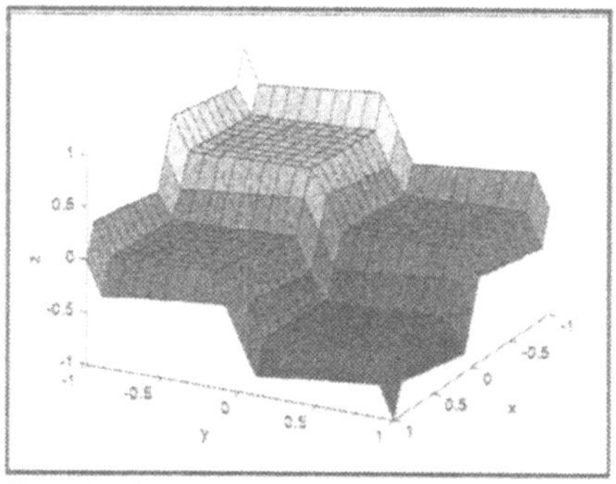

Fig. 18. Graphical illustration of the output surface for Goguen fuzzy implication.

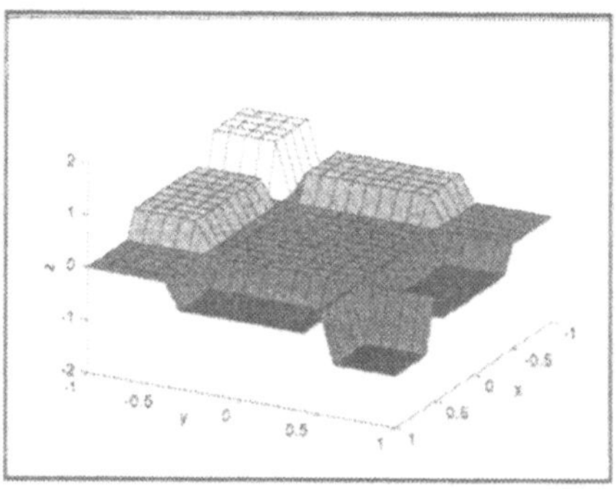

Fig. 19. Graphical illustration of the output surface for Zadeh fuzzy implication.

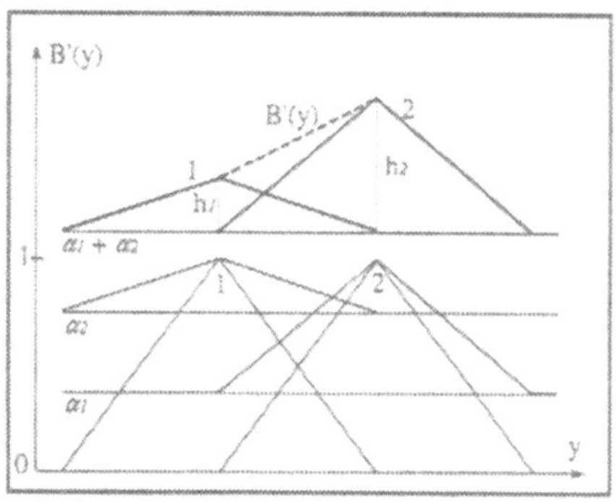

Fig. 20. An illustration of the equivalence of inference results (Reichenbach f.imp. versus Larsen's product).

5. Numerical examples

A fuzzy knowledge base presented in Fig 11 is taken as a basis of numerical calculation carried out here. Such a knowledge base consisting of 9 fuzzy if-then rules may have practical meaning, e.g. in fuzzy control. Each rule consists of two premises (e.g. error and change of error) in the antecedent part of the rule and one conclusion (e.g.control) in consequent part. The fuzzy sets representing possible values of the respective linguistic variables are also shown in Fig. 11.

Table 2. Values of quality indexes.

Implication name	λ_{MSE}	λ_{MAX}
Kleene-Dienes	0.005428	0.1463
Reichenbach	0	0
Lukasiewicz	0.000524	0.0446
Gödel	0.043745	0.4737
Standard Sequence (Sharp)	0.066836	0.9997
Goguen	0.039267	0.4593
Zadeh	0.054069	0.7500
Fodor	0.000287	0.0418

For all numerical examples of this section the 'and' connective is considered to be an algebraic product. The equivalence described in section 4 can be illustrated using the above mentioned kwnoledge base. Considering Reichenbach fuzzy implication with normalized arithmetic sum as the aggregation operation and defuzzifier of MICOG$_\alpha$ type (α's are computed from the formula (35)), the equivalence of inference results with those obtained on the basis of Larsen's product is shown in Fig 20. The equivalence of inference results based on Lukasiewicz fuzzy implication and Mamdani's minimum can be shown in a similar way.

The rule base depicted in Fig. 11 was tested by means of a complete set of singletons for the reason of fuzzy modeling of the function z = f(x,y) = -(x + y) / 2. Eight fuzzy implications (c.f. Table 1) were investigated in modeling the above mentioned function using the normalized arithmetic sum as an aggregation operation and defuzzifier of MICOG$_\alpha$ type with α's computed from formula (35) as well.

The resulting surfaces are presented in Figs 12 to 19. These surfaces correspond to the surfaces obtained from the conjunctive based inference system. The quality indexes (λ_{MSE}, λ_{MAX}) characterizing the quality of inference system may be defined as:

$$\lambda_{MSE} = \frac{1}{IJ}\sum_{i=1}^{I}\sum_{j=1}^{J}\left[I(x_i, y_j) - \frac{-(x_i + y_j)}{2}\right]^2$$
$$\lambda_{MAX} = \max_{i,i}\left|I(x_i, y_j) - \frac{-(x_i + y_j)}{2}\right| \quad \textbf{(38)}$$

The values of the above mentioned indexes are gathered in Table 2. As expected, both indexes for Reichenbach fuzzy implication are equal to zero. It can be seen that for Lukasiewicz implication the values of indexes are the same as for Mamdani's inference system. It can be noticed that in this example of modeling only four fuzzy implications (Kleen-Dienes, Reichenbach, Lukasiwicz and Fodor) applied in the inference system deliver reasonable results.

The programming tool applied to these investigations was FDSS Fuzzy-Flou and Fuzzy Logic toolbox for Matlab systems. Special procedures (m-files) concerning fuzzy implications and modified COG methods were written for the above mentioned toolbox.

6. Conclusions

In this paper the applicability of fuzzy implications in approximate reasoning has been investigated. Based on these investigations a specific type of equivalence of inference results using fuzzy implication interpretation and conjunctive interpretation of the if-then rules has been shown. Such equivalence is important regarding the inference algorithm construction. The inference algorithms based on conjunctive operators in some cases seem to be faster and easier to build than the algorithms of fuzzy implication based inference system. For future research, the corresponding equivalence between other fuzzy implications and conjunctive operators with respect to inference should be determined.

References

1. Z. Cao, A. Kandel, Applicability of some fuzzy implication operators, Fuzzy Sets and Systems 31 (1989), pp. 151-186,
2. O.Cordon, F. Herrera, A. Peregrin, Applicability of the fuzzy operators in the design of fuzzy logic controllers, Fuzzy Sets and Systems 86 (1997), pp. 15-41,
3. E. Czogala, R. Kowalczyk, Investigation of selected fuzzy operations and implications in engineering, Fifth IEEE Int. Conf. on Fuzzy Systems, (1996), pp. 879-885,
4. D. Dubois, H. Prade, Fuzzy sets in approximate reasoning, Part 1: Inference with possibility distributions, Fuzzy Sets and Systems 40 (1991), pp. 143-202,
5. D. Dubois, H. Prade, What are fuzzy rules and how to use them, Fuzzy Sets and Systems 84 (1996), pp. 169-185,
6. J.C. Fodor, On fuzzy implication operators, Fuzzy Sets and Systems 42 (1991), pp. 293-300,
7. J.C. Fodor, Contrapositive symmetry of fuzzy implications, Fuzzy Sets and Systems 69 (1995), pp. 141-156,
8. J.C. Fodor, M. Roubens, Fuzzy Preference Modelling and Multicriteria Decision Support (Kluwer, Dordrecht, 1994),
9. E. Kerre, A comparative study of the behavior of some popular fuzzy implication operators on the generalized modus ponens, in: L. Zadeh and J. Kacprzyk, Eds., Fuzzy Logic for the Management of Uncertainty (Wiley, New York, 1992), pp. 281-295,
10. H.Maeda, An investigation on the spread of fuzziness in multi-fold multi-stage approximate reasoning by pictorial representation - under sup-min composition and triangular type membership function, Fuzzy Sets and Systems 80 (1996), pp.133 - 148,
11. E. Trillas, L. Valverde, On implication and indistinguishability in the setting of fuzzy logic, in: J. Kacprzyk and R.R Yager (Eds.), Management Decision Support Systems using, Fuzzy Sets and Possibility Theory, (Verlag TÜV Rheinland, Köln, 1985), pp. 198-212,
12. S. Weber, A general concept of fuzzy connectives, negations and implications based on t-norms and t-conorms, Fuzzy Sets and Systems 11 (1983), pp. 115-134,
13. R. R. Yager, On the interpretation of fuzzy if-then rules, Applied Intelligence 6 (1996), pp. 141-151,

On the Semantics of Fuzzy Linguistic Quantifiers*

Helmut Thiele

University of Dortmund, Department of Computer Science I,
D-44221 Dortmund, Germany
Phone: +49 231 755 6152
Fax: +49 231 755 6555
E-Mail: thiele@ls1.informatik.uni-dortmund.de
WWW: http://ls1-www.informatik.uni-dortmund.de

1 Some Notations and Fundamental Definitions

For definiteness we start with some notations and definitions.

By $\mathbb{I}$ and $\mathbb{N}$ we denote the set of all integers and non-negative integers, respectively. The set of all real numbers and the set of all non-negative real numbers are termed by $\mathbb{R}$ and $\mathbb{R}^+$, respectively. The set of all real numbers r with $0 \leq r \leq 1$ is denoted by $\langle 0, 1 \rangle$. For an arbitrary subset S of $\langle 0, 1 \rangle$ we denote the infimum and the supremum of S with respect to $\langle 0, 1 \rangle$ by $\inf S$ and $\sup S$, respectively. Note that for the empty set $\emptyset$ we get $\inf \emptyset = 1$ and $\sup \emptyset = 0$.

Let U be an arbitrary (crisp) set (in the usual sense of set theory). Then it is well-known that the power set $\mathfrak{P}U$ (i. e. the set of all subsets of U) forms a complete atomistic BOOLEan algebra with respect to the intersection $\cap$, the union $\cup$, the empty set $\emptyset$ as zero element, the set U as unit element and the sets $\{x\}$ $(x \in U)$ as atoms. For $\mathfrak{S} \subseteq \mathfrak{P}U$ the infimum and the supremum of $\mathfrak{S}$ with respect to the subset relation $\subseteq$ is denoted by $\operatorname{Inf} \mathfrak{S}$ and $\operatorname{Sup} \mathfrak{S}$, respectively. Note, if $\mathfrak{S}$ is empty then we have $\operatorname{Inf} \mathfrak{S} = U$ and $\operatorname{Sup} \mathfrak{S} = \emptyset$.

Let n be a non-negative integer with $n \geq 1$. Furthermore, let $U_1, \ldots, U_n$ be arbitrary (crisp) sets. Then by $U_1 \times \cdots \times U_n$ we denote the CARTESIan product of the sets given, i. e. the set of all n-tuples $[x_1, \ldots, x_n]$ with $x_1 \in U_1, \ldots, x_n \in U_n$. If $U_1 = \cdots = U_n = U$ then we denote $U_1 \times \cdots \times U_n$ by U^n.

The cardinal number of an arbitrary set S is denoted by $\operatorname{card} S$. Note that for arbitrary sets S, S' the equation $\operatorname{card} S = \operatorname{card} S'$ holds if and only if there exists a bijection between S and S'.

An (n-ary) two-valued (or BOOLEan) predicate π on $[U_1, \ldots, U_n]$ is a mapping

$$\pi : U_1 \times \cdots \times U_n \rightarrow \{0, 1\}$$

* This research was supported by the Deutsche Forschungsgemeinschaft as part of the Collaborative Research Center "Computational Intelligence" (531)

where 1 and 0 play the roles of the logical values *true* and *false*, respectively. The set of all two-valued predicates on $[U_1, \dots, U_n]$ is denoted by $\Pi(U_1, \dots, U_n)$.

Furthermore, a subset $R \subseteq U_1 \times \cdots \times U_n$ is called an (n-ary) relation on $[U_1, \dots, U_n]$, hence $\mathfrak{P}(U_1 \times \cdots \times U_n)$ is the set of all (n-ary) relations on $[U_1, \dots, U_n]$.

Obviously, there exists a bijection between $\Pi(U_1, \dots, U_n)$ and $\mathfrak{P}(U_1 \times \cdots \times U_n)$, hence the equation $\operatorname{card} \Pi(U_1, \dots, U_n) = \operatorname{card} \mathfrak{P}(U_1 \times \cdots \times U_n)$ holds.

A (n-ary) continuous-valued (or ŁUKASIEWICZ or fuzzy) predicate ρ on $[U_1, \dots, U_n]$ is a mapping

$$\rho : U_1 \times \cdots \times U_n \to \langle 0, 1 \rangle \, .$$

The set $\langle 0, 1 \rangle$ is interpreted as the set of all logical values. In fuzzy logic ρ is also called fuzzy relation. For $n = 1$ and $U_1 = U$ mappings

$$F : U \to \langle 0, 1 \rangle$$

are termed fuzzy sets on U, i.e. we do not distinguish between a fuzzy set and its membership function.

The set of all fuzzy predicates on $[U_1, \dots, U_n]$ is denoted by $\mathrm{F}\Pi(U_1, \dots, U_n)$.

In order to exclude undesirable exceptions we assume that all sets $U_1, \dots, U_n$ considered are non-empty throughout the paper.

2 On Quantifiers in Two-valued Logic

Assume that there are non-empty sets U_j^i aggregated in the form

$$\mathfrak{U} = \left[\left[U_1^1, \dots U_{m_1}^1 \right], \dots, \left[U_1^n, \dots U_{m_n}^n \right] \right]$$

where $m_1, \dots, m_n, n \in \mathbb{N}$ and $m_1 \geq 1, \dots, m_n \geq 1$, $n \geq 1$.

We call $\mathfrak{U}$ a type and following A. MOSTOWSKI [21], N. RESCHER [26,27] and L. A. ZADEH [45] we define

Definition 2.1
Q is said to be a general two-valued (or BOOLEan) quantifier of the type $\mathfrak{U}$ $=_{def}$ $Q : \Pi \left(U_1^1, \dots U_{m_1}^1 \right) \times \cdots \times \Pi \left(U_1^n, \dots U_{m_n}^n \right) \to \{0, 1\}$.

Remarks

1. The definition above means that a quantifier is a second order predicate. This "philosophy" is the basis for the following considerations.

2. For a semantical analysis of the quantifier concept it is not necessary to introduce any formalized language or calculus. So, for instance, one can easily realize that in [17] the introduction and the use of the formalized first order logic is redundant.
3. To illustrate this general definition let U and U' be non-empty sets. We consider the type $\mathfrak{U} = [[U], [U']]$ and define for $\pi : U \to \{0,1\}$, $\pi' : U' \to \{0,1\}$

$$H(\pi, \pi') =_{def} \begin{cases} 1 & \text{if } \operatorname{card}\{x \mid x \in U \land \pi(x) = 1\} \\ & \qquad = \operatorname{card}\{x' \mid x' \in U' \land \pi'(x') = 1\} \\ 0 & \text{else.} \end{cases}$$

Obviously, this is the well-known HÄRTIG-quantifier introduced by K. HÄRTIG in [11] and applied in foundations of arithmetics. See also [12].
4. For simplification of the notions and notations in the following we consider only the special case $m_1 = 1$ and $n = 1$. For our purposes this restriction can be made without essential loss of generality. Therefore for a given non-empty set U we define

Definition 2.2
Q is said to be a general two-valued (or BOOLEan) quantifier on U
$=_{def}$ $Q : \Pi(U) \to \{0,1\}$.

From theory and applications of the two-valued logic the quantifiers "for every" and "there exists" are well-known and very often used. We denote these quantifiers by ALL and EX, respectively, and define them as follows where $\pi : U \to \{0,1\}$.

Definition 2.3

1. $\mathrm{ALL}(\pi) =_{def} \begin{cases} 1 & \text{if } \{x \mid x \in U \land \pi(x) = 1\} = U \\ 0 & \text{else} \end{cases}$
2. $\mathrm{EX}(\pi) =_{def} \begin{cases} 1 & \text{if } \{x \mid x \in U \land \pi(x) = 1\} \neq \emptyset \\ 0 & \text{else} \end{cases}$

They share the important property of extensionality which we define for arbitrary BOOLEan quantifiers on U as follows.

Definition 2.4
Q is said to be extensional
$=_{def}$ There exists a mapping q with

$$q : \{\{0,1\}, \{1\}, \{0\}\} \to \{0,1\}$$

such that for every $\pi \in \Pi(U)$,

$$Q(\pi) = q\{\pi(x) \mid x \in U\}.$$

Obviously, there are exactly eight extensional BOOLEan quantifiers. They can be characterized by the following table.

	q_1	q_2	q_3	q_4	q_5	q_6	q_7	q_8
$\{0\}$	0	0	0	0	1	1	1	1
$\{1\}$	0	0	1	1	0	0	1	1
$\{0,1\}$	0	1	0	1	0	1	0	1

The functions q_3 and q_4 characterize the quantifiers "for every" and "there exists", respectively. Using the BOOLEan functions non and et defined by

$$\text{non}(0) = 1, \text{non}(1) = 0$$

and

$$\text{et}(0,0) = \text{et}(0,1) = \text{et}(1,0) = 0, \text{et}(1,1) = 1$$

we can state that for every $S \subseteq \{0,1\}$ with $S \neq \emptyset$ one has

$$\begin{aligned} q_6(S) &= \text{non}(q_3(S)) \\ q_5(S) &= \text{non}(q_4(S)) \\ q_7(S) &= \text{non}(q_2(S)) \\ \text{and} \qquad q_2(S) &= \text{et}(q_4(S), \text{non}(q_3(S))). \end{aligned}$$

We think that the "semantic meaning" q_1 and q_8 is clear. So, we have a complete overview of all BOOLEan extensional quantifiers. Furthermore, we see that q_3 and q_4 are the iterations of the BOOLEan functions et and vel, respectively, where vel is defined by

$$\text{vel}(0,0) = 0, \text{vel}(0,1) = \text{vel}(1,0) = \text{vel}(1,1) = 1.$$

Now, in applications of two-valued logic one can find a lot of important quantifiers which are not extensional in the sense of definition 2.4.

Examples are where $\mathfrak{k}$ is an arbitrary cardinal number greater than 0:

- "there are at least $\mathfrak{k}$ elements such that ... "
- "there are at most $\mathfrak{k}$ elements such that ... "
- "there are exactly $\mathfrak{k}$ elements such that ... "
- "there are infinitely many elements such that ... "
- "there are at most finitely many elements such that ... "
- "for almost all elements ... "

Now, we introduce $\text{EX}_\mathfrak{k}$, $\text{EX}_\mathfrak{k}!$, $\text{EX}_\mathfrak{k}!!$, EXI, EXF!, and AMA as denotations for the quantifiers described above.

Then for a non-empty set U and $\pi : U \to \{0,1\}$ we define

Definition 2.5

1. $\mathrm{EX}_{\mathfrak{t}}(\pi) =_{def} \begin{cases} 1 & \text{if } \operatorname{card}\{x \mid x \in U \wedge \pi(x) = 1\} \geq \mathfrak{t} \\ 0 & \text{else} \end{cases}$

2. $\mathrm{EX}_{\mathfrak{t}}!(\pi) =_{def} \begin{cases} 1 & \text{if } \operatorname{card}\{x \mid x \in U \wedge \pi(x) = 1\} \leq \mathfrak{t} \\ 0 & \text{else} \end{cases}$

3. $\mathrm{EX}_{\mathfrak{t}}!!(\pi) =_{def} \begin{cases} 1 & \text{if } \operatorname{card}\{x \mid x \in U \wedge \pi(x) = 1\} = \mathfrak{t} \\ 0 & \text{else} \end{cases}$

4. $\mathrm{EXI}(\pi) =_{def} \begin{cases} 1 & \text{if } \{x \mid x \in U \wedge \pi(x) = 1\} \text{ is infinite} \\ 0 & \text{else} \end{cases}$

5. $\mathrm{EXF}!(\pi) =_{def} \begin{cases} 1 & \text{if } \{x \mid x \in U \wedge \pi(x) = 1\} \text{ is finite} \\ 0 & \text{else} \end{cases}$

6. $\mathrm{AMA}(\pi) =_{def} \begin{cases} 1 & \text{if there exists a finite set } V \subseteq U \text{ such that} \\ & \qquad \{x \mid x \in U \wedge \pi(x) = 1\} \supseteq U \setminus V \\ 0 & \text{else} \end{cases}$

All these quantifiers are *not* extensional in the sense of definition 2.4 but they have the common property that for an arbitrary $\pi \in \Pi(U)$ the value $Q(\pi)$ of such a quantifier Q only depends on the "cardinality" of π, i. e. on $\operatorname{card}\{x \mid x \in U \wedge \pi(x) = 1\}$.

Hence we define

Definition 2.6
Q is said to be a cardinal quantifier on U

$$=_{def} \forall\pi\forall\pi'(\pi, \pi' \in \Pi(U) \\ \wedge \operatorname{card}\{x \mid x \in U \wedge \pi(x) = 1\} = \operatorname{card}\{x \mid x \in U \wedge \pi'(x) = 1\} \\ \rightarrow Q(\pi) = Q(\pi'))$$

Proposition 2.1
For every non-empty U, the quantifiers $\mathrm{EX}_{\mathfrak{t}}$, $\mathrm{EX}_{\mathfrak{t}}!$, $\mathrm{EX}_{\mathfrak{t}}!!$, EXI, EXF!, and AMA are cardinal quantifiers on U.

Proof
Obvious by definition. ∎

With respect to generalizations of definition 2.6 to fuzzy logic we define

Definition 2.7
The BOOLEan predicates π and π' on U are said to be isomorphic
$=_{def}$ there exists a bijection β on U such that for every $x \in U$,

$$\pi(x) = \pi'(\beta(x)).$$

Then we can state the following

Proposition 2.2
For every $\pi, \pi' \in \Pi(U)$ the statements 1, 2, and 3 are pairwise equivalent:

1. π and π' are isomorphic.
2. $\text{card}\{x \mid x \in U \wedge \pi(x) = 1\} = \text{card}\{x \mid x \in U \wedge \pi'(x) = 1\}$
3. there exists a bijection β between the sets $\{x \mid x \in U \wedge \pi(x) = 1\}$ and $\{x \mid x \in U \wedge \pi'(x) = 1\}$.

Now, let us discuss the quantifiers

- EXI (there exist at least infinitely many elements such that ...)
- EXF! (there are at most finitely many elements such that ...)
- AMA (for almost all elements ...)

These quantifiers are well-known from classical mathematics, in particular, the quantifier AMA plays an important role in analysis, for instance in defining the convergence of sequences and rows.

Obviously, we get where $\neg\pi$ is defined by $(\neg\pi)(x) =_{def} \text{non}(\pi(x))$ for every $x \in U$

Proposition 2.3
For every U and every $\pi \in \Pi(U)$,

1. $\text{EXI}(\pi) = 1 - \text{AMA}(\neg\pi)$
2. $\text{EXF!}(\pi) = \text{AMA}(\neg\pi)$

But with respect to finite U these quantifiers are completely unapplicable because we get the following proposition.

Proposition 2.4
If U is finite then for every $\pi \in \Pi(U)$,

1. $\text{EXI}(\pi) = 0$
2. $\text{EXF!}(\pi) = 1$
3. $\text{AMA}(\pi) = 1$.

Proof
The assertions 1 and 2 are trivial. In order to prove 3 choose as V the finite set U, then $U \setminus V$ is empty, hence the condition

$$\text{for every } x \in U \setminus V,\ \pi(x) = 1$$

holds trivially. ■

Example

Assume that my class consists of 100 students. During our lunch I informed my colleagues by the following sentence: "In my lecture this morning almost all students of my class were present." What is the meaning of this sentence? Or, more correctly, what is the logical value of this sentence? Using the "classical" interpretation of this quantifier expressed by definition 2.5 we get that this sentence is always true independent of the fact whether in my lecture this morning 0, 21, 74 or even 100 students were present.

To overcome these difficulties caused by finite U we could try to introduce a correct semantics as follows.

Assume U is finite. Fix a natural number c with $0 \leq c \leq \operatorname{card} U$. Then define for $\pi : U \to \{0, 1\}$

Definition 2.8

$$\mathrm{AMA}'(\pi) =_{def} \begin{cases} 1 & \text{if } \operatorname{card}\{x \mid x \in U \wedge \pi(x) = 1\} \geq c \\ 0 & \text{else.} \end{cases}$$

In our example above we assumed $\operatorname{card} U = 100$. Maybe we have fixed $c = 95$.

In this case the sentence "In my lecture this morning almost all students of my class were present" is *true* if 95 (or more) students were present and *false* if 94 (or less) students were present. So, this interpretation leads to a "semantic paradox" which is unacceptable even in "common sense" communication. This paradox becomes more and more unacceptable if $\operatorname{card} U$ and c are growing, for instance, if $\operatorname{card} U = 600$ and $c = 570$.

The difficulties described can be eliminated to a certain extent if we admit more than two logical values, for instance, all real numbers of $\langle 0, 1 \rangle$, as it is usual in fuzzy logic.

Returning to our example this means if n $(0 \leq n \leq 100)$ students were present then the logical value of the sentence considered could be defined as $\frac{n}{100}$, hence $\frac{n}{100} \in \langle 0, 1 \rangle$.

Generalizing these ideas for a finite U we could define

Definition 2.9

$$\mathrm{AMA}''(\pi) =_{def} \frac{\operatorname{card}\{x \mid x \in U \wedge \pi(x) = 1\}}{\operatorname{card} U}$$

We have to underline that this definition of a logical value is arbitrary to a certain extent and cannot be justified by mathematical reasons. That means if φ fulfills the conditions $\varphi : \langle 0, 1 \rangle \to \langle 0, 1 \rangle$, $\varphi(0) = 0$, $\varphi(1) = 1$, and φ is increasing then instead of $\frac{n}{100}$ one could also choose the number $\varphi\left(\frac{n}{100}\right)$ as the logical value. Which function φ one has to choose only depends on the special application one has in mind.

So, we define a new quantifier AMA^* as follows.

Definition 2.10

$$\mathrm{AMA}^*(\pi) =_{def} \begin{cases} \mathrm{AMA}(\pi) & \text{if } U \text{ is infinite} \\ \mathrm{AMA}''(\pi) & \text{if } U \text{ is finite} \end{cases}$$

Let $\mathfrak{k}$ be an arbitrary cardinal number greater than 0. Then we can introduce a generalization of the quantifier AMA to

- "for every element, excluding a set of elements with a cardinal number less than $\mathfrak{k}$"

We denote this quantifier by $\text{ALL-EXC}_{\mathfrak{k}}$ and define

Definition 2.11

$$\text{ALL-EXC}_{\mathfrak{k}}(\pi) =_{def} \begin{cases} 1 & \text{if } \exists V(V \subseteq U \wedge \operatorname{card} V < \mathfrak{k} \\ & \qquad \wedge \{x \mid x \in U \wedge \pi(x) = 1\} \supseteq U \setminus V) \\ 0 & \text{else.} \end{cases}$$

Obviously, we get the following

Proposition 2.5

1. $\mathrm{ALL}(\pi) = \text{ALL-EXC}_1(\pi)$
2. $\mathrm{AMA}(\pi) = \text{ALL-EXC}_{\aleph_0}(\pi)$
3. For $n \in \mathbb{N}$ and $n \geq 1$,

$$\text{ALL-EXC}_1(\pi) \leq \cdots \leq \text{ALL-EXC}_n(\pi) \leq \cdots \leq \text{ALL-EXC}_{\aleph_0}(\pi)$$

4. If $n \in \mathbb{N}$, $n \geq 1$, and $\operatorname{card} U < n$, then for every $\pi : U \to \{0,1\}$, $\text{ALL-EXC}_n(\pi) = 1$.

Assertion 4 shows that for the quantifier $\text{ALL-EXC}_n(\pi)$ we can observe the same effect for $\operatorname{card} U < n$ as we have for AMA if U is finite.

Now, we turn over to the quantifier

- "for the most elements ... "

denoted by MOST. Following N. RESCHER [26,27] we define

Definition 2.12

$$\mathrm{MOST}(\pi) =_{def} \begin{cases} 1 & \text{if } \exists V(V \subseteq U \wedge \operatorname{card} V < \operatorname{card}(U \setminus V) \\ & \qquad \wedge \{x \mid x \in U \wedge \pi(x) = 1\} \supseteq U \setminus V) \\ 0 & \text{else.} \end{cases}$$

We have the following

Proposition 2.6

1. If $\operatorname{card} U > \aleph_0$ then for every $\pi : U \to \{0,1\}$,

$$\mathrm{AMA}(\pi) \leq \mathrm{MOST}(\pi).$$

2. If $\operatorname{card} U = \aleph_0$ then for every $\pi : U \to \{0,1\}$,

$$\mathrm{AMA}(\pi) = \mathrm{MOST}(\pi).$$

3. If $\operatorname{card} U < \aleph_0$ (hence U is finite) then for every $\pi : U \to \{0,1\}$,

$$\mathrm{MOST}(\pi) = 1 \text{ if and only if } \operatorname{card}\{x \mid x \in U \wedge \pi(x) = 0\} < \operatorname{card}\{x \mid x \in U \wedge \pi(x) = 1\}.$$

Proof

ad 1 Obvious by definitions.

ad 2 This follows from the fact that a cardinal number less than $\aleph_0$ is a non-negative integer.

ad 3

I ($\leftarrow$). Assume $\mathrm{MOST}(\pi) = 1$. Hence there exists a set $V \subseteq U$ such that $\operatorname{card} V < \operatorname{card}(U \setminus V)$ and $\{x \mid x \in U \wedge \pi(x) = 1\} \supseteq U \setminus V$. From the last inclusion we get

$$\operatorname{card}(U \setminus V) \leq \operatorname{card}\{x \mid x \in U \wedge \pi(x) = 1\},$$

hence

$$\operatorname{card} V < \operatorname{card}\{x \mid x \in U \wedge \pi(x) = 1\}.$$

Furthermore, from $\{x \mid x \in U \wedge \pi(x) = 1\} \supseteq U \setminus V$ we obtain $\{x \mid x \in U \wedge \pi(x) = 0\} \subseteq V$, hence $\operatorname{card}\{x \mid x \in U \wedge \pi(x) = 0\} < \operatorname{card} V$, consequently $\operatorname{card}\{x \mid x \in U \wedge \pi(x) = 0\} < \operatorname{card}\{x \mid x \in U \wedge \pi(x) = 1\}$.

II ($\rightarrow$). Assume $\operatorname{card}\{x \mid x \in U \wedge \pi(x) = 0\} < \operatorname{card}\{x \mid x \in U \wedge \pi(x) = 1\}$. Define $V =_{def} \{x \mid x \in U \wedge \pi(x) = 0\}$. Then $U \setminus V = \{x \mid x \in U \wedge \pi(x) = 1\}$, hence $\operatorname{card} V < \operatorname{card}(U \setminus V)$ and $\{x \mid x \in U \wedge \pi(x) = 1\} \supseteq U \setminus V$ holds.

■

Remarks on proposition 2.6

1. If $\operatorname{card} U > \aleph_0$ then assertion 1 fits our intuitive expectations. Furthermore, in this case there are $\pi : U \to \{0,1\}$ such that $\mathrm{AMA}(\pi) < \mathrm{MOST}(\pi)$.
2. Assertion 2 is frustrating because for domains U with $\operatorname{card} U = \aleph_0$ one cannot accept that in this case the quantifiers AMA and MOST coincide. We are faced with the (unsolved) problem how to modify the definition of AMA and/or MOST for domains with $\operatorname{card} U = \aleph_0$. Maybe measure theory can help, but we do not discuss this problem in the paper presented.

3. Assertion 3 is completely counter-intuitive because of the following two reasons.
First, assume that $\operatorname{card} U = 1000$. Furthermore, let $\pi_1, \pi_2 : U \to \{0,1\}$ with $\operatorname{card}\{x \mid x \in U \wedge \pi_1(x) = 1\} = 500$ and $\operatorname{card}\{x \mid x \in U \wedge \pi_2(x) = 1\} = 501$. Then we get

$$\begin{aligned} & \mathrm{MOST}(\pi_1) = 0 \\ \text{and} \quad & \mathrm{MOST}(\pi_2) = 1. \end{aligned}$$

This result must be valued as a "semantical paradox" and cannot be accepted.
Second, we expect for every $\pi : U \to \{0,1\}$

$$\mathrm{AMA}(\pi) \leq \mathrm{MOST}(\pi)$$

as stated in assertion 1 for U with $\operatorname{card} U > \aleph_0$. But for π_1 we have

$$\mathrm{MOST}(\pi_1) < \mathrm{AMA}(\pi_1)$$

in contrast to our intuition.

So adopting the idea of modifying AMA to AMA* we define a new quantifier MOST* as follows.

Definition 2.13

$$\mathrm{MOST}^*(\pi) =_{def} \begin{cases} \mathrm{MOST}(\pi) & \text{if } U \text{ is infinite} \\ \sqrt{\mathrm{AMA}''(\pi)} & \text{if } U \text{ is finite.} \end{cases}$$

The introduction of the quantifier MOST* can be justified by the following

Proposition 2.7
For every $U \neq \emptyset$ and every $\pi : U \to \{0,1\}$, $\mathrm{AMA}^*(\pi) \leq \mathrm{MOST}^*(\pi)$.

Proof
Obvious by definition. ■

Now, we try to define the quantifier

- "for many elements ... "

denoted by MANY.

Definition 2.14

$$\mathrm{MANY}(\pi) =_{def} \begin{cases} 1 & \text{if } \exists V(V \subseteq U \wedge \operatorname{card} V \leq \operatorname{card}(U \setminus V) \\ & \qquad \wedge \{x \mid x \in U \wedge \pi(x) = 1\} \supseteq U \setminus V) \\ 0 & \text{else.} \end{cases}$$

Proposition 2.8

1. For every U and every $\pi : U \to \{0,1\}$,
$$\mathrm{MOST}(\pi) \le \mathrm{MANY}(\pi).$$
2. If U is finite then for every $\pi : U \to \{0,1\}$,
$$\mathrm{MANY}(\pi) = 1 \text{ if and only if } \operatorname{card}\{x \mid x \in U \wedge \pi(x) = 0\} \le \operatorname{card}\{x \mid x \in U \wedge \pi(x) = 1\}.$$

Proof
ad 1 Obvious by definitions.
ad 2 Like assertion 3 of proposition 2.6.

■

Remarks on proposition 2.8

1. Assertion 1 fits our intuition.
2. Assume $\operatorname{card} U = 1000$, $\operatorname{card}\{x \mid x \in U \wedge \pi_1(x) = 1\} = 500$, $\operatorname{card}\{x \mid x \in U \wedge \pi_2(x) = 1\} = 499$. Then $\mathrm{MANY}(\pi_1) = 1$, but $\mathrm{MANY}(\pi_2) = 0$ which is a counter-intuitive result. Therefore we put

Definition 2.15
$$\mathrm{MANY}^*(\pi) =_{def} \begin{cases} \mathrm{MANY}(\pi) & \text{if } U \text{ is infinite} \\ \sqrt{\mathrm{MOST}(\pi)} & \text{if } U \text{ is finite.} \end{cases}$$

Proposition 2.9
For every $U \neq \emptyset$ and every $\pi : U \to \{0,1\}$,
$$\mathrm{AMA}^*(\pi) \le \mathrm{MOST}^*(\pi) \le \mathrm{MANY}^*(\pi).$$

Remark on definitions 2.13 and 2.15 Instead of $\sqrt{\ }$ we could also use functions $\varphi, \psi : \langle 0,1\rangle \to \langle 0,1\rangle$ with $\varphi(1) = \psi(1) = 1$ and $\forall r (r \in \langle 0,1\rangle \wedge 0 \le r < 1 \to r < \varphi(r) \wedge r < \psi(r))$.

3 A Typology of Quantifiers

The following considerations are based only on the set $\{0,1\}$ and the set $\langle 0,1\rangle$ of logical values, respectively.

Remember that $\Pi(U)$ and $\mathrm{F}\Pi(U)$ are the sets of all mappings $\pi : U \to \{0,1\}$ and $F : U \to \langle 0,1\rangle$, respectively.

Definition 3.1

1. Q is said to be a crisp-crisp quantifier (or a quantifier of type I) on U $=_{def}$ $Q : \Pi(U) \to \{0,1\}$

2. Q is said to be a crisp-fuzzy quantifier (or a quantifier of type II) on U $=_{def}$ $Q : \Pi(U) \to \langle 0,1 \rangle$
3. Q is said to be a fuzzy-crisp quantifier (or a quantifier of type III) on U $=_{def}$ $Q : \mathrm{F}\Pi(U) \to \{0,1\}$
4. Q is said to be a fuzzy-fuzzy quantifier (or a quantifier of type IV) on U $=_{def}$ $Q : \mathrm{F}\Pi(U) \to \langle 0,1 \rangle$

For every $i \in \{\mathrm{I}, \mathrm{II}, \mathrm{III}, \mathrm{IV}\}$ the set of all quantifiers of type i on U is denoted by $\mathrm{QUANT}(U, i)$.

Let Q_1, Q_2 and Q_3, Q_4 be quantifiers of type II on U and of type IV on U, respectively. Then we define

Definition 3.2
1. $Q_1 \subseteq Q_2$
   $=_{def}$ For every $\pi \in \Pi(U)$, $Q_1(\pi) \leq Q_2(\pi)$.
2. $Q_3 \subseteq' Q_4$
   $=_{def}$ For every $F \in \mathrm{F}\Pi(U)$, $Q_3(F) \leq Q_4(F)$.

Proposition 3.1
1. $[\mathrm{QUANT}(U, \mathrm{I}), \subseteq]$ and $[\mathrm{QUANT}(U, \mathrm{III}), \subseteq']$ are complete BOOLEan algebras.
2. $[\mathrm{QUANT}(U, \mathrm{II}), \subseteq]$ and $[\mathrm{QUANT}(U, \mathrm{IV}), \subseteq']$ are complete DEMORGAN algebras.

Quantifiers of type I have been extensively investigated in two-valued logic. Methods for their finer classification are sketched in section 2 as extensional and cardinality quantifiers, respectively.

Quantifiers of type II are introduced in section 2 in order to formulate definitions for "almost all", "most" and "many" which fit our intuition.

Quantifiers of type III are two-valued predicates on $\mathrm{F}\Pi(U)$ indicating two-valued properties of a given fuzzy set $F : U \to \langle 0,1 \rangle$, for instance, that

- F is normal
- F is empty
- F is finite, i. e. its support is finite

etc. The study of such predicates as quantifiers (of type III) has still to be tackled.

Quantifiers of type IV play an important role in fuzzy logic and have been investigated in many papers. Therefore we shall consider such quantifiers in the rest of this paper.

4 The Concept of a General Fuzzy Quantifier

As in section 2 we start with an arbitrary type

$$\mathfrak{U} = \left[\left[U_1^1, \dots U_{m_1}^1\right], \dots, \left[U_1^n, \dots U_{m_n}^n\right]\right]$$

of non-empty universes U_j^i.

Again following MOSTOWSKI, RESCHER and ZADEH we define

Definition 4.1
FQ is said to be a general fuzzy quantifier of type $\mathfrak{U}$
$=_{def}$ $FQ : \mathrm{F}\Pi\left(U_1^1, \dots, U_{m_1}^1\right) \times \dots \times \mathrm{F}\Pi\left(U_1^n, \dots, U_{m_n}^n\right) \to \langle 0, 1\rangle$.

As in section 2 we restrict our considerations to the special case $n = 1$ and $m_1 = 1$ and put

Definition 4.2
FQ is said to be a general fuzzy quantifier on U
$=_{def}$ $FQ : \mathrm{F}\Pi(U) \to \langle 0, 1\rangle$.

Generalizing the property of extensionality we put

Definition 4.3
A fuzzy quantifier FQ on U is said to be extensional
$=_{def}$ There exists a mapping fq with

$$fq : \mathfrak{P}\langle 0, 1\rangle \setminus \{\emptyset\} \to \langle 0, 1\rangle$$

such that for every $F : U \to \langle 0, 1\rangle$,

$$FQ(F) = fq\,\{F(x)\,|\,x \in U\}\,.$$

Very well-known because of their importance are the extensional fuzzy quantifiers "fuzzy-all" and "fuzzy-exists" denoted by FALL and FEX. For every $F : U \to \langle 0, 1\rangle$ they are defined as follows.

Definition 4.4
1. $\mathrm{FALL}(F) =_{def} \inf\{F(x)\,|\,x \in U\}$
2. $\mathrm{FEX}(F) =_{def} \sup\{F(x)\,|\,x \in U\}$

In contrast to two-valued logic where we have exactly eight extensional quantifiers on U in fuzzy logic there exist uncountably many extensional fuzzy quantifiers on U.

An overview and a systematic theory of this class of quantifiers does not exist up to now.

Now, we switch to the definition and investigation of cardinal fuzzy quantifiers, i. e. fuzzy quantifiers for which the value $FQ(F)$ only depends on the "cardinality" of F. Therefore in many papers one can find the conception that in order to define cardinal fuzzy quantifiers first of all one has to define the cardinality of F (see, for instance, [17]). Then faced with an entangling plenty of different definitions of a cardinality of a fuzzy set the authors do not find an approach to a lucid theory of cardinal fuzzy quantifiers.

The starting point of our considerations is the philosophy that for defining the concept of cardinal fuzzy quantifier we do not need the cardinality of F, but we only need that fuzzy sets F and G have the "same" cardinality, expressed by a suitable equivalence relation for fuzzy sets. But with respect to this approach we can adopt corresponding concepts from classical (two-valued) set theory and algebra. Assume F and G are fuzzy sets on U.

Definition 4.5

1. F and G are said to be isomorphic ($F \approx_{iso} G$)
   $=_{def}$ there exists a bijection β of U such that for every $x \in U$, $F(x) = G(\beta(x))$.
2. F and G are said to be cardinality equivalent ($F \approx_{card} G$)
   $=_{def}$ for every $r \in \langle 0, 1 \rangle$ the equation
   $$\mathrm{card}\,\{x \,|\, x \in U \wedge F(x) = r\} = \mathrm{card}\,\{x \,|\, x \in U \wedge G(x) = r\}$$
   holds.
3. F and G are said to be value equivalent ($F \approx_{val} G$)
   $=_{def}$ $\{F(x) \,|\, x \in U\} = \{G(x) \,|\, x \in U\}$

Proposition 4.1
The binary relations $\approx_{iso}$, $\approx_{card}$, and $\approx_{val}$ are equivalence relations on $\mathrm{F}\Pi(U)$.

Proposition 4.2
For arbitrary fuzzy sets F and G on U we have

1. $F \approx_{iso} G$ if and only if $F \approx_{card} G$
2. If $F \approx_{card} G$, then $F \approx_{val} G$.
3. The inversion of 2 does not hold, in general.

Proposition 4.3
A general fuzzy quantifier FQ on U is extensional if and only if for every fuzzy set F and G on U the condition $F \approx_{val} G$ implies $FQ(F) = FQ(G)$.

Now, we define

Definition 4.6
A general fuzzy quantifier FQ on U is said to be a cardinal fuzzy quantifier
$=_{def}$ for every fuzzy set F and G on U the condition $F \approx_{card} G$ implies $FQ(F) = FQ(G)$.

Proposition 4.4

1. If a general fuzzy quantifier FQ on U is extensional then FQ is a cardinal fuzzy quantifier.
2. A general fuzzy quantifier FQ on U is a cardinal fuzzy quantifier if and only if FQ is "invariant" with respect to isomorphic fuzzy sets, i. e. if for every fuzzy set F and G on U the condition $F \approx_{iso} G$ implies $FQ(F) = FQ(G)$.

5 On the Fuzzification of the Quantifiers EXI, EXF!, AMA, MOST, and MANY

First, we consider only the quantifiers EXI, EXF!, and AMA.

We define fuzzy versions of these quantifiers as follows where $F : U \to \langle 0,1\rangle$, and $\neg F$ is defined by $(\neg F)(x) =_{def} 1 - F(x)$ for every $x \in U$.

Definition 5.1

1. $\mathrm{FEXI}(F) =_{def} \sup\{\inf\{F(x)\,|\,x \in V\}\,|\,V \subseteq U \wedge V \text{ is infinite}\}$
2. $\mathrm{FEXF!}(F) =_{def} \inf\{\inf\{F(x)\,|\,x \in V\}\,|\,V \subseteq U \wedge V \text{ is finite}\}$
3. $\mathrm{FAMA}(F) =_{def} \sup\{\inf\{F(x)\,|\,x \in U \setminus V\}\,|\,V \subseteq U \wedge V \text{ is finite}\}$

Proposition 5.1
The fuzzy quantifiers FEXI, FEXF!, and FAMA are cardinal fuzzy quantifiers.

Proof
By definition and proposition 4.4. ■

Proposition 5.2
For every $F : U \to \langle 0,1\rangle$,

1. $\mathrm{FEXI}(F) = 1 - \mathrm{FAMA}(\neg F)$
2. $\mathrm{FEXF!}(F) = \mathrm{FAMA}(\neg F)$

Proof
By definitions and properties of inf and sup. See also proposition 2.3. ■

Proposition 5.3
For every $\pi : U \to \{0,1\}$,

1. $\mathrm{FEXI}(\pi) = \mathrm{EXI}(\pi)$
2. $\mathrm{FEXF!}(\pi) = \mathrm{EXF!}(\pi)$
3. $\mathrm{FAMA}(\pi) = \mathrm{AMA}(\pi)$

Proof
The assumption $\pi : U \to \{0,1\}$ implies $\pi : U \to \langle 0,1\rangle$. ■

Proposition 5.4
If U is finite then for every $F : U \to \langle 0,1\rangle$,

1. $\mathrm{FEXI}(F) = 0$
2. $\mathrm{FEXF!}(F) = 1$
3. $\mathrm{FAMA}(F) = 1$

Proof
Obviously by definitions. ■

Remark Like proposition 2.4 this result is also counter-intuitive. Therefore we generalize the definition 2.10 of AMA* for fuzzy sets $F : U \to \langle 0,1\rangle$ as follows.

Definition 5.2

$$\mathrm{FAMA}^*(F) =_{def} \begin{cases} \mathrm{FAMA}(F) & \text{if } U \text{ is infinite} \\ \frac{1}{\operatorname{card} U} \cdot \sum\limits_{x\in U} F(x) & \text{else} \end{cases}$$

Remark The definition of $\mathrm{FAMA}^*(F)$ for finite U is closely related to the relative sigma count where the (non-relative) sigma count was introduced by De Luca and Termini in order to define a ("scalar") cardinality of a fuzzy set F on a finite universe U.

With respect to proposition 5.2 we put for every $F : U \to \langle 0,1\rangle$

Definition 5.3

1. $\mathrm{FEXI}^*(F) =_{def} 1 - \mathrm{FAMA}^*(\neg F)$
2. $\mathrm{FEXF!}^*(F) =_{def} \mathrm{FAMA}^*(\neg F)$

Proposition 5.5
The fuzzy quantifiers FAMA*, FEXI*, and FEXF!* are cardinal fuzzy quantifiers.

Proof
Using the definitions. ■

Proposition 5.6
For finite universes U the fuzzy quantifier FAMA* is self-dual, i. e. for every $F : U \to \langle 0,1\rangle$,

$$1 - \mathrm{FAMA}^*(\neg F) = \mathrm{FAMA}^*(F),$$

hence

$$\mathrm{FEXI}^*(F) = \mathrm{FAMA}^*(F).$$

Proof
If U is finite then by definition of FAMA* we have for every $F : U \to \langle 0,1\rangle$

$$\begin{aligned} 1 - \mathrm{FAMA}^*(\neg F) &= 1 - \frac{1}{\operatorname{card} U} \cdot \sum_{x\in U} (1 - F(x)) \\ &= 1 - \frac{1}{\operatorname{card} U} \cdot \left(\operatorname{card} U - \sum_{x\in U} F(x)\right) \\ &= 1 - 1 + \frac{1}{\operatorname{card} U} \cdot \sum_{x\in U} F(x) = \frac{1}{\operatorname{card} U} \cdot \sum_{x\in U} F(x) \\ &= \mathrm{FAMA}^*(F) \end{aligned}$$

■

Now, we consider the quantifiers MOST and MANY.

We generalize the two-valued definitions 2.12 and 2.14 for MOST and MANY, respectively, as follows.

Definition 5.4

1. FMOST(F) $=_{def} \sup\{\inf\{F(x) \,|\, x \in U \setminus V\} \,|\, V \subseteq U \wedge \operatorname{card} V < \operatorname{card}(U \setminus V)\}$
2. FMANY(F) $=_{def} \sup\{\inf\{F(x) \,|\, x \in U \setminus V\} \,|\, V \subseteq U \wedge \operatorname{card} V \leq \operatorname{card}(U \setminus V)\}$

Proposition 5.7

1. If $\operatorname{card} U > \aleph_0$ then for every $F : U \to \langle 0, 1 \rangle$,

$$\text{FAMA}(F) \leq \text{FMOST}(F) \leq \text{FMANY}(F).$$

2. If $\operatorname{card} U = \aleph_0$ then for every $F : U \to \langle 0, 1 \rangle$,

$$\text{FAMA}(F) = \text{FMOST}(F) \leq \text{FMANY}(F).$$

Proof

Like proposition 2.6. ■

Remark For finite U we get the same counter-intuitive results as described in the remarks on proposition 2.6 and on proposition 2.8. Therefore we define

Definition 5.5

1. $\text{FMOST}^*(\pi) =_{def} \begin{cases} \text{FMOST}(\pi) & \text{if } U \text{ is infinite} \\ \sqrt{\text{FAMA}^*(\pi)} & \text{if } U \text{ is finite.} \end{cases}$
2. $\text{FMANY}^*(\pi) =_{def} \begin{cases} \text{FMANY}(\pi) & \text{if } U \text{ is infinite} \\ \sqrt{\text{FMOST}^*(\pi)} & \text{if } U \text{ is finite.} \end{cases}$

Proposition 5.8

For every U and every $F : U \to \langle 0, 1 \rangle$,

$$\text{FAMA}^*(F) \leq \text{FMOST}^*(F) \leq \text{FMANY}^*(F).$$

Remark The remarks made on definition 2.13 and 2.15 are also applicable to definition 5.5.

6 On t-Quantifiers and s-Quantifiers

We start with the (trivial) observation that the extensional fuzzy quantifiers FALL and FEX can be generated by iteration of the t-norm min and the s-norm max, respectively. Basis of this iterative construction is the fact that both of the functions min and max are commutative and associative.

If we accept that beside the functions min and max other t- and s-norms play an important role both in theory and practice we are faced with the problem to consider and to apply iterations of such norms. Infinite iterations of t- and s-norms lead to the concept of t-quantifier and s-quantifier, respectively [30].

Let φ be an arbitrary function with $\varphi : \langle 0,1\rangle^2 \rightarrow \langle 0,1\rangle$, in special cases let φ be a t-norm or an s-norm. By induction on the integer $n \geq 1$ we define an n-ary function $\varphi^n : \langle 0,1\rangle^n \rightarrow \langle 0,1\rangle$ as follows where $r_1, \ldots, r_n, \ldots \in \langle 0,1\rangle$.

Definition 6.1

1. $\varphi^1(r_1) =_{def} r_1$
2. $\varphi^{n+1}(r_1, \ldots, r_{n+1}) =_{def} \varphi(\varphi^n(r_1, \ldots, r_n))$

Remark We underline that for formulating definition 6.1 as well as for formulating the following definitions 6.2 and 6.3 we do not need any additional properties of the function φ.

Only for formulating and proving corresponding theorems we shall introduce certain assumptions.

Now, using the infinite sequence of the functions $\varphi^1, \ldots, \varphi^n, \ldots$ we define the "fuzzy-all-quantifier" FALL(φ) and the "fuzzy-ex-quantifier" FEX(φ) generated by the function φ.

As an appropriate abbreviation we introduce SET(φ, F).

Definition 6.2

$$\mathrm{SET}(\varphi, F) =_{def} \left\{ \varphi(F(x_1), \ldots, F(x_n)) \middle| \begin{array}{l} n \in \mathbb{N} \wedge n \geq 1 \wedge x_1, \ldots, x_n \in U \\ \wedge \forall i \forall j (1 \leq i < j \leq n \rightarrow x_i \neq x_j) \end{array} \right\}$$

Then we define

Definition 6.3

1. $\mathrm{FALL}(\varphi)(F) =_{def} \inf \mathrm{SET}(\varphi, F)$
2. $\mathrm{FEX}(\varphi)(F) =_{def} \sup \mathrm{SET}(\varphi, F)$

The generating procedure from φ to FALL(φ) and FEX(φ) can be hard if the set SET(φ, F) is infinite.

Obviously, we have the following

Lemma 6.1

1. If φ is a t-norm and $\mathrm{supp}\, \neg F$ is finite then SET(φ, F) is finite.
2. If φ is an s-norm (t-conorm) and $\mathrm{supp}\, F$ is finite then SET(φ, F) is finite.

Therefore we introduce the following weakly generated fuzzy quantifiers WFALL(φ) and WFEX(φ) as follows.

Definition 6.4

1. $\mathrm{WFALL}(\varphi)(F) =_{def} \begin{cases} \inf \mathrm{SET}(\varphi, F) & \text{if } \operatorname{supp} \neg F \text{ is finite} \\ 0 & \text{else.} \end{cases}$
2. $\mathrm{WFEX}(\varphi)(F) =_{def} \begin{cases} \sup \mathrm{SET}(\varphi, F) & \text{if } \operatorname{supp} F \text{ is finite} \\ 1 & \text{else.} \end{cases}$

Remark By definition we obtain that for every U and every $F : U \to \langle 0, 1\rangle$,

1. $\mathrm{WFALL}(\varphi)(F) \leq \mathrm{FALL}(\varphi)(F)$ and
2. $\mathrm{FEX}(\varphi)(F) \leq \mathrm{WFEX}(\varphi)(F)$.

In [20] one can find necessary and sufficient conditions for φ such that WFALL(φ) coincides with FALL(φ) and WFEX(φ) with FEX(φ), respectively.

In order to investigate whether a fuzzy quantifier FQ can be generated by a function φ in the sense of definition 6.3 or definition 6.4 we define the generation of a binary function $\varphi : \langle 0, 1\rangle^2 \to \langle 0, 1\rangle$ by a given fuzzy quantifier FQ on U.

Remember that $\boldsymbol{\emptyset}$ and $\boldsymbol{U}$ are fuzzy sets such that for every $x \in U$,

$$\boldsymbol{\emptyset}(x) = 0$$
$$\text{and} \quad \boldsymbol{U}(x) = 1$$

hold. Remember furthermore that for arbitrary fuzzy sets F and G the relation $F \subseteq G$ is defined by $\forall x(x \in U \to F(x) \leq G(x))$. For arbitrary $r \in \langle 0, 1\rangle$, $F : U \to \langle 0, 1\rangle$, and $x, y \in U$ we define

$$F\langle x := r\rangle (y) =_{def} \begin{cases} r & \text{if } y = x \\ F(y) & \text{if } y \neq x. \end{cases}$$

Furthermore, for $r, s \in \langle 0, 1\rangle$ and $x, y \in U$ with $x \neq y$ we put

$$F\langle x, y := r, s\rangle =_{def} (F\langle x := r\rangle)\langle y := s\rangle .$$

Now, we assume that $\operatorname{card} U \geq 2$. We fix $x, y \in U$ with $x \neq y$. With respect to the fixed elements x and y we define a t-generated binary function $TF_{x,y}(FQ)$ and an s-generated binary function $SF_{x,y}(FQ)$ as follows where $r, s \in \langle 0, 1\rangle$.

Definition 6.5

1. $TF_{x,y}(FQ)(r, s) =_{def} FQ(\boldsymbol{U}\langle x, y := r, s\rangle)$
2. $SF_{x,y}(FQ)(r, s) =_{def} FQ(\boldsymbol{\emptyset}\langle x, y := r, s\rangle)$

For describing t-quantifiers and s-quantifiers, respectively, we introduce the following axioms.

1. TBORDER (the border condition for t-quantifiers)

$$\forall x \forall r (x \in U \wedge r \in \langle 0,1\rangle \rightarrow FQ(U \langle x := r\rangle) = r)$$

2. SBORDER (the border condition for s-quantifiers)

$$\forall x \forall r (x \in U \wedge r \in \langle 0,1\rangle \rightarrow FQ(\emptyset \langle x := r\rangle) = r)$$

3. MONOT (the monotonicity)

$$\forall F \forall G (F, G \in \mathrm{F}\Pi(U) \wedge F \subseteq G \rightarrow FQ(F) \leq FQ(G))$$

4. COM/ASS (the combined commutativity and associativity)

$$\begin{aligned} &\forall x \forall y \forall F \forall G (x, y \in U \wedge F, G \in \mathrm{F}\Pi(U) \\ &\quad \rightarrow FQ(F \langle x := FQ(G)\rangle) = FQ(G \langle y := FQ(F \langle x := G(y)\rangle)\rangle)) \end{aligned}$$

5. TWCOM/ASS (the t-weak combined commutativity and associativity)

$$\begin{aligned} &\forall x \forall y \forall F \forall G (x, y \in U \wedge F, G \in \mathrm{F}\Pi(U) \wedge \operatorname{supp} \neg F, \operatorname{supp} \neg G \text{ are finite} \\ &\quad \rightarrow FQ(F \langle x := FQ(G)\rangle) = FQ(G \langle y := FQ(F \langle x := G(y)\rangle)\rangle)) \end{aligned}$$

6. SWCOM/ASS (the s-weak combined commutativity and associativity)

$$\begin{aligned} &\forall x \forall y \forall F \forall G (x, y \in U \wedge F, G \in \mathrm{F}\Pi(U) \wedge \operatorname{supp} F, \operatorname{supp} G \text{ are finite} \\ &\quad \rightarrow FQ(F \langle x := FQ(G)\rangle) = FQ(G \langle y := FQ(F \langle x := G(y)\rangle)\rangle)) \end{aligned}$$

So, we define

Definition 6.6

1. FQ is said to be an (extensional) t-fuzzy-quantifier
   $=_{def}$ FQ is an (extensional) fuzzy quantifier which satisfies the axioms TBORDER, MONOT, and TWCOM/ASS.
2. FQ is said to be an (extensional) s-fuzzy-quantifier
   $=_{def}$ FQ is an (extensional) fuzzy quantifier which satisfies the axioms SBORDER, MONOT, and SWCOM/ASS.

We have the following theorems.

Theorem 6.2
If φ is a t-norm then

1. FALL(φ) is an extensional t-fuzzy quantifier on U and
2. for every $x, y \in U$ with $x \neq y$, $TF_{x,y}(\mathrm{FALL}(\varphi)) = \varphi$.

Theorem 6.3
If FQ is an extensional t-fuzzy quantifier on U then for every $x, y \in U$ with $x \neq y$,

1. $TF_{x,y}(FQ)$ is a t-norm and
2. $\text{FALL}(TF_{x,y}(FQ)) = FQ$.

Theorem 6.4
If φ is an s-norm (t-conorm) then

1. $\text{FEX}(\varphi)$ is an extensional s-fuzzy quantifier on U and
2. for every $x, y \in U$ with $x \neq y$, $SF_{x,y}(\text{FEX}(\varphi)) = \varphi$.

Theorem 6.5
If FQ is an extensional s-fuzzy quantifier on U then for every $x, y \in U$ with $x \neq y$,

1. $SF_{x,y}(FQ)$ is an s-norm and
2. $\text{FEX}(SF_{x,y}(FQ)) = FQ$.

Definition 6.7
1. FQ is said to be a modified (extensional) t-fuzzy-quantifier
   $=_{def}$ FQ is an (extensional) fuzzy quantifier which satisfies the axioms TBORDER, MONOT, and COM/ASS.
2. FQ is said to be a modified (extensional) s-fuzzy-quantifier
   $=_{def}$ FQ is an (extensional) fuzzy quantifier which satisfies the axioms SBORDER, MONOT, and COM/ASS.

Theorem 6.6
If φ is a t-norm then

1. $\text{WFALL}(\varphi)$ is a modified extensional t-fuzzy quantifier on U and
2. for every $x, y \in U$ with $x \neq y$, $TF_{x,y}(\text{WFALL}(\varphi)) = \varphi$.

Theorem 6.7
If FQ is a modified extensional t-fuzzy quantifier on U then for every $x, y \in U$ with $x \neq y$,

1. $TF_{x,y}(FQ)$ is a t-norm and
2. $\text{WFALL}(TF_{x,y}(FQ)) = FQ$.

Theorem 6.8
If φ is an s-norm (t-conorm) then

1. $\text{WFEX}(\varphi)$ is a modified extensional s-fuzzy quantifier on U and
2. for every $x, y \in U$ with $x \neq y$, $SF_{x,y}(\text{WFEX}(\varphi)) = \varphi$.

Theorem 6.9
If FQ is a modified extensional s-fuzzy quantifier on U then for every $x, y \in U$ with $x \neq y$,

1. $SF_{x,y}(FQ)$ is an s-norm and
2. $\mathrm{WFEX}(SF_{x,y}(FQ)) = FQ$.

Adopting the concept of compactness used for entailment operators in formalized languages we define for fuzzy quantifiers FQ on U.

Assume $F : U \to \langle 0,1 \rangle$, $V \subseteq U$, $r \in \langle 0,1 \rangle$, and $x \in U$.

Definition 6.8

$$F_V^r(x) =_{def} \begin{cases} F(x) & \text{if } x \in V \\ r & \text{if } x \in U \setminus V \end{cases}$$

Definition 6.9

1. FQ is said to be t-compact
$$=_{def} \forall F(F \in \mathrm{F}\Pi(U) \wedge FQ(F) > 0 \rightarrow \exists V(V \subseteq U \wedge V \text{ is finite} \wedge FQ(F) = FQ(F_V^1)))$$
2. FQ is said to be s-compact
$$=_{def} \forall F(F \in \mathrm{F}\Pi(U) \wedge FQ(F) < 1 \rightarrow \exists V(V \subseteq U \wedge V \text{ is finite} \wedge FQ(F) = FQ(F_V^0)))$$

Then we have the following theorems.

Theorem 6.10
FQ is a modified extensional t-fuzzy quantifier on U if and only if FQ is a t-compact extensional t-fuzzy quantifier.

Theorem 6.11
FQ is a modified extensional s-fuzzy quantifier on U if and only if FQ is an s-compact extensional s-fuzzy quantifier.

Acknowledgement

The author wishes to thank ULRICH FIESELER for his help in preparing the manuscript.

References

1. J. BARWISE and R. COOPER. *Generalized Quantifiers and Natural Language.* Linguistics and Philosophy **4**, 159–219, 1980.
2. J. BARWISE and F. FEFERMAN (editors). *Model-Theoretic Logics.* Perspectives in Mathematical Logics. Springer-Verlag, 1985.
3. P. BOSC and L. LIETARD. *Monotonic quantified statements and fuzzy integrals.* In: *Proc. 1st Internat. Joint Conf. of NAFIPS, IFIS and NASA*, pages 8–12, 1994.

4. Didier Dubois and Henri Prade. *Fuzzy cardinality and the modeling of imprecise quantification.* Fuzzy Sets and Systems **16**, 199–230, 1985.
5. Didier Dubois and Henri Prade. *On fuzzy syllogisms.* Computational Intelligence **4**, 171–179, 1988.
6. J. van Eijck. *Generalized quantifiers and traditional logic.* In: J. van Benthem et al. (editors), *Generalized Quantifiers, Theory and Applications.* Foris, 1985.
7. Kurt Gödel. *Die Vollständigkeit der Axiome des logischen Funktionenkalküls.* Monatshefte für Mathematik und Physik **37**, 349–360, 1930.
8. Siegfried Gottwald. *A Note on Fuzzy Cardinals.* Kybernetika **16**, 156–158, 1980.
9. Siegfried Gottwald. *Fuzzy Sets and Fuzzy Logic. Foundations of Application—from a Mathematical Point of View.* Vieweg, Braunschweig, Wiesbaden, 1993.
10. R. Hähnle. *Commodious axiomatization of quantifiers in multiple-valued logic.* In: *The Twenty-Sixth International Symposium on Multiple-Valued Logic*, Santiago de Compostela, Spain, May 29–31, 1996.
11. K. Härtig. *Über einen Quantifikator mit zwei Wirkungsbereichen.* In: *Proceedings*, pages 31–36, Tihany, Hungary, 1962.
12. Kurt Hauschild. *Zum Vergleich von Härtigquantor und Rescherquantor.* Zeitschrift für Mathematische Logik und Grundlagen der Mathematik **27**, 255–264, 1981.
13. L. Hella. *Definability hierarchies of generalized quantifiers.* Ann. Math. Logic 1990.
14. L. Kalmár. *Contributions to the reduction theory of the decision problem. Fourth paper: Reduction to the case of a finite set of individuals.* Acta Mathematica Academiae Scientiarum Hungaricae **2**, 125–142, 1951.
15. H. J. Keisler. *Logic with the Quantifier "there exists uncountably many".* Ann. Math. Logic **1**, 1–93, 1970.
16. P. Lindström. *First order predicate logic with generalized quantifiers.* Theoria **32**, 186–195, 1966.
17. Yaxin Liu and Etienne E. Kerre. *An overview of fuzzy quantifiers. (I). Interpretations.* Fuzzy Sets and Systems **95**, 1–21, 1998.
18. Yaxin Liu and Etienne E. Kerre. *An overview of fuzzy quantifiers. (II). Reasoning and applications.* Fuzzy Sets and Systems **95**, 135–146, 1998.
19. Aldo De Luca and Settimo Termini. *A definition of a non-probabilistic entropy in the setting of fuzzy sets theory.* Information and Control **20**, 301–312, 1972.
20. Radko Mesiar and Helmut Thiele. *On T-quantifiers and S-quantifiers.* To appear.
21. A. Mostowski. *On a generalization of quantifiers.* Fundamenta mathematicae **44**, 12–36, 1957.
22. Vilém Novák. *Fuzzy Sets and Their Applications.* Adam Hilger, Bristol, Philadelphia, 1989.
23. P. Peterson. *On the Logic of Few, Many and Most.* Notre Dame J. Formal Logic **20**, 155–179, 1979.
24. Henri Prade. *A note on the evaluation of conditions involving vague quantifiers in presence of imprecise or uncertain information.* Bull. Stud. Exchanges Fuzziness Appl. (BUSEFAL) **32**, 1987.

25. D. Ralescu. *Cardinality, quantifiers, and the aggregation of fuzzy criteria.* Fuzzy Sets and Systems **69**, 355–365, 1995.
26. N. Rescher. *Plurality-quantification (abstract).* The Journal of Symbolic Logic **27**, 373–374, 1962.
27. N. Rescher. *Many-valued Logic.* McGraw-Hill Book Company, 1969.
28. R. Rovatti and C. Fantuzzi. *s-norm aggregation of infinite collections.* Fuzzy Sets and Systems **84**, 255–269, 1996.
29. Helmut Thiele. *On Fuzzy Quantifiers.* In: *Proceedings: Fifth International Fuzzy Systems Association World Congress '93*, volume I, pages 395–398, Seoul, Korea, July 4–9, 1993.
30. Helmut Thiele. *On T-Quantifiers and S-Quantifiers.* In: *The Twenty-Fourth International Symposium on Multiple-Valued Logic*, pages 264–269, Boston, Massachusetts, May 22–25, 1994.
31. Helmut Thiele. *On the Concept of Cardinal Number for Fuzzy Sets.* In: *EUFIT '94—European Congress on Fuzzy and Intelligent Technologies*, volume 1, pages 504–516, Aachen, Germany, September 20–23, 1994. Invited Paper.
32. Helmut Thiele. *On Fuzzy Quantifiers.* In: Z. Bien and K. C. Min (editors), *Fuzzy Logic and its Applications, Information Systems, and Intelligent Systems*, pages 343–352. Kluwer Academic Publishers, Dordrecht, 1995.
33. B. A. Trakhtenbrot. *On the algorithmic unsolvability of the decision problem in finite domains (in Russian).* Dokl. Akad. Nauk SSSR **70**, 569–572, 1950.
34. Dag Westerståhl. *Quantifiers in Formal and Natural Languages.* In: D. Gabbay and F. Guenthner (editors), *Handbook of Philosophical Logic*, volume IV, pages 1–131. Reidel, Dordrecht, 1989.
35. Maciej Wygralak. *Vaguely Defined Objects.* Kluwer Academic Publishers, Dordrecht, 1995.
36. Ronald R. Yager. *Quantified propositions in a linguistic logic.* International Journal of Man Machine Studies **19**, 195–227, 1983.
37. Ronald R. Yager. *Reasoning with fuzzy quantified statements, part I.* Kybernetes **14**, 233–240, 1985.
38. Ronald R. Yager. *Connectives and Quantifiers in Fuzzy Sets.* Fuzzy Sets and Systems **40**, 39–75, 1991.
39. Ronald R. Yager. *Families of OWA operators.* Fuzzy Sets and Systems **59**, 125–148, 1993.
40. Ronald R. Yager, S. Ovchinnikov, R. M. Tong and H. T. Nguyen (editors). *Fuzzy Sets and Applications — Selected Papers by L. A. Zadeh.* John Wiley & Sons, New York, 1987.
41. Lotfi A. Zadeh. *A computational approach to fuzzy quantifiers in natural language.* Comp. Math. Appl. **9**, 149–184, 1983.
42. Lotfi A. Zadeh. *A computational theory of dispositions.* In: *Proc. 1984 Int. Conference Computational Linguistics*, pages 312–318, 1984. See also [47].
43. Lotfi A. Zadeh. *A theory of commonsense knowledge.* In: H. J. Skala et al. (editors), *Aspects of Vagueness*, pages 257–295. Reidel, Dordrecht, 1984.
44. Lotfi A. Zadeh. *Syllogistic reasoning as a basis for combination of evidence in expert systems.* In: *Proceedings of IJCAL*, pages 417–419, Los Angeles, CA, 1985.
45. Lotfi A. Zadeh. *Syllogistic reasoning in fuzzy logic and its application to usuality and reasoning with dispositions.* IEEE Transactions on Systems, Man, and Cybernetics **15**, 754–763, 1985.

46. Lotfi A. Zadeh. *Dispositional logic and commonsense reasoning.* In: *Proceedings of the Second Annual Artificial Intelligence Forum*, pages 375–389, Moffett-Field, CA, 1987. NASA—Ames Research Center.
47. Lotfi A. Zadeh. *On computational theory of dispositions.* International Journal of Intelligent Systems **2**, 39–63, 1987.
48. Lotfi A. Zadeh. *PRUF — A Meaning Representation Language for Natural Languages.* In: Yager et al. [40], pages 499–568.
49. Lotfi A. Zadeh. *Test-score semantics as a basis for a computational approach to the representation of meaning.* In: Yager et al. [40], pages 655–684.
50. Lotfi A. Zadeh. *Dispositional logic.* Appl. Math. Lett. **1**, 95–99, 1988.

Evaluating Linguistic Expressions and Functional Fuzzy Theories in Fuzzy Logic

Vilém Novák

University of Ostrava
Institute for Research and Applications of Fuzzy Modeling
Bráfova 7, 70100 Ostrava 1, Czech Republic

and

Institute of the Theory of Information and Automation
Academy of Sciences of the Czech Republic
Pod vodárenskou věží 4, 186 02 Praha 8, Czech Republic

Irina Perfilieva

Moscow State Academy of Instrument Making
Stromynka 20, 107846 Moscow, Russia

Abstract

In this paper, we introduce a new mathematical model of the meaning of the basic linguistic trichotomy, which are the canonical words "small", "medium" and "big". The model is based on the concept of *horizon* as elaborated in the Alternative Set Theory. Such a model makes also possible to include naturally the linguistic hedges which form a consistent class of functions. Each linguistic hedge is thus characterized by one number only.

Then it is shown that continuous functional dependences between x and y can be described (precisely or approximately) by the collections of logical formulas of implicative form with predicates interpreted by fuzzy sets with meaning of the basic linguistic trichotomy. It demonstrates the expressive power of modified by linguistic hedges membership functions of fuzzy sets from the basic triplet.

1 Introduction

One of the most important features of fuzzy set theory which made it very attractive for applications is its potential for modelling of the meaning of natural language expressions. Most works done on this topic either continue directly, or have been inspired by the works of L. A. Zadeh (see e.g., [23, 24, 25, 26]). He focused on some parts of natural language, mostly those which correspond to the so called *evaluating linguistic expressions*, i.e. the expressions which characterize position on an ordered scale.

[0]This work has been supported by the grant 201/96/0985 of the GA ČR, partially by COST Action 15 and also partially by ZI 104/27-1 (part 436 RUS 113/197/O(R)).

In this paper, we deal with two problems. First, we propose the model of the meaning of simple *linguistic evaluating expressions* of the form

$$\langle\text{linguistic modifier}\rangle\langle\text{atomic term}\rangle, \tag{1}$$

which is based on modification of the corresponding fuzzy sets.

The second problem elaborated in this paper is formalization of the linguistic characterization of functions in fuzzy logic and their approximation properties.

The *atomic terms* in (1) characterize various properties of objects such as "small, medium, big, slim, stout, sour, sweet", etc. The *linguistic modifiers* (often called also *linguistic hedges*) specify various nuances of properties. In general, they modify the meaning of the atomic terms before which they stand. The leading role among them is played by words such as "very, extremely, roughly ", etc.

It is easy to see that these properties form ordered linguistic scales. Inherent vaguenes of the above considered terms then makes us possible to characterize the set of objects using three basic atomic terms, namely ⟨small, medium, big⟩, ⟨slim, normal, stout⟩, etc. As *canonical*, we take the triple ⟨small, medium, big⟩.

The deliberation leading to our model of the meaning of (1) is based on the concept of *horizon* and its *shift*. Starting from this, we obtain the model of the meaning both of the basic linguistic triple as well as of the linguistic modifiers using specific fuzzy sets. This approach makes possible to give systematic representation of (1) by a unified parametric class of membership functions. The mathematical outcome of this approach is that all the membership functions modeling the meaning of the evaluating expressions (1) are composed of simple functions of two kinds, called Z- and S-functions. We will mention also practical applications of this theory.

2 The meaning of simple evaluating linguistic expressions

2.1 Basic linguistic triple of atomic terms

2.1.1 The concept of horizon and finite numbers

The accepted form of the membership functions modelling the meaning of the basic linguistic triple are Z-, S- and Π-functions (see Fig. 1). Notable on their form is the following: first, there is a kernel consisting of the elements which surely have the property in concern (i.e., elements which are surely "small, medium" or "big"). Second, when getting farther from the kernel (to the right or left), the truth that the elements have this property decreases until the point is reached when it vanishes completely. Let us remark that this course is justified by the intuition and some psychological experiments. The functions used in order to expres the described course are mostly of one of the three kinds: linear, quadratic, and exponential.

However, the question raises, whether is it possible to find also other arguments in favour of the above described course and possible, the used functions. To this goal, we will employ the concept of *finite numbers* which seems to be related to the meaning of the atomic term *small*. The working mathematical model of finite and infinite numbers can be found, for example, in the Alternative

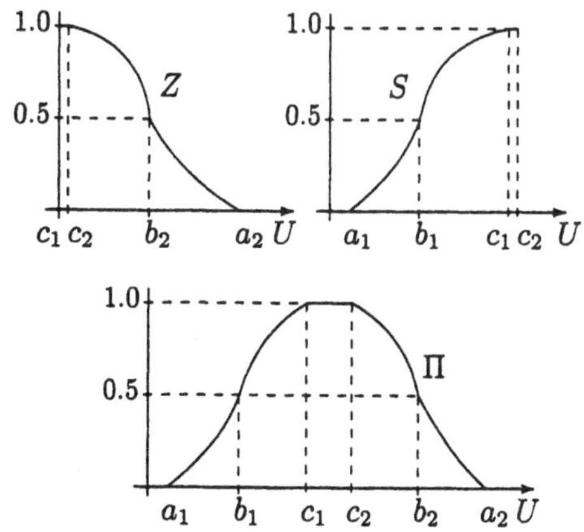

Figure 1: Typical membership functions of the basic linguistic triple.

Set Theory (AST) [22] and in non-standard analysis (cf. [4]), and a simplified one not leaving classical mathematics is constructed also in fuzzy logic.

Let us briefly mention the main idea of finite and infinite numbers in these theories. In classical set theory, infinity is taken as imposibility to reach the end; whatever number is at our disposal but we cannot regard the end of the inifinite set of all numbers. On the other hand, the AST begins with the observation that big finite numbers behave as infinite ones (for demonstration, see [22]). We come to a new understanding of infinity and therefore, we may distinguish between finite and infinite numbers. The infinity of some number n stems from our *inability to verify* whether n is finite. For example, there is no direct way how to verify that the number 1, 000, 000, 005 is indeed finite[1]. Hence, some (classically finite!) numbers are thus finite and some are infinite. However, there is no clear border between them and, consequently, there is no last finite number. We may distinguish finite numbers from infinite ones but we are not able to say about *each* number whether it is finite or not. Note that the finiteness is there a synonym for transparency, i.e. when seeing a finite number, we are able to verify easily that this is indeed the case. The fundamental concept on the basis of which finite numbers are constructed in AST is that of *horizon*, which represents the border between finite and infinite numbers. The horizon is seen by the *observer* (identified with the number 0). Precise specification of the position of the horizon, however, is not possible[2].

In this paper, we use these ideas for construction of the meaning of the basic linguistic triples. This provides us with a unified way how the membership functions can be constructed. Furthermore, the model of linguistic modifiers is naturally included in a way to extend the unification of membership functions to all (or, at least, a wide subclass of) evaluating expressions of the form (1).

For our purposes, the direct application of the AST is unnecessary and therefore, we use fuzzy logic to obtain a possible mathematical model of the horizon

[1]Sitting and counting, say 1, 000, 000, 005 sticks would be ungrateful work with uncertain ending — could we be sure that we did not make a mistake?

[2]All these concepts and much more have been explained in detail in [22] and from the point of view of natural language discussed also in [15].

and finite numbers. Its idea follows the principles discussed above, i.e. that finiteness of a number means the *ability to verify* it. This may be imagined, for example, as a necessity to count a number of lines written on a paper. For numbers 0 or 1, we immediately see that this is indeed the case (we immediately see no or one line). However, verification that x is finite does not generally imply that we will be able to verify finiteness of $x+1$ with the same effort. Verification of the finiteness of the latter requires to repeat the same procedure we did for x. For example, if we verify that 1000 is finite by counting one thousand lines then verification that 1001 is also finite means that we have to count one line more, i.e. our effort to verify finiteness of 1001 is a little (imperceptibly) greater than that for 1000. In fuzzy logic, we will measure this effort by the *degree of truth*, i.e. less effort means higher truth degree and vice-versa.

Let $\mathbb{FN}(x)$ denote the proposition "the number x is finite". Then the above discussion justifies the formula $\mathbb{FN}(x) \Rightarrow \mathbb{FN}(x+1)$ to be true only in a degree $1-\varepsilon$ where ε is some small number. Starting from this, we may formally construct the fuzzy set of finite numbers — the numbers laying between the observer identified with 0 and the horizon.

The formal demonstration that such a procedure is reasonable is given by the following theorem.

Theorem 1 *Let T be a fuzzy theory which includes Peano arithmetics and $\varepsilon > 0$. Let $\mathbb{FN}$ be a new predicate. Then the fuzzy theory*

$$T^+ = T \cup \{{}^1/\mathbb{FN}(0), {}^{1-\varepsilon}/(\forall x)(\mathbb{FN}(x) \Rightarrow \mathbb{FN}(x+1), {}^1/(\exists x)\neg\mathbb{FN}(x)\}$$

is a conservative extension of T.

For details and the proof see [13, 15]. The theory T^+ conservatively introduces a predicate $\mathbb{FN}$ which has the properties assumed for finite numbers, namely that 0 is surely finite, that $\mathbb{FN}(x) \Rightarrow \mathbb{FN}(x+1)$ is not surely true and, finally, that there surely exists a number which is not finite.

When interpreting $\mathbb{FN}$ from this theorem, we obtain the following formula for the *fuzzy set* $\mathbb{FN}$ of finite numbers:

$$\mathbb{FN}(x) = \max\{0, (1-\varepsilon)^x\} = \max\{0, 1-\varepsilon x\} \tag{2}$$

where the power is taken with respect to the Łukasiewicz product defined by

$$a \otimes b = \max\{0, a+b-1\}, \qquad a, b \in [0,1].$$

In [15], several important properties of such fuzzy set are also demonstrated.

The *position of the horizon* is given by the least x such that $\mathbb{FN}(x) = 0$. We easily see that the bigger is ε, the sooner we reach the horizon, i.e. $\mathbb{FN}(x) = 0$ for smaller x. Thus, the magnitude of the number ε determines the "distance of the horizon" from 0.

Due to formula (2), the horizon is approached linearly by uniform decreasing of the truth of $\mathbb{FN}(x)$ with the increase of x. However, it follows from our discussion that the effort to verify finiteness could increase more rapidly when moving farther from the observer. Consequently, the approach to the horizon might be non-linear. Formula (2) can be made non-linear when considering ε to be dependent on x, i.e. ε is taken as a function $\varepsilon : \mathbb{R} \longrightarrow \mathbb{R}$. Then (2) takes the form

$$\mathbb{FN}(x) = \max\{0, 1-\varepsilon(x)\cdot x\}. \tag{3}$$

The $\varepsilon(x)$ will be called the *horizon approach* function.

2.1.2 Canonical membership functions of "Small" and "Big"

In this section, we apply the above reasoning to the model of the linguistic meaning of the linguistic expressions (1). The existence of the basic linguistic triples demonstrates that people always tend to classify three positions on an ordered scale, namely "the leftmost" (the smallest), "the rightmost" (the biggest), and "in the middle". This observation has also been experimentally verified, e.g. in [10]. Hence, we may find three points on which we base this classification.

Let an ordered universe U be given. Without loss of generality, we put

$$U = [u, v] \subseteq \mathbb{R} \tag{4}$$

where $\mathbb{R}$ is the real line. The above considered three points ("leftmost", "rightmost" and "center") are u, v and $s \in U$, $u < s < v$, respectively. We put $L = [u, s]$ and $R = [s, v]$. Observe that the point s needs not necessarily lay in the exact middle of $[u, v]$. The reason is that big values are less distinguishable than small ones (cf., e.g., the discussion in [6]).

The meaning of *small* is obtained when realizing that the border of small numbers lays "somewhere to the right from u". The *u is the position of the observer* and there is no last small number — we may encounter only horizon of small numbers runnig "somewhere towards big ones". Thus, small numbers behave similarly as finite ones and it seems natural to identify the former with the latter.

Using (3), we will construct the *canonical fuzzy set $Sm \underset{\sim}{\subset} L$ of small* (numbers) with the membership function given by

$$Sm(x) = 1 - \varepsilon_{Sm}(x, a, c)x \tag{5}$$

where $\varepsilon_{Sm} : L \longrightarrow [0, 1]$ is a non-decreasing parametric function with the parameters $a, c \in L$, $c \leq a$ such that

$$\varepsilon_{Sm}(x, a, c) = \begin{cases} 0 & \text{for } x \leq c, \\ \text{increasing} & \text{for } c < x < a, \\ 1 & \text{for } a \leq x. \end{cases}$$

The interval $[u, c]$ is the set of *numbers being surely small*, i.e. $Sm(x) = 1$ for $x \in [u, c]$. Similarly, the interval $[a, s]$ is the set of numbers surely not being small, i.e. $Sm(x) = 0$ for $x \in [a, s]$.

As mentioned, the horizon approach function $\varepsilon_{Sm}(x, a, c)$ "implements" the idea of approaching the horizon. The bigger $\varepsilon_{Sm}(x, a, c)$ is, the shorter is our way to it. By setting specific formulas for $\varepsilon_{Sm}(x, a, c)$, we obtain various concrete membership functions. Note that in general, they will be Z-functions.

The atomic term "big" is not a complement of "small" but its *antonym*. Therefore, big numbers also behave as finite ones but taken in the reversed ordering from the rightmost side of the universe. To achieve this, we take the ordering of U reversely and change the position of the oberver from u to v. The horizon of *big* then lays "somewhere to the left from v". Of course, it may not be in the same distance from the observer as the horizon of small ones. Thus, the corresponding horizon approach function ε_{Bi}, in general, differs from ε_{Sm}.

The *canonical fuzzy set* of *big* (numbers) $Bi \underset{\sim}{\subset} R$ is given by

$$Bi(x) = 1 - \varepsilon_{Bi}(x, a, c)x \tag{6}$$

where $\varepsilon_{Bi} : R \longrightarrow [0,1]$ is a non-increasing parametric function with the parameters $a, c \in R$, $a \le c$ such that

$$\varepsilon_{Bi}(x,a,c) = \begin{cases} 1 & \text{for } x \le a \\ \text{decreasing} & \text{for } a < x < c, \\ 0 & \text{for } c \le x. \end{cases}$$

The interval $[c, v]$ is the set of *numbers being surely big*, i.e. $Bi(x) = 1$ for $x \in [c, v]$ and $[s, a]$ is the set of numbers surely not being big, i.e. $Bi(x) = 0$ for $x \in [s, a]$. By setting specific formulas for $\varepsilon_{Bi}(x,a,c)$, we obtain concrete membership functions, being generally S-functions.

2.1.3 Canonical membership function of "Medium"

In the case of the atomic term "medium", the observer is placed in the center $s \in U$ (cf. (4)). The horizon is spread both to the left as well as to the right from it. Hence, we may find two points $c^1_{Me} \le s \le c^2_{Me}$ and analogously as above define the *canonical fuzzy set* $Me \subseteq U$ of *medium* numbers given by

$$Me(x) = \begin{cases} 1 - \varepsilon^1_{Me}(x, a^1, c^1)x & \text{for } x \in L, \\ 1 - \varepsilon^2_{Me}(x, a^2, c^2)x & \text{for } x \in R \end{cases} \tag{7}$$

where ε^1_{Me} and ε^2_{Me} are parametric functions fulfiling the following conditions:

1. $\varepsilon^1_{Me} : L \longrightarrow [0,1]$ is a non-increasing parametric function with the parameters $a^1, c^1 \in L$, $a^1 \le c^1$ such that

$$\varepsilon^1_{Me}(x,a^1,c^1) = \begin{cases} 1 & \text{for } x \le a^1 \\ \text{decreasing} & \text{for } a^1 < x < c^1, \\ 0 & \text{for } c^1 \le x. \end{cases}$$

2. $\varepsilon^2_{Me} : R \longrightarrow [0,1]$ is a non-decreasing parametric function with the parameters $a^2, c^2 \in R$, $c^2 \le a^2$ such that

$$\varepsilon^2_{Me}(x,a^2,c^2) = \begin{cases} 0 & \text{for } x \le c^2, \\ \text{increasing} & \text{for } c^2 < x < a^2, \\ 1 & \text{for } a^2 \le x. \end{cases}$$

The interval $[c^1_{Me}, c^2_{Me}]$ is the set of *numbers being surely medium*, i.e. $Me(x) = 1$ for $x \in [c^1_{Me}, c^2_{Me}]$.

The canonical membership functions (5), (6) and (7) serve as a basis for derivation of the mentioned accepted form of the membership functions Z, S and Π-curves, respectively. It has always been accepted that and Z and S functions are special cases of the Π-one. However, the opposite understanding — that the latter is composed of the formers — is also possible. Therefore, "medium" can be understood as a composed term of the form

$$medium = medium^1 \; OR \; medium^2$$

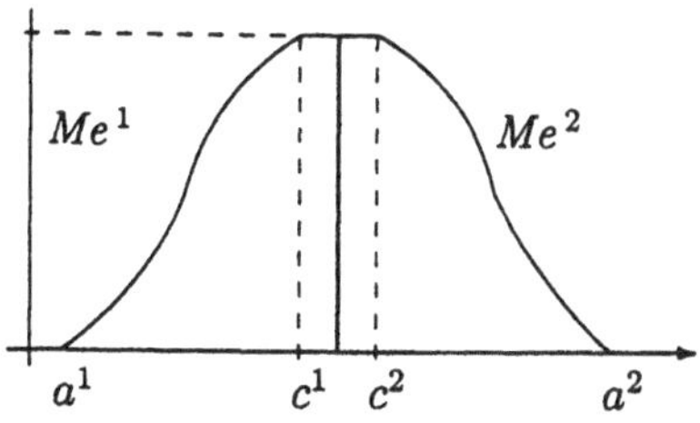

Figure 2: Membership function of "medium = medium[1] OR medium[2]" composed of two adjacent S and Z curves.

where "medium[1]" and "medium[2]" are atomic terms with the meaning analogous to the meaning of the terms "big" and "small" respectively (cf. Fig. 2). The fuzzy set Me in (7) is then the union of two fuzzy sets

$$Me = Me^1 \cup Me^2$$

defined by the corresponding two cases in (7).

Note 1 Let us remark that *fuzzy numbers* are generally accepted to be triangular fuzzy sets where the peak corresponds to the given number. For example "about 25" is represented by a triangular number with the peak in 25. Due to our approach, also fuzzy numbers can be explained in the same way as the term "medium". Thus, we obtain a unique representation for all the basic atomic terms as well as for a wider class of evaluating linguistic expressions which includes also fuzzy numbers.

2.1.4 Concrete membership functions of basic atomic terms

Concrete shapes of the membership functions depend on the form of the horizon approach function $\varepsilon(x, c)$. We will consider three basic kinds of membership functions, namely linear, quadratic and exponential ones which lead to the well known membership function widely used in applications.

For the term "small", the corresponding membership functions are the following.

(a) *linear*

$$Sm(x) = \begin{cases} 1 & \text{if } 0 \le x \le c \\ \frac{a-x}{a-c} & \text{if } c \le x \le a \\ 0 & \text{if } a < x \end{cases}$$

(b) *quadratic*

$$Sm(x) = \begin{cases} 1 & \text{if } 0 \le x \le c \\ 1 - \frac{1}{2}\left(\frac{x-c}{b-c}\right)^2 & \text{if } c \le x \le b \\ \frac{1}{2}\left(\frac{a-x}{a-b}\right)^2 & \text{if } b \le x \le a \\ 0 & \text{if } a < x \end{cases}$$

(c) *exponential*

$$Sm(x) = \begin{cases} 1 & \text{if } 0 \le x \le c \\ e^{-k(x-c)^2} & \text{if } c < x \end{cases}$$

where $u \le a \le b \le c \le v$ are parameters specifying position of the corresponding curve in the universe $U = [u, v]$. The parameter b is auxiliary and may be missing (cf. Fig. 1 and 3).

These functions can be obtained from (5) by putting:

$$\varepsilon_{Sm}(x,a,c) = \begin{cases} 0 & \text{for } x \le c, \\ \frac{x-c}{x(a-c)} & \text{for } c < x < a, \\ 1 & \text{for } a \le x, \end{cases} \qquad (Sm \text{ linear}) \tag{8}$$

$$\varepsilon_{Sm}(x,a,b,c) = \begin{cases} 0 & \text{for } x \le c, \\ \frac{(x-c)^2}{2x(b-c)^2} & \text{for } c < x < b, \\ \frac{2(a-b)^2-(a-x)^2}{2x(a-b)^2} & \text{for } b < x < a \\ 1 & \text{for } a \le x, \end{cases} \qquad (Sm \text{ quadratic}) \tag{9}$$

$$\varepsilon_{Sm}(x,a,c) = \begin{cases} 0 & \text{for } x \le c, \\ \frac{1-e^{-k(x-c)^2}}{x} & \text{for } c < x < a, \\ 1 & \text{for } a \le x. \end{cases} \qquad (Sm \text{ exponential}) \tag{10}$$

Similarly, the correspoinding membership functions for *big* have the horizon approach functions as follows:

$$\varepsilon_{Bi}(x,a,c) = \begin{cases} 0 & \text{for } c \le x, \\ \frac{c-x}{x(c-a)} & \text{for } a < x < c, \\ 1 & \text{for } x \le a, \end{cases} \qquad (Bi \text{ linear}) \tag{11}$$

$$\varepsilon_{Bi}(x,a,b,c) = \begin{cases} 0 & \text{for } c \le x, \\ \frac{(c-x)^2}{2x(c-b)^2} & \text{for } b < x < c, \\ \frac{2(b-a)^2-(x-a)^2}{2x(b-a)^2} & \text{for } a < x < b, \\ 1 & \text{for } x \le a, \end{cases} \qquad (Bi \text{ quadratic}) \tag{12}$$

$$\varepsilon_{Bi}(x,a,c) = \begin{cases} 0 & \text{for } c \le x, \\ \frac{1-e^{-k(c-x)^2}}{x} & \text{for } a < x < c, \\ 1 & \text{for } x \le a. \end{cases} \qquad (Bi \text{ exponential}) \tag{13}$$

The membership functions for *medium* are obtained analogously.

The linear membership functions of the basic triple of atomic terms have trapezoidal shape depicted on Fig. 3. The other two have the shape depicted on Fig. 1 (exponential, however, has the disadvantage of asymptotical approaching of the x axis, which is not favourable behavior).

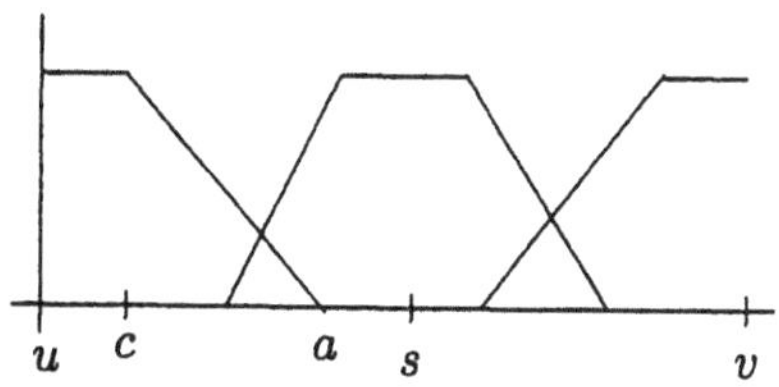

Figure 3: The meaning of the basic triple of atomic terms if the horizon approach function $\varepsilon(x, a, c)$ gives linear membership functions (trapezoidal shape).

2.2 Linguistic hedges

2.2.1 Existing models of linguistic hedges

The model of the meaning of natural language in fuzzy set theory works especially for adjectives and nouns. Verbs are omitted due to their extreme complexity[3].

L. A. Zadeh proposed in his works the model of the meaning of the linguistic hedges using certain transformations of the membership functions. More exactly, if $A \underset{\sim}{\subseteq} U$ is a fuzzy set assigned to the word $\mathcal{A}$ and $\mathcal{M}$ is a linguistic hedge so that $\mathcal{MA}$ is a linguistic expression then its meaning is a fuzzy set

$$M(\mathcal{MA}) = m(A) \tag{14}$$

where m is a transformation assigned to $\mathcal{M}$ which acts on the membership function A. The first studied linguistic hedge was the hedge *very*. The transformation assigned to it is the operation $CON(a)$ defined by $CON(a) = a^2$, $a \in [0, 1]$. For example, the meaning of *very small* is the membership function A^2_{Sm} where A_{Sm} is the fuzzy set assigned to the word *small*. The effect of such modifier is depicted on Fig. 4.

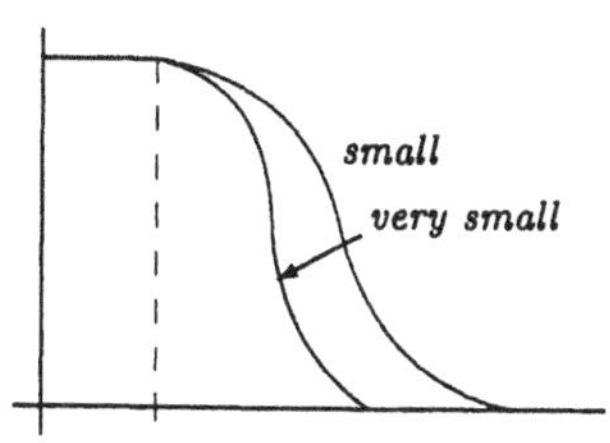

Figure 4:

Later on, L. A. Zadeh proposed the model of some other hedges [23]. He used several classes of functions which can be combined in various ways. Modifications of his theory have been proposed, e.g., in [1, 11, 14].

G. Lakoff in his detailed linguistic analysis [11] demonstrated that the above model does not fit well the real linguistic effect. The hedge *very* and other similar

[3]The only elaborated mathematical model known to the author, which includes also the meaning of verbs, is presented in his book [15].

ones should steepen the membership function as well as *shift it*. Furthermore, the shifting depends on the kind of adjective so that there is a difference between the modification of the adjectives *small* and *big* (see Fig. 5).

Modification of Zadeh's proposal aiming at fulfilling the above requirements was proposed in [14]. Due to it, the meaning of $\mathcal{MA}$ above is computed using the composition of functions

$$M(\mathcal{MA}) = \nu_{\mathcal{M}} \circ A \circ \zeta_{\mathcal{M}} \tag{15}$$

where $\nu_{\mathcal{M}} : [0,1] \longrightarrow [0,1]$ is a modification function and $\zeta_{\mathcal{M}} : U \longrightarrow U$ is a shifting function. For example, the hedge *very* is determined using the functions

$$\nu_{very}(a) = CON(a) = a^2, \qquad a \in [0,1],$$

and

$$\zeta_{very} = x + (-1)^k d \,\|\operatorname{Ker}(A)\|$$

where $k = 1$ for $\mathcal{A} :=$ '*small*', $k = 2$ for $\mathcal{A} :=$ '*big*', d is a shifting factor (experimentally it has been found that $d \in [0.25, 0.4]$) and $\|\operatorname{Ker}(a)\|$ is the width of the kernel of A, i.e., $\operatorname{Ker}(A) = \{x \mid Ax = 1\}$ (for details and other hedges, see [14]). This model behaves in accordance with Lakoff's discussion. However, it is fairly complicated and thus, most authors incorrectly stick to the original Zadeh's proposal.

Shifting of the membership function as a method for realization of the linguistic hedges is proposed also by B. Bouchon in [1]. Her approach considers only linear membership functions.

2.2.2 A horizon shifting model of linguistic hedges

What does it mean "very small"? The hedge *very* makes the meaning of *small numbers* more accurate. *Very small* numbers are small but there are small numbers which are not very small. A very small number is closer to 0 and, therefore, it is more transparent. Of course, the set (interval) of "surely very small numbers" is smaller than that of "surely small ones". In other words, the *horizon of very small numbers is closer to the observer than that of small ones.* This suggests to consider the meaning of the expression *very small* in the same way as small simply by changing the horizon approach function $\varepsilon_{Sm}(x,a,c)$.

We will introduce a new special parameter corresponding to the given hedge. Hence, the fuzzy set *VeSm* modeling the meaning of *very small numbers* is given by

$$VeSm(x) = 1 - \varepsilon'_{Sm}(x,a,c,\sigma_V)x \tag{16}$$

where $0 < \sigma_V < 1$ is some parameter such that $\varepsilon'_{Sm}(x,a,c,\sigma_V) > \varepsilon_{Sm}(x,a,c)$. Since $\varepsilon_{Sm}(x,a,c)$ can be understood as a special case of $\varepsilon'_{Sm}(x,a,c,\sigma_V)$ with the parameter $\sigma_V = 1$, we will omit the apostrophe in the sequel.

The function (16) realizes both the required actions: it shifts the horizon closer and steepens the membership function (cf. Fig. 5). Note that $[u, \sigma_V c] \subset [u, c]$, i.e., the interval of surely very small numbers is shorter than that of surely small numbers.

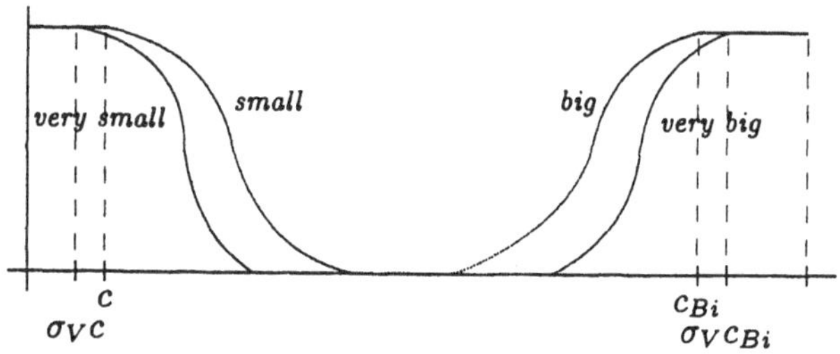

Figure 5: The effect of the horizon shifting model of the hedge "very". Note that the membership function of *big* is shifted to the right.

Opposite effect, i.e. shifting the horizon farther from the observer, is encountered for the hedges such as *more or less, roughly*, etc. In general, we speak about hedges with *narrowing effect* (very, highly, etc.) and those with *widening effect* (more or less, roughly, etc.).

Let $\mathcal{M}$ denote a linguistic hedge. Then, applying it to the atomic term *small* in (5), we generally get

$$\mathcal{M}Sm(x) = 1 - \varepsilon_{Sm}(x, a, c, \sigma_{\mathcal{M}})x \tag{17}$$

where $a, c \in L$ and $\varepsilon_{Sm}(x, a, c, \sigma_{\mathcal{M}}) : L \longrightarrow [0,1]$ is a parametric function with the parameters $c \leq a$ such that

$$\varepsilon_{Sm}(x, a, c, \sigma_{\mathcal{M}}) = \begin{cases} 0 & \text{for } x \leq \min\{\sigma_{\mathcal{M}}c, s\}, \\ \text{increasing} & \text{for } \min\{\sigma_{\mathcal{M}}c < x < \min\{\sigma_{\mathcal{M}}a, s\}, \\ 1 & \text{for } \min\{\sigma_{\mathcal{M}}a, s\} \leq x \end{cases}$$

where $x \in [u, s]$ and moreover,

$$\varepsilon_{Sm}(x, a, c, \sigma_{\mathcal{M}}) \geq \varepsilon_{Sm}(x, a, c, \sigma'_{\mathcal{M}})$$

for $\sigma_{\mathcal{M}} \leq \sigma'_{\mathcal{M}}$ and $\varepsilon_{Sm}(x, a, c, 1) = \varepsilon_{Sm}(x, a, c)$.

The parameter $\sigma_{\mathcal{M}}$ works as follows: $\sigma_{\mathcal{M}} = 1$ when no hedge in (1) is present (we may also speak about *empty hedge*). Furthermore, $0 < \sigma_{\mathcal{M}} < 1$ for $\mathcal{M}$ being the hedge with narrowing effect and $1 < \sigma_{\mathcal{M}}$ for $\mathcal{M}$ being the hedge with widening effect.

The interval $[u, \min\{\sigma_{\mathcal{M}}c, s\}]$ is the set of *numbers being surely $\mathcal{M}$ small*, i.e. $\mathcal{M}Sm(x) = 1$ for $x \in [u, \min\{\sigma_{\mathcal{M}}c, s\}]$. Similarly, the interval $[\min\{\sigma_{\mathcal{M}}a, s\}, s]$ is the set of numbers surely not being $\mathcal{M}$ small, i.e. $\mathcal{M}Sm(x) = 0$ for $x \in [\min\{\sigma_{\mathcal{M}}a, s\}, s]$. Each linguistic hedge is thus characterized by one parameter σ only.

Similarly we proceed for the linguistic hedges of *big* and *medium*, where we have

$$\mathcal{M}Me = \mathcal{M}Me^1 \cup \mathcal{M}Me^2.$$

Note that there is no linguistic hedge with narrowing effect applied to the atomic term *medium*.

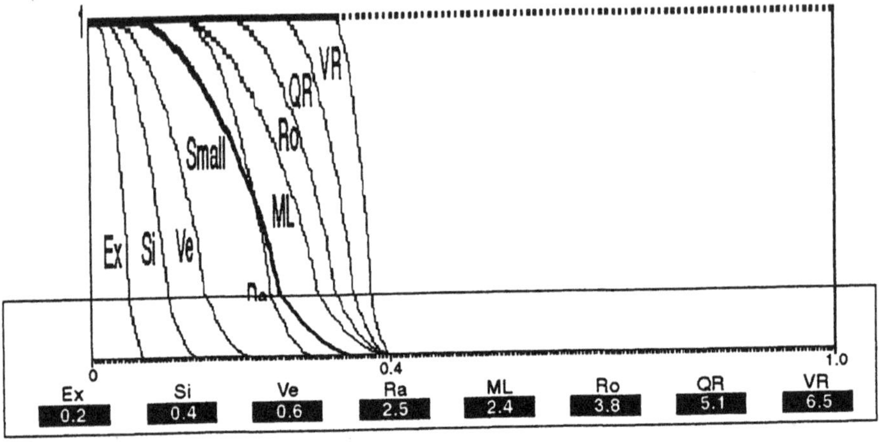

Figure 6: The effect of the hedges *extremely*, *significantly*, *very*, *more or less roughly*, *quite roughly* and *very roughly* for the atomic term "small". Included is also the hedge *rather*, but this is exceptional and does not belong to the class of the previous ones.

2.2.3 Linguistic hedges for specific types of membership functions

The horizon approach functions for the atomic term "small" when linguistic modifiers are included have the following form:

Sm linear:

$$\varepsilon_{Sm}(x,a,c,\sigma_{\mathcal{M}}) = \begin{cases} 0 & \text{for } x \leq \sigma_{\mathcal{M}}c, \\ \frac{x-\sigma_{\mathcal{M}}c}{x\sigma_{\mathcal{M}}(a-c)} & \text{for } \sigma_{\mathcal{M}}c < x < \sigma_{\mathcal{M}}a, \\ 1 & \text{for } \sigma_{\mathcal{M}}a \leq x, \end{cases} \tag{18}$$

Sm quadratic:

$$\varepsilon_{Sm}(x,a,c,\sigma_{\mathcal{M}}) = \begin{cases} 0 & \text{for } x \leq \sigma_{\mathcal{M}}c, \\ \frac{(x-\sigma_{\mathcal{M}}c)^2}{2x\sigma_{\mathcal{M}}^2(b-c)^2} & \text{for } \sigma_{\mathcal{M}}c < x \leq \sigma_{\mathcal{M}}b, \\ \frac{2\sigma_{\mathcal{M}}^2(a-b)^2-(\sigma_{\mathcal{M}}a-x)^2}{2x\sigma_{\mathcal{M}}^2(a-b)^2} & \text{for } \sigma_{\mathcal{M}}b \leq x < \sigma_{\mathcal{M}}a, \\ 1 & \text{for } \sigma_{\mathcal{M}}a \leq x, \end{cases} \tag{19}$$

Sm exponential:

$$\varepsilon_{Sm}(x,a,c,\sigma_{\mathcal{M}}) = \begin{cases} 0 & \text{for } x \leq \sigma_{\mathcal{M}}c, \\ \frac{1-e^{-k(x-\sigma_{\mathcal{M}}c)^2}}{x} & \text{for } \sigma_{\mathcal{M}}c < x < \sigma_{\mathcal{M}}a, \\ 1 & \text{for } \sigma_{\mathcal{M}}a \leq x. \end{cases} \tag{20}$$

This model has been implemented in the software system called Linguistic Fuzzy Logic Controller (LFLC). Its theory is presented, for example in [18].

The behaviour of a few kinds of hedges used in it including the values of the corresponding parameters $\sigma_{\mathcal{M}}$ is depicted on Fig. 6. The membership functions are quadratic, which seem to fit best all the linguistic requirements. The universe is $[u, v] = [0, 1]$ and the center s is set to $s = 0.4$. There are also few successful applications of LFLC in the control of real processes.

The horizon approach functions (18), (19) and (20) for the terms "big" and "medium" are defined analogously. Let us stress, however, that the values of $\sigma_{\mathcal{M}}$ are not unique. They depend on the definition of the modified membership function as well as on the kind of the atomic term in concern, i.e. they should differ for the atomic terms "small", "medium" and "big". This is a necessary tax for the more realistic behaviour[4]. Let us also mention that this theory opens a promising way for finding effective learning procedures which could concentrate on finding the optimal values of the parameters $\sigma_{\mathcal{M}}$.

2.3 Class of functions modeling the meaning of evaluating terms

It follows from the previous discussion that simple evaluating expressions (1) have the meaning which can be modeled using fuzzy sets with membership functions taken from the class of fuctions described in this section.

Let a set (interval) $[p, q] = \{x \mid x \in U, p \leq x \leq q\}$ be given where U is, by assumption, an ordered set of elements. Then the following class contains all the functions using which membership functions of the meaning of the simple evaluating expressions (1) can be constructed:

$$\mathcal{Z}([p, q]) = \{Z, S \mid Z, S : [p, q] \longrightarrow [0, 1]\} \tag{21}$$

where Z, S are functions given by

$$Z(x, a_Z, c_Z, \sigma_Z) = 1 - \varepsilon_Z(x, a_Z, c_Z, \sigma_Z)x, \tag{22}$$

$$S(x, a_S, c_S, \sigma_S) = 1 - \varepsilon_S(x, a_S, c_S, \sigma_S)x \tag{23}$$

where $a_Z, c_Z, a_S, c_S \in [p, q]$, $\sigma_Z, \sigma_S > 0$ and

$$\varepsilon_Z(x, a_Z, c_Z, \sigma_Z) : [p, q] \longrightarrow [0, 1],$$
$$\varepsilon_S(x, a_S, c_S, \sigma_S) : [p, q] \longrightarrow [0, 1]$$

are functions with the following properties:

(a) Denote $u_Z = \min\{\sigma_Z c_Z, q\}$ and $v_Z = \min\{\sigma_Z a_Z, q\}$. Then $\varepsilon_Z(x, a_Z, c_Z, \sigma_Z)$ is a parametric function such that

$$\varepsilon_Z(x, a_Z, c_Z, \sigma_Z) = \begin{cases} 0 & \text{for } x \leq u_Z, \\ \text{increasing} & \text{for } u_Z < x < v_Z, \\ 1 & \text{for } v_Z \leq x, \end{cases}$$

(b) Denote $u_S = \min\{\sigma_S c_S, q\}$ and $v_S = \min\{\sigma_S a_S, p\}$. Then $\varepsilon_S(x, a_S, c_S, \sigma_S)$ is a parametric function such that

$$\varepsilon_S(x, a_S, c_S, \sigma_S) = \begin{cases} 1 & \text{for } x \leq v_S, \\ \text{decreasing} & \text{for } v_S < x < u_S, \\ 0 & \text{for } u_S \leq x. \end{cases}$$

[4] All these problems are already solved in LFLC.

Both functions are, moreover, decreasing with respect to σ, i.e.

$$\varepsilon(x, a, c, \sigma) > \varepsilon(x, a, c, \sigma')$$

for $\sigma < \sigma'$. The functions from the class $\mathcal{Z}([p, q])$ are depicted in Fig. 7.

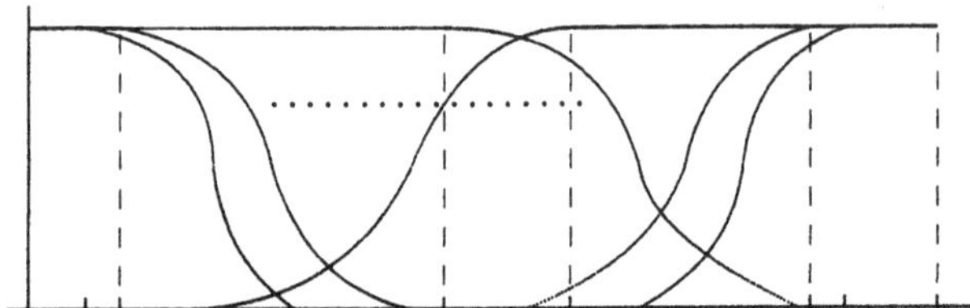

Figure 7: Scheme of the class of functions from $\mathcal{Z}([p, q])$. The σ' has narrowing and σ'' widening effect (this is marked for Z-functions only).

The $\varepsilon_Z, \varepsilon_S$ are special parametric functions (horizon approach functions) providing concrete shapes of the membership functions of the the meaning of simple evaluating linguistic expressions (1).

The outcome of this approach is that these membership functions are formed using only two forms of functions from the class $\mathcal{Z}([p, q])$. Furthermore, the use of them is well justified to fit both the results of the linguistic analysis as well as the intuition.

3 Representation of continuous functions using formulas containing linguistic terms

3.1 Expressional ability of the 'computing with words' methodology

Amazing ability of fuzzy logic formulas to represent functional dependencies does not surprize specialists thanks to the results on fuzzy logic controllers to be universal approximators (see [3, 2, 7, 9]). This technique is based on the representation of continuous functions using fuzzy logic formulas of special type. It is notable that this kind of representation is a result of formalization of expert rules used for the control of simple dynamic processes, such as steam engine, etc. For more complicated controlled objects, however, one kind of expert knowledge is insufficient.

As often happens, the experience has been generalized and a mechanism of elaboration of dependencies of various kind (expert data and knowledge, algebraic expressions) has been expressed in a form of logical formulas comprizing sets implications between antecedent and succedent. The fundamental part of this mechanism is based on making use of properties of logical operations being general for all algebraic systems interpreting fuzzy logic. It has been demonstrated that the class of algebraic systems based on any of the three basic t-norms (minimum, Łuksiewicz product and ordinary product) has a sufficient expressing power for approximation of continuous functions.

The secondary part of this mechanism is based on the choice of basic membership functions interpreting fuzzy logic predicates in antecedents and succedents. In the existing literature on the approximate description of functions by fuzzy logic formulas, these membership functions are generalized characteristic functions of certain areas in the universe without any other specificity. A consequent of this is unlimited extension of the number of the used logical formulas (in the form of implications) necessary for approximation of the given dependence with a given precision. In some sense, this makes impossible a direct use of the approximation result in the practice. Hence, we face a problem of effective representation of dependencies using logical formulas, i.e. how to find a minimal number of them.

We solve this problem in this paper by choosing basic membership functions reflecting the specificity of the given dependence. These basic functions serve also as interpretations of the meaning of words forming the above introduced canonical linguistic triple ("small, medium, high").

To fit the concrete dependence, it is necessary to modify the membership functions of the basic triple. We will show that using linguistic modifiers introduced in the previous section, it is possible to represent effectively an arbitrary continuous function, monotonous on finite number of intervals, using logical formulas formed from the basic functions of the type mentioned above. Consequently, this representation is possible using the simple evaluating linguistic expressions (1).

The obtained result means that the 'computing with words' methodology has an expressing power comparable, for example, with polynomial or other representations. However, the possibility to use linguistic expressions in the description of the dependence makes this methodology significantly attractive for the applications.

3.2 Normal forms for fuzzy logic formulas

To achieve the results outlined in the previous section, we will work with formulas in the form of implications $A(x) \Rightarrow B(y)$, where $A(x)$ is an atomic formula or equals to a conjunction of atomic formulas and $B(y)$ is an atomic formula. Let us have a collection of such kind of formulas

$$\{A_i(x) \Rightarrow B_i(y) \mid 1 \leq i \leq N\}. \tag{24}$$

We aim at proving that continuous functional dependences between x and y can be logically described (precisely or approximately) by those collections. We obtain this result by successive solution of the following tasks:

(i) interpretation of (24) by a fuzzy relation;

(ii) transformation of a fuzzy relation to a function;

(iii) reverse representation of a function by a collection of fuzzy logic formulas;

(iv) generalization of (iii) to some special class of functions.

In this section, we consider task (i) and show how the collection (24) can be interpreted by a fuzzy relation in the universe $X \times Y$.

Let $A_i(x), B_i(y)$ be atomic formulas with one variable being interpreted by the corresponding fuzzy sets on some universes X and Y, respectively. As the strict distinction between formulas and their interpretations is not necessary in this paper, we will employ the same symbols also for fuzzy sets. Hence, $A_i \underset{\sim}{\subset} X$ and $B_i \underset{\sim}{\subset} Y$ express that $A_i(x), B_i(y)$ are interpreted by the respective fuzzy sets. We will work with these representations only, in the sequel. Using this agreement, (24) is represented by a fuzzy relation in the universe $X \times Y$.

There are two basic general forms how (24) can be realized. They generalize the common disjunctive and conjunctive normal forms (cf. [20], and also [7]), namely

$$\bigvee_{i=1}^{N} (A_i(x) * B_i(y)) \tag{25}$$

and

$$\bigwedge_{i=1}^{N} (A_i(x) \rightarrow_* B_i(y)) \tag{26}$$

where $*$ denotes some t-norm and $\rightarrow_*$ the implication operator adjoint to $*$.

When viewed as functions of independent variable x and dependent variable y, expressions (25) and (26) define fuzzy relations on $X \times Y$. Both these relations are used as interpretations of the set of logical formulas (24).

Due to results in the theory of t-norms (cf., for example, [8]), the following t-norms are sufficient for representation of all continuous t-norms.

$$a * b = a \wedge b = \min(a, b), \qquad a \rightarrow_G b = \begin{cases} 1 & \text{if } a \leq b, \\ b & \text{if } b < a. \end{cases}$$

$$a * b = a \otimes b = \max\{0, a + b - 1\}, \qquad a \rightarrow_L b = 1 \wedge (1 - a + b).$$

$$a * b = a \cdot b \qquad a \rightarrow_P b = \begin{cases} 1 & \text{if } a \leq b, \\ \frac{b}{a} & \text{if } b < a. \end{cases}$$

where $\rightarrow_G, \rightarrow_L, \rightarrow_P$ are the corresponding adjoints.

3.3 From fuzzy relations to functions

Let $X, Y \subseteq \mathbb{R}$ be subsets of the set of real numbers and $R \underset{\sim}{\subset} X \times Y$ be a fuzzy relation corresponding to normal form (25) or (26) for some fixed t-norm $*$. We show the way how the relation $R(x, y)$ can be transformed to a function $f_R : X \longrightarrow Y$ (and it will be a solution of the task (ii)).

Let $x^0 \in X$ be an arbitrary but fixed element in X. Consider $R(x^0, y)$ and note that it defines a membership function of some fuzzy set in Y. To define a function f_R it is sufficient to choose one element from $R(x^0, y)$ and correspond it to x^0. We will do it following the procedure of defuzzification. Recall that $DF : \mathcal{F}(Y) \longrightarrow Y$ is a defuzzification function where $\mathcal{F}(Y)$ is the set of all fuzzy sets on Y, when it assigns an element y^0 to the fuzzy set $R(x^0, y)$ by a certain procedure so that

$$y^0 = DF(R(x^0, y)).$$

The function f_R we are looking for can be defined by

$$f_R : x^0 \mapsto DF(R(x^0, y)).$$

We call this function as *function realized by fuzzy relation R* or, we can say also that *fuzzy relation R defines the function* f_R.

In the sequel we will restrict ourselves to the defuzzification function such that

$$DF(B(y)) = \inf\{y \mid B(y) = \sup_{u \in Y} B(u)\}.$$

3.4 Representation of continuous and piecewise monotone functions

In the previous section we showed that a collection of fuzzy logic formulas can represent a function. Precisely this fact makes fuzzy logic applicable in many areas. But choosing a fuzzy logic representation of a function, one should know how to obtain its algorithm and how to evaluate a complexity of such kind of representation. To answer these questions, we associate the complexity of a fuzzy logic representation of a function with a number of formulas in the representing collection (24).

In this section we show, how is it possible to obtain a precise representation of a function by non-excessive collections of fuzzy logic formulas. It will be a solution of the task (iii). For the simplicity, we consider the case of functions with one variable.

Theorem 2 *To any continuous and strictly monotonous real-valued real function* $f(x) : [a, b] \longrightarrow \mathbb{R}$ *there are fuzzy sets* $A_1, A_2 \underset{\sim}{\subset} [a, b]$ *and* $B_1, B_2 \underset{\sim}{\subset} f([a, b])$ *such that the collection of fuzzy logic formulas*

$$\{A_i(x) \Rightarrow B_i(y) \mid 1 \leq i \leq 2\},$$

describes a function $f_R(x) : [a, b] \longrightarrow \mathbb{R}$ *and the fuzzy relation in the conjunctive normal form (see (26))*

$$R(x, y) = \bigwedge_{i=1}^{2} (A_i(x) \rightarrow B_i(y))$$

defines $f_R(x)$ *in such a way that* $f_R(x) = f(x)$ *for every* $x \in [a, b]$.

PROOF: The proof is constructive and can be used as a basis for an algorithm. Fix a t-norm t and let $\rightarrow$ be its ajoint implication. Since $f(x)$ is continuous and monotonous on $[a, b]$ it defines a one-to-one correspondence between $[a, b]$ and $[f(a), f(b)]$. Therefore, the inverse function $f^{-1}(y)$ exists.

Assume that $f(x)$ monotonously increases. The proof consists in construction of membership functions of the fuzzy sets A_1, A_2 and B_1, B_2 in such a way that the equality $f_R(x) = f(x)$ is fulfiled for all $x \in [a, b]$. We suggest two possible solutions.

1. Membership functions for the fuzzy sets A_1, A_2 and B_1, B_2 are the following:

$$A_1(x) = 1 - \frac{x-a}{b-a}, \qquad A_2(x) = \frac{x-a}{b-a}, \qquad x \in [a, b], \tag{27}$$

$$B_1(y) = 1 - \frac{f^{-1}(y) - a}{b-a}, \quad B_2(y) = \frac{f^{-1}(y) - a}{b-a}, \quad y \in [f(a), f(b)]. \tag{28}$$

Let $x^0 \in [a, b]$ be an arbitrary, but fixed element. We show that $f_R(x^0) = f(x^0)$. Indeed,

$$A_1(x^0) \to B_1(y) = 1 \quad \text{iff} \quad A_1(x^0) \le B_1(y) \quad \text{iff} \quad 1 - \frac{x^0 - a}{b - a} \le \frac{b - f^{-1}(y)}{b - a}$$
$$\text{iff} \quad y \le f(x^0);$$
$$A_2(x^0) \to B_2(y) = 1 \quad \text{iff} \quad A_2(x^0) \le B_2(y) \quad \text{iff} \quad \frac{x^0 - a}{b - a} \le \frac{f^{-1}(y) - a}{b - a}$$
$$\text{iff} \quad f(x^0) \le y.$$

Thus,

$$R(x^0, y) = 1 \quad \text{iff} \quad f(x^0) = y,$$

and then

$$\sup_y R(x^0, y) = R(x^0, f(x^0)) = 1.$$

By the definition,

$$f_R(x^0) = DF(R(x^0, y)) = f(x^0).$$

2. The second variant of membership functions of the fuzzy sets A_1, A_2 and B_1, B_2 is the following:

$$A_1(x) = 1 - \frac{f(x) - f(a)}{f(b) - f(a)}, \qquad A_2(x) = \frac{f(x) - f(a)}{f(b) - f(a)}, \qquad x \in [a, b],$$
$$B_1(y) = 1 - \frac{y - f(a)}{f(b) - f(a)}, \qquad B_2(y) = \frac{y - f(a)}{f(b) - f(a)}, \qquad y \in [f(a), f(b)].$$

Analogously as above, let $x^0 \in [a, b]$ be an arbitrary, but fixed element. We show that $f(R(x^0)) = f(x^0)$. Indeed,

$$A_1(x^0) \to B_1(y) = 1 \quad \text{iff} \quad A_1(x^0) \le B_1(y)$$
$$\text{iff} \quad 1 - \frac{f(x^0) - f(a)}{f(b) - f(a)} \le 1 - \frac{y - f(a)}{f(b) - f(a)} \quad \text{iff} \quad y \le f(x^0);$$
$$A_2(x^0) \to B_2(y) = 1 \quad \text{iff} \quad A_2(x^0) \le B_2(y)$$
$$\text{iff} \quad \frac{f(x^0) - f(a)}{f(b) - f(a)} \le \frac{y - f(a)}{f(b) - f(a)} \quad \text{iff} \quad f(x^0) \le y.$$

The rest follows the same way as above. □

To extend the class of functions which are non-excessively realized by fuzzy relation R we introduce the following definition.

Definition 1 *By a piecewise monotonous function f on a compact U we mean a function, for which there exists a finite partition of U such that the restriction of f to each set from the partition is strictly monotonous.*

We again consider only the case of functions with one variable.

Theorem 3 *For any continuous and piecewise monotonous real-valued real function $f(x) : [a, b] \longrightarrow \mathbb{R}$ there exist a number N and fuzzy sets $A_{i1}, A_{i2} \subsetneq$*

$[a,b]$ and $B_{i1}, B_{i2} \underset{\sim}{\subset} f([a,b])$, $1 \le i \le N$, such that the collection of fuzzy logic formulas

$$\{A_{ij}(x) \Rightarrow B_{ij}(y) \mid 1 \le i \le N,\ 1 \le j \le 2\},$$

describes a function $f_R(x) : [a,b] \longrightarrow \mathbb{R}$ and the fuzzy relation in the conjunctive normal form (see (26))

$$R(x,y) = \bigwedge_{i=1}^{N} \bigwedge_{j=1}^{2} (A_{ij}(x) \rightarrow B_{ij}(y))$$

defines $f_R(x)$ in such a way that $f_R(x) = f(x)$ for every $x \in [a,b]$.

PROOF: Since $f(x)$ is continuous and piecewise monotonous on $[a,b]$, there exists a finite partition of $[a,b]$ into a finite number of subintervals $J_1, \ldots, J_N$ such that the restriction $f|J_i$, $1 \le i \le N$, to each set from the partition is strictly monotonous. In accordance with Theorem 2, for each such restriction there exist fuzzy sets $A_{i1}, A_{i2} \underset{\sim}{\subset} J_i$ and $B_{i1}, B_{i2} \underset{\sim}{\subset} f(J_i)$ such that the fuzzy relation

$$R_i(x,y) = \bigwedge_{j=1}^{2} (A_{ij}(x) \rightarrow B_{ij}(y))$$

defines a function $f_{R_i}(x)$ such that $f(x) = f_{R_i}(x)$ for all $x \in J_i$.

We extend the definitions of the membership functions $A_{ij}(x), B_{ij}(y)$, $1 \le i \le N$, $1 \le j \le 2$, to $[a,b]$ and $f([a,b])$, by setting them equal to 0 outside of J_i and $f(J_i)$, respectively. Consider the fuzzy relation

$$R(x,y) = \bigwedge_{i=1}^{N} \bigwedge_{j=1}^{2} (A_{ij}(x) \rightarrow B_{ij}(y))$$

where $x \in [a,b]$, $y \in f([a,b])$ and $A_{ij}(x), B_{ij}(y)$ are the extensions. Since any arbitrary $x^0 \in [a,b]$ belongs to exactly one subinterval J_i (except for the bounds of subintervals) then not more than two membership functions $A_{i1}(x), A_{i2}(x)$ ($A_{i-1,2}(x), A_{i1}(x)$ or $A_{i2}(x)$, $A_{i+1,1}(x)$, $2 \le i \le N-1$, for internal bounds) can differ from 0 in x^0. Thus,

$$R(x^0, y) = R_i(x^0, y),\ y \in f(J_i),$$

and then

$$f_R(x^0) = f_{R_i}(x^0) = f(x^0).$$

□

Corollary 1 *Let conditions of Theorem 3 be satisfied and in addition, let $f(x)$ be monotonously increasing or decreasing on the whole interval $[a,b]$. Then there exist fuzzy sets $A_1, \ldots, A_{N+1} \underset{\sim}{\subset} [a,b]$ and $B_1, \ldots, B_{N+1} \underset{\sim}{\subset} f([a,b]$ such that*

$$R(x,y) = \bigwedge_{i=1}^{N+1} (A_i(x) \rightarrow B_i(y))$$

defines $f_R(x)$ in such a way that $f_R(x) = f(x)$ for every $x \in [a,b]$.

PROOF: We show only the case when $f(x)$ is monotonously increasing. Consider the membership functions $A_{ij}(x), B_{ij}(y)$, $1 \le i \le N$, $1 \le j \le 2$, constructed in Theorem 3 and define new ones as follows:

$$\begin{aligned} A_1(x) &= A_{11}(x), \\ A_i(x) &= A_{i-1,2}(x) \vee A_{i,1}(x), \\ A_{N+1}(x) &= A_{N2}(x), \end{aligned}$$

and analogously for $B_1(y), B_i(y), B_{N+1}(y)$, $2 \le i \le N-1$. It is easy to verify that

$$\bigwedge_{i=1}^{N+1} (A_i(x) \to B_i(y)) = \bigwedge_{i=1}^{N} \bigwedge_{j=1}^{2} (A_{ij}(x) \to B_{ij}(y)).$$

□

3.5 Representation of functions and computing with words

In this subsection we jointly consider linguistic and functional points of view on fuzzy sets and combine results from the previous sections. We show that each continuous function defined on a compact set can be realized or approximated by fuzzy relation with membership functions similar to those from the basic triplet *small, medium, big*. This fact precisely means that having at disposal three given linguistic labels and the set of linguistic hedges, it is possible to construct a collection of logical formulas (based only on their combinations) and a fuzzy relation using which we can construct a function which either fits precisely or approximately each continuous function.

Similarly as above, we start with a continuous piecewise monotonously increasing function $f(x)$ defined on interval $[a,b] \subseteq \mathbb{R}$. From Corollary 1 we see that to realize such a function by a fuzzy relation, we need membership functions of three types in the universe X divided into N subintervals $[a_1,b_1],\dots,[a_N,b_N]$, namely

$$A_1(x) = 1 - \frac{f(x)-f(a_1)}{f(b_1)-f(a_1)}, \qquad x \in [a_1,b_1],$$

$$A_i(x) = \begin{cases} \frac{f(x)-f(a_{i-1})}{f(b_{i-1})-f(a_{i-1})}, & \text{for } x \in [a_{i-1},b_{i-1}], \\ 1-\frac{f(x)-f(a_i)}{f(b_i)-f(a_i)}, & \text{for } x \in [a_i,b_i], \end{cases} \qquad 2 \le i \le N,$$

$$A_{N+1}(x) = \frac{f(x)-f(a_N)}{f(b_N)-f(a_N)}, \qquad x \in [a_N,b_N].$$

Similarly, we divide the universe Y into N subintervals

$$[f(a_1),f(b_1)],\dots,[f(a_N),f(b_N)]$$

and obtain the membership functions

$$B_1(y) = 1 - \frac{y-f(a_1)}{f(b_1)-f(a_1)}, \qquad y \in [f(a_1),f(b_1)],$$

$$B_i(y) = \begin{cases} \frac{y-f(a_{i-1})}{f(b_{i-1})-f(a_{i-1})}, & \text{for } y \in [f(a_{i-1}),f(b_{i-1})], \\ 1-\frac{y-f(a_i)}{f(b_i)-f(a_i)}, & \text{for } y \in [f(a_i),f(b_i)], \end{cases} \qquad 2 \le i \le N,$$

$$B_{N+1}(y) = \frac{y-f(a_N)}{f(b_N)-f(a_N)}, \qquad y \in [f(a_N),f(b_N)].$$

Note, that the character and form of these membership functions depend on the character and form of the function $f(x)$. Consider different cases for $f(x)$.

1. The function $f(x)$ is piecewise linear and monotonously increasing. In this case it is not difficult to see that:

   - the membership functions $A_1(x), B_1(y)$ are precisely described and expressed by a modified linguistic term "small",
   - the membership functions $A_i(x), B_i(y)$, $2 \leq i \leq N$, are precisely described and expressed by a modified linguistic term "medium",
   - the membership functions $A_N(x), B_N(y)$ are precisely described and expressed by modified linguistic term "big".

   We verify this on the example of $A_1(x), B_1(y)$. Let $f|[a_1, b_1](x) = kx + l$. Then

   $$A_1(x) = 1 - \frac{k(x - a_1)}{k(b_1 - a_1)} = 1 - \frac{x - a_1}{b_1 - a_1} = \frac{b_1 - x}{b_1 - a_1},$$

   $$B_1(y) = 1 - \frac{f^{-1}(y) - a_1}{b_1 - a_1} = 1 - \frac{\frac{y-l}{k} - a_1}{b_1 - a_1} = \frac{(kb_1 + l) - y}{(kb_1 + l) - (ka_1 + l)},$$

   i.e. we obtain the linear membership functions of simple evaluating linguistic expressions as discussed in Sections 2.1.4 and 2.2.3.

2. The function $f(x)$ is continuous and monotonously increasing on $[a, b]$, but not necessarily piecewise linear. It is well known that for the given function and each $\epsilon > 0$ there exist a partition of $[a, b]$ into a finite number of subintervals $J_1, \ldots, J_N$ and a piecewise linear function $f^L(x)$ such that $f^L|J_i$ is linear and

   $$|f(x) - f^L(x)| \leq \epsilon$$

   holds for for all x. It follows that $f^L(x)$ admits a represetation by some fuzzy relation R^L with the membership functions expressed by (linear) fuzzy sets representing the meanings of simple evaluating terms (1). Thence, the original function $f(x)$ admits an approximation by R^L.

3. The function $f(x)$ is continuous on $[a, b]$ but the character of monotonicity can be different. Then for the given function and each $\epsilon > 0$ there exists a piecewise linear function $f^L(x)$ which approximates $f(x)$ on the whole interval $[a, b]$ with the precision ϵ. In this case, a fuzzy relation R^L defining function $f^L(x)$ can be constructed on the basis of Theorem 3 rather than on its corollary. It means that membership functions characterized by a modified term "medium" can be missing. With this restriction, the fuzzy relation R^L approximately defines $f(x)$.

So far, we have exploited only linear membership functions among those modeling the meaning of the simple evaluating linguistic expressions (1). The non-linear (quadratic or exponential) membership functions are used mainly for approximation. It is necessary to point out that the approximation of continuous functions based on fuzzy relation with non-linear membership functions is more preferable because it enables to reduce the number of formulas in (24) and fits better the linguistic environment. A precise formulation of this problem and its solution will be done in the future paper.

On the other hand, if we stick on the precise discription of the given function $f(x)$, have have to employ the membership functions constructed in accordance with Theorem 3. However, these may not necessarily have the form suggested for the basic lingistic terms *small, medium, big*, even if they are modified due to the theory presented in Section 2.

4 Discussion

In this paper, we have proposed a horizon shifting method for computation of the linguistic hedges which technically leads to parametric classes of membership functions. The method meets the requirements of linguists, i.e., that the membership function should be shifted as well as modified its steepness. Furthermore, it has a potential for further development because it affects the basic parameters of the defined membership functions in a unified way and using one parameter only. Thence, the potential for effective learning is open.

The expressing power of basic linguistic terms together with modifiers has been demonstrated on the example of the representation of an arbitrary continuous piecewise monotonous function. The obtained result means that the methodology of 'computing with words' is comparable, for example, with polynomial or other representations. However, the possibility to use linguistic expressions in the description of functions makes this methodology significantly attractive for the applications.

To conclude, let us remark the following. In this paper, we have elaborated the model of the meaning of linguistic expressions in a traditional way, which is purely extensional understanding of the semantics of the linguistic expressions. This means that their semantics is explained only on the basis of the groupings (i.e., fuzzy sets) of elements falling into the meaning of the expressions in concern. This is correct and quite well working in various applications of fuzzy set theory. However, the groupings vary in various contexts and in time and therefore, the extensional approach is often criticized by linguists. A more realistic theoretically well founded interpretation of the linguistic semantics must take the intension (property) into consideration (cf., e.g. [21]). However, pure fuzzy set theory is unable to fit this requirement. It is a challenge to find a formal apparatus capable to model both the intension as well as extension of the linguistic semantics including its vagueness (fuzziness). Promising in this respect seems to be *fuzzy logic in broader sense* (see [17, 19]) which is an extension of the fuzzy logic in narrow sense[5]. Fuzzy logic in broader sense attempts to elaborate methods of approximate reasoning including the formal model of linguistic meaning. A more elaborated theory of the meaning of the evaluated linguistic expressions developed in the frame of fuzzy logic in broader sense is a task of future work.

[5]Presentation of fuzzy logic in narrow sense can be found, for example, in [5, 17] and elsewhere.

References

[1] Bouchon-Meunier, B.: *Fuzzy logic and knowledge representation using linguistic modifiers.* In: Zadeh, L.A. and J. Kacprzyk: **Fuzzy Logic for the Management of Uncertainty**, J. Wiley, New York 1992.

[2] Buckley, J. J. and Y. Hayashi, *Fuzzy input-output controllers are universal approximators*, Fuzzy Sets and Systems **58**(1993), 273–278.

[3] Castro, J., *Fuzzy Logic Controllers are Universal Approximators*, IEEE Trans. on Systems, Man, and Cybernetics **25**(1995), 629–635.

[4] Davis, M.: **Applied nonstandard analysis.** J. Wiley, New York 1977.

[5] Hájek P.: **Metamathematics of fuzzy logic**. Kluwer, Dordrecht (to appear).

[6] Klawonn, F., *Fuzzy sets and vague environments*, Fuzzy Sets and Systems **66**(1994), 207–221.

[7] Klawonn, F. and V. Novák: *The Relation between Inference and Interpolation in the Framework of Fuzzy Systems.* Fuzzy Sets and Systems **81**(1996), 331–354.

[8] Klement, E. P., Mesiar, R. and E. Pap. **Triangular Norms**. Monograph in preparation.

[9] Kosko, B., *Fuzzy Systems as Universal Approximators*, Proc. IEEE Conf. on Fuzzy Systems, San Diego 1992, 1153–1162.

[10] Kuzmin, V. B.: *About semantical structure of linguistic hedges: an experimental hypothesis.* BUSEFAL 24, 1986, pp. 117–125.

[11] Lakoff, G.: *Hedges: A study in meaning criteria and logic of fuzzy concepts*, J. Philos. Logic **2**(1973), 458–508.

[12] Lee, J. and Chae, S.: *Analysis on function duplicating capabilities of fuzzy controllers.* Fuzzy Sets and Systems **56**(1993), 127–143.

[13] Novák, V.: *Sorites-like First-order Fuzzy Theories.* Proc. of IIIrd IFSA Congress, Seattle 1989.

[14] Novák, V., **Fuzzy Sets and Their Applications**, Adam–Hilger, Bristol, 1989.

[15] Novák, V., **The Alternative Mathematical Model of Linguistic Semantics and Pragmatics**, Plenum, New York, 1992.

[16] Novák, V.: *Towards Formalized Integrated Theory of Fuzzy Logic.* In: Bien, Z, and K. Min (eds.), **Fuzzy Logic and Its Applications to Engineering, Information Sciences, and Intelligent Systems**, Kluwer, Dordrecht 1995, 353–363.

[17] Novák, V.: *Paradigm, Formal Properties and Limits of Fuzzy Logic.* Int. J. of General Systems **24**, 1996.

[18] Novák, V.: *Linguistically Oriented Fuzzy Logic Controller and Its Design.* Int. J. of Approximate Reasoning 1995, **12**(1995), 263–277.

[19] Novák, V. and I. Perfilieva: *On Logical and Algebraic Foundations of Approximate Reasoning.* Proc. FUZZ-IEEE'97, Barcelona, 693–698.

[20] Perfilieva, I.: *Fuzzy logic normal forms for control law representation* In: Fuzzy Algorithms for Control Engineering — from misunderstanding to benefits and challenges. Eds. H. B. Verbruggen, H. J. Zimmermann, 1998 (to appear).

[21] Sgall, P., Hajičová, E., Panevová J., **The meaning of the sentence in its semantic and pragmatic aspects**, D. Reidel, Dordecht 1986.

[22] Vopěnka, P.: **Mathematics in the Alternative Set Theory**. Teubner, Leipzig 1979.

[23] Zadeh, L.A.: *A fuzzy-set-theoretic interpretation of linguistic hedges.* J. Cyber. **2**(1972), 2–34.

[24] Zadeh, L.A.: *Quantitative Fuzzy Semantics*, Inf. Sci.,**3**(1973), 159–176.

[25] Zadeh, L.A.: *The concept of a linguistic variable and its application to approximate reasoning I, II, III*, Inf. Sci., **8**(1975), 199–257, 301–357; **9**(1975), 43–80.

[26] Zadeh, L. A. *Test-score semantics for natural languages and meaning representation via PRUF.* In: Rieger, Burghard, **Empirical Semantics I**. Dr. N. Brockmayer, Bochum, 1981.

5

COMPUTING WITH WORDS: NUMERICAL ASPECTS

Calculation over Verbal Quantities[1]

Milan Mareš[1] and Radko Mesiar[2]

[1] Institute of Information Theory and Automation
Academy of Sciences of the Czech Republic
P.O. Box 18, 18208
Prague 8, Czech Republic

E-mail: mares@utia.cas.cz

[2] Faculty of Civil Engineering
Slovak Technical University
Radlinského 11
81368 Bratislava, Slovak Republic

E-mail: mesiar@cvt.stuba.sk

Summary. Some verbal expressions represent quantitative data of essentially vague character and manipulation with them is frequently of computative type. This computation with words can be represented by fuzzy quantities. Nevertheless, each verbal quantitative expression is a combination of two components – of a quantitative one which connects it with some numerical (or quantitative) value, and of a semantic one which reflects its logical (or qualitative) features. The paper continues authors' previous works in mathematical modelling of these two components and discussing their properties and interpretations.

1. Heuristic Introduction

Verbal expressions representing quantitative data are as old as the mathematical thinking and many historical documents include technological, medical or geographical instructions in which vague verbal data are dealt. In spite of their fundamental position among mathematical concepts the verbal quantitative data were not essentially investigated and their mathematical meaning was not formalized. Fuzzy set theory appears to be an adequate formal tool for handling the computing with words. This paper is to extend, discuss and interpret a fuzzy set theoretical model of verbal quantities which was partly formulated in the authors' previous papers, namely in [10, 7, 9]. In this introductory section we heuristically analyze the structure and intuitive properties of the modelled fuzzy quantities.

[1] Particular parts of the research the results of which are summarized in this paper were partly supported by the Key Project of the Academy of Sciences of the Czech Republic No. 1, by the Grant Agency of the Czech Republic, grant No. 402/96/0414, by the EU PHARE Project No. P95–2014–R, and by the Ministry of Education, Youth and Sports of the Czech Republic project No. VS96063.

1.1 Verbal Quantity

By *verbal quantity* we intuitively understand any verbal expression offering quantitatively oriented information. If $x, y \in R$ are real values then typical verbal quantities are *"approximately x"*, *"much more than y"*, *"something between x and y "* but also expressions like *"many"*, *"few"*, *"several"*, *"enormous"* and many others. These examples illustrate some general properties of vagueness connected with the referred concept:

- Some verbal quantities are related to a real number which represents their most expected (i.e. one of modal) value, e.g., "about x", "approximately y", etc. We can speak about *"referred value"*.
- In some other cases there is no specific referred value and the verbal expression itself describes some quantitative attributes, like "very small", "big", "rarely", etc. In fact, even such verbal quantities have some mostly expected values but these are closely connected with actual application and can be very variable.
- Finally, there exist verbal quantities which are related to some real number but this number is not their modal value (frequently does not belong to possible values of the considered verbal quantity at all). For example "almost x", "much more than y", "something between x and y", and others. An attempt to model these verbal quantities was done in [10]. Anyhow, it is worth a thorough reconsideration if they represent specific pure type of quantity or if they are results of algebraic operation (addition or multiplication) of crisp value and a verbal quantity with nonspecified referred value, e.g.

  "a bit more than x"= $x +$ "a bit",

  "many times more than y"= $y\times$ "many",

  or a result of logical operation with verbal quantities, like

  "something between x and y"="more than x" $\wedge$ "less than y".

The previous examples of various types of verbal quantities illustrate also one basic fact which should be respected by any of their models.

Postulate 1. Any verbal quantity is a composition of two types of phenomena: a quantitative value (specified or unspecified) and a semantic expression specifying the distribution of its vagueness.

This bipolarity of verbal quantities also implies the duality of their handling. Their processing includes both, arithmetical and logical (semantic) types of manipulation.

1.2 Processing Verbal Quantities

Verbal presentation of quantitative attributes is not only descriptive. It is also possible to process them in several ways. This processing can be, generally, of one of the following three types:

- *Arithmetic operations* which regard mainly the quantitative components of verbal quantities ("add several grains of ... to 2 handfuls of ..., "repeat as many times as possible", etc.)
- *Logical relations* which deal with their semantic components and specific descriptions of the distribution of vagueness ("not less than x and not much more than y", "approximately x or y times", etc.)
- *Structural relations* which respect the mutual relations between fuzzy quantities, namely their orderings which can regard their quantitative ("many" is usually more than "a few") as well as semantic ("near to x" is usually a narrower specification than "not very far from x") components. (For example, "choose the one of several vague quantities which is most similar to x".)

Observing the verbal quantities, their structures and their processing it is possible to formulate the next empirical postulate of their modelling.

Postulate 2. Quantitative and semantic meaning of verbal quantities is very relative. It can differ due to particular application, to actual situation or to the referred crisp value.

The previous empirical conclusion is quite obvious, "approximately x" reflects different extent of possible values if $x = 5$ and for $x = 5000$, "much money" means something different for national economist and for a family budget, "near approximation of x" in scientific experiment differs, for the same x, due to the technical quality of laboratory device, etc.

1.3 Structure of Verbal Quantities

Respecting the previous heuristic discussion of verbal quantities we may conclude some framework ideas about the formal model.

Evidently, fuzzy set and, especially, fuzzy numbers (fuzzy quantities) theory appears to be an adequate mathematical representation of the vagueness existing in verbal quantitative data.

There exists a disproportion unseparable from the fuzzy set theoretical approach to verbality. Namely, there exist only a finite, quite limited, number of verbal expressions but a very rich class of fuzzy quantities usable for their modelling. It justifies the following postulate.

Postulate 3. Verbal quantities can be modelled by fuzzy quantities, where every verbal quantity corresponds to a class of the fuzzy ones. The choice of the actual one to be applied depends on the modelled situation and its subjective evaluation by the user of the model.

The fuzzy set theoretical model of verbal quantity should respect its dualism mentioned above. Its quantitative and semantic component, and also the individual vagueness of the source of the considered quantities. The superposition of these characteristics enables the choice of the unique fuzzy quantity representing the relevant verbal expression in a given application. It means that fuzzy quantity representing a verbal one is determined by:

Crisp numerical value. expressing the typical, or reference, value of the verbal quantity. It is called also the **crisp core** of the verbal quantity. It need not be exactly specified and if it is then it is one of modal values of the fuzzy quantity.

Generator of the verbal data. which characterizes the distribution of the vagueness over real line. Different sources of verbal data are more or less vague (or, vice versa, reliable) for different areas of their possible values. Such generators are called **generating functions (scales)** and they are defined as continuous strictly increasing functions defined on the real line.

Structure of vagueness in verbal expression. describing the proportions of the vagueness which is present in the words. It is defined as a function on the real line with values in the unit interval, and it represents an in certain sense normalized membership function of the fuzzy quantities expressing the vagueness of the words used in the verbal quantity. It is called the **shape generator**. Every word can be described by a class of shape generators (in some sense similar) and the choice of the actual one depends on the subjective view on the realized application.

The existence and essential qualitative difference of these components of verbal quantities implies also qualitatively different approach to their processing.

The "crisp core" as deterministic numeric value, if it is specified, is naturally handled by deterministic arithmetic methods. As follows from the above heuristic discussion, the reference value can be identified with modal value of the membership function of the fuzzy quantity representing the considered verbal quantity. If there exist more modal values then the choice of the very one belongs to the subjective interface between the actual verbal expression and mathematical formalism of fuzzy quantities. If the "reference value" is evidently out of the modal values (or even out of the support set of the chosen fuzzy quantity), e.g. in fuzzy expressions like "rather more than ...", then such verbal expression can be presented as a result of operation (algebraic or logical) with standard verbal quantities whose "reference" and "modal" values do not differ (e.g., "rather more than x" can be presented as a sum of "near x" and "a few" or "exactly x" and "a few").

The "generating functions" can be processed in two ways due to the processing the generated data. The algebraic operations with data can be reflected by analogous processing of their sources which properly modifies their distribution of uncertainty (cf. [9]). On the other hand, it is possible to combine different sources of one datum in order to minimize the vagueness. These combinations do not correspond to algebraic operations and are of rather more functional character.

Finally, the "shape generators" describe the semantic meanings of words used in the verbal quantities in the sense of the specific distributions of vagueness by means of formal mathematical concepts ("normalized" membership functions). Their semantic ground demands rather (fuzzy) logical approach and the application of various logical operations or operations of in some sense similar structure.

2. Fuzzy Quantity

Fuzzy set theory offers effective tools for modelling vagueness which is typical for verbal expressions. The concept of fuzzy quantities (cf. [6, 3, 8]) appears to be an adequate formal representation of colloquial quantitative information which we have called here "verbal quantity". More detailed presentation of fuzzy quantities (or fuzzy numbers) is summarized in [6, 8] and [3]. Here, we briefly recall their formal definition and classical approach to operations with them based on the so-called *"extension principle"*.

Let us denote by R the set of real numbers. By a *fuzzy quantity* we call any fuzzy subset a of R with membership function $\mu_a : R \longrightarrow [0,1]$ such that

$$\exists ccx_a \in R : \mu_a(x_a) = 1. \tag{2.1}$$

A real number x_a in (2.1) is called a *modal value* of a. The set of all fuzzy quantities is denoted by $I\!R$.

The *extension principle* (cf. [3] and also [8] or [6]) allows to extend the algebraic operations with real numbers to fuzzy quantities from $I\!R$. Here, we recommend the definition of addition and multiplication. If $a, b \in I\!R$ are fuzzy quantities then their *sum* $a \oplus b$ and *product* $a \odot b$ are also fuzzy quantities in $I\!R$, and

$$\begin{aligned}
\mu_{a\oplus b}(x) &= \sup_{y\in R} \left(\min(\mu_a(y), \mu_b(x-y))\right), \qquad x \in R, &(2.2)\\
\mu_{a\odot b}(x) &= \sup_{y\in R, y\neq 0} \left(\min(\mu_a(y), \mu_b(x/y))\right), \qquad x \in R,\ x \neq 0, &(2.3)\\
\mu_{a\odot b}(0) &= \max(\mu_a(0), \mu_b(0)). &(2.4)
\end{aligned}$$

Definitions can be simplified if one of the input fuzzy quantities is a real number. Namely, for $r \in R$, $a \in I\!R$, $r+a$ and $r \cdot a$ are fuzzy quantities, where

$$\begin{aligned}
\mu_{r+a}(x) &= \mu_a(x-r), \quad x \in R, &(2.5)\\
\mu_{r\cdot a}(x) &= \mu_a(x/r), \quad x \in R,\ r \neq 0, &(2.6)
\end{aligned}$$

$$\begin{aligned}
\mu_{0\cdot a}(x) &= 1 \quad \text{for} \quad x = 0 &(2.7)\\
&= 0 \quad \text{for} \quad x \neq 0.
\end{aligned}$$

The properties of these operations are summarized and discussed in [8] and [6]. In the context of this paper, it is essential only to mention that those properties are not as convenient as the analogous ones valid for crisp numbers. Moreover, application of (2.1),(2.2) and (2.3) generally increases the extent of possible values of the results. Namely, if we denote for $a \in I\!R$ the number $\Delta(a) \in R$ by

$$\Delta(a) = \sup(x : \mu_a(x) > 0) - \inf(x : \mu_a(x) > 0) \geq 0 \qquad (2.8)$$

then

$$\Delta(a \oplus b) = \Delta(a) + \Delta(b).$$

This increase of the extent of vagueness is natural but in the applications of algorithms with many algebraical operations it can become enormous.

It is worth noting that the historical experience with vague verbal data and their processing frequently shows something rather different. Application of vague verbal instructions including quantitative components, e.g., in traditional technologies, traditional herb medicine, geographic knowledge of discovering expeditions and others, usually leads to satisfactory stationary results with quite acceptable degree of vagueness. It seems that its increase is somehow compensed by the way of realization of the algorithms, or, in other words, that the realized "algebraic" operations do not strictly respect the formalism of the extension principle.

3. Verbal Quantity

The heuristic discussion in Section 1 has already introduced the basic principles of the formal model of verbal quantity suggested in this paper (in a rather narrower version also in [7, 10]) and in [9].

3.1 Representation of Verbal Quantities

Let us consider a triple

$$(x_a, f_a, \varphi_a), \qquad (3.1)$$

where: x_a is a real number, f_a is a strictly increasing continuous mapping of R in R such that $f_a(0) = 0$, φ_a is a mapping of R in $[0, 1]$ such that $\varphi_a(0) = 1$.

Definition 1. Let (x_a, f_a, φ_a) be a triple introduced by (3.1), let $a \in I\!R$ be fuzzy quantity with membership function μ_a, where

$$\mu_a(x) = \varphi_a(f_a(x) - f_a(x_a)), \quad x \in R. \qquad (3.2)$$

Then we say that μ_a is *generated* by (x_a, f_a, φ_a). Real number x_a is called the *crisp core* of a, function f_a is called the *scale* (or *generating function*) of a and φ_a is the *shape generator* of a. The triple (x_a, f_a, φ_a) is called the *generator* of a.

Let us assume that a verbal quantitative expression A, which describes the vagueness specificable by φ_a, is generated by a source described by f_a and connected with reference value of x_a (explicitely specified or subjectively derived from the context). Then the fuzzy quantity a generated by means of (3.2) is said to be a *representation* of A.

Remark 1. Function μ_a generated by (3.2) is a membership function of a fuzzy quantity and x_a is its modal value.

3.2 Formal Processing

Fuzzy quantities generated by (3.2) can be processed like any other fuzzy quantities or, even more generally, as fuzzy subsets of R they can be processed like any other fuzzy sets. Due to the bipolar nature of verbal quantities mentioned in Postulate 1, two approaches to them are admissible. As quantitative concepts they can be dealt by the extension principle and related operations, e.g., (2.2),(2.3),(2.4). As semantic expressions they can be processed by means of logical operations. The first case regards verbal combinations like "approximately x plus approximately y" or "several times nearly x". The second case can be regarded to expressions like "approximately divisible by 100" (i.e. "approximately 100 or approximately 200 or ..."), "rather more than x but not exceeding y", where $x < y$ (i.e. "rather more than x and not more than y") and others. It is not difficult to see that the results of such operations are also verbal quantities but, in some cases, with rather complex structure.

Definition 2. Let A be a verbal quantity represented by fuzzy quantity a with membership function μ_a. Then we say that A is *elementary* fuzzy quantity iff there exists a real number $x_a \in R$ such that

$$\mu_a(x) \quad \text{is increasing for } x < x_a, \tag{3.3}$$

$$\mu_a(x) \quad \text{is decreasing for } x > x_a. \tag{3.4}$$

If there is no such x_a then A is called a *composed* verbal quantity.

Remark 2. If A is represented by $a \in \mathbb{R}$ and a is generated by (x_a, f_a, φ_a) using (3.2) then A is elementary if $\varphi_a(x)$ is increasing for $x < 0$ and decreasing for $x > 0$. In such case the crisp core x_a is the value which satisfies (3.3) and (3.4).

Lemma 1. Let A, B be elementary verbal quantities represented by fuzzy quantities $a, b \in \mathbb{R}$, respectively, and let $r \in R$. Then verbal quantities represented by $a \oplus b, a \odot b, r + a$ and $r \cdot a$ are elementary as well.

Proof. The statement follows from (3.2), strict monotonicity of f_a and f_b and from (2.2),(2.3) and (2.4).

The logical operations with verbal quantities and their fuzzy representations need not fulfill the property mentioned in the previous lemma. Logical disjunction of two elementary verbal quantities

$$C = A \vee B$$

is also represented by a fuzzy quantity c with

$$\mu_c(x) = \max(\mu_a(x), \mu_b(x)), \quad x \in R,$$

but μ_c does not generally preserve the monotonicity (3.3),(3.4) of μ_a and μ_b. Moreover, if we consider logical conjunction

$$D = A \wedge B$$

of two verbal quantities and if we attempt to represent it by some fuzzy quantity $d \in I\!R$, then its membership function μ_d would not be defined by

$$\mu_d(x) = \min(\mu_a(x), \mu_b(x))$$

as it generally does not fulfill (2.1) and, consequently, $d \notin I\!R$. It means that manipulations with verbal quantities, namely in the case of logical operations, cannot mechanically repeat the classical formalism of fuzzy logic or fuzzy algebra. Their reflections of quantitative or logical relations should respect the specificity of the quantitative verbal expressions. One of possible approaches is presented in the following section.

4. Processing of Generators

The alternative approach to the processing of verbal quantities which could be more adequate to the combined structure of verbal quantities and their fuzzy representatives, namely the superposition of crisp core, generating function and shape generators, was suggested in [9, 7] and [10].

4.1 Motivation of the Combined Processing

The specific structure of verbal quantity enables specific formal approach to its components which influences also the handling of the fuzzy quantities representing it. The main specificity is based on the following idea.

Fuzzy quantity representing verbal data is defined by three mathematical objects – crisp core, generating function and shape generator. Each of them is connected with a vide class of potential fuzzy quantities and only their superposition (3.2) specifies the formal membership function of the final one. In many practical situations the applied algorithms include some algebraical and logical operations where the input verbal quantities have their generating functions (sources of the data), shape generators (used words) and the crisp cores (reference values). It could be profitable to derive, according to the operations used in the algorithm, some final pattern of the output verbal quantities, namely their generating function and shape generator which describe the vagueness of the verbal output. Then the algorithm can be in any of its applications used for the crisp cores, only. It represents a relatively easy manipulation with crisp real numbers. Its result – the output crisp core can be attached to the general pattern of the output and the triple defining the resulting fuzzy quantity and by means of it the resulting verbal quantity will be complete.

In such procedure, the manipulation with generating functions represents rather the quantitative component of the realized operations, meanwhile the composition of the shape generators represents the logical or semantic one.

4.2 Quantitative Procedures

The essential part of quantitative handling of verbal quantity generated by a triple (3.1) is realized via the classical deterministic computation with the crisp cores which results into the crisp core of the generator of the output fuzzy quantity and related verbal quantity.

However, certain deal of quantitative manipulation is also connected with the generating functions. It follows from the fact that operations with fuzzy quantities (their addition or multiplication, for instance) means also some kind of composition of the vagueness of the input elements. Frequently, the vagueness of the output is larger than the vagueness of inputs, as we have already mentioned in Section 2 (cf. formula (2.8)). This composition of vagueness should be reflected by a relation between the reliability (or vagueness) of the input data sources (generating functions), the type or realized computational operations and the reliability (or vagueness) of the final output generating function as a representative of the output data emission. It means that it is desirable to define some operations with generating functions as counterparts of analogous operations with verbal quantities and their fuzzy representants.

This problem was studied in [9, 10] already and the results achieved there can be briefly referred below.

Let us denote by $\mathcal{F}$ the set of all *generating functions*, i.e. strictly increasing continuous functions with $f(0) = 0$ for any $f \in \mathcal{F}$. If $f, g \in \mathcal{F}$ and $r \in R, r > 0$, then we define the operations of addition, multiplication and crisp product denoted by $f \boxplus g$, $f \boxtimes g$ and $r \cdot f$, respectively, by

$$
\begin{aligned}
(f \boxplus g)(x) &= \left(f^{-1} + g^{-1}\right)^{-1}(x), && (4.1)\\
(f \boxtimes g)(x) &= \left(f^{-1} \cdot g^{-1}\right)^{-1}(x) \cdot \operatorname{sign}(x), && (4.2)\\
(r \cdot f)(x) &= f(x/r) \cdot \operatorname{sign}(r), \quad \text{for } r \neq 0, && (4.3)
\end{aligned}
$$

where f^{-1} denotes the inverse function to f and $\operatorname{sign}(x) = 1$ for $x > 0$, $\operatorname{sign}(x) = -1$ for $x < 0$, $\operatorname{sign}(0) = 0$.

Lemma 2. If $f \in \mathcal{F}$ and $r \in R$, then

$$(r \cdot f)(x) = (r \cdot f^{-1})^{-1}(x) \cdot \operatorname{sign}(r).$$

Proof. Evidently, under the assumption $f \in \mathcal{F}$

$$r \cdot f^{-1}(x) = f^{-1}(x/r) \quad \text{and} \quad (f^{-1}(x/r))^{-1} = f(x/r).$$

Remark 3. If $f,g \in \mathcal{F}$, $\alpha,\beta \in R, \alpha,\beta > 0$, $f(x) = \alpha \cdot x, g(x) = \beta \cdot x$, then obviously

$$(f \boxplus g)(x) = \frac{\alpha \cdot \beta}{\alpha + \beta} x, \quad (f \boxtimes g)(x) = \alpha \cdot \beta \cdot \sqrt{|x|} \cdot \mathrm{sign}(x).$$

Remark 4. If $f,g \in \mathcal{F}$, $\alpha,\beta \in R$, $f(x) = |x|^{\alpha} \cdot \mathrm{sign}(x)$, $g(x) = |x|^{\beta} \cdot \mathrm{sign}(x)$, then, obviously,

$$(f \boxtimes g)x = |x|^{\frac{\alpha \cdot \beta}{\alpha + \beta}} \cdot \mathrm{sign}(x).$$

The operations over $\mathcal{F}$ defined by (4.1),(4.2) and (4.3) fulfil some properties analogous to the algebraic processing of real numbers. They were summarized in [9, 10], and the next statement briefly recollects the most significant ones of them.

Theorem 1. The set of generating functions $\mathcal{F}$ is closed with respect to the operations (4.1),(4.2) and (4.3), and, moreover, for $f,g,h \in \mathcal{F}$, $r_1, r_2 \in R$ such that $r_1 \cdot r_2 > 0$

$$\begin{aligned} f \boxplus g = g \boxplus f, \quad f \boxtimes g = g \boxtimes f, \\ f \boxplus (g \boxplus h) = (f \boxplus g) \boxplus h, \quad f \boxtimes (g \boxtimes h) = (f \boxtimes g) \boxtimes h, \\ r_1 \cdot (f \boxplus g) = (r_1 \cdot f) \boxplus (r_1 \cdot g), \\ (r_1 + r_2) \cdot f = (r_1 \cdot f) \boxplus (r_2 \cdot f), \\ (r_1 \cdot r_2) \cdot f = r_1 \cdot (r_2 \cdot f), \\ f \boxtimes (g \boxplus h) = (f \boxtimes g) \boxplus (f \boxtimes h). \end{aligned}$$

Proof. The proof is given in [10], the particular equalities follow from (4.1),(4.2) and (4.3), immediately.

The specific form of generating functions does not admit to introduce some concepts like the 0-element, 1-element, opposite and reciprocal elements and their classical properties in a natural way. Anyhow, even the relations summarized in Theorem 1 offer effective tools for processing generating functions in order to reflect quantitative operations with verbal (or fuzzy) quantities generated by the functions from $\mathcal{F}$.

The classical theory of fuzzy quantities shows special position of so called 0-symmetric fuzzy quantities, i.e., quantities whose membership function μ fulfills

$$\mu(x) = \mu(-x) \quad \text{for all} \quad x \in R. \tag{4.4}$$

They can play the role of "fuzzy zeros" (cf. [8]) in algebra of fuzzy quantities. The following remark shows that such "zeros" naturally follow also from the model considered here.

Remark 5. Let $f, g \in \mathcal{F}$ be generating functions such that

$$f = g \boxplus (-1 \cdot g). \tag{4.5}$$

Then $f(-x) = -f(x)$ for any $x \in R$. If the shape generator φ in (3.2) is symmetric, $\varphi(-x) = \varphi(x)$ for all $x \in R$ then any fuzzy quantity $a \in I\!R$ generated by the triple $(0, f, \varphi)$ is 0-symmetric in the sense of (4.4).

Evidently, for general $f \in \mathcal{F}$ and crisp core $x_a = 0$ the generated fuzzy quantity need not be 0-symmetric.

4.3 Combination of Data Sources

The next processing of verbal quantities and their generators have more qualitative than quantitative character. As it was already mentioned above, the generating functions from $\mathcal{F}$ represent the sources of vague data and their vagueness which is, by means of shape generators φ and generating formula (3.2), transformed into the membership functions of particular fuzzy quantities.

Generally, for a given φ, the higher the derivative of f is in a neighbourhood of some crisp core x_a, the "narrower" is the support set of the generated membership function and, consequently, the less vague the generated fuzzy quantity is.

In practical situations, different sources of data are more or less reliable in different segments of their domain. If we, for example, consider generating functions $f, g \in \mathcal{F}$ such that

$$\begin{aligned} f(x) &= x && \text{for} \quad x \in R, \\ g(x) &= 2x && \text{for} \quad x \in [-2, 2], \\ &= x/2 - 3 && \text{for} \quad x \in (-\infty, -2], \\ &= x/2 + 3 && \text{for} \quad x \in [2, \infty) \end{aligned}$$

then g generates less vague (more reliable) data in the neighborhood of 0 meanwhile the data generated by f are less vague in certain distance from 0. If there exist two or more sources of data then it can be rational to combine their using. If it is sufficient to use only one generating function then the best strategy is to use the least vague one for every part of real line.

Theorem 2. Let $f, g \in \mathcal{F}$ be generating functions. Then there exists exactly one generating function $h \in \mathcal{F}$ with derivative h' such that

$$h'(x) = \max(f'(x), g'(x))$$

for all $x \in R$ except a set with zero Lebesgue measure.

Proof. Due to the monotonicity of f, g, their derivatives f', g' exist almost everywhere in Lebesgue measure, and they are non-negative. Put

$$\begin{aligned} h^*(x) &= \max(f'(x), g'(x)) && \text{if both } f'(x) \text{ and } g'(x) \text{ exist,} \\ &= 0 && \text{otherwise.} \end{aligned}$$

Then $h^* \geq 0$ and it is integrable. Now, we put

$$h(x) = \int_0^x h^*(x) \mathrm{d}x,$$

where the right-hand-side is the Lebesgue integral. Obviously, $h \in \mathcal{F}$ and $h' = h^*$ almost everywhere in the Lebesgue measure.

Some other applications demand some form of conformity of two or more data sources from the point of view of their reliability. Such situation may appear when some data are to be confirmed from two (or more) sources simultaneously. In such case the reliability of the resulting data source may be defined as the minimal reliability of the sources composing the final one.

Theorem 3. Let $f, g \in \mathcal{F}$ be generating functions. Then there exists exactly one generating function $h \in \mathcal{F}$ such that

$$h'(x) = \min(f'(x), g'(x))$$

for all $x \in R$ except a set with zero Lebesgue measure.

Proof. The proof is completely analogous to the previous one.

The construction of generating functions with maximal or minimal derivative and, consequently, maximal or minimal reliability of the generated data, is not the single possibility of the combinations of those functions. In some practical applications, it appears adequate to the situation to consider a convex combination of generating functions. Such approach corresponds to the case when some data are parallelly produced by two or more sources (e.g., subjective estimations of experts) and these sources are respected with different weights. If $f, g \in \mathcal{F}$ and $\alpha \in [0, 1]$ then it is possible to define a real valued function

$$h(x) = \alpha \cdot f(x) + (1 - \alpha)g(x), \quad x \in R. \tag{4.6}$$

Remark 6. Function h defined by (4.6) is a generating function, $h \in \mathcal{F}$.

Remark 7.. Let $f, g, h \in \mathcal{F}$, $\alpha \in [0, 1]$ fulfill (4.6). Then $h'(x) = \alpha f'(x) + (1 - \alpha)g'(x)$, $x \in R$.

The previous remark shows that the convex combination of generating functions leads to analogous combination of the vagueness of the generated data.

4.4 Processing of Semantic Sense

The qualitative component of the verbal variables is expressed prevailably by the *shape generators* – the φ_a component in (3.1). We denote the set of all shape generators by Φ and remember, that shape generator is, generally, any mapping $\varphi : R \rightarrow [0,1]$ such that $\varphi(0) = 0$. Moreover, as follows from Section 3.1 (Definition 2) a shape generator can be called *elementary* iff $\varphi(x)$ is increasing for $x < 0$ and decreasing for $x > 0$. Shape generators which are not elementary will be called *composed*, and they can appear as result of some logical operations with elementary verbal quantities, mainly, as result of "or" operation (e.g., "rather less than x or rather more than y, $x < y$", "approximately divisible by 100" which is "approximately 100 or approximately 200 or approximately 300 or ...").

Lemma 3. Set of shape generators Φ is an ordered set with ordering relation

$$\varphi^{(1)} \succeq \varphi^{(2)} \quad \text{iff} \quad \varphi^{(1)}(x) \geq \varphi^{(2)}(x) \quad \text{for all } x \in R$$

for $\varphi^{(1)}, \varphi^{(2)} \in \Phi$. There exist minimal element $\varphi^{(0)} \in \Phi$ and maximal element $\varphi^{*} \in \Phi$ such that

$$\varphi^{(0)}(0) = 1, \quad \varphi^{(0)}(x) = 0 \quad \text{for } x \neq 0,$$
$$\varphi^{*}(x) = 1, \qquad\qquad \text{for all } x \in R.$$

Proof. The relation defined in the statement is an ordering, it is reflexive $\varphi \succeq \varphi$ for any $\varphi \in \Phi$, semi-antisymmetric, $\varphi^{(1)} \succeq \varphi^{(2)}$ and $\varphi^{(2)} \succeq \varphi^{(1)}$ implies $\varphi^{(1)} = \varphi^{(2)}$ for $\varphi^{(1)}, \varphi^{(2)} \in \Phi$, and transitive, $\varphi^{(1)} \succeq \varphi^{(2)}$ and $\varphi^{(2)} \succeq \varphi^{(3)}$ implies $\varphi^{(1)} \succeq \varphi^{(3)}$, as follows from the properties of real-valued functions. Moreover, it is evident that, for any $\varphi \in \Phi$, $\varphi \succeq \varphi^{(0)}$ and $\varphi^{*} \succeq \varphi$.

It is natural to connect very general quantitative words without explicite reference value (like: "many", "several", "sufficiently large", etc.) with shape generators φ which are in this ordering "higher" than the shape generators connected with specified values (like "approximately x_a", etc.).

Composition of shape generators is any mapping $C : \Phi \times \Phi \rightarrow \Phi$. It can *preserve the elementarity*, i.e. the monotonicity on the negative and positive part of the domain. On the other hand, some composition rules, e.g., $C(\varphi^{(1)}, \varphi^{(2)}) = \varphi$ defined by

$$\varphi(x) = \max(\varphi^{(1)}(x), \varphi^{(2)}(x + \alpha)), \quad x \in R, \ \alpha \neq 0 \tag{4.7}$$

does not preserve the elementarity. It can be a formal representation of the verbal expression of logical operation *"or"* between verbal expressions represented by $\varphi^{(1)}$ and $\varphi^{(2)}$ applied to the crisp cores $x_{(1)}$ and $x_{(2)} = x_{(1)} - \alpha$. The above example also illustrates one of many channels in which subjective approach incomes in the fuzzy set theoretical model of verbal expressions. Equality (4.7) can be substituted by

$$\varphi^{(0)}(x) = \max\left(\varphi^{(1)}(x-\alpha), \varphi^{(2)}(x)\right) \tag{4.8}$$

which also models the disjunction of verbal expressions represented by $\varphi^{(1)}, \varphi^{(2)}$. In both cases, for fuzzy quantities generated by (3.2) from

$$(x_a, f_a, \varphi) \quad \text{and} \quad (x_a, f_a, \varphi^{(0)}),$$

there exist at least two modal values but in one case they are $(x_a - \alpha, x_a)$ meanwhile in the complementary case they are $(x_a, x_a + \alpha)$. Both approaches are formally very similar, but the resulting fuzzy quantities with membership functions $\mu_a, \mu_a^{(0)}$ can differ due to the form of f_a in the neighbourhood of $x_a, x_a - \alpha, x_a + \alpha$. The choice of these two eventualities must follow from the non-mathematical evaluation of the modelled situation.

The definition of the composition operation allows many special types of composing the shape generators. Some of them are connected with the ability of the composition rules to reduce or increase the vagueness being present in the model.

Definition 3. We say that a composition C of shape generators is contractive iff for any $\varphi^{(1)}, \varphi^{(2)} \in \Phi, \varphi = C(\varphi^{(1)}, \varphi^{(2)})$ implies

$$\varphi^{(1)} \succeq \varphi, \quad \varphi^{(2)} \succeq \varphi.$$

Remark 8. C is contractive, iff for all $\varphi = C(\varphi^{(1)}, \varphi^{(2)})$ and for all $x \in R$

$$\varphi(x) \leq \min(\varphi^{(1)}(x), \varphi^{(2)}(x)).$$

Theorem 8. If the composition of shape generators C is contractive, if $\varphi^{(1)}, \varphi^{(2)}, \ldots \in \Phi$ and if we denote by $\psi^{(1)}, \psi^{(2)}, \ldots \in \Phi$ the shape generators

$$\psi^{(1)} = C\left(\varphi^{(1)}, \varphi^{(2)}\right), \quad \psi^{(n)} = C\left(\psi^{(n-1)}, \varphi^{(n+1)}\right), \quad n = 2, 3, \ldots,$$

then the sequence $\{\psi^{(n)}\}_{n=1}^{\infty}$ is convergent.

Proof. The statement immediately follows from Remark 8 and from the boundedness of shape generators.

Typical examples of the contractive composition shape generators are minimum and product composition rules

$$\varphi(x) = \min\left(\varphi^{(1)}(x), \varphi^{(2)}(x)\right), \quad x \in R, \tag{4.9}$$

$$\varphi(x) = \varphi^{(1)}(x) \cdot \varphi^{(2)}(x), \quad x \in R. \tag{4.10}$$

Each of them reflects certain type of logical conjunction of phenomena verbally described by expressions whose mathematical model is represented by $\varphi^{(1)}$ and $\varphi^{(2)}$. The second one of them is connected with some kind of their independence (like in the probabilistic case) meanwhile (4.9) can be connected with their relatively strong dependence.

Definition 4. We say that a composition C of shape generators is expansive iff for any $\varphi^{(1)}, \varphi^{(2)} \in \Phi, \varphi = C(\varphi^{(1)}, \varphi^{(2)})$ implies

$$\varphi \succeq \varphi^{(1)} \quad \text{and} \quad \varphi \succeq \varphi^{(2)}.$$

Remark 9. C is expansive iff for all $\varphi = C(\varphi^{(1)}, \varphi^{(2)})$ and all $x \in R$

$$\varphi(x) \geq \max\left(\varphi^{(1)}(x), \varphi^{(2)}(x)\right).$$

Theorem 5. If the composition of shape generators C is expansive, if $\varphi^{(1)}, \varphi^{(2)}, \ldots \in \Phi$ and if we denote by $\psi^{(1)}, \psi^{(2)}, \ldots \in \Phi$ the shape generators

$$\psi^{(1)} = C\left(\varphi^{(1)}, \varphi^{(2)}\right), \quad \psi^{(n)} = C\left(\psi^{(n-1)}, \varphi^{(n+1)}\right), \quad n = 2, 3, \ldots,$$

then the sequence $\{\psi^{(n)}\}_{n=1}^{\infty}$ is convergent.

Proof. The statement follows immediately from Remark 9 and from the fact that $\varphi(x) \leq, \leq 1$, for all $x \in R$, $\varphi \in \Phi$.

Typical examples of expansive composition of shape generators are maximum and probabilistic addition composition rules

$$\varphi(x) = \max\left(\varphi^{(1)}(x), \varphi^{(2)}(x)\right), \qquad x \in R, \tag{4.11}$$

$$\varphi(x) = \varphi^{(1)}(x) + \varphi^{(2)}(x) - \varphi^{(1)}(x) \cdot \varphi^{(2)}(x). \tag{4.12}$$

These composition rules reflect certain type of logical disjunction of phenomena verbally described by expressions whose mathematical model is represented by $\varphi^{(1)}, \varphi^{(2)}$.

The following statement offers a formal explanation of the fact mentioned above (e.g., in the last paragraph of Section 2), namely of the rapid increasing of formal vagueness of results if the extension principle is used.

Lemma 4. The extension principle based composition rule

$$\varphi(x) = \sup_{y \in R}\left(\min(\varphi^{(1)}(y), \varphi^{(2)}(x-y))\right) \tag{4.13}$$

is expansive.

Proof. Formula (4.13) can also be written as

$$\varphi(x) = \sup_{\substack{y,z \in R \\ y+z=x}}\left(\min(\varphi^{(1)}(y), \varphi^{(2)}(z))\right).$$

It means that pairs $(0, x)$ and $(x, 0)$ belong to relevant pairs (y, z). As $\varphi^{(1)}(0) = \varphi^{(2)}(0) =$
$= 1$, the corresponding minima for $(0, x)$ and $(x, 0)$ are $\varphi^{(2)}(x)$ and $\varphi^{(1)}(x)$, respectively. The supremum means that

$$\varphi(x) \geq \max\left(\varphi^{(1)}(x), \varphi^{(2)}(x)\right)$$

and Remark 9 implies the statement.

5. Conclusive Summary – the Role of Subjectivity

The adequacy of fuzzy numbers to the modelling of vagueness of quantitative verbal expressions appears congent. Anyhow, the class of fuzzy numbers is evidently much larger and its structure is much more sophisticated than the class of words describing quantitative phenomena, their relations and operations with them. It means that, wishing to model verbal quantities by fuzzy numbers, we have to admit that each verbal expression corresponds to a relatively wide set of fuzzy numbers (or fuzzy quantities). The choice of a single fuzzy number from the class of those corresponding to a given verbal expression depends on the actual context of the realized application, and it will be always rather subjective.

In the classical theory of fuzzy numbers, each of them is represented by its membership function. If the fuzzy numbers (and operations with them) represent verbal expressions then the construction of their membership functions has to be derived from the quantitative and qualitative (semantic) content of the related words including the quality of their sources.

In the preceding sections, the formal representation of the quantitative verbal expressions is realized by means of a triple consisting of crisp core (determining the numerical value referred by the words), scale (characterizing the qualities of the source of verbal data), and shape generator (describing "normalized" form of the membership functions and representing the qualitative component of the expression). In formulas, verbal quantitative expression A is represented by a fuzzy quantity $a \in \mathbb{R}$ with membership function μ_a. This membership function is generated, by means of (3.2) from the triple $(x_a, f_a, \varphi_a) \in R \times \mathcal{F} \times \Phi$.

The first subjective input into the formal model takes place in the choice of the generating triple. If the verbal expression A refers more than one numerical value which can be modal values of μ_a then it is necessary to choose the one of them which will be the crisp core x_a. Moreover, if the verbal expression regards only general quantities (like "several", "many", etc.) the crisp core is to be subjectively chosen and substituted into the model. This choice can, with respect to the form of f_a for a given φ_a, influence the definitive form of μ_a. Also the choice of f_a is, at least in certain degree, dependent on the subjective evaluation of the reliability (vagueness) of the modelled source of data in different segments of its domain. The greater or smaller expected accuracy of the produced data can be expressed by higher or lower value of its first derivative in the relevant part of real line but only rarely the exact values of this derivative (and the running of the generating function) is exactly derivable from the situation. The last component, the shape generator, is least given by some non-personal rules. Formal description of the possibilities distribution corresponding to words like "approximately", "much more than", "almost", "several" and others is expected to possess some frame properties like symmetry or asymmetry, existence of one or more modal values, or in some cases also the extent of the support set. But the exact shape results from the subjective evaluation of the modelled situation by the author of the model. In spite of all this subjectivity the generation of membership functions μ_a from the generating triple appears more respecting the objective features of the situation than direct subjective choice of μ_a. Moreover, the repetitive application of this construction guarantees quite acceptable consistency of the obtained fuzzy quantities and proportions among them.

Another way in which subjectivity influences the final form of the chosen model is the processing of generating functions and shape generators.

In correspondence with the modelled situation and with the type of described operations with the verbal expressions, the generating functions can be processed in the algebraic way (cf. (4.1),(4.2) and (4.3)) or they can be combined due to Theorems 2 and 3. They can be also combined, as described in Remark 7, and there may exist situations in which also some other operations over $\mathcal{F}$ can be rational. For example, in the cases in which there is only one source of all input data there can exist rational reasons for respecting this source also on the output of the procedures and to use only one generating function $f \in \mathcal{F}$ in the whole model.

The processing of shape generators also admits certain degree of subjectivity. The composition of shape generators reflects quite rich structure of logical and semantical relations between verbal descriptions of quantitative vagueness. Some of the composition rules are closely connected with logical operations and they can be, consistently with the generally accepted fuzzy set theoretical methods, defined by means of minima and maxima. Some of them reflect more complex relations and they can be defined in a proportionally complex way (e.g., by an analogy of the extension principle). From the general point of view, the variety of the composition rules rather explains the variable exactness of the results of manipulation with vague verbal quantities in real situations which is mentioned in the introductory sections.

The general model of fuzzy quantities based on their generating from the triple (x_a, f_a, φ_a) and, namely, the processing of fuzzy quantities derived from the processing of the generator triples offers much wider scale of possible approaches to the fuzziness than the classical concepts of fuzzy quantities (or even the triangular or trapezoidal fuzzy numbers) and their processing in terms of extension principle (or elementary manipulation with triangular and trapezoidal fuzzy numbers). Only some of the specific instances of the general model are near to the traditional conceptions.

The generating functions most similar to the classical view on the vagueness of numbers are, probably, the linear ones

$$f(x) = x \tag{5.1}$$

or, more generally,

$$f(x) = \alpha \cdot x, \quad \alpha > 0, \tag{5.2}$$

even if the most realistic reflection of the development of vagueness of the data sources is probably represented by smooth functions with decreasing first derivative like

$$f(x) = \log(1 + |x|) \cdot \mathrm{sign}(x) \tag{5.3}$$

or

$$\begin{aligned} f(x) &= \sqrt{(x+1)} - 1, & x \geq 0, \\ &= -\sqrt{(|x|+1)} + 1, & x < 0, \end{aligned} \tag{5.4}$$

or even

$$\begin{aligned} f(x) &= \alpha \cdot \left(1 - \left(\tfrac{1}{2}\right)^{x}\right), & \alpha > 0,\ x \geq 0, \\ &= -\beta \cdot \left(1 - \left(\tfrac{1}{2}\right)^{-x}\right), & \beta > 0,\ x < 0. \end{aligned} \tag{5.5}$$

The simplest, and for many practical applications quite satisfactory shape generator is the triangular one as it was used, e.g., in [4]

$$\varphi(x) = \max(0, 1 - |x|) \tag{5.6}$$

or, more generally,

$$\begin{aligned} \varphi(x) &= \max(0, 1 - \alpha x) & \text{for } \alpha > 0,\ x \geq 0, \\ &= \max(0, 1 + \beta x) & \text{for } \beta > 0,\ x < 0. \end{aligned} \tag{5.7}$$

Definitional equation (5.6) combined with (3.2) leads to the membership function

$$\mu_a(x) = \max\left(0, 1 - |f(x_a) - f(x)|\right), \quad x_a \in R$$

and for linear generating function (5.1) it means the triangular membership function

$$\mu_a(x) = \max(0, 1 - |a_a - x|).$$

Processing such simple models in some cases leads to analogous results like the classical approach to fuzzy numbers.

Theorem 6. Let $f \in \mathcal{F}$ be linear (5.1), let $\varphi \in \Phi$ be triangular $\varphi(x) = \max(0, 1 - |\beta x|)$, $x \in R$, $\beta > 0$, and let C be the extension-principle-composition rule

$$C(\varphi, \varphi) = \sup_{y \in R} \left(\min(\varphi(y), \varphi(x - y))\right).$$

Then for any $x_a \in R$ the membership functions μ_a and μ_a^* generated by $(x_a, f \boxplus f, \varphi)$ and $(x_a, f, C(\varphi, \varphi))$, respectively, are equal,

$$\mu_a(x) = \mu_a^*(x), \quad x \in R.$$

Proof. Under the assumptions of the theorem $g(x) = x/2$ for

$$g(x) = (f \boxplus f)(x),$$
$$\psi(x) = C(\varphi,\varphi)(x) = \max\left(0, 1 - \left|\tfrac{\beta}{2}x\right|\right),$$

and, consequently,

$$\begin{aligned} \mu_a(x) &= \varphi(g(x_a) - g(x)) = \max\left(0, 1 - \left|\frac{\beta x_a}{2} - \frac{\beta x}{2}\right|\right) = \\ &= \max\left(0, 1 - \frac{\beta}{2}|x_a - x|\right) = \varphi\left(f(x_a) - f(x)\right) = \mu_a^*(x). \end{aligned}$$

The previous statement contributes to a more general question, namely under which assumptions the generators $(x_a, f, C(\varphi,\varphi))$ and $(x_a, P(f,f), \varphi)$, where P is a binary operation with scales, lead (via (3.2)) to the same membership function μ_a.

References

1. B. DeBaets, M. Mareš, R. Mesiar: On the invariance of classes of shape generators. In: Proceedings of EUFIT'97. Verlag Mainz, Aachen 1997, Vol. 1, 10–14.
2. B. DeBaets, M. Mareš, R. Mesiar: Fuzzy zeroes and indisguishability of real numbers. In: Proceedings of 5th Fuzzy Days – International Conference on Computational Intelligence. Dortmund 1997 (Ed.: B. Reutsch). Springer Verlag, Berlin 1997, 299–303.
3. D. Dubois, H. Prade: Fuzzy numbers: an overview. In: J. Bezdek (Ed.): Analysis of Fuzzy Information. CRC–Press, Boca Raton 1987, Vol. I, 3–39.
4. J. Jacas, J. Recasens: Fuzzy numbers and equality relations. In: Proceedings of IEEE'93 on Fuzzy Systems, San Francisco 1993, 1298–1301.
5. A. Kaufmann, M.M. Gupta: Introduction to Fuzzy Arithmetics. Van Nostrand, New York 1985.
6. M. Mareš: Computation Over Fuzzy Quantities. CRC–Press, Boca Raton 1994.
7. M. Mareš, R. Mesiar: Composition of shape generators. Acta Mathematica et Informatica Universitatis Ostraviensis. University of Ostrava 1996, 37–45.
8. M. Mareš: Weak arithmetics of fuzzy numbers. Fuzzy Sets and Systems, 1997, to appear.
9. M. Mareš, R. Mesiar: Processing of sources of fuzzy quantities. In: Proceedings of IPMU'96, University of Granada 1996, Vol. I, 359–363.
10. M. Mareš, R. Mesiar: Vagueness of verbal variable. In: Soft Computing of Financial Engineering (Eds.: J. Kacprzyk, R. Ribeiro, R.R. Yager, H.-J. Zimmermann). Physica Verlag, to appear.
11. Proceedings of International Panel Conference on Soft and Intelligent Computing, (Ed. J. Kóczy). Technical University of Budapest, Budapest 1996.

Aggregation of Linguistic Information Based on a Symbolic Approach

M. Delgado, F. Herrera, E. Herrera-Viedma, J.L. Verdegay and M.A. Vila

Department of Computer Science and Artificial Intelligence, University of Granada
18071 - Granada, Spain

Summary. A summary on the symbolic basic arithmetic operators and aggregation operators of linguistic information developed by the authors is presented. In particular, label addition, label difference, product of a label by a positive real number, and convex combination of labels are shown as the symbolic basic arithmetic operators, and two aggregation operators of linguistic information built using those tools are described. The first one, called the Linguistic Ordered Weighted Averaging operator, is used to deal with linguistic information with equal importance, and the second one, called the Linguistic Weighted Averaging operator, is used to deal with weighted linguistic information.

1. Introduction

The *"linguistic approach based on fuzzy sets"* has given very good results for modeling qualitative information. It has been widely used in different fields, as for example, "information retrieval" [2], "clinical diagnosis" [6], "marketing" [35], "risk in software development" [26, 27], "technology transfer strategy selection" [4], "education" [25], "decision making" [3],... It is an approximate technique in its essence, which represents qualitative aspects as linguistic values by means of *linguistic variables*, that is, variables whose values are not numbers but words or sentences in a natural or artificial language [36]. Each linguistic value is characterized by a *syntactic value* or *label* and a *semantic value* or *meaning*. The label is a word or sentence belonging to a linguistic term set, and the meaning is a fuzzy number of a universe of discourse.

In any fuzzy sets based application of the linguistic approach, the combination (in a general sense) of linguistic values (labels) is needed. Two approaches may be used to cope with this task:

- The first one is based on the "Extension Principle", and it allows us to aggregate and compare labels through computations on the associated membership functions, but it is well known that by using extended arithmetic operations to handle fuzzy numbers, the vagueness of results increases step by step and the shape of membership functions does not keep when the linguistic variables are interactive. Thus, the final results of those methods are fuzzy sets which do not correspond to any label in the original term set. If one finally wants to have a label, then a "linguistic approximation" is needed [6, 28].

- The second kind of approach is the *symbolic one*, which acts by direct computation on labels [10, 13, 24, 32, 34], only taking into account the meaning and properties of such linguistic assessments, with independence of their semantic representation. From this point of view in most situations the results of symbolic aggregation operators of labels may be summarized in one table or as simple procedures [10]. Symbolic methods seem to be the more "natural" ones when the linguistic approach is used, because the linguistic assessments are just approximations which are given and handled if obtaining more accurate values is impossible or unnecessary. Futhermore, they are computationally simple and may be easily applied in user-driven interactive systems.

Although the symbolic linguistic approach has been used extensively, we miss a global study which analyzes from its basical typical tools to the new techniques by direct application. To bridge that gap this paper summarizes some issues for symbolic aggregation of linguistic information presented by the authors. We review a particular symbolic approach on arithmetic operators [10], which includes a formal and general definition of a label space and a basic arithmetic of labels composed by the following aggregation tools of labels: *label addition, label difference, product of a label by a real number, and convex combination of labels.* After that, we introduce two aggregation operators of linguistic information, which are built using the mentioned symbolic aggregation tools:

1. the *Linguistic Ordered Weighted Averaging (LOWA)* operator [24], which is used to combine non-weighted linguistic information, and
2. the *Linguistic Weighted Averaging (LWA)* operator [13], which is used to combine weighted linguistic information and is proposed as a generalization of the LOWA operator applied to combine linguistic information provided by information sources with different importance.

Consequently, the paper is structured as follows: Section 2 presents a review of the symbolic basic arithmetic operators; Section 3 shows the LOWA and LWA operators; and finally, some concluding remarks are pointed out.

2. A Symbolic Approach for Basic Arithmetic Operators

In this section, we present the arithmetic of labels which is composed of different symbolic aggregation tools. To do so, a particular linguistic framework, called "generalized label space" is used . Firstly, we present this linguistic framework, and then, the arithmetic operators.

2.1 The Generalized Label Set

The linguistic context considered in [10] is a simple but simultaneously general one characterized by a certain semantic representation of the labels according to the following hypothesis.

Hypothesis 1. *Let X be the interval $[x_1, x_2] \subseteq \mathcal{R}$ ($\mathcal{R}$ stands for real number set), where x_1 or x_2 may be $-\infty$ or $+\infty$ respectively, and $\mathcal{H} = \{p_i\}$ $i \in M \subset \mathcal{Z}$ ($\mathcal{Z}$ stands for integer number set) be a finite and totally ordered term set on X in the usual sense [1]. Any label p_i will represent a possible value for a linguistic real variable, that is a vague property or constraint on X. According to Zadeh [36], each label has a semantic representation as a fuzzy set of X. M reflects the order of $\mathcal{H}$ and we will denote by i_0 and i_m its first and last elements, respectively.*

Hypothesis 2. *The semantic of any label $p_i \in \mathcal{H}$ is given by an LR fuzzy interval $(a_i, b_i, c_i, d_i)_{LR}$, indicating the first two paremeters the interval in which the membership value is 1 and the third and fourth parameters the left and right widths[12]. Furthermore,*

1. *$\forall i$, $i \neq i_0$, $i \neq i_m$, p_i is symmetric, that is $L(\cdot) = R(\cdot)$; $c_i = d_i = k$.*
2. *$a_{i_0} = x_1$, $c_{i_0} = 0$, $d_{i_0} = k$, $b_{i_m} = x_2$, $d_{i_m} = 0$, $c_{i_m} = k$. If $x_1 \neq -\infty$ or $x_2 \neq +\infty$ then $(b_{i_0} - a_{i_0}) = k'$ or $(b_{i_m} - a_{i_m}) = k'$, respectively.*
3. *$\forall i$, $(a_{i+1} - b_i) = k''$. Additionally if $i \neq i_0$ and $i \neq i_m$, $(b_i - a_i) = k'$.*
4. *$e = k' + k'' \geq k$.*

As it was shown in [10], a lot of examples, about money, risk, etc., can be found to confirm that *"when labels are aggregated, the referential set changes and thus, if we assume the term set keeps, then the semantic representation of labels changes."*

Then, according to these ideas, in order to achieve a good definition for aggregation tools, in [10] was proposed the following generalized label space to express the linguistic assessments, which provides a new flexible semantic for labels being adaptive to the number of operations already made.

Definition 2.1. *Let $\mathcal{H}$ be the label set with basic semantic given by hypotheses 1 and 2. The "generalized label space" based on $\mathcal{H}$ is the cartesian product:*

$$\mathcal{G} = \mathcal{H} \times \mathcal{Z}^+,$$

where $\mathcal{Z}^+$ stands for the non-negative integer set. Any $(p_i, k) \in \mathcal{G}$ will be called a generalized label and must be interpreted as the label p_i with semantic given by: $k \otimes (a_i, b_i, c_i, d_i)_{LR}$, where the product is the classical one of a real positive number by a fuzzy number, that is,

$$\forall x \in \mathcal{G};\ x = (p_i, k) \simeq (ka_i, kb_i, kc_i, kd_i)_{LR}.$$

Let us observe k represents the number of times that the scale changes that will correspond with the number of aggregations which have been made.

The basic label set is $\mathcal{H} = \{(p_i, 1),\ i \in M\}$. We shall consider $(p_i, h),\ h > 0$, when we are using the linguistic term p_i in some situation where the magnitude to be qualified appears h times "greater" than the initial one, for example: time to carry out h tasks, money to be obtained from h investment, etc...

Generalized labels with $h = 0$ will appear in relation with the difference between labels in the same scale, or to aggregate labels without changing the scale, in particular, when we need to linguistically express the comparison between (p_i, d) and (p_j, d), $i,\ j \in M,\ d > 0$.

2.2 Arithmetic of Generalized Labels

Using as linguistic framework the above generalized label space, in [10] was defined an arithmetic of generalized labels, which is composed of the following four aggregation tools of linguistic information: label addition, label difference, product of label by a real number, and convex combination of linguistic labels. Below they are described.

Definition 2.2. *Let $(p_i, t), (p_j, h) \in \mathcal{G}$ two generalized labels to be aggregated with positive t and h. The addition of both generalized labels is the generalized label $(p_s, t + h)$, obtained according to*

$$(p_i, t) \oplus (p_j, h) = (p_s, t + h),$$

where

$$s = round((ti+hj)/(t+h)) = \begin{cases} \lfloor \frac{(ti+hj)}{(t+h)} \rfloor & \text{if } |\frac{(ti+hj)}{(t+h)} - \lfloor \frac{(ti+hj)}{(t+h)} \rfloor| \leq 0.5 \\ \lfloor \frac{(ti+hj)}{(t+h)} \rfloor + 1 & \text{otherwise.} \end{cases}$$

Definition 2.3. *Let $(p_i, t), (p_j, h) \in \mathcal{G}$ and suppose either $\{t > h;\ t(i - i_0) \geq h(j - i_0);\ t(i_m - i) \geq h(i_m - j)\}$ or $\{t = h;\ i_0 \leq i - j \leq i_m\}$ holds. The difference between both generalized labels is the generalized label (p_s, l) given by*

$$(p_i, t) \ominus (p_j, h) = (p_s, l),$$

where

$$\begin{array}{lll} l = t - h & \text{and } s = round(\frac{(ti+hj)}{(t+h)}) & \text{if } t > h \\ l = 0 & \text{and } s = i - j & \text{otherwise.} \end{array}$$

Definition 2.4. *Let $(p_i, t) \in \mathcal{G}$ and let v be a positive integer number. The product $v \otimes (p_i, t)$ is given by*

$$v \otimes (p_i, t) = (p_i, vt) \quad \text{if } t > 0$$

$$v \otimes (p_i, 0) = (p_s, 0) \quad \text{with } s = \begin{cases} i_0 & \text{if } vi < i_0 \\ i_m & \text{if } vi > i_m \\ vi & \text{otherwise.} \end{cases}$$

Definition 2.5. *Let $(p_i, t) \in \mathcal{G}$ and $\alpha \in (0,1)$. The product $\alpha \otimes (p_i, t)$ is the generalized label (p_s, t) where $s = round(\alpha i)$.*

Definition 2.6. *Let $(p_i, t) \in \mathcal{G}$ be and $\gamma \in \mathcal{R}$, $\gamma > 0$. The product $\gamma \otimes (p_i, t)$ is given by*

$$\gamma \otimes (p_i, t) = \begin{cases} v \otimes (p_i, t) \oplus \alpha \otimes (p_i, t) & \text{if } v > 0 \\ \alpha \otimes (p_i, t) & \text{otherwise.} \end{cases}$$

where $v = |\gamma|$ and $\alpha = \gamma - v$.

Definition 2.7. *Let $(p_i, t), (p_j, t) \in \mathcal{G}$ and $\gamma \in [0,1]$. (Without losing generality we shall admit $j > i$). The convex combination $\gamma \otimes (p_j, t) \oplus (1-\gamma)(p_i, t)$ is the generalized label (p_c, t) given by*

$$(p_c, t) = (p_i, t) \oplus \gamma \otimes ((p_j, t) \ominus (p_i, t)).$$

Definition 2.8. *Let $(p_{i(k)}, t) \in \mathcal{G}, k = 1, 2, \ldots, K$ be and assume $i(K) \leq i(K-1) \leq \ldots, \leq i(1)$ without loss of generality. For any set of coefficients $\{\lambda_k \in [0,1],\ k = 1, 2, \ldots, K,\ \sum \lambda_k = 1\}$ the convex combination of these K generalized labels is the one given by*

$$\begin{aligned} &\mathcal{C}\{\lambda_k, (p_{i(k)}, t),\ k = 1, 2, \ldots, K\} = \\ &= \ \lambda_1 p_{i(1)} \oplus (1-\lambda_1)\mathcal{C}(\beta_h, (p_{i(h)}, t),\ h = 2, \ldots, K), \end{aligned}$$

where

$$\beta_h = \lambda_h / \Sigma_2^K \lambda_k, h = 2, \ldots, K.$$

3. Two Aggregation Operators: LOWA and LWA

From the above symbolic basic arithmetic operators of generalized labels, LOWA [24] and LWA [13] operators can be introduced. They are proposed to combine non-weighted and weighted linguistic information, respectively, and they can be described assuming the following linguistic context.

The linguistic framework used here is similar to that given in Subsection 2.1, but it does not consider the scale changes. In particular, in [18, 24] is proposed to use label sets with an odd cardinal, representing the middle term an assessment of "approximately 0.5", with the rest of the terms being placed symmetrically around it and the limit of granularity 11 or no more than 13 [1]. The semantic of the elements in the label set is given by fuzzy numbers defined on the [0,1] interval, which are described by membership functions. Because the linguistic assessments are just approximate ones given by the experts, we can consider that linear trapezoidal membership functions are good enough to capture the vagueness of those linguistic assessments, since it may be impossible or unnecessary to obtain more accurate values. This representation is achieved as above by the 4-tuple, (a_i, b_i, c_i, d_i). Furthermore, the term set, $S = \{s_0, \ldots, s_T\}$, must have the following characteristics:

1) The set is ordered: $s_i \geq s_j$ if $i \geq$ j.
2) There is the negation operator: Neg$(s_i) = s_j$ such that $j = T$-i.
3) Maximization operator: Max$(s_i, s_j) = s_i$ if $s_i \geq s_j$.
4) Minimization operator: Min$(s_i, s_j) = s_i$ if $s_i \leq s_j$.

For example, this is the case of the following set of nine labels:

VH	$Very\_High$	$(1, 1, 0, 0)$
H	$High$	$(.98, .99, .05, .01)$
MH	$Moreorless\_High$	$(.78, .92, .06, .05)$
$FFMH$	$From\_Fair\_to\_Moreorless\_High$	$(.63, .80, .05, .06)$
F	$Fair$	$(.41, .58, .09, .07)$
$FFML$	$From\_Fair\_to\_Moreorless\_Low$	$(.22, .36, .05, .06)$
ML	$Moreorless\_Low$	$(.1, .18, .06, .05)$
L	Low	$(.01, .02, .01, .05)$
VL	$Very\_Low$	$(0, 0, 0, 0)$

In this linguistic context, the following two aggregation operators of linguistic information are defined.

3.1 The LOWA Operator

The *LOWA operator* [24] is based on the OWA operator defined in [31] and the previously defined convex combination of generalized labels.

Definition 3.1. *Let $A = \{a_1, \ldots, a_m\}$ be a set of labels to be aggregated, then the LOWA operator, ϕ, is defined as*

$$\phi(a_1, \ldots, a_m) = W \cdot B^T = \mathcal{C}^m\{w_k, b_k, k = 1, \ldots, m\} =$$

$$= w_1 \odot b_1 \oplus (1 - w_1) \odot \mathcal{C}^{m-1}\{\beta_h, b_h, h = 2, \ldots, m\}$$

where $W = [w_1, \ldots, w_m]$, is a weighting vector, such that,

1. *$w_i \in [0, 1]$ and,*
2. *$\Sigma_i w_i = 1$,*

$\beta_h = w_h / \Sigma_2^m w_k$, $h = 2, \ldots, m$, and $B = \{b_1, \ldots, b_m\}$ is a vector associated to A, such that,

$$B = \sigma(A) = \{a_{\sigma(1)}, \ldots, a_{\sigma(n)}\}$$

where,

$$a_{\sigma(j)} \leq a_{\sigma(i)} \;\forall\, i \leq j,$$

with σ being a permutation over the set of labels A. $\mathcal{C}^m$ is the convex combination operator of m labels (without scale change parameter), and if m=2, then it is defined as

$$\mathcal{C}^2\{w_i, b_i, i = 1, 2\} = w_1 \odot s_j \oplus (1 - w_1) \odot s_i = s_k, \quad s_j,\ s_i\ \in\ S,\ (j \geq i)$$

such that

$$k \ = \ min\{T, i \ + \ round(w_1 \cdot (j - i))\}$$

where $b_1 = s_j,\ b_2 = s_i$.
If $w_j = 1$ *and* $w_i = 0$ *with* $i \neq j\ \forall i$, *then the convex combination is defined as:*

$$\mathcal{C}^m\{w_i, b_i, i = 1, \ldots, m\} = b_j.$$

An extension of this operator combining numerical and linguistic information has been developed in [8].

How to calculate the weighting vector of LOWA operator, W, is a basic question to be solved. Any possible solution will depend on the application context. For example, in the case of group decision making problems a possible solution is that the weights represent the concept of *fuzzy majority* in the aggregation of LOWA operator using *fuzzy linguistic quantifiers* [37]. Yager proposed an interesting way to compute the weights of the OWA aggregation operator, which, in the case of a non-decreasing proportional fuzzy linguistic quantifier, Q, is given by this expression [31]:

$$w_i = Q(i/n) - Q((i-1)/n), i = 1, \ldots, n,$$

being the membership function of Q, as follows:

$$Q(r) = \begin{cases} 0 & \text{if } r < a \\ \frac{r-a}{b-a} & \text{if } a \leq r \leq b \\ 1 & \text{if } r > b \end{cases}$$

with $a, b, r \in [0, 1]$. Some examples of non-decreasing proportional fuzzy linguistic quantifiers are: "most" $(0.3, 0.8)$, "at least half" $(0, 0.5)$ and "as many as possible" $(0.5, 1)$. When a fuzzy linguistic quantifier, Q, is used to compute the weights of LOWA operator, ϕ, it is symbolized by ϕ_Q. Similarly happens for the I-LOWA operator, i.e., in this case it is symbolized by ϕ_Q^I.

The LOWA operator is a rational aggregation operator. It verifies the following properties and axioms of any acceptable aggregation operator [18]: *increasing monotonous, "orand" operator, unrestricted domain, unanimity or idempotence, positive association of social and individual values, independence of irrelevant alternatives, citizen sovereignty, neutrality with respect to alternatives, and neutrality with respect to voters.*

Some applications of the LOWA operator guided by fuzzy majority can be found in group decision making problems, with main emphasys on selection processes [14, 16, 18] and consensus models [17, 19, 20, 21].

3.2 The LWA Operator

Here, we analyze the LWA operator [13] that allows us to aggregate linguistic weighted information.

Let $\{(c_1, a_1), \ldots, (c_m, a_m)\}$ be a set of weighted opinions such that a_i shows the opinion of an expert e_i, assessed linguistically on the label set, S, $a_i \in S$, and c_i the importance degree of expert e_i, assessed linguistically on the same label set S, $c_i \in S$.

As it is well known[5] if we want to aggregate weighted information we have to define two aggregations:

- the aggregation of importance degrees ($\{c_1, \ldots, c_m\}$) of information, and
- the aggregation of weighted information, which combines information with its importance degrees.

The first aspect consists of obtaining a collective importance degree from individual importance degrees that characterizes the final result of the aggregation operator. In the LWA operator, as the importance degrees are linguistic values, the aggregation of importance degrees is solved using the LOWA operator guided by the concept of fuzzy majority.

The aggregation of weighted information involves the transformation of the weighted information under the importance degrees and the final aggregation of the transformed information. The transformation form depends upon the type of aggregation of weighted information being performed [33]. In [29, 30] Yager discussed the effect of the importance degrees in the types of aggregation "MAX" and "MIN" and suggested a class of functions for importance transformation in both types of aggregation. For MIN type aggregation he suggested a family of "t-conorms" acting on the weighted information and the negation of the importance degrees, which presents the non-increasing monotonic property in the weights. For MAX type aggregation he suggested a family of "t-norms" acting on weighted information and the importance degree, which presents the non-decreasing monotonic property in the importance degrees.

In [33] Yager proposed a general specification of the requirements that any *importance transformation function*, g, must satisfy for any type of the aggregation operator. The function, g, must have the following properties:

1. if $a > b$ then $g(c, a) \geq g(c, b)$
2. $g(c, a)$ is monotone in c
3. $g(0, a) = ID$
4. $g(1, a) = a$.

with a, $b \in [0, 1]$ expressing the satisfaction with regards to a criterion, $c \in [0, 1]$ the importance degree associated to the criterion, and "ID" an identity element, which is such that if we add it to our aggregations it doesn't change the aggregated value.

- Condition one means that the function g is monotonically non-decreasing in the second argument, that is, if the satisfaction with regards to the criteria is increased the overall satisfaction shouldn't decrease.
- The second condition may be viewed as a requirement that the effect of the importance be consistent. It doesn't specify whether g is monotonically non-increasing or non-decreasing in the first argument, but must be one of these. It should be denoted that conditions three and four actually determine the type of monotonicity obtained from two. If $a >$ ID, the $g(c, a)$ is monotonically non-decreasing in w, while if $a <$ ID, then it is monotonically non-increasing.
- The third condition is a manifestation of the imperative that zero importance items don't effect the aggregation process.
- The final condition is essentially a boundary condition which states that the assumption of all importances equal to one effectively is like not including importances at all [33].

Before defining the LWA operator, let us present the following two families of linguistic connectives [13] and an extension of the LOWA operator, the *Inverse LOWA* operator [13]:

1. **Linguistic conjunction functions ($LC^{\rightarrow}$).**
   These linguistic conjunction functions are monotonically non-decreasing t-norms in the importance degrees:
   a) *The classical MIN operator:*
   $$LC_1^{\rightarrow}(c, a) = MIN(c, a).$$
   b) *The nilpotent MIN operator:*
   $$LC_2^{\rightarrow}(c, a) = \begin{cases} MIN(c, a) & \text{if } c > Neg(a) \\ s_0 & \text{otherwise.} \end{cases}$$
   c) *The weakest conjunction:*
   $$LC_3^{\rightarrow}(c, a) = \begin{cases} MIN(c, a) & \text{if } MAX(c, a) = s_T \\ s_0 & \text{otherwise.} \end{cases}$$
2. **Linguistic implication functions ($LI^{\rightarrow}$).**
   These linguistic implication functions are monotonically non-increasing in the importance degrees:
   a) *Kleene-Dienes's implication function:*
   $$LI_1^{\rightarrow}(c, a) = MAX(Neg(c), a).$$
   b) *Gödel's implication function:*
   $$LI_2^{\rightarrow}(c, a) = \begin{cases} s_T & \text{if } c \leq a \\ a & \text{otherwise.} \end{cases}$$

c) *Fodor's implication function:*

$$LI_3^{\rightarrow}(c,a) = \begin{cases} s_T & \text{if } c \leq a \\ MAX(Neg(c), a) & \text{otherwise.} \end{cases}$$

Definition 3.2. *An Inverse-Linguistic Ordered Weighted Averaging operator(I-LOWA operator), ϕ^I, is a type of LOWA operator, in which*

$$B = \sigma^I(A) = \{a_{\sigma(1)}, \ldots, a_{\sigma(n)}\}$$

where,

$$a_{\sigma(i)} \leq a_{\sigma(j)} \ \forall\, i \leq j.$$

If m=2, then C^2 is defined as

$$C^2\{w_h, b_h, h = 1, 2,\ b_1 \leq b_2\} = w_1 \odot s_j \oplus (1 - w_1) \odot s_i = s_k,$$

$$k \ = \ min\{T, i \ + \ round(w_1 \cdot (j - i))\}.$$

with $b_1 = s_j, b_2 = s_i,\ \ s_j,\ s_i\ \in\ S,\ \ j \leq i$.

Considering the aforementioned ideas and assuming a label set, S, to express the information and the importance degrees, in [13] it is presented the LWA operator, with its respective aggregation operators and transformation functions:

1. Aggregation operator: LOWA or I-LOWA.
2. Transformation function: $g_{(\text{LOWA})} \ = \ LC^{\rightarrow}(c,a)$ or $g_{(\text{I-LOWA})} \ = \ LI^{\rightarrow}(c,a)$.

It is based on the combination of the LOWA and I-LOWA operator with several *linguistic conjunction functions* ($LC^{\rightarrow}$) and several *linguistic implication functions* ($LI^{\rightarrow}$), respectively. Therefore, the LWA operator is a type of fuzzy majority guided weighted aggregation operator, which may be viewed as a generalization of the LOWA operator.

Definition 3.3. *The aggregation of the set of weighted individual information, $\{(c_1, a_1), \ldots, (c_m, a_m)\}$, according to the LWA operator, Ω, is defined as a weighted collective information, (c_E, a_E), such that*

$$(c_E, a_E) = \Omega[(c_1, a_1), \ldots, (c_m, a_m)],$$

where the importance degree of the group opinion, c_E, is obtained as

$$c_E = \phi_Q(c_1, \ldots, c_m),$$

and, the opinion of the group, a_E, is obtained as

$$a_E = f[g(c_1, a_1), \ldots, g(c_m, a_m)],$$

where $f \in \{\phi_Q, \phi_Q^I\}$ is an linguistic aggregation operator of transformed information and g is a importance transformation function, such that,

$$g \in \{LC_1^{\rightarrow}, LC_2^{\rightarrow}, LC_3^{\rightarrow}\} \text{ if } f = \phi_Q, \text{ and } g \in \{LI_1^{\rightarrow}, LI_2^{\rightarrow}, LI_3^{\rightarrow}\} \text{ if } f = \phi_Q^I.$$

As it was commented in [13], when the aggregation operator, f, is the I-LOWA operator, ϕ_Q^I, and given that ϕ_Q^I is an aggregation operator with characteristics of a MIN type aggregation operator, then we decide to use the linguistic implication functions, $LI^{\rightarrow}$, as the transformation function type. Something similar happens when f is the LOWA operator ϕ_Q. It can be observed that the LWA operator tries to reduce the effect of elements with low importance. To do so, when $f = \phi_Q$, the elements with low importance are transformed into small values and when $f = \phi_Q^I$ the elements with low importance are transformed into large values.

In [13] are presented some evidences of rationality of the LWA operator.

Applications of the LWA operator have been developed in multi-criteria [13], group decision making [22], information gathering on the Internet [7] and personnel management problems [23].

4. Concluding Remarks

In this paper, we have reviewed the symbolic basic arithmetic operators. These have a great potential for solving problems with linguistic information, because they define an appropriate linguistic framework for designing aggregation operators. A clear example of their application are the two aggregation operators of linguistic information defined using them, the LOWA and LWA operators. These aggregation operators allow us to aggregate linguistic non-weighted and weighted information, respectively, having a great range of application.

References

1. P.P. Bonissone and K.S. Decker, Selecting Uncertainty Calculi and Granularity: An Experiment in Trading-off Precision and Complexity, in: L.H. Kanal and J.F. Lemmer, Eds., *Uncertainty in Artificial Intelligence* (North-Holland, 1986) 217-247.
2. G. Bordogna and G. Pasi, A Fuzzy Linguistic Approach Generalizing Boolean Information Retrieval; a Model and Its Evaluation, *J. of the American Society for Information Science* **44** (1993) 70-82.
3. G. Bordogna, M. Fedrizzi and G. Passi, A Linguistic Modelling of Consensus in Group Decision Making Based on OWA Operators, *IEEE Transactions on Systems, Man, and Cybernetics* **27** (1997) 126-132.
4. P. Chang and Y. Chen, A Fuzzy Multicriteria Decision Making Method for Technology Transfer Strategy Selection in Biotechnology, *Fuzzy Sets and Systems* **63** (1994) 131-139.
5. W. Cholewa, Aggregation of Fuzzy Opinions: An Axiomatic Approach, *Fuzzy Sets and Systems* **17** (1985) 249-259.
6. R. Degani and G. Bortolan, The Problem of Linguistic Approximation in Clinical Decision Making, *Int. J. of Approximate Reasoning* **2** (1988) 143-162.

7. M. Delgado, F. Herrera, E. Herrera-Viedma, M.J. Martin-Bautista and M.A. Vila, Combining Linguistic Information in a Distributed Intelligent Agent Model for Information Gathering on the Internet, in: J. P.P. Wang, Ed., *Computing with Words* (John Wiley & Son, 1997). To appear.
8. M. Delgado, F. Herrera, E. Herrera-Viedma and L. Martínez, Combining Numerical and Linguistic Information in Group Decision Making, *Information Sciences* (1997). To appear.
9. M. Delgado, J.L. Verdegay and M.A. Vila, Linguistic Decision Making Models, *Int. J. of Intelligent Systems* **7** (1992) 479-492.
10. M. Delgado, J.L. Verdegåy and M.A. Vila, On Aggregation Operations of Linguistic Labels, *Int. J. of Intelligent Systems* **8** (1993) 351-370.
11. M. Delgado, J.L. Verdegay and M.A. Vila, A Model for Linguistic Partial Information in Decision Making Problems, *Int. J. of Intelligent Systems* **9** (1994) 365-378.
12. D. Dubois and H. Prade, *Fuzzy and Systems Theory and Applications*, (Academic Press, New York, 1980).
13. F. Herrera and E. Herrera-Viedma, Aggregation Operators for Linguistic Weighted Information, *IEEE Transactions on Systems, Man, and Cybernetics* **27** (1997) 646-656.
14. F. Herrera, E. Herrera-Viedma and J.L. Verdegay, A Sequential Selection Process in Group Decision Making with Linguistic Assessment, *Information Sciences* **85** (1995) 223-239.
15. F. Herrera, E. Herrera-Viedma and J.L. Verdegay, Aggregating Linguistic Preferences: Properties of LOWA Operator, *Proc. 5th IFSA World Congress*, Sao Paulo, 1995, 153-156.
16. F. Herrera, E. Herrera-Viedma and J.L. Verdegay, A Linguistic Decision Process in Group Decision Making, *Group Decision and Negotiation* **5** (1996) 165-176.
17. F. Herrera, E. Herrera-Viedma and J.L. Verdegay, A Model of Consensus in Group Decision Making under Linguistic Assessments, *Fuzzy Sets and Systems* **78** (1996) 73-87.
18. F. Herrera, E. Herrera-Viedma and J.L. Verdegay, Direct Approach Processes in Group Decision Making Using Linguistic OWA Operators, *Fuzzy Sets and Systems* **79** (1996) 175-190.
19. F. Herrera, E. Herrera-Viedma and J.L. Verdegay, A Rational Consensus Model in Group Decision Making using Linguistic Assessments. *Fuzzy Sets and Systems*, **88** (1997) 31-49.
20. F. Herrera, E. Herrera-Viedma and J.L. Verdegay, Consensus Based on Fuzzy Coincidence for Group Decision Making in Linguistic Setting, in: J. Kacprzyk, H. Nurmi and M. Fedrizzi, Eds., *Consensus Under Fuzziness* (Kluwer Academic Publishers, 1997) 121-146.
21. F. Herrera, E. Herrera-Viedma and J.L. Verdegay, Linguistic Measures Based on Fuzzy Coincidence for Reaching Consensus in Group Decision Making, *Int. J. Approximate Reasoning* **16** (1997) 309-334.
22. F. Herrera, E. Herrera-Viedma and J.L. Verdegay, Choice Processes for Non-Homogeneous Group Decision Making in Linguistic Setting, *Fuzzy Sets and Systems* (1997). To appear.
23. F. Herrera, E. Lopez, C. Mendaña and M.A Rodriguez, A Linguistic Decision Model for Personnel Management Solved with a Linguistic Biobjective Genetic Algorithms, Technical Report 97119, Dept. of Computer Science and A.I, University of Granada (1997).

24. F. Herrera and J.L. Verdegay, Linguistic Assessments in Group Decision, *Proc. 1th European Congress on Fuzzy and Intelligent Technologies*, Aachen, 1993, 941-948.
25. C.K. Law, Using Fuzzy Numbers in Educational Grading System, *Fuzzy Sets and Systems* **83** (1996) 311-323.
26. H.M. Lee, Group Decision Making Using Fuzzy Sets Theory for Evaluating the Rate of Aggregative Risk in Software Development, *Fuzzy Sets and Systems* **80** (1996) 261-271.
27. H.M. Lee, Applying Fuzzy Set Theory to Evaluate the Rate of Aggregative Risk in Software Development, *Fuzzy Sets and Systems* **80** (1996) 323-336.
28. M. Tong and P. P. Bonissone, A Linguistic Approach to Decision Making with Fuzzy Sets, *IEEE Transactions on Systems, Man and Cybernetics* **11** (1980) 716-723.
29. R.R. Yager, A New Methodology for Ordinal Multiple Aspect Decision Based on Fuzzy Sets, *Decision Sciences* **12** (1981) 589-600.
30. R.R. Yager, A Note on Weighted Queries in Information Retrieval Systems, *J. of the American Society of Information Sciences* **38** (1987) 23-24.
31. R.R. Yager, On Ordered Weighted Averaging Aggregation Operators in Multicriteria Decision Making, *IEEE Transactions on Systems, Man, and Cybernetics* **18** (1988) 183-190.
32. R.R. Yager, Fuzzy Screening Systems, in: R. Lowen, Ed., *Fuzzy Logic: State of the Art* (Kluwer Academic Publishers, 1993) 251-261.
33. R.R. Yager, On Weighted Median Aggregation, *Int. J. Uncertainty, Fuzzines and Knowledge-Based Systems* **2** (1994) 101-113.
34. R.R. Yager, An Approach to Ordinal Decision Making, *Int. J. of Approximate Reasoning*, **12** (1995) 237-261.
35. R.R. Yager, L.S. Goldstein and E. Mendels, FUZMAR: An Approach to Aggregating Market Research Data Based on Fuzzy Reasoning, *Fuzzy Sets and Systems* **68** (1994) 1-11.
36. L. A. Zadeh, The Concept of a Linguistic Variable and its Applications to Approximate Reasoning. Part I, *Information Sciences* **8** (1975) 199-249, Part II, *Information Sciences* **8** (1975) 301-357, Part III, *Information Sciences* **9** (1975) 43-80.
37. L. A. Zadeh, A Computational Approach to Fuzzy Quantifiers in Natural Languages, *Computers and Mathematics with Applications* **9** (1983) 149-184.

6

GENERAL FRAMEWORKS FOR COMPUTING WITH WORDS

Object Networks : A Computational Framework to Compute with Words

R.R. Gudwin and F.A.C. Gomide
DCA-FEEC-UNICAMP, CAIXA POSTAL 6101
13.083-970 – CAMPINAS – SP – BRASIL
E-MAILS: gudwin@dca.fee.unicamp.br
gomide@dca.fee.unicamp.br

ABSTRACT: In this work, we introduce a framework as a modeling and implementation tool to compute with words. The basis of the framework is a computational model called object networks. We present the mathematical concept of objects, generic objects and fuzzy objects. The interaction of these elements composes object systems. In particular, emphasis is given on a special class of object systems, the object networks. They are proposed here as a dynamic software architecture suitable for handling the issues involved when computing with words, but independent of the specific numerical algorithms used. The object networks architecture is easily translated into computer programs, and support explanatory databases build upon atomic pieces of information and from the query entered, among other important features. It is also shown how object networks manage semantics of linguistic, semiotic terms, to provide higher level linguistic computations. Illustrative examples are also included.

1 Introduction

Words are the elementary granules of information used by humans to communicate with each other, using sentences from a natural or artificial language. The information conveyed by those sentences can be of two types. The first type is related to the appearance and position where given words take place in sentences. This type of information considers grammatical aspects only, disregarding the concepts embedded in each word by itself. The second type of information is just the information that a word can carry by itself, i.e., its meaning as isolated granules of information. This type of information is addressed as words semantics. The grammatical aspects of words were studied extensively during the earlier periods of artificial intelligence. The semantic aspects were enhanced only recently, within the study of fuzzy sets, linguistic variables and fuzzy logic[1].

But how can humans use words to communicate each other? How do they represent and perform computations with them ? This is a basic question addressed by semiotics[2]. Let us look at figure 1.

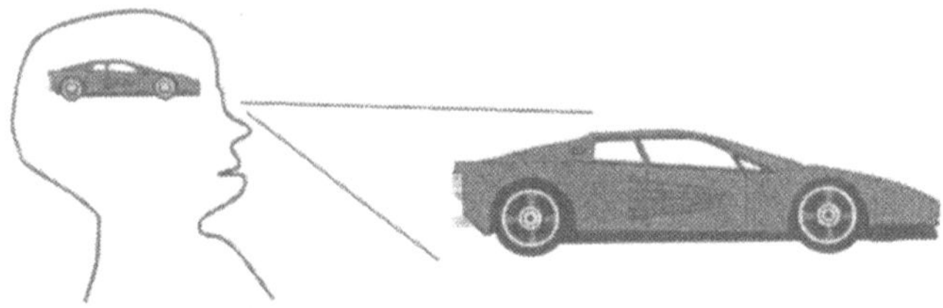

Figure 1 – Concept Formation

After being in contact with a phenomenon of the real world, humans create an internal representation for the observed phenomenon. Further, humans associate this representation to a word that summarizes and labels the concept. When presented to the word, they first recognize the word by itself, as illustrated in figure 2.

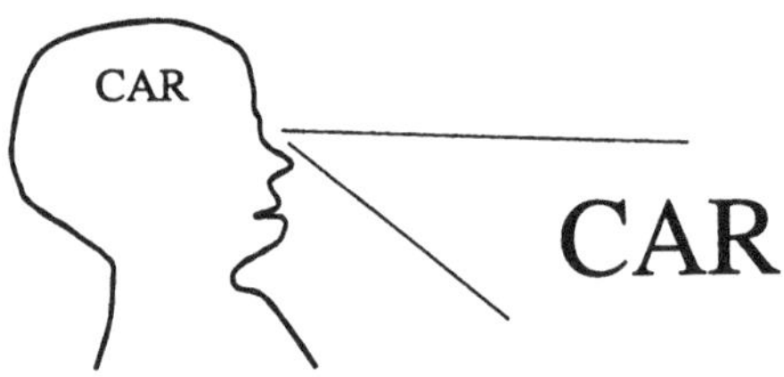

Figure 2 – Word Recognition

In a second step, the recognition of the word leads to the understanding of the concept (figure 3).

When communicating, the use of words is an optimization of information transfer, because it does not need to detail the concept being conveyed, but uses the previous contact of each subject with the phenomenon, sharing experiences to transfer the information. Some problems could arise if the semantic of words is not exactly the same for two different humans, but to be effective they must share some similarity (figure 4).

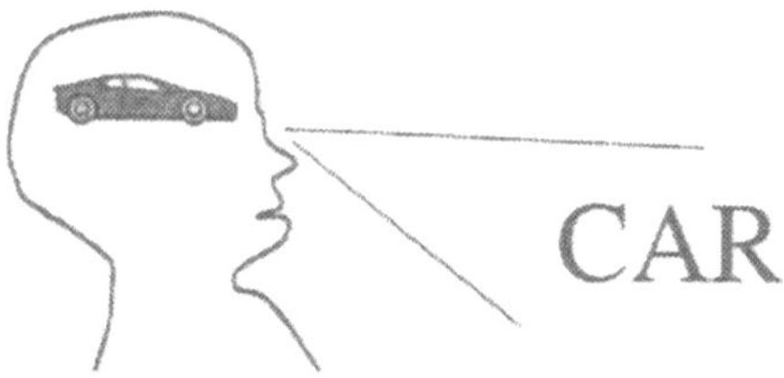

Figure 3 – Symbol Interpretation

Figure 4 – Different Symbol Interpretation

From the computational point of view, one of the objectives of computing with words is to allow computers communicate with humans, using this semiotic paradigm, i.e., grounding the concepts being held by words. This can be achieved by allowing the computer to share experiences with humans. In this sense, computers should process sensory information to develop internal representations for phenomena from environment.

The study of sign processing in general, within the scope of computers, is addressed by the field of Computational Semiotics[3,4,5,6,7] . There, the different types of phenomena existing in the world are categorized in a taxonomy of types of knowledge, and a formal representation is proposed for them. In this work, we use the Computational Semiotics paradigms to focus on the use of words instead general signs. We show how the main tool within Computational Semiotics, the object network, is used to model the different types of concepts that can be acquired from environment.

In next section, we introduce the main concepts to be used: objects, generic objects, fuzzy objects, meta-objects, object system and object network. In section 3, we address the paradigm of "computing with words", through the view of computational semiotics and object networks and in section 4 we illustrate on how object networks can be used to implement other paradigms within the context of soft computing. Section 5 ends with the conclusions.

2 Objects

The main element in the modeling tool to be addressed here is the object, and its extensions, generic object and fuzzy object. We address objects in two different views. In the first, we present the conceptual object, i.e., the conceptual specification of objects. Next, we present a formal model that implements this specification. With this formal representation, we study the interaction among objects to compose object systems and a particular kind of object system, the object network.

2.1 The Conceptual Object

Our concept of object[8] is closely related to its intuitive physical meaning. Ontologically, an object is an entity of the real world and is characterized by its properties. The properties are its attributes[9] . Based on a frame of reference, it is possible to find attributes distinguishing different objects. Thus attributes describe the objects. This view of objects does not consider that, in addition to its existence, the objects also "act" in real world. Therefore, a mathematical concept of object must model its active aspect.

The conceptualization of object cannot, in principle, be made in an independent way. Although we can imagine the existence of an object by itself, we should also consider its capability to interact with different objects. In other words, to introduce the main concepts about objects, we have to discuss object systems. An object system is a set of interacting entities. The object components which allow interaction are shown in figure 5.

Each active object is assumed to have two types of interfaces: input and output interfaces, as in figure 5. The input interface is composed by a collection of gates (input gates). Within an object we find its internal states. These states are divided in four regions. The first is a copy of the input interface whereas the second comprises internal variables. The third region is a copy of the output interface whereas the fourth region is a set of transformation (internal) functions. The output interface is composed by a collection of output gates.

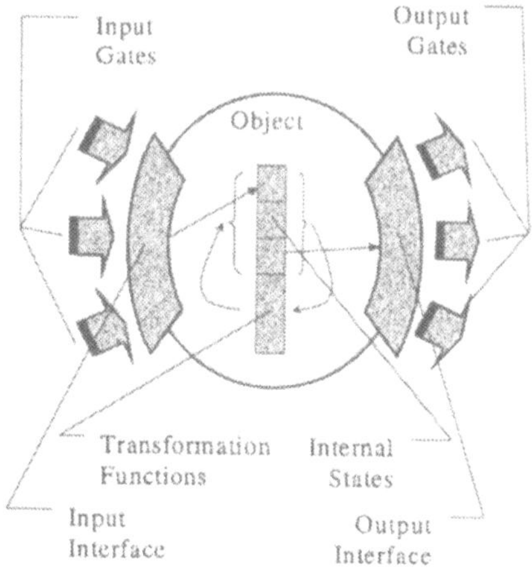

Figure 5 – The Conceptual Object

The interaction among objects is regulated by a mechanism called triggering, and is performed by active objects. In this mechanism, some objects are first bound to the active object, through the input gates, starting what is called the assimilation phase. In this phase, the active object copies the internal states of binding objects to its internal states. After assimilation, the bounded objects can be destroyed or released back to the system. If they are destroyed, then we have a destructive assimilation (or consumption). Otherwise, we have a non-destructive assimilation. In the second phase of triggering, the active object uses one of the transformation functions to change its internal states. Both, input and output, are parts of the internal states. This is called the transformation phase. After the transformation phase, some of the internal states of the active object are copied into the output interface. Next, another set of objects is bound to the output gates, and their internal states are changed to those present in the output interface. This last phase is called either generation phase, or regeneration phase, depending on the objects that are bound to output gates. If the bounded objects are existing objects, then this process is called regeneration because it alters the internal states of bounded objects. However, this last phase can also create a new object, not part of the object system. In this case, the last phase creates this new object, fills its internal states with the information of the output interface, and releases it to the system. This process is called generation.

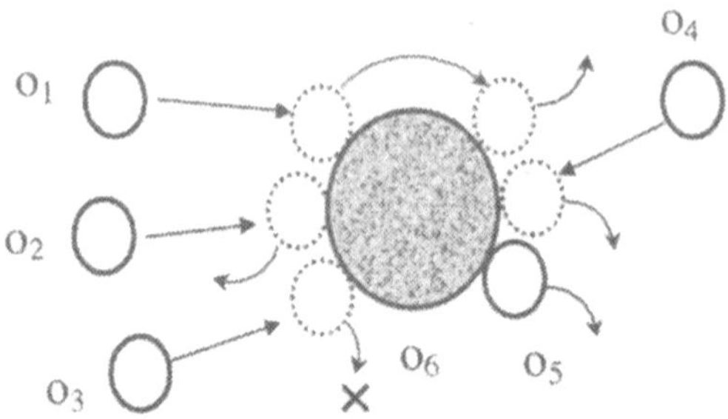

Figure 6 – Object Interactions

The triggering mechanism may allow different kinds of behavior, as illustrated in figure 6. In this example, object o_6 is the active object performing the triggering process. Objects o_1, o_2 and o_3 are the objects to be assimilated in the triggering. Objects o_1 and o_4 are regenerated, and o_5 is generated. Note that o_1 is, at the same time, assimilated and regenerated. Object o_2, after assimilation, is released back to the system but o_3 is destroyed.

To control the triggering process, there is a special function associated with each object called the selection function. This function decides which objects are to be bound to input gates, which objects are to be bound to output gates, and which internal function is to be used in the triggering process. The control strategy of an object system is dictated by the selection functions.

Note, however, that the selection functions do have some restrictions. These restrictions concern the transformation functions requirements, as well as some problems involving synchronization. Each transformation (internal) function requires a minimum set of objects to start the triggering procedure. Therefore, the selection function must consider the simultaneous availability of all objects needed to enable a transformation function. The synchronization problems that may appear are related to multiple active objects binding the same object. For assimilation bindings, there should be a guarantee that only one active object is performing a destructive assimilation. If some assimilated object is also being regenerated, it must be regenerated by only one active object. And cannot be destructively assimilated in this case. In this sense, there should be a global policy for the selection functions, assuring that those constraints are satisfied.

With an appropriate implementation of selection functions, objects can become autonomous entities, i.e., independent of an external synchronization mechanism. Synchronism, despite being useful sometimes, is not a requirement in object systems. The behavior of real objects, with asynchronous and parallel activities can be modeled. Note that both assimilated and (re)generated objects are not necessarily passive. This allows adaptive and self-organizing systems to be modeled by object systems.

2.2 *The Formal Object*

Here, we introduce the concepts and definitions used as a formal background for further developments. The focus here is on the main issues and definitions only. For a more in depth coverage and detailed examples illustrating the main definitions stated below, the reader is referred to the work of Gudwin[3,4,5,6,7] . The definitions assume a discrete set N associated with time instants, or algorithm steps when convenient. Extensions to the continuous case may be possible, but it will not be considered here. Usually N is the set of natural numbers, but in general it can be any countable set.

A remark concerning notation: no distinction between a function and its graph will be made. Therefore, both $f : A \rightarrow B$ and $f \subset A \times B$ will be used to express a function f.

Definition 1 – **Tuples :** Let $q_1 , q_2 , \dots , q_n$ be generic elements of the sets $Q_1 , Q_2 , \dots , Q_n$ respectively. A tuple is a structure joining $q_1 , q_2 , \dots , q_n$ into a single element denoted by $q = (q_1 , q_2 , \dots , q_n)$.

A tuple with n elements is an n-tuple, or tuple for short. The elements of a tuple are called components. They can be identified by the indices associated with the order in which they appear. Note that a tuple component can be itself a tuple. In this case they are called complex tuples. For example $q = (q_1 , (q_{21} , q_{22} , q_{23}), q_3 , q_4 , q_5)$ is a complex tuple. To simplify notation we may assign $q_2 = (q_{21} , q_{22} , q_{23})$ turning the original tuple into $q = (q_1 , q_2 , q_3 , q_4 , q_5)$.

Definition 2 - **Tuple Arity:** Let $q = (q_1 , q_2 , \dots , q_n)$ be a tuple. The **arity** of q, Ar(q), is the number of tuple's components: Ar(q) = n.

Definition 3 - **Reference Index:** Let q be tuple. To identify an individual component of q we associate a reference index to each of its element. For a simple tuple the reference index will be a number i, $1 \leq i \leq Ar(q)$. For a complex tuple the reference index will be a simple tuple i with each element i_k corresponding to a sub-index of level k. The value of the sub-indices ranges between one and the arity of the tuple at level k. The reference index can also be used to identify the domain of the components.

Definition 4 - **Induction Formula :** Let $q = (q_1, q_2, \dots, q_n)$ be a tuple and k be an expression defined by the following syntax: $k \leftarrow [\, i \,]$; $i \leftarrow i\, , i$; $i \leftarrow [\, i\, , i \,]$, where i is a reference index of q. The expression k is called an induction formula.

Definition 5 - **Induction of a tuple:** Let $q = (q_1, q_2, \dots, q_n)$ be a tuple in $Q = Q_1 \times \dots \times Q_n$ and k be an induction formula. The induction of q according k is defined as the new tuple $q_{(k)}$ induced by the induction formula. The induced tuple $q_{(k)}$ is found from k by changing brackets and each reference index i_j into parenthesis and q_{i_j} of the original tuple q. The domain $Q_{(k)}$ of $q_{(k)}$ is found similarly.

Definition 6 - **Sub-tuple:** A tuple $q_{(k)}$ is called a sub-tuple of q if k has only one pair of brackets, and each reference index in k is unary and appears only once in k.

Definition 7 – **Relation:** If $R_1, \dots, R_n$ are sets and $R = \{(r_{i1}, \dots, r_{in})\}$, $i = 1, \dots, M$, is a set of M tuples with arity $n > 1$ such that $\forall i \in \{1, \dots, M\}$, $\forall k \in \{1, \dots, n\}$, $r_{ik} \in R_k$, then the set R, $R \subseteq R_1 \times \dots \times R_n$ is a relation in $R_1 \times \dots \times R_n$,

Definition 8 – **Projection:** Let $R = \{r_i\}$, $r_i = (r_{i1}, \dots, r_{in})$ be an n-ary relation in $R_1 \times \dots \times R_n$ and k be an induction formula with unary indices $k = [k_1, k_2, \dots, k_m]$, $k_i \in \{1, \dots, n\}$, $k_i \neq k_j$, if $i \neq j$, $i = 1, \dots, m$, $j = 1, \dots, m$, $m \leq n$. The projection of R on $R_{k_1} \times \dots \times R_{k_m}$,denoted by $R \downarrow R_{k_1} \times \dots \times R_{k_m}$ (alternatively, $R_{(k)}$) is the relation obtained by the union of all sub-tuples $r_{i(k)} = (r_{ik_1}, \dots, r_{ik_m})$ of R originated from the induction of R's tuples according to k, $R_{(k)} = \cup\, r_{i(k)}$.

Definition 9 - **Free Projection:** Let $R = \{r_i\}$, $r_i = (r_{i1}, \dots, r_{in})$ be an n-ary relation defined in $U = R_1 \times \dots \times R_n$ and k be an induction formula. The free projection of R in $U_{(k)}$, $R \downarrow U_{(k)}$ (alternatively, $R_{(k)}$) is the relation obtained by the union of all sub-tuples $r_{i(k)}$ originated by the induction of the tuples from R according to k: $R_{(k)} = \cup\, r_{i(k)}$.

NOTE: Free projection is a generalization of projection. Recall that in a projection, the induction formula has unary indices only. This implies in tuples defined only over the main dimensions of the original tuple. In free projection, any element, in whatever level of a tuple, can be used to define the inducted tuple. Clearly, with the proper induction formula free projection becomes standard projection.

Definition 10 - **Cylindrical Extension:** Let $R = \{ (r_{i1}, r_{i2}, \dots, r_{in}) \}$ be an n-ary relation in $R_1 \times \dots \times R_n$. The cylindrical extension P of R in $P_1 \times \dots \times P_m$, denoted by $P = R\uparrow P_1 \times \ldots \times P_m$, where $\forall k \in \{1, \ldots, n\}\ \exists P_j = R_k$, $1 \le j \le m$, is the greatest (in the sense of the greatest number of elements) relation $P \subseteq P_1 \times \ldots \times P_m$ such that $P \downarrow R_1 \times \ldots \times R_n = R$.

NOTE: As in projection, the order of elements in tuples of the cylindrical extension it is not the same as in the original tuples.

Definition 11 – **Junction:** Let R and S be two relations in $R_1 \times \ldots \times R_n$ and $S_1 \times \ldots \times S_m$, respectively, and $P = P_1 \times \ldots \times P_o$ an universe where $\forall i \in \{1, \ldots, n\}\ \exists P_k = R_i$, and $\forall j \in \{1, \ldots, m\}\ \exists P_h = S_j$, $o \le n + m$. The junction of R and S under P, denoted by $R * S\ |_P$, is $R * S\ |_P = R\uparrow P \cap S\uparrow P$.

NOTE: If there is a $R_i = S_j$ then there may be only one set P_k with elements in tuples of R*S. In this case, for the tuples to be included in junction, the value of such element in the tuple in R and S should be the same (see first example).
NOTE: If $\forall i,j$, $R_i \neq S_j$, then $R*S\ |_P \downarrow R_1 \times \ldots \times R_n = R$ and $R * S\ |_P \downarrow S_1 \times \ldots \times S_m = S$.

Definition 12 – **Variable:** Let N be a countable set with a generic element n (comprising some type of time measure), and $X \subseteq U$. A variable x of type X is a function $x : N \rightarrow X$. Note that a function is also a relation and hence it can be expressed as a set. Thus, $x \subset N \times X$.

Definition 13 - **Composed Variable:** Let x be a variable of type X. If the elements of X are n-tuples with n > 1, then x is called a composed variable (or structure).

The value of a composed variable, at a particular instant of time, will always be a tuple. The individual value of each sub-element of this tuple can be obtained by its reference index, the field of the variable. If $X = X_1 \times \ldots \times X_n$, then each field of x can be viewed as a free projection on $N \times X_i$, i.e., it is a standard variable of type X_i.

Definition 14 – **Class:** A class C is a set whose elements c_i are tuples of the type:

$$(v_1, v_2, \ldots, v_n, f_1, f_2, \ldots, f_m),\ n \ge 0,\ m \ge 0$$

where $v_i \in V_i$, and f_j are functions

$$f_j : \mathop{\times}_{p \in P_j} V_p \rightarrow \mathop{\times}_{q \in Q_j} V_q .$$

Here $\times$ means the Cartesian product, $P_j \subseteq \{1, \ldots, n\}$ and $Q_j \subseteq \{1, \ldots, n\}$.

Definition 15 – **Object:** Let C be an non-empty class and c be a variable of type C. Thus c is an object of class C.

It is worth noting that an object, as a variable, supports objects composed by parts which are objects themselves. In addition, if n=1 and m=0 then the tuple reduces to a single element. Hence a standard variable (a primitive object) is an object. For an empty class n=m=0 and there is no object. Clearly structures are also objects. As it will be seen later, a structure is a passive object.

Definition 16 - **Instance of an Object:** Let c be an object of class C. The instance c(n) is the value of c at n.

C is a set of tuples. Therefore the instance of an object is an element of C, i.e. a tuple.

Definition 17 - **Superclass and Subclass:** Let C be a class. The set D whose elements are sub-tuples of the elements of C belonging to the same universe, and each element in C is associated with one element of D and D is itself a class, is called a superclass of C. In this case C is a subclass of D.

Note that a class can be defined from primitive classes. Since class is a relation, another class can be generated by the cylindrical extension of a class, by the junction of two or more classes, or by both junction and a cylindrical extension. In all cases, the primitive classes are superclasses of the newly generated class. Moreover, for a given a class its cylindrical extension is a subclass of itself. The junction of two classes is a subclass of both of them. Any class is a subclass of empty class. Therefore a hierarchy of classes is induced by projections, junctions and cylindrical extensions (figure 7).

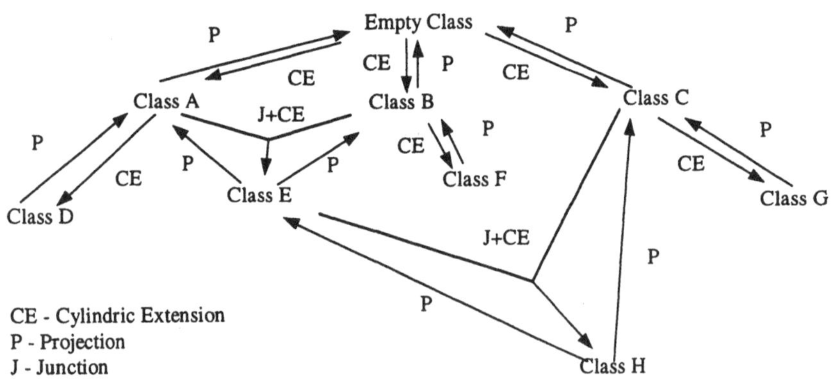

Figure 7 - Example of Class Hierarchy

Definition 18 - **Sub-object:** Let c be an object of class C and d an object of class D a superclass of C. If for any n the instance of d is a sub-tuple of the instance of c, then d is a sub-object of c.

In other words, d is the free projection of c in $N \times D$, i.e. $d = c \downarrow N \times D$.

Definition 19 - **Active and Passive Objects:** An object c of a class C is called an active object if $m > 0$. If $m = 0$, then c is a passive object.

Definition 20 - **Input Interface:** Let c be an active object of a class C and I a superclass of C, defined by:

$$I = \bigtimes_i V_i, \forall i \in \{1,\ldots,n\} \text{ such that} \begin{cases} \exists f_j,\ 1 \le j \le m \text{ where } i \in P_j \\ \forall f_l,\ 1 \le l \le m \quad i \notin Q_l \end{cases}$$

The input interface i of the object c is the passive object generated by the free projection of c in $N \times I$, i.e. $i = c \downarrow N \times I$.

Definition 21 - **Function Specific Input Interfaces:** Let c be an active object of class C, i its input interface, and I^j a superclass of I and C such that :

$$I^j = \bigtimes_i V_i, \forall i \in \{1,\ldots,n\} \text{ such that, for } f_j, i \in P_j \text{ and } \forall l \in \{1,\ldots,m\},\ i \notin Q_l$$

The specific input interface for function j of c, i^j, is the free projection of c in $N \times I^j$.

Note that $i^j = c \downarrow N \times I^j = i \downarrow N \times I^j$. If the elements of class C have m functions, then there exist m function specific input interfaces. Each i^j is a sub-object of i and c.

Definition 22 - **Output Interface:** Let c be an active object of class C and O a superclass of C characterized by:

$$O = \bigtimes_i V_i, \forall i \in \{1,\ldots,n\} \text{ such that} \begin{cases} \exists f_j, 1 \le j \le m \text{ where } i \in Q_j \\ \forall f_l,\ 1 \le l \le m \quad i \notin P_l \end{cases}$$

The output interface o of object c is the passive object generated by the free projection of c in $N \times O$, i.e. $i = c \downarrow N \times O$.

Definition 23 -**Function Specific Output Interfaces:** Let c be an active object of a class C, o its output interface, and O^j is a superclass of O and C such that :

$$O^j = \bigtimes_i V_i, \forall i \in \{1,...,n\} \text{ such that for } f_j\ i \in Q_j \text{ and } \forall l \in \{1,...,m\}, i \notin P_l$$

The output interface specific for function j of c, o^j, is the free projection of c in $N \times O^j$.

Clearly, $o^j = c \downarrow N \times O^j = o \downarrow N \times O^j$ and if the elements of class C have m functions, then there exist m function specific input interfaces. Each o^j is a sub-object of o and c.

Definition 24 - **Existence of Objects:** An object c is said to exist at n if the function which maps instances of c in C is defined for $n \in N$.

Definition 25 - **Temporal Restriction for Objects:** Let N be a set of time instants, S a class and o:N→S an object of type S. Let $N' \subseteq N$. The temporal restriction of object o to N', denoted by $o \Downarrow N'$ corresponds to the object o':N→S such that if $(n,s) \in o$ and $n \in N'$, $(n,s) \in o'$. Otherwise, $(n,s) \notin o'$.

Definition 26 -**Set Variable:** Let N be an enumerable set, with a generic element n and $X \subseteq U$ a subset of U. We define a **set variable** x of type X as a function $x : N \rightarrow 2^X$.

Definition 27 - **Generic Object:** Let C be a non-empty class. Let c be a set variable of type C. The variable c is called a **generic object** of class C.

Definition 28 - **Case of a Generic Object:** Let c be a generic object of class C. An object c' of type C is said to be a case of generic object c if $\forall n \in N$, $c'(n) \in c(n)$.

Definition 29 - **Fuzzy Object:** Let N be an enumerable set with a generic element n, X a class, $\tilde{X}$ a fuzzy set defined onto X and $2^{\tilde{X}}$ the set of all fuzzy sets onto X. We define a **fuzzy object** x of type X as a function $x : N \rightarrow 2^{\tilde{X}}$.

If X is a passive class, $X = X_1 \times ... \times X_m$, $\tilde{X}$ will be, in general, an m-ary fuzzy relation. In some cases, it is interesting to use not a generic fuzzy relation, but a fuzzy relation formed by the cartesian product of different fuzzy sets. In this case, $\tilde{X}$ may be represented by a tuple of m fuzzy sets. If X is an active class, $\tilde{X}$ would consider as fuzzy only the fields that are not functions. The m-ary fuzzy relation, in this case, will be represented by the (fuzzy) cartesian product of all elements that are not functions. Note that a fuzzy object can represent any (standard) object $o = \{ (n,x) \mid \forall n \in N, x \in X\}$ if we take, for each $n \in N$, a fuzzy set that is a singleton in $x \in X$. Since a passive object corresponds to a fuzzy relation, it is possible to define operations involving fuzzy objects. The same occurs with active objects, because the operations are related with non-function fields only.

Definition 30 - **Union of Fuzzy Objects:** Let x' and x'' be two fuzzy objects of type X, defined in N such that $\forall n \in N$, if x'(n) is defined, x''(n) is also defined. The union x of x' and x'' is a fuzzy object such that $\forall n \in N$, $x(n) = x'(n)\ S\ x''(n)$, where S is a matrix operator which applies a triangular co-norm, element to element, in the m-ary relational matrices. Operator S applies only to non-function fields of the corresponding tuples.

Definition 31 - **Intersection of Fuzzy Objects:** Let x' and x'' be two fuzzy objects of type X, defined in N, such that $\forall n \in N$, if x'(n) is defined, x''(n) is also defined. The intersection x of x' and x'' is a fuzzy object such that $\forall n \in N$, $x(n) = x'(n)\ T\ x''(n)$, where T is a matrix operator which applies a triangular norm, element to element, in the m-ary relational matrices. Again, operator T applies only to the non-function fields of the tuples.

For the sake of computational implementation, it is important to stress that both generic objects and fuzzy objects can be transformed into objects. Suppose that the values of their instances (which are sets or fuzzy sets) are represented by discriminating functions, functions that are approximated by multilayer neural networks. We can generate a standard object whose attributes are the parameters of such neural network. In this case, we represent a generic object (or a fuzzy object), by a standard object. To use a generic knowledge in this form, however, the arguments used to manipulate it must be modified to deal with generic/fuzzy objects in such a representation.

Definition 32 - **Meta-Object:** Let N be an enumerable set, with a generic element n; V be an enumerable set where each $v \in V$ is a variable of type N defined over the occurrence space T, $v : T \rightarrow N$; R be a set of restrictions for the values of variables V (possibly empty) and X be a class. A **meta-object** x of type X is a function $x : V \rightarrow X$.

Definition 33 - **Instance of a Meta-Object:** Let x be a meta-object of type X. An **instance** of x is an object x' where the variables of x are substituted for the values provided by specific instances of such variables in the occurrence space.

Definition 34 - **Occurrence of a Meta-Object in an Object:** Consider an object o from class X, and a meta-object o' from class X'. An occurrence o'' of meta-object o' in o is an object o'' such that o'' is at the same time a sub-object from an instance of o' and a temporal restriction of a sub-object of o.

When the restriction R for a meta-object is not empty, domain variables may have restrictions to its values. One way of representing restrictions is by means of algebraic equations and/or inequations using domain variables. In this case the occurrence of meta-objects in objects does consider such restrictions for the determination of possible instances for the meta-object.

Following the definition, an occurrence does not need to be, necessarily, a meta-object instance, but any sub-object of the former. With this, from the same meta-object there may be different occurrences in different objects, with each object from a different class, but sharing a field of the instance of the meta-object.

Definition 35 - **Occurrence of a Meta-Object in a Generic Object:** Let x be a generic object from class X, and x' a meta-object from class X'. An occurrence x'' of the meta-object x' in x is an object x'' such that x'' is an occurrence for any case of x.

Definition 36 - **Occurrence of a Meta-Object in a Fuzzy Object:** Let o be a fuzzy object from class X, and o' a meta-object from class X'. An occurrence o'' of the meta-object o' in o is a fuzzy object o'' such that o'' corresponds to the intersection of a sub-object from an instance of o', described as a fuzzy object by means of singletons, and a temporal restriction of a fuzzy sub-object of o.

Definition 37 - **Generic Meta-Object:** Let N be an enumerable set, with generic element n, V be an enumerable set, where each $v \in V$ is a variable of type N, R be a set of restrictions on the variables of V (possibly empty) and X be a class. A **generic meta-object** x of type X is a function $x : V \to 2^X$.

Definition 38 - **Case of a Generic Meta-Object:** Let x be a generic meta-object from class X. A meta-object x' of type X is a case of generic meta-object x if $\forall v \in V, x'(v) \in x(v)$.

Definition 39 - **Occurrence of a Generic Meta-Object in an Object:** Assume x as a generic meta-object of type X and x' an object of type X'. An occurrence x'' of x in x' is an object x'' such that x'' is an occurrence of any case of x in x'.

Definition 40 - **Occurrence of a Generic Meta-Object in a Generic Object:** Let x be a generic meta-object of type X and x' a generic object of type X'. An occurrence x'' of x in x' is a generic object x'' such that x'' is the union of all occurrences of any case of x in cases of x'.

Definition 41 - **Occurrence of a Generic Meta-Object in a Fuzzy Object:** Let x be a generic meta-object of type X and x' a fuzzy object of type X'. An occurrence x'' of x in x' is a fuzzy object x'' such that x'' is the intersection of a sub-object of x, viewed as fuzzy object, and a temporal restriction of a sub-object of x'.

Definition 42 - **Fuzzy Meta-Object:** Let N be an enumerable set, with a generic element n, V be an enumerable set, where each $v \in V$ is a variable of type N, R be a set of restrictions over the variables in V (possibly empty), X a class, $\tilde{X}$, a fuzzy set defined over X and $2^{\tilde{X}}$, the set of all fuzzy sets defined on X. A **fuzzy meta-object** x of type X is a function $x : V \rightarrow 2^{\tilde{X}}$.

Definition 43 - **Occurrence of a Fuzzy Meta-Object in an Object:** Let x be a fuzzy meta-object of type X and x' an object of type X'. An occurrence x'' of x in x' is a fuzzy object x'' such that x'' is the intersection of a sub-object of x and a temporal restriction of a sub-object of x' described as a fuzzy object.

Definition 44 - **Occurrence of a Fuzzy Meta-Object in a Generic Object:** Let x be a fuzzy meta-object of type X and x' a generic object of type X'. An occurrence x'' of x in x' is a fuzzy object x'' such that x'' is the intersection of a sub-object of x and a temporal restriction of a sub-object of x' described as a fuzzy object.

Definition 45 - **Occurrence of a Fuzzy Meta-Object in a Fuzzy Object:** Let x be a fuzzy meta-object of type X and x' a fuzzy object of type X'. An occurrence x'' of x in x' is a fuzzy object x'' such that x'' is the intersection of a sub-object of x and a temporal restriction of a sub-object of x'.

2.3 *Interaction Among Objects*

After formally defining the concepts involving objects, we now proceed to define the concepts necessary to provide objects interaction.

Definition 46 - **Generation and Destruction of Objects:** An object is generated at n if it does not exist at n and does exist at n+1. An object is destroyed (destructively assimilated) at n if it does exist at n but does not exist at n+1.

Definition 47 - **Enabling Scope of Functions:** Consider an active object c from a class $C = \{ (v_1, v_2, \dots, v_n, f_1, f_2, \dots, f_m) \}$, a function f_j of C, and i^j an input interface specific for function f_j. Let β be the arity of instances of i^j, gi an input index function for f_j, $gi : \{1, \dots, \beta\} \rightarrow \{1, \dots, n\}$ mapping each component from instances of the input interface specific for f_j to a component in instances of c, and $B = \{0,1\}$. An enabling scope for f_j is a set of tuples $H = \{(h_t, b_t)\}$, $t = 1, \dots, \beta$, where h_t is an object of class $V_{gi(t)}$ and $b_t \in B$ is a boolean value indicating if object h_t should ($b_t = 1$) or should not ($b_t = 0$) be destroyed when c triggers.

Definition 48 - **Generative Scope of Functions:** Assume an active object c of class $C = \{ (v_1, v_2, \dots, v_n, f_1, f_2, \dots, f_m) \}$, a function f_j of C, an output interface o^j specific or function f_j, α the arity of instances of o^j, and an output index function for f_j, $go : \{1, \dots, \alpha\} \rightarrow \{1, \dots, n\}$ mapping each component from instances of output interface specific for f_j to a component in instances of c. A generative scope for f_j is a set of objects $S = \{s_u\}$, $u = 1, \dots, \alpha$, where s_u is an object of class $V_{go(u)}$.

Definition 49 - **Enabling of an Active Object:** An active object of class C is enabled at n if all objects belonging to an enabling scope of one of its functions f_j do exist at n. Function f_j is said to be enabled at n.

Definition 50 - **Triggering of an Active Object:** Consider the following:

a)-an object c from a class C,

b)- the instance of c at n, $c(n) = (v_1(n), \dots, v_n(n), f_1(n), \dots, f_m(n))$,

c)-a function f_j of c at n, enabled by $H = \{(h_t, b_t)\}$,

d)-a generative scope $S = \{s_u\}$ for f_j such that if $s \in S$, then or s does not exist at n, or $s \in H$,

e)-p, the number of values such that $k \in P_j$, $k = 1, \dots, n$, (P_j from def. 14)

f)-a domain index function $gd : (1, \dots, p\} \rightarrow \{1, \dots, n\}$ for f_j,

g)-the projection of f(.) on V_k, $f(.)\downarrow V_k$,

h)-β, α, gi e go as before.

Triggering an active object at n means:

1)- determination of c's instance at instant n+1, given the instance of c at n and the instances of h_t at n:

$$v_i(n+1) = \begin{cases} v_i(n) & \text{if } i \notin P_j \text{ and } i \notin Q_j \\ h_{gi^{-1}(i)}(n) & \text{if } i \in P_j \text{ and } i \notin Q_j \\ f_j(w_1, \dots, w_b)\downarrow V_i & \text{if } i \in Q_j \end{cases}$$

$$\text{where } w_r = \begin{cases} h_{gi^{-1}(gd(r))}(n), & \text{if } gd(r) \in P_j \\ v_{gd(r)}(n), & \text{if } gd(r) \notin P_j \end{cases}$$

2)- destruction ($b_t = 1$) of object h_t, $(h_t, b_t) \in H$, at n,

3)-generation, at n, of the objects of S those do not exist at n,

4)-determination of the instances of the objects of S, at n+1, according to the instances of c at n+1:

$$s_u(n+1) = v_{go(u)}(n+1)$$

2.4 *Object Systems*

Knowing what objects are and which mechanisms allow objects interaction we can define an object system.

Definition 51 - **Object System:** Assume the following:

a)-c_i are objects of class C_i, $i = 1, \ldots, \delta$,

b)-$\mathcal{C} = \bigcup_i c_i$,

c)-$\Theta_i = \{0, \ldots, m_i\}$ where m_i is the number of functions for object c_i,

d)-$B = \{0,1\}$,

e)-γ_i, $0 \le i \le \delta$, $\delta > 0$, are selection functions $\gamma_i : N \to 2^{\mathcal{C} \times B} \times 2^{\mathcal{C}} \times \Theta_i$ which, for each object c_i at n, select an enabling scope H_i, a generative scope S_i and a function index such that $\forall(c,b) \in H_i$, if $b = 1$, then $(\forall k \neq i)((c,1) \notin H_k)$, $\forall c \in S_i$, $(\forall k \neq i)(c \notin S_k)$ and $(\forall k)((c,1) \notin H_k)$. H_i is an enabling scope and S_i is a generative scope for function $\gamma_i(n) \downarrow \Theta_i$. If c_i is a passive object or, at n $\nexists H_i \neq \varnothing$ or $\nexists S_i \neq \varnothing$, then $\gamma_i(n) = (\varnothing, \varnothing, 0)$. The third index is null to indicate that no function is to be executed. The meaning of these conditions are grasped as follows. An object of an enabling scope programmed to be destroyed must be destroyed by only one active object. If an object is part of a generative scope of an active object, then it cannot be in any other generative scope. If the object in question is passive, or if active it does not have an enabling scope for any of its functions, then its selection function must do nothing.

An object system Ω is a set of pairs $\{\omega_i\}$, $\omega_i = (c_i, \gamma_i)$, such that :

1)-for n=0, there exists at least one ω_i with an object c_i defined,

2)-for n>0 all active objects c_i with $\gamma_i(n) \neq (\varnothing, \varnothing, 0)$, i.e. objects whose selection functions are in the form $\gamma_i(n) = (H_i, S_i, j)$ may trigger according to its enabling scope H_i and the generative scope S_i, using its j-th internal function,

3)-for $n>0$, all objects c_i which exist at n and do not have its instance at $(n+1)$ determined by item 2, may have $c_i(n+1) = c_i(n)$.

The definition of an object system may be viewed from two different perspectives. In the first, it provides a recursive way to build an object system. In the second view, when comprising a given collection of objects, it works as a specification. To call a given set of objects an object system, the values of its instances (and their existence at different times) should be associated with each other according to the laws of triggering and regeneration of objects given by items 2 and 3 of definition 51. These laws determine, at each time instant, the values of the instances (or its inexistence) based on their previous values. The objects that interact at each instant are determined according to the selection functions, which define the enabling scopes, the generative scopes, and the functions to be triggered for each active object. Therefore, the selection function plays a fundamental role in the object system dynamics.

Objects are functions and there are, in principle, no restrictions on their form. For a set of objects the functions can be any. An object system has, as opposed to a set of objects, a clear recursive nature. The recursiveness is not simple because objects may be *partial* functions, i.e. they do not have to be defined for any value of its domain. This leads to the fundamental question about the computability[8,9] of object systems, certainly a desirable property. An object system being computable means that we can determine, for each $n \in N$, the values of the instances for the existing objects at n. Conditions for computability of object systems are given as follows. Assume Ω an object system with a finite number of elements ω_i, with all its selection functions γ_i computable, and all internal functions of all objects c_i of ω_i computable. Then Ω is computable. These are sufficient conditions only. An object system does not need to necessarily have a finite number of objects to be computable. If for adjacent instants n and n+1 the number of existing objects is finite, then the system is computable.

An object system fulfilling the previous conditions can be viewed as the limit of a (possibly infinite) sequence of objects systems Ω_1, Ω_2, ... , each Ω_i with a finite number of objects defined on a finite and incremental domain N_i. That is: $N_0 = \{0\}$, and $N_i = N_{i-1} \cup \{i\}$. Consequently, each object system Ω_i is computable and the whole sequence is computable as well. The infinite object is the i-th element of this sequence when $i \rightarrow \infty$. Hence, the object system is computable, although infinite.

2.5 *Object Network*

An object network is a special type of object system in which additional restrictions concerning interactions are included. To distinguish object network and object system let us assume places and arcs whose roles are similar to those used in Petri nets[10,11] context. Objects in places can only interact with objects in places connected through arcs. Thus, at each instant, the objects defined should be at one place. For each place there is a set of places connected with through input arcs. These places are called the input gates of the place. Analogously, each place has a set of places connected with it by means of output arcs, called output gates. For each field of output interface of objects in this place there should exist one corresponding output gate. With those conditions we can see that, for each place, there should be only objects of the same class. Remember that objects can be of two types: passive and active. Passive objects do not have functions in its tuples and are only used to store information. Active objects do have functions in its tuples, and perform the task of transitions in the object network. Each place can only have objects of the same class. In this sense, we can say that there are passive and active places if the objects that can be put in a place are passive or active, respectively. Apart of those special characteristics, an object network is similar to an object system.

Object networks can be put in a graphical form, with places being represented by circles and arcs by lines. Passive places are indicated by circles. Active places are indicated by double circles, and instances of objects by black tokens, as in figure 8.

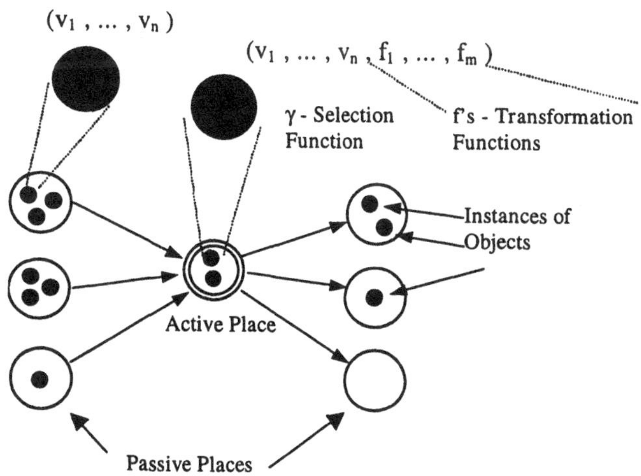

Figure 8 : Example of an Object Network

Observe that, differently than in Petri nets, the tokens are instances of objects that have individuality, i.e., they are not a marking on the place, but are related to objects with attributes and eventually transforming functions. Again, active objects, which perform the role of transitions, are also mobile and changeable. This gives an object net great power of representation, allowing modeling of systems that are not suitable to be modeled by Petri nets, e.g., adaptive systems.

As for an object system, the basic behavior in an object network is the triggering of active objects. Triggering an active object corresponds to the generation of new instances of objects in places directly connected to the place where the active object is through output arcs. To be triggered, an object must first have an enabling scope, that is, a set of object instances put in the input gates, enabling one of the object functions. To select an enabling scope, there is a selection function that selects, from the object instances available, those that are to be used for triggering. After triggering, object instances may be put in one ore more output gates of the place where the active object is. This is also determined by the selection function. The object instances used as an enabling scope may (or not) be destroyed for the next time instant.

Definition 52 - **Object Network:** Assume the following:

a)- a set of classes $\Sigma = \{C_i\}$

b)- a set of objects $\mathcal{C} = \{c_i\}$, where c_i are objects from a class C_i , $C_i \in \Sigma$, $0 \leq i \leq \delta$, $\delta > 0$.

c)- $\Pi = \{\pi_i\}$ a set of places π_i

d)- A , a set of arcs $A = \{a_i\}$

e)-η a node function $\eta : A \to \Pi \times \Pi$

f)-ξ a localization function $\xi : N \times \mathcal{C} \to \Pi$, which relates to each object $c \in \mathcal{C}$, for each instant n, a place π.

g)-$F(\pi)$ a mapping $\Pi \to 2^{\Pi}$, defined by $F(\pi) = \cup \pi_k$ where $k \in K$, $K = \{k \mid \exists a_j \in A \text{ such that } \eta(a_j) = (\pi_k,\pi)\}$.

h)-$V(\pi)$ a mapping $\Pi \to 2^{\Pi}$, defined by $V(\pi) = \cup \pi_k$ where $k \in K$, $K = \{k \mid \exists a_j \in A \text{ such that } \eta(a_j) = (\pi,\pi_k)\}$.

i)- $X(\pi)$ a mapping of connections $\Pi \to 2^{\Pi}$, such that $X(\pi) = F(\pi) \cup V(\pi)$.

j)-$\Xi = \Xi(\pi)$ a mapping of classes $\Pi \to \Sigma$, such that $\forall \pi \in \Pi$ for each field v_i of input interface of objects from class $\Xi(\pi)$, being v_i an object from class C, $\exists \pi_k$, $\pi_k \in F(\pi)$, such that $\Xi(\pi_k) = C$, and for each field v_i of output interface of objects from class $\Xi(\pi)$, being v_i an object from class C, $\exists\pi_k$, $\pi_k \in V(\pi)$, such that $\Xi(\pi_k) = C$.

k)- i^i the input interface of an object from class $\Xi(\pi_i)$.

l)-o^i the output interface of an object from class $\Xi(\pi_i)$.

m)-∂_i the number of fields in i^i and ρ_i the number of fields in o^i.

n)-the function fpi_i the attribute function for input gates of objects which are at a place π_i, defined $fpi_i : \{1, \dots, \partial_i\} \rightarrow A$ and $fpi = \{fpi_i\}$.

o)-$fpo_i = \{1, \dots, \rho_i\} \rightarrow A$ the attribute function for output gates of objects that are at a place π_i and $fpo = \{fpo_i\}$

p)-$\Theta_i = \{0, \dots, m_i\}$, where m_i is the number of function for object c_i

q)-$\gamma = \{\gamma_i\}$, $0 \le i \le \delta$, $\delta > 0$, which elements are selection functions $\gamma_i : N \rightarrow 2^{\mathcal{C} \times B} \times 2^{\mathcal{C}} \times \Theta_i$ that for each object c_i, in an instant n, select an enabling scope H_i, a generative scope S_i and the index for the function to be executed by the object, having as a restriction that $\forall(c,b) \in H_i$, $\xi(n,c) = \pi$, $\pi \in F(\xi(n,c_i))$, if $b = 1$, $(\forall k \neq i)((c,1) \notin H_k)$, $\forall c \in S_i$, $\xi(n+1,c) = \pi$, $\pi \in V(\xi(n,c_i))$, $(\forall k \neq i)(c \notin S_k)$ and $(\forall k)((c,1) \notin H_k)$. More than that, H_i should be an enabling scope and S_i should be a generative scope for function f_k, $k = \gamma_i(n) \downarrow \Theta_i$. If c_i is a passive object or, for a given n, $\nexists H_i \neq \emptyset$ or $\nexists S_i \neq \emptyset$ then $\gamma_i(n) = (\emptyset, \emptyset, 0)$. The third index being 0 does mean that no function is going to be executed. Those conditions are analogous to the selection function for an object system, added by the following conditions: Any object belonging to the enabling scope of another object should be connected to the place where the active object is by an input arc. Any object belonging to the generative scope of an active object should be put in a place that is connected to the place where the active object is by means of an output arc.

An object network $\Re$ is a tuple $\Re = (\Sigma, \Pi, \Xi, A, \eta, fpi, fpo, \mathcal{C}, \xi, \gamma)$, such that:

1)- an objects system $\Omega = \{(c_i, \gamma_i)\}$ is determined by choosing $c_i \in \mathcal{C}$ and $\gamma_i \in \gamma$, $0 \le i \le \delta$,

2)-for each object $c_i \in \mathcal{C}$ with a function f_j being triggered at n, being this object at n at a place $\pi = \xi(n,c_i)$, the objects s_i^k belonging to the generative scope S_i indicated by $\gamma_i(n)$ should have a localization function defined by:

$$\xi(n+1,s_i^k) = \pi^k$$

where π^k should be such that $\eta(fpo_\pi(k')) = (\pi,\pi^k)$ and k' is the index of the k-th field of the input interface specific to function f_i of c_i referred at the output interface of c_i.

Similarly to an object system, an object network can be seen as a specification comprising the trajectories over time for a given set of objects. In the same way, an important class of object networks are those that are computable. Again, we can determine a computable object network iteratively, generating a sequence of object networks $\mathfrak{R}_0$, $\mathfrak{R}_1$, ... , where each $\mathfrak{R}_i$ contains a finite number of objects, defined over incremental domains N_i . Each object network from the sequence is equivalent to the previous, being its objects added by a temporal instance, according to the laws of triggering, the selection function defined for the last instance and the localization function. The procedure is similar to the one used for objects systems with infinite number of objects, included the conditions for localization functions. With this methodology, one can determine, for each instant $n \in N$, the instance of any object that exists in n. The initial objects network from the sequence, $\mathfrak{R}_0$ has a special denomination, being called the kernel of an object network. In its kernel, objects and localization functions are defined only for instance n=0, and the selection function should be computable, being described by an algorithm γ'.

Definition 32 - **Kernel of an Object Network:** We define the kernel of an object network as an objects network $\mathfrak{R}_0 = (\Sigma, \Pi, \Xi, A, \eta$, fpi, fpo, $\mathcal{C}^0$, ξ^0 , $\gamma)$, where

- Σ, Π, Ξ, A, η , fpi and fpo are as in the Definition of objects network and
- $\mathcal{C}^0 = \{c_i'\}$ is a set of objects defined only for n=0.
- ξ^0 is a localization function $\xi^0 : N \times \mathcal{C}^0 \rightarrow \Pi$, defined only for n=0.
- γ is a selection function determined by means an algorithm γ'.

Starting with a kernel, new finite object networks are computed in sequence. Each algorithm step generates a new network that is, fundamentally, the previous one increased by the definition of new values for $\mathcal{C}$, ξ and γ . The new $\mathcal{C}$ is the old one plus the objects to be generated at step n, according to γ. The new ξ is also the old one, defined now also for instant n, again according to γ. The algorithm γ' incrementally defines function γ. At each step the algorithm defines new instances for the current objects and new values for localization function and selection function such that for each instant n, we obtain new $\mathcal{C}$, ξ and γ corresponding to a new finite objects network. Finite networks correspond to some element of such a sequence. Infinite networks (both networks with a finite number of objects, defined in infinite domains, or networks with an infinite number of objects), are considered as the limit element i of the sequence, when $i \rightarrow \infty$. An example of such algorithm is described in figure 9. Note that each new network in the sequence includes the previous one increased by the definition of a new time instant.

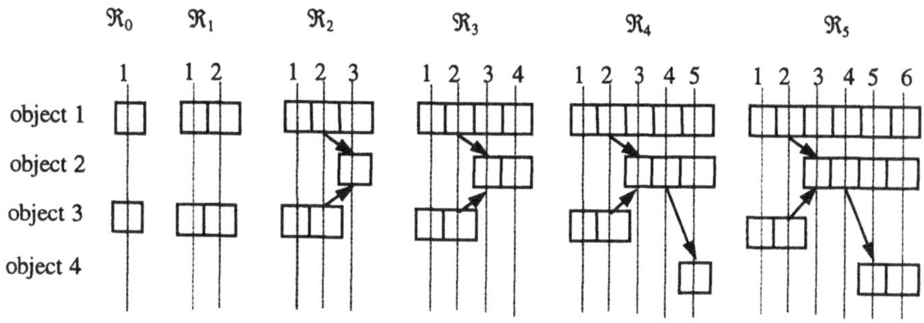

Figure 9 - Example of an Evolution Sequence

For a detailed example of the main procedures to assemble an object network, see the work of Gudwin[3,4,7].

2.6 *Using Meta-Objects within Object Networks*

To use meta-objects (and its generic and fuzzy extensions) in the framework of object networks, we have to convert them to objects. But first, all objects that are to be related to the meta-objects have to be modified to handle some kind of memory. This is showed in figure 10.

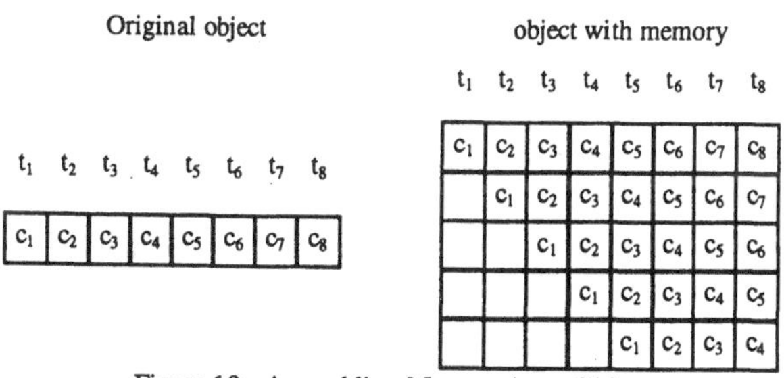

Figure 10 - Assembling Memory in an Object

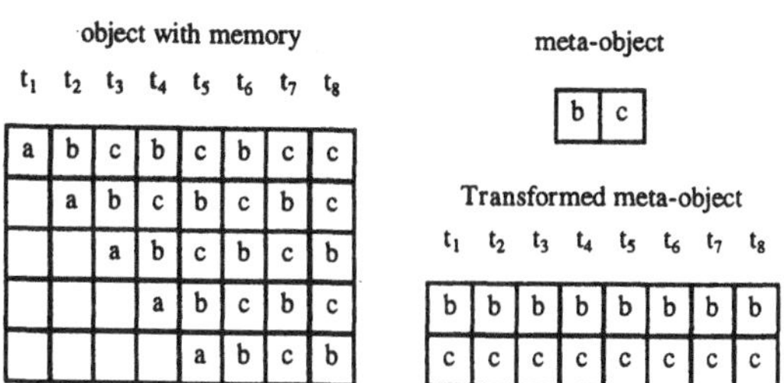

Figure 11 - Transformation of a meta-object into an object

Once the related objects are equipped with memory, we can modify the meta-object to become an object. This transformation is shown in figure 11.

Now, to check the occurrence of a meta-object in an object (and its variations), we use an active object that is fed both with the modified meta-object and the object with memory. Its active function is responsible for doing the respective computations.

The use of meta-objects with two variables is particularly useful to represent events, i.e. sudden changes between two states. But other types of occurrences do exist, as e.g. a unitary occurrence that represents a single state. This kind of occurrence is useful, e.g., to obtain information about some attribute of the object during its existence. Meta-objects with more than 2 variables are used to represent tendencies or behaviors as, e.g., an increasing or decreasing behavior, or a periodic behavior. The formal model herein stated allows the representation of occurrences with all those subtle differences.

3 Computing with Words

Words may represent a huge variety of concepts from real world. These concepts are of different natures and originate different types of knowledge. In a natural language, words are classified by the type of meaning they can be assigned to. We may have words representing adjectives, substantives, verbs, prepositions, adverbs, etc. In computational semiotics, these meanings are referred to as rhematic iconic pieces of knowledge. Among them, the most important ones, concerning computability, are adjectives, substantives and verbs. Adjectives are related to some quality associated to an entity, being described within computational semiotics as sensorial rhematic knowledge. Substantives are related to individuals or entities of the real world, being described within computational semiotics by the object type of knowledge. And finally, verbs are related to a dynamics involving the entities of real world, being modeled within computational semiotics by a type of knowledge called occurrence knowledge.

Current approaches of computing with words only deal with the semantics of adjectives or, in other words, qualities. Qualities are modeled by values assigned to linguistic variables, represented by fuzzy sets. For example, consider the following fuzzy proposition:

P1 = Carol lives near Mary

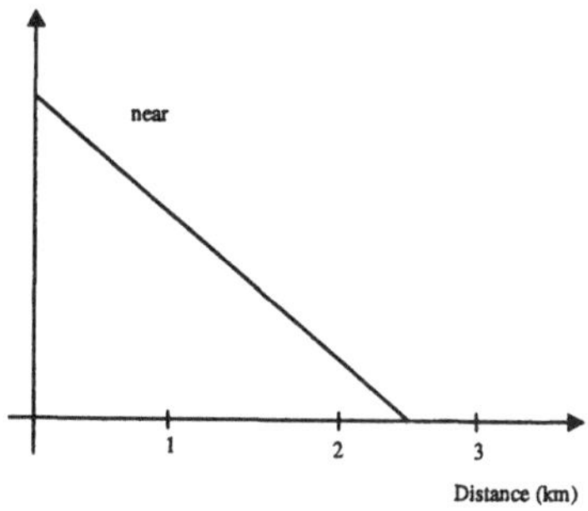

Figure 12 – Model for Fuzzy Proposition

If we use the fuzzy set of figure 12 to model such a proposition, we are in fact not modeling the whole proposition, but only the quality "near". All other words are only grammatically modeled, in the sense that they have to appear in the proposition to let it make sense. But we are not modeling neither "Carol", nor "live", or "Mary". The same is true with a rule like:

P2: If oven temperature is high then cooking time should be small

In this case, we are using a fuzzy relation R to represent the proposition, e.g., R= high × small (figure 13).

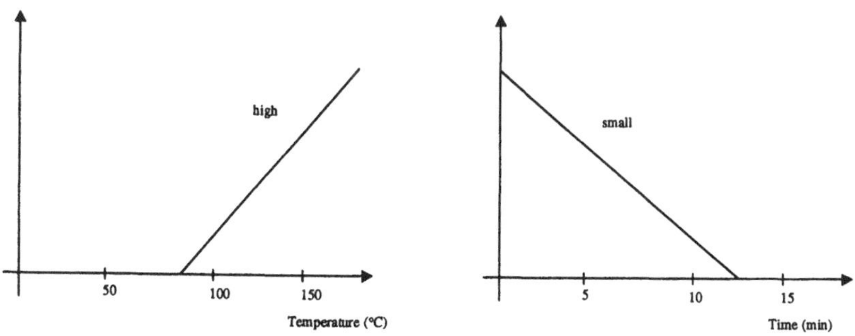

Figure 13 – Model for Fuzzy Proposition

Note that the semantics of "oven", "temperature", "time" and "cooking" are not modeled.

Object Networks, differently from the current approaches, provide a framework where not only quality is processed, but also entity and entity dynamics. In the next subsection, we show an example of an object network to compute with words according to the currently known approach. Subsequently we suggest on how other types of meaning may be addressed under the scope of computational semiotics.

3.1 Computing Qualities

In this example, we have two linguistic variables, oven_temperature and cooking_time. The oven temperature has its universe within 0 and 200°C range, and the cooking time within 0 and 20 minutes. These linguistic variables are used to build a very simple fuzzy rule base, as follows:

RB: If oven_temperature is low then cooking_time is large
If oven_temperature is moderate then cooking_time is medium
If oven_temperature is high then cooking_time is small

This rule base expresses (linguistically) the relation about the temperature of the oven and the time that should be used in cooking some item. Observe that both are qualities associated with other linguistic concepts. The oven_temperature is a quality (an attribute) associated with the oven, and the cooking_time is a quality associated to the dynamic process of cooking some food. Note that oven_temperature by itself doesn't give too much information of what is an oven at all. Similarly, cooking_time is not too informative about the process of cooking.

The problem here is how to compute the cooking time, using as input information about the oven temperature and the given linguistic rule base. We may consider two different outputs for this problem. The first is a specific time, e.g. to program the timer of an automatic oven. The other one is a linguistic output, to be used e.g., as an advice to the user.

The first step in solving this problem is to frame it into the object network formalism. For this purpose, let it be the following classes:

$C_1 = \{(s_1)\}$ – Class of Symbols, where $s_1 \in S$ and S is the set of words.

$C_2 = \{(s_2, i_1)\}$ – Class of Labeled Icons, where $s_2 \in S$ and $i_1 \in I$, where I is the set of all fuzzy sets of a universe.

$C_3 = \{(s_3, (s_4, i_2), i_3, f_1)\}$ – Class of Symbol-Icon Converters, where $s_k \in S$, $i_k \in I$ and $f_1 : S \times (S \times I) \rightarrow I$ is a partial function $f_1(s_3,(s_4,i_2)) = \begin{cases} i_2, \text{if } s_3 = s_4 \\ \text{not defined, otherwise} \end{cases}$, which puts its result in i_3.

$C_4 = \{(i_4)\}$ – Class of Fuzzy Sets (Unlabeled Icons), where $i_4 \in I$

$C_5 = \{(r_1)\}$ – Class of Fuzzy Rule Bases, where $r_1 \in R$ is a fuzzy rule base, and R is the set of all fuzzy rule bases.

$C_6 = \{(i_5, r_2, i_6, f_2)\}$ – Class of Inference Engines, where $i_k \in I$, $r_2 \in R$, and f_2 is a function that performs the fuzzy composition of i_5 and r_2, putting the result in i_6.

$C_7 = \{(i_7, v_1, f_3)\}$ – Class of Defuzzifiers, where $i_7 \in I$, $v_1 \in V$, V is a real value, and f_3 is a function $f_3 : I \rightarrow V$, that performs the defuzzification of the fuzzy set in i_7.

$C_8 = \{(v_2)\}$ – Class of Real Values, where $v_2 \in V$.

$C_9 = \{(i_8, (s_5, i_9), s_6, f_4)\}$ – Class of Icon-Symbol Converters, where $i_k \in I$, $s_k \in S$ and $f_4 : I \times (S \times I) \rightarrow S$ is a partial function $f_4(i_8, (s_5, i_9)) = \begin{cases} s_5, \text{if } i_8 = i_9 \\ \text{not defined, otherwise} \end{cases}$, which puts the result in s_6.

Next, consider the following object network, represented by its kernel $\mathfrak{R}_0$:

$\mathfrak{R}_0 = (\Sigma, \Pi, \Xi, A, \eta, fpi, fpo, \mathcal{C}^0, \xi^0, \gamma)$

$\Sigma = \{C_1, C_2, C_3, C_4, C_5, C_6, C_7, C_8, C_9\}$

$\Pi = \{\pi_1, \pi_2, \pi_3, \pi_4, \pi_5, \pi_6, \pi_7, \pi_8, \pi_9, \pi_{10}, \pi_{11}\}$,

$\Xi = \{ (\pi_1, C_1), (\pi_2, C_2), (\pi_3, C_3), (\pi_4, C_4), (\pi_5, C_5), (\pi_6, C_6), (\pi_7, C_4), (\pi_8, C_7), (\pi_9, C_8), (\pi_{10}, C_9), (\pi_{11}, C_1)\}$

$A = \{a_1, a_2, a_3, a_4, a_5, a_6, a_7, a_8, a_9, a_{10}, a_{11}\}$,

$\eta = \{ (a_1, (\pi_1, \pi_3)), (a_2, (\pi_2, \pi_3)), (a_3, (\pi_3, \pi_4)), (a_4, (\pi_4, \pi_6)),$
$(a_5, (\pi_5, \pi_6)), (a_6, (\pi_6, \pi_7)), (a_7, (\pi_7, \pi_8)), (a_8, (\pi_8, \pi_9)),$
$(a_9, (\pi_7, \pi_{10})), (a_{10}, (\pi_2, \pi_{10})), (a_{11}, (\pi_{10}, \pi_{11}))\}$

$fpi_{\pi 3} = \{(1, a_1), (2, a_2)\}$, $fpo_{\pi 3} = \{(1, a_3)\}$

$fpi_{\pi 6} = \{(1, a_4), (2, a_5)\}$, $fpo_{\pi 6} = \{(1, a_6)\}$

$fpi_{\pi 8} = \{(1, a_7)\}$, $fpo_{\pi 8} = \{(1, a_8)\}$

$fpi_{\pi 10} = \{(1, a_9), (2, a_{10})\}$, $fpo_{\pi 10} = \{(1, a_{11})\}$

In this example, we assume the following initial set of objects:

$\mathcal{C}^0 = \{c_1, c_2, c_3, c_4, c_5, c_6, c_7, c_8, c_9, c_{10}, c_{11}, c_{12}\}$,

Where

$c_1 = \{(0, (\text{"high"}))\}$, is an object of type C_1, put in π_1, and corresponding to the word used as an input, in this case the word "high".

c_2 = { (0, ("low",mf_1)) }, is an object of type C_2, put in π_2, and corresponding to one of the labeled icons present at the iconic knowledge base.
c_3 = { (0, ("moderate",mf_2)) }, is an object of type C_2, put in π_2, and corresponding to one of the labeled icons present at the iconic knowledge base.
c_4 = { (0, ("high";mf_3)) }, is an object of type C_2, put in π_2, and corresponding to one of the labeled icons present at the iconic knowledge base.
c_5 = { (0, ("small",mf_4)) }, is an object of type C_2, put in π_2, and corresponding to one of the labeled icons present at the iconic knowledge base.
c_6 = { (0, ("medium",mf_5)) }, is an object of type C_2, put in π_2, and corresponding to one of the labeled icons present at the iconic knowledge base.
c_7 = { (0, ("large",mf_6)) }, is an object of type C_2, put in π_2, and corresponding to one of the labeled icons present at the iconic knowledge base.
$c_8 = \{ (0, (Def_s ,(Def_s,Def_i), Def_i ,f_1)) \}$, is an object of type C_3, put in π_3, and corresponding to a symbol-icon converter. The values $Def_i \in I$ are default values for icons, and $Def_s \in S$ are default values for symbols. They are needed because the tuples values are related to input and output interfaces, not already used in the previous iterations.
$c_9 = \{ (0, (rb)) \}$, is an object of type C_5, put in π_5, and rb is the fuzzy rule base to be used.
$c_{10} = \{ (0, (Def_i ,Def_{RB} , Def_i , f_2)) \}$, is an object of type C_6, put in π_6, and corresponding to the inference engine.
$c_{11} = \{ (0, (Def_i ,Def_v , f_3)) \}$, is an object of type C_7, put in π_8, and corresponding to the defuzzifier. $Def_v \in V$ is a default real value.
$c_{12} = \{ (0, (Def_i ,(Def_s,Def_i), Def_s ,f_4)) \}$, is an object of type C_9, put in π_{10}, and corresponding to the icon-symbol converter.

Then, the corresponding localization function becomes:

$$\xi^0 = \{ (0, c_1 , \pi_1), (0, c_2 , \pi_2), (0, c_3 , \pi_2), (0, c_4 , \pi_2), (0, c_5 , \pi_2), (0, c_6 , \pi_2), (0, c_7 , \pi_2), (0, c_8 , \pi_3), (0, c_9 , \pi_5), (0, c_{10} , \pi_6), (0, c_{11} , \pi_8), (0, c_{12} , \pi_{10}) \}$$

The selection function, allowing the transition for the first step is:

$$\gamma (0) = \{\gamma_1 , \gamma_2 , \gamma_3 , \gamma_4 , \gamma_5 , \gamma_6 , \gamma_7 , \gamma_8 , \gamma_9 , \gamma_{10} , \gamma_{11} , \gamma_{12} \}$$
$$\gamma_8(0) = (\{(c_1,1), (c_4 , 0)\} , \{c_{13} \}, 1)$$
$$\gamma_1(0) = ... = \gamma_7(0) = \gamma_9(0) = ... = \gamma_{12}(0) = (\varnothing, \varnothing, 0)$$

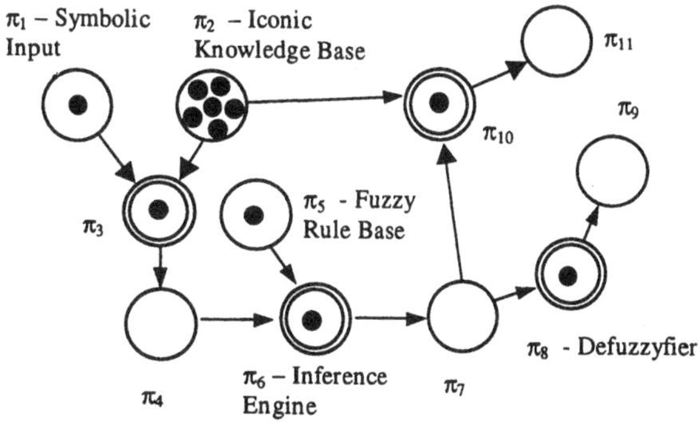

Figure 14 - Object Network at step 0

Observe that using this selection function, object c_1 is destroyed from step 0 to step 1, but object c_4 is only non-destructively assimilated. They are used by object c_8 to generate a new object c_{13} (an icon), at π_4 . With this, at step 1, the object network stays like in figure 15.

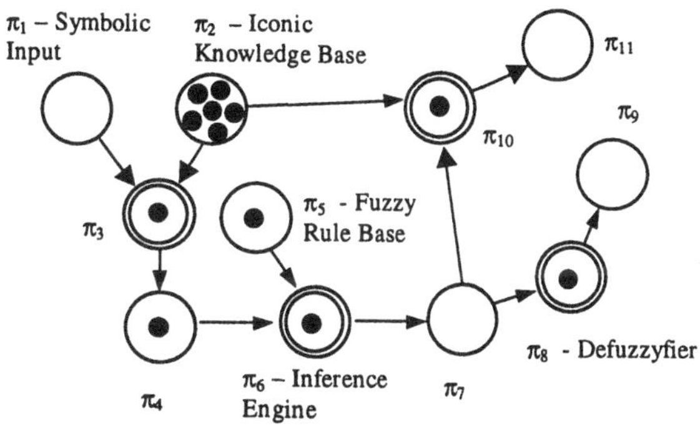

Figure 15 - Object Network at step 1

At step 1, the existing objects are:

$\mathcal{C}^1 = \{ c_2 , c_3 , c_4 , c_5 , c_6 , c_7 , c_8 , c_9 , c_{10} , c_{11} , c_{12} , c_{13} \}$,

Objects c_2 , c_3 , c_4 , c_5 , c_6 , c_7 did not suffer any modification. The instance of c_8 for step 1 becomes:

$c_8 (1) =$ (“high” ,(“high”,mf_3), mf_3 ,f_1)

Objects c_9 , c_{10} , c_{11} , c_{12} have not been modified.

Object c_{13} is a new object of type C_4 , and its instance for step 1 is:

$c_{13}(1) = (mf_3)$

The localization function, at step 1 becomes:

$$\xi^1 = \{ (1, c_2, \pi_2), (1, c_3, \pi_2), (1, c_4, \pi_2), (1, c_5, \pi_2), (1, c_6, \pi_2), (1, c_7, \pi_2), (1, c_8, \pi_3), (1, c_9, \pi_5), (1, c_{10}, \pi_6), (1, c_{11}, \pi_8), (1, c_{12}, \pi_{10}), (1, c_{13}, \pi_4) \}$$

The selection function, enabling the transition to step 2 (figure 16) is:

$$\gamma(1) = \{ \gamma_2, \gamma_3, \gamma_4, \gamma_5, \gamma_6, \gamma_7, \gamma_8, \gamma_9, \gamma_{10}, \gamma_{11}, \gamma_{12}, \gamma_{13} \}$$
$$\gamma_{10}(1) = (\{(c_{13},0), (c_9, 0)\}, \{c_{13}\}, 1)$$
$$\gamma_2(1) = \ldots = \gamma_9(1) = \gamma_{11}(1) = \ldots = \gamma_{13}(1) = (\varnothing, \varnothing, 0)$$

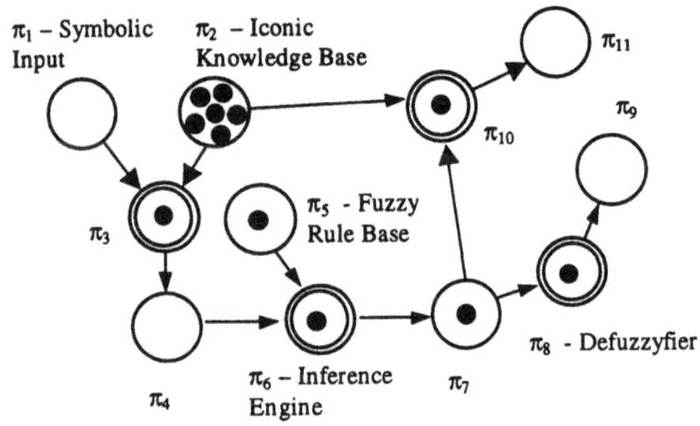

Figure 16 - Object Network at step 2

This selection function takes object c_{13}, uses its information together with the information within c_9 to compute a new fuzzy set (an icon), and store this new information again in c_{13}, that is moved to π_7.

At step 2, the existing objects remain the same:

$$\mathcal{C}^2 = \{ c_2, c_3, c_4, c_5, c_6, c_7, c_8, c_9, c_{10}, c_{11}, c_{12}, c_{13} \},$$

Objects c_2, c_3, c_4, c_5, c_6, c_7, c_8, c_9 did not suffer any modification. The instance of c_{10} for step 2 becomes:

$c_{10}(2) = (mf_3, rb, mf_x, f_2)$, where mf_x is the result of fuzzy composition involving mf_3 and rb, performed by function f_2. Objects c_{11} and c_{12} also didn't have any modification. Object c_{13} receives a new value, after being conducted from π_4 to π_7: $c_{13}(2) = (mf_x)$

The localization function at step 2 becomes

$\xi^1 = \{ (2, c_2, \pi_2), (2, c_3, \pi_2), (2, c_4, \pi_2), (2, c_5, \pi_2), (2, c_6, \pi_2), (2, c_7, \pi_2),$
$(2, c_8, \pi_3), (2, c_9, \pi_5), (2, c_{10}, \pi_6), (2, c_{11}, \pi_8), (2, c_{12}, \pi_{10}), (2, c_{13}, \pi_7) \}$

The selection function, which allows the transition to step 3 (figure 17) is:

$\gamma(2) = \{ \gamma_2, \gamma_3, \gamma_4, \gamma_5, \gamma_6, \gamma_7, \gamma_8, \gamma_9, \gamma_{10}, \gamma_{11}, \gamma_{12}, \gamma_{13} \}$
$\gamma_{11}(2) = (\{(c_{13},1)\}, \{c_{14}\}, 1)$
$\gamma_{12}(2) = (\{(c_{13},0), (c_5, 0)\}, \{c_{15}\}, 1)$
$\gamma_2(2) = \ldots = \gamma_{10}(1) = \gamma_{13}(1) = (\varnothing, \varnothing, 0)$

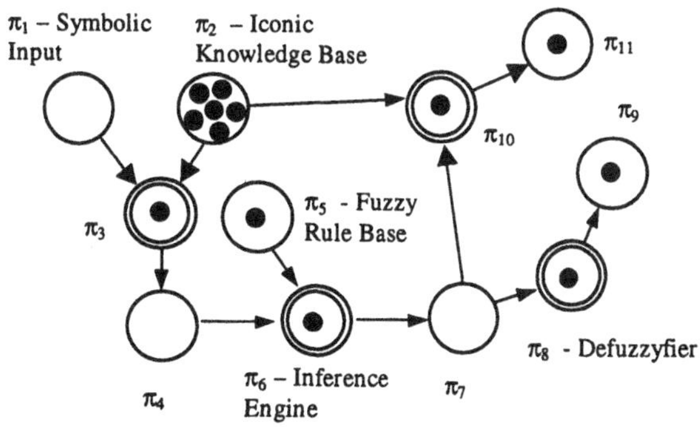

Figure 17 - Object Network at step 3

With these selection functions, object c_{13} is both used to generate a new object c_{14}, (put at π_9 - the defuzzification measure of mf_x) and a new object c_{15}, put at π_{11} (the most plausible linguistic term associated with the membership function mf_x).

With this selection function, at step 3, the existing objects become:

$\mathcal{C}^3 = \{ c_2, c_3, c_4, c_5, c_6, c_7, c_8, c_9, c_{10}, c_{11}, c_{12}, c_{14}, c_{15} \}$,

Objects c_2, c_3, c_4, c_5, c_6, c_7, c_8, c_9, c_{10} did not suffer any alteration. The instance of c_{11} and c_{12} for step 3 becomes:

$c_{11}(3) = (mf_x, x, f_3)$

$c_{12}(3) = (mf_x, (\text{"small"}, mf_4), \text{"small"}, f_4)$

Objects c_{14} and c_{15} get the following instances:

$c_{14}(3) = (x)$

$c_{15}(3) = (\text{"small"})$

Both c_{14} and c_{15} are solutions for the example problem stated.

3.2 *Other Types of Meaning*

Meaning modeling for other types of words different from qualities is still an open question. Computational semiotics provides a tool for assigning such a meaning for some types of substantives (entities) and some types of verbs (entities dynamics), but mechanisms for performing computations using such a representation are under development. In this section, we illustrate on how we may use objects and meta-objects to do such a task.

Consider, e.g., that we want to assign a meaning to the word "oven". To do this, we have to find a collection of attributes that adequately represent the concept of an oven. Suppose that we acquaint that the following list is a good set of such attributes: Width (w), Height (h), Depth (d), Weight (p), Color (c), Temperature (t), number of heaters (nh), Cleaning State (cl), Age (a), Conservation State (cs). Then, to fully describe an oven in a particular instant of time, we may use a tuple like:

$$(w,h,d,p,c,t,nh,cl,a,cs)$$

But, to fully describe an oven, we have to consider not only a description for the current time instant, but also to its whole existence in the real world, during different periods of time. For different instants, some of the attributes may have a different value than the current one. So, to fully model the word "oven", we have to use a mathematical object. Let O be a class, given by $O = \{ (w,h,d,p,c,t,nh,cl,a,cs) \}$. Then, an object o of type O is said to be a model for an oven from the real world. Notice that each of oven's attributes, may be modeled by a number, a set of numbers or a fuzzy set. Depending on each case, we may have a standard object, a generic object or a fuzzy object.

Consider now that we want to assign a meaning to the verb "to warm". The main meaning for such a word is that, for some entity of the world, there should be an attribute, measuring a temperature, and there must be a change for this temperature, from one value, somewhat classified as small, to other value considered large. This meaning can be represented using a meta-object.

For example, let us define a class $C = \{(t)\}$, (notice that it is a superclass of O), and define a fuzzy meta-object w of class C given by:

$$w = \{(v_1, \text{small}), (v_2, \text{large})\},$$

where small and large are two fuzzy sets defined on the universe of temperatures. This meta-object can be represented by table 1 below:

	v_1	v_2
t	small	large

Table 1 – Generic Meta-object warmed

Note that once the meta-object is defined, it can be used with an object to make a phrase make sense. For example, "to warm" may be used with any other substantive, which is modeled by an object that has "temperature" among its attributes. In this case, variables v_1 and v_2 are substituted by instants of time, in the object description, to establish a correspondence with the dynamic behavior "to warm", assuring that it really happened in the object history through time.

It is important to stress that the examples presented in this sub-section are only a sketch on how effectively using the meaning of substantives and verbs in computing. It is also worth to mention that the computations envisioned here will certainly use the kind of techniques addressed so far, using the current computing with words paradigm. What we actually claim is that object networks are a very suitable tool to do computations concerning words. They not only are able to perform the computations which have been already proposed in the literature, but introduce a formalism that suggests extensions to be made in order to enhance the representation power of the paradigm.

4 Computational Intelligence and Object Nets

The same framework used in last section to perform computation with words, can be used to model other types of paradigms within computational intelligence[12] and soft computing[13] .

In this section, we briefly suggest how we can use object networks to model neural networks and evolutionary systems.

4.1 Neural Networks

Figure 18 shows the representation of a self-organizing neural network by an object network. Note that this neural network has two main arguments[6] . The deductive argument works during the feedforward phase when it generates an output from an input. The learning function is an inductive argument that performs the self-organization of the neural network. It acts considering the input, and modifying the neural structure (e.g., the weights and offsets of the neural net) to perform learning.

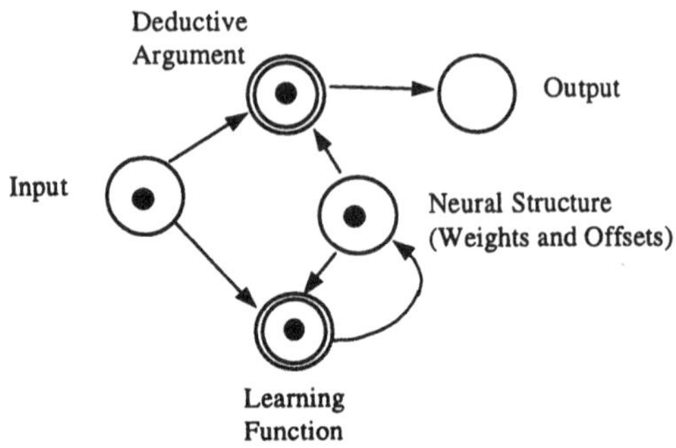

Figure 18 – Self-Organizing Neural Network

Other types of neural networks (like supervised neural networks) would have a similar representation including, in this case, a place for the desired output feeding the learning function argument.

4.2 Evolutionary Systems

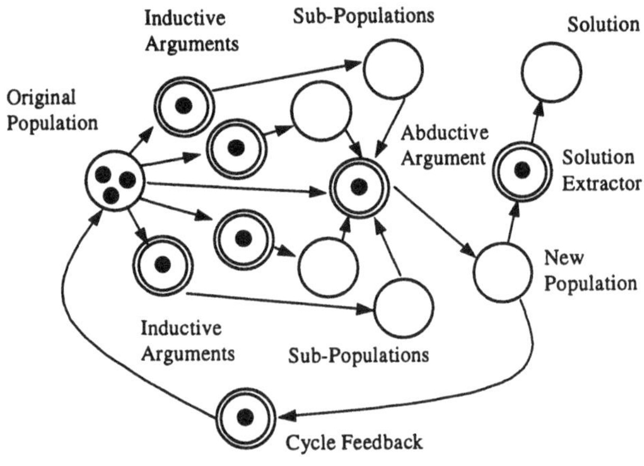

Figure 19 – Evolutionary System

An example of an evolutionary system is given in figure 19. In this example, there is an original population used as input for four inductive arguments (performing crossover, mutation, inductive mutation, etc.), generating new sub-populations. The four new sub-populations are used in conjunction with the original population to feed an abductive argument that will choose the new population (and destroy the old one). The best individual of this new population is extracted by an abductive argument to generate a solution, and the new population is redirected again to the beginning through a feedback deductive argument that simply moves the new population from the new population place to the original population place.

5 Conclusion

The notion of object network has been introduced with the purpose to provide a modeling and implementation framework for computing with words. Beginning with the mathematical concept of objects, generic objects and fuzzy objects, we addressed their interaction to each other, composing object systems. A special class of object systems, the object networks was emphasized, proposed here as a dynamic software architecture suitable for handling the issues involved when computing with words, independently of the specific numerical algorithms used. An example of an object network performing computations with words was detailed. We also suggested how object networks may manage semantics of linguistic, semiotic terms, to provide higher level linguistic computations.

The main conclusions are that object networks, addressed within the context of computational semiotics, are a very suitable tool to perform computation with words. Object networks provide a representation for the current approaches in this field, and suggest extensions to increase the representation power of such a paradigm.

Acknowledgements

The second author acknowledges CNPq, the Brazilian National Research Council for grant #300729/86-3.

References

1. L.Zadeh, "Fuzzy Logic = Computing with Words" – *IEEE Transactions on Fuzzy Systems*, pp. 103-111, vol. 4, no. 2, May (1996).
2. C.S. Peirce, *Collected Papers of Charles Sanders Peirce* - vol I - Principles of Philosophy; vol II - Elements of Logic; vol III - Exact Logic; vol IV - The Simplest Mathematics; vol V - Pragmatism and Pragmaticism; vol. VI - Scientific Metaphysics - edited by Charles Hartshorne and Paul Weiss - Belknap Press of Harvard University Press – (Cambridge, Massachusetts, 2nd printing, 1960).

3. R.R.Gudwin and F.A.C.Gomide, *Computational Semiotics : An Approach for the Study of Intelligent Systems - Part I : Foundations* – (Technical Report RT-DCA 09 – DCA-FEEC-UNICAMP, 1997).
4. R.R.Gudwin and F.A.C.Gomide, *Computational Semiotics : An Approach for the Study of Intelligent Systems - Part II : Theory and Application* – (Technical Report RT-DCA 09 – DCA-FEEC-UNICAMP, 1997).
5. R.R.Gudwin and F.A.C.Gomide, *An Approach to Computational Semiotics* – (Proceedings of the ISAS'97 – Intelligent Systems and Semiotics : A Learning Perspective – International Conference – Gaithersburg, MD, USA - 22-25 September, 1997).
6. R.R.Gudwin and F.A.C.Gomide, *A Computational Semiotics Approach for Soft Computing* – (Proceedings of the IEEE SMC'97 – IEEE International Conference on Systems, Man and Cybernetics - Orlando, FL, USA - 12-15 October, 1997).
7. R.R.Gudwin and F.A.C. Gomide, "Object Network : A Formal Model to Develop Intelligent Systems" in *Computational Intelligence and Software Engineering*, J.Peters and W. Pedrycz (Eds.) – World Scientific, 1998.
8. A.Snyder, "The Essence of Objects:Concepts and Terms" - *IEEE Software*, pp. 31-42, Jan. (1993).
9. Y. Wand, "A Proposal for a Formal Model of Objects" - *in Object-Oriented Concepts, Databases and Applications*, W. Kim and F. Lochovsky, eds., (ACM Press, New York, pp. 537-559, 1989).
10. K.Jensen, - "Coloured Petri Nets : A High Level Language for System Design and Analysis" - *Lecture Notes in Computer Science 483 - Advances in Petri Nets*, pp. 342-416, (1990).
11. T.Murata, - "Petri Nets : Properties, Analysis and Applications" - *Proceedings of the IEEE*, vol. 77, n. 4, April (1989).
12. J.Zurada, R.J.Marks II, and C.J.Robinson, - *Computational Intelligence - Imitating Life* – (IEEE Press, USA, 1994).
13. L.Zadeh, – "Soft Computing and Fuzzy Logic", *IEEE Software*, vol. 11, n. 6, pp. 48-56, (1994).

Study on a Framework for Solving Ill-defined Problem Using Patterns and Symbols

Yoichiro Hattori , Takeshi Furuhashi

Dept. of Information Electronics, Nagoya University
Furo-cho, Chikusa-ku, Nagoya 464-01, Japan
email: {hattori, furu}@bioele.nuee.nagoya-u.ac.jp

Abstract

Both symbolic information processing and pattern information processing are important for intelligent information processing. Patterns and symbols constitute concepts. A new function is expected to be realized by interaction between patterns and symbols. The authors have proposed a two-layered network which consists of a pattern layer and a symbol layer for the realization of the processing of patterns and symbols. In the symbol layer, nonlinear dynamics is introduced and retrieval of patterns and symbols related to inputted vague patterns has been achieved.

In this paper, a new definition of pattern is introduced, and inference using patterns and symbols is discussed in a framework for solving ill-defined problem. Kohonen model is applied to self-organization of patterns and symbols from extracted features from inputted information. The two-layered network is applied to implement the framework. Experiments are done to show that the patterns are self-organized, and the retrieval of related patterns to the inputted patterns is achieved.

1 Introduction

This paper studies computation through interactions between patterns and symbols. Both symbolic and pattern information processing are very important for intelligent information processing. Patterns and symbols are inseparable information which constitute concepts. It is expected that a new function will be realized by interaction between patterns and symbols.

Takagi et al.[1] proposed Conceptual Fuzzy Set (CFS). The CFS is a set of labels with activation values for representing various meanings of a label by other labels with grades of activation. The CFS was a pioneering concept for exploring new development of fuzzy logic. However, this fuzzy set does not treat patterns whose spatial distributions have meanings. Sun[2] also proposed integration of rules and connectionism for robust common sense reasoning. Rule application is modeled at the conceptual level by a symbolic process and fine-grained similarity matching is modeled at the subconceptual level by a subsymbolic process. This model did not treat patterns nor contain dynamics of interactions between patterns and symbols. Sakurai and Omori[3] proposed an architecture for symbol and pattern interactions for image understanding. Omori and Yamanashi[4] proposed PATON: a model of concept consisting of a pattern and a symbol layer. These models in [3] and [4] treated only crisp patterns.

The authors[5] have proposed a two-layered associative memory network consisting of a pattern layer and a symbol layer for the realization of the new processing of patterns and symbols. The non-linear dynamics[6] which can cause chaotic vibrations is incorporated into the association in the symbol layer. The associations in the pattern layer and the symbol layer interact with each other. The authors[7, 8] have also proposed a multi-module network whose basic modules are the two-layered networks. However, the patterns and symbols used in this model was given a priori.

In this paper, a new definition of pattern is introduced, and inference using patterns and symbols is discussed in a framework for solving ill-defined problem. Kohonen model is applied to self-organization of patterns and symbols from extracted features from inputted information. The two-layered network is applied to implement the framework. The self-organized patterns by Kohonen model are inputted into the pattern layer of this two-layered network. Generation and testing of candidates for an unknown inputted information by interactions between patterns and symbols are done to solve the ill-defined problem by this network.

2 What are Patterns and Symbols?

For pattern recognition, how to treat vagueness of information is an important problem. Generally, features are extracted from inputted image data, and the image is recognized based on the extracted features after, for example, the principal component analysis is done. Figure 1 and 2 illustrate a simple example of features and feature space. The sizes of fish $v_1 \sim v_6$ are extracted. These features are plotted in the feature space as shown in Fig.2. Recognition is done by using distances in the feature space. The problem here is that it is hard to extract features which have no correlations with each other. It is almost impossible to find a matrix mapping the feature space into an orthogonal space. In this study, a feature vector is treated as a pattern not as a point in the feature space. The "pattern" is defined as a set of feature vectors belonging to a class and the "symbol" is regarded as a label of the pattern in this study.

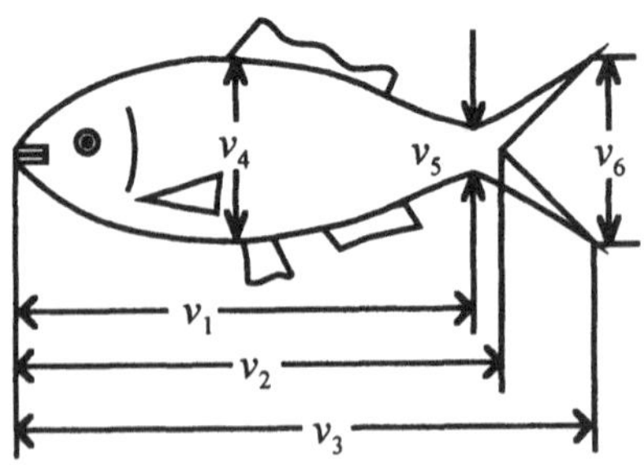

Fig.1 Extraction of Features

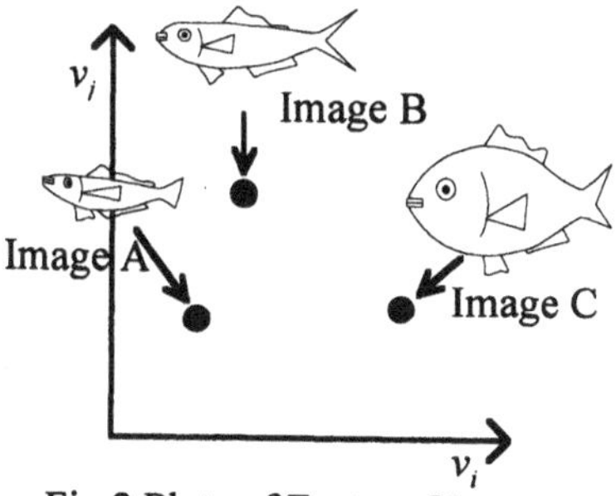

Fig.2 Plots of Feature Vectors

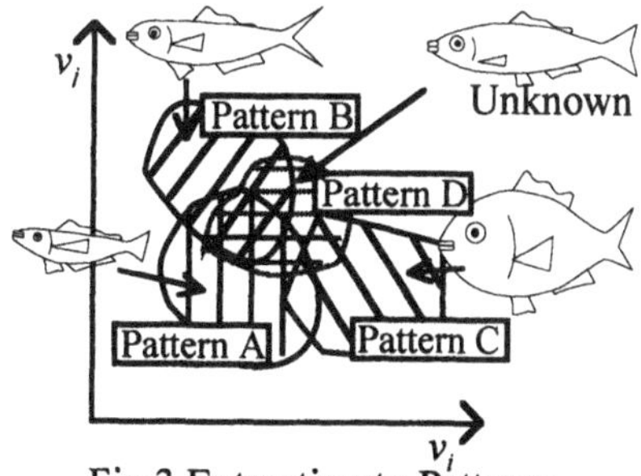

Fig.3 Extraction to Patterns

Fig.3 illustrates an example of the patterns *A*, *B*, and *C* which are sets of feature vectors belonging to the images *A*, *B*, and *C*, respectively. The reason why the patterns are defined in this manner is that multiple distances can be defined between these patterns. It is assumed that the pattern *D* is generated from an unknown image, and the related patterns to the unknown pattern *D* are evaluated from various points of view. The recognition from the nonlinear features is regarded as an ill-defined problem. In this paper, a framework for solving the ill-defined problem which generates candidates for the inputted unknown image by treating multiple distances between patterns is studied.

3 Framework for Solving Ill-defined Problems

Fig.4 shows a general framework for solving ill-defined problems. In the case where obtained data is not enough to identify a solution, a hypothesis is generated based on this insufficient data, and then the hypothesis is tested by comparison with the input. This process is to determine a class of an inputted unknown image. Successful generation of candidates by repetition of generation and testing of hypotheses is expected.

Fig.5 shows a framework proposed in this paper. This framework consists of three blocks: hypothesis generation block, hypothesis testing block, and feature pattern generator. Patterns which are generated from feature vectors representing each classes, based on the distribution of learning data, are memorized in the hypothesis testing block. When an unknown image is

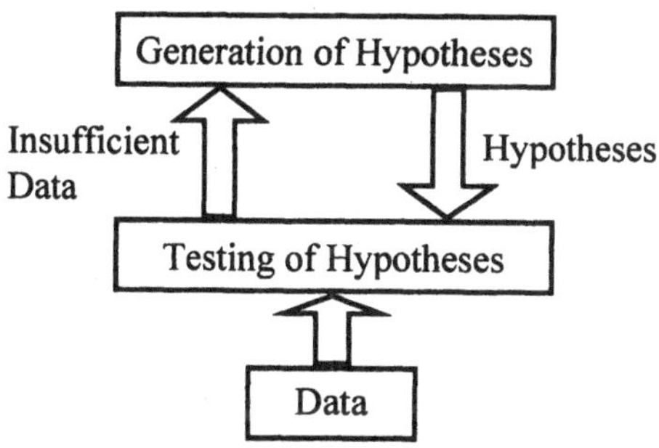

Fig.4 Framework for Solving Ill-defined Problems

inputted, features are extracted from the inputted image, and a feature pattern is generated from the extracted feature vector. In the hypothesis generation block, a symbol is inferred as a candidate based on the distances between feature patterns. The hypothesis testing block tests the generated hypothesis through a pattern inference between the feature pattern generated from the inputted image and the memorized pattern corresponding to the candidate symbol. Candidates for an inputted image are generated by repetition of this generation and testing process.

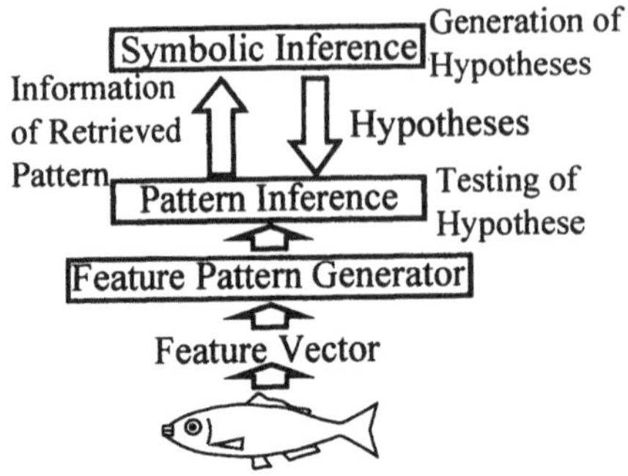

Fig. 5 Framework for Solving Ill-defined Problem Using Patterns and Symbols

3.1 Symbolic Inference

A symbols is assigned to a memorized pattern as its label. After generation of a new pattern from an unknown inputted image, the symbolic inference is initiated. Each symbol receives information from the new pattern. This information contains various distances between the new pattern and the memorized patterns, for example, distances between the centers of gravity, the degree of overlapping areas and so on. Then, a symbol is inferred as a hypothesis for the unknown image by using if-then rules or a neural network with nodes of symbols. This hypothesis is tested by the pattern inference in the hypothesis testing block. Each symbols, then, receives new information from the retrieved pattern by the pattern inference, and the symbolic inference is repeated.

3.2 Pattern Inference

The system memorizes patterns corresponding to each class in advance. The pattern generated from the unknown inputted image is the initial pattern. The symbol inferred in the hypothesis generation block is tested by the pattern inference. The information of the memorized pattern corresponding to the inferred symbol is added to the initial pattern. The pattern inference is the association of patterns using multiple distances between the patterns. This addition of information from the symbol is regarded as a guide for the pattern inference. If the unknown inputted pattern modified by the hypothesis is similar to a memorized pattern, the memorized pattern is retrieved in a relatively short time. This means that the hypothesis indicated by the symbol is correct. If it is not similar, the hypothesis might not be correct. Another hypothesis will be generated from the result of this hypothesis testing.

4 Proposed System

The authors[7, 8] have proposed a multi-module network shown in Fig.6 for the realization of the new processing of patterns and symbols. Its basic modules are three layered networks. Each module consists of a pattern layer for handling patterns and two symbol layers for handling symbols, and infers through interactions between a retrieved pattern and a retrieved intermediate symbol. In this network, inferences from a pattern to another pattern and from a symbol to another symbol and between patterns and symbols are done. It is difficult for the single module to infer a meaning in the case where a pattern can be interpreted into plural meanings. In the multi-module network, a combination of patterns in each module can determine the meanings of the patterns. The intermediate symbols in each module are assigned to combinations of patterns to represent their meanings. This model has abstract symbols corresponding to the combinations of the intermediate symbols, and inference between the intermediate symbol layer and the top symbol layer is also done.

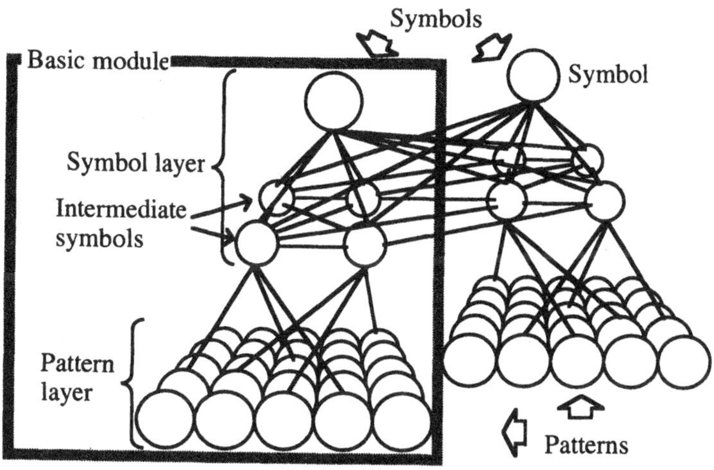

Fig.6 Multi-Module Network

In this paper, the model shown in Fig.6 is regarded as a basic configuration for implementing the framework for the solution of ill-defined problems. The basic module shown in Fig.7 is proposed. The basic module consists of a feature pattern generator and a three-layered associative memory network. The three-layered associative memory network consists of a pattern layer for the hypothesis testing and symbol layers for the hypothesis generation. In Fig.7, the top symbol layer and other modules are omitted for simplicity. The units in the symbol layer in the proposed basic module corresponds to intermediate symbols in the multi-module network, and each external input into a unit in the symbol layer in the proposed basic module is regarded as a sum of stimulations from both abstract symbols and intermediate symbols in the other modules in the multi-module network. In this paper, this basic module is applied to a primitive experiment to determine the class of a two-dimensional vector extracted from an unknown image.

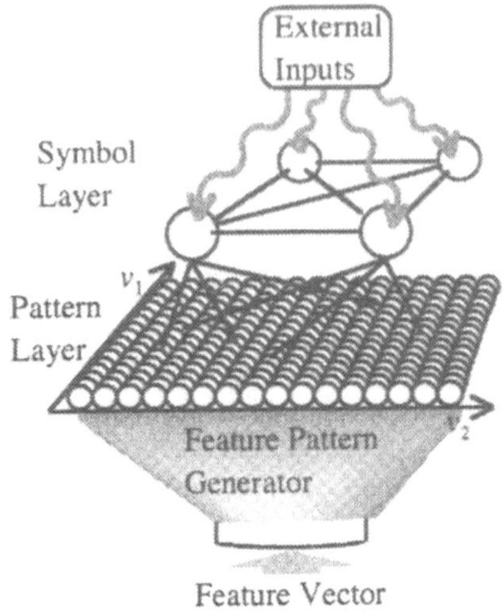

Fig.7 Proposed Model

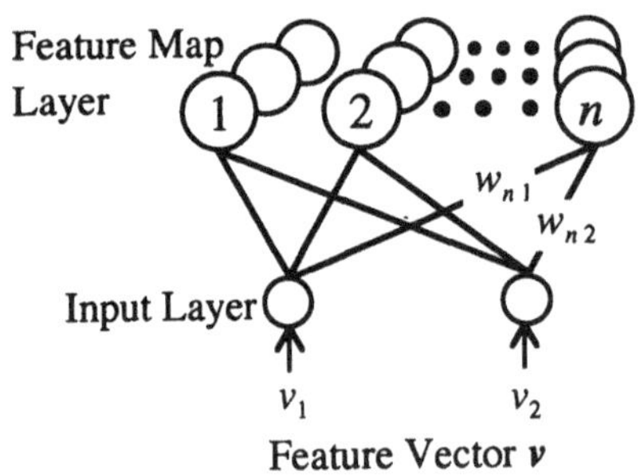

Fig.8 Kohonen Model

4.1 Learning of Feature Pattern Generator

Fig.7 shows an example in the case where two-dimensional feature vectors are available. All the units in the pattern layer are located in the two-dimensional feature space uniformly. When an image is inputted into this system, a feature vector is obtained from the image. The feature vector is extended to a feature pattern. In this paper, Kohonen's self-organizing feature map (SOM)[9] is applied to the generation of the feature pattern. Kohonen model is one of the most popular neural networks and can map an inputted n-dimensional vector into two-dimensional space in the feature map layer topologically by its learning algorithm. Fig.8 shows Kohonen model for inputs of two-dimensional feature vectors. This model consists of an input layer and a feature map layer, and each feature value is inputted into each unit in the input layer. Units in the feature map layer are located in a two-dimensional lattice and each unit has weighted connections with all the units in the input layer. In this model, the distance between two units in the feature map layer is related to the Euclidian distance between two inputted feature vectors. The connection weights between the two layers are determined by frequency of occurrence of feature vectors given as learning data.

This map is generated by a learning algorithm of Kohonen model. A two-dimensional feature vector $\boldsymbol{v}$ is assumed to be obtained from an information. The Euclidian distances between the feature vector $\boldsymbol{v}$ and the weight vectors $\boldsymbol{mw}_i = (mwx_i, mwy_i)$ of unit i in the feature map layer are calculated. Then, the unit c in the feature map layer which has the smallest Euclidian distance is sought. The distance is given by

$$\left\| v - mw_c \right\| = \min_i \left\{ \left\| v - mw_i \right\| \right\} \tag{1}$$

The unit c is the winner, and the weight vectors in the neighborhood space are changed by the following equation:

$$mw_i(t+1) = mw_i(t) + \alpha(t) h_{ic}(t) \left\{ v(t) - mw_i(t) \right\} \tag{2}$$

where t is an integer and represents the discrete-time, h_{ic} is the neighborhood function, and α is the learning rate expressed as follows:

$$h_{ic}(t) = \exp\left(\frac{d(i,c)^2}{\sigma^2} \right) \tag{3}$$

$$\alpha(t+1) = \alpha(t) \cdot \left(\frac{\alpha_f}{\alpha_i} \right)^{\frac{1}{t_{\max}}} \tag{4}$$

where $d(i, j)$ is the Euclidian distance between the unit i and j, and σ is the neighborhood-radius expressed by

$$\sigma(t+1) = \sigma(t) \cdot \left(\frac{\sigma_f}{\sigma_i} \right)^{\frac{1}{t_{\max}}} \tag{5}$$

$t_{\max}$ in eqs.(4) and (5) is the learning time, α_i and α_f are the initial and final values of learning rate, respectively, σ_i and σ_f are the initial and final values of the neighborhood-radius, respectively.

After the feature map is trained by this learning algorithm, a feature pattern is generated.

4.2 How to Generate Feature Pattern

Fig.9 shows how to generate a feature pattern from a feature vector. The following method is to reflect the distribution of occurrence probability of the memorized data in the neighborhood of the new inputted data. When a feature vector extracted from an unknown image is inputted, the winner unit c is fired. Units i within R radius from the winner unit c are fired. Their outputs som_i are given by

$$som_i = \begin{cases} 1 & \left(d(i,c) \leq R\right) \\ 0 & \left(d(i,c) > R\right) \end{cases} \tag{6}$$

The inverse mapping of this circle in the feature map layer is shown in Fig.9(iii). This area is considered to be activated. This area is the feature pattern for the inputted vector and is directly mapping onto the pattern layer in the three-layered associative memory network as shown in Fig.9(iv).

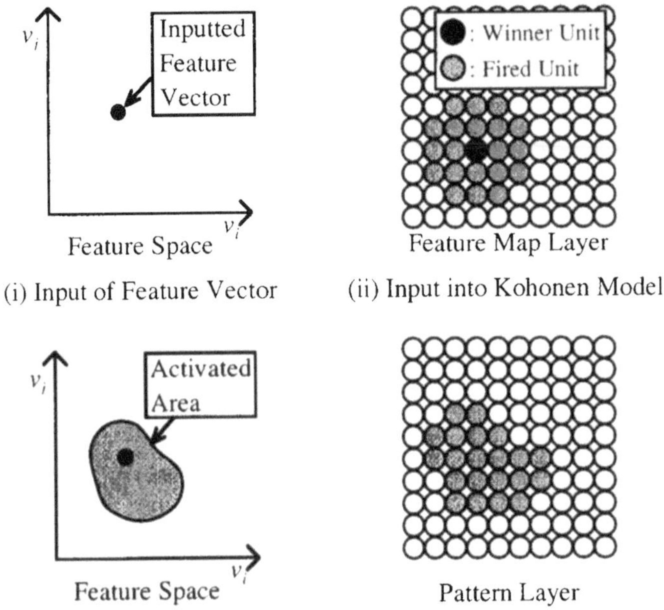

(i) Input of Feature Vector (ii) Input into Kohonen Model

(iii) Activation of Feature Space (iv) Input into Pattern Layer

Fig.9 Generation of Feature Pattern from Feature Vector

4.3 Learning of Two-layered Network

The pattern layer is an associative memory network, and it memorizes patterns by Hebbian law. Inference between patterns with multiple distances is done in this layer.

A unit in the symbol layer is assigned to a memorized pattern. All the units in the pattern layer have unidirectional connections to each unit in the symbol layer, and the connection weight psw_{ij} to the unit i in the symbol layer from the unit j in the pattern layer is determined by the following equation:

$$psw_{ij} = p_j \tag{7}$$

where p_j is the output (1 or -1) of the unit j in the pattern layer. On the other hand, each unit in the symbol layer has another unidirectional connections with some of the units in the pattern layer which are randomly selected at the rate of a constant value (<1). The connection weight spw_{ji} to the unit j in the pattern layer from the unit i in the symbol layer is given by

$$spw_{ji} = p_j. \tag{8}$$

The connection between units i and m in the same symbol layer has inhibitory weight. The degree of the inhibition can be determined by various distances between the classes, for example, the distance between the centers of gravity of patterns and so on.

4.4 Pattern and Symbolic Inferences

First of all, a feature pattern is generated in the feature pattern generator from a feature vector extracted from an inputted image. Then, the feature pattern is inputted into the pattern layer in the two-layered associative memory network.

(a) Symbolic Inference

In the process of the symbolic inference, the unit i in the symbol layer has a stimulation from the units in the pattern layer α_i and a inhibition from the units in the symbol layer. The internal state u_i is determined by the differential equation (9). The nonlinear term f in eq.(9) is given by eq.(10), and causes unstable oscillation of u_i.

$$m\ddot{u}_i + f(\dot{u}_i, \omega t) + ku_i = \varepsilon \sum_m sw_{im} s_m + d_3 \alpha_i + d_4 \beta_i \tag{9}$$

$$f(\dot{u}, \omega t) = \left[d_0 \sin(\omega t) + d_1\right]\dot{u} + d_2 \dot{u}^2 \operatorname{sgn}(\dot{u}) \tag{10}$$

where m, k, ω, d_0, d_1, d_2, d_3, and d_4 are coefficients, s_m is the output of the unit m in the symbol layer, sw_{im} is the connection weight between units i and m in the symbol layer. The nonlinearity can be controlled by the value of d_2. s_m is given by

$$s_m = \frac{1}{1 + \exp\left(-u_m\right)} \tag{11}$$

α_i is a ratio of overlapping area between the inputted pattern and the memorized pattern corresponding to the symbol i, and this information is given to the symbol i by eq.(12) through connections between the two layers.

$$\alpha_i = \frac{2overlap_i(k)}{area_i + area(k) - overlap_i(k)} - 1 \tag{12}$$

where $area_i$ is the number of units whose outputs are 1 in the pattern layer when the memorized pattern i is assumed to be retrieved, $area(k)$ is the number of units whose outputs are 1 at the time k, and $overlap_i(k)$ is the number of overlapping units of $area_i$ and $area(k)$ at the time k. β_i is an external input into the symbol i which is assumed to be a sum of stimulations from abstract symbols and intermediate symbols in the other modules in the multi-module network shown in Fig.6.

The internal states of the units in the symbol layer are determined at every step of calculation of the nonlinear differential equation (11), and the memorized symbol of the unit in the symbol layer that has the largest output is the winner. The winner symbol influences the pattern inference.

(b)Pattern Inference

In the process of the pattern inference, when the unit i in the symbol layer is the winner in the symbolic inference, an output of the unit j in the pattern layer is given by

$$p_j(k+1) = \begin{cases} spw_{ji} \text{ (if } spw_{ji} \neq 0) \\ 1 \left(\text{if } \sum_l pw_{lj} p_l(k) \geq 0 \text{ and } spw_{ji} = 0\right) \\ -1 \left(\text{if } \sum_l pw_{lj} p_l(k) < 0 \text{ and } spw_{ji} = 0\right) \end{cases} \tag{13}$$

where pw_{lj} is the connection weight between unit l and unit j in the pattern layer. When spw_{ji} is not 0, i.e. there is a connection from unit i in the symbol layer to unit j in the pattern layer, the state p_i of unit i is set at spw_{ji}, i.e. the same state as in the case where the memorized pattern i is assumed to be retrieved. When spw_{ji} is 0, the unit i is stimulated by randomly selected units l in the same pattern layer. In this stimulation, not all the units in the pattern layer are used in order to prevent the pattern inference from being trapped into one particular pattern[10]. Then, α is updated, and the symbolic inference is done again. Association is repeated by these two kinds of inferences.

5 Experiment

5.1 Experimental Condition

In this paper, a simple experiment was done using the proposed system. Vectors $\boldsymbol{a} = (a_1, a_2)$ were assumed to be observed instead of real images. The feature vectors $\boldsymbol{v} = (v_1, v_2)$, which should be extracted from the real images, were assumed to be generated by the following equations:

$$v_1 = \frac{a_1^{\frac{4}{5}} + 0.05\sin\left(2a_2{}^2 \times 2\pi\right) + 0.05}{1.1} \tag{14}$$

$$v_2 = \frac{a_2^{\frac{3}{2}} + 0.05\sin\left(2a_1{}^2 \times 2\pi\right) + 0.05}{1.1} \tag{15}$$

where a_1 and a_2 were in the range of (0, 1). Eight classes in (a_1, a_2)-space shown in Fig.10 were assumed to be observed. The centers of the areas corresponding to eight classes are (0.3,0.3), (0.4,0.3), (0.35,0.4), (0.7,0.3), (0.6,0.6), (0.7,0.7), (0.3,0.7), and (0.6,0.5). In each class, the probability of occurrence of $\boldsymbol{a}$ is inversely proportional to the distance from each center. In this experiment, the distance sl_{ij} between classes i and j is regarded as the distances between the centers of areas corresponding to the classes i and j.

In this experiment, the number of units in the feature map layer is 1024 (=32x32). The number of units in the pattern layer is 256 (=16x16) and the number of units in the symbol layer is 8.

The learning of weighting vectors of Kohonen model used in the feature pattern generator is done by using feature vectors $\boldsymbol{v}$ calculated from randomly selected $\boldsymbol{a}$ by eqs.(16) and (17). The feature pattern generated from the vector $\boldsymbol{a}$ was inputted into the pattern layer every 30 steps. The step is the interval of Runge-Kutta calculation of the differential equation in eq.(11). The constants in eqs.(11) and (12) were set at $m = 1.0$, $\omega = 0.24$, $k = 1.0$, $\varepsilon = 0.1$, $d_0 = 1.0$, $d_1 = -2.0$, $d_3 = 0.8$, $d_4 = 2.0$. The connection weight sw_{ij} between unit i and j in the symbol layer is in proportion to the distance sl_{ij} between classes i and j.

$$sw_{ij} = -\frac{sl_{ij}}{\sqrt{2}} \tag{18}$$

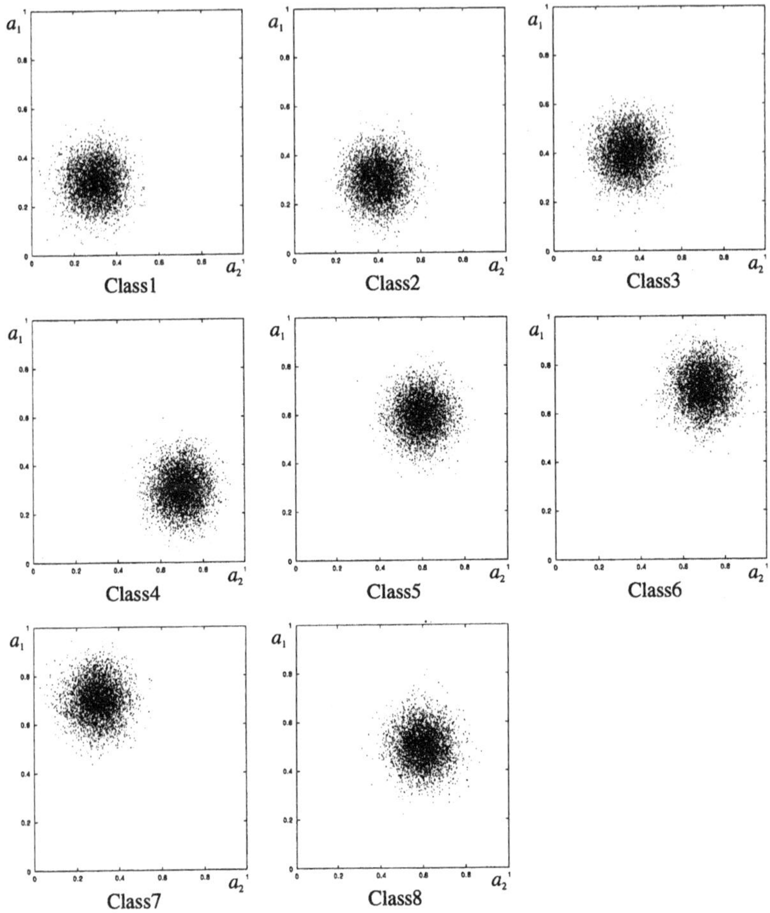

Fig.10 Vectors $\boldsymbol{a}$ belonging to each classes

5.2 Experimental Result

Fig.11 shows memorized patterns in the pattern layer corresponding to the classes shown in Fig.10 respectively. Fig.12 shows the feature pattern generated from the new input vector $\boldsymbol{a} = (0.5, 0.45)$.

Fig.13 shows a series of association in the pattern layer as well as in the symbol layer in the case where the nonlinearity in eq.(9) was middle ($d_2 = 6.0$) and only the symbol 1 had an external input (i.e. $\beta_1 = 1.0$ and $\beta_{i \neq 1} = 0$) at every step. The top figure in each box is the retrieved pattern in the pattern layer. The winner symbol is indicated by the corresponding class number. Multiple candidates for the inputted pattern were generated successively by the inference with nonlinear dynamics in the two-layered network. The retrieved patterns corresponding to the symbols of candidates were similar to the inputted pattern in Fig.12 and the

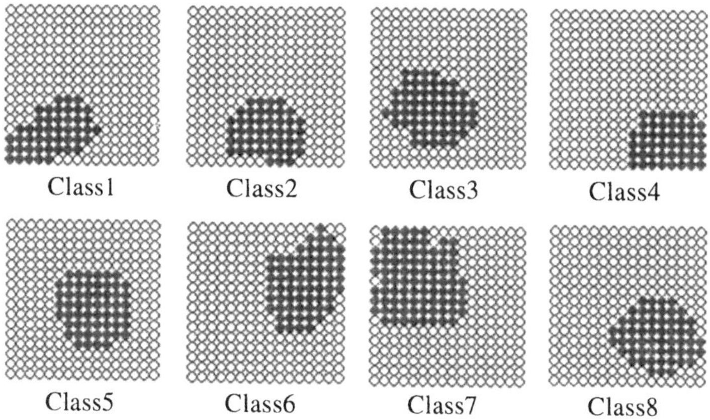

Fig.11 Memorized Patterns

memorized pattern belonging to the class 1.

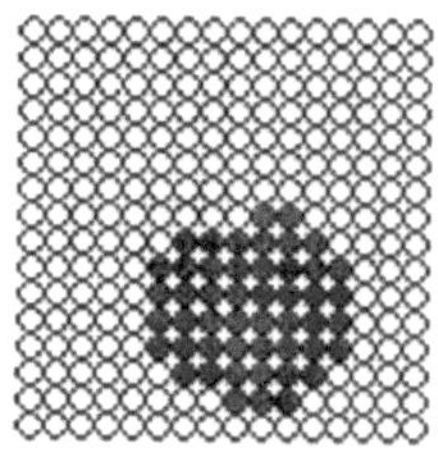

Fig.12 Input Pattern

Frequency of occurrence of each symbol for 10,000 steps were counted in order to show the effects of the external input into a symbol and the nonlinear dynamics in the symbolic inference. The histograms in Fig.14 show the emergent frequencies of symbols in the case where the external input into units in the symbol layer did not exist. Fig.14(a) is the case where the nonlinearity was small ($d_2 = 7.0$) and (b) is the case where it was large ($d_2 = 5.0$). In both cases, the emergent frequencies of the symbol 3, 5, and 8 were relatively higher because the memorized patterns corresponding to these symbols were similar to the inputted pattern. The larger the nonlinearity became, the symbols became easy to be retrieved even if the corresponding patterns were not so similar. The histograms in Fig.15 shows the emergent frequencies of symbols in the case where the external input into symbol 1 existed (i.e. $\beta_1 = 1.0$ and $\beta_{i \neq 1} = 0$). Fig.15(a) is the case where the nonlinearity was small ($d_2 = 8.0$), (b) and (c) are the cases where it was middle ($d_2 = 6.0$) and large ($d_2 = 5.0$), respectively. In all cases, the emergent frequency of symbol 1 was the highest. The frequencies were also relatively higher if the corresponding patterns were similar to pattern 1 and the inputted pattern. In this case, the larger the nonlinearity became, the symbols also became easy to be retrieved even if the corresponding patterns were not so similar. These results mean that the search for candidates is done in detail around the external input if the nonlinearity is small, and the search is done roughly in the wider space if the nonlinearity is large.

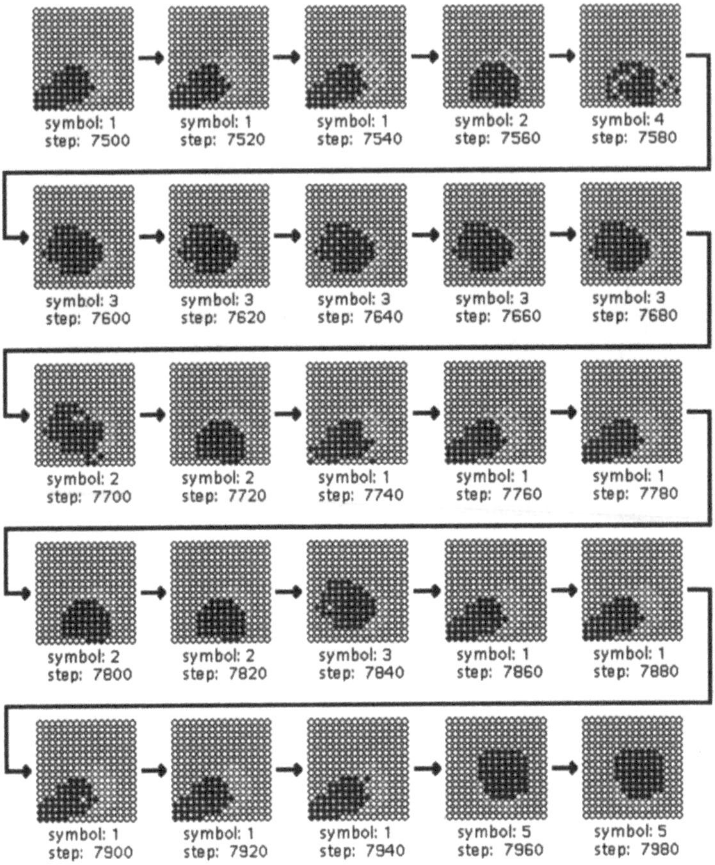

Fig.13 Behavior of Association in Two-layered Network

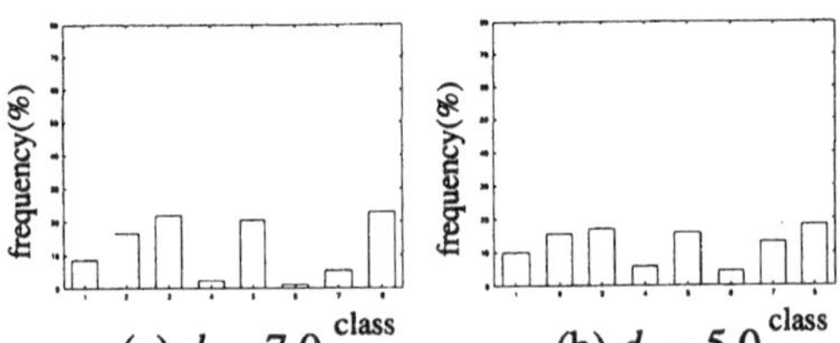

(a) $d_2 = 7.0$ (b) $d_2 = 5.0$

Fig.14 Emergent Frequency of Symbols without External Input into Symbols

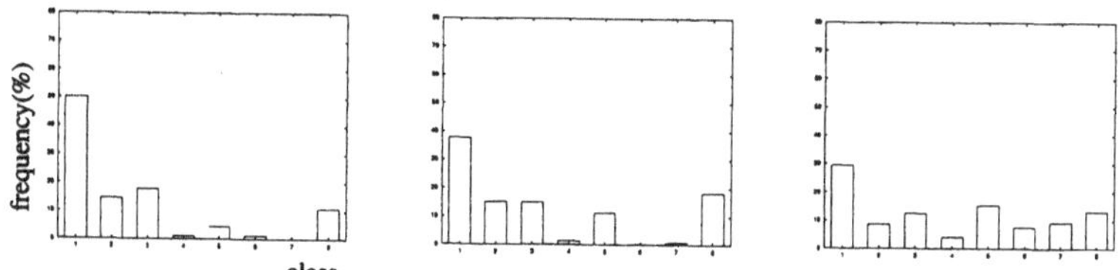

(a) $d_2 = 8.0$ (b) $d_2 = 6.0$ (c) $d_2 = 5.0$

Fig.15 Emergent Frequency of Symbols with External Input into Symbol 1

6 Conclusion

This paper studied a framework for solving ill-defined problems. A multi-module network which had been proposed for the realization of processing of patterns and symbols was regarded as a model to implement the framework. This paper proposed a new basic module. The model consisted of a feature pattern generator and a three-layered associative memory network. A primitive experiment was done to show the capability of the proposed network to generate various candidates of related patterns for the inputted unknown image.

The framework for solving the ill-defined problems needs a measure to control the search space. This control can be done by using an attention mechanism[8] which can automatically shift range and precision of search. Discovering a proper solution from combinations of candidates is realized by using a multi-module network[7, 8] whose modules are the proposed ones.

References

[1]T. Takagi, T. Yamaguchi, M. Sugeno, "Conceptual Fuzzy Sets", Proc. of Int'l Fuzzy Eng. Symposium'91, pp.261-272 (1991).

[2]R. Sun, "Integrating Rules and Connectionism for Robust Common Sense Reasoning", John Wiley Sons, Inc. (1994)

[3]N. Sakurai and T. Omori, "Image Recognition with Cooperation of Symbolic Inference and Neural Networks", Proc. of Int'l Conf. on Artificial Neural Network'92 (1992).

[4]T. Omori, N. Yamanashi, "PATON: A Model of Concept Representation and Operation in Brain", Proc. of Int'l Conf. on Neural Network'94, pp.2227-2232 (1994).

[5]T. Furuhashi, Y. Hattori, Y. Uchikawa, "Associative Memory for Patterns and Symbols and its chaotic Retrieval", Proc. of 11th Fuzzy System Symposium, pp.749-752 (1995).

[6]J. Tani, "Proposal of Chaotic Steepest Descent Method for Neural Networks and Analysis of Their Dynamics", The transactions of the IEICE vol.J74-A,

No.8, pp.1208-1215 (1991).
[7]Y. Hattori, T. Furuhashi, Y. Uchikawa, "Multi-module Network for Association of Vague Patterns and symbols", Proc. of IIZUKA '96, pp.612-615 (1996).
[8]Y. Hattori, T. Furuhashi, "An Inference Method Using Vague Patterns with Multiple Meanings and Attention Mechanism", Journal of Japan Society for Fuzzy Theory and Systems vol.9, No.4, pp.496-504 (1997).
[9]T. Kohonen, "Self-Organizing Maps", Springer Verlag (1995).
[10]S. Nara, P. Davis, "Chaos and Intelligent Information Processing", JustSystem (1994).

From Expert Words Directly to Numerical Simulations: Group-Theoretic Approach to Computing with Words in Information/Intelligent Systems

Vladik Kreinovich, Brian Penn, and Scott Starks
NASA Pan-American Center for
Earth and Environmental Studies
University of Texas at El Paso
El Paso, TX 79968, USA
emails vladik@cs.utep.edu, bpenn@geo.utep.edu,
sstarks@utep.edu

Abstract

In many real-life situations, e.g., when making an environmental decision, it is important to be able to predict long-term consequences of different decisions. Very often, these predictions must be done in the situation where the only available information consists of expert rules, which are formulated by words from natural language. One possible way to transform these expert words into numerical simulation (leading to prediction) is to use the fuzzy control methodology. However, there is a problem with using this methodology: it invokes replacing each word by a membership function, and this replacement drastically increases the required computer space (and thus, increases the computation time), i.e., it "de-granulates" the original compact description. It is, therefore, desirable to get from the original words directly to numerical simulations, thus avoiding this de-granulation.

In seeking this direct transformation, we will use the experience of modern physics, where symmetry groups are a tool that enables to compress complicated differential equations into compact form. In our previous papers, we have shown that the symmetry group approach can be used to find optimal membership functions, optimal t-norms and t-conorms, and optimal defuzzification procedures. In this paper, we show that the same approach can also be used to combine these steps and produce an (optimal) direct transformation from words to numerical results.

1 From Expert Words to Numerical Simulations: Necessity

For many complex systems, long-term predictions are necessary. In the 20 century, there have been many situations in which an environment-related decision, that seemed, at first, to be very reasonable and successful, turned out, in the long run, to have been a mistake. Such decisions include the use of pesticides (e.g., DDT), the design of some river dams, etc.

To avoid such mistakes, we must be able to predict long-term consequences of each decision.

Numerical simulations are needed. The ideal situation is when we have an *analytical* formula that would enable us to *exactly* predict the consequences of each decision. However, in reality, such formulas are extremely rare. In most cases, we have to rely on *numerical simulations* instead.

Often, expert words are the only information we have. In some cases, we know the differential or difference equations that describe the system. However, in many other cases, especially for environmental systems, we do not know the exact equations. Instead, we have the informal *expert knowledge*.

This knowledge is usually formulated in terms of rules that use only words from natural language, such as: "if x increases, then y slightly decreases".

We must transform (fuzzy) expert words into (crisp) numerical simulations. Thus, to make meaningful decisions, we must somehow transform the (fuzzy) expert words that describe the system's dynamics, into crisp equations that would enable us to run numerical (computer) simulations of the consequences of different possible decisions.

2 From Expert Words to Numerical Simulations: How It Is Done Now

2.1 For the desired translation, we can use the experience of fuzzy control

There is an area where the methodology of transforming expert rules (like the one described above) into numerical formulas has been already successfully developed: the area of *intelligent control* based on fuzzy expert rules.

The corresponding *fuzzy control* methodology was first developed by Mamdani in [21, 22] (for the latest overview, see, e.g., see, Klir and Yuan [11], Nguyen and Walker [32], and Nguyen and Sugeno [31]). So, we can use this methodology to transform expert words into numerical simulations.

2.2 Fuzzy control methodology: in brief

Why explain. This paper has three main objectives:

- to explain the fuzzy control methodology and how it can be used for simulations;
- to explain the problems with applying this methodology to simulations, and
- to propose a better methodology.

Thus, fuzzy control methodology is crucial for us, and so, we will briefly describe this methodology for those readers who are not 100% familiar with it (readers familiar with fuzzy control can skip this explanation). In this explanation, we will only describe the *simplest* (basic) version of fuzzy control.

Rules. In the fuzzy control methodology, we start with expert rules of the type

$$\text{If } x_1 \text{ is } A_{r1}, \ldots, \text{ and } x_n \text{ is } A_{rn}, \text{ then } u \text{ is } B_r.$$

Here:

- $x_1, \ldots, x_n$ are inputs, i.e., parameters whose values we measure in order to decide what control to apply (e.g., the position and velocity of a spaceship);
- u is the desired control (e.g., the force applied to the spaceship);
- $r = 1, \ldots, R$ is the rule number, and
- A_{ri} and B_r are words from natural language that are used in r-th rule, like "small", "medium", "large", "approximately 1", etc.

To transform these rules into a precise control strategy $u = u(x_1, \ldots, x_n)$, we do the following:

First stage. First, we describe the words A_{ri} and B_r in numerical terms. In fuzzy control methodology, we usually describe each such word by a *membership function* $\mu_{ri}(x_i)$ (or, correspondingly, $\mu_r(u)$), i.e., a function that describes, for each x_i, to what extent the experts believe this very value x_i to satisfy the corresponding property A_{ri} (e.g., to what extent the experts believe that x_i is small).

These degrees of belief run from complete disbelief (x_i does not satisfy the property A_{ri}) to complete belief, i.e., from "false" to "true". In the computer, "false" is usually represented by 0, and "true" by 1. Therefore, in most implementations, the membership functions take values from 0 to 1.

Second stage. Next, for each input $(x_1, \ldots, x_n)$, and for each possible value, we describe to what extent i-th rule holds, i.e., to what extent it is true that

x_1 satisfies the property A_{r1}, *and* x_2 satisfies the property A_{r2}, ..., *and* x_n satisfies the property A_{rn}, *and* u satisfies the property B_r.

We have $n + 1$ statements $A_{r1}(x_1), \ldots, A_{rn}(x_n), B_r(u)$, and for each of these statements, we know its "degree of belief" ("truth value"). We are interested in the degree of belief of their "and"-combination (disjunction) $A_{r1}(x_1) \& \ldots \& A_{rn}(x_n) \& B_r(u)$.

If all the combined statements were known to be exactly true or exactly false, then we would be able to use the known "and" operation for Boolean truth values. Thus, what we need is to generalize the traditional Boolean "and" operation, that is well defined for truth values from the set $\{0, 1\}$, to the entire interval $[0, 1]$.

Many such generalizations have been proposed; they are usually called "and"-operations, or *t-norms*. Two most widely used examples of t-norms are $a\&b = \min(a, b)$ and $a\&b = a \cdot b$.

In terms of a t-norm &, the degree of belief that r-th rule is applicable is equal to $b_r = \mu_{r1}(x_1) \& \ldots \& \mu_{rn}(x_n) \& \mu_r(u)$.

Third stage. To compute, for given $x_1, \ldots, x_n$, and u, the degree of belief that this u is a reasonable control for the given $x_1, \ldots, x_n$, we must estimate the degree of belief that one of the rules is applicable, i.e., that *either* the first rule is applicable, *or* the second rule is applicable, etc.

We know the degree of belief b_r that each rule is applicable, so, to combine them, we need an extension $\vee$ of the Boolean "or"-operation to the interval $[0, 1]$. This extended "or"-operation is usually called a *t-conorm*.

The most widely used t-conorms are $a \vee b = \max(a, b)$ and $a \vee b = a + b - a \cdot b$. So, for each u, we can estimate the desired degree of belief as $\mu(u) = b_1 \vee \ldots \vee b_R$.

Fourth stage. After the previous step, for every possible value u, we get the degree of belief $\mu(u)$ that u is a reasonable control. We need to use the membership function $\mu(u)$ to choose a single value $\bar{u}$ that corresponds to the given $x_1, \ldots, x_n$. The transformation from the (fuzzy) membership function $\mu(u)$ to a single (crisp) value $\bar{u}$ is called a *defuzzification*.

In fuzzy control, one of the most widely used defuzzification procedures is the following *centroid defuzzification*:

$$\bar{u} = \frac{\int u \cdot \mu(u)\, du}{\int \mu(u)\, du}.$$

Conclusion. As a result of this methodology, we get, for each set of values $x_1, \ldots, x_n$, a certain control; in mathematical terms, we describe control as a *function* of the inputs: $u = u(x_1, \ldots, x_n)$. This function is called a *control strategy*.

Successes of fuzzy control methodology. The resulting *fuzzy control* is used in various areas ranging from appliances (camcorders, washing machines, etc.) to automatically controlled subway trains in Japan to cement kilns to regulating temperature within the Space Shuttle.

2.3 How we can apply fuzzy control methodology to transform expert words into numerical simulation

Let $x_1, \ldots, x_n$ be parameters that describe the current state of a system that we are trying to simulate.

Expert formulate the rules that describe, for each of these variables (i.e., for each i from 1 to n), how the rate of change $u = \dot{x}_i$ of this variable depends on the values of this and other parameters. For example, a rule can be: "if x_1 is small, and x_2 is large, then u should be small".

The above-described methodology will then allow us to transform these rules into a numerical formula $u = f_i(x_1, \ldots, x_n)$. Since $u = \dot{x}_i$, we get a system of differential equations $\dot{x}_i = f_i(x_1, \ldots, x_n)$, whose simulation describes the long-term consequences of the given decision.

3 First Problem with the Existing Approach: The Problem of Choice

3.1 Formulation of the problem, and why it is important

The problem. On each step of the described methodology, we have lots of choices:

- we can choose different membership functions to represent different words;
- we can use different t-norms to represent "and";
- we can use different "or"-operations to combine degrees of belief in different rules; and
- finally, we can use different defuzzification procedures.

In principle, we can make all these choices based on *knowledge elicitation techniques*, i.e., based on the detailed interviews with experts. However:

- this detailed elicitation takes too much time, and,
- in reality, although we can force experts to make their statements more precise (this is exactly what knowledge elicitation is about), the resulting numbers will represent not so much expert knowledge, but the (rather arbitrary) result of our forcing. All the knowledge that expert can describe is already contained in the (fuzzy) rules, and although we can extract additional numbers from the experts, these numbers will not represent any additional knowledge.

Of course, we must use *some* knowledge elicitation, e.g., we must describe at least the range of what the experts mean by "small". However, with this *partial* knowledge elicitation, there are still lots of possible choices that are consistent with experts' knowledge.

It is very important to make the right choice. Different choices can lead to a drastically different quality of the resulting control or simulation, so making the right choice is very important.

3.2 How this choice is currently done in fuzzy control: general idea

For *control*, the choice can made based on different criteria; e.g., we should make choices for which:

- either the *smallest* number of rules is needed, on average, to approximate the given control with a given accuracy; or,
- the resulting control is *the best* according to the chosen criterion (i.e., is the most *stable*, or the most *smooth*, etc.).

Let us briefly describe the situations in which the best choice is known.

3.3 Best choice in the sense of best approximation

Choice of membership functions. The authors of [23, 24] compared the quality of the approximation achieved by using different shapes of membership functions. Their numerical experiments have shown that in almost all test situations, the best approximation if we use the "sinc" membership function $\sin(x)/x$.

The paper [12] contains a partial explanation of this result: namely, it is proven that in linear approximation, the function $\sin(x)/x$ is indeed the best (in some reasonable sense). It is desirable to extend this explanation to the general (non-linear) case.

Choice of "and" and "or" operations. In [41], is is shown that the choice of the product $a \cdot b$ as an "and" operation leads to a better approximation than the choice of the minimum $\min(a, b)$.

Choice of defuzzification. In [41], is is shown that the above choice of the centroid defuzzification leads to a better approximation than the *Mean of Maximum* defuzzification.

3.4 Best choice in the sense of best control

Choice of membership functions. The most *robust* membership functions (i.e., the least sensitive to the inaccuracy of the input data) are piecewise-linear ones [25, 28].

This result explains why the piecewise-linear membership functions are, at present, most frequently used.

Choice of "and" and "or" operations. (These results are (mainly) summarized in [18, 19, 25, 28, 39, 4].)

- If we are looking for the *most stable* control, then the best choice is to use $f_{\&}(a,b) = \min(a,b)$ and $f_{\vee}(a,b) = a + b - a \cdot b$ [18, 19, 39, 17].
- If we are looking for the *smoothest* control, then the best choice is to use $f_{\&}(a,b) = a \cdot b$ and $f_{\vee}(a,b) = \min(a,b)$ [18, 19, 39].
- If we are looking for the control that is *most robust* (i.e., least sensitive to the inaccuracy with which we measure the membership functions), then, depending on what exactly we are looking for, we can get two different results:
  - if we are looking for the control that is the most robust *in the the worst case*, then the best choice is to use $f_{\&}(a,b) = \min(a,b)$ and $f_{\vee}(a,b) = \max(a,b)$ [27, 29, 25, 28, 32];
  - if we are looking for the control that is the most robust *in the average*, then the best choice is to use $f_{\&}(a,b) = a \cdot b$ and $f_{\vee}(a,b) = a + b - a \cdot b$ [30, 25, 28, 32];
  - instead of minimizing the *average* error, we can try to minimize the corresponding *entropy* [36, 37, 38, 17, 14, 15]:
    * if we use the *average* entropy (in some reasonable sense), we get the same pair of optimal functions as for average error;
    * for an appropriately defined *worst-case* entropy the optimal operations are $f_{\&}(a,b) = \min(a,b)$ and $f_{\vee}(a,b) = a + b - a \cdot b$.
- Finally, if we are looking for the control that is the *fastest to compute*, then the best choice is to use $f_{\&}(a,b) = \min(a,b)$ and $f_{\vee}(a,b) = \max(a,b)$ [20].

Choice of defuzzification. In [18, 19, 17, 14], we show that the optimal defuzzification is given by the centroid formula.

3.5 A general description of known choices

These optimization results are in good accordance with the general *group-theoretic* approach that enables us to classify techniques that are optimal relative to arbitrary reasonable criteria [18, 19, 39, 4, 26].

Namely, we are looking for the *best* (*optimal*) choices. Normally, the word "best" is understood in the sense of some *numerical* optimality criterion. However, in our case of *fuzzy* choice, it is often difficult to formulate the exact *numerical* criterion. Instead, we assume that there is an *ordinal* criterion, i.e., that we can compare arbitrary two choices, but that we cannot assign numerical values to these choices. It turns out that in many cases, there are reasonable symmetries, and it is natural to assume that the (ordinal) optimality criterion is invariant with respect to these symmetries. Then, we are able to describe all choices that are optimal with respect to some invariant ordinal optimality criteria.

Right now, we are simply describing the main idea; in the next section, we will return to this idea, and describe it in more detail.

4 Second Problem with the Existing Approach: De-Granulation

What causes this problem. The second problem with the existing fuzzy-control approach is caused by its very nature, namely, by the fact that in this approach, the originally compact representation – in terms of words – is then replaced by a representation in terms of membership functions.

This replacement causes problems.

Too much computer space. The necessity to represent every term by a *function* drastically increases the computer space that is necessary to store the corresponding information.

Too much time. This increase in storage space, in turn, drastically increases the computation time.

The problem re-formulated. We can reformulate this problem as follows: the fuzzy control methodology "de-granulates" the original compact description, and this de-granulation causes an unnecessary increase in computation time.

5 Our Main Idea

Direct transformation is desirable. In view of the above problem, it is desirable to get from the original words *directly* to numerical simulations, thus avoiding this de-granulation.

Let us borrow from the experience of modern physics and use symmetries. In seeking this direct transformation, we will use the experience of modern physics, where symmetry groups are a tool that enables to compress complicated differential equations into compact form (see, e.g., [10, 34, 40]). For example:

- Maxwell's equations of electrodynamics consist of *four* different differential equations for two vector fields: electric field $\vec{E}$ and magnetic filed $\vec{B}$.

- However, if we take into consideration that these equations are invariant with respect to Lorentz transformations (that form the basis of Special Relativity) then we can compress these equations into *two*: $F_{ab}^{;b} = j_a$, and $F_{ab,c} + F_{bc,a} + F_{ca,b} = 0$.

Moreover, the very differential equations themselves can be uniquely deduced from the corresponding symmetry requirements [8, 9, 13, 16] (see also [5, 6, 7]).

It is possible to use symmetry. As we have mentioned, in our previous papers, we have shown that the symmetry group approach can be used to find optimal membership functions, optimal t-norms and t-conorms, and optimal defuzzification procedures.

It is therefore reasonable to expect that the same approach can also be used to *combine* these steps and produce an (optimal) *direct* transformation from words to numerical results.

6 From the General Idea to Precise Methodology: Motivations, Definitions, and Results

6.1 Motivations

We must choose a family of functions. For each situation, and for each i from 1 to n, we must find a function $f_i(x_1, \ldots, x_n)$ that describes the dependence of the rate change $\dot{x}_i$ on the current values $x_1, \ldots, x_n$: $\dot{x}_i = f_i(x_1, \ldots, x_n)$.

In different situations, we will need different functions. Thus, one of our objectives is to describe the functions f_i that correspond to different expert knowledge. In other words, we must select a *family of functions.*

Comment about notations. In the following text, we will denote families of functions by capital letters, such as F, F', G, etc.

Reasonable conditions on the desired family of functions, and what these conditions lead to. For a complex system, we usually have many independent processes that lead to the change in x_i. These processes can be present separately or at the same time.

> For example, the increase in ozone pollution can be caused by industrial pollution, or by frequent thunderstorms.

If the first factor leads to the rate $f(x_1, \ldots, x_n)$, and the second factor leads to the rate $f'(x_1, \ldots, x_n)$, then both factors together lead to the rate $f(x_1, \ldots, x_n) + f'(x_1, \ldots, x_n)$.

Thus, if two functions are reasonable (i.e., belong to the desired family F), their sum should also be reasonable (i.e., should also belong to the same family F). In mathematical terms, the family F should be *closed under addition.*

The second condition on the desired family F follows from the fact that the intensity of a process can change. Thus, if $f(x_1, \ldots, x_n)$ is a reasonable rate of change, then for every real number λ, the product $\lambda \cdot f(x_1, \ldots, x_n)$ is also a reasonable rate of change:

- the values $\lambda \in (0,1)$ describe the *decreased* intensity;
- the values $\lambda > 1$ describe the *increased* intensity; and
- the values $\lambda < 0$ describe the *reversed* process.

Thus, if $f \in F$, then $\lambda \cdot f \in F$.

Together with the first condition, we can conclude that if the functions $f_1, \ldots, f_m$ belong to F and $c_1, \ldots, c_m$ are real numbers, then the linear combination $f = c_1 \cdot f_1 + \ldots + c_m \cdot f_m$ must also belong to the family F. In mathematical terms, the family $\mathcal{F}$ must be a *linear space.*

It is known, from linear algebra, that linear spaces can be described as follows: every linear space has a subset $\{e_1, e_2, \ldots\}$ called a *basis*, such that every element e from the linear space can be represented as a linear combination of elements from this basis: $e = c_1 \cdot e_1 + c_2 \cdot e_2 + \ldots$ The smallest possible number of elements in this basis is called a *dimension* of the linear space.

In principle, some spaces are infinite-dimensional, but with an infinite basis, we can represent an arbitrary function of n variables; so, if we want our family to be meaningful, we must restrict ourselves only to *finite-dimensional* linear spaces, i.e., to linear spaces F formed by functions of the type $f(x_1, \ldots, x_n) = c_1 \cdot e_1(x, \ldots, x_n) + \ldots + e_m \cdot e_m(x_1, \ldots, x_m)$, where $e_j(x_1, \ldots, x_n)$ are fixed functions, and c_j are arbitrary real numbers.

For such families, choosing the family means choosing the corresponding m functions $e_1(x_1, \ldots, x_n), \ldots, e_m(x_1, \ldots, x_n)$.

We must choose the best family of functions. We want to select the *best* transformation from expert words to functions. This means, in particular, that we are interested in choosing the *best* family of functions.

What is a criterion for choosing a family of functions? What does it mean to choose a *best* family of functions? It means that we have some *criterion* that enables us to choose between the two families.

Traditionally, optimality criteria are *numerical*, i.e., to every family F, we assign some value $J(F)$ expressing its quality, and choose a family for which this value is maximal (i.e., when $J(F) \geq J(G)$ for every other alternative G). However, it is not necessary to restrict ourselves to such numeric criteria only.

For example, if we have several different families F that have the same prediction ability $P(F)$, we can choose between them the one that has the minimal computational complexity $C(F)$. In this case, the actual criterion that we use to compare two families is not numeric, but more complicated:

> *A family F_1 is better than the family F_2 if and only if*
>
> – *either* $P(F_1) > P(F_2)$,
>
> – *or* $P(F_1) = P(F_2)$ *and* $C(F_1) < C(F_2)$.

A criterion can be even more complicated.

The only thing that a criterion *must* do is to allow us, for every pair of families (F_1, F_2), to make one of the following conclusions:

- the first family is better with respect to this criterion (we'll denote it by $F_1 \succ F_2$, or $F_2 \prec F_1$);
- with respect to the given criterion, the second family is better ($F_2 \succ F_1$);
- with respect to this criterion, these families have the same quality (we'll denote it by $F_1 \sim F_2$);
- this criterion does not allow us to compare the two families.

Of course, it is necessary to demand that these choices be consistent.

> For example, if $F_1 \succ F_2$ and $F_2 \succ F_3$ then $F_1 \succ F_3$.

The criterion must be final, i.e., it must pick the unique family as the best one. A natural demand is that this criterion must choose a *unique* optimal family (i.e., a family that is better with respect to this criterion than any other family).

The reason for this demand is very simple:

- If a criterion *does not choose* any family at all, then it is of no use.
- If *several* different families are the best according to this criterion, then we still have a problem to choose among those best. Therefore we need some additional criterion for that choice, like in the above example:

  > If several families $F_1, F_2, \ldots$ turn out to have the same prediction ability ($P(F_1) = P(F_2) = \ldots$), we can choose among them a family with minimal computational complexity ($C(F_i) \to \min$).

  So what we actually do in this case is abandon that criterion for which there were several "best" families, and consider a new "composite" criterion instead: F_1 is better than F_2 according to this new criterion if:

  – either it was better according to the old criterion,

- or they had the same quality according to the old criterion and F_1 is better than F_2 according to the additional criterion.

In other words, if a criterion does not allow us to choose a unique best family, it means that this criterion is not final, we'll have to modify it until we come to a final criterion that will have that property.

The criterion must not change if we change the measuring units for one of the variables x_i. The exact mathematical form of a function $f_i(x_1, \ldots, x_n)$ depends on the exact choice of units for measuring $x_1, \ldots, x_n$. If, for some j, we replace a unit for measuring x_j by a new unit that is λ_j times larger, then the same physical value that was previously described by a numerical value x_j will now be described, in the new units, by a new numerical value $\tilde{x}_j = x_j/\lambda_j$. For example, if we replace centimeters by inches, with $\lambda_j = 2.54$, then $x_j = 5.08$ cm becomes $\tilde{x}_j = x_j/\lambda_j = 2$ in.

How will the dynamical equations $\dot{x}_i = f_i(x_1, \ldots, x_{j-1}, x_j, x_{j+1}, \ldots, x_n)$ change if we use the new unit? In terms of $\tilde{x}_j$, we have $x_j = \lambda_j \cdot \tilde{x}_j$, and thus, we have $\dot{x}_i = f_i(x_1, \ldots, x_{j-1}, \lambda_j \cdot x_j, x_{j+1}, \ldots, x_n)$. In other words, if we change the measuring unit for x_j, the same dynamics that was originally represented by a function $f_i(x_1, \ldots, x_{j-1}, x_j, x_{j+1}, \ldots, x_n)$, will be described, in the new units, by a function
$\tilde{f}(x_1, \ldots, x_n) = f_i(x_1, \ldots, x_{j-1}, \lambda_j \cdot x_j, x_{j+1}, \ldots, x_n)$.

If we make a similar replacement of the measuring units for several quantities x_j, so that x_1 is replaced by a unit that is λ_1 times larger, x_2 by a unit that is λ_2 times larger, etc., then each function $f_i(x_1, \ldots, x_n)$ will be replaced by a new function $\tilde{f}_i(x_1, \ldots, x_n) = \lambda_i^{-1} \cdot f_i(\lambda_1 \cdot x_1, \ldots, \lambda_n \cdot x_n)$.

It is reasonable to assume that the relative quality of different families should not change if we simply change the units, i.e., if the family F is better than a family G, then the transformed family $\tilde{F}$ should also be better than the family $\tilde{G}$.

We are now ready for the formal definitions.

6.2 Definitions

Definition 1. *Let two positive integers $n, m \geq 1$ be fixed, and let $i \leq n$.*

- *By a family F, we mean a collection of m differentiable function $e_1(x_1, \ldots, x_n), \ldots, e_m(x_1, \ldots, x_n)$.*
- *We say that a function $e(x_1, \ldots, x_n)$ belongs to the family F (and that F contains the function $e(x_1, \ldots, x_n)$) if this function can be represented as a linear combination of the functions e_j, i.e., if there exist m real numbers $c_1, \ldots, c_m$ for which, for all x_k, $e(x_1, \ldots, x_n) = c_1 \cdot e_1(x_1, \ldots, x_n) + \ldots + c_m \cdot e_m(x_1, \ldots, x_m)$.*
- *Two families F and G are considered equal if they contain the same functions.*

Denotation. *Let's denote the set of all possible families by* Φ.

Comment. In order to formalize the notion of an optimality criterion, we must describe that for some pairs of families, F is better than G, and for some other pairs, F is not better than G. To describe this "relation" it better, we must, thus, describe the *set* of all possible pairs (F, G) for which F is better than G. In mathematics, if a set Φ is given:

- the set of all pairs (F_1, F_2) of elements $F_1 \in \Phi$, $F_2 \in \Phi$, is usually denoted by $\Phi \times \Phi$.
- An arbitrary subset R of a set of pairs $\Phi \times \Phi$ is called a *relation* on the set Φ. If $(F_1, F_2) \in R$, it is said that F_1 and F_2 are in relation R; this fact is denoted by $F_1 R F_2$.

Definition 2. *A pair of relations* $(\prec, \sim)$ *on a set* Φ *is called consistent if it satisfies the following conditions, for every* $F, G, H \in \Phi$:

(1) *if* $F \prec G$ *and* $G \prec H$ *then* $F \prec H$;

(2) $F \sim F$;

(3) *if* $F \sim G$ *then* $G \sim F$;

(4) *if* $F \sim G$ *and* $G \sim H$ *then* $F \sim H$;

(5) *if* $F \prec G$ *and* $G \sim H$ *then* $F \prec H$;

(6) *if* $F \sim G$ *and* $G < H$ *then* $F < H$;

(7) *if* $F \prec G$ *then it is not true that* $G \prec F$, *and it is not true that* $F \sim G$.

Comment. The intended meaning of these relations is as follows:

- $F \prec G$ means that with respect to a given criterion, G is better than F;
- $F \sim G$ means that with respect to a given criterion, F and G are of the same quality.

Under this interpretation, conditions (1)–(7) have simple intuitive meaning:

(1) if G is better than F, and H is better than G, then H is better than F;

(2) every alternative F is of the same quality as itself;

(3) if G is of the same quality as F, then F is of the same quality as G;

(4) if F is of the same quality as G, and G is of the same quality as H, then F is of the same quality as H;

(5) if G is better than F, and H is of the same quality as G, then H is also better than F;

(6) if H is better than G, and F is of the same quality as G, then H is better than F;

(7) if G is better than F, then F cannot be better than G and F cannot be of the same quality as G.

Definition 3. *Assume a set Φ is given. Its elements will be called alternatives.*

- *By an optimality criterion, we mean a consistent pair $(\prec, \sim)$ of relations on the set Φ of all alternatives.*
  - *If $F \succ G$ we say that F is better than G;*
  - *if $F \sim G$ we say that the alternatives F and G are equivalent with respect to this criterion.*
- *We say that an alternative F is optimal (or best) with respect to a criterion $(\prec, \sim)$ if for every other alternative G either $F \succ G$ or $F \sim G$.*
- *We say that a criterion is final if there exists an optimal alternative, and this optimal alternative is unique.*

Comment. In this paper, we will consider optimality criteria on the set Φ of all families.

Definition 4. *Let $\vec{\lambda} = (\lambda_1, \ldots, \lambda_n)$ be a tuple of positive real numbers.*

- *By a $\vec{\lambda}$-rescaling of a function $f(x_1, \ldots, x_n)$ we mean a function $\tilde{f}(x_1, \ldots, x_n) = \lambda_i^{-1} \cdot f_i(\lambda_1 \cdot x_1, \ldots, \lambda_n \cdot x_n)$.*
- *By a $\vec{\lambda}$-rescaling of a family of functions F we mean the family consisting of $\vec{\lambda}$-rescalings of all functions from F.*

Denotation. *$\vec{\lambda}$-rescaling of a family F will be denoted by $R_{\vec{\lambda}}(F)$.*

Definition 5. *We say that an optimality criterion on Φ is unit-invariant if for every two families F and G and for every vector $\vec{\lambda}$, the following two conditions are true:*

i) if F is better than G in the sense of this criterion (i.e., $F \succ G$), then $R_{\vec{\lambda}}(F) \succ R_{\vec{\lambda}}(G)$;

ii) if F is equivalent to G in the sense of this criterion (i.e., $F \sim G$), then $R_{\vec{\lambda}}(F) \sim R_{\vec{\lambda}}(G)$.

Comment. As we have already remarked, the demands that the optimality criterion is final and unit-invariant are quite reasonable. At first glance they may seem rather trivial and therefore weak, because these demands do not specify the exact optimality criterion. However, these demands are strong enough, as the following theorem shows:

6.3 Main result

Theorem. *If a family F is optimal in the sense of some optimality criterion that is final and unit-invariant, then every function $f_i(x_1, \ldots, x_n)$ from this family F is a linear combination of the functions of the type*

$$x_1^{\alpha_1} \cdot \ldots \cdot x_n^{\alpha_n} \cdot \ln^{k_1}(x_1) \cdot \ldots \cdot \ln^{k_n}(x_n),$$

where α_j are complex numbers, and k_j are non-negative integers.

Comment. The above expression can be re-formulated without complex numbers; in this case, the basic functions are of the type

$$x_1^{\alpha_1} \cdot \sin(\beta_1 \cdot \ln(x_1) + \varphi_1) \cdot \ldots \cdot x_n^{\alpha_n} \cdot \sin(\beta_n \cdot \ln(x_n) + \varphi_n) \cdot \ln^{k_1}(x_1) \cdot \ldots \cdot \ln^{k_n}(x_n),$$

where α_j, β_j, and φ_j are real numbers, and k_j are non-negative integers.

In particular, for $n = 1$, we get the following result:

Corollary 1. *For $n = 1$, if an m-dimensional family F is optimal in the sense of some optimality criterion that is final and unit-invariant, then every function $f(x)$ from the family F is equal to a linear combination of the functions of the type $\ln^p(x) \cdot x^\alpha \cdot \sin(\beta \cdot \ln(x) + \varphi)$, where p is a non-negative integer, α, β and φ are real numbers.*

Corollary 2. *Let a 2-dimensional family F be optimal in the sense of some optimality criterion that is final and unit-invariant. Then, every function $f(x)$ from the family F has one of the following forms:*

1. $f(x) = C_1 \cdot x^{\alpha_1} + C_2 \cdot x^{\alpha_2}$;
2. $f(x) = C_1 \cdot x^\alpha + C_2 \cdot x^\alpha \cdot \ln(x)$;
3. $f(x) = C \cdot x^\alpha \cdot \sin(\beta \cdot \ln(x) + \varphi)$.

Comment. The optimal families that we have just described are exactly the ones that were described, on a semi-heuristic basis, by Ludwig von Bertalanffy in his General System Theory (see, e.g., his books [2, 3]).

Bertalanffy mainly considered equations of the *first* type. These so-called *Bertalanffy equations* turned out to be very adequate for describing growth in biology (namely, the growth of individual organisms and of their organs), so adequate that they are routinely used by fisheries in England and Japan and by by the Food and Agriculture Organization (FAO) of the United Nations. The following particular cases of the Bertalanffy equation describe the simplest growth processes:

- For $\alpha_1 = 1$, $C_1 > 0$, and $C_1 = 0$, we get the equation $\dot{x} = C_1 \cdot x$ that describe an *exponential* growth $x(t) = C \cdot \exp(C_1 \cdot t)$.

- For $\alpha_1 = 1$, $\alpha_2 = 2$, $C_1 > 0$, and $C_2 < 0$, we get the equation $\dot{x} = C_1 \cdot x - |C_2| \cdot x^2$ that describes a so-called *logistic curve* that starts with an exponential growth but then flatters out. For this particular growth function, the growth equation also admits an explicit solution

$$L(t) = \frac{1}{K + A \cdot b^t}.$$

Equations of the *second* type were originally proposed by Gompertz (for $\alpha = 1$). These equations describe, e.g., such growth processes as *population dynamics* (see, e.g., [33]),

Thus, our general approach provides a precise mathematical justification for the (highly successful) semi-heuristic formulas of von Bertalanffy's general system theory.

6.4 How to use this result: examples

Example 1. If an increase in x_1 leads to a slower increase rate of x_2, this means that we have a term in $\dot{x}_2 = f_2(x_1, \ldots, x_n)$ that is decreasing with x_1. Since this terms should be monotonic, it should not contain sines, and therefore, it should be of the form $C \cdot x_2^{\alpha} \cdot \ln^k(x_2)$. The exact values of the coefficients must be determined in one of the following two ways:

- either by showing the expert the results of different values and asking this expert to choose the most appropriate value;
- or by tuning the resulting simulation to the actual recorded behavior of the system that we are simulating.

Example 2. Similarly, if we know that, e.g., x_3 starts decreasing if both x_1 and x_2 are present, then we should add, to f_3, terms of the type $-x_1^{\alpha_1} \cdot x_2^{\alpha_2}$, maybe with logarithmic terms as well.

What did we gain? At first glance, there still seems to be a lot of freedom of choice, and this is inevitable, because we are developing a general formalism that should cover many different systems. However, we did gain a lot:

- initially, we had the choice of choosing several arbitrary *functions* (membership function, etc.);
- now, we only need to choose a few *parameters*.

We have less choice, thus, more granularity, and less computation time.

7 Case Study: Sedimental System

This idea was used in geology, for simulating a *sedimentary system* (for details, see [35]). We tried a simplified system in which the state is characterized by the following three parameters:

- $x_1 = h$ is the hinterland elevation,
- $x_2 = s$ is the sealevel elevation, and
- $x_3 = r$ is the sediment transport rate.

Several reasonable rules can be formulated about the evolution of these three variables; e.g.:

- on one hand, sediment transport erodes the hinterland and eventually reduces its elevation;
- on the other hand, it causes isostatic uplift and thus, after a longer period of time, increases the hinterland elevation.

These two rules lead to the terms $-k_1 \cdot r(t-\Delta_1)^{\alpha_1} + k_2 \cdot r(t-\Delta_2)^{\alpha_2}$ in $\dot{x}_1(t)$, where Δ_i are the appropriate time delays.

After transforming all other rules into the corresponding terms, we got a system of differential equations, for which the numerical simulation is in very good accordance with the geological data.

Acknowledgments. This work was supported in part by NASA under cooperative agreement NCCW-0089, by NSF grants No. DUE-9750858 and EEC-9322370, and by the Future Aerospace Science and Technology Program (FAST) Center for Structural Integrity of Aerospace Systems, effort sponsored by the Air Force Office of Scientific Research, Air Force Materiel Command, USAF, under grant number F49620-95-1-0518.

References

[1] R. E. Bellman. *Introduction to Matrix Analysis*, McGraw-Hill, New York, 1970.

[2] L. v. Bertalanffy, *Perspectives on general system theory*, G. Braziller, N.Y., 1975.

[3] L. v. Bertalanffy, *General system theory* (G. Braziller, N.Y., 1984.

[4] B. Bouchon-Meunier, V. Kreinovich, A. Lokshin, and H. T. Nguyen, "On the formulation of optimization under elastic constraints (with control in mind)", *Fuzzy Sets and Systems,* 1996, Vol. 81, No. 1, pp. 5–29.

[5] A. Finkelstein, O. Kosheleva, and V. Kreinovich, "Astrogeometry, error estimation, and other applications of set-valued analysis", *ACM SIGNUM Newsletter*, 1996, Vol. 31, No. 4, pp. 3–25.

[6] A. Finkelstein, O. Kosheleva, and V. Kreinovich, "Astrogeometry: towards mathematical foundations", *International Journal of Theoretical Physics*, 1997, Vol. 36, No. 4, pp. 1009–1020.

[7] A. Finkelstein, O. Kosheleva, and V. Kreinovich, Andrei Finkelstein, Olga Kosheleva, and Vladik Kreinovich, "Astrogeometry: geometry explains shapes of celestial bodies", *Geombinatorics*, 1997, Vol. VI, No. 4, pp. 125–139.

[8] A. M. Finkelstein and V. Kreinovich, "Derivation of Einstein's, Brans-Dicke and other equations from group considerations," *On Relativity Theory. Proceedings of the Sir Arthur Eddington Centenary Symposium, Nagpur India 1984*, Vol. 2, Y. Choque-Bruhat and T. M. Karade (eds), World Scientific, Singapore, 1985, pp. 138–146.

[9] A. M. Finkelstein, V. Kreinovich, and R. R. Zapatrin, "Fundamental physical equations uniquely determined by their symmetry groups," *Lecture Notes in Mathematics*, Springer-Verlag, Berlin-Heidelberg-N.Y., Vol. 1214, 1986, pp. 159–170.

[10] *Group theory in physics: proceedings of the international symposium held in honor of Prof. Marcos Moshinsky, Cocoyoc, Morelos, Mexico, 1991*, American Institute of Physics, N.Y., 1992.

[11] G. Klir and B. Yuan, *Fuzzy sets and fuzzy logic: theory and applications*, Prentice Hall, Upper Saddle River, NJ, 1995.

[12] O. Kosheleva, "Why Sinc? Signal Processing Helps Fuzzy Control", *SC-COSMIC, South Central Computational Sciences in Minority Institutions Consortium, Second Student Conference in Computational Sciences*, October 25–27, 1996, El Paso, TX, Abstracts, pp. 19–21.

[13] V. Kreinovich. "Derivation of the Schroedinger equations from scale invariance," *Theoretical and Mathematical Physics*, 1976, Vol. 8, No. 3, pp. 282–285.

[14] V. Kreinovich, "Random sets unify, explain, and aid known uncertainty methods in expert systems", in J. Goutsias, R. P. S. Mahler, and H. T. Nguyen (eds.), *Random Sets: Theory and Applications*, Springer-Verlag, N.Y., 1997, pp. 321–345.

[15] V. Kreinovich, "Maximum entropy and interval computations", *Reliable Computing*, 1996, Vol. 2, No. 1, pp. 63–79.

[16] V. Kreinovich and L. Longpré, "Unreasonable effectiveness of symmetry in physics", *International Journal of Theoretical Physics*, 1996, Vol. 35, No. 7, pp. 1549–1555.

[17] V. Kreinovich, H. T. Nguyen, and E. A. Walker, "Maximum entropy (MaxEnt) method in expert systems and intelligent control: new possibilities and limitations", In: K. Hanson and R. Silver, Eds., *Maximum Entropy and Bayesian Methods, Santa Fe, New Mexico, 1995*, Kluwer Academic Publishers, Dordrecht, Boston, 1996, pp. 93–100.

[18] V. Kreinovich, C. Quintana, and R. Lea, "What procedure to choose while designing a fuzzy control? Towards mathematical foundations of fuzzy control", *Working Notes of the 1st International Workshop on Industrial Applications of Fuzzy Control and Intelligent Systems*, College Station, TX, 1991, pp. 123–130.

[19] V. Kreinovich, C. Quintana, R. Lea, O. Fuentes, A. Lokshin, S. Kumar, I. Boricheva, and L. Reznik, "What non-linearity to choose? Mathematical foundations of fuzzy control", *Proceedings of the 1992 International Conference on Fuzzy Systems and Intelligent Control*, Louisville, KY, pp. 349–412.

[20] V. Kreinovich and D. Tolbert, "Minimizing computational complexity as a criterion for choosing fuzzy rules and neural activation functions in intelligent control". In: M. Jamshidi, C. Nguyen, R. Lumia, and J. Yuh (Editors), *Intelligent Automation and Soft Computing. Trends in Research, Development, and Applications. Proceedings of the First World Automation Congress (WAC'94), August 14–17, 1994, Maui, Hawaii*, TSI Press, Albuquerque, NM, Vol. 1, pp. 545–550.

[21] E. H. Mamdani, "Application of fuzzy algorithms for control of simple dynamic plant", *Proceedings of the IEE*, 1974, Vol. 121, No. 12, pp. 1585–1588.

[22] E. H. Mamdani, "Application of fuzzy logic to approximate reasoning using linguistic systems", *IEEE Transactions on Computing*, 1977, Vol. 26, pp. 1182–1191.

[23] S. Mitaim and B. Kosko, "What is the best shape for a fuzzy set in function approximation?", *Proceedings of the Fifth IEEE International Conference on Fuzzy Systems FUZZ-IEEE'96*, New Orleans, September 8–11, 1996, Vol. 2, pp. 1237–1243.

[24] S. Mitaim and B. Kosko, "Fuzzy function approximation and the shape of fuzzy sets", *Proceedings of the World Congress on Neural Networks WCNN'96*, September 1996.

[25] H. T. Nguyen and V. Kreinovich, "Towards theoretical foundations of soft computing applications", *International Journal on Uncertainty, Fuzziness, and Knowledge-Based Systems*, 1995, Vol. 3, No. 3, pp. 341–373.

[26] H. T. Nguyen and V. Kreinovich, *Applications of continuous mathematics to computer science*, Kluwer, Dordrecht, 1997.

[27] H. T. Nguyen, V. Kreinovich, B. Lea, D. Tolbert, "How to control if even experts are not sure: robust fuzzy control", *Proceedings of the Second International Workshop on Industrial Applications of Fuzzy Control and Intelligent Systems*, College Station, December 2–4, 1992, pp. 153–162.

[28] H. T. Nguyen, V. Kreinovich, B. Lea, and D. Tolbert, "Interpolation that leads to the narrowest intervals, and its application to expert systems and intelligent control", *Reliable Computing*, 1995, Vol. 3, No. 1, pp. 299–316.

[29] H. T. Nguyen, V. Kreinovich, and D. Tolbert, "On robustness of fuzzy logics". *Proceedings of IEEE-FUZZ International Conference*, San Francisco, CA, March 1993, Vol. 1, pp. 543–547.

[30] H. T. Nguyen, V. Kreinovich, and D. Tolbert, "A measure of average sensitivity for fuzzy logics", *International Journal on Uncertainty, Fuzziness, and Knowledge-Based Systems*, 1994, Vol. 2, No. 4, pp. 361–375.

[31] H. T. Nguyen and M. Sugeno (eds.), *Handbooks of Fuzzy Systems. Vol. VI: Fuzzy Modeling and Control*, Kluwer Academic, 1997 (to appear).

[32] H. T. Nguyen and E. A. Walker, *A first course in fuzzy logic*, CRC Press, Boca Raton, FL, 1997.

[33] A. G. Nobile, L. M. Riccardi, L. Sacerdote, "On a class of difference equations modeling growth processes", In: L. M. Riccardi and A. C. Scott, *Biomathematics in 1980*, North-Holland, Amsterdam, 1982, pp. 217–244.

[34] P. J. Olver, *Equivalence, invariants, and symmetry*, Cambridge University Press, Cambridge, N.Y., 1995.

[35] B. S. Penn and J. W. Harbaugh, *DYNASED: a model for tightly coupled sedimentary systems*, NASA PACES Center, El Paso, TX, Technical Report, 1996.

[36] A. Ramer and V. Kreinovich, "Maximum entropy approach to fuzzy control", *Proceedings of the Second International Workshop on Industrial Applications of Fuzzy Control and Intelligent Systems*, College Station, December 2–4, 1992, pp. 113–117.

[37] A. Ramer and V. Kreinovich, "Information complexity and fuzzy control", Chapter 4 in: A. Kandel and G. Langholtz (Eds.), *Fuzzy Control Systems*, CRC Press, Boca Raton, FL, 1994, pp. 75–97.

[38] A. Ramer and V. Kreinovich, "Maximum entropy approach to fuzzy control", *Information Sciences*, 1994, Vol. 81, No. 3–4, pp. 235–260.

[39] M. H. Smith and V. Kreinovich, "Optimal strategy of switching reasoning methods in fuzzy control", Chapter 6 in H. T. Nguyen, M. Sugeno, R. Tong, and R. Yager (eds.), *Theoretical aspects of fuzzy control*, J. Wiley, N.Y., 1995, pp. 117–146.

[40] *Symmetries in physics: proceedings of the international symposium held in honor of Prof. Marcos Moshinsky, Cocoyoc, Morelos, Mexico, 1991*, Springer-Verlag, Berlin, N.Y., 1992.

[41] X.-J. Zeng and M. G. Singh, "Approximation accuracy analysis of fuzzy systems as function approximators," *IEEE Trans. on Fuzzy Systems*, 1996, Vol. 4, pp. 44–63.

8 Appendix: Proof

This proof is based on the following auxiliary result of independent interest:

Proposition. *If an optimality criterion is final and unit-invariant, then the optimal family* F_{opt} *is also unit-invariant, i.e.,* $R_{\vec{\lambda}}(F_{opt}) = F_{opt}$ *for every vector* $\vec{\lambda}$.

Proof of the Proposition. Since the optimality criterion is final, there exists a unique family F_{opt} that is optimal with respect to this criterion, i.e., for every other F:

- either $F_{opt} \succ F$
- or $F_{opt} \sim F$.

To prove that $F_{opt} = R_{\vec{\lambda}}(F_{opt})$, we will first show that the re-scaled family $R_{\vec{\lambda}}(F_{opt})$ is also optimal, i.e., that for every family F:

- either $R_{\vec{\lambda}}(F_{opt}) \succ F$
- or $R_{\vec{\lambda}}(F_{opt}) \sim F$.

If we prove this optimality, then the desired equality will follow from the fact that our optimality criterion is final and therefore, there is only one optimal family (so, since the families F_{opt} and $R_{\vec{\lambda}}(F_{opt})$ are both optimal, they must be the same family).

Let us show that $R_{\vec{\lambda}}(F_{opt})$ is indeed optimal. How can we, e.g., prove that $R_{\vec{\lambda}}(F_{opt}) \succ F$? Since the optimality criterion is unit-invariant, the desired relation is equivalent to $F_{opt} \succ R_{\vec{\lambda}^{-1}}(F)$, where by $\vec{\lambda}^{-1}$, we denoted a tuple $(\lambda_1^{-1}, \ldots, \lambda_n^{-1})$. Similarly, the relation $R_{\vec{\lambda}}(F_{opt}) \sim F$ is equivalent to $F_{opt} \sim R_{\vec{\lambda}^{-1}}(F)$.

These two equivalences allow us to complete the proof of the proposition. Indeed, since F_{opt} is optimal, we have one of the two possibilities:

- either $F_{opt} \succ R_{\vec{\lambda}^{-1}}(F)$,
- or $F_{opt} \sim R_{\vec{\lambda}^{-1}}(F)$.

In the first case, we have $R_{\vec{\lambda}}(F_{opt}) \succ F$; in the second case, we have $R_{\vec{\lambda}}(F_{opt}) \sim F$. Thus, whatever family F we take, we always have either $R_{\vec{\lambda}}(F_{opt}) \succ F$, or $R_{\vec{\lambda}}(F_{opt}) \sim F$. Hence, $R_{\vec{\lambda}}(F_{opt})$ is indeed optimal and thence, $R_{\vec{\lambda}}(F_{opt}) = F_{opt}$. The proposition is proven.

Let us now prove the theorem. Since the criterion is final, there exists an optimal family $F_{opt} = \{c_1 \cdot e_1(x_1, \ldots, x_n) + \ldots + c_m \cdot e_m(x_1, \ldots, x_n)\}$. Eaxh of the corresponding functions $e_j(x_1, \ldots, x_n)$ belongs to the family F_{opt} (for $c_j = 1$ and $c_k = 0$ for $k \neq j$).

Due to the Proposition, the optimal family is unit-invariant, i.e., $F_{opt} = R_{\vec{\lambda}}(F_{opt})$. In particular, this means that for very j, and for every $\vec{\lambda}$, we have $R_{\vec{\lambda}}(e_j) \in F_{opt}$, i.e.,

$$e_j(\lambda_1 \cdot x_1, \ldots, \lambda_n \cdot x_n) =$$
$$c_{j1}(\vec{\lambda}) \cdot e_1(x_1, \ldots, x_n) + \ldots + c_{jm}(\vec{\lambda}) \cdot e_m(x_1, \ldots, x_n). \tag{1}$$

for some values c_{jk}. If we take m different values of $(x_1, \ldots, x_n)$, then the corresponding equations (1) form a system of m linear equations to determine m coefficients $c_{j1}(\vec{\lambda}), \ldots, c_{jm}(\vec{\lambda})$. The well-known Cramer's rule describes the solution of a system of linear equation as a ratio of two determinants and thus, as a differentiable function of the coefficients and right-hand sides of these equations. Since $e_j(x_1, \ldots, x_n)$ are differentiable functions, we can thus conclude that the functions $c_j(\vec{\lambda})$ are differentiable too.

Since both sides of the equation (1) is differentiable, let us pick an arbitrary $l = 1, \ldots, n$, differentiate both sides with respect to λ_l, and then substitute $\lambda_l = \ldots = \lambda_n = 1$. As a result, we get the following system of differential equations:

$$x_l \cdot \frac{\partial e_j}{\partial x_l}(x_1, \ldots, x_n) = \sum_{k=1}^{m} c_{jkl} \cdot e_k(x_1, \ldots, x_n), \tag{2}$$

where we denoted

$$c_{jkl} = \frac{\partial c_{jk}(\lambda_1, \ldots, \lambda_n)}{\partial \lambda_l}_{|\lambda_1 = \ldots = \lambda_n = 1}$$

This equation can be further simplified if we use new variables $X_j = \ln(x_j)$, for which $dx_l/x_l = dX_l$. In terms of these new variables, $x_j = \exp(X_j)$, and the values $e_j(x_1, \ldots, x_n)$ take the form $e_j(x_1, \ldots, x_n) = E_j(X_1, \ldots, X_n)$, where we denoted $E_j(X_1, \ldots, X_n) = e_j(\exp(X_1), \ldots, \exp(X_n))$. In terms of the new function $E_j(X_1, \ldots, X_n)$, the equation (2) takes the following form:

$$\frac{\partial E_j}{\partial X_l}(X_1, \ldots, X_n) = \sum_{k=1}^{m} c_{jkl} \cdot E_k(X_1, \ldots, X_n). \tag{3}$$

If we fix all the variables but one (e.g., except for X_1), we conclude that the functions $E_1(X_1), \ldots, E_m(X_1)$ satisfy a system of linear differential equations with constant coefficients. A general solution of such a system is well known (see, e.g., [1]): it has a form

$$E_j(X_1) = \sum C_{jp} \cdot \exp(\alpha_p \cdot X_1) \cdot X_1^{k_p}, \quad (4)$$

where α_p are complex numbers (eigenvalues of the coefficient matrix), C_p are complex numbers, and k_p are non-negative integers.

If we take into consideration the dependence on X_2, then all the coefficients of the formula (4) should depend on X_2, i.e.,

$$E_j(X_1, X_2) = \sum C_{jp}(X_2) \cdot \exp(\alpha_p(X_2) \cdot X_1) \cdot X_1^{k_p(X_2)}. \quad (5)$$

Since the dependence on X_2 is smooth (hence, continuous), and k_p is an integer, we conclude that k_p is a constant: $k_p(X_2) = k_p$. The dependence on all other coefficients on X_2 can be determined from the fact that, similarly to (4), for a fixed X_1, we must have a similar expression in terms of X_2:

$$E_j(X_2) = \sum C'_{jp} \cdot \exp(\alpha'_p \cdot X_2) \cdot X_2^{k'_p}. \quad (6)$$

Thus, the only possible dependence of C_{jp} on X_2 is a dependence of the type $\exp(\alpha'_p \cdot X_2) \cdot X_2^{k'_p}$, and the only possible dependence of α_p on X_2 is linear, i.e., we get

$$E_j(X_1, X_2) = \sum C_{jp} \cdot \exp(\alpha_{p1} \cdot X_1 + \alpha_{p2} \cdot X_2 + \alpha'_p \cdot X_1 \cdot X_2) \cdot X_1^{k_{p1}} \cdot X_2^{k_{p2}}. \quad (7)$$

We started with the system (3). This system remains similar if we make a linear change of variables, e.g., if we replace X_1 and X_2 by $X'_1 = X_1 + X_2$ and $X'_2 = X_1 - X_2$. Therefore, we would like to get a similar formula (7) in the new variables. If $\alpha'_p \neq 0$, we get the undesired quadratic term in the exponential expression. Thus, $\alpha'_p = 0$, and (7) take the form

$$E_j(X_1, X_2) = \sum C_{jp} \cdot \exp(\alpha_{p1} \cdot X_1 + \alpha_{p2} \cdot X_2) \cdot X_1^{k_{p1}} \cdot X_2^{k_{p2}}. \quad (7)$$

Similarly, if we take into consideration the dependence on all n variables X_k, we conclude that

$$E_j(X_1, \ldots, X_n) = \sum C_{jp} \cdot \exp(\alpha_{p1} \cdot X_1 + \ldots + \alpha_{pn} \cdot X_n) \cdot X_1^{k_{p1}} \cdot \ldots \cdot X_n^{k_{pn}}. \quad (8)$$

Substituting $X_k = \ln(x_k)$ into this formula (8), we get the desired expression for $e_j(x_1, \ldots, x_n)$:

$$e_j(x_1, \ldots, x_n) = \sum C_{jp} \cdot x_1^{\alpha_{p1}} \cdot \ldots \cdot x_n^{\alpha_{pn}} \cdot \ln^{k_{p1}}(x_1) \cdot \ldots \cdot \ln^{k_{pn}}(x_n).$$

The theorem is proven.

Studies in Fuzziness and Soft Computing

Vol. 25. J. Buckley and Th. Feuring
Fuzzy and Neural: Interactions and Applications, 1999
ISBN 3-7908-1170-X

Vol. 26. A. Yazici and R. George
Fuzzy Database Modeling, 1999
ISBN 3-7908-1171-8

Vol. 27. M. Zaus
Crisp and Soft Computing with Hypercubical Calculus, 1999
ISBN 3-7908-1172-6

Vol. 28. R.A. Ribeiro, H.-J. Zimmermann, R.R. Yager and J. Kacprzyk (Eds.)
Soft Computing in Financial Engineering, 1999
ISBN 3-7908-1173-4

Vol. 29. H. Tanaka and P. Guo
Possibilistic Data Analysis for Operations Research, 1999
ISBN 3-7908-1183-1

Vol. 30. N. Kasabov and R. Kozma (Eds.)
Neuro-Fuzzy Techniques for Intelligent Informations Systems, 1999
ISBN 3-7908-1187-4

Vol. 31. B. Kostek
Soft Computing in Acoustics, 1999
ISBN 3-7908-1190-4

Vol. 32. K. Hirota and T. Fukuda
Soft Computing in Mechatronics, 1999
ISBN 3-7908-1212-9

SPRINGER NATURE

GPSR Compliance

The European Union's (EU) General Product Safety Regulation (GPSR) is a set of rules that requires consumer products to be safe and our obligations to ensure this.

If you have any concerns about our products, you can contact us on ProductSafety@springernature.com

In case Publisher is established outside the EU, the EU authorized representative is:

Springer Nature Customer Service Center GmbH
Europaplatz 3
69115 Heidelberg, Germany

Kolibri 360 GmbH
Ferdinand-Jühlke-Straße 7
99095 Erfurt, Deutschland
produktsicherheit@kolibri360.de